ERNST KRAUSE · RICHARD STRAUSS

ERNST KRAUSE

RICHARD STRAUSS

THE MAN AND HIS WORK

CRESCENDO PUBLISHING COMPANY
BOSTON

V

Standard Book Number 87597-024-9
Library of Congress Card Number 78-77591
Printed in Germany
© of the English edition by Collet's (Publishers) Ltd. London
First United States registration 1969
Crescendo Publishing Company, Boston

Music is an exalted art!
Only reluctantly does it serve the illusion of the theatre.
Not illusion!
The stage reveals to us the secret of reality.
As though in a magic mirror we perceive ourselves.
The theatre is the impressive symbol of life.

("Capriccio," Scene 9)

FOREWORD

THE CENTENARY OF THE BIRTH OF RICHARD STRAUSS sees this book in its third German edition. The personality and work of this German composer have become the objects of new love and respect–reason enough for the author to revise yet again a book which originally appeared in 1955. The basic concept of the book has remained unaltered, but its contents have been brought into line with the findings of the most recent Strauss research, and it has been extended by the addition of new material and by reference to new sources. In many places it has virtually become a new book.

It should again be emphasized that this is not, strictly speaking, a biography. The book represents an attempt to come to grips with the composer's life and works. His life, bounded within the confines of bourgeois existence, scarcely needs to be dealt with again in great detail. Everything worth knowing about Richard Strauss the man can best be presented in conjunction with a consideration of his works. The attempt will be made to examine this rich œuvre in detail and at the same time as a whole, as one of the last offshoots of the bourgeois musical culture of Germany and Europe. The research work and the conclusions to which it has led are based on many years of familiarity with the material, and of personal contact with the composer. The extent to which his life's work can be expected to outlive his own age and surroundings can be estimated on the basis of the present-day situation concerning that part of his music which has survived the death of its composer.

We do not yet stand at a sufficient distance to be able to pass a final judgement on Strauss's works, but certain new aesthetic standards, associated with the development of artistic realism, are of assistance in an attempt to evaluate the music. The reader will find all he needs in the documentary material presented here, which includes hitherto unpublished letters dating from the end of Strauss's life, to enable him to build up as objective a picture as possible of the composer's work. In cases where familiarity with Strauss's art has given rise to subjective expressions of opinion, these are intended only to throw new light on undoubted facts. The work and influence of this composer speak for themselves.

An appendix provides a survey of factual material, including all the names, data and references not given in the body of the text. Musical examples as adjuncts to the text were considered unnecessary, in view of the existence of analyses and introductions to the works. Illustrations, too, appeared to be required only in small numbers. New features of this edition include details of the scoring of the orchestral works, and an international Strauss discography.

I could not have undertaken this task but for the helpful encouragement of Strauss enthusiasts and authorities. I received especially valuable assistance from Dr. Franz and Alice Strauss (Garmisch), Dr. Willi Schuh (Zürich), and from music publishers and recording companies, which willingly supplied me with study material. The number of kind helpers in the German Democratic Republic, elsewhere in Germany and in other countries, is great. My most sincere thanks go out to them all.

Berlin, end of 1962   E. K.

PERIOD AND SURROUNDINGS

THE WORK OF RICHARD STRAUSS, WHICH ROMAIN Rolland once described as the "last great event in European music," is already part of musical history. Strauss stood at the end of an era of bourgeois art, not at the beginning of a new age. His death on the 8th September 1949 has to be regarded as marking the close of the period of late-romantic development. Clearly the middle of this century witnessed the final extinction of a musical culture which was a manifestation of bourgeois society. Strauss went on working until, in the music of his eighties, he achieved a new clarity of spirit, and until, in his last songs with orchestra, he looked death in the face. Then his race was run.

Viewing his work as a whole we cannot but recognize, despite setbacks, the fruits of a life fulfilled. The master of the age of psychology, the tonal magician and man of many parts was at the same time the last in the succession of musicians who brought together in their thinking and feeling all the forces of past centuries. Forms and styles blended together. The elements of music became the last means of giving expression to high spiritual aspirations. Strauss's greatness made itself felt without effort. There was something over-ripe about it–the pure reflection of the individual romantic artist surrounded by the reality of everyday life in his time. Even in those among his works which once appeared revolutionary, such as "Don Juan" and "Salome," which represented the musical "progress" of their time, his function in musical history is felt to be one of summing up, of bringing to a close. When he had carried the process of dissolving traditional harmony to its furthest limits in the dissonances of "Elektra," he threw the rudder hard over to change the course of development.

His work is not something lifeless which merits only historical

9

consideration. It is actual, fully alive in the reality of the opera house and concert hall. His principal works are performed in Berlin and Vienna, Moscow and New York–in all countries and continents where Strauss's music has been cultivated and admired ever since it first appeared. His popular operas and tone poems belong to the "solid core" of the repertoire of opera companies and orchestras all over the world. While Mahler the symphonist exceeded him in the determination with which he pursued ethical ideals, and Puccini had an even greater power over opera audiences, Strauss the bourgeois humanist succeeded in combining human feeling with the power of melodic expression in such a way as to create the deep and widespread effect on which his worldwide fame was founded. The German master musician Richard Strauss, who loved his native land and always felt himself to be a representative of his people, belonged as a composer of international stature to *all* peoples. The fact that he, to whom it was granted to speak the "international language" of music, became regarded as the representative of a vague "worldwide society" is one of the great misunderstandings in the evaluation of his personality. It is not given to many artists to see something of their immortality growing up during their lifetime, but Strauss was one of the few. It is seldom that anything doomed to quick extinction survives for more than a generation. Strauss's music has already proved that its survival is assured. His œuvre, whose validity was more than once questioned by his opponents during his lifetime, has withstood the changes of the times. His death has not halted the progress of his music, but has in fact spread it even further afield. How many of those who turned their backs on Strauss during the turbulent days following the First World War have since returned to him! His work and its impact have destroyed the myth that great artists are not recognized until a hundred years after their death.

Nevertheless his work calls for examination. What Thomas Mann once said of Schoenberg, that the curve of his life clearly veered "between adulation and neglect," is also true of Strauss. Undoubtedly he made it difficult to trace a straight line of development, with the abundance of his works, and the many demands he makes on both performer and listener. Strauss never ceased to surprise; whether working in the contrasting media of opera, symphonic or chamber music he constantly alternated between tension and repose. He needed ever new impetus, whether from life or from literature. He was not like Wagner, seeking throughout his mature life to create a complete whole, with a particular theme such as the idea of redemption recurring again and again. The heart of Strauss's music is comparable to the secret of Ariadne: *transformation.* A master of the programmatic symphony and of music drama, he is regarded as a leading exponent of naturalism. His works also, however, contain elements of realism which reflect the social truths of particular eras of cultural history. Strauss's personality set him apart from the sickly artistic movement which dominated central Europe about the turn of the century, and which found expression to an alarming degree in the decadence which was itself a product of the breakdown of European society before the First World War. The basis of his work directed toward Eros is "sympathy with life"; it is something of this world. He proved that it is possible to swim against the current if one has sufficient strength.

His music is not an art of expression but of representation. There are works in which the son of prosperous middle-class parents felt himself closely linked with the ordinary people, in which he proved his sympathy for the poor and oppressed, or was concerned with painting a clear picture of the life of the community. There are also works in which Strauss rejected reality, seeking refuge in dreams and visions, looking backwards rather than forwards; indeed he, who stood apart from the religious outlook on life, sometimes drew upon elements and figures of fate with which he himself had scarcely anything in common. Such contradictions resulted in the last analysis from the inconsistency of bourgeois life and of the imperialistic era which it supported. It was his flight into an idealistic, "literary" world remote from real life which endangered certain of his works. Nevertheless it would be difficult to divide the works he left us into those for the broad mass of the people and those for "connoisseurs" and snobs. "Ariadne," a spirited compound of feelings and artistry, was originally conceived as an opera for the elite among audiences, but it now delights a far wider circle. Then again "Salome," which Strauss considered suitable for only "a few of the largest court theatres," went into the repertoire of opera houses both large and small all over the world. On the other hand the Viennese ballet "Schlagobers," which

11

was intended to appeal to the taste of the general public, like many of the songs written in a popular vein, received only a few performances. In the case of Strauss the voice of the people was decisive.

The consciousness that he was working in accordance with the German musical tradition was strong in Strauss. It is an unmistakable fact that the young composer, having turned first to the symphonic poem of Hector Berlioz and Franz Liszt, was unable to prevent himself, led on by the poetic idea of pure programme music, from erring further and further into the decorative and descriptive sphere of the later monumental tone poems, combining blatantly illustrative with genuinely musical elements. It is also unmistakable that the young Wagnerian progressed from the echoes of Bayreuth in "Guntram" and "Feuersnot" to the "nervous counterpoint" of "Salome" and "Elektra," which are free from the direct influence of Wagner, only to strive immediately afterwards toward the essentially musical ideals of "Der Rosenkavalier," "Ariadne" and "Die Frau ohne Schatten"–a path which was to lead him as far as the tonal baroque world of "Die ägyptische Helena." The lyrically transfigured, autumnally sweet closing stage of this uncommonly rich succession of works within the wide realm of opera seems to begin with "Arabella" and to continue into the dramatic and instrumental works of Strauss's final period, with classical longing surrounded by late-romantic blossoms. In actual fact the stylistic development of Strauss the epicurean can be traced right back to "Don Juan," that stroke of genius of a twenty-four-year-old composer; his entire life's work consists of variations and refinements on this style with its roots in psychology, by which he sought to conquer "a modest stretch of new territory"–since "Ariadne," at least, he drew again and again on his own vocabulary. The fluctuations and changes in Strauss both as man and musician were a result of his relationship to the reality of social life. The fact that he was able to rise above setbacks and difficult times (he showed signs of weariness on occasion during the 'twenties) to soar to new heights of achievement testifies to his unbroken artistic power, which was itself a product of his strength of will. While he represented the most vital aspects of the musical style current at the turn of the century (a style often corresponding to the snobbish attitude of society during the age of imperialism),

12

at the same time proclaiming human values and spreading happiness, he managed to overcome all obstacles and arrive at the threshold of modernity. Surrounded by dissolution and decay, he certainly shows in his work that he was fully aware of the world around him, but his music itself is not marked by dissolution. Though Strauss did not set foot in a new land, he caught a glimpse of a better world in many of his works, and went steadily forward. However, his forward progress was not what technicians consider to represent advance, as it carried with it the obligation to look back with far-seeing eyes. He, whose last years of development were independent of the immense struggles and decisions going on in the world around, built on the great humanitarian ideals of classicism. The "last of the great line of full-blooded German musicians which extended from Handel by way of Beethoven and Brahms to our own times" (Stefan Zweig) saw many of his works accepted as classics in his lifetime, and they represent a part of the cultural heritage of the German people, which present and future generations have a duty to cherish.

During his long life Strauss wrote seventeen stage works (operas and ballets), fourteen major orchestral works, six works of the concerto type, chamber music, and a great many songs and other smaller pieces. Tireless in his urge to create, incomparable in his craftsmanship, honourable in his expression of feelings, self-confident in his life, subjective and reflecting his times in his choice of subjects, he was a truly German composer in a troubled age of social upheaval and stylistic change. His field of activity was divided in an almost unique manner between the great musical centres of Germany and Austria: Munich, Weimar, Berlin, Dresden and Vienna. Before following in detail the "trail" which he left behind him both as musician and man, before the works and their underlying programmes are examined, it is necessary to say something about the times during which the young Strauss grew up. In order to give an idea of the surroundings in which he developed during the course of a long life some account must be given of the background of society.

*

The middle-class revolution of 1848 and 1849 had ended in defeat. Progressive elements fought in vain for the unity and democratic rebirth of Germany, then a general sense of disappointment descended on the German people. Nevertheless the consequences of the two years of revolution went deeper than was the case in France. For the first time the idea of a united Germany had been voiced; the relative strengths of the will of the people and of the governments in power could be gauged far more accurately than had been the case previously. The revolutionary concept of society had been born. The change which began to come over the community in mid-century found expression in the class antagonism which marked the growth of *capitalism*. When the hard years of the post-revolutionary depression were at last over, new hopes of German unity began to arise among both middle-class and working class people. One of the aims of the revolution of 1848, national unity, was actually attained—but in a very imperfect manner: a German Empire under Prussian leadership. This was no solution of the problem arrived at with the support of the people, let alone by the people themselves, but one imposed from above, directed by the ruling class at the expense of the ordinary people! This development began with the Customs Union and the accession of Wilhelm I in January 1861. A year later Bismarck made a significant statement in the Prussian Chamber of Deputies: "The great questions of the age are not to be decided by speeches and majority decisions, but by iron and blood." From that point the political road ran inevitably toward the Franco-Prussian war and to the Imperial Coronation at Versailles in 1871.

Undoubtedly a great step forward had been taken toward the unity, might and greatness of Germany. But who could fail to recognize the wide discrepancy between the splendid outward structure and the inward hollowness of this aggressive State machine? The so-called "good old days" about which the elderly delight to ramble on when they are in the mood were in reality a time of rapid *decay*. In the fields of politics, economics, and last but not least culture, the German Reich presented a picture of threatening crisis at the turn of the century. Behind the complacent façade of an apparently flourishing middle class, behind the "results of satisfaction with superficial sociology" (Rilla) closer examination revealed cracks in the crumbling walls which could scarcely be concealed, and which indicated the questionable stability of the entire structure of the existing social order. During the last third of the 19th century the agricultural and bourgeois Germany of former days rapidly developed into a modern industrial state. In the stifling atmosphere of this "prison of the spirit" with its censorship, avarice, place-hunting and resentful servility Wilhelm II reigned from 1888 onwards as "Emperor by the Grace of God." Under his ægis there was completed toward the turn of the century the ominous development of German capitalism into an internationally controlled monopoly system, *imperialism* in its own right, with its powerful business firms, in private hands, exploiting the masses, its typical structure of cartels, trusts, combines and syndicates. All the power of capitalism was concentrated within the vast banking houses. Business ability became greed for profit. At the same time the Junkers, the wealthy landowners, influenced middle-class citizens to adopt their reactionary-imperialistic attitude. In place of a drawing together of bourgeois elements with the increasingly powerful working class to oppose the power-hungry forces of reaction (as occurred, for example, in Russia), there was an open league of monopoly capitalism and the Junkers against the working class.

German imperialism is shown up in all its shame by a comparison between the ruling class with its unbridled desire for expansion and its sabre-rattling, and the oppressed, downtrodden masses of the ordinary people. Those who were at the bottom of the social ladder in the "splendid" days of the Kaiser's Germany saw only the shabby reverse side of the glittering façade of the upward-striving bourgeoisie. The conditions of vast numbers of workers and craftsmen were unbelievably wretched. They bore out Schiller's statement that the poverty-stricken need food and clothing before they can concern themselves with cultural matters. It was only slowly, first and foremost through the writings of Karl Marx and Friedrich Engels, that the proletariat became conscious of a right to demand a change in the established order. The inarticulate longings of the working man and woman for freedom from the dominating forces of corruption, oppression and destruction, for new ideals of human greatness, human dignity and human love, were directed into channels of social aspiration. Meanwhile the disparity between the different strata of society became even more acute. Class-conscious workers who strove for a voice in State and industry, while

15

still unable significantly to influence the condition of the country as a whole, had banded together in trade unions, and after a time they managed to take up the struggle on the political level through the Social Democratic Party. In 1890 the Socialists, fighting stubbornly, achieved a great success in the Reichstag elections. The German labour movement made its voice heard: it compelled the government to repeal the anti-socialist laws and brought about the dismissal of their author Bismarck. But this important victory of the working class was not to prove lasting. The Social Democratic leaders betrayed the trust placed in them, and there followed an act of political "reconciliation" between labour and the capitalist system which served only to speed up imperialistic policies and to weaken the proletariat. Many progressively-inclined people welcomed the unification of the nation while shutting their eyes to the price which had been paid for it–the price of democracy . . . were vital economic and at the same time cultural matters not at stake? "Work alone creates wealth and culture" wrote Wilhelm Liebknecht in 1900. "A country which really intends to attain cultural heights must increase its inner strength by work. To organize work reasonably and rightly is the great cultural task of mankind."

The pompous arrogance and ambition of the period found expression in the Kaiser's policy of expansion backed by *military might*. The world had suddenly become too small, and it seemed that a new distribution of the sources of raw materials and of world markets could be brought about only by the use of armed force. While the armament industry received vast orders for the expansion of the army and navy, paid for out of the compensation exacted from France after the war of 1870, the likelihood of hostilities was everywhere increasing as a result of the exploitation of other nations. An incident in Morocco all but led to the outbreak of a European war. The Bagdad railway, that vast undertaking initiated by the German Bank, opened the way to the oil wells of the Persian Gulf, where the struggle for power between German and British imperialism approached the point of decision. German nationalism, with its flag waving, sabre rattling and heel clicking, its concept of true manliness and its blind obedience, was moving rapidly toward its first great clash with reality. European society with its crumbling morality was rushing toward an abyss whose proximity it pos-

16

sibly guessed at but of whose nature it had as yet no conception. Those who had no ideal for which to strive existed only for themselves, enjoying life to the full, making it an end in itself. *Life* was the goal of life–and what life! A dance round the golden calf, a dance on the rim of a volcano ... That was the age.

*

Culture, as the reflection of the period, cannot be separated from it. What had become of the revolutionary elan which had inspired Beethoven's "Fidelio," or of the humanistic fire of the "Ninth"? What remained of the progressive message of Heine, Gutzkow, Freiligrath, Börne and Büchner? German idealism of the early 19th century had been directed toward freedom of the mind and the establishment of a progressive society. These fine, deeply humanistic aims were falsified even by some of the romanticists into expressions of reaction, and were watered down by the mass of the middle classes until they had become no more than empty phrases. Then the "glorious" victories of 1866 and 1870 turned what little remained of these high ideals, the noblest produced in Germany since the Reformation, into relics hardly worth remembering. It was clear to everyone that the middle of the century, which saw the first performances of Schumann's "Genoveva" and Wagner's "Lohengrin," marked the close of the era of impassioned romanticism. German romanticism was at once reactionary and progressive, veering between idealism and reality. Its attitude to the world manifested itself in the works of the writers Jean Paul, Ludwig Tieck and Novalis, with their emphasis on death as the real meaning of life. This idea was carried furthest in the pessimistic philosophy of Schopenhauer, with his disavowal of the world. In their quest after subjects to stir the popular imagination and reflect nature, romantic artists frequently chose themes from German mythology –their works helped to instil national consciousness into the minds of the increasingly prominent middle classes.

The artistic fruits of what is termed "late romanticism" were even further removed from classicism. The musical creations of that period were increasingly remote from the powerful vitality which animates genuine folk art. The same was true, during the post-revolutionary period, in all branches of the arts, and it was in these surroundings that Wagner, Hebbel and Nietzsche worked. At the same time the national opera of the people was making its way, assisted by favourable conditions, in Italy and Russia, and new progressive elements in literature, the products of critical realism, were flourishing in Russia, and later in France and England, but not at first in Germany. While in Italy the "maestro della rivoluzzione italiana," Giuseppe Verdi, clearly recognized signs of decay and the threatened decline of the middle class when he wrote his patriotic works, Wagner expressed the aspiration toward national unity in "Die Meistersinger."

The ideological chaos of the Kaiser's reign was demonstrated by the yawning gulf which separated the "great political splendour" of the Reich and the paucity of important creative artistry in Germany from the time of the foundation of the Empire. The period produced a supposed culture of its own, unconnected with national traditions, which reflected inner *emptiness* and *stagnation.* The official art of Imperial Germany was the pompously decorated counterpart of the ostentatious age which saw progress in the spread of capitalism. "Naturalistic artists" restricted themselves to depicting in crude colours the bourgeoisie and the things favoured by a society in decline. (Similar work could have been undertaken for other, more positive reasons!) Later there followed as a product of the general decadence the representatives of symbolism, mysticism, expressionism and even formalism—they were to place an even greater distance between themselves and the ordinary people. All genuinely realistic reflection of life and its problems in art was regarded by the upper classes as being suspect, the product of "inferior feelings." The gulf between art and the people was indeed a feature of the era. A last tawdry brilliance, redolent of morbid luxury, surrounded the "courtly" music, literature and painting, whose beauty-drunk untruthfulness and empty pathos were characteristic of "fin de siècle" art. The fact that this age of decadence also produced certain positive achievements, that from time to time something really new was created, does not alter the overall picture of an era of crisis and artistic mediocrity.

At that time there was not a major artist in Germany who failed to recognize the opposition of capitalism—yet how few could see through capitalism as a system! It is, however, a great mistake to equate this doomed official art of the Kaiser's Reich (which was on a level with the all-too-familiar oil paintings in reproduction, plaster busts and cheap copies of ornate buildings dating from the same period) with the true, forward-looking *culture of the people,* which was not a hollow sham but was really alive. The culture of the Kaiser's Germany lacked the spur of artistic opposition, which normally helps to create the spirit of the age. While artists of one kind reflected the spiritual vacuum of the times in post-romantic forms, in the glorification of superhuman exploits and of racial pride with a greater or lesser degree of personal satisfaction, those of the other kind, clearly aware of the feverish condition of imperialistic society, acted as what Carl Sternheim described as a "physician to the body of the age." To an ever increasing extent the milieu of the socially "inferior" classes became the subject of works of art. It must be admitted, however, that the artistic materials were almost exclusively those of bourgeois humanism, Marxist social criticism appearing only occasionally on the periphery. The majority of musicians, poets and painters who retained freshness and independence of mind consciously depicted the unhealthy condition of society. Many of them, like Oscar Wilde, sought their material not in life but in books, pictures, and even products of the decadence of their age, while others, such as the representatives of the "school of youth," strove to escape from reality. In both cases the spectacle was one of flight from the function of criticising the age into the realm of aesthetics—as something inevitable and unavoidable. What the artist of that time recognized and represented as "truth" very rarely corresponded to the truths of everyday life. One of the signs of a sceptical outlook on the world around was the fact that the real tensions of community life and the newly released social forces were considered and commented upon only marginally.

Who were the creative *musicians* who helped to fashion the liberal-individualistic era inside and outside the borders of Germany? Who were the composers able to set positive values against the decline of German national culture and of middle-class sensibility? The historical and philosophical crisis of the era attained its fullest expression in the music dramas of Richard Wagner. His œuvre, a vital contribution to the German "national opera," only in part represented opposition to the Reich's claim to domination. The fighter at the Dresden barricades had become a friend of princes and a "State Musician" (Marx), though in the end he turned his back on the "Second" Reich and its Chancellor. Wagner the man was realist enough to turn the situation to his own advantage, whatever his personal feelings toward the Hohenzollern rulers may have been. However, Wagner was at the same time what Thomas Mann aptly described in his Zürich lecture of 1937 as the "unique revolutionary" whose "true dreams and intentions extended beyond the age of the bourgeoisie," an "artistic power politician" who wanted to conquer the world and did in fact conquer the 19th century. In his essay "The artistic work of the future" he demanded of the individual arts, released from their original alliance, that they should give up their independent development and return to close association. Through Wagner's "Gesamtkunstwerk," whose effect still continues to be felt today, and which was an epoch-making event in the history of artistic creation, German opera received an infusion of new blood such as it had not known since Gluck, Mozart and Weber.

Few signs of any cultural achievements on the same plane can be observed in the circle around Wagner and his followers. His most fervent admirers who saturated the Bayreuth music drama in bombast and mysticism, Felix Draeseke, August Bungert, Max von Schillings and others, failed to achieve any widespread effect. The "New Germans," too, followers of Berlioz and Liszt who held themselves apart from the "traditionalist" Brahms, failed to create any very lasting impression, with the exception of the finely sensitive Peter Cornelius. From the east Rimsky-Korsakoff, the master of romantic atmosphere painting, gave international music new colours of Russian nationalism. In later years such music, at the hands of the French impressionist Claude Debussy, entered into the sphere of the over-refined art of nervous tension. About the end of the century Max Reger and Hans Pfitzner raised their voices (though at first they were heard only in Germany): the one was a late-romanticist with the dual attitude of an artist deeply sensitive to feeling who was at the same time a strict formalist where structure was concerned, the other the prototype of the "last romanticist" showing all the signs of dreaminess, absorption in thought, and mysticism. The neo-classical innovations of Ferruccio Busoni were the concern of only a comparatively small professional circle, while Arnold

Schoenberg, that unique prophet of disenchanted, anti-romantic music, together with his school, soon formulated a culture of the abstract isolated from society. There remains the ethically great artistry of Gustav Mahler, whose symphonies with their human-istic programmes do not describe but bear witness. They are personal utterances on the spiritual plane–in fact symbols. Such idealism, which often went hand in hand with a natural striving after the simplicity of music-making "in the folksong style," did not, however, obscure the darker side of life; expansion of the means of musical expression culminated in the despairing "Welt-schmerz" of the Eighth Symphony and "Das Lied von der Erde."

All these so essentially different composers (whose appear-ance within a few years must nevertheless be regarded as a rare piece of good fortune) derived little inspiration from the social questions of the world around them. With a few excep-tions they avoided referring in their works to the struggle to build a better world. To a far greater extent than the writers, sculptors and painters, the musicians remained in their accepted sphere in which fame and privations, success and failure were the sum of life, a life in which music was often debased to the status of merchandise. Nothing rousing or admonitory was to be heard in most of the armour-plated, naturalistically conceived scores of the period. New musical forms were almost always intended to fulfil the requirements of bourgeois musical festivals and concerts. The striving after mass effects was expressed in superficially overblown, monstrous forms. "There is too much music in Germany" was Romain Rolland's conclusion at the turn of the century.

The most understandable and convincing mode of utterance in an era dominated by capitalism and nearing exhaustion re-mained the language and form of *literature.* There was an aston-ishingly long list of poets and writers who deliberately turned their backs on the reactionary, military spirit of the age, who depicted the life of middle-class society realistically, and at the same time subjected it to critical scrutiny. Even in the 'nineties the young Gerhart Hauptmann entered the arena of the social drama of the day. In the field of naturalism, which had little to offer as regards subject matter, but in which there had sprung up a new relationship between observation and artistic creation

21

born of the times, there began to gather momentum a movement which held the mirror up to narrow-minded philistinism and the self-appointed arbiters of conduct in all walks of life. Admittedly the dangers of becoming bogged down in a mere description of things, and of placing undue emphasis on details, were ever-present. The audiences at the court theatres in the days prior to the First World War, seeking nothing but amusement, rejected this representation of truth as they were unconcerned with such matters—except that they found the "immorality of the lower classes" interesting. The vital factor to such people was dazzling theatrical effectiveness. When Hauptmann replaced real life by idealistic creations of the imagination in his later dramatic and epic works, they were unable to follow him.

Another great German writer displayed admirable courage in expressing his opinion of the growing power of the nouveaux riches: Thomas Mann. His novels and essays threw light on the principal pillars of the bourgeois age whose downfall he clearly foresaw, although he felt himself strong enough "to withstand the end of the bourgeois era" (Rilla). In his famous essay on Goethe Thomas Mann wrote: "The middle-class citizen is lost, and will fall a victim of the new world which is to come, unless he succeeds in freeing himself from the fatal love of comfort and the life-denying ideologies which still dominate him, and boldly declares himself for the future . . ." The process of critical examination of the age was carried even further by Heinrich Mann. This great realist, following a sound artistic instinct, strove constantly to renew himself by listening to the progressive voice of the people. Finally it can scarcely be denied that the literature of other lands made a decisive contribution to the shedding of light on the culture of Imperial Germany. Such literature included the writings of the French critical realists from Balzac to Flaubert, works from the north including Ibsen's "Ghosts" and the fiercely disputed novels of Knut Hamsun, together with the works of the Austrian aesthetes Hugo von Hofmannsthal and Stefan Zweig.

Then there was the soulless pathos of the epoch of the Makart bouquets. Romain Rolland wrote: "Germany had hardly become a world power when it found the voice of Nietzsche and of the hallucinated artists of secession." The development of painting during the period was determined less by the romantic coulisses

22

of Arnold Böcklin, Hans Makart's concept of fleshly beauty, and the hollow décor of Franz Stuck, than by the sensuous glow of colours created by Lovis Corinth or Max Slevogt. But how far removed from the neo-romantic spirit of the times were the clarity of Max Liebermann's brushwork and the expressive language of Edvard Munch! The influence from France of such impressionistic masters as Corot, Manet, and above all Cézanne influenced the painting of Europe. The tendency of the artistic profession toward ornamentation, like the design of new town buildings, belonged to the dawning century, which was experiencing a rapid transformation. We should not forget what was happening in other fields in the Europe of that time: Planck's Quantum Theory, the investigation of cathode rays, the association of radio activity with the breaking down of atoms, the flying box-kite of the Wright brothers, Zeppelin's airships, the racing car . . .

Was this age really *poor?* Poor in material things certainly not–but poor in spiritual values. Those permitted the honour of strutting past His Majesty represented to the outside world the decadence of the era, while clear-thinking minds with progressive ideas were accused of endangering "culture." The way to make the philistine tremble on his plush sofa was to declare war on the reactionary spirit of the age. With Gerhart Hauptmann's "Vor Sonnenaufgang" of 1889 a generation striving to change obsolete conditions hammered at the doors of the theatre. In the same year Detlev von Liliencron published his "Contemporary Poems," and in Weimar the sensuous power in the tone poem of a young "storm and stress" composer shocked the philistines . . . Well-known writers, producers, actors and men of learning raised their voices against the era's increasing antagonism to life. The age saw a tragi-comic gulf widening between general moral instability on the one hand and the demands of an inflexible code of behaviour on the other, with the result that the confidence of the average citizen was shaken. What sort of an age was this in which violent contradictions existed so close to each other? . . . The might of the Reich and the increasing power of the proletariat, the Kiel Navy Week and the first May Day meeting in Berlin, the Wagner Festivals at Bayreuth and the "Free Theatre" in Berlin, the "Philosophy of the Unconscious" and "Das Kapital"! One can either admire or reject such con-

23

trasts of a "nervous" period—they created the crisis of society which formed the background to the rise of a musician of world stature.

*

The life of Richard Strauss began a few weeks after Meyerbeer's death in the year which saw the war waged by Prussia and Austria against Denmark, six years before the Franco-Prussian war which led to the unification of Germany, and it ended four years after the close of the second of the two catastrophic world wars. It therefore extended over periods whose political and intellectual characteristics appear irreconcilable. The world in which Strauss's music originated was that of the Kaiser's Empire, the Weimar Republic, and the Nazi regime. At the age of seven the young Strauss, in his native city of Munich, followed the news of the seemingly glorious foundation of the "Second Reich" at Versailles. In 1914 the prosperous edifice began to tremble, and thirty years later the aged composer, who had long since lost all sympathy with the pseudo-culture of brownshirt imperialism, was a witness in Garmisch to the total collapse of Hitler's "Third Reich." (It is worth recalling that "Don Juan" appeared in 1889, the year which witnessed the birth of the man who was to lead Germany into the abyss.) At the dawn of a new age of which Strauss, marked by illness and old age, was scarcely aware, he died in his native Upper Bavaria on the 8th September 1949.

Five days before the birth of Richard Georg Strauss on the 11th June 1864, Richard Wagner had moved to Munich at the invitation of King Ludwig II of Bavaria. A few months after young Richard had drawn his first breath the rehearsals for the world première of "Tristan" began not far from his birthplace (Altheimer Eck 2, toward the rear of the Pschorr property—the house was partially destroyed at the end of the last war, was restored, but has now, disgracefully, been marked down for demolition). Strauss's father Franz, the principal horn player of the Court Orchestra, also assisted at that second birth of great importance to musical history. Strauss was eighteen when he heard from his father, in Munich, of Wagner's death, and at first he probably did not realize what a deep, lasting wound that event was to cause him. He was ten years old when Hugo von Hofmannsthal, his artistic colleague of later years, was born, thirty

The birthplace: Altheimer Eck 2 in Munich

when his friend and mentor Hans von Bülow died. In that same year the first dramatic work by the up-and-coming composer, "Guntram," with its fervent homage to Wagner, had its world première at Weimar, his future wife Pauline de Ahna appearing as Freihild, and the young Wagnerian was able to

25

introduce himself at Bayreuth as conductor of "Tannhäuser." To complete the circle: he conducted "Parsifal" in Bayreuth at the age of seventy, and "Tristan" in Dresden on the 50th anniversary of Wagner's death. The "misunderstood genius" of the Kaiser's day, at first feared and later praised as an avant-gardist, became suspect from 1919 onward as an "impossible archreactionary" by the younger generation pressing impulsively onward; he was almost completely isolated from the immense social upheavals of the years following the Second World War. Such were the changes of fortune during the lifetime of this musician who founded his work on the ideal of musical "progress" during the bourgeois-imperialistic age, who later changed, yet remained essentially the same. What altered was not so much Strauss as the listener who shared in his art. He went his way calmly, until far into his old age an example of creative power worthy to be ranked with Goethe.

BEGINNINGS

AT THE COMPOSER'S CRADLE IN THE OLDEST PART OF the backward, conservative Munich of 1864 Court Orchestra and Pschorr Beer, art and middle-class prosperity came together. The father Franz Joseph Strauss was certainly a man of many parts. The principal horn player of the Court Opera and professor at the Royal Academy, he not only had a virtuistic command of his instrument (a "Joachim of the horn"), but had also mastered several other instruments, and was active as a composer; even at the age of eighty he wrote ten trios for Bavarian posthorns. He was generally admired as one of the finest horn players of his time, although he was at first unwilling to take part in the world premières of Wagner's music dramas in Munich and at the Bayreuth Festivals. ("He is an intolerable fellow, but when he plays it is impossible to be angry with him," Bülow remarked.) His strongly conservative attitude, which detected the hand of "Mephisto Richard Wagner" in everything which lay outside the classical orbit, determined the course of young Richard's musical education. The mother, Josephine Strauss, who was also musical, was a member of the wealthy Munich Pschorr family of brewers, who were patrons of the arts; Franz Strauss had married her, as his second wife, at the end of August 1863. Strauss later wrote of his father in his "Recollections": "He was a so-called character. He would have considered it dishonest ever to alter his opinion once he had made his mind up in an artistic matter, and right into his old age I could never persuade him to accept my view if it differed from his." It has been proved that Franz Strauss came of peasant stock. Richard Strauss's grandfather was a policeman in the little town of Parkstein in the Upper Palatinate, and Strauss spoke of the family's possible "Bohemian origins." This may perhaps account

27

for a certain resemblance to the music of Dvořák which has recently been noticed in some of Strauss's later works, in particular the blossoming string melos of "Daphne." Far more important genealogically than the line bearing the name Strauss which was to become familiar all round the world was his descent from the family of his grandfather's wife, Maria Anna Kunigunda Walter. For generations her ancestors had held the post of tower warder, which carried with it the task of supervising the municipal music.

"With a father's joyful heart I have the honour to inform you, my dear father-in-law, that yesterday, Saturday, at six in the morning, my dear, good wife presented me with a healthy, plump, pretty baby boy, and at the same time I have the greatest pleasure in letting you know that mother and son are both well." So runs the letter in which Franz Strauss announced the arrival of his first child to the Pschorr family. "The birth of my dear little fellow took place quite quickly and happily. On Friday evening we hadn't the slightest inkling that my good wife would be brought to bed during the night, so I was most astonished when I . . . arrived home a little later, to find that everything had been prepared for the birth . . . Our little boy has made us very happy, as you can well imagine."

Little Richard had a carefree childhood. The Altheimer Eck home proving too small for the little Strauss family, they moved to a house in the Sonnenstrasse. (This house no longer exists). According to his mother the future composer showed his musicality even as a baby, reacting to the sound of the French horn with smiles, and to that of a violin with tears. At the age of four he had his first piano lessons from his mother; not long afterwards the teaching was taken over by the virtuoso harpist August Tombo, a friend and colleague of Strauss's father in the Court Orchestra, and by the pedagogue Carl Niest, while the father's cousin Benno Walter gave the eight-year-old boy his first instruction in violin playing. When he was six his parents took the evidently musical boy to see performances of "Der Freischütz" and "Die Zauberflöte" at the National Theatre. At the same age Richard began to attend an elementary school, the Cathedral School, and composed his first pieces: the so-called "Schneider Polka," a Christmas song, a waltz, and even an overture for orchestra. When he composed the Polka he was still

28

unable to write it out himself–his father had to do it for him, and his mother wrote in pencil at the bottom: "Copied out by Papa." In the case of the Christmas song his mother had to write the words under the notes, as the "composer," who was just old enough to go to school, could "draw" the notes, but could not tackle the German script. Faced by such natural gifts, the parents insisted on a higher classical education. Thanks to private coaching the young Strauss was able to obtain a place in the second class of the Royal Ludwig Gymnasium, which he attended from 1874 until 1882. He did not find learning difficult, his teachers liked and encouraged him. ("Keen and persevering, but over-hasty, lacking prudence; despite evident liking and talent for music does not neglect any subjects except mathematics," ran the school report on him at the beginning of his final year there). He then continued his studies at the University of Munich, where he read philosophy, aesthetics and artistic history for two terms. In later life Strauss frequently stressed the advantages of a classical education.

Among the immediate records of this sunny springtime of life the recently published memoirs of Strauss's only sister Johanna von Rauchenberger, who was three years his junior, are of delightful freshness and perceptiveness. "From his earliest youth onward Richard avidly collected experiences of every kind, especially those from nature, a great many of which were offered by our holidays. My father chose to spend the holidays in high-lying districts, as the air there helped to combat the tendency toward asthma brought on by his career as a horn player. A remote, unpretentious spot in the Pustertal, Sillian, near Ampezzo-Cortina-Toblach, was the paradise where for many years we enjoyed happy periods of freedom. Even the wonderful trip across the Brenner eighty years ago was an experience of the first order. And as in the lines of Uhland's poem (the text of Richard's first song) 'An innkeeper so kind and good of late has made me welcome.' He provided us with pleasant accommodation and the most excellent attention. The innkeeper of the 'Black Eagle' even got hold of a piano for Richard–that was splendid! His first visit was to the parson, for permission to play the organ; then to the teacher, with whom he made music; then to the doctor, to go fishing with him in the Drau–things he longed to do, and which made him really happy. Excursions to lonely valleys among the peaks, then coffee with whipped cream and little cakes ... There were innumerable joys and freedom which ever remained implanted in Richard's heart, to reappear in his music ... It was the simplicity, peace, and chance of quiet contemplation with none of the complications of present-day life which had so great an effect on Richard. ... Our dear father, who loved us children deeply, was stern and quick-tempered, so with Richard's forceful temperament there were some difficulties. Mother, who was of rare goodness, modesty and simplicity of heart, tried to smooth everything over and keep things which would cause trouble from Father's sharp eyes–sometimes my sisterly tears resolved such differences."

Meanwhile Strauss's musical training went on steadily under his father's guidance, side by side with his studies at school and university. At the age of eleven he became a pupil of the Munich Court Conductor Friedrich Wilhelm Meyer, who instructed him so thoroughly in theoretical subjects, harmony, musical form and instrumentation, that it proved unnecessary for him to attend the Academy of Music. By the time he was sixteen he knew all there was to know about counterpoint, "from plain and double to quadruple," and fugue. Strauss always expressed his appreciation for the systematic nature of his musical training: "My father insisted strongly that I should study the old masters. It is impossible to understand Wagner and the moderns unless one has studied the classics." Nevertheless Strauss may be considered to have been, in the higher sense, self-taught.

The boy's amazing creative power and joy in composing, demonstrated by a great many youthful works, most of which were not published, pointed to a solidly-based talent. Strauss learned musical craftsmanship as though it were child's play, and he was very soon to get beyond the stage of youthful experiments. He was also lucky in being able to hear his music performed. When Franz Strauss first included a piece by his son in the programme of a "musical entertainment" given by the amateur orchestra "Wilde Gung'l" which he conducted, the following report appeared in a Munich paper: "A Gavotte by Richard Strauss was shown to be receiving its first performance, and it met with a favourable reception. After repeated calls the composer was led on by the Chairman of the Association–it was the 14-year-old son of Herr Strauss, the conductor. He will certainly do honour

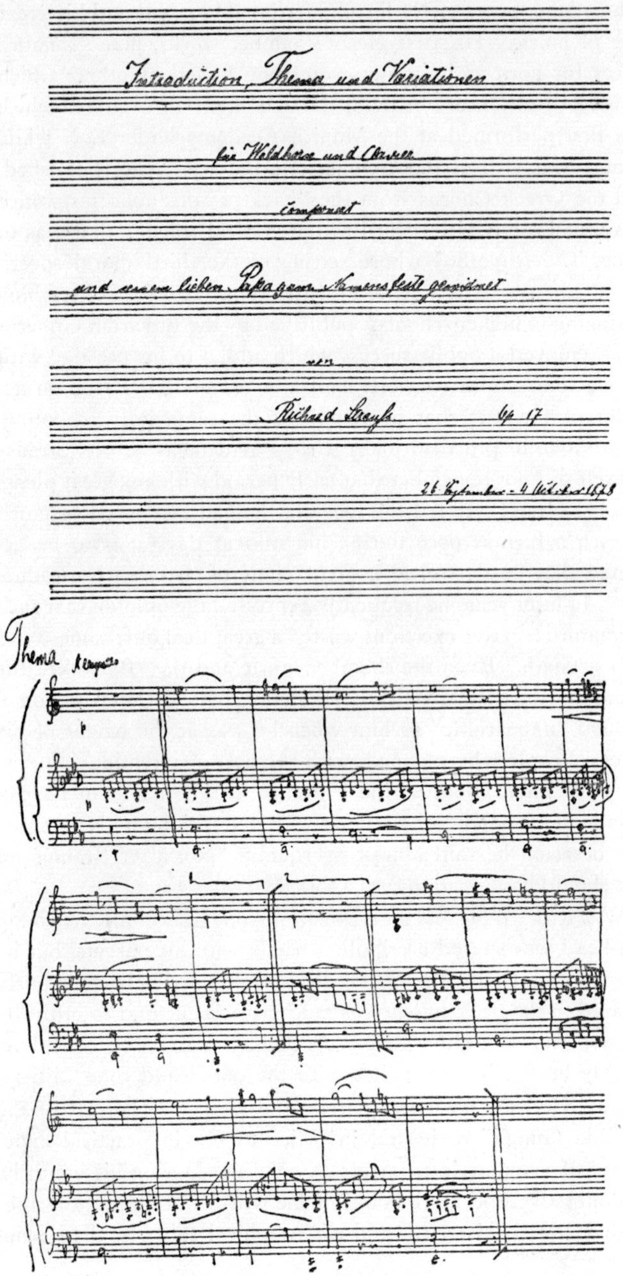
Introduction, Thema und Variationen
für Waldhorn und Clavier
componirt
und seinem lieben Papa zum Namensfeste gewidmet
von
Richard Strauss
Op 17
26 September - 4 Oktober 1878
Thema

to his name, by virtue of his unquestionable talent and his great love of music." His first pieces–chamber works, piano sonatas, pieces for horn and clarinet–were soon joined by others which pointed to the future Strauss: the Symphony in D minor which was first performed at the Munich Academy under Levi while Strauss was still at the Gymnasium, but was never published, and the Greek Chorus from the "Elektra" of Sophocles, which was remarkable with regard to the musical tragedy that was to come. The schoolboy whose setting of the third choral speech from "Elektra" was accepted for the book "Aid for the teaching of singing in higher schools," published by the Bavarian Government, enjoyed a public success which added to his prestige with his classmates and teachers. This was all the more true on account of the fact that he remained the same jolly schoolboy whose love of practical jokes was as evident as before. Strauss himself did not remember that early period with any great pleasure. He often regretted the fact that he had composed so much at such a furious pace during his student days–it is to be assumed that he destroyed a great many of these early productions. In later years he frequently expressed the opinion that such premature creative exertions waste "a great deal of freshness and also strength." Even the chamber music and the "Burleske" for piano and orchestra, which bears many signs of things to come, seemed "unbearable" to him when he was at the height of his career. People who planned, with the best of intentions, to perform the Piano Quartet, the Violin or Cello Sonatas or the Serenade in his honour always met with opposition on his part. On one occasion he said almost brusquely: "No, after Brahms no one should have written such a thing."

Was Richard Strauss a *darling of fortune*? Certainly the young hot-head was spared a crippling battle with his parents, but he was no infant prodigy. All he did and planned was consciously related to the need to learn as much as possible and to profit by the experience of older people. At the Gymnasium he "was thoroughly bored, but stuck it out to the end," and that "did no harm." He took an active part in the weekly rehearsals of the "Wilde Gung'l" orchestra, in order to obtain practical experience of as many instruments as possible. During his youth he undoubtedly read more books of the world's literature, together with many on historical and philosophical subjects, than Schubert or Bruckner, to mention but two examples, read during their whole lives. When he paid his first lengthy visit to Berlin (financed by his father) in the winter of 1883 he took advantage of every opportunity which offered itself to widen his mental horizon in the spheres of opera, concerts, literature and the visual arts. No rewards without industry. Nevertheless, despite the apparent certainty with which the young Strauss pursued and attained his goals, he was not spared contradictions and struggles within himself.

Among the major figures of his youth pride of place must go to Hans von Bülow, Alexander Ritter and Ludwig Thuille. The great conductor Bülow has been reproached for wilfulness in matters of tempo and dynamics, and for his habit of making pauses for breath, but his leading role in the creation of the "modern" interpretation of Beethoven and Brahms is unquestionable. He revised his original opinion of the young Strauss ("No genius, I am convinced, but a run-of-the-mill talent" he declared after studying the five piano pieces Op. 3) when he received the eighteen-year-old composer's Serenade for Wind Instruments, which he took into the permanent repertoire of the Meiningen orchestra. Bülow then recognized in him an "uncommonly gifted young man. ... by far the most striking personality since Brahms. ... versatile, eager to learn, firm and tactful, in short a first-rate force." (Letter to Hermann Wolff). To Strauss himself Bülow wrote significantly that he was one of the "exceptional musicians" who "have the stuff in them to occupy the highest positions at once." Through his influence young Strauss became acquainted with Brahms, in whose works he immersed himself, not without some scepticism. (To his father he referred at that time to the "miserable instrumentation" of the symphonies). In 1884 Franz Strauss brought his son's Suite for Wind Instruments to the great conductor's notice, and Bülow insisted that the young composer himself should conduct the world première, which was given in Munich by the Meiningen Court Orchestra. Lacking any training in conducting, "in a kind of twilight," as he put it, "with the feelings of a sleepwalker," Strauss carried out his task, coming out of the affair very creditably. When it became necessary to find a reliable deputy for the frequently absent Court Conductor, Bülow and his "Theatre Duke," the art-loving Georg II, chose the twenty-one-year-old

Strauss. That same autumn, having written to the publisher Spitzweg about "the astonishing certainty with which Strauss at once wielded the baton," the master was able to hand over to his gifted pupil the sole responsibility for the direction of the orchestra. It was from his time at Meiningen, with its atmosphere of vigorous music making, that his reputation as a born conductor dates. Strauss's gratitude to Bülow was expressed in almost idolatrous admiration. In his "Reminiscences of Hans von Bülow" (1919) he described him as the "model of all the shining virtues of the interpretative artist," despite the fact that Bülow, the egocentric, had later cooled off in his attitude to the younger man.

The German-Russian musician Alexander Ritter, who was then at Meiningen, using the powers of persuasion which were part of his nature, drew Strauss into the orbit of his ideal composers Berlioz, Liszt and Wagner. Strauss was indebted to this "New-German" composer of long-forgotten folk operas and symphonic poems, who was leader of the Court Orchestra, for a great deal of intellectual stimulus. "Ritter was extraordinarily well read in all philosophical works, in literature both old and new," Strauss wrote in his autobiographical notes. "His influence was something in the nature of a rushing wind." When Strauss left Meiningen in the spring of 1886 to become third conductor of the Munich Court Opera, Ritter went with him as a devoted colleague. By contrast to Ritter, who remained an adherent of Strauss up to the time of their differences of opinion in connection with "Guntram," Strauss's boyhood friend Thuille was unable to keep pace with his impetuous progress for long. The dedication of "Don Juan" no longer meant much to him. In later years this sensitive musician and teacher of composition set to music two sentimental opera libretti by Otto Julius Bierbaum ("Lobetanz" and "Gugeline") which had originally been intended for Strauss.

*

Some of the great composers have demonstrated all the facets of their personal style in their youth—this was so in the cases of such masters as Mozart, Mendelssohn and Verdi. On the other hand there are musicians who abound in talent, but who succeed only gradually in filling the outward forms of music with contents of really deep significance; the young Richard Strauss undoubtedly belonged to the second category. The opus 1 of the twelve-year-old boy, a "Festmarsch" for orchestra which was printed by Breitkopf & Härtel on behalf of his uncle Georg Pschorr (who no doubt felt honoured by the dedication to himself), and such early chamber music as the String Quartet in A major, the Cello Sonata and the Five Piano Pieces give no hint of the "progressive" element in German music of that period. This music possesses considerable melodic warmth, but its waters are still unruffled, and it follows traditional classical-romantic lines. In view of the shortage of good cello music a thought should be spared occasionally for the Cello Sonata (at whose first performance at Dresden in December 1883 with the composer at the piano he made his first contact with what was later to be the city of Strauss premières). The delightful Serenade in E♭ for 13 wind instruments, inspired by Mozart, a short piece which skilfully exploits the varied colour values of the wind instruments, is also to be met with occasionally in the concert hall; it is quite impossible to detect the composer of "Salome" in its tradition-based musical language. The Suite for 13 wind instruments (which was not published until 1911), with its evident joy in music making, represents a clear step forward. Critical opinion was first divided to any great extent in connection with the musically fresh Violin Concerto, which was played for the first time by Strauss's teacher Benno Walter, and whose preliminary sketches the young composer had noted down in his mathematics exercise book. While some valued its enchanting, elegant virtuosity, and even Hanslick referred to "unusual talent," it appeared to others too superficially rapturous in its melodies. Stylistically related to this work is the Violin Sonata in E♭ dating from the period when Strauss was in Munich as a conductor. This piece, which is still effective today, owes more than usual to Schumann, while its delicately-felt Notturno is distinguished by its Chopinesque poetry.

Strauss's student years also saw the composition of the Eight Songs to texts by Gilm, the First Horn Concerto in E♭, and the Symphony in F minor. The songs included the first "popular successes" of the young Strauss, who was then only eighteen: "Zueignung" and "Allerseelen." The Concerto, written as a tribute to the great skill of his father (60 years later Strauss composed a second work of this type) is an early example of certainty in the creation of fine melody, and it shows a genuine sense of form, savouring to the full a feeling for the sounds of nature reminiscent of Weber. The songlike themes are characteristic of the later Strauss in their soaring breadth of conception. The Symphony, which found a friendly advocate in Bülow (". . . really very important, original, formally mature"), still lacks the Straussian tonal idiom; what it says is not strikingly unusual, but it says it in an attractive manner. A work which takes a worthy place in the sphere of late-romantic chamber music yet which gives an indication of many things to come in the naturalness of its music-making and the splendid verve of its expressive language is the Piano Quartet in C minor. The twenty-year-old composer submitted it in a competition arranged by the Berlin Tonkünstlerverein, and it won the first prize. Strauss's partiality to deriving inspiration for his instrumental and vocal works from the realm of literature is demonstrated in his early "Wandrers Sturmlied" after the poem by Goethe– "a work constructed in the manner of Brahms, in which conscious use is made of conventional ideas" (Rolland). It is characteristic of that early period, which bore witness to certainty of craftsmanship rather than independence of ideas. Nevertheless it points forward to the harshness of "Macbeth," and its conclusion ("Sehr ruhig"–very calm) suggests the rapture of "Don Juan."

It was not until four years after its composition at Meiningen that Strauss let his friends see the *"Burleske"* for piano and orchestra. He gave the first information about this work in a letter written to his parents in November 1885; writing later to his mother he referred to it for the sake of simplicity as his "Piano Concerto." This, the only one of the youthful works written in the traditional form of a sonata movement to hold its own among the instrumental works of the following years, was not as personal as the later tone poems, but was their equal in the embodiment of high spirits and virtuosity; the manner in which the specifically Straussian element makes itself felt above the still strongly Brahmsian basis of the work is most fascinating. (The keen-eared listener will notice in the last bars of a solo cadenza the motif of "Liebessehnsucht" from "Tristan"–a first hint of the coming approach to Wagner.) The piquant charm of the solo part, with the cheerful competition of four timpani and orchestra, has made the "Burleske" a pianistic showpiece. This work owes its personality to the sprightly, dancelike first theme of the timpani, which recurs again and again throughout the piece, sometimes boldly assertative, sometimes fluttering gracefully. Von Bülow, for whom the work was written, at first declared it to be unplayable. "Every bar a different position of the hand; do you think I'm going to sit down for a month to study so refractory a piece?" But Eugen d'Albert, to whom it was finally dedicated, mastered it easily. His experiences with the "Burleske," which Strauss once described as "pure nonsense," declaring later that it was "miserably orchestrated," and to which he gave no opus number, hardly served to encourage the young composer. A Rhapsody in C♯ minor for piano and orchestra, on which he had begun work at Meiningen, remained unfinished.

*

So the musical characteristics of Richard Strauss, the thoughtful craftsman in touch with the world around, were relatively quickly established. In contrast to the narrowly provincial background against which Mahler and Reger grew up, Strauss was soon aware of the artistic aspirations within the community of the South German cultural metropolis, the seat of a music-loving royal dynasty. During the period of his life spent under the careful guidance of his parents the young artist, who received friendly encouragement from all sides, met more great intellectual figures than others did during a whole lifetime. It is doubtful, though, whether he came into contact with the political and social movements of his day. Certainly Strauss learned the meaning of hardship in his contacts with friends of his youth. The hitherto rather uncritical romanticist, whose thoughts were in field, wood and meadow, unexpectedly developed into a musician with ideas of his own concerning art and the world, who attracted the attention of the musical experts. A "Richard III," as Bülow jokingly called him. ("There is no II"). A portent.

"THE GREAT OPPORTUNIST"

FUNDAMENTALLY A MAN OF THIS WORLD: SO RICHARD
Strauss presents himself to later generations. His was a musical
life built on middle-class foundations. The last great composer
of a dying epoch (though not lacking in self-irony), the wholesale exporter of German musical concepts for a great many years,
the man through whom European music of his time leaped
ahead of all the other arts, may undoubtedly be considered the
standard bearer of his day. He was its representative. He was
not, however, an active force influencing the course of historical
events at the time when capitalism entered into the last stages of
imperialism. He represented international prestige and middle-
class artistic craftsmanship—no burning cultural ideal such as
Wagner's aspiration toward a national theatre, or Verdi's toward Italian unity. With him the centre of the stage was occupied
by the work itself, a shining monument to creative power in music. As in the case of almost every other musician of the late romantic age, the signs of conservatism, of links with the old order,
were stronger in Strauss than were those of the forward-driving
impulse of progressive society fighting for the future. In a bourgeois world ruled by the profit motive he created his intellec-
tual-material existence. While the world declined into chaos he
built up what was, all in all, impregnable security for himself
and his work.

It was Mahler who first described Strauss as the *"great opportunist"*–not without justification. His life was perfectly ordered, divided without effort between the two poles of a very
full career as an international conductor, and the Buon Retiro
of his country house at Garmisch. He was remarkably receptive
to events around him, and extremely good at adapting himself
to changed circumstances. He was the musician in tune with the

39

times, carried forward by the momentum of the world around him. Strauss observed everything that went on in the realm of European art from Paris to Moscow, and assessed its value to himself. Everything on the intellectual-philosophical horizon reached him either through personal conversation or through the medium of literature. At every period of his long life he was (sometimes without appreciating the consequences) in accord with his times. To turn his back completely on a State system with which he was out of sympathy would have been foreign to his conciliatory nature. The fact that he did not degenerate into a spineless slave of his times was due to his independence of the fashions and moral judgements of the age. He did not, as a musician, succumb to the temptations of the morbidly reactionary state of society, thanks to the dithyrambic verve of "Don Juan" and "Ariadne," the healthy power of "Rosenkavalier" and the scintillating spiritual qualities of "Don Quixote" and "Capriccio." Strauss was altogether unique.

In what light did he see the world? He did not despise it with that repudiation of material things characteristic of the bourgeois intelligentsia of that epoch. He saw the world without illusions, as he sought to create a *"colourful reflection of life."* ("In its colourful reflection we have life" says Faust). What he depicted in his operas and tone poems sprang from vital, sensuous observation. He accepted fully Hofmannsthal's saying that "Man perceives in the world only what is already in him, but he needs the world in order to perceive *what* is in him: however, action and suffering are necessary to that." In Strauss's case these ideas found expression in the boldly asserted principle of the late-romantic psychological attitude to music, which places the subjective experience rather than the universally valid idea at the centre of the picture. Even the individualistic artist Strauss felt the importance of playing his part in the "education of mankind" in Goethe's sense; his contribution to the "destiny of Germany" lay, as he wrote during the last months of his life (to Julius Kopsch), referring to a widely-read book on Goethe, not in the active political field but in his work. His aim was to use this work to help better the world. His idealistic artistic purpose led him to the conclusion that the only purpose of this life was, in his own words, "to make art possible." The finest fruits of this outlook on life are the human warmth and the living fire which glow through his works. Not for long did he seek to reconcile freedom of expression and receptiveness to spiritual things with the comfortable materialism of a dying bourgeois world. Strauss would not have developed, during the years prior to the First World War, into the great humanist of "Ariadne" and above all of "Frau ohne Schatten" had he remained rooted to the paucity of ideas of certain of his early tone poems and operas. He overcame the "sluggish stream of the time," to quote the significant words of one of the Hölderlin Hymns.

Flight from mankind, a typical characteristic of the age of "l'art pour l'art," was foreign to this composer whose mind was open to all living things. He was concerned with speaking to the *whole* human being. He criticized the theories of those followers of Schoenberg who allowed their twelve-tone compositions to become a purely private matter among themselves, and he had nothing in common with the strange individualists who were indifferent to the question of whether their artistic message was understood by the public. Quite rightly Strauss, a composer of this world, did not write *against* the public as the abstract and formalistic artists did; he wrote *for* his listeners. He was concerned with what Thomas Mann propounded in his "Doktor Faustus" as the possible new aim of musical aesthetics: to free music from its "splendid isolation," to remove it from its "lonely contact with an educated elite, the 'public', and to find the way to mankind." The fact that a series of special trains had to be run from Berlin, Leipzig and Prague for the Dresden performances of "Rosenkavalier" in 1911, and that evening after evening thousands of people flocked to the box office when his popular operas were to be performed, interested Strauss in all its social implications. It was quite clear to him that the growth of opera required the participation of *all* classes of society. The introduction which Strauss wrote in 1903 for the first number of the series "Die Musik" which he edited ("Beethoven" by Göllerich) has the character of a profession of faith: "Art is an artificial product," he wrote. "Its mission is not to lead a self-satisfied, isolated existence in accordance with arbitary laws, or those which were formulated merely to fulfil a temporary need but which were later proclaimed to be 'eternal'; its natural purpose is rather to testify to the culture of ages and peoples." Strauss attacked the pale aesthetes "to whom only outward, formalistic

41

things are accessible, while (short-sighted through their lack of productivity) they either completely ignore what is really important or pay only very superficial attention to it." He declared the "error of those who regard as the essential element of music only a more or less mechanical formalism" to have been overcome, and concluded: "The fact of the direct relationship between life and art has been demonstrated irrefutably by the lives of the great masters and by their masterpieces."

Anyone who reads today Strauss's essay "Is there a progressive party in music?," which had an alarming effect when it appeared in 1907, must consider the artistic-political circumstances of that time. "Welcome to all who 'strive and exert themselves'" –but beware all those who seem to need a fashionable catchphrase, referred to by Strauss as "tempting titles such as 'Leader of the modernists' or 'Head of the Progressive Party'." ... Strauss answered the question posed by his title with a clear No. "Even the close circle of Wagnerians were merely a group of like-thinking disciples whose aim was to explain and propagate the master's ideas, to eliminate misunderstandings, to rouse those who were indifferent, to confirm those of good will in their opinions, and to drive opponents away. In the event, however, these partisans have been unable to turn progress in the way they intended, as the driving and in the last analysis decisive force, which helped Richard Wagner, like every other great innovator, to final victory, was the great mass of the ordinary public. In its natural, untrained receptiveness to every new and significant artistic achievement it has generally proved itself the reliable supporter of every progressive idea ... provided that is has not become prejudiced through bitter criticism or the machinations of rivals. . . . In view of the fact, repeatedly confirmed by history, that a great artistic figure is accepted instinctively by the general public almost as a fact of nature, although they may not form any clear idea of his aims, the activities of any small group of experts forming what might be described as a progressive party are not of decisive importance."

He wrote later: "The principal consideration is the compelling contact between the creative genius and the *mass* of people ranging far ahead of any party or group. One should only beware of becoming confused by the fact that the same broad public gives as much tumultuous applause to things which are effort-

42

lessly pleasing, easily understandable and even banal as it gives
to works which are artistically significant, novel, and ahead of
their time. The public has, in fact, two souls. It has not, however,
a third—for the public has not the slightest understanding of, or
interest in, art which is neither immediately accessible nor compelling to an outstanding degree. That is the reason for the many
disappointments of earnestly striving artists whose enemies cannot accuse them of banality, while their friends cannot claim
that they possess a great deal of really compelling power . . ."
In view of such opinions what is one likely to think about the
origins of Strauss's more popular-sounding melodic ideas, his
"melodious lumps of sugar?" Did he not in fact compose, as he
once wrote to Fritz Busch (apologizing for the saccharine sweetness of the Db major melody of Da-ud in "Die ägyptische Helena") quite consciously for the *broad public?* "Believe me, the
ordinary people wouldn't go to 'Tannhäuser' if it didn't contain 'O star of eve'." What Leopold Mozart wrote in the album
of the young Salzburg genius: "You must be popular!" was also,
fortunately, taken to heart by Strauss. However, in his case this
had nothing to do with a "calculation of effect," doing violence
to his talent merely "to please the public," against which Tschaikowsky warned Nadeshda von Meck in one of his letters. Quite
apart from statements of his intentions made privately, it is
clear from Strauss's music that it needs to appeal to large numbers of listeners. Unfortunately, however, his choice of opera
libretti repeatedly led him into the realm of mythological symbolism, which remains a closed book to the masses. That involved
his creative work in a conflict which was insoluble.

It was impossible for Strauss, in an age of contradictions, to
arrive at a clear estimation of the relationship between *art and
the people,* between the ideological preparation and the practical realization of a project. He had no certain knowledge of
the fact that the class struggle of the proletariat would create
a social order leading to an entirely new relationship between
cultural riches and the working man. He saw only the prosperous patrons of the arts, intoxicated by their successes in capital-
istic speculation, and the bourgeoisie following admiringly in
their footsteps; his eyes were closed to the historic role of the
working class. But at least Strauss owed a great deal to his
knowledge of how ordinary people think and feel; at least he

was conscious of the doubtful value of a society which made much of its "culture," but which, in its easy-going complacency, actually represented the negation of progress ... (How aptly the aged composer described the contrasts between different theatre-goers in a letter to Joseph Gregor. He wrote scathingly of Frau Alphonse Rothschild in Vienna, who "saw one of the silliest operettas thirty-two times in one winter," while "my chauffeur and Anna the housekeeper prefer 'Die Meistersinger' to 'The Merry Widow' if they have the choice.") Could Strauss doubt the fact that every artistic concept was bound to penetrate the sphere of social economics? Practical experience proved irrefutably that a great many of his operas and orchestral works, whose intellectual-musical structure had been related to the characteristics of bourgeois society under the Kaiser and the Weimar Republic, were able to achieve wide popularity and international standing to a surprising degree.

The young artist who, after the elemental breakthrough of "Don Juan," had turned to Schopenhauer, Nietzsche and Stirner, who had created "Guntram" and "Zarathustra," soon freed himself from the tragic pessimism of those philosophers of a dying century. He was not in the least degree attracted to Gobineau's racial theory, or to the "purifying force" of the mystical Wagner in "Parsifal" (which he valued highly only as a musical work). From then on nothing affected, gloomily meditative or sickly was characteristic of the young Strauss. The same Nietzsche whose ideas had strongly influenced him at first now saw in Strauss "one of those who have all the attributes of the modern soul, but who are strong enough to make them wholesome." The experience of classical civilization came to mean more and more to him. The world of antiquity, Goethe's Weimar, and the consummate romanticism of "Tristan"–those were his new ideals. Through his whole career we can trace a line of development which changed him from a revolutionary intoxicated with new-found sensuous power at the turn of the century into the classicist, recalling Goethe, of his full maturity. In Strauss's attitude to life his acceptance of the laws of *classical beauty,* of the ideals of Winckelmann and the formal concepts of Goethe, became increasingly evident, combined with a critical attitude to the culture of his own day. During his last years, too, he frequently referred to Plato's world of ideas, the "origins of forms projected into the visible world." His work had its own foundations.

Where did Strauss stand with regard to *religion?* Christianity meant hardly anything to him. "While I was in Egypt I became acquainted with the works of Nietzsche, whose polemic against the Christian religion seemed to come to me straight from the heart. Ever since my fifteenth year I had had an unconscious antipathy toward that religion, which frees its followers (through confession) from responsibility for their actions, and I now found this antipathy strengthened and given solid foundations," he wrote in the papers left behind at his death. The young musical dramatist gave clear expression to this attitude in "Guntram." When Guntram says: "My life is governed by the law of my spirit. My God speaks to me only through myself" he is expressing, to a great degree, the ideas of the freethinking poet-composer. It is not mere chance that not a single sacred composition exists among all his works. Only in the "Deutsche Motette" did Strauss, completely in sympathy with the mildly devotional words of Rückert: "Creation has gone to rest, O watch in me," sing with pious conviction. He had no personal interest in the "chaste Joseph, who seeks God" in "Josephslegende," and it was difficult for him to find music for anything he considered boring. It is only in the "adoration of eternal, glorious nature" that we can find religion in Strauss. (He intended originally to follow the impressions of nature in the "Alpensinfonie" by a second part devoted to spiritual impressions, an "Antichrist"). Those who are familiar with "Daphne" know that its loveliest music springs from an inner sense of the omnipotence of nature. During the correspondence which Strauss exchanged with Hofmannsthal over a period of thirty years the Christian (and thus the religious) element is completely excluded by that of classical paganism—just as there is no reference to the ideas of socialism. To an ever increasing extent Strauss was possessed by the "longing for Hellenism," the Grecian sense of life, Greek mythology and the Grecian landscape, which not only determined his thinking, but became what was virtually a religion to him. It is in relation to this avowal of a "religion of classicism" (in the sense of the book by Leopold Ziegler) that we should consider the aphorism which the aged Strauss wrote in a book on Nietzsche and Burckhardt which he had borrowed from Schuh: "Christianity had to be invented in order that, following Phidias, the Kolmar Altar could be fashioned, the Sistine Chapel painted, and the 'Missa solemnis' and 'Parsifal' written." There is no need of more than a passing reference to the fact that Strauss was not a member of any religious denomination at the time of his death. The Creator spiritus lived in his music.

The "opportunist" could also act "inopportunely." One of the most attractive characteristics of this composer, whose financial security was assured even in his early years, was the fact that his sense of justice impelled him to protest against failures to appreciate past genius. When Wagner's autobiography was published in 1911 Strauss wrote about it to Hofmannsthal: "A really gripping book, which one cannot put down without being moved. What creative power despite a really desperate life, whose course represents one of the darkest chapters in German cultural history!" It was certainly not to be taken as a matter of course that the Munich Court Conductor and General Musical Director to Kaiser Wilhelm II should take an active interest in the plight of the working class, and should be one of the first to turn to the new *Soziallyrik* of the 'nineties as inspiration for some of his songs. Nor was that all: the young Court Conductor did not hesitate to perform these challenging songs "Der Arbeitsmann" ("We have a bed, we have a child, my wife"), the "Lied an meinen Sohn" and "Lied des Steinklopfers" to words by Dehmel and Henckell in public with Ludwig Wüllner—to the horror of certain circles. Naturally enough the comfortably-situated relation of the rich Munich brewer Pschorr did not become a socialist, but he had a sense of social justice; petty, narrow-minded thinking was abhorrent to him. Undoubtedly, too, the famous composer and conductor was shown in a favourable light by the fact that in an essay written at that time he vigorously supported the claims then being made by orchestral musicians. "Has anyone ever been heard to refer in Parliament to the overwork and starvation wages of our worthy orchestral players and chorus singers?" Later on, as director of the Vienna State Opera from 1919 until 1924, Strauss remained true to the idea that all who worked for the Opera were his colleagues. When he took up office, and Franz Schalk greeted him in the presence of the entire company, Strauss replied in these highly characteristic words: "Above all I am grateful for the trust in me which you have expressed ... I will strive with all the influence I possess to improve and safeguard your social status, and to bring about the fulfilment of your demands, especially the claims of those who now have to contend with hardship: the orchestra, chorus, ballet and stage staff ..." It is tragic to recall that Strauss was finally forced out of his work in Vienna, where he had always been conscious of his responsibility, by the opposition of petty bureaucracy. His resignation came shortly after his sixtieth birthday, principally as a result of official refusal to provide a rehearsal stage and a storehouse for scenery. On account of a rehearsal stage ... Was Strauss embittered? It almost seemed as though he were not: "Now I ask you only to believe that I am neither angry nor bitter, but always remember with the greatest pleasure the happy hours which I have been allowed to spend in artistic labours at the State Opera ..."

Although Strauss had no lack of work in his dual functions as a creative and interpretative artist, he took up most energetically at the turn of the century the question of obtaining better protection of authors' rights for German composers. Was he concerned only with his personal interests in this long-drawn-out affair, which was to assure creative musicians of their independence, so that they became free from parasitic patrons and speculators, and all the "blessings" of the capitalist system? Strauss knew perfectly well that there were thousands of people in the world of music who were growing rich solely as the result of the labour of others. The foundation of the *"Genossenschaft deutscher Tonsetzer,"* which he undertook in conjunction with his old friend the lawyer and musician Friedrich Rösch, together with Hans Sommer, in 1898, was an important step forward toward providing material security for the independent creative musician. Only gradually did those of Strauss's colleagues who at first felt themselves threatened recognize the social purpose of the new copyright law which Strauss and Rösch proposed to the Reichstag. Only gradually did the two men, with their broad view of artistic sociology, gain understanding for their pioneering work in a hitherto neglected field–a progressive action which helped to release the creative musician from the hands of profiteers. Until that time the publishers had been accustomed to purchasing artistic works lock, stock and barrel, to become their own property. Strauss, fighting as a champion of the rights of

47

composers (the parliamentarian Eugen Richter had railled at him as a "musical agrarian"), stood at that time in the forefront of the movement for social advance in his profession. There was in fact a parallel: "Worker against employer, creative artist against publisher" (Kopsch). "While the goal of the manual workers was to obtain real influence over their social conditions by the free exercise of their capacity to work, so the intellectual creative workers, headed by the composers under the leadership of Richard Strauss, also sought the right to dispose of the fruits of their labours as they wished, in order to build a firm foundation for their existence amid the turbulent economic conditions of the day."

There could be no doubt that material things were here being made to serve spiritual ends. One does not become a composer in order to make money, but it is necessary to earn sufficient money if one is to be a composer. It was, however, inevitable in the long run that the ideas of the commercial music "trade" of the Kaiser's Empire should infect the musicians in their struggle for professional security. The battle was renewed and intensified in 1903 on the founding of the "AFMA" (Institute for musical performing rights, which was set up in conjunction with the "Genossenschaft" to deal with the regulation of royalties), and especially in 1915 at the birth of "GEMA" (Society for the distribution of musical performing rights). The task now was to break down the resistance of the publishers and concert agents. The publishers, in particular, would not agree that all members, not the individual, should have the advantage of performing rights. When Rösch died before his time in 1925 Strauss spoke these words at his graveside: "Rösch has struggled with the lawgivers for the rights of German composers, and it is to him they owe their dignity and their independence in dealing with publishers ... We can repay him only by carrying on the work in accordance with his intentions, never losing sight of the goal which he pointed out to us, and never diverging an inch from the road he marked out."

The goal toward which the "Genossenschaft" had been struggling ever since its foundation was the extension of the period for which a work was protected by copyright to fifty years. Even in 1928 when an international conference was held in Rome neither the German government nor the publishers could be per-

The composer of "Don Juan"
Painting by Leopold von Kalckreuth (1889)

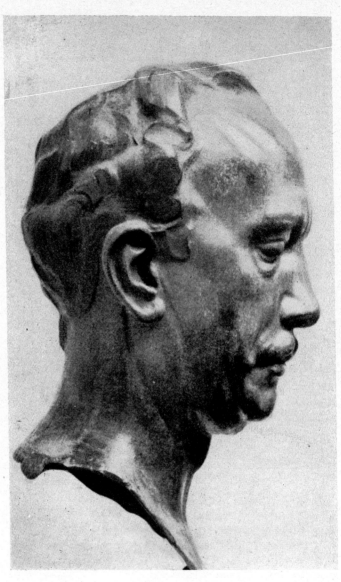

At the turn of the century
Bust by Hugo Lederer (1903)

suaded to agree to the wishes of the composers. After a delay of half a century the period of copyright protection in Germany was finally altered to conform to the Berne Convention at the end of 1934. Julius Kopsch gave an authentic account of the circumstances in which this step, highly important to the German composers, was taken: "At the 1934 Bayreuth Festival Strauss conducted 'Parsifal', and Hitler, who attended one of the performances, took the opportunity to establish contact with the foremost musician of Germany. He asked Strauss to tell him what he wanted in his professional capacity. Strauss demanded: 1. the introduction of the fifty year copyright protection period in Germany, 2. a guarantee by law that 'Parsifal' was to be performed only at Bayreuth, in accordance with Wagner's wishes, and 3. effective protection against the mutilation of important artistic works by unscrupulous arrangers and plunderers... Strauss at once phoned me from Bayreuth and asked me to draft a law to cover the third point he had raised. The question of the extension of the copyright period was taken up energetically by the Ministry of Propaganda, on Hitler's instructions. I soon learned, however, that the wily minister was preparing a solution of the problem which would serve only his *own* interests: the period of protection was to be extended from 30 to 50 years, but the royalties for the additional years would be paid not to the composers' estates but to a special fund set up and administered by the Ministry of Propaganda." The fact that Strauss finally obtained what he wanted was due partly to his energetic handling of the affair, partly to his skilful tactics. During a conversation the Bavarian Minister of Justice Frank pointed out how difficult it would be to obtain what Strauss wanted from Hitler against the wishes of Goebbels. There was, however, one argument which would undoubtedly be decisive with Hitler: the information that the Nazis had once pressed for the extension of the period of copyright protection in the Reichstag *before* their seizure of power. And so it was. The fifty year protection period became law in Germany without a parliamentary debate, and Strauss's "second life's work" had been crowned with success.

The importance which Strauss placed on the question of the legal protection of artistic works against damaging exploitation is also emphasized by the appeal which he published during the 'thirties: "With regard to the protection of the material interests of authors improvements have been effected ... On the other hand it must be emphasized that the protection of their artistic works themselves still leaves much to be desired. A work of art should be inviolable. Therefore the proposed protection of the rightful personal interests of the work's author is not sufficient; we demand that the same period of protection shall be enjoyed by the work of art itself, so that the spiritual riches of our people and of other nations will be preserved inviolate. This demand is concerned with protection against distorting arrangements, against mutilation of any other kind, against plagiarism and the theft of the ideas of others for financial gain. Exploitation of works of art is theft of the nation's spiritual wealth, and must be punishable as such ..." Words of gold, which are still valid today! "As long as something like 'Lilac Time' is possible no one can say that composers have any real protection," he used to say.

Another source of controversy was the annual festival of the "ADMV" (General German Musical Association), founded by Liszt in 1861. Here again it was Strauss who succeeded in reversing the hitherto conservative policy in the choice of modern works to be performed, so that the original intention of the Association's statute to "further the progressive development of German musical life" would be honoured. A comparison between the names of the unknown composers whose works were played at previous festivals and those represented after Strauss had been elected as President in 1901 shows the extent of the change. Mahler, Reger, Pfitzner, Schillings and many others had works performed at the festivals, and Strauss's helpful attitude was of great assistance to them. He also exerted himself on behalf of contemporary composers in connection with the "Modern Concerts" which he gave with the "Tonkünstler Orchester" in Berlin. How free from critical arrogance, how considerate his views were on the work of another composer (in this case only a second-rate talent) can be seen from these words: "Let time be the judge! No matter if a man is over-praised—it is better for twenty to be regarded too highly than for one to have the way barred to him. The main thing is that a man has the will and ability to do something..." He was gratified to know that he had "brought a few able young talents into the light of day" ... No one was surprised, though, when the immensely busy composer resigned from the presidency of the ADMV after a few years. Even Strauss could not prevent its festivals from becoming to an ever increasing extent the exclusive concern of the connoisseurs.

*

In order to understand why such works as "Don Juan" and "Feuersnot" gave rise to so much perplexity in their early years one must read the childishly agitated reports published at the time of their appearance, reports whose moral indignation seems incomprehensible today. When the young Strauss, inspired by a poem by Lenau, wrote his tone poem "Don Juan" with its impassioned protest against the repression of sensuality by the narrow-minded bigotry of society, there was much turning up of noses in reactionary and Court circles. Then when "Feuersnot" infected the opera house with the poison of the young rebel's "immoral" attack on bigotry and prudery not a few people seemed to despair of Strauss. During the negotiations concerning the world première of this work at the Berlin Court Opera a violent dispute arose between the management and Strauss, who was at that time Court Conductor. The affair ended with an angry letter to the administrative director Pierson (who was later to play an inglorious role in another connection). "In consequence of all these facts I take the liberty of concluding the matter by informing you with respectful thanks that I hereby renounce once and for all both the honour of having 'Feuersnot' performed for the first time at the Berlin Opera House, and also the distinction of seeing any of my other dramatic works presented there." Strauss transferred the right to give the world première to the energetic Ernst von Schuch in Dresden, and he stood by his refusal to offer the first showing of any of his later operas to Berlin. He recognized clearly the great advantages of the Dresden Opera as the place for world premières. Especially after the death of the Jesuitically-minded King Georg of Saxony, conditions in Dresden were very encouraging for modern developments in the theatre and in the arts generally. In addition the atmosphere of Dresden, where the arts were really appreciated, seemed far more propitious for a Strauss première than that of the metropolis of Berlin. Following the "Feuersnot" episode, in 1902, the Empress, narrow-minded in her rigidly pious outlook, even pressed for Strauss's dismissal. The young musical dramatist had also to fight in Dresden against many objections on professedly moral grounds. Shortly before the first performance he felt obliged to address this appeal to Schuch: "Please do not tone anything down. To take away the opera's sharp teeth would be to invite a 'success through misunderstanding'. I gladly renounce that: rather a resounding failure with a few good coarsenesses and satisfying smacks in the eye for the whole pack of philistines, to purify the brain and the gall . . ."

Strauss's relationship to the former Imperial Court represents a chapter of its own in his life. The foremost musician of the "German Reich" had no very high opinion of the Hohenzollerns. He could afford to remain outside the sunshine of the Kaiser's favour, sunshine in which many people now forgotten basked. He calmly ignored the Kaiser's well-known remark "The whole movement doesn't suit me," and he made no secret of the fact that he for his part had little sympathy with the official taste in artistic matters (the Kaiser was enraptured by Meyerbeer's "L'Etoile du Nord"). There was a wide gulf between the narrow-minded puritanism of the Court clique and Strauss's free outlook on life. Only once, having been persuaded by the Crown Prince, did the Kaiser attend a performance of a Strauss opera, "Rosenkavalier," which he left with the words: "That's no music for me!" He was even less able to understand "Salome." After reading the libretto he said to his opera director Georg Hülsen-Haeseler: "I'm sorry that Strauss has composed this 'Salome'; apart from this I like him very much, but he will do himself *terrible* damage with it." (To which Strauss added in his "Recollections:" "The proceeds from that 'damage' enabled me to build my villa at Garmisch.") The Kaiser permitted "Salome" to be performed at the Berlin Court Opera only after Hülsen had conceived the "brilliant" idea of showing the Star of Bethlehem rising in the night sky at the end of the work, in order to placate sensitive tastes. As though the Princess of Judaea turned into a Christmas fairy! The Kaiser's reaction to "Elektra" was also worth mentioning. An aide-de-camp of the Kaiser sent one of the fiercely critical reviews which this latest "shocking" work of its composer had received to the opera director, with the covering note: "H. M. believes that you agree with this man."

The experiences with "Rosenkavalier" at the Court Operas in Dresden and Berlin were tragi-comic. Scarcely was the brilliantly successful Dresden première over when Schuch decided to make wholesale cuts in the bawdy narrative of Ochs, and these cuts were also made in Berlin. Strauss's protest was of a forcefulness which left nothing to be desired. "This is no way to treat an artist. This is the sort of treatment meted out by a sergeant major of the guards ... You write that the cuts in 'Rosenkavalier' amount to only fifteen minutes. Is it worth destroying the architecture of an artistic work to save fifteen minutes? That's all nonsense, there's really a different reason. A nobleman who behaves on the stage in the way that very many noblemen behave at Court and in country society is not a pleasant spectacle in the eyes of the aristocratic General Director. An imperial chamberlain must not be a common boor. Therefore the cuts. Not because it's too long. Herr von Hülsen has admitted the fact to me" (letter to Schuch) ... But while a sense of proportion was preserved in Dresden, the Kaiser's Court found so many "repulsive" and "dubious" things in Hofmannsthal's libretto that Hülsen begged the master "to run his hand over the whole, toning down and refining." In the end the Director himself set about the task of revising the libretto so as to make it "acceptable for a Court Theatre." What havoc such a large bed might not create in the Imperial mind ... ! It is also strange to recall that at another court theatre the first singer offered the role of the Marschallin asked to be excused from appearing in the "suggestive" atmosphere of this piece.

"I've nourished a fine serpent at my breast" the Kaiser once remarked to Schuch apropos Strauss's "modernity." The Kaiser's acceptance of the dedication of two marches by Strauss, quite unmartial in character, put the coolly correct relationship between the Monarch and his General Musical Director on a more friendly footing for the time being. "Most humbly dedicated to His most gracious Majesty Kaiser Wilhelm II, in deepest homage." This dedication may not have flowed readily from the pen of the generally by no means servile Strauss, who had showed his independence in no uncertain a manner in a letter to the Meiningen Court Chamberlain. However, the Kaiser had to commission his "court operas" in the style of "Roland von Berlin" from Leoncavallo and similar prominent composers of the day.

53

It is a fact that Strauss not only quickly fell in line with the new course taken by the Weimar Republic, but also came to terms with the questionable cultural policy of the Nazi regime in 1933. His social or (to put it more clearly) political conduct appeared open to criticism principally during the first years of the regime, when for a time he undertook the responsibilities of the President of the "Reichsmusikkammer." Almost seventy years of age, he probably believed that by virtue of his authority and his attitude he could work for understanding and conciliation. ("I have accepted the office of President of the Reichsmusikkammer only in order to prevent worse things from happening," he wrote apologetically to Stefan Zweig.) At a time when the very existence of German culture was in the balance, when what was needed was an effective protest against Nazi tyranny such as would have been within Strauss's power to make, his strength of will, like that of so many other artists at that time, failed him. Not until far too late (in the summer of 1935) did he draw the only correct conclusions; from then on he was active only in his capacity as President of the "Permanent Council for the International Association of Composers," founded in 1934. Yet what an unreliable "German Foreign Minister in musicis" he had been! How had Strauss ever been able to come to an understanding with "brownshirt culture?" His difficulties began within the inner circle of his own family: his daughter-in-law and grandchildren suffered under the Nazi racial laws, as did his Jewish friends, his publisher, and many other fellow-workers. Nazi decrees had begun to affect his life and work in many ways, often petty but most disturbing, and he was compelled to recognize them as manifestations of a State fundamentally opposed to culture. The extent to which Strauss had, in his own mind, cut himself off from the Nazis even as early as the autumn of 1934 is shown by a letter he wrote to Kopsch: " I cannot possibly be in Berlin on the 16th October. In any case nothing will come of these meetings. I hear that the paragraph concerning Aryans is to be tightened up, and 'Carmen' banned! In any event I, as a creative artist, do not wish to take an active part in any further foolishness of this kind ... My time is too precious for me to waste it by associating myself with this amateurish nonsense."

Would the Nazis accept the fact that the foremost musician

of Germany had chosen as the librettist of his latest comic opera "Die schweigsame Frau" the "non-Aryan" Stefan Zweig, to be the successor of Hofmannsthal (who had died in 1929)? Strauss soon began to realize how much opposition the opera and its first production would have to contend with. As Zweig wrote in his memoirs: "The party leaders put off coming to a decision as long as they possibly could, but at the beginning of 1935 they had to make up their minds once and for all whether to go against their own law or against the greatest musician of the age. The full score, vocal scores and libretti had long since been printed, the costumes had been ordered by the Dresden State Opera, the casting was complete and the work had even been rehearsed, yet the conflict of opinions was still unresolved. Although it may seem like a mad dream, the 'Schweigsame Frau' affair finally became a national sensation." Probably in order to avoid laying himself open to ridicule abroad, Hitler finally gave permission for the world première to take place at Dresden in the summer of 1935, but he announced at the last moment that he would not be present. The fact that the Propaganda Ministry ordered Zweig's name to be omitted from the posters and press notices ("Freely adapted from Ben Jonson") spoke for itself. Nevertheless the composer, who at a concert held at Vichy that autumn in memory of Dukas dared to acknowledge the French composer's Jewish blood, and who kept up his correspondence with Jewish friends abroad all through those dark days, saw to it that Zweig's name was printed in its rightful place on the programmes.

The catastrophe followed. A letter which Strauss sent Zweig on the 17th June, under the influence of the unsavoury events which were accompanying the preparations to produce the opera, was intercepted by the Gestapo on its way to Marienbad. It contained unmistakable expressions of strong distate for the newly appointed management of the Dresden Opera and for the Nazi regime. Strauss had stated quite categorically that he would not allow himself to be overruled by anyone in artistic matters which were his concern, and had insisted that Zweig should also write the libretto for his next opera. This ominous letter contained the following passage: "Do you believe I have ever, in any of my activities, been motivated by that fact that I am—perhaps, qui le sait?—of pure German blood? Do you

55

think Mozart consciously composed 'Aryan' music? To me there are only two classes of people: those with talent and those with none." The consequences were drastic: not only was "Die schweigsame Frau" taken off after the third performance in Dresden, but everywhere else, too, this "silent woman" was silenced in earnest, and had to go into the "concentration camp of the Reichstheaterkammer" (Strauss). Bitterly resentful and gnashing his teeth, a prisoner of his own bourgeois freedom, the deeply offended composer let the course of events, and the degradation which they represented for him, flow over him. A giant brought down by dwarfs! "Things have come to a sorry pass when an artist of my standing has to ask a cub of a minister what he is permitted to compose and perform. I feel I belong among servants and waiters, and almost envy my Stefan Zweig who is being persecuted on account of his race," wrote Strauss in a testamentary note which dates from shortly after the world première. He wrote to the Viennese cultural historian Joseph Gregor: "Moreover I am so depressed in spirit that I doubt whether I shall ever be able to compose another note..." The fact that the master determined to treat his librettist with the respect and consideration due to him is demonstrated by his approach to Zweig for a new opera libretto. "You are my librettist and remain my librettist"–a loyal effort which was given up only when the endangered writer withdrew of his own accord. Even when, on Zweig's recommendation, Gregor became his successor, help and advice was sought of the persona ingrate. Right up to the time of "Danae" and "Capriccio" Zweig influenced the construction of the libretti.

The "Schweigsame Frau" affair marked the beginning of a policy of reticence in official circles concerning everything said and done by the aged composer. On the other hand Strauss, who had regained his freedom of spirit, chose the path of Lavieren, and was glad to know that his works were still performed in the Third Reich, where opera was in high favour. "The world looks rather different from the picture of it which you see in your study at Garmisch, Herr Dr. Strauss," the mistrustful Goebbels is said to have remarked. "Unfortunately," replied Strauss, "unfortunately it does look different..." Some time later, when the composer asked, on account of his great age, that air-raid victims should not be billetted in his house, and the local Nazi leader pointed out how many refugees from bombing there were, Strauss replied: "If I'd had my way no one would have had to die . . . !" The extent to which relations between him and the Nazi regime had become strained was evident at the time of Strauss's 80th birthday, which passed off very quietly indeed by comparison with other cultural "events" of that period. Only in Vienna and Dresden were unofficial Strauss birthday performances given on the initiative of Furtwängler, and the music critics were instructed by the authorities to write only about the works, not the personality of the man who was being "honoured." (Siegfried Melchinger threw some light on the macabre scene at that time: "A special performance was given in Vienna in 1944 to mark Strauss's 80th birthday. At the end of the performance the crowds pressing to leave the State Opera were not allowed out of the building as 'Reichsleiter' von Schirach had not yet left. I stood hemmed in by a solid wall of people behind the barrier blocking the doorway. Once I turned round, and saw a tall man standing behind me, holding a young boy by each hand. It was Richard Strauss with his grandsons.") From 1943 onward the secret police refused him a permit to enter Switzerland, where he would have liked to live, and was it really nothing but a coincidence that Goebbels ordered all the German and Austrian theatres to close down, in accordance with his "total war" decree, just before the world première of "Die Liebe der Danae" was to have taken place at Salzburg? All that could be given, in August 1944, was a "dress rehearsal before invited guests" . . . The naively despicable way in which the Nazis sought to reduce Strauss's personal standing was demonstrated clearly enough in official publications of the period. For example a book entitled "Men of Germany, 200 pictures and biographies" (published by Ernst Steiniger, Berlin, in 1938) dealt with prominent figures in the national and intellectual life of Germany up to the end of the first world war. The subjects chosen included Bismarck, Krupp and Ludendorff, and among composers Bruckner, Wolf and Reger–but one would search in vain for Strauss, whom Goebbels described as a "decadent neurotic," in their company.

*

Strauss and his opponents . . . Just as he carried the solution of the "Confusion in Music" ad absurdum with his introduction to the magazine "Der Morgen," aimed at Draeseke, so he exposed his critical adversaries to deadly ridicule by means of the discordant music dedicated to them in "Heldenleben." Nowhere else did he lash the deeds and misdeeds of his opponents so mercilessly as in this tone poem. ("Very shrill and penetrating" he marked the complaints of the flutes.) Strauss always had effective means of dealing with such contemporaries, without

"The Hero's Adversaries" (1898)

reacting to "uncomprehending and malicious criticism" in any way that was beneath his dignity. He dealt with Draeseke, Riemann, Louis and Göhler, his embittered foes at the turn of the century, Storck, who fulminated against "Der Rosenkavalier," and in later years with an impatient musical writer in Hamburg, whom he described with bitter irony in a letter to the author written during his last years as "Herr morning-and-evening-editions Hanslick." "Let us go on working in silence!" It is characteristic that even as the young composer of "Taillefer" he remarked apropos Bierbaum's scathing article on this work: "Oh yes, life's very interesting when one views it from *above*" . . . At the age of fifty-seven Strauss gave vent most wittily to his annoyance over certain disagreements in his dealings with music publishers. (Beethoven had called them "poachers"). As Strauss had failed to provide a promised volume of songs, the firm of Bote & Bock threatened a court action. In reply Strauss composed as an "outlet for artistic temperament" his satirical song cycle "Krämerspiegel" (Mirror of Tradesmen) to words by Alfred Kerr, and headed it with a motto which may be freely translated:

> The merchants stifle music's breath,
> A plague throughout the nation.
> Their dealings bring to music *death,*
> To them—*transfiguration.*

The "merchants" were the directors of the company Bote, Bock, Hase and Schott, and their names were referred to directly in the titles of the songs. When these Berlin publishers realized that the piece was a satirical attack on the unscrupulous practices of certain members of their profession they refused point-blank to publish it. (Cassirer brought it out at his own expense in 1921.) In order to settle the matter Strauss provided instead an album containing settings of three songs of Ophelia from "Hamlet", and three pieces from the "Books of the Anger of Rendsch Nameh" from Goethe's "West-östlicher Divan." These songs, uncomfortable, spiky, and as short as possible, expressions of his own lack of sympathy with the post-war period and its greed, are no less revealing of the relationship between the artist and the "art market" at a critical stage in the development of society. "Have I ever told you how to wage war?"

On the opera stage it was really only in "Feuersnot" that Strauss crossed swords with his "adversaries." (Even in the autobiographical "Intermezzo," with its naive self-criticism of the contents and form of marriage, he dealt very gently with the world outside the family.) The satire of "Feuersnot" is directed against a target of no great immediacy to the general listener: the narrow-minded citizens of Strauss's native Munich who had shown a great deal of animosity toward Richard Wagner, and

59

little appreciation for Strauss himself. In a bitter address delivered by Kunrad to the citizens of a Munich of legendary times, the librettist Ernst von Wolzogen included the lines:

> His daring (Wagen) was all too much for you,
> So you drove *Wagner* out of your gates

and continued with a play of words on his own name, emphasizing the hostility of conservative Munich to progress in the arts.

*

Although always in touch with his times, Strauss wrote few works which can be related to day by day political events. After "Feuersnot" he avoided entering the arena of personal or political disputes in his major works. Had he not raised his sights in this way he could scarcely have written such highly artistic works as his greatest operas are—creations whose spiritual message is not always easy to grasp, and which were conceived as music for "connoisseurs and music lovers," to use the expression popular in middle-class artistic circles. Only a few of his large-scale works were written with a view to immediate mass effect such as matched the nationalism and pomposity of the Kaiser's Reich. Apart from the military marches, the Royal and Parade marches and the "Bardengesang" there were only such occasional compositions as the "Festmusik" to mark the golden wedding of the Grand Duke Alexander of Weimar, and the "Feierlicher Einzug" written for the Knights of the Order of St. John. After 1933 the only works written to celebrate events in an increasingly ominous age were the "Japanische Festmusik" for the 2,600th anniversary of the Imperial dynasty of Japan, and the "Olympische Hymne" for the 1936 Olympic Games in Berlin.

On a higher ethical plane Strauss dealt with problems of the stability of human society in his opera "Friedenstag." In his first opera the young author/composer had spoken out on behalf of the idea of *peace* in the song of peace sung by his hero Guntram ("I see peace-in the roseate evening sky it soars aloft on angels' wings, a seraph, protecting lands and seas!"). Then in the summer of 1938, with the world on the brink of another descent into the abyss, the aged composer again posed the question: war or peace? Should war really be the last resort in deciding the destiny of nations? Strauss wanted to show the painful birth of the spirit of peace, after a time of dreadful national chaos and misery, in a single episode of the Thirty Years' War. We share the final struggle of the commandant of a beleaguered and starving town, the bitter determination of the officer who puts his duty before even the desperate plight of the townspeople. However, the fact that peace does not finally have to be achieved by a struggle, but comes out of the blue like a miracle at the last moment, is the great failing of Joseph Gregor's libretto, which is now known to have been derived from an idea of Stefan Zweig. It is ridiculous to link "Friedenstag" with the "National Socialist ethos," as was, unfortunately, done on the occasion of the world première in Munich (Strauss, who was normally very careful in such matters, evidently omitted to demand the removal of the passage in question from the programme book). No one who understands Strauss and his attitude to the question can doubt that what was nearest to his heart in the composition of this work was the apotheosis of peace triumphant over blind heroism... In the case of "Die Liebe der Danae," too, this unique opera, whose subject is the corrupting power of gold in the hands of those who have subjected themselves to it, does not belong ideologically among the works in which the aged composer sought or found a way of escape.

It seems hardly credible today that during the First World War Strauss was so evidently untouched by the stresses of the day that he sank himself in the wholly unreal fairy-tale world of "Die Frau ohne Schatten," wrote a new operatic prologue to his "Ariadne," and finally descended from the heights of artistry to the everyday prose of his private "Intermezzo." Such complete artistic isolation seems astonishing. On closer examination, however, one comes upon personal statements which indicate that Strauss (in contrast to other famous exponents of bourgeois musical culture) regarded the times in a highly critical light. At the beginning of the war, for example, Strauss refused to add his signature to a chauvinistic manifesto put out by the German intellectuals. At that time he wrote to Hofmannsthal (to whom he normally mentioned the war only in passing): "In the midst of all the unpleasantness... of these days assiduous *work* is the only salvation," and "Only working can console us, only working can help us to win through." However, in a revealing letter dating from 1916 in which Strauss wrote of his "great talent for operetta," considering that he could be the "Offenbach of the 20th century," he demanded a "political-satirical parody of the most biting kind" based on the experiences and figures of the First World War–what a bold plan, unfortunately never carried out! Finally the following, written to his friend during the third year of the war, gives a clear picture of Strauss's human and artistic feelings against the background of the times: "It is sad that the mature, serious and artistic purposes of those working diligently must be so greatly influenced by people to whom the 'great times' are only an excuse to bring their own mediocre achievements to the fore, people who see in these times a good opportunity to decry real artists as hollow aesthetes and bad patriots, who forget that during peacetime I wrote my 'Heldenleben,' the 'Bardengesang,' battle songs and military marches, but now remain respectfully silent in the face of the great events, while they, taking advantage of the situation, use patriotism as a cloak under which to further their dilettantish ambitions. It is nauseating to read in the papers about the regeneration of German art twenty years after the most German of artists, Richard Wagner, was being derided as a 'romantic hothead,' and to read how the youth of Germany will return from this 'noble war' purified and strengthened, when in fact we can be glad if the poor wretches, having been cleansed from lice and bugs, and cured of all their diseases, can ever again become accustomed to a life free from slaughter."

However, the finest and clearest proof of Strauss's blameless attitude and frame of mind during the war years is the remarkable letter which he wrote on the 12th February 1917 to Romain Rolland, who was then working for the Red Cross in Switzerland. In this letter to the progressive French writer, whom he later described in a dedication as the "heroic fighter against all infamous forces working for the downfall of Europe," and who responded by calling his friendship with Strauss "one of the greatest gifts which fate has bestowed on me," he wrote: "I am extremely sorry that your health has prevented you from coming to Berne. I am sure that my performances would have given you pleasure, and perhaps 'Ariadne' would have changed to some extent your opinion of German music in general as I see it stated in 'Jean-Christophe.' I hope the warm sun of Lake Geneva will soon restore you to health. I hope to return to Switzerland in May to conduct some Mozart, and perhaps I will have the pleasure of seeing you again. I look forward to a personal conversation with you as a source of joy and comfort, since I have had the satisfaction of seeing from your excellent article in how many points of general human principles we agree, despite the love which each bears for his own fatherland, and his admiration for our brave troops in the field. We artists, in particular, must attempt to retain our ability to recognize beauty and nobility wherever it is to be found, and to serve the cause of *truth,* which will eventually shine as a light through the darkness and the thick web of lies and deceit in which the bemused world now seems to be enmeshed. I have heard from many quarters in Switzerland, to my grief, the most shocking reports of the inhuman treatment of the poor German prisoners of war, who have been subjected to indignities, insults, and even torture by your fellow-countrymen. How different from the treatment of prisoners in Germany, England, or even Italy, from where there have been no complaints! I wish that men like you could create a better and more convincing basis for your personal work of mercy and reconciliation in enemy territory. Wouldn't that give you satisfaction? I have not yet spoken to anyone about this idea, but I believe that with my connections it would be possible to invite you to visit us at Garmisch in the spring, and to enable you to form some impressions of our people in wartime. I have asked the German Embassy in Berne to forward to me any letters which might be sent to me there, so you can simply send your letters there in an outer envelope addressed to the Embassy..." Is that the letter of an artist who, wholly isolated from the world, wants nothing but luxury, and endeavours with his music to provide diversion from the stresses of the war years? How regrettable that the suggested meeting, amid the noise of warfare, destruction, and the hatred of nation against nation, between two great intellectual figures of Germany and France, never took place!

Meanwhile Strauss resumed work on his "Frau ohne Schatten" after a long break. It is revealing to notice how his initial patriotic view of the war (at the end of the sketches for the first act he had written: "Finished on the 20th August 1914, the day of the victory at Saarburg. Hail to our splendid, brave troops!")

very quickly cooled down into an outright rejection of the "accursed war." The profound humanism of this opera cannot in fact be separated from the personal experience of the war years. "The child of pain was born amid sorrow and tribulation during the war, after a certain Bavarian Major D. had shown his human goodness by preventing the premature conscription of my son ... These wartime worries left their mark on the score, especially toward the middle of the third act, in the shape of a certain over-excitement, which finally 'discharged' itself in the melodrama," we read in Strauss's "Recollections." The fact that, unlike Pfitzner's "Palestrina" which dates from the same period, "Die Frau ohne Schatten" is not a work of resignation but of confidence in the happiness and future of mankind, gives this opera a significance far outliving the age of its composition.

This work, with its high aspirations and its message of peace, caused far less surprise to Strauss's contemporaries than the gay Viennese ballet which followed. Certainly there was some justification in regarding Strauss's ballet "Schlagobers" (the Viennese name for whipped cream), written during the hungry days which followed the end of the war, as a sign that the composer was out of touch with the real needs of the period of inflation. ("Surely I have the right to compose the music that suits me ...") Is the situation altered by the fact that Strauss intended to do what he could to help promote a Franco-German alliance by incorporating in his Viennese ballet a liaison between Mlle. Marianne and Michel–a project which was soon given up? The all-too personal "Intermezzo" was also bound to antagonize many people in the difficult early post-war period ... However, Strauss again provided convincing proof of his fine human feeling at the time of the founding of the Weimar Republic, when existing values were overthrown and new artistic aims declared which were contrary to his own intentions. For example in 1920 he wrote an appeal on behalf of the idea of the Salzburg Festival, which included the following statement: "The Salzburg Festspielhaus ... is to be a symbol, full of the light of truth and the reflection of culture ... All Europe will know that our future lies in art, and especially in music ... In these days when the gods of the mind are far fewer than those of material things, and when egoism, envy, hatred and mistrut seem to rule the world, he who supports our proposals will be doing a good work,

Father and Son (1904)

At the conductor's desk of the Vienna Opera
Etching by Alois Kolb (1920)

and contributing substantially toward the revival of brother-
liness and love of our neighbour."

By the time Strauss, with the wisdom of eighty years, enchanted
a world once again beset by war with his "Capriccio," he had
become a changed man. Was he indifferent to the heavy blows
of the Second World War which was still raging, and to the
destruction of the world which he had known? Was he unmoved
by the desperate plight of the German people who were being
led along the road to a national fiasco? He, who loved the world,
nature, and his fellow human beings, was hard hit, seeing only
too clearly the disaster looming ahead. Spells of pessimism overcame this man who had always relished life. Had he merely
persuaded himself that he was contented? He was beset by
doubts whether, coming after Wagner, he had really been able
to enrich the world's treasury of music. With benumbed senses
yet in full consciousness he experienced in an almost physical
sense the blood-red nights of devastation which destroyed irrev-
ocably many of the cultural treasures of Germany. With the
sarcasm of a worldy-wise observer who had a sense of history
he made the following diary entry in 1945: "In 1939 I wrote:
The Mark of Brandenburg has been returned to the Reich. In
the meantime the puffed-up frog Prussia, also known as Greater
Germany, has been burst, and Germany's political role is played
out. The parallel with the destruction of Athens by Sulla is incredible. I have read today that even Luther said 'Germany is
a thing of the past!' He had not seen the ruins of modern Germany ..."

He was overwhelmed first and foremost by the news that the
most historic *opera houses in Berlin, Munich, Dresden and
Vienna* (in this order) had fallen victim to the Anglo-American
air raids shortly before the end of the war. In a letter to Willi
Schuh Strauss gave spontaneous expression to his grief on the
loss of the National Theatre in Munich. "I am desolate: poor
Krauss! Years of most valuable artistic work in ashes! Perhaps
sorrow and despair make us babble on too much. But the burning of the Munich Court Theatre, where 'Tristan' and 'Die
Meistersinger' received their first performances, where I first
heard 'Freischütz' 73 years ago, where my good father sat at the
first horn desk for 49 years ... it was the greatest catastrophe of my
life; there is no possible consolation, and at my age no hope."

Six months later, when congratulating his younger grandson on his birthday, he again referred to the personal tragedy. To a greater extent than almost any other document this letter bears witness to the feelings of Strauss the man in relation to personal responsibility for the nation's cultural heritage. "Your 12th birthday coincides with the grievous event of the almost complete destruction of the beautiful imperial city. 165 years ago people regarded the Lisbon earthquake as a turning point in history, ignoring the greater significance of the first performance of Gluck's "Iphigenie in Aulis," which marked the conclusion of a process of musical development that had lasted for 3000 years and called down from heaven the melody of Mozart, revealing the secrets of the human spirit to a greater extent than thinkers have been able to over the course of thousands of years. Likewise when you remember your last birthday you should always think with loathing of the barbarians whose dreadful deeds are reducing our lovely Germany to ruins and ashes. Perhaps you will understand what I am saying as little as your brother does. If you read these sad lines again in 30 years' time, think of your grandfather, who exerted himself for nearly 70 years on behalf of German culture and the honour and renown of his fatherland . . ." This sense of personal sorrow was never to leave Strauss at the end of an "eighty-year lifetime of honourable and good German artistic labours." "How often I think with deep grief of the beautiful Dresden Opera House, hallowed by Carl Maria von Weber and Richard Wagner, which was also, under the incomparable Schuch, the birthplace of my works," he wrote to the author from Ouchy in 1946, and a few weeks before his death he was not ashamed of the "tears of sorrow" which he had shed "over all that was destroyed in these places of culture." Shortly before the end of the war, in silent recollection of those monuments to great European musical culture, and of long years of triumph, the now "inopportune" composer created the most significant work of his old age–the elegiac tone poem "Metamorphosen."

ACKNOWLEDGMENT TO LIFE

MODERN BOURGEOIS MUSIC IS INSEPARABLE FROM signs of decadence. This will always be the case when the culture of a dying class of society confronts that of an oppressed class fighting for power. A culture is decadent (in the sense of the "Décadence" about which Nietzsche wrote) when it is isolated from the living force of the will of the people, having as its aim a spontaneous, anarchistic dissolution of artistic values hitherto accepted. Does this apply to Richard Strauss, the exponent of bourgeois society and leader of the young German secession movement? Is it not, on the contrary, correct to say that while he succumbed temporarily to the attractions of morbid subjects far removed from life, he merely represented the decadent world without falling victim to it? True, many highly talented artists with a bourgeois background, at least during the first thirty years of this century, finding themselves in some way at odds with middle-class society around them, had recourse to forms of expression springing from contemporary decadence. It is, however, significant that after the perverse enormities of "Salome" and "Elektra" Strauss was forced to decide: was he to remain permanently on the dark or on the sunny side of life? Romain Rolland had addressed himself very forcibly to the composer of "Salome": "In the European world of today there is an unbridled urge toward decadence and suicide (taking different forms in France and Germany); beware of making it your own. Whatever has to die, let it die—and *live* yourself!" Strauss wanted to live. Ideas which had seemed to be like exotic blooms in the fading light at the turn of the century, and had clouded his senses for a time, were soon recognized to be unhealthy by this son of the Bavarian soil. Strauss, the vital, easily overcame the sickly pessimism of an age which produced so much monstrosity and bombast with the direct beauty of his "Rosenkavalier" music. Although he used the techniques of decadent art he had long since returned to himself—to a healthy relationship with the world. The road which Thomas Mann made the composer Adrian Leverkühn travel in his novel "Doktor Faustus"—the pact with evil, isolation, nihilism and ruin—was not that of the musician Strauss, who declared himself, as a latter-day standard bearer of classical culture, for *life* and *humanism*. As he assured Rolland in 1924, he intended to spread light and the sun, to give freely of himself in his art. "I want to spread joy, I need it . . ." There we have it.

Thomas Mann described the nature of late bourgeois music as "abstract and mystical," but these characteristics of modernism have no validity with Strauss. His decorative splendour represents a neo-baroque concept of sound. His intoxication through the sensuous appeal of sheer sound sometimes approached a power complex, but it was never the product of an ice-cold intellect or deep-seated loathing of the world. His listeners never stray into the late-Wagnerian garden of mystic longing for death, from which labyrinth very few find their way out. The triumphant, convincing qualities of Strauss's work amid the unrest and crises of "modern" music during the early years of the century, the power of his personality and his artistic will, were founded on the fact that his particular kind of vital bourgeois art does not create its effect in one direction from a marginal point, but in many directions from a centre. Its very essence resides in dialectic exchanges between the vital attributes of the creative work, in exploring to the full all viewpoints of the operatic and symphonic scenes. No matter whether we are considering the youthful, volcanic fire of "Don Juan," the suddenly soaring love music of "Rosenkavalier," or the baroque splendour of the "Deutsche Motette," what a sense of confident vigour this music gives, what joy in giving expression to a nature founded on happiness, what intimate contact with life, and what belief in the enhancing of all human qualities! With Strauss there is scarcely any suggestion of the isolation of the bourgeois artist, or of a gulf between art and life. His work springs not from dark forebodings but from radiant consciousness, not from the anguished question but from the positive answer, not from a tragic struggle but from the satisfaction of achievement. The profound study of the world which marked the visionary and demoniac character of Wagner gave place in the epicurean Strauss to a poetic temperament backed by eminent intellectual and artistic ability. Even in the opera whose subject is the struggle for the earthly shadow, his music strove for streaming light. The words of Ricarda Huch: "O life, O beauty" are his motto.

With his easy-going nature and his sensitive feeling for all aspects of life Strauss combined that utter clarity of thought and action which can only be the expression of a healthy disposition. Nothing weary, remote from life spoke out of those eyes which Stefan Zweig said were probably more alert than those of any other musician he had ever seen. "Not demoniac, but somehow clear-sighted, the eyes of a man who recognized his mission to the last detail." Countless recollections of Strauss the man tell of the cheerful naivety which characterized his attitude to life. (A later chapter will be devoted entirely to "Strauss the man"). His creative work was rooted in pure joy in the sensuous appeal of all things. Related as he was to Ludwig Thoma and Ludwig Ganghofer, that which was natural and close to the soil was nearer to him than hothouse artistry ever was. The full-blooded melodies of Barak or Mandryka with their overflowing life correspond to his uncomplicated personality far more than the psychologically fluctuating motif fragments of the Tetrarch Herod and his depraved daughter. The powerful intellect which distinguishes the mature Strauss in particular virtually demands the extreme contrast of great and primitive naivety. These characteristics were joined by an effervescent wit: he had a rich sense of free, liberating humour and a love of tricks worthy of his Till Eulenspiegel. It was that roguish streak in his nature which carried him, over the course of his long life, more and more consciously away from the veiled region of "Zarathustra" and the darkly tragic shadows of "Salome" and "Elektra." It was such inward happiness which Goethe once said must reside in the highest secular art.

All in all, Strauss remains within the best traditions of German romanticism: in his love of nature (from which he derived the inspiration in his early days for the piano pieces "Auf stillem Waldespfad" and "Heidebild"), in his links with his homeland ("Feuersnot," "Alpensinfonie"), and in his feeling for fairy

69

tales ("Frau ohne Schatten"). As man and musician he saw the world through the eyes of a bourgeois humanist. In his gay, realistic works he saw it before the richly-coloured background of artistic history, and in other works as the "last fulfilment of Grecian longing." In his efforts to enchant the listeners he went so far as to create an illusory world to provide contrast to his real one. What Brecht describes as the culinary nature of later bourgeois opera appears otherwise in the works of Strauss. Does he not appeal, in his best realistic works, equally to feeling and understanding? Does he not always associate with the sense of ecstasy, which he never spurns, clarity of thought?

On the occasion of Strauss's 60th birthday, when many leading personalities in the cultural life of Germany paid tribute to him and his work, Gerhart Hauptmann published this eloquent dedication: "The great musician Richard Strauss is a western European through and through, but at the same time he is wholly German. A child of the imperial era, he is nevertheless sounder than that age, and even during the war when sickliness was rife his art remained as healthy as ever. None of the questioning and morbidity of Dostoievsky or Strindberg is contained in it or can permeate it. It is free from Catholic mysticism, since Strauss's eye and art delight in the wonders of the world that can be seen, heard and felt. The best of his music is like blossoms and fruits. Just as they spring from the mystery of the tree, so it is with this music. Naturally it also has roots beneath the earth, but, like the tree, it shows only what is above the surface, shows it in conjunction with mountains, valleys, winds and clouds, linked with human destiny under the light of the sun."

*

It will be well at this point to relate particular concepts of progressive musical aesthetics with the work of Strauss. (Although it would be a mistake to ascribe to him ideological intentions unknown to him and his period.) In view of the fact that all music must have a content, the first question concerning every class of work, including those of the bourgeois era, must relate to its *contents*, what it has to say on the plane of ideas and emotions. If the contents are based on poetic origins, on a clearly established or merely imagined "programme," the "programmatic"

70

element of this particular work is expressed in it. Every piece of music has a living content, though this is often difficult to express in words. If the content, which derives from the choice of subject, is progressively constructive, humanistic, then the composer is addressing his message to human beings, and his intention is to create a realistic work. A programme demands the adoption of a realistic principle. If, however, the content of a work is anti-humanitarian, mystic, or otherwise negative in character, we have to do with a formalistic production. This aloof offspring of "modernism," remote from the ordinary people, destroys form and disfigures reality. Naturalism differs from the "typical characters in typical circumstances" of realism in that it gives only the external reflection of certain natural events and conditions of life, which press for very detailed musical description. Realism and formalism, both of which are the signs of an artistic attitude and not of a particular style, are most sharply contrasted. The bounds of naturalism, which musicians, writers and painters had observed since the 'nineties, could not be mapped out with any precision.

The reflection of reality and the quest for musical form are the criteria for a realistic work of art. What few idealistic musical writers, in particular Hanslick with his aesthetic of "tönend bewegte Form" ventured to dispute, has since been generally accepted as music of "inner values" or of "pure expression of the spiritual." Naturally this individualistic "inner life" remains a highly unclear concept, remote from the community as a whole. Music is really a universally understandable language, a form of communication between human beings, a reflection of life in its broadest form, of nature and of the community. In contrast to other artistic media, however, music creates a picture of man, "reproducing his changes of emotional state and disclosing his experiences" (Wanslow). The form, the illustrative quality of realistic music cannot be separated from the characteristics of melody, including its national colouring. Such melodic features represent only one element, though a very important one, with whose help the composer models reality. Musical form and melodic character are never ends in themselves, but means to express human conflict and characteristics, on the basis of a genuine relationship to both tradition and modern concepts. On the other hand the naturalistic reproductions which frequently descend to

71

being "mere stereotyped copies of a collection of details" (E. H. Meyer) generally represent no more than purely illustrative musical imitations of fortuitous objects in the world around.

The question is: where does Strauss stand in this respect–in his youth a representative of the progressive movement, and later the prophet of the neo-baroque and neo-classical ideals? His music is predominantly naturalistic in conception, but in the objective effect of its mirroring of social conditions it is realistic. (Erhardt formulated this fact as follows: "The Strauss œuvre is rationalistic in conception, idealistic in intention, realistic in execution.") It is indisputable that the symphonic poems, in particular, contain innumerable naturalistic features. The programmes on which they are based bear witness to no progressive ideas; they belong to their times, are often private and untypical, and to a great extent provide the impetus for purely descriptive music–though it should be emphasized that the naturalistic principle by no means rules out full-blooded melody and the employment of abundant means of musical expression. At the same time, however, the early tone poems and most of the dramatic works also show the hand of the *realist*. Works based on subjects from cultural history often contain clear indications of concern with social conditions, and express humanistic ideals of universal validity. Those are the works in which Strauss did not merely produce a naturalistic copy of reality, but, from his own standpoint, represented it realistically–with the aesthetic properties of musical form. They are works in which the elements of naturalism are found again on a higher plane of realism–the "erreichte Soziale" as Hofmannsthal once put it. Hence the division of Strauss's music into two parts: those works which correspond to the spirit of the age, and those which run counter to it. That is the great problem of his work as a whole.

It is undoubtedly true that Strauss, pledged to beauty, obeying the laws of an art of natural growth which was linked with tradition yet in touch with present times and universally understandable, was a declared enemy of every kind of formalism. With him human values, *mankind,* are at the centre of the picture: music without a concrete "purpose," a definite "programme" of some kind, appeared unthinkable to him. "I have long recognized," he wrote "that when composing I am unable to write anything without a programme to guide me." Strauss was thus consciously setting himself apart from the representatives of the over-ripe bourgeois attitude which desired to "take back" all the positive values (to adopt the expression employed by Thomas Mann in "Doktor Faustus") which music possesses today. From the *"poetic idea"* Strauss pressed on to the formal architecture and tonal landscape of his tone poems. As a musical dramatist he undoubtedly derived inspiration from the poetic word, from his historical subject on whose reality he could build and create something of value, or from the living story or myth. (The composer's enthusiastic letter in which he informed Hofmannsthal of the completion of the Empress's solo scene in "Die Frau ohne Schatten" is very revealing in this respect: "Everything full of variety," the text is brilliant, composes itself fabulously easily, gives continual stimulus . . .") The themes which aroused his imagination varied greatly between the symphonic and dramatic fields. While a masculine "hero" gave the decisive impetus to the composition of most of the tone poems, in the case of the operas it was generally the "cruel, enchanting female heart with its incomprehensible changes" which Zerbinetta mentions. On the basis of the poetic word Strauss formed the typical characters and musical personalities of his most successful opera figures.

It is no new observation that this composer of a succession of realistic stage works dealing with "characteristics and relationships of the material world perceived by the senses" preferred to draw on literary works and those of cultural history, that such works are therefore based largely on reflections of reality, and the adoption or quotation of existing objective attitudes to historical circumstances, and that the contents of the works frequently approximate to an appearance of social reality. It is undoubtedly true that the episodes on which Strauss directed his spotlight are not of great moment in themselves. What interest, for example, have people of today in the social-psychological situation in the Vienna of 1750 and 1860, the settings of "Der Rosenkavalier" and "Arabella"? The composer's imagination was aroused by the historical milieu (whose tensions often sprang from the realm of literature), and clothed the social unreality of the figures and situations with the reality of music. Strauss, like Tschaikowsky, wanted "living people and not puppets." He sought the "world of relationships," and a style of music drama with roots both in the human community and in the stage's own representation of the world. His best works held the mirror up to society. (In his naturalistic productions, too, there had been a reflection of reality, but it had been unconscious and insignificant.) He depicted the world around with his sense of actuality by creating a realistic, often satirical representation of prominent characteristics, which he drew with all their foibles and failings. Nevertheless we cannot find impassioned denunciation in his works, despite the clarity with which he saw life around him. Although he was aware of the decaying state of society his insight was not sufficient for him to alter the bourgeois outlook to which he had been brought up. Like Hauptmann, Liebermann, and most contemporaries of his class, he got no further than sympathy in his attitude to the proletariat. That was his tragedy, and it reduced the validity of even some of his realistic works.

An important factor with Strauss was his romantic sense of *personal involvement,* which frequently led to his presentation of an heroic or idyllic vision of his own bourgeois life. The unusual thing was not that he wrote on the basis of personal experience, but that in fact the greater part of his music actually grew from situations of his private life. This pronounced subjectivity of Strauss as an individual musician isolated from the ideas of the community as a whole was part of the heritage of Berlioz and Nietzsche to which the young composer long remained committed. It is true that this young storm and stress artist had little of Macbeth about him, he was certainly no Don Juan, and at the time when he wrote "Tod und Verklärung" he had hardly ever been seriously ill. However, even in his early tone poem "Aus Italien" he passed on to the listener his impression of the natural events of spring in Italy, together with a turbulent description of Neapolitan life, and no one but Strauss himself could be behind the mischievous declaration of war against puffed-up philistinism in "Till Eulenspiegel."

His works mirrored the man and his outlook on life to an ever increasing extent. As time went on he gave fuller rein to the urge, typical of the age, to project himself as his own dramatist and producer. The world-conquering artist wrote his challenging "Heldenleben" in full consciousness of his powers. The man who had attained the joy of an idyllic home life immortalized it in the "Sinfonia domestica," and who but Strauss himself guides the listener among the peaks and glaciers of the "Alpensinfonie," the panorama of his beloved mountains which could be seen from his Garmisch home? Is it not true to say that Strauss the man appears even more clearly in the dramatic works? The autobiographical element was not always presented to the eyes and ears of the public as palpably as in the trivialities of his private "commedia domestica" the opera "Intermezzo," but "Feuersnot" (Kunrad), "Die Frau ohne Schatten" (Barak), "Die schweigsame Frau" (Morosus) and "Capriccio" (La Roche) all contain self-portraits of the composer in less obvious forms. Strauss reacted in his own dramatic way to the widespread complaints against the subjective character of his works, some of which are not free from traces of self-glorification: "Chevalley advises me against always composing myself. Do you know a composer who has ever composed anything but himself? Funny people, these aestheticians!" (Letter to Bernhard Schuster, 1905). After a performance of the "Sinfonia domestica" in Strasbourg he wrote to Rolland: "I don't see why I shouldn't make a symphony about myself. I find myself quite as interesting as Napoleon or Alexander." Later, in his last memoranda of 1949, the aged composer was to refer to Goethe, in whose work people had long been accustomed to seeking "relationships between the writer's personal experiences and the work in every sentence." He could also have quoted Goethe's phrase "Poetical content is the content of one's own life."

As early as the period of "Salome" Romain Rolland was perceptive enough to recognize the subjective nature of Strauss's musical impulse. "The impression I have of you—perhaps I am mistaken—is that you are lyrical by nature. You draw brilliantly upon your own personality (and everything which closely or distantly resembles it). As you possess, in addition to your genius, a wealth of understanding and a very strong will, you are always able to comprehend and represent other characters or passions you do not share—but from outside, without really feeling them yourself. Take for example Jokanaan. I have the clear impression that you did not really share the faith of that wild prophet. You were able to portray his faith strongly and correctly—but a little abstractly, and with no truly personal accent . . . When you speak in your own name, as in the 'Domestica' or 'Heldenleben,' you attain an incomparable richness and intensity of feeling and expression. When you speak in the name of Herod or John the Baptist you are creating a powerfully-built work, but you are not, in my opinion, speaking for eternity . . ."

*

It will always remain a mystery how an artist who was known to enjoy using the most prosaic everyday language in his private life declared himself in his music for the beguiling *sensuousness* of life. No one could doubt that Richard Strauss the bourgeois, with his vital personality and knowledge of the world, was behind the healthy melodic charm of the love music in "Der Rosenkavalier" and "Ariadne," and the quieter amorous enchantment of "Arabella." It is quite clear that the most fascinating female characters in his operas, ranging from Freihild to Madeleine, whose blossoming melodies wholesomely embody many aspects of the feminine psyche, are far removed from the amoral sensuality of a society in decay. "I cannot conceive that the spirit of music is other than the spirit of love"–that sentence of Wagner applies also to the work of Strauss, at whose centre there stands the human being possessed by pure love. Only very rarely did Strauss replace love by the unbridled sexual urge. The eroticism which appears in "Feuersnot," in "Salome" and "Josephslegende," with their vivid musical portrayal of a woman inflamed by desire, came from the pen of an artist who was untouched by the lures of vice, whose life was not governed by "adventures." The sensual passion which he could express in such intoxicating floods of sound was a creation of his brain alone. Strauss was no dissolute artist–he needed no erotic stimulus. It is characteristic of Strauss that all his sense of the happiness of pure, true love sprang from his lifetime of companionship with Pauline de Ahna. From the time when he wrote the dewy-fresh, deeply-felt songs Op. 27 as a gift for his "beloved Pauline" on the occasion of their wedding in Weimar on the 10th September 1894, he chose his "more beautiful half" (as Hanslick described this excellent lieder singer at her first appearance in Vienna) as the mainspring of his works again and again. Without the experience of this "really happy marriage" there could have been no "Heldenleben" or "Sinfonia domestica," not to mention "Intermezzo" with its lightly disguised capricious cross-patch Christine-

Pauline. In their naturalness and candour these fruits of Strauss's marriage are often quite disarmingly naive. That is, however, typical of Strauss, whose open-heartedness was as evident as his geniality. What he needed was a wife who would keep him at his work (even though it was no doubt sometimes with the energetic methods of a general's daughter).

From early on in his career his music was criticized as lacking depth. Not all such comments are to be taken as seriously as the practical advice of his father, a severe critic as he followed Richard's career with no little scepticism: "I hope you will be convinced by the performance of your work ("Don Juan") that in future you must be more sparing and careful in your use of the brass, and must concern yourself less with inner brilliance and more with inner content. Colour is still only a means to an end . . . In all your things reflection comes to the fore, or at least that is what I always feel . . ." Writers referred to Strauss's "boundless and uncontrolled hunt for tone pictures" and his "stammering intoxication with sound" (Hanslick), to the "Colossus with feet of clay" (Riemann) and to "overheating of the artistic temperament" (Bekker). More recent writers, including Adolf Weissmann and Alfred Einstein, have also made critical evaluations of this kind on occasion. Rolland, who was so just a man, once wrote in connection with the "Sinfonia domestica" of "parade music, which is always drilled to create an effect," attributing this to the "abominable influence of the theatre," with which Strauss was conspiring (though at that time only as a conductor). Thomas Mann once compared the "Salome" meteor to the gaily swishing ball of a musical skittle alley . . . Such statements may have had a damaging effect on Strauss's music, but they did not rob his inspired individual style of one iota of its radiance. To deny this music its ethical power would be to bring it down to the level of mere entertainment, and to show Strauss in a completely false light as a spiritless vulgarian. If "metaphysics" implies a sense of the intangible mysteries of life and "ethos" refers to the artist's relationship to the forward-driving forces, then even Strauss's music is a symbol and reflection of a high spiritual and human order in the sense of Goethe, even though, as Rolland tried to show in his account of Strauss's life, he was "indifferent to the eternal, universal attributes of human nature." Mahler, with intuitive foresight, attempted to give an account of Strauss with reference to the impression made by "Salome": "Under a pile of rubble there is a volcano, a subterranean fire, not a mere firework. The same is probably true of Strauss's whole personality. That is why it is so difficult to separate the chaff from the wheat where he is concerned ... I cannot make rhyme or reason of this fact, and only feel that the voice of the 'Erdgeist' makes itself heard from the centre of genius, having chosen its dwelling not in accordance with human taste but to fulfil its unfathomable needs ..."

Strauss was no moralist in the accepted sense of the word. He was not the man for Wagner's musical philosophy (the exception of his "Zarathustra" only serves to prove the rule), for Bruckner's religious fervour or for the "Weltgefühl" of the seeker Mahler. The demoniac undercurrents of "Don Giovanni" were as remote from his work as the transformation of the "Tristan" Liebestod. His ethos expressed itself as the product of an absolutely factual attitude to the world, plumbing no depths of "inwardness" and "Weltabgewandtheit." Nevertheless to him (in the words of the Composer in the Prologue to "Ariadne") music was the "most holy of the arts." In a gradually increasing brightness of spirit he depicted in his symphonies and dramatic works images and moods which represented the spiritual reflexes of sensuous reality or vital imagination. Richard Specht and other biographers were mistaken when they divided Strauss's works, on such a basis, into the "transcendental" and the "ciscendental." In reality Strauss's finest melodies have *breadth, height and depth*. The music which forms a hymn to the splendour of the world also reveals, behind that brilliant exterior, a great deal concerning human secrets and destinies. He makes the boldest style of the music dramatist, the most colourful palette of the painter in sound "simple" when he is concerned with capturing the music of the human spirit. His is not the simplicity of the primitive, who can express himself only crudely owing to a lack of imagination and ability, but the simplicity of one who has attained the ultimate degree of wisdom. This was the case with the Marschallin, as it was with Barak and Morosus, Daphne and Danae. Anyone who remembers Daphne's wonderful transformation, in which the human voice is freed from all earthly ties, or the breathtaking melodic purity and depth of the orchestral interlude in C major ("Jupiter's renunciation") from "Danae" will understand what is meant. There need be no hesitation in applying to Strauss's own musical outlook the words which he dedicated to Mozart in 1944. He wrote then that the ideal perfection of Mozart's vocal lines was something: ". . . not to be perceived with the eyes or comprehended with the brain, a divine quality to be sensed only by those into whose ear it has breathed: Plato's Eros, floating between heaven and earth, revealing the ultimate secrets of the human soul."

Little feeling and an inclination towards triviality? . . . Ever since the appearance of "Ständchen" and "Cäcilie" such phrases have cropped up regularly in considerations of Strauss's style. Since "Josephslegende," the "Alpensinfonie" and "Die ägyptische Helena" people have juggled with similar phrases to describe that element of Strauss's tonal language which was directed towards splendour of colour and broad effect. No doubt Strauss considered some of his music principally as sensuous background sound rather than as the result of melodic-expressive inspiration. He succumbed more than once to the danger of writing "something to feel" at the request of his Munich relatives. Rolland warned Strauss against "taking over certain dubious melodies, which may create the desired dramatic effect, but which are certainly not the expression of genuine passions . . ." Some mediocre passages in his songs, the scene by the bedside of little Franzel in "Intermezzo" and "Helena's awakening" may be mentioned as examples of Strauss's occasional lapses into writing melodies of inferior quality. (However, as Strauss later remarked, the word "Kitsch" is a favourite one among people who, like the fox who said "sour grapes", are envious of the effectiveness of the "Tannhäuser" and "Oberon" Overtures, or Schiller's "Räuber".) It is easy to differentiate between the ear-tickling, all-too blissfully melodious Strauss style and the full-blooded melos of Straussian cantilena with a spiritual content. Nevertheless a work of art without its share of genuine feeling would be inconceivable, and many a work of Strauss, seemingly extrovert, takes on an inner significance. All his typical "pearls" of melody, his many pictures in white and gold with their enchanting vivacity or poise, came from the depths of his heart and were fashioned by the strength of his Bavarian constitution. There is no doubt that spiritual riches resulted when Strauss drew inspiration from the springs of folksong.

79

It cannot be said that his music shows any signs of superficial speculation, mass production, mere routine or the like. Strauss, to whom routine meant the "death of true art", composed as one to whom life itself was the greatest sensation, and who often enough succeeded, as man and musician, in representing and interpreting it. He defended himself passionately against those who accused him of inartistic or frivolous tendencies. "When people accuse me of writing in too complicated a way–the devil take them! I can't express what I have to say more simply, although I strive for the greatest possible simplicity: a real artist doesn't strive for originality . . ." After Bülow had conducted "Don Juan" unsuccessfully in Berlin, a performance which the audience "could not understand," the young composer, writing to his father, made this significant statement: "I intend to serve my art honourably, and I am not afraid of failures so long as I am certain that my message is presented to the public correctly. A success on any other basis is of no account to me, indeed it is repugnant." Considerable importance may be attached to Strauss's words when, at forty, he wrote of himself as a composer: "One can't be this person today and another tomorrow, but must always be as God has made one." Two further principles of his attitude to art, which speak for him: "First comes art, and other considerations come afterwards" (1912), and "I have been sincere at every moment of my life, and I have never written a work with the intention of gaining a reputation as a futurist or revolutionary" (1923). Despite isolated lapses into the commonplace, did Strauss not seek and find the way to the heights of art again and again? What Hofmannsthal wrote to the composer after first hearing the music of "Helena": "The after-effect of the music is really magical; everything is so effortless and full of light, despite its great, pure seriousness" is applicable to all the works representing a synthesis of the heritage of Wagnerian romanticism carried to its highest point of musical development, and the growing effort to attain classical proportion. Such a synthesis occurred for the last time in the four posthumous songs with orchestra which are based on poems by Eichendorff and Hermann Hesse–music of spiritual refinement, of tranquillity in sound.

A less able man, a merely versatile talent, an enjoyer of differents gifts, would have become a feeble aesthete in Strauss's

80

place. But this healthy musician was no aesthete–greatly though he attracted literary aesthetic natures. He was a man who felt himself to be part of a living, progressing German culture. Although in his artistic sphere Strauss accepted only the "colourful reflection" of life's most beautiful attributes, he did not labour under the delusion that the world of reality was to be rejected, that life rose to its highest point only in beauty and pleasure. His operas and orchestral works made this quite clear. Elegy was not for him; his work did not lose itself either in dreams or in visions of a Utopia; he did not falsify the meaning of existence. (Only "Tod und Verklärung," not one of his strongest works, echoes Schopenhauer's concept of suffering on earth and victory in paradise). It is worth while to live and to help create the art of one's own time . . . With what words does La Roche in "Capriccio," the director with a sense of the reality of the theatre, speak of the opera of the future . . .?

> I will people my stage with human beings,
> Human beings like us
> Who speak our language!
> Their sorrows shall touch us
> And their joys move us deeply!
> Go to it, you hero of the writing desk!
> Create works which prove to me
> That you can bring new life to the theatre.

THE HERITAGE

As STRAUSS GREW IN YEARS AND WISDOM HE BECAME increasingly conscious of the fact that he was an heir to the great historical achievements of the 18th and 19th centuries. Without his natural indebtedness to forms handed down from the past —not only in the works of his youth—and to the great classical and romantic heritage, the picture of him would be unthinkable and incomplete. It was the spiritual wave of those brilliant musical eras, of which he never for a moment lost sight, which carried him and his work into the present day. He accepted the inspiration which he received from the musical culture of all Europe as a German, and formed it with his fine feeling for the subtlest spiritual impulses. With firm fidelity and the energy natural to him Strauss upheld the music of the masters who, he was convinced, represented an organic development of music after Beethoven: the Frenchman Berlioz, the Hungarian Liszt, and first and foremost the German Richard Wagner, his real predecessor. Neither classicism nor true romanticism but the second romantic era provided the soil which nourished the seeds of his art. During the course of a century the classical picture of music had changed greatly. The outlines of the musical structure had gradually become less clear-cut, the delineation less precise, while the colours had taken on an ever-increasing lustre. The essentials of this development led to the work of Wagner. Nevertheless Strauss was no imitator: from "Don Juan" onward every bar showed his own handwriting. When he had once recognized the fact that it was in the music of these masters, not that of Schumann and Brahms, that his starting point lay, his own musical language suddenly made itself heard. Instead of taking the well-trodden path of imitation of Beethoven's symphonies and of their "renowned follower" (Brahms), he sought

6*

his own way, which scarcely altered right up to the time of his fullest maturity. Wholly aware of the past, he nevertheless strode onward. Strauss was one of the last of the great era of German romantic musicians. He was its consummator.

*

His love and reverence for the ideals of Mozart's artistry influenced all his work. In the smile of *Mozart,* but also in his knowledge of the unfathomable depths of life and his expression of bitter sorrow, Strauss saw the embodiment of classicality in music. That sense of happiness on a new level of genuine human experience, that lucidity and transparency of sensuous sound– were they not the finest thing he had to give? What would his music be without the pearls and prickles of "Till Eulenspiegel", without the sweetness and lustre of "Der Rosenkavalier?" Tenschert called Strauss's link with Mozart a "relationship by choice." It was even more: an allegiance of the heart. "I cannot write about Mozart, I can only worship him!" Strauss replied when he was asked to write an introduction to the book "Mozart and Munich." His enthusiasm was not by any means limited to a particular period of his life. Even while still at the Gymnasium in Munich he wrote to his friend Thuille describing the Jupiter Symphony as "the most splendid work I have yet heard ... During the final Fugue I thought I was in heaven." From this enthusiasm it was no very long distance to the great achievements of the masterly interpreter of Mozart, the born conductor of "Figaro" and re-discoverer of "Così fan tutte" ("Not only unique among Mozart's dramatic masterpieces, but a pearl of the entire range of comedy prior to Richard Wagner's 'Meistersinger' "). He did not indulge in romantic nuances and personal interpretations: at a spirited tempo, with the witty commentary of his accompaniments to the secco recitatives, Mozart was presented in the best and purest manner possible. Strauss was never able to do enough for the works of the Salzburg master. Fritz Busch wrote in his memoirs that Strauss once happened to come in to a rehearsal of the Mozart Clarinet Concerto in Dresden. "For a long time after the rehearsal we talked about the miracle of Mozart. Strauss declared the G minor String Quintet to be music at its highest point of perfection ever

84

attained. He himself had been an outstanding pianist, and related happily how he had played one of Mozart's piano concertos under Bülow at Meiningen. He often told me I should present a cycle containing all 28 of the master's piano concertos, every one of which, he said, was more beautiful than the others..." It is also known that when he was in his eighties, and had withdrawn from the cares of public life, he immersed himself at home in listening to and studying Mozart's chamber music. Time thus spent was, to him, a real strengthening of the heart.

Strauss and Mozart: complete self-absorption in the happy yet deeply-feeling art, the respect for formal laws, the individual sense of sound and sonority which had distinguished Mozart. An artist of similar disposition, who from his youth upward had devoted himself to the art he loved with all his being, made himself into an instrument to serve the composer he idolized. He experienced the same longing for the innocent realm of music that led his contemporary Mahler to the folk song. This was the essence of Strauss's music which, despite its sensuous warmth, was in the last analysis light-footed, winged and elastic, shorn of all problematic elements. He regarded his beloved master Mozart as having "solved all problems before they are posed", writing that his "passion has been stripped of everything earthly." Once when Oscar Bie was talking to Strauss about the latter's new works, the composer closed the conversation by saying: " 'You know, Mozart was the one to succeed there. Let's go in and play some Mozart!' So he sat down at the piano and played a quartet by Mozart with his two delicate hands, caressing the instrumental lines and becoming enraptured by the melodic ideas..." On another occasion, during the Second World War, when Strauss attended a quartet recital in Munich, he exclaimed movingly: "How I should like to be able to compose as simply as that!" Strauss gave expression to his boundless love of Mozart in these words: "Listen to the wonderful growth of a Mozartian melody! You think it's the end, but it goes on and on. Ah yes, melody!" He wrote one of his last appreciations of Mozart in 1944: "Almost immediately (after Bach) there followed the miraculous Mozart with his perfection and absolute idealization of the melody of the human voice–I might refer to the Platonic "idea" and "ideal" not to be perceived with the eye or comprehended by the mind, something divine which can be sensed only by those into whose ear it has breathed ..."

Anyone who wishes to compose in the spirit of Mozart must be true to himself. A copy of Mozart's own idiom like the "Symphonie classique" to which Serge Prokofieff gave such intellectual polish would have been foreign to Strauss's' nature. (His additions to the arrangement which he made of "Idomeneo" are to be regarded as creative homage to Mozart.) The Mozartian grace and warmth which Strauss poured into his own music from his earliest days, or more correctly from the time of the "Burleske" for piano and orchestra, were to be of decisive importance to a great many of his works. The bright exuberance of the tonal language, the Apollonian serenity of melody came like a beam of sunlight from the realm which Mozart had made his own. The "Mozartian change of direction" in Strauss's development as an opera composer clearly came between "Elektra" and "Rosenkavalier"–"The Mozartian spirit rose unbidden before me, but I have remained true to myself." It would be a mistake to overlook the fact that even the early tone poems contain an abundance of Mozartian features. The influence of Mozart is evident in the epilogue to "Till," even more clearly in the meditative F major and G major melodies, based on thirds, of the "Sinfonia domestica," and in the flexible tone moulding and changing face of "Don Quixote." This spirit came to Strauss from a related nature whose sunlike radiance dispelled the surrounding gloom. In his old age he sought the smile of Mozart in his last instrumental works, heading the Second Sonatina for wind instruments: "In homage to the divine Mozart at the end of a life filled with gratitude."

In the sphere of opera the "Mozartian line" can be followed clearly from the time of the serenely festive "comedy for music" (this description itself comes from Mozart) "Der Rosenkavalier." The sweet, poignant enchantment, the gaiety of the healthy sensuousness which surround this score so captivated Strauss himself that he rejected outright Hofmannsthal's suggestion that they should again seek out the terrible forces of the Oresteia. Instead they created "Ariadne", with its form influenced by Mozart and its wealth of lovely melody. From that time onward Strauss never departed from the same general style in his dramatic works. It was particularly clear in the slenderly-fashioned Aithra scenes of "Helena", the finely-chiselled music of human feelings in "Arabella", and the brilliantly constructed ensembles of "Die schweigsame Frau," right up to the "line of absolute beauty" in the late works "Daphne," "Die Liebe der Danae" and "Capriccio." The manner in which Strauss, at the height of his mastery, transformed the scenes of an opera libretto into musical scenes, creating music to be sung and played which was sensitive yet effervescent, would not have been possible without Mozart. What Strauss saw as his goal was what Max Mell once wrote of Hofmannsthal's aspirations: "To win back the serenely light, Mozartian element for German opera." The listener who recognizes only the familiar examples of Mozart's influence in "Der Rosenkavalier" (e. g. the breakfast music and the closing duet) will find many more if he looks elsewhere. The facts that "Rosenkavalier" and "Schweigsame Frau" would be inconceivable without "Figaro," that there are relationships between the significant masquerades of "Ariadne" and "Così fan tutte" and also, in many respects, between "Ariadne" and "Die Zauberflöte," and that "Frau ohne Schatten" with its humanistic purity may be regarded as a continuation of "Die Zauberflöte," impress themselves on every opera lover. "Capriccio," too, derives from a Mozartian idea: the theory and practice of the opera theatre are discussed in his early singspiel "Der Schauspieldirektor."

*

While Mozart represented to Strauss a part of his own nature, Richard *Wagner* was the Temple of the Grail through which he moved as his life progressed. His reverence for the spiritual and artistic greatness of Wagner the musician became more and more profound. His was not, however, the veneration of an unfruitful epigone; in his youthful "Guntram" he had approached his great model closely, but he was a mature artist in his own right, who had created a position for himself in the realm of music. "I believe," he wrote on his 50th birthday, "that I have learned from Wagner all there is to be learned. Opera composition on the basis of the union of text and music, Wagner's handling of recitative, must provide every modern musician with both examples and models. I do not think I have failed to study anything in that respect, yet I have not fallen into the error of imitation." Later, in 1933, after he had conducted "Parsifal" at the Bayreuth Festival, he wrote to Winifred Wagner of the "reverential payment of the immense debt" which he owed "to the great master, in my heart, for all that he gave to the world and to me in particular." In the same year he replied to a question put by a Dresden newspaper: "The only fitting attitude to him is one of respectful silence, and propaganda through deeds." Stefan Zweig wrote in his memoirs about Strauss's creative relationship to Wagner, whom, unfortunately, he had never known personally. In a conversation on opera Strauss said he knew well enough that opera was really finished as an art form. He regarded Wagner as so tremendous a summit as to be insurmountable. " 'But,' he added with a Bavarian laugh, 'I have got out of the difficulty by making a detour round the foot of the mountain' . . ." Another significant statement: "With the B major chord at the end of 'Tristan' romanticism is at an end for 200 years: we must see about starting somewhere else."

Strauss's youthful works were still rooted in the traditional classical and romantic forms. It was not only that hardly any Wagnerian influence can be detected in his early period–for a long time he was "completely unable to understand" Wagner's works at all. Undoubtedly the conservative training which he received from his father, who taught the boy first and foremost "to love and admire the classical masters of composition," was responsible for the course matters took. Even when he was fifteen, and had become acquainted with the gigantic Wagnerian music dramas in the standing-room places of the Munich Court Theatre, he considered the high-lying violins in the "Lohengrin" Prelude "dreadfully sweet and sickly." The only thing which impressed him in "Tannhäuser" was the scenic transformation from the Venusberg to the Wartburg Valley–on the subject of the music he was silent. "Siegfried" caused him boredom and displeasure. "I tell you you've not the slightest idea of the confusion there is in it . . . My ears were humming with those monstrosities of chords, if they can still be called chords at all," and he added rashly that in ten years' time no one would know who Richard Wagner was . . . It was only slowly that the phenomenon of Wagner penetrated into his consciousness. Through "forbidden study of the score of 'Tristan'" the young Munich music student at last found his way into that wonderful work, and later also into the "Ring" of the master whom he had hitherto rejected out of hand. "I still remember very well how, at about the age of seventeen, I began feverishly turning over the pages of 'Tristan,' intoxicated with enthusiasm – which cooled off only when I tried again, at a performance of the work, to find confirmation of the impressions my eyes and my mind's ear had received on reading the score. Fresh disappointments and doubt, then back to the score, until at last it was clear to me that it was the discrepancy between a mediocre performance and the intention of the great master as I pictured it from the printed music which prevented the work from sounding to me as I had already heard it in my imagination ... After my eyes had been opened in this way I became (despite all the warnings about the 'Bayreuth swindler' which I received from my old uncle) a 'complete Wagnerian' ..." The day would come when Wagner became recognized as the "true musical classicist" ...

"So times change" – Strauss himself made this observation in a report, which he sent to his father, of rehearsals for "Tristan" at Weimar in 1891. Prior to that, when he was convalescing at Feldafing with his uncle Pschorr following a severe attack of inflammation of the lungs, he had written to Arthur Seidl: "Dying may not be so bad, but I should first like to conduct 'Tristan.' " It was not long before the young enthusiast (who had taken part in "Tristan" rehearsals as musical assistant at Bayreuth as early as 1889) was able to write jubilantly to Cosima Wagner: "I have now conducted 'Tristan' for the first time; it was the most wonderful day of my life!" Later, when he saw the sunset beyond the cliffs during a sea voyage to England, he was overwhelmed by reminiscences of "Tristan." ... No other work in the whole history of music filled Strauss with such a sense of utter reverence and passionate involvement, except perhaps "Lohengrin," over which even as a mature composer he could "weep like a baby." All through his life it was not the "Ring," with whose monumental pathos he was never completely in sympathy, but "Tristan" which he extolled most fervently. A few weeks before the jubilee performance of "Tristan" which he conducted at Dresden in 1933, the "last act of homage to a really great man," Busch wrote to him: "Just think, 'Tristan' is beginning to be less of a draw at the box office." The

The beginning and end of "Tristan"
compressed into four bars (1946)

following answer reached him from Garmisch: "Even if only *one* person pays for a seat at 'Tristan' it must be performed for him, because he must be the last surviving German!"

An idea of the breadth and depth of the experience which "Tristan" represented to him, and of the work's place in musical history, is given in the letter which Strauss wrote in 1935 to his friend Joseph Gregor in Vienna, after reading Gregor's book "World history of the theatre": "Further to your ideas about the relationship between Schiller and Goethe (one of your best chapters!) and your particularly acute observation that you regard 'Iphigenie' as the work 'which gave the world theatre the last spiritual creation of form, which has never been achieved again,' I must, as a musician and dramatic composer, ask permission to make a modest criticism. That last 'spiritual creation of form' – thanks to music – was not only equalled but even exceeded in 'Tristan.'... It was granted only to the universal genius Richard Wagner to combine the perfect art of the theatre, the incomparable architecture of Schiller's dramatic works... with the inner questioning of Goethe's intellectual masterpieces. This he did in 'Tristan,' which does not, as you believe, represent the 'dazzling resurrection' of romanticism, but the end of all romanticism, as it brings into focus the longing of the entire 19th century, longing which is finally released in the 'Tag- und Nachtgespräch' and in 'Isolde's Liebestod.'... 'Tristan' is the ultimate conclusion of Schiller and Goethe, and the highest fulfilment of a development of the theatre stretching over 2,000 years."

It is fascinating to observe how Strauss the sensuous attempted to explain the nature of the experience created by the Wagnerian music drama from the standpoint of absolute sound. As early as 1889 he had written to Dora Wihan after a performance of the "Tannhäuser" Overture under Bülow: "I still tremble when I think of the actual sound!" In his letter to Gregor Strauss he made no mention of the validity of the leitmotiv technique or of the principle of the "Gesamtkunstwerk." He found warm words, however, for the instrument which "alone is capable of representing by symbols meaningful only to feelings attuned to them that incommensurable element (something which is beyond the range of the understanding) about which the aged Goethe spoke"–namely the romantic orchestra of Wagner. "Only. with the invention and extremely skilful use of the modern orchestra did the world theatre rise to the highest pitch of perfection." Strauss echoed this glowing opinion of Wagner in 1940. "The modern orchestra does not merely underline, explain or remind –it gives the music's very content, discloses the original vision, and tells the innermost truth. . . . I can never hear enough of the revelations of this (Wagner) orchestra; I am constantly discovering new beauties, and each time I am indebted to him for new perception." It was only after he had acquired the wisdom of old age that he could sum up his attitude to Wagner in such simple, unambiguous words. The extent of Strauss's intensive study of the subtle tonal relationships in the music of "Tristan" is indicated by the modifications of dynamics which he made in his score of the work at Weimar in 1891, and most of which he observed in later years.

As a result of his revelation of Wagner the young "storm and stress" composer pledged himself passionately to the master of "Lohengrin" and "Tristan" in his "Guntram." It is scarcely believable that this music, which leans so heavily on Wagner even down to details of melody and harmony, was composed by the same man who, in the tone poem "Don Juan," had overcome Wagnerian pathos in a sudden upsurge of energy. The Singspiel "Feuersnot," too, could not have existed without the model of "Die Meistersinger," although a good deal of frivolity was also evident here. (The last page of the draft score of "Guntram" bears the significant note "Deo Gracia! And to the holy Wagner," while the final page of "Feuersnot" bears the words

Page of a letter to Dora Wihan (1889)

"Completed on the birthday and to the greater glory of the 'Almighty,' Charlottenburg, 22nd May 1901"–Richard Wagner!) From then onward the character of Strauss's operatic works followed a curve of development whose starting point was the influence of Wagner. This curve moved to bold new conquests in the field of naturalistically heightened tragedy: "Salome" and "Elektra;" on to the classical-realistic comedy enchantment of

"Rosenkavalier" and to the filigree chamber music style of "Ariadne;" back to the mystical baroque world of "Frau ohne Schatten" and "Helena." There were excursions into the realm of comedy with "Arabella," "Schweigsame Frau" and "Capriccio," and glances back to the beginnings in "Daphne" and "Danae' ... It was in fact a remarkable detour, this course taken by his life's work for the theatre, but the influence of the Bayreuth master can be traced all through–there was no mere imitation, but a personal process of continued development. There were the technique of psychological motifs, the new ability to blend instrumental colours, the art of throwing light on the characters through variations of instrumental tone and the handling of the voices, the formal clarity and beauty of proportions, the balance between emotional and lyrical elements derived from "Tristan," and many other things. Weissmann referred aptly to the "sensuous glow of Wagner which Strauss fills with expression." (Although Strauss's most strongly personal melodic characteristics derive not from Wagner but from folk music sources.) Strauss extended and refashioned the world of Wagnerian music drama by passing beyond the typically Wagnerian sources of conflict, and he gave formal stability to what had been in danger of becoming shapeless at the hands of Wagner's mere imitators. It was a natural consequence of Strauss's characteristics as a dramatic composer that he should restore to post-Wagnerian opera the forms of aria, duet and strictly-constructed ensembles. The Rhinemaidens became the trio of nymphs in "Ariadne," and Wotan's "Abschied" became the "Majaerzählung" in "Danae."

Who knows whether Strauss would have found his way to the relaxed, transparent overall style of his later works had Hofmannsthal not been tireless in his attempts to win back the light, serene, Mozartian element for the German music drama! When, after "Frau ohne Schatten," the poet begged his friend finally to give up the heavy Wagnerian style, the composer replied: "Your cry of distress ... has touched me to the heart and has opened the door to an entirely new landscape where, guided by 'Ariadne,' and in particular the new Prologue, I hope to find myself in the realm of the un-Wagnerian opera of the play of human feelings. I now see the way straight in front of me, and I am grateful to you for opening my eyes to the possibility. ... I promise you I have now taken off the Wagnerian musical ar-

93

mour for good . . ." For good? It was not the "heitere Mythologie" of "Die Liebe der Danae" which was preferred at that time, in 1920, but the Wagnerian drama of ideas "Die ägyptische Helena," in which Hofmannsthal once again plunged into the world of alliteration. Nevertheless the poet again raised his voice imploringly when work had begun on "Arabella" a few years later. From the poetic and musical points of view the new work was to be related to "Rosenkavalier," but it should be "even lighter, even more Frenchified, if I may so express myself –even further from Wagner." For the last time the poet wanted to help his friend with his suggestions. . . . Both in the scenes of Gaea and of Peneios in "Daphne" and in the Wotan-like pathos of Jupiter in "Danae" Strauss did, however, return to the romantic splendour of the tonal realm of Wagnerian mythology. (There is, too, a striking reminiscence of the motif of the Rhinemaidens in the Second Sonatina for wind instruments.) In these pathetic echoes of the world of the "Ring," which was no longer his own, he was returning in a new, radiant, purified manner, "in a nobler garment to the same point" from which he had started out.

*

More than the mere name linked him with the Viennese waltz king Johann *Strauß*. Although no family relationship has so far been shown to exist between the two composers, the same spark of natural musicality shone out of each of them, and they had the same open outlook on life. From childhood onward Richard Strauss had been on good terms with the Viennese waltz. In later years, like many other great musicians (Wagner referred to the waltz king as the "most musical skull of the century–") he had a sincere admiration for the Strauß whose name was spelt with the German ß, the composer of "Die Fledermaus" and the "Tritsch-Tratsch Polka." "To me Johann Strauß is, among all who are divinely gifted, the most lovable bringer of pleasure. This first, general idea may serve as motto for the feelings I have for that remarkable man. In particular I revere the naturalness of Johann Strauß's inborn gifts. . . . To me he was one of the last who had primary ideas. Yes, his was a primary, primitive, naturally melodic talent, that was it . . ." Strauss frequently conducted the classics among operettas in Berlin and Vienna, and in the concerts which he conducted with the Vienna Philharmonic he did not consider it beneath him, despite opposition in some quarters, to present a swirling Strauß waltz. About the turn of the century the Viennese expressed surprise that Strauss conducted an "Elite" open-air concert. He was not slow to reply: "What my great namesake did so often here in Vienna I can also do without dishonour."

When one remembers that the two masters, who met only once in Munich at the time of "Till," had very different geographical backgrounds and that there was a great contrast in the social structures underlying their music, their waltzes often have an astonishing amount in common. In his "Rosenkavalier," above all, "Johann Wagner," as Bülow aptly called his young friend, proved himself a serious rival of the waltz king. What Strauss wrote were not always artistically stylized Viennese waltzes like the "Tanzlied" of his tone poem "Zarathustra" and the agreeable ländlers in "Feuersnot": in "Rosenkavalier," and again in the Grundlsee scene of "Intermezzo" he wrote real Viennese "Gstanzerln," which do not for a moment deny their origins among the ordinary people. Strauss was never ashamed of the relationships (even if they were distant) between the Ochs Waltz and the "Dynamiden" Waltz of Joseph Strauß, and between the Mariandl theme "Nein, nein! I trink kein Wein!", of such importance to the closing Trio, and the "Blue Danube." He made something quite different from the material. What delights the listener in a waltz by Richard Strauss, apart from the rich melodic invention and the velvet-soft Viennese idiom, with sighing thirds and sixths, is the original treatment of the waltz rhythm, the varying of the stereotyped three-four time by means of "rhythmic counterpoint." The virtuistic service to which the waltzes are put to depict Ochs's predicament in the last act could become tonal reality only by the use of such artistic means. There were two other stage works in which the Viennese waltz played a leading part. However, while in the ballet "Schlagobers" it has clearly descended from the hayloft to the salon, it appears in the ball scene of "Arabella" as the pale reflection of a pleasure-seeking, morbid, no longer vital Vienna. The verve and charm of the "Rosenkavalier" Waltz were also to elude Strauss in the waltz "München," one of his late works.

*

Now for a brief account of his creative relationship with *other masters*. In his "Deutsche Motette" Strauss demonstrated his reverence for the highly developed polyphonic art of 17th century composers, Schütz in particular. He was a follower of Gluck in the re-vivifying of an unacademic concept of classical antiquity, as he showed in his youthful arrangement of "Iphigénie en Tauride" and in many important aspects of his own works ranging from "Elektra" to "Danae" and "Capriccio." He named as the "patron saint of this theoretical comedy" in his foreword to the score of "Capriccio" the "great reformer of the art of composition Gluck." It was not until very late in his life that he found his way to the great Bach. (At the age of twenty-three he wrote to Bülow that to him the B minor Mass was "very boring," and that "apart from wonderful counterpoint" he could find in it "no trace of the living sense of passion.") He was, however, an adherent of Beethoven in the general sense that he was closely drawn to that most human of musicians. At the age of sixty he wrote the festival play "Die Ruinen von Athen," making free use of themes by Beethoven. The composer of "Friedenstag" crowned that opera with a scenic cantata which was clearly influenced by the related dramatic situation in "Fidelio"; over and above that there is no doubt that the Finale was conceived in accordance with the formal model of classical opera. The aged master who expressed his deepest feelings in the spiritually transfigured world of "Metamorphosen" was moved to the composition of this melancholy tone poem by the theme of the Funeral March from the "Eroica." His relation to Beethoven was one of love and reverence. When a Viennese paper asked him to make a statement about the master during the Beethoven year 1927, Strauss replied tersely that he did not consider himself entitled to move a vote of thanks to Beethoven . . .

Among other musical forerunners Mendelssohn made his influence felt in the early fantasy "Aus Italien," and later in certain sentimental melodic phrases of "Sinfonia domestica," "Salome," and the "middle period" operas. Strauss described Weber, who influenced the shape of his motifs (beginning of "Don Juan") and his handling of the orchestra, as the "instrumental poet and expounder of colour" who had succeeded in "developing the choir of instruments into groups with a soul of their own and finally into eloquent individual voices." Fleet-

96

ing resemblances to the highly theatrical works of Meyerbeer (in 1902 he had an unexpected success with "Robert le Diable" in Berlin) were used by opponents of Strauss in an attempt to draw false parallels between these composers of very different types. There is, however, no denying the importance of the impulse which the rapidly developing young composer of programme music received from Berlioz and Liszt. Berlioz's brilliant "Symphonie fantastique" ushered in the era of the symphonic poem, so characteristic both musically and sociologically of bourgeois art. The reasons for Strauss's enthusiasm for Berlioz are not far to seek: the subjective expressive language of his music and his virtuistic orchestral technique. When Strauss was concerned with filling the idealistic-poetic world of the Lisztian tone poems with new, personally observed contents, he derived his inspiration from an intimate knowledge of the works of Berlioz. "So little artistic skill and so much poetry, so little counterpoint and so much music," the young Strauss had written about Liszt's "Heilige Elisabeth." And when he informed his uncle Carl Hörburger of the existence of a new tone poem, "Macbeth," he did not forget to add: ". . . but not from Liszt . . ." Mention has already been made of the important human and artistic influence of Alexander Ritter. Strauss last made a clear acknowledgment to Brahms in "Aus Italien" and "Macbeth." As early as 1889 he had irreverently described the elder composer as the "Holy, leathern Johannes," and a few years later he turned his back on Brahms's music for good. Bizet's "Carmen" and Verdi's "Falstaff," two of the "greatest masterworks of all times," were among his favourite operas. On the other hand Strauss, at twenty, described "Aida" as "Indian music," and in his old age he called Verdi's "Macbeth" a "joke." Certain weak melodic characteristics of Saint-Saëns and Massenet were to play a part in the mature operas. He admired the colourful Russian style of Rimsy-Korsakoff ("Scheherazade"). Debussy's impressionism meant a great deal to him; he was proud of having introduced the "Nocturnes" in Berlin. Occasional echoes of Rubinstein's lyricism have been detected in Strauss's songs.

It is scarcely surprising, in view of Strauss's receptiveness to all the world had to offer, that the garden of his art should also have seen the blossoming of an abundance of other styles. Do not the tenor aria in "Rosenkavalier," with which the stylistic imitation of earlier musical eras begins, and the sonnet in "Capriccio" echo the southern cantilenas of Porpora and Giordani in every detail? Is there not something Italian about the god Bacchus, and later Apollo? Surely Zerbinetta's ornate aria comes straight from the land of coloratura! Are influences of Schubert not evident in the trio of nymphs in "Ariadne" and in the lyrical blossoms of "Daphne" and "Danae," and do certain songs and the moonlight music in "Capriccio" not suggest Schumann? Strauss achieved real triumphs of playing with styles, juggling with generations of musical history and indulging in witty anachronisms, in the buffo artistry of "Die schweigsame Frau." He re-composed two early Italian vocal pieces, which he probably found in Riemann's "History of Music with Examples": in the "singing lesson" of Act 3 an aria from Monteverdi's "Poppea" makes its appearance, followed soon afterwards by the duet "Dolce Amor" from the "dramma per musica" "Eteocle e Polinece" by Legrenzi. All these, together with old English allemandes, are presented with immense skill in a highly personal form. And who could fail to follow with smiles the perfectly proportioned, effervescent Finale à la Rossini which the seventy-year-old Strauss lets loose on the surprised listeners at the end of Act 1? From the time of "Ariadne" onward Strauss had a partiality for amusing tricks of this kind: one remembers the delightful obeisance to the art of Lully in the music to "Der Bürger als Edelmann," and the various pieces in the Dance Suite after Couperin. An unfeigned love for these French courtly composers of the 17th and 18th centuries accompanied him throughout his whole life. Unconcerned with differences of period and style, Strauss summoned up the spirits of musical history to prove his mastery in the blending of contrasting elements. His ability in this field has seldom been equalled.

*

Where did he stand with regard to the *folksong*? Is it not a fact that a composer's attitude to folk music indicates his relationship to the community? The importance of the German folk song to Strauss has been underestimated by most of his biographers. Certainly it is true that in an era of imperialism out of touch with the ordinary people folksong, the simple and above all stirring, forward-driving songs of the working class were pushed into the background. The folksong was hardly ever so greatly threatened in the nation's life as it was during those years. It played only a secondary role in the works of the great, and it was not without significance that Wagner, as an old man, spoke of the "irreconcilability" of the elements of folksong. Not that it could ever be wholly forgotten. Such composers as Brahms, and later Mahler, Pfitzner and Haas sensed and savoured it lovingly–like a "beautiful dream to which one scarcely dares surrender oneself" (Knepler). It is an astonishing fact that the longing to return to the folksong, to purity, simplicity and clarity, became all the stronger as the orchestral apparatus became more complex and overwhelming toward the turn of the century. While well-to-do bourgeois society increasingly demanded a flood of sumptuous sound, the representative composers of the age realized that salvation could come only from the folk song and folk dance. A creative method which did not shrink from embellishing the charming simplicity of folksong in the romantic manner and placing it in a setting of opulent luxury was undoubtedly approaching the folk song by a roundabout route via modern art-psychology and civilization, and could not be equated with the direct, natural and naive approach of the classical masters to folk music. Nevertheless there was a definite relationship to the songs of the people, and this is clear in the works of Strauss.

The connection with folk song and folk dance was a source of inspiration to him at times when he was not working on the highest plane of pure artistry but was representing historical or near-contemporary reality. In the event Strauss never again got "down to earth," in music of both immense popular appeal and clarity of ideas, to the extent that he had in the delightful waltz sequences from "Der Rosenkavalier." A musician of high culture and a healthy outlook on the world was here concerned with the fundamentals of the Viennese "Dreher" and related dance forms from the dance hall "Beim Sperl," the home of three-four time. What would remain of the Mediterranean panorama of "Aus Italien" without the Neapolitan popular song "Funiculi-funicula" by Denza, played as a fiery tarantella? What would the virtuistic gymnastics of "Till Eulenspiegel" amount to if Strauss had not placed an irresistible "Gassenhauer" in the mouth of his mischievous hero, or the operatic satire "Feuersnot" without the old Munich melodies "Solang der alte Peter," "Mir san net von Pasing" and "Gut'n Morgen, Herr Fischer!" The peasant dances from the Upper-Palatine in "Schlagobers," the Bavarian "Gestampften" at the country dance in "Intermezzo" and the quick polka of the yodelling Fiakermilli in "Arabella" show Strauss singing and playing amid the people of southern Germany and Austria, whose music he had studied diligently. The delicious closing duet of the young lovers in "Rosenkavalier" is clearly modelled on the lovely folksong style of "Heideröslein."

The stream of folklore flows particularly strongly in "Arabella"–in this respect, too, the historically artistic counterpart to the realistic "Wienerische Maskerad" dating from 22 years earlier. Strauss, at the height of his powers, was inspired by south-Slavonic folk songs to write such warm-blooded, attractively "folky" melodies as the Duet in F of Arabella and Zdenka "Aber der Richtige, wenn's einen gibt für mich" in the first act, and the Duet in E of Arabella and Mandryka "Du wirst mein Gebieter sein" in the second act, with the poetical cadence of its orchestral postlude. (Strauss took the two melodies from the volume of songs "South-Slavonic Folk Melodies, collected and set with piano accompaniment, edited by Franjo Ksaverije Kuhač, Agram 1878/82".) It would be useless to expect to find in these melodies derived from folksong an attempt to make up for dwindling inventive powers. They grew naturally out of the Austro-Hungarian dialect of the work. In Strauss's original sketches he quoted the first eight bars of the original form of the melody used in the first duet. How instructive it is to see the changes he subsequently made from the third bar onward! Instead of the strictly symmetrical construction of the original he adapted the music to the ebb and flow of a freely varied form of the melodic cantilena–and despite this transformation he remained true to the character of Slavonic folksong. At the world première of "Arabella" Clemens Krauss underlined the folk music flavour of the duet between the two sisters by adding mandolines to the tremolo of the violins. Unfortunately this measure to emphasize the national colouring was not included in the score.

"I know of no greater cause of happiness for a composer than to have written a simple song which, fifty years later, has become a folk song, so that the name of its creator has been forgotten . . ." Not only when Strauss made use of particular folk melodies but also when he invented his own melodies and rhythms in folksong style his music found its way to the ear of the people. The important thing is not to "quote" from German or other folk songs, but to "create" in their spirit, not to take something, a melody or dance form, from folk art and then to live at its expense, but to make the characteristics of folk music so much one's own that they exercise a fructifying effect on one's own style. "I take the first two bars of a beautiful old folk song and develop them in my own way to form substantial structures," Strauss told Max Marschalk. Here we have an example of the dialectic process of change which is a common feature of the national art of all countries in the recent history of music. Certain turns of melody sung by Mandryka in "Arabella" ("Mein sind die Wälder" or "Kommen meine Verwalter: was ist's mit unserm Herrn?") could pass at any time for Hungarian or Rumanian folk songs, they are so "genuine," so close to the Magyar music of the people. As regards the art of creating atmosphere through folk music, too, "Arabella" is a work apart. For example Arabella's "Über seine Felder wird der Wagen fahren" at the beginning of the last act is wholly in the character of folksong, and bears witness to a deep love for the music of the people. It is always true to say that Strauss adopted the diatonic simplicity of folksong melodies when he was concerned with expressing very intimate, human feelings. Examples include the sweetly flowing theme of the child's birth in the "Sinfonia domestica" or the straightforward melodies of Barak in "Die Frau ohne Schatten" and of Morosus in "Die schweigsame Frau." (On the other hand the high pathos of the lyrical melodies of "Helena," for example, is far removed from folksong.) Strauss's approaches to folklore are always to be seen in connection with the subject matter of his symphonic and dramatic works. This is so, for example, of the rough "Old German" style of the "Reiterlied" of the Commandant in "Friedenstag" ("Zu Magdeburg in der Reiterschlacht"). When Strauss invoked the spirit of folk music in his last operas, what resulted was straightforward music of noble feeling. In "Danae" we are charmed by an abundance of vocal music of high artistry, and in particular by the heartfelt, Mendelssohnian warmth of the charming Duet in B♭

between Danae and Midas in the third act: "So führ ich dich mit sanfter Hand ins neue, in der Liebe Land." The composer, approaching eighty, had discovered the perfect expression of the spirit of folk music.

In the field of Strauss's lieder the folk song lies, as it were, behind a veil of artistry. Strangely enough, although Strauss constantly sought the simplicity of folk art in these small-scale lyrical works, he generally remained rooted to the style of his youth, which held him back from his ideal. When the young master sang his dewy-fresh "Morgen" or his deeply-felt "Ich trage meine Minne" he achieved the desired effect through a conscious simplicity of melodic character. However, such songs (in particular the "Ständchen") all too easily verge upon the sphere of popular trash, and fail to measure up to the criterion of genuine folk art. Indeed, not many of the songs can really be considered to belong to the class of folk songs. The most valuable pieces in this category include the few songs from "Des Knaben Wunderhorn," among them the roguish "Für fünfzehn Pfennig," the graceful "Himmelsboten zu Liebchens Himmelsbett" and the blunt "Junggesellenschwur," together with the naively fragant "Ich wollt' ein Sträusslein binden" from the Brentano Songs. They represent the late-romantic, individually fashioned artistic folk song, but even they are by no means free from nervous modern tensions of colour which are foreign to the genuine folk song.

*

What an abundance of points of contact with lesser and greater masters of musical history! What a tremendous task of consciously adopting and subordinating within the development which Strauss always regarded as the last offshoot of the romanticism of "Tristan"! His life and work were a single process of stylistic assimilation. Scarcely any other musician has so imbibed the powers of classical and romantic masterworks, and has transformed them into something new, with such creative vitality. He alone has the right to compose who has drawn upon his great heritage, yet seeks his own road. Strauss was the leaven of several generations of musicians—but no starting point of a particular *"school"* like his contemporaries Reger and Schoenberg. (Strauss was active as a teacher only toward the end of his period in Berlin.) The "Straussian elements, the luminosity of sound and the sensuous vibrancy of his music, left their mark from the outset only in the sphere of eclecticism. Such men as Emil Nikolaus von Reznicek, Joseph Marx, Franz Schmidt, Bernhard Sekles and Walter Braunfels adopted from Strauss the brilliance of his orchestral technique and the externals of certain of his procedures (the celesta effect depicting the silver rose in "Rosenkavalier," for example, has been copied hundreds of times), without equalling their original in spirit, wit, or melodic substance. Strauss's tonal physiognomy, his rapid shifts of harmony and his sensitive feeling in the use of colour were not without influence on most of the musical personalities of the dawning century, for example the Englishmen Elgar and Delius, the Czech Suk, the Poles Szymanowski and Karlowicz, the Frenchmen Dukas and Ravel, the Italian Respighi, the Hungarian Bartók and the Swede Alfvén. Debussy, Reger and Mahler owed a good deal to Strauss, both as composer and conductor, while such powerful representatives of new national musical styles as the Moravian Janáček and the Finn Sibelius went their own ways. If "Straussian" elements are noticed even in the ballet "Ondine" and the "Nachtstücke und Arien" composed by the dodecaphonist Henze since his return to romanticism, this does not deny them a fascination of their own. Stravinsky represents a case apart. He has put it on record that during his early days he made a careful study of the scores of "Salome" and "Elektra," but later, in an interview which he gave in 1958 for example, he has spoken about Strauss in a highly derogatory manner. ("'Ariadne' made me want to scream.") Be that as it may, Strauss cannot be overlooked as a phenomenon of his times . . .

I preserve the things of value that we possess,
I support the art of our forbears . . .
Where are the works which speak to the heart of the people,
Which reflect its soul?
Where are they?
I cannot find them, however much I seek.
Only pale aesthetes confront me,
They mock at the old and create nothing new!

What a wealth of self-assurance and scepticism are contained in these words of the theatre director La Roche in "Capriccio," words which shed light on Strauss's own attitude to the music of the generations coming after him! ... "I believe only in music," he once wrote. "Instead of different schools we should talk about genuine and false talents. It is an excellent thing to seek for that which is new and, whenever possible, to speak in new words never heard before, but so far ..." He gave voice to his misgivings concerning every attempt to replace the old musical values by the new values of de-romanticized sound bereft of feeling. The whole intellectually frigid *"New Music"* movement after the First World War remained a closed book to Strauss. ("I have been numbered among the old, the has-beens, for a long time now, so I cannot be expected to understand the compositions of these gentlemen—and to be quite candid I don't understand them"), and the movement's supporters could do nothing with Strauss. When a "young composer," concealing the identity of the iconoclast Paul Hindemith, asked for his renowned colleague's verdict on a new work performed at the first Donaueschingen Music Festival in 1921, Strauss was not slow to reply: "My dear fellow, I believe you have enough talent to enable you to compose in a different manner." When Stravinsky, in a manifesto, proclaimed the "New Objectivity," Strauss replied that mathematics certainly represented a basic element of music, but not the only one ... He loathed jazz, which was incomprehensible to him, describing it as "Music at the Court of Attila." However Strauss, an individualist to an extent which seemed almost mythical in his later years, undoubtedly possessed the ability to recognize anything genuinely new within what he considered were the bounds of real music. So vital a work as Carl Orff's "Carmina burana" won his unqualified praise. "The purity of style," he wrote to the composer after the Vienna performance in 1943, "and the unaffected musical language, free from any posing and any digressions to left or right, make me certain that you will give the stage a valuable work when you find a subject to suit your nature. It is only in the theatre that I can see the future development of which you speak to be possible ..." The aged composer referred in his last writings to certain neo-classical currents of the day. The old was still new to him ... Modern music, new music? The master's reply speaks for itself: "Modern? What does 'modern' mean? Give the word a different significance! Have ideas like Beethoven's, write contrapuntally like Bach, orchestrate like Mozart and be genuine and true children of your own times, then you will be modern!"

THE WORKSHOP

A WHOLE SERIES OF PHOTOGRAPHS SHOW STRAUSS AT
the writing desk in the study of his home at Garmisch, writing
out his scores. There he sits in a comfortable position, a man
who does not create notes from the sweat of his brow, but who
busies himself, to his own satisfaction, with the exercise of his
musical craftsmanship. To him composition was never a matter
of anguish and struggle, but the very reason for his existence,
and its fulfilment. "Je ne travaille pas, je m'amuse"–that phrase
of the French sculptor Maillol was a favourite of Strauss's in
his later years. "Genius is industry," Schopenhauer is said to
have remarked. "But industry and the will to work are also inborn, not merely put on," the composer wrote at the age of seventy. This fact alone enables us to understand how, in addition
to his innumerable duties as an opera director and conductor, he
was able to leave such a wealth of creative work behind him.

Genius is industry–Strauss proved that to be true. When we
consider the works he composed over a period of seven decades
what strikes us first is the extent of this output. Tirelessly he
piled score on score; many of them contain on each page the
thirty staves or more required when writing for all the resources of the full modern orchestra, and every page is covered with
the composer's handwriting, delicate and wonderfully expressive of character. It should not be forgotten that a Strauss opera
contains about three times as many notes as an opera by Mozart.
It is also worth noting that Strauss wrote out each of his fifteen
operas and two ballets, his fourteen major orchestral works and
his songs with orchestra three times: first the draft written in
pencil in his little, battered sketch books which he carried around
with him, generally thrust carelessly in a coat pocket; then came
the piano score, written in ink, and finally the full score, con-

taining few erasures, in which every detail of the work was ready for print. What an enormous volume of painstaking labour, often extending over several years, this entailed! It is highly instructive to consider Strauss's proverbial productivity from the viewpoint of an artistic "time and motion study." Everyone who ever had an opportunity to witness a working day in the life of Strauss the composer and conductor will have been astonished not only by the fluent hand but by the unique economy of his actions and by his gift of making the best possible use of every minute. Apart from his creative work his daily tasks included dealing with a vast amount of correspondence (nearly always writing his own letters with pen and ink), and reading libretti which had been sent to him. Even his few holidays were regarded, at most, as an escape from business commitments—the creative work went on uninterrupted. "Work is a constant and never tiring source of enjoyment, to which I have completely dedicated myself" (1886).

In the lecture on Strauss which he gave at Berlin in 1957 Joseph Gregor spoke amusingly about the master's technique of composition: "He made no use of the piano, and didn't even hum over what he was writing." He described Strauss's method of instrumentation: "With the aid of a ruler the barline was drawn most accurately across the 30 or 50 staves on the page. He began not with the basses, the fundamental orchestral part which many musicians would use as their starting point, but with the piccolo, then he proceeded to fill in all the instrumental parts in the bar on which he was working, from the top of the page down to the bottom. When that bar was completed the ruler was again placed across the 30 to 50 staves, another barline was drawn, and once again there followed the process which I once compared to an old man clambering across a rocky slope. Imagine, if you can, such astonishing command of the tonal picture, not only in its vertical details but also in the relationship between each part and its neighbours. All this went on in conjunction with a tonal scheme which was only then taking shape, and with the need to keep the whole course of a musical episode, an opera scene or a movement of a concert work, constantly in mind. In answer to my perplexed question why he did not begin with the lowest parts as was customary, he replied that one could naturally do so, but that there would be a danger, when working upward from the bottom of the page, of smudging ink which was still wet with one's sleeve. . . ."

It is worth while examining the versatility of the life and work of the musician Strauss. He never considered himself, by calling or inclination, to be solely a composer. A worthy successor to the great Dresden reformers Weber and Wagner, he always wanted to be concerned with the life and practical work of the opera theatre. He did not simply compose for voices and instruments, he felt the need to master every aspect of the setting in which his music was to unfold itself. Strauss was a man both of ears and eyes. In his work for the theatre he was always interested in the idea of the "Gesamtkunstwerk." How much time and effort even the young opera conductor at Weimar devoted to problems of production and décor! His correspondence with Ritter at that time gives a clear idea of his multiplicity of duties: "Now that I have some peace after a ceaseless round of activities as a conductor, solo repetiteur, scenic artist, stage director and theatre tailor, I can give my mind to the duties of my private life again, and . . ." (here he informed his friend of his engagement). Especially during the years after the First World War when he had complete authority as director of the Vienna State Opera, Strauss concerned himself with every detail of the organization, both artistic and technical. He would sometimes even order a sofa or chair to be removed from the set of a production with which he himself had no direct concern, because he considered it to be stylistically out of place. As late as 1948 his concept of opera in all its aspects was reflected in a passage from a letter in which he greeted Joseph Keilberth as one of the few "baton wavers" who "look up from the score, trumpets and trombones, to see what is going on beyond the prompt box." Strauss, the complete man of the theatre, also expressed his views in his numerous publications dealing with questions of a better and healthier organization of the machinery of opera. Prominent among these were his "Anregungen eines Städtebund-Theaters" (1914) and "Erwägungen zum Opernspielplan" (1922). He considered an "experimental institute" to be less important than a "kind of academy where a selected repertoire would be brought to performance in the most perfect manner possible." Right into his old age Strauss concerned himself with the simplification of the German opera sys-

109

tem. During the war he evolved a plan to take opera out of the "state theatres" with their mixed repertoire of operas, operettas and plays, and to present it at a few centres devoted solely to opera. His "Artistic Testament" which he gave Karl Böhm in 1945 dealt with the structure of a national opera organization similar to those which have since been created in Moscow and Prague, to mention two typical examples. Not many opera composers possessed or possess such clear and well-informed views regarding artistic perception and practice.

Almost independently of the meteoric ascent of the young tone poet there proceeded the development of the highly gifted conductor. In Meiningen, Munich, Weimar, and Munich again from 1894, audiences discovered with surprise that this slim musician, whose health was endangered by various illnesses, proved to have a most promising talent at the conductor's desk. ("One stands up, and can do it," Mottl's explanation of the secret of conducting, applied to him perfectly.) Then he took over the conducting of "Tannhäuser" at Bayreuth–what an important assignment for a musician only just thirty years old! We should not, however, ignore the difficulties which faced the young conductor, especially in his "dear native city," in the shape of "intrigues, hatred and envy." "It's really not possible to stay in this swamp any longer!" he wrote to Bülow, and in a letter to Dora Wihan which is in the possession of the present author: "... after three years of breathing swamp vapour, fresh air really does one good. It will be very hard to go away from Munich, from my family and from two friends such as Ritter and Thuille to whom I have become attached in a way you could scarcely imagine, but I must go, because my whole future depends on my avoiding falling a victim to the Munich swamp fever. . . . Where am I going? To Weimar! Together with Lassen and under Bronsart as Director! That's a good exchange for Munich. In Weimar, the town of the future, the place where Liszt worked for so long! I hope for a *very* great deal there!"

In later life Strauss liked to give an account of his early days as a conductor. "I was not (in my first period in Munich) a particularly good conductor! Although I was adept at filling a breach–even at that time I took over an opera by Rheinberger –I lacked routine experience, in which far less talented colleagues had the advantage over me, and my determination to

110

abide by my "own tempi" often stood in the way of the required smooth running of the performance. This led to some cases of the familiar lack of co-ordination between singers and orchestra, all the more so on account of the fact that the operas which I was given to conduct at that time did not interest me enough to encourage me to study them in sufficient detail; they really needed a great deal of careful preparation prior to the rehearsals, and I found this far too boring in the case of such works as 'Nachtlager von Granada' and 'Martha.' ... My second engagement at Munich (as Court Conductor, at first together with Levi) suffered mainly from the friction between Possart (Court Theatre), who was well disposed toward me, and Perfall (Court Music Direction), whose attitude to me became more and more hostile as new works of mine ('Eulenspiegel', 'Zarathustra') appeared. ... In any event I conducted 'Tristan' and 'Meistersinger' in Munich, and improved my technique, although much was still to be desired. ... In 1898 I was offered a position for life in Munich, but at the last moment Perfall wanted to reduce the salary already agreed upon. As Weingartner had resigned from the Berlin Opera I seized my opportunity and went to Berlin. Hochberg and Pierson appointed me Court Conductor (together with Muck), and I never had any reason to regret my association with Berlin; all my experiences were happy, and I was received with a great deal of encouragement and hospitality. ..."

At the beginning of October in that year Strauss arrived in the German capital, which was a great musical centre. "Berlin is a charming city; my wife has rented a fine house there (Knesebeckstraße 30). ... People have made the most flattering attempts to keep me (in Munich), in fact I am beginning to be extremely popular here–but it's too late!" At the beginning of November Strauss appeared for the first time at the conductor's desk of the "Lindenoper", directing a performance of "Tristan." During the eight months of the 1898/99 season he conducted no fewer than 71 performances of 25 different operas, including "Freischütz," "Euryanthe," "Lohengrin" and a cycle of the "Ring," and in his second season he conducted 90 performances of 30 works. In all, the Berlin audiences had the chance to see the eminent composer conducting 700 performances over a period of ten years. His position in Berlin, which had been pre-

111

ceeded by a season as conductor of the Berlin Philharmonic Orchestra (1894/95, following the death of Bülow), was the first appointment as a conductor which gave him an opportunity to exercise all his authority both as artist and organizer. (In his contract he was allowed holidays of eight weeks in the summer and four weeks in the winter, with an annual salary of 18,000 marks and a pension after ten years of service.) Strauss continued this operatic work, as General Music Director from 1908, until 1910, from then onward conducting only the symphony concerts, directing a certain number of opera performances as a guest conductor. It should never be forgotten that during the turmoil of 1918, the year of revolution, he again sprang into the breach at the Berlin Opera, "as an act of self-sacrifice, for pure love of his art and the call of old loyalties." Eleven months later, after the founding of the new "State Theatre," in the expectation that his office would become subordinate to the "Oberregisseur" of long standing Georg Droescher, he withdrew from the artistic direction. At the beginning of 1919 he conducted a few more performances, including his first "Parsifal," then he succumbed to the lure of the Vienna Opera.

What Strauss once later mentioned to Schuh as ideal, "creative work regarded as almost a secondary matter beside a real career as a conductor" became reality for him early in his life. It corresponded to his maxim that the artist must have a firm economic basis of his existence in order to be able to engage in creative work. How strongly Strauss felt himself drawn to his conducting! Nothing demonstrates this more clearly than the letter which he sent to the sceptical Hofmannsthal shortly before he was appointed to be director of the Vienna Opera: "So I tell you it was my innermost desire, for thirty years, to obtain an authoritative artistic post as head of a major court opera theatre. It never came my way–possibly because I was always regarded as the opposite to the routinists so much in favour, possibly because it was considered that as an all-too independent artistic personality, a composer of repute, I could not be trusted to have as much interest as a purely interpretative musician for the ordinary work of the theatre with its everyday requirements. So it is that after twenty years of work in Berlin, with. ... Count Hülsen, impervious to all persuasion, opposing every effort on my part to gain a share in the direction of the institution, I have

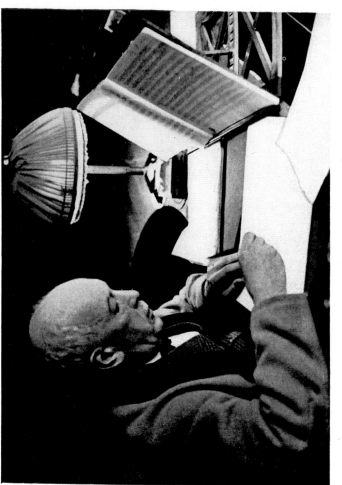

During the instrumentation of "Die schweigsame Frau" in Garmisch (1934)

"Der Bürger als Edelmann"
First page of the score of the Overture (1911)

become what you now so severely censure. What holds me in Berlin is the duty to keep a father's loving hand on the performances of my own works at the foremost musical establishment of Germany, together with the joy of having a splendidly disciplined orchestra which is perfectly attuned to me; being constantly in contact with this instrument of mine, like Antaeus, I gain fresh stimulus for my work as a composer . . ."

It is clear to every intelligent person how much work such positions involved, how the musical direction of Germany's foremost opera house alone claimed the *entire* man. . . . But that was not all! Despite his many commitments Strauss extended his field of activity to an ever increasing extent. He also conducted concerts regularly in Berlin; he appeared as a guest conductor in London and Madrid, in Paris and New York. He pressed Schuch to keep to the proposed date for the Dresden world première of "Salome," as he was to conduct in Moscow two days later. . . . His travelling was increased still further by the fact that he never disdained to add lustre to performances of his works even in smaller music centres (e. g. Plauen and Darmstadt) by taking part himself. Not until the autumn of 1919 when, after overcoming opposition in some quarters, he took over the direction of the Vienna Opera in conjunction with Franz Schalk, did the furious tempo of his existence seem to be too much for him. He left Vienna, with its perpetual rivalries and struggles against officialdom, in the summer of 1924; like his predecessor Mahler he had found himself virtually compelled to withdraw. Schalk became the sole director. From then on Strauss avoided a permanent position with any opera company or orchestra. He restricted himself to agreements for guest appearances, sometimes spread over a long period, which allowed him sufficient free time. He soon came to an amicable agreement with Schalk on this basis, enabling him to work in Vienna from time to time.

The fantastic volume of work to which Strauss was accustomed during the days of his heaviest commitments is indicated by the following: "In Berlin I conducted concerts consisting entirely of unfamiliar works with the mediocre Tonkünstler Orchestra for three years, really hard work compared with the Opera! I might mention the following in passing as a typical day's work: 11 o'clock until 2 'Don Juan' orchestral rehearsal,

3 until 6 Bruckner Third Symphony, 'Tristan' in the evening..."
In February 1904, when Strauss went to America to conduct the
world première of the "Sinfonia domestica" in New York as
part of a whole series of concerts devoted to his works, he reported cheerfully to Schillings: "Twenty-one concerts with about
twenty orchestras got through in four weeks, together with travelling day and night, dinners in my honour and other damned
nonsense." Strauss did not even mention the fact that his engagements also included a whole series of lieder recitals with his
wife. Also revealing was a letter which he wrote, at the age of
sixty, to Ludwig Karpath while on his tour of South America.
"My first stay in Buenos Aires was very pleasant. . . . I obtained
excellent performances of 'Salome' and 'Elektra.' . . . Just think
how the people here work: Thursday afternoon general rehearsal
'Elektra,' Friday 'Elektra.' Culminating point of the work:
Sunday afternoon performance of 'Salome,' in the evening 'Elektra,' both under my very own direction, in which, for example,
Frau Dahmen sang an outstanding Salome in the afternoon and
Chrysothemis in the evening. And both were good performances,
by no means slovenly or tired." (Strauss evidently did not think
of himself at all).

How was Strauss the composer to have his say in the midst of
such a round of activities? . . . In the same letter in which he
gave details of his work as a conductor on the tour with a wealth
of detail characteristic of him, and in which he repeatedly mentioned how "well he was," there is also a reference to the activity of the creative musician. He wrote, quite casually: "I have
already written thirty pages of the score of my new opera 'Intermezzo.' Hope to get to near the end of the work here." He did.
He wrote on the final page of the score: "Buenos Aires, 23rd
August 1923." . . . Strauss possessed to a high degree the ability
to plan accurately. When writing his major operas he would
advise the publishers when he expected to be able to deliver
each act, almost to the day. The same disciplined division of the
working day which he considered a necessary condition for artistic effectiveness as a conductor and man of the theatre applied also to the composer. While his "rehearsal sheets," on
which his plans were often laid down weeks ahead, were both
feared and admired, there were "aesthetes" in plenty who were
scandalized by his hard-headed planning of creative work. More

114

Draft rehearsal schedule for the world première of "Elektra" at Dresden. Bottom right: Additions in Schuch's handwriting.

than once Strauss surprised the musical world by completing his extensive scores even *before* the date he had set as his target. For example he wrote to his mother from Luxor in January 1893, at the time of "Guntram": "I work from 10 until 1 every day: the instrumentation of the first act is going ahead slowly but surely. From 3 until 4 I work again. . . . About 6 it's cool and dark; then I write letters or work until 7. I hope to finish the instrumentation of the first act here. The second act will follow in Sicily, and by next Christmas, I believe, everything will be ready." (In fact Strauss completed "Guntram" as early as September.) What an astonishing command of organization is demonstrated, for example, by the letter sent to Schuch in December 1907: "I am busy with 'Elektra' (50 pages of score are already written), and I definitely hope to be finished a year from today ..." (In actual fact "Elektra" was finished months before that.) Then there was the letter sent to Fritz Busch in September 1931: "'Arabella' third act is ready in rough sketches; score will be another two years or so! Will probably be finished when I reach seventy." (The première took place at Dresden in July 1933.) When we learn that Strauss needed only a bare two months for the composition of the complex Prologue to "Ariadne," and see from the manuscript of "Metamorphosen" that the eighty-one-year-old composer needed exactly a month to write the hundred or so pages of the score of this work, we get some idea of his ability to work with concentration.

Only external circumstances such as the difficulties presented by the two world wars delayed the world premières of his operas; in the cases of only two large-scale orchestral works, the Symphony in E♭ of 1925 and the tone poem "Die Donau," intended as a "tribute in music" to the Vienna Philharmonic on its hundredth birthday, was he unable to achieve what he had in mind. Work on both came to a standstill before the sketches were completed. In all other instances he completed his scores as planned. ... "Don't talk to me about works that have never been finished! ... Only if something is completed can it claim to be a work of art. Anything unfinished is the result of disparity between intention and ability. ... We have enough to do concerning ourselves with completed works. This worship of torsos is false romanticism and leads nowhere!"

The main thing was that Strauss, restless and yet so consciously living, always felt he had an obligation to the world as a *creative* artist. From his Weimar period onward he kept to a definite routine in his work as a composer: the actual process of composition took place during the summer months in Marquartstein and later in his home at Garmisch, the time-consuming activity of instrumentation during the months of his duties as a conductor and on journeys, in Berlin, Vienna, in hotels or at friend's houses. Not until his old age could he dispose of his time exactly as he pleased. Viewing his œuvre as a whole, one notices a temporary slackening off in the intensity of his creative work during the years when he was director of the Vienna Opera. Apart from that, however, the furious tempo of his existence never endangered his joy in the production of new works. On the contrary Strauss, like such other great masters of opera as Mozart, Weber, Wagner and Verdi, was only half himself unless, before the completion of a dramatic work, he already had the libretto of the next one in his hands. He liked to order matters in advance so that any break would be avoided (he had no very high opinion of a "creative pause"). In his old age this untiring man could not work fast enough. Once the rough sketches of an opera were complete he wanted to begin composing the next, and to get down to the instrumentation of the first, which Strauss considered merely as so much manual work, when he had time later. When the Dresden Opera Director Alfred Reucker expressed concern that this practice would delay the completion of "Arabella," he received the following humorous reply from Garmisch: "I'll get that together all right, even if I pass the age of seventy, but whether I'll have any good ideas after that–who can tell?"

*

Strauss at work. . . . Scarcely anyone described the master's *"Workshop"* as aptly as his close colleague Stefan Zweig. "This 'working' is a very strange process with Strauss. Nothing daemonic, none of the artist's fever of inspiration here, nothing of the fits of depression and desperation such as we know from accounts of Beethoven and Wagner. Strauss works factually and coolly, he composes–like Johann Sebastian Bach and all sublime craftsmen of their art–calmly and regularly. At nine o'clock in the morning he sits down at his desk and resumes his composition at exactly the spot where he had left off the day before... working without a break until twelve or one o'clock. In the afternoon he plays skat, writes out two or three pages of the full score, and invariably conducts at the theatre in the evening. Any kind of nervousness is foreign to him; his artistic intellect is always equally bright and clear by day and night. When the servant knocks on the door, bringing him his evening dress for conducting, he goes to the theatre and conducts with the same

117

certainty and as calmly as he has played skat in the afternoon, and the inspiration begins again at exactly the same spot next morning. This is because, to quote Goethe, Strauss 'commands' his ideas. . . ."

All his life the best ideas came to him out of cheerful relaxation. "It's strange that everything I've done casually, with my left hand, has turned out particularly well," he remarked to Willi Schuh. This may, however, seem to contradict other statements by Strauss to the effect that the current of his imagination was made to flow more strongly "by spiritual excitement, also anger and annoyance." "The melodic idea which descends on me suddenly out of the sky, which appears without having to be prompted by any outward event or any personal emotion–the latter is also likely to be a direct cause, as I have often experienced from quite different types of excitement unrelated to art–comes straight into the mind unannounced, uninfluenced by the understanding" ("Vom melodischen Einfall," 1940). This is the kind of circumstance in which the young "Composer" in the Prologue to the second version of "Ariadne" conceives the idea of the sweet melody of dawning love. He sings: "I was annoyed by an insolent lackey, it flashed by–then the tenor boxed the wigmaker's ears–and I had it!"

Nothing was further from Strauss's nature than achievement as a result of hard compulsion. "Liberation through work," he wrote at the time of Mahler's death on a piece of paper containing notes concerning his "Alpensinfonie," and in a letter dating from the period of "Helena" he referred to "agreeable birth pangs." "Strauss is in a real fever of work on the second act of 'Helena'; he told me he often stays up late into the night in order to capture his ideas," Hofmannsthal wrote to Carl Jakob Burckhardt. The main theme of "Rosenkavalier" was written down in great haste on a telegram form. . . . Every kind of romantic rapture in composition was foreign to Strauss. When Gregor wrote a great spate of words about his work on "Daphne" the far more factual Strauss replied: "Above all be on your guard against the dangerous enthusiasm, true and genuine though it is, with which you have written the piece. Such products are neither compatible with sober artistic understanding, nor capable of arousing the same feelings in the audience. . . ." A great deal is born of the unerring aim of genius. For example in "Salome," shortly before the execution of Jokanaan, there occurs a mysterious, mystical chord which found its way into musical history as a harmonic curiosity ("cacophony" as it was termed at that time). Strauss was asked how he had discovered this chord. "That? I just hacked it out!" A great many other instances of that kind could be quoted. In common with Mozart and Schubert, Strauss was not disturbed in his composing by the noisy surrounding world of family and friends, in fact they gave him new ideas. "What I'm doing is so agreeable," he once exclaimed to an unexpected visitor, "that I can leave it, and go back to it whenever I like." And when he was told how slowly and painfully an eminent colleague had worked at his latest great opera he said: "Why does he compose at all if he finds it so difficult!"

This calmness of a natural creative ability, with the man never standing in the way of the artist, is typical of Strauss. "I write at a work table which looks exactly the same as all other tables, either in a house coat or in an English cheviot suit," he once rambled on rather ironically to a reporter. "I am never feverishly excited.... One must be master of oneself in order to keep that ever changing, ever moving chessboard called the orchestra under control. The head that composed 'Tristan' must have been as cold as marble...." His statement to David Evans was similar: "I compose everywhere, on walks or journeys, eating or drinking, at home or elsewhere, in noisy hotels, in my garden, in railway trains. My sketch book never leaves my side, and as soon as a motif strikes me I write it down. One of the most important melodies of 'Rosenkavalier' occurred to me while I was playing a Bavarian card game..." There were abundant proofs of this ability to conjure up musical ideas at seemingly unsuitable moments.

We now know that the musical *"idea"* cannot come, as bourgeois psychology imagines, from a vacuum or from the subconscious mind. Or have all great composers really left themselves at the mercy of chance or relied on a gift of grace at the moment when they needed their initial inspiration? The real "impulse" may not depend on any direct act of will on the part of the composer—indeed, every idea represents an "effect" which must necessarily have been preceded by a "cause." This cause can, however, only occur in a propitious combination of personal and social circumstances, and impressions received from life.

119

("The psychological peculiarities of musical creation consist of the many, sometimes scarcely perceptible, connections between the creative process and life around," according to Jarustowski.) The idea received like a sudden flash of light should be regarded as the decisive impulse of the creative *"must,"* in order to avoid any error.

In common with all great masters Strauss was not content with the musical idea as it occurred to him. With the help of a "perfectly functioning brain" (to quote Bernard Shaw) he did everything possible to assist the process by means of intensive "work through the understanding." The best clues to the transformation of an as yet imperfect idea, swiftly noted down, to a perfectly moulded musical theme are given by the sketch books. A sight of the original libretti with Strauss's annotations is also of great interest. He often made a note of ideas which came to him as he was reading the text. Frequently what first formed in his mind were merely vague ideas of motifs and general musical characteristics expressing a particular dramatic situation or conflict of wills; often he would merely indicate the tonality which his inner ear heard at a particular passage.... Karl Böhm has given an exact account of this unusual occurrence at the first encounter between a genius and the work which was to be: "One afternoon in Garmisch we were lying side by side in easy chairs waiting to see the text of the opera 'Daphne'—which Strauss later dedicated to me—and which Franz Strauss, his son, brought down to us from the study where Gregor was working. Strauss read it through, then handed it over to me. I became aware of something almost incredible which seemed to take me right into the process of creation itself. On the margins of the pages—I repeat, after reading the text for the first time—Strauss had jotted down notes concerning rhythms, generally also the tonality, and in sections concerning several characters precise indications of the musical form. And he had needed, for what was already a creative activity, scarcely any more time than it took to read through the text...."

It seems certain that in Strauss's case the creative act was not something which started at any particular time on any particular day. He allowed a period of time to elapse after the first germ of the idea had been implanted in his mind; during that period the idea first became firmly established and then took on clear melodic shape. What is generally considered to be the act of "composition" began with Strauss when he set to work on page 1 of the piano sketches. His works were not only brilliantly "conceived," but were "worked over" thoroughly in his mind. It was clear to him from his early youth that he could not simply rely on the "idea," but that one had to learn to assist the creative powers by intellectual means. ("This dilettantish rigmarole about inspiration and workmanship–in connection with theatrical impotentias whose 'inspiration' is no inspiration at all in most cases, and whose technical 'workmanship' is often clumsy in the extreme–should be completely ignored," Strauss wrote to the present author in 1936). It was his technical skill which built up the overall structures of his works, enabling him to achieve the naturalness of his programmatic orchestral works and the psychological drawing of the characters in his operas.

Unlike Wagner, Strauss repeatedly gave illuminating accounts of his method of composition. Of more consequence than the answers he gave to the questionnaire sent to composers by Hausegger and Bahle are many passages in his letters to friends and colleagues. "Musical ideas, like new wine, must be kept for a time, and can be taken out only after they have been given time to ferment and mature. I often write down a motif or a melody, then put it away for a year. When I return to it I find that quite unconsciously something in me–the imagination–has been at work on it. . . . Before I note down even the slightest sketch for an opera I allow the text to permeate my mind for at least six months and take root within me, so that I am wholly familiar with the situations and characters. Only then do I allow musical ideas to enter my head. The preliminary sketches become more elaborate sketches which are written down, worked on, put into shape as a piano score and worked on again, often up to four times. This is the difficult part of the work. I finally write the score in my study, straight through and without effort, working up to twelve hours a day. I have long recognized that when composing I am unable to write anything without a programme to guide me" (Evans).

The following statement is based on conversations with Marschalk. (The reader should note that by the "shape" of a work Strauss meant something different from the interpretation put on the word in the sphere of progressive musical aesthetics.) "I work on melodies for a very long time; a great distance separates the first idea from the final melodic shape. Yes, the melodic shape; everything is taught at conservatoires except (in sufficient detail) motif construction, which appears to me to be the most important thing of all. The motif is a matter of inspiration; it is an idea, and most people content themselves with it, although true art shows itself only in the development of the idea. What matters is not the beginning of the melody but its continuation, its development into a perfect melodic shape ... Building it up naturally requires talent, but this is also one of the most difficult technical problems. We no longer have fresh brains, with so long a road of development behind us, and we must be very careful how we go about the work. Two bars of a melody occur to me spontaneously, so I spin it out and write a few more bars, but I soon sense inadequacies, and I lay one foundation stone after another until at last I find the right version. That sometimes takes a long time, a very long time. A melody which seems to have been born in a moment is almost always the result of laborious work...." This confession should not lessen our astonishment at the power of Strauss's inspiration, quite the reverse.

Strauss wrote about the origins of his songs: "Musical ideas have prepared themselves in me—God knows why—and when, as it were, the barrel is full a song appears in the twinkling of an eye as soon as I come across a poem more or less corresponding to the subject of the imaginary song while glancing through a book of poetry. If, however, the flint does not strike a spark at the decisive moment, if I find no poem corresponding to the subject which exists in my sub-conscious mind, then the creative urge has to be re-channelled to the setting of some other poem which I think lends itself to music. It goes slowly, though, because the music which had developed spontaneously has to be reshaped if it is to see the light of day. I resort to artifice, the melody flows sluggishly, and I have to use all my technique to produce something which will stand up to stern self-criticism."

In the papers which Strauss wrote in his old age he again formulated what music represented to him—although at that late stage of his thinking and feeling he gave no answer to the question of a totally unexpected "inspiration." "What is a musical idea? In general a motif, a melody which suddenly occurs to me, without being summoned by my understanding, especially in the morning immediately after waking, or in a dream. . . . Has my imagination been at work on its own during the night, without my conscious knowledge, without leaving a 'recollection' (Plato)?" And again "My own experience: if, during the evening, I get stuck at a certain point while composing, and no further progress seems possible despite a great deal of hard thinking, I close the piano or my sketch book, go to sleep, and when I wake in the morning I know how to continue. Through what spiritual and physical process?"

One of the remarkable features of this process is the fact that in the first instance Strauss merely indicated the outlines of most of his finest melodic ideas; they blossomed out into fully-fashioned melodies and took on their final form only at the dramatically decisive moment. This technique, which can be found to a lesser extent in Wagner (Isolde's Liebestod) and Bruckner, was developed and refined in a masterly way by Strauss. It occurs in the hesitant introduction to the melodic "events" of the Epilogue in "Heldenleben," in the D♭ major cantilena of the concluding Trio of "Rosenkavalier" and in the deeply-felt Watchmen's Song from "Frau ohne Schatten." It is encountered in a striking form in "Arabella": when the Countess comes down the staircase at the beginning of Act 2 and walks toward Mandryka we hear for the first time the striking succession of chords which later unfolds as a musical reminiscence of sensuous beauty during Arabella's last important meeting with her lover. Indeed this economy with which Strauss presented his ideas in the right light, enabling him to create their harmonic setting and weave them together, accounts for a good deal of the effectiveness of his music. His scores were almost always written in close connection with their programme or subject, "in the correct sequence." One well-known exception: Strauss added Salome's Dance to the score after the rest of the opera was complete. Apart from that instance he probably departed from the original order only in the case of "Die schweigsame Frau": it must be presumed from Fritz Busch's account of a play-through of the opera from the piano sketches in February 1933 that the lyrical epilogue of old Morosus was included in the first stages of composition, and that the overture was added after the completion of the opera proper. It would be pointless to attempt to show that any difference in quality exists between such works as "Don Juan" and "Rosenkavalier" which were composed at great speed, and others such as the "Alpensinfonie," "Die Frau ohne Schatten" and "Intermezzo" which took many years to germinate, merely because one work flowed more freely under his hand than another. Small-scale works of less artistic importance were often composed at a sitting immediately after Strauss had happened, purely by chance, to read the poem. He once mentioned specifically in this connection "Traum durch die Dämmerung" and "Der Stern." In the cases of several planned operas, one to have been based by Ernst von Wolzogen on Cervantes and another by Hofmannsthal after Calderón among others, it proved advisable after a time to subject the project to a critical examination, which led to its abandonment. The contrasts between the subjects chosen by Strauss, above all as an opera composer, are really astonishing. Not only was "Elektra" followed by "Rosenkavalier" and "Frau ohne Schatten" by "Schlagobers"–while still occupied with the heroic Finale of "Friedenstag" Strauss began to search for an ironic subject.

The striving after artistic perfection, the quest for and struggle to capture the last ounce of valid expression are characteristics which appear in almost all Strauss's important works. Before he sketched the fugato Prelude to the last act of "Rosenkavalier" he is said to have composed a dozen fugues in accordance with the strict rules of the old masters. He repeatedly revised the score of the tone poem "Macbeth" before it took on its final form. Three times he rewrote the Klytemnestra scene in "Elektra" before it satisfied him, and even so apparently light a task as the composition of the skat scene of "Intermezzo" was in reality no easy matter, as is shown by a piano sketch marked "Fourth Version." In such cases, as his own severest critic, Strauss wrote the unmistakable word "schlecht" (bad) on the border of the page. "When writing the Klytemnestra scene I hesitated and interrupted the work until I hit on the right note. I generally sit down and try over my idea. If it goes right at once everything is plain sailing. If not, I prefer to stop right away." (From a conversation reported by Oscar Bie.) And in 1914, in connection with the first sketches of "Frau ohne Schatten": "So far I am very dissatisfied with myself; I have made the highest demands on myself, but what I have done to date only partially measures up to my expectations." No suggestion of mere routine even in ripe old age–Strauss confessed that he had subjected the completed rough draft of "Danae" to a further searching examination.... Extensive studies of cultural and artistic history accompanied the writing of most of Strauss's stage works. Each score concealed serious and responsible preparatory work. Strauss's correspondence with Romain Rolland shows how much scientific perception he brought to bear on the literary and spiritual contents of Oscar Wilde's "Salome." He asked the French writer's advice on innumerable points concerning cultural history and phonetics.

The manner in which Strauss collaborated with his librettists reveals a great deal about him and his work. In actual fact Strauss set scarcely a single libretto to music in the form in which he had received it from his literary colleague. This man who, as in all other matters of life and art, knew exactly what he wanted, not only chose his subjects himself, but took a prominent part in deciding the final form which the libretti were to take. (Only in the case of "Die schweigsame Frau" were his alterations to the text unimportant.) There was almost always a tedious round of discussions, with ideas passed backwards and forwards until the artistic collaboration could stand up to the severest criticism in every detail. The chapters dealing with the individual operas will show that it made a great deal of difference to the creative process whether the librettist was Hofmannsthal, Zweig or Gregor. It can easily be seen that the musician had the deciding word from "Rosenkavalier" right through to "Capriccio," above all in the construction of the concluding scenes. Strauss accepted the same responsibility for subject, treatment, libretto and stage effect that we hear of in the case of Verdi. Strauss possessed the striking ability to sum up the essence of a new opera subject instantly, although it generally originated in the form of a loosely-knit account, and at the same time so to shape it that it took on a firmly constructed form in his mind.

Three Crown witnesses have their say.... Hofmannsthal on the first conversation with Strauss, concerning "Rosenkavalier": "His manner of listening was truly productive. I felt as though he were assigning unborn music to the characters who as yet scarcely existed. Then he said: 'We'll do that!' " ... Zweig on

his first meeting with the composer of "Die schweigsame Frau":
". . . it was a pleasant surprise to me how quickly, how clear-sightedly Strauss agreed to all my proposals. I would never have supposed him to possess such an immediate grasp of artistic problems, and such astonishingly thorough knowledge of dramaturgy. Even while one was relating a story to him he would give it dramatic shape and at once–an even more astonishing fact–adapt it within the limits of his own ability, which he recognized with an almost uncanny clarity of perception. . . . After we had agreed upon the basic outlines he gave me another piece of advice. He said he would give me absolute freedom, as he was never inspired by an opera libretto which was tailored to measure in advance, like those of Verdi, but only by a really poetic work. . . ." And finally Gregor, who laid various ideas before Strauss in 1935, including those of "Friedenstag," "Daphne" and, even at that early stage, "Danae": "While the mist of an afternoon of heavy rain swirled about outside, he read the six sheets of paper. . . . I still remember with great clarity that he did not spend more than two minutes on any of the sheets, and he did not read any of them through a second time. While still reading he put three aside, then he gave them back to me with the remark that they would interest him as dramatic subjects. Within a quarter of an hour the programme of work for a period which has now lasted for four years had been laid down."

*

Strauss fell victim to some amusing little accidents when he simply could not write quickly enough in his desire to complete a score. For example in "Rosenkavalier," which he wrote at almost Rossinian speed ("I'm getting through it like a knife through butter") he twice set a passage of the text wrongly. In the first instance he composed a stage direction of Hofmannsthal's: the statement that Ochs was to address the Marschallin "diskret und vertraulich" (discreetly and confidentially), as part of the sung text, so that Ochs now introduces his Leopold to the Marschallin with the words: "Darf ich das Gegenstück diskret vertraulich dero sauberm Kammerzoferl präsentieren?" In the second instance Strauss, in his eagerness to get on with the composition, failed to observe the placing of a comma. In the or-

126

iginal text the words of Faninal's Major-Domo were: "Der hochadelige Bräutigamsvater, sagt die Schicklichkeit, muß ausgefahren sein, bevor der silberne Rosenkavalier vorfährt." Strauss
misplaced the comma by one word: "Der hochadelige Bräutigamsvater sagt, die Schicklichkeit muß ausgefahren sein, bevor . . ." When his attention was drawn to this fact, he is said to
have replied: "Well I've composed it like that, we'll leave it as
it is!" A truly Straussian remark, even if it should prove to be
apocryphal! Later, in "Helena," he noticed a similar mistake
himself, and replaced the stage direction "Schon im halben
Schlaf" (already half asleep) which he had inadvertently composed, by other words. Then there was the harmless slip in the
score of "Die schweigsame Frau" which has afforded amusement to musical historians. During the scene of the second act
in which the "priest" and the "notary" enter, Strauss introduces
them with an attractive Allegro from the Fitzwilliam Virginal
Book, the famous collection of early English keyboard music;
he had the misfortune to misread the word "Anton." as the actual name of the composer of the piece.

Strauss leads his listeners into the realm of musical *humour,*
now wholly intentional in its effect, by means of numerous musical quotations and self-quotations. ("If I were discreet I wouldn't
be called–Till," he wrote at the age of eighty.) His sense of humour is easily seen as a product of his pleasure in the cheerful
things of life. There is in fact an amusing vein of humour running through many of his tone poems and operas–a sparkling
rondo of his popular themes, a gay "Quid-pro-quo" of contrapuntal complexities. Ever since the time when the young Strauss
of the "Burleske" had made very amusing parodistic use of the
storm motif from "Die Walküre," it was evident that he had
a roguish wit. How many cross-references there are in the symphonic poems, in particular "Heldenleben," in which the section
entitled "The Hero's works of peace" brings together motifs
from a wide range of earlier important works by Strauss, while
"Heldenleben" itself is quoted in "Intermezzo!" How brilliantly
Strauss wove these reminiscences into the texture of his scores,
with scarcely a join to be detected! During the spendid dinner
of Herr Jourdain in "Der Bürger als Edelmann" the second
course is "lamb cutlet in the Italian manner," and Strauss introduces the motif of the bleating of sheep from "Don Quixote."

127

The Munich declaration of war of "Feuersnot" ("Der stellt sich euch immer auf's neu' zum Strauß") is clearly related to the war theme from "Guntram," and at the discussion on opera in "Capriccio" between the poet Oliver and the musician Flamand there are echoes of tenderly stylized melodic lines from the mythological worlds of "Ariadne" and "Daphne"–all these quotations are highly significant. Almost more striking are the examples of borrowings from other masters. (Only a composer of equal stature can quote from the works of another.) Who would fail to recognize the Valhalla theme in "Feuersnot," or would be in doubt about the identity of the wine served at Jourdain's table when Strauss quotes the swirling theme of the Rhine from "Das Rheingold"? Who would need to be told what opera is referred to when the singer in "Intermezzo" speaks of "tremendously energetic rehearsing," and a swift counterpoint in the orchestra reveals the fact that it is evidently "Figaro" which is being rehearsed? "Die schweigsame Frau" contains a rich abundance of quotations from various chapters of musical history. At the point when the old foe to noise and music Morosus hurls abuse at the noises all round him Strauss makes a real cats' chorus of excerpts from many different sources. The piccolo plays the Waltz from "Faust," flutes and oboes the hunt motif from "Tannhäuser," the "Trompeter von Säckingen" (from the opera by Nessler) blares out his "Behüt dich Gott," and while the glockenspiel recalls "Die Zauberflöte" the violins add yet a fifth melody, reminiscent of the Ländler from "Der Freischütz. . . ."

All these are products of his "Merry Workshop," to which, at the age of eighty, he dedicated his Second Sonatina for Wind. It will be clear to every attentive listener how much serious work lay behind such laughing philosophy, how much honest receptiveness to the artistic world around. The hallmarks of Strauss's music making are not the self-consumption, the struggling and questioning of Mahler. Strauss was the last of the great musicians whose work streamed from a great spring. It was not that, like King Midas, he could turn everything he touched to gold, but brilliance and beauty glowed under his hands. Whenever he gave his music to the community he spread warmth, help and healing.

Strauss himself needed *warmth and light* when composing.

The country house at Garmisch (photographed in March 1954)

The study, in which most of the works from "Elektra" onward were composed

"I don't like being in the half-dark, I like light," he told Schuh, and forty years earlier he had said to Albert Gutmann, explaining why he had expressed the wish to retire to Ceylon: "Why Ceylon in particular? Because it's warm there. I need a great deal of warmth." Ever since his childhood, when he became acquainted with the beauties of the Alpine landscape on excursions, and after the journeys which he made to Italy, Greece and Egypt between 1886 and 1894 in order to strengthen his weakened constitution, the experience of nature in the south remained in the foreground of his mind. "The love of Greece and of antiquity has remained with me and has steadily increased since... I was able to travel to Egypt for eight months, and prior to that spent three weeks in Greece. From the moment when, sailing from Brindisi in an Italian steamer, I came within sight of Corfu and the blue mountains of Albania I have remained a German Grecian, and I can look back on artistic works such as 'Elektra,' 'Ariadne,' 'Ägyptische Helena,' 'Daphne' and 'Liebe der Danae' which pay homage to the genius of the Grecian people. . . ." The radiantly bright springtime of the Mediterranean filled Strauss with longing all through his life. Romain Rolland related how he saw Strauss on an "icy April day in Charlottenburg," and how the composer had told him, with a sigh, that he "couldn't compose anything during the winter, he was nostalgic for the light of Italy. . . ." Rolland added: "This nostalgia found its way into his music."

In Greece and Egypt in November 1892. . . . Gifted with alert powers of observation, the twenty-eight-year-old pilgrim to the south made many attempts to preserve the impressions of the journeyings of this half year. During the first weeks he kept a diary, whose style is indicated by the following brief extracts: "Greece! A great civilization is no more! No Olympic festivals, none of Dionysus, but the blue sea, with its eternal serenity, beats in greedy waves upon a land bright with a sad radiancy, deserted by the gods and the muses! These mountains still stand in the deceptive brightness of the sun; when will this spring, too, be benumbed to ice and night?" (6th November). ". . . Monday the 12th, at 5 p.m., left Corfu, to Patras at 5 a.m. on Tuesday, at 3 p.m. in Olympia! Exalted by the divine peace of this revered place, I give thanks to my genius that has brought me safely here. Amid the most gentle hills, between Alpheios and Kladeios, is the holy place which a great people created to its gods, winning for itself everlasting renown . . . What harmony in Olympia: nature, the gentle hills, the serene sky, the blessed solitude and the temple with its decorations etc." ". . . Splendid July weather. Donkey ride to the citadel. Alabaster mosques and the Mosque of Sultan Hassan; great dimensions and strange, but with no real artistic effect after the Grecian temples. I feel as though I already knew Egypt, and it begins to dawn upon me how little can permanently capture the imagination if it comes to us from outside, without *artistic* effect. The life of exotic peoples–our interest in it quickly dies away if there is not always something new and more striking to see. Nature is more lasting in its effect because it is far more varied, but in the long run all that holds the attention is what man himself creates and adds to nature; artistic work or the presentation of the artistic works of others, our great geniuses . . ." (29th November).

Strauss was also homesick for Vienna . . . From the "Rosen-kavalier" period onward he had a deep love for things Viennese, Austrian. The brightness of Viennese baroque art attracted him. The charm of the Viennese meant far more to this son of Munich than the narrow-mindedness of his compatriots. (It was no mere chance that his librettists Hofmannsthal, Zweig and Gregor were all members of the Viennese cultural circle.) He wrote his "Festliches Präludium" for the Viennese, and he laid the unusual gift of his "Schlagobers" on their table. He set "Austria" by Wildgans, and Weinheber's poems "St. Michael" and "Blick vom oberen Belvedere." Finally he intended to crown his tone poem "Die Donau," which remained incomplete, with a tribute to Vienna (again, the words are by Weinheber):

> How shall I sing to thee, much-loved city?
> How control my heart that it does not weep
> Before a scene of so much beauty? . . .

The master's confession that his artistic imagination was not roused "as is often believed, by impressions on the senses, observation of beauties of nature, or the heightened atmosphere of a poetic landscape," but that the translation of such effects into musical images occurred rather through "labour of the understanding, therefore transmitted, not direct," is surprising, but

130

may be doubted as an objective fact. Was even the schoolboy not inspired by an excursion to a noisy "Mountain Tour" on the piano? And did the fiery opening themes of "Don Juan" not occur to him when, during a later trip to Italy, he saw the courtyard of the monastery of St. Anthony in Padua? The direct influx of experiences from nature into the orchestral fantasy "Aus Italien" is even less open to question. "I have never," he wrote in a letter to Bülow, "really believed in inspiration through beauties of nature; amid the Roman ruins I learned better, and ideas came flying." The "Alpensinfonie," too, would be unthinkable without the spiritual reflections and feelings released by the experience of nature amid the mountains of his homeland, and transformed into music. In order "to bring back a few beautiful melodies for the second act of 'Helena'," the sixty-two-year-old composer made a trip to Greece. What he expressed in the poetic tonal enchantment of "Daphne" was described by Gregor, conscious of the musician's inner links with the Hellenic world, as an "invocation of nature." The more the ageing composer was drawn to the blue skies and sunshine, the more gentle lustre of colours and seraphic graciousness of expression he had to bestow in his late works ... "Cherry trees do not blossom in the winter, and no more are musical ideas born when nature is bleak and cold. I am a great nature lover. Therefore it is to be expected that I should do my best creative work amid the Bavarian mountains in spring."

*

Richard Strauss at the *conductor's desk* ... His conducting, right into his old age, was a thing of influencing by suggestion, an electrifying experience. The role which the interpreter played in this life dedicated to music is to be understood with reference to his especial relationship to the artistic "world." The man who, as a composer, gave the orchestra a new abundance of colour, himself felt the urge to transform his art into actual sound. The composer whom the call of music took all over the world assisted personally in the realization of his works by opera companies, orchestras, and finally also radio organizations. By the time he was forty he could write, not without pride, that he had "conducted the orchestras of almost all the civilized world." As

[Handwritten letter in German — Strauss's message to the Dresden State Orchestra]

Caption: Strauss congratulates the Dresden State Orchestra (1948)

early as 1886 the newly-appointed third conductor at the Munich Opera directed "Jean de Paris," "Un Ballo in Maschera" and "Così fan tutte," although (in the composer's own words) "Troubles and pleasures alternated in the career of this greenhorn who went his own way," and after holding his second post in Munich he was able to move swiftly to the top of the ladder with his appointments in Berlin and Vienna. Until the very end

132

der mein Lebenschaffen nicht zuletzt durch die aufopfernden
Leistungen der Kapelle zum schönsten Erfolge verdankt.
Als die Fülle der herrlichsten Erinnerungen meiner Künstlerischen
Laufbahn während der Klänge dieses Meisterwerkes floß
von diesem Gefühle innigster Dankbarkeit und Bewunderung
war, mit denen ich jedes Mal zuletzt im Juni 1944
aus der geliebten Kapelle schied.

Möge in uns zwiespältiger Zeit, in der schon mein
Intermezzo zur Uraufführung erlebte, die Staatskapelle
glücklich, freudig und unter Lorbeer blühen, ebenbürtig
400 jährigen Ruhmes!

        In alter treuer Anhänglichkeit

           Richard Strauss

of his life he felt himself to be linked with the precious cultural
heritage of the German orchestras. He had particularly close
ties of affection with the Vienna Philharmonic, and, from the
time of the first Dresden performance of "Don Juan" in 1890,
with the Dresden Orchestra, about which he wrote to his father
that the "sound of the magnificent orchestra was splendid." On
the occasion of the four-hundredth anniversary of the Dresden

State Orchestra he sent this "first opera orchestra of the world" a letter which gave convincing expression to his feelings. "I consider it a rare privilege that it has been granted to me to offer my most sincere and heartfelt good wishes to so magnificent an artistic body on this happy anniversary . . . From the abundance of most glorious recollections extending over my whole life, the sound of this masterly orchestra always awakens new feelings of most profound thankfulness and admiration. . . ."

Strauss the conductor changed over the course of the years. When he was a lanky young man of twenty-one his father had to warn him against "making snake-like gestures" and "fooling about" while conducting, and Rolland wrote of the "young, tall, rather elegant German artist" who "did a frantic dance while conducting." The dominant characteristic of the mature orchestral conductor of later years was, on the contrary, his habit of remaining calm and factual even in impassioned music. In fact no conductor could be more straightforward and economical in his gestures. Strauss would walk to the conductor's desk with his usual dignified self-possession. It was clearly to be seen how the music within him became transformed into bodily expression, the skilled exercise of his baton technique. Face and figure remained statuesque; it was only close to him that one could sense the vibration of his nerves, the radiation of magnetic forces. No one escaped the hypnotic power of his eye, and his small, spare, sometimes vigorous strokes of the baton made the sound take wing and glow with light. He was able to achieve masterpieces of performance almost solely with his right hand. Strauss did not gesticulate with both arms like so many prima donnas and gymnasts of the rostrum; he merely extended his right wrist, reserving his left hand (which he liked to keep in his waistcoat pocket) for making occasional indications of especial importance. "Conducting with one's tie" was Strauss's own term for this highly refined technique. Clarity of intention was the principal quality of his artistry as a conductor; his gestures always remained rounded and springy even when marking accents. Thus it was that orchestras always played so lightly and naturally under Strauss, accompanying, when required to do so, with such sympathy and sovereign control. Hence the fact that the tonal picture was so remarkably compressed and clean, so smooth and yet full of inexplicable depths beneath a polished surface. That

134

was the reason, too, why everyone on the stage felt so confident under the direction of this musician par excellence.

The most remarkable fact about Strauss the conductor is appreciated only by those who realize that here was a musician who, as a power in the creative field, had all the potentials of a flashy

The Berlin Court Conductor: Drawing by Eduard Grützner (1904)

star conductor, but who was in fact a model of the conductor who devotes himself solely to the service of the music. His technique was a far cry from that of the conductors of the school of Nikisch, who attempted to indicate by their actions what the orchestra should express, while romantic conductors of the type still to be met with today developed the visual aspect of their art to the point of virtuosity–Strauss referred in a letter to his parents to the "most disgusting rostrum exhibitionism which, for the sake of its beloved vanity, no longer respects any composer's intentions." We must realize what it meant in an age when, generally speaking, the decorative was considered beautiful, that here was a man from whom nothing was further than demonstrative show, whose every gesture was calculated to serve the purpose of the work he was conducting, instead of distracting attention away from it. That was always Strauss's intention, whether as an as yet inexperienced beginner at Meiningen, or later as the renowned General Musical Director of Berlin and a world-famous guest conductor. This ability of the composing conductor Strauss to put everything creative which was in him to the service of interpretation is remarkable. (Although it is, to some extent, repeated today in the cases of Stravinsky and Egk). Indeed, Strauss was so concerned, as a true colleague, to promote the works of others that he sometimes gave the impression of standing at a distance from his own music, and was consequently criticized for being too remote.

The most remarkable variety of opinions were current concerning Strauss, the masterly conductor whose full significance only gradually came to be recognized. It may be that the full force of his musicality came fully into play only when he conducted works by composers in some way akin to himself: it is well known which were his favourite children, and which were those that gave him no pleasure. The devotion of this great musician to the genius of Mozart and Wagner extended very strongly to the interpretation of their works. His performances in Munich, of "Figaro" and "Così fan tutte" in particular, belonged in their polished beauty, their precision without pedantry, their combination of sovereign power and serenity, of technical accomplishment and inner spirituality, and in the feeling which they conveyed of the all-embracing presence of the Anima Mozartiana, to the finest fruits of opera interpretation in this century. His "Tristan" was always a most personal confession: the listener at so magical a performance heard something which can be conceived only in terms of an elemental creative process. Strauss was always concerned to shape the music, at the dictates of both feeling and intellect, "correctly" in every detail, with no suggestion of a personal attitude intruding. In this respect he differed fundamentally from his admired mentor Bülow (although he had written to Ritter in 1892: "If only I knew how I should begin to conduct 'objectively'!"). It was always his purpose to simplify the seemingly complicated nature of the score, to transform it into the naive expression of the sheer joy of music making. His tempi in Mozart and Wagner, which were often very quick, sometimes gave rise to criticism. But did Wagner not warn against attempting to prove anything about music by means of figures? Tempi the metronome lays down need not represent the absolute "rule" for the interpretative musician, quite apart from the fact that no metronome markings exist for classical works prior to Beethoven. "Only our music critics have authentic information about them, direct from Olympus" remarked Strauss shortly before his death.

With the exception of his years at the Berlin and Vienna Operas, during which Strauss conducted a great many works of the international repertoire ranging from Pergolesi's "La serva padrona" to Schillings's "Mona Lisa," and his period with the Berlin Symphony Orchestra when he exerted himself with remarkable elan on behalf of music which was then modern, he restricted his conducting, in his later years, to Mozart and Wagner, the symphonies of Beethoven–and his own works. He was one of the rare cases of a composer who was his own best interpreter. In the years of his maturity and old age he brought out, both as composer and conductor, the chamber music and Mozartian elements, and he clarified the musical picture by preserving the brio and the dramatic accents of his own works. He had an alert sense of the subtle values of his own scores, emphasizing not so much their Dionysian fervour as the fascination of their finesse in details. This was the same discretion in revealing the tonal picture, the "Sistine objectivity," which he considered the Prelude to "Parsifal" required. A consideration of the most important Strauss conductors of recent decades will indicate that the art of subtle differentiation of elements and of tonal simplification has remained the hallmark of the truly valid Strauss performance. The names are worth mentioning here: the Germans and Austrians Ernst von Schuch, Leo Blech, Hans Knappertsbusch, Fritz Busch, Erich Kleiber, Clemens Krauss, Karl Böhm, Franz Konwitschny, Joseph Keilberth, Herbert von Karajan and Rudolf Kempe, and in the international sphere the Dutchman Willem Mengelberg, the Englishman Sir Thomas

137

Beecham, the Rumanian Georges Georgescu, the Italian Victor de Sabata, the Greek Dimitri Mitropoulos, the American Eugene Ormandy and the Hungarian Georg Solti.

How far removed from the time beaters whom Wagner examined so critically under the magnifying glass in his essay "On Conducting" are these modern conductors! Spirit and feeling become essential parts of a re-creative will watched over by the intellect. "The best music making comes when you conduct calmly," Strauss used to say, and the words he used in connection with Schuch, whom he always acknowledged as a model, apply equally to himself: "... calmly master the demons." His re-creative imagination was most clearly at work in connection with music which represented a particularly personal utterance. "Salome" was the opera he conducted most frequently, on account of its immense concentration. In addition the "Sinfonia domestica," "Alpensinfonie," "Elektra," "Ariadne" and "Arabella" were among the favourite children of Strauss the conductor, and at his hands they became feats of the flexible revelation of values characteristic of him. Although other conductors have often sinned against Strauss through their raptures of extravagant tone colour and their muddy textures, Strauss himself wiped these away with effortless virtuosity. Even things in these scores which appear to be less the fruits of inspiration than the outcome of technical brilliance took on intensive life under such direction. The orchestra began to talk, sing and laugh in innumerable secondary melodies. The tempo and style of performance reflected to an ever greater degree the character of his music making: the work of a musical architect, never doctrinaire and never overburdened with unnecessary rehearsals. When in later years he was asked about this or that work which he had not himself conducted for a long time he replied: "I have no more ambition as a conductor; I conduct only for opera directors who are friends of mine, and then only such works as gain by my presenting them to the public." He said of "Rosenkavalier": "I haven't wanted to conduct it myself for many years–it tires me out too much, and it gives me little pleasure as I have conducted it too often."

Every conductor is surely aware of the delightful "Ten Golden Rules" which Strauss is said to have devised after a performance of "Intermezzo" under Knappertsbusch in Munich.

"... You should not perspire while conducting, but the audience should become warm.... Never look encouragingly at the brass, except to give them a quick glance at an important entry.... On the other hand never let the horns and woodwind out of your sight: if you hear them at all they are too loud.... If you think the brass are not playing loudly enough reduce their tone by two more degrees.... It is not enough for you yourself to hear every word of the singers, which you know by heart: the *audience* must be able to follow without trouble. If they don't understand the words they go to sleep.... Always accompany the singer so that he can sing without straining.... When you believe you have reached the ultimate prestissimo take the tempo twice as fast. (Twenty years later Strauss corrected himself: take the tempo half as fast.) ... Remember that you are not conducting for your own amusement, but for the enjoyment of your listeners...." Thus spake Richard Strauss.

*

Glad though Strauss was to conduct his own music, he had no desire to promote his personal interests through the medium of the *written word*. He wrote very little about his own works. It was not until the last years of his life that he wrote with a delicate, mellow humour short reminiscences of his father, his formative years, and the first performances of several of his operas. When, in 1907, he was misguided enough to edit the artistic periodical "Der Morgen" for a time he referred in the foreword to his "almost insurmountable aversion to the activity of authorship." "It is one of my basic principles that we should let our deeds and works speak for us, but not words...." Nevertheless when he took up arms on the questions of copyright protection, interpretation, and musical education, he wrote a great deal in support of his views. His forewords to "Intermezzo" and "Capriccio" are among the most thought-provoking and instructive statements of a composer's views on the artistic realization of a dramatic work since Gluck's introduction to "Alceste." His notes concerning stylistic, unadulterated interpretation of the masterworks of Mozart, Beethoven, Weber and Wagner, too, should be in the hands of every conductor and devotee of music. ("You always have something to say when you write, whether in notes or letters," Bülow had written to the young musician). Strauss felt a strong inner compulsion to put into words his relationships to the great figures of German music. It is known that he wrote several lengthy articles on the occasion of the 25th anniversary of Wagner's death, but he did not consider any of them to be worthy of publication. There was also talk of the first draft of an essay on Mozart designed to appear in a "propylaeum" series, devised in conjunction with Specht (1920). And what a unique musicological document the musical world could have expected if Strauss, at seventy, had carried out his intention of producing, as a companion to the publication of Beethoven's conversation books, his own biography of the composer! ". . . Strauss spoke privately about Beethoven (in his opinion no conductor since Bülow knows how to perform the works). Writing a book on Beethoven and the correct interpretation of Beethoven seemed to him at that time to be more important than writing his own scores" (Schnoor).

Less light is thrown on Strauss's intellectual gifts in the literary field by the two opera libretti he wrote for himself–the Wagnerian alliterations of "Guntram" and the everyday dialogue of the auto-biographical "Intermezzo," than by the letters to Hofmannsthal which were published in 1926 and 1952. Here the man and musician Strauss, one of the most conscientious and industrious letter writers of his generation, revealed himself as he really was: pressing, impatient and demanding when artistic matters were at stake, temperamental, and sometimes even crude, despite his efforts to accommodate himself to the delicate sensitivity of Hofmannsthal, who was ten years younger than himself. By comparison with the poetically tempered tone of Hofmannsthal's letters those of the musician are couched in the factual style of the "employer." This correspondence dating from between 1907 and 1929 which has been published (as were the correspondence with Bahr–dating over an even longer period–in 1947, with Bülow in 1953, with Strauss's parents in 1954, with Gregor in 1955, with Zweig in 1957 and with Krauss in 1963) was a continuing source of intellectual stimulus suggesting the exchanges of opinion between Goethe and Schiller. Probably, in fact, there has never been so lively and fruitful an examination of the whole question of opera dramaturgy since E. T. A. Hoffmann's fictional dialogue "The poet and the composer." The field of discussion covered in this prolonged exchange of ideas is that

"Experiences of conducting": from a notebook (1944)

of the classical artistic values insofar as they are of service to the theatre; saga and mythology have a prominent place. The most rewarding aspect of these letters is the fact that they were created in a world of the living and practical exercise of the arts–reading them provides valuable flashes of insight into the minds and workshops of the two men who pledged themselves to the cause of a national blossoming of German opera despite the dissimilarity of their natures and the contradictions of a relationship poised between warm friendship and antagonism. It is all the more to be regretted that their collaboration to develop realistic opera of their day became a not entirely harmonious marriage.

THE ELEMENTS OF STYLE

My concern is with *melody*.
It reveals deeper things, the unimaginable!
In *one* chord you experience a world!
The composer Flamand in "Capriccio"

STRAUSS SCORES ARE STILL STUDIED TODAY; THE SE-crets of his epicurean tonal language with its melodic, harmonic and rhythmic attractions are still being probed, and many musicians school themselves, even though their sympathies may lie elsewhere, in the sensuous magic of his handling of the orchestra. The most important information concerning his rich and varied œuvre and his stylistic characteristics is given not by his verbal or written statements or by his far-reaching revision of Berlioz's treatise on instrumentation, but by his works themselves. Only when we pass from isolated facets of his creative career to consider the overall picture can we discover the specific Strauss "*style*," in which melody, harmony and rhythm are blended into a single *entity*. The words of the theatre director La Roche apply to Strauss: "In the realm of my stage they all *serve*."

It was not chance but inner compulsion which determined the course of his work. The question whether Strauss was primarily an instrumental or a vocal composer is not decisive: he created lasting works in both media. Nevertheless is it not true that the opera composer, who placed many contrasting styles alongside one another in "Rosenkavalier," advanced to a compelling stylistic synthesis in "Ariadne" and "Frau ohne Schatten," while the road of the composer of programme music extending from "Don Juan" to the "Alpensinfonie," seen as a whole, led him not to an ascent of the mountains, but rather to a descent? At the age of fifty, after trying his hand at all the traditional forms of expression, he devoted himself to opera—no longer to the

143

world of the fierce passions of Salome and Elektra but to the beautiful landscapes of the opera of pure music. His was a style of colour and lustre, comprehensible to all, the style of a lively spirit, a "homo ludens," soaring ecstatically, and by now only occasionally pathetic. It was a flexible, individual style, animated by a keen perception of artistic values, whose seeds had lain in the first endeavours of the "Burleske" for piano and "Aus Italien," and which had taken on firm contours in the overwhelming breakthrough of "Don Juan," later to become tensely dramatic at times and eventually, in the hands of the master of rich experience, to reach its apotheosis on a plane of spiritual sublimity. It is true that this refining of the stylistic elements was accompanied from the time of the middle period works (dramatic and symphonic) by a lessening of effectiveness as far as the general public was concerned. Now that Strauss's music has become common property it is scarcely possible to give sufficient recognition to the courage and generative power which he demonstrated in the creation and shaping of his personal musical language, with its atmospheric and psychological roots.

The instinct of the musician Strauss, which was tried and strengthened, purified and refined by long years of practical experience, did not lead him along a predictable path. His creative work, its character determined by constantly fresh subjects, was always in a process of change. Change and metamorphosis wherever one looks within the realm of his works! Metamorphosis does not mean repeating the same thing by means which have proved effective, but ever saying something new. All through his life Strauss acknowledged the need of that *audacity* without which, according to Goethe, no talent is possible: in this case audacity with regard to stylistic means and tonal management. All through his life, too, his great intelligence never checked his naive joy in acts of daring, or a delight in achievement which spurred him on to discover and traverse unknown territory. The scores, ranging from "Till" to "Metamorphosen," from "Salome" to "Capriccio," have enough to tell about such adventures of style. The polytonal passages of "Elektra" belong to these adventures as do the stylized semiseria of "Ariadne," the unhappy combination of bourgeois small talk and symphonic commentary of "Intermezzo," and the witty reanimation of the spirit of Italian opera buffa in "Die schweigsame Frau." The style changed in accordance with the subject, the different content giving rise to the need for new means of expression. It will be seen that within the same stylistic sphere each work was treated in a manner of its own, dependent on its subject matter. The same composer who created music of blossoming sensuous beauty did not hesitate to pen blatant examples of realism including descriptions of running blood and of the neighing of wild horses. "I always strove to find the style best suited to the inner nature of the work. I am convinced that every work must be written in a different language, and must wear clothes made especially for it. . . ." In a letter to Zweig he confessed that it was "always a rather long time" before he could "get into the spirit of the work and hit upon the particular style required. . . . Once half an act is sketched my invention works by itself."

Such pleasure in constantly changing is granted only to genius, for a talent merely varies itself. It always moves in the same circle, and woe to the possessor of such a talent if he reaches old age. Genius (a word reserved for those who are dead) climbs from step to step, and it alone can lead to a genuine "last period" style. Talent creates from *one* spring, but genius from *many,* and the remarkable fact is that they all flow out of the same ground. Thus it is that Strauss's works never lost the common attributes of his personal style. We now know that his "transformations" consisted only of changes of direction and effect, relating to content and form, that each of his works is genuine and "Straussian," but that the same artistic force reflects a different phase of development in each. (The law governing this development, as in the case of Wagner, is one of inbreeding, since, from the time of his first successful tone poems and operas, Strauss restricted himself almost exclusively to developing his own style.) The "style" as such, with concentrated melodic power as the principal factor in the creation of the musical effect, the combination of pictorial realism and naturalistic tone painting, with simple or subtle musical gestures marked by lyricism or turbulence, deep feeling or effervescent wit–this style which is uniquely free from friction yet not over-smooth, aesthetically beautiful yet not bloodless, bright and serene in its very nature, was born while Strauss was still young, and proved to be lasting. His music could undoubtedly be described as German, in the best sense, with a pronounced south German accent. (The fact that his part of the country is a gateway to Italy and France is indicated by those works of his which are full of light and graceful charm.) Without changing the essentials of his art Strauss made his way from the music drama to the opera of pure music, from Wagner to Mozart, completing the journey with "Rosenkavalier." He succeeded in creating, without apparent effort, the astonishing compound of elements of rococo styliza- tion, Viennese farce, opera buffa and operetta found in that "comedy for music" without seriously endangering the overall unity of style. It is the language of music to whose natural living strength, serenity and luminosity nothing human is foreign, which has, in the words of Kierkegaard, "erotic-sensuous originality as its absolute object," and whose power of expression penetrates to all regions of the spirit. This stylistic aspect of Strauss the seeker after beauty, with his many discoveries in the realms of melody, harmony, form and orchestral colour (in common with his actual technique of composition) has not yet been examined with great thoroughness. This can be attempted here only in general terms, by the use of stylistic analysis and stylistic com- parisons to throw light on the basic characteristics of Strauss's artistic technique.

*

"My concern is with melody...." No one can be oblivious to the fresh spring of the musical *idea* when listening to Strauss's music. Darius Milhaud once remarked that the life span of an opera depends on the richness of the melodic substance which it contains, and Serge Prokofieff said: "I love melody and regard it as the most important element of music." Even Stravinsky, in the wisdom of his full maturity, had to confess in his "Poetics of Music" that "Melody must retain the highest position in the hierarchy of the elements...." The fact that the composer of "Don Juan," "Ariadne" and "Die Frau ohne Schatten" was one of the most gifted of all composers since Mozart and Schubert as regards melodic inspiration would be disputed only by his most determined opponents. Strauss's naive musical nature only very seldom renounced the most basic artistic element of music– melody. Indeed, does there not seem to be an acute danger in

146

some of his later works of the melody being allowed to occupy the centre of the picture to an excessive degree? The musician Strauss always proved himself youthfully fresh and vigorous in works created at a propitious time of real inspiration. When, however, the melodies flowed from his pen sluggishly and hesitantly the resulting music was undoubtedly less strongly invented and experienced on the basis of the original idea.

Strauss, who thought in terms of musical symbols, was concerned primarily with the formative melodic idea and the musical shape. It made no difference in principle to the value of the theme or motif whether it was for an orchestral or stage work, whether it was to be employed as symphonic building material or as an element of musical-dramatic architecture. What Strauss stated in 1929 to be the pre-requisite of really artistic programme music, that "its creator must be primarily a musician with ideas and the ability to fashion structures," whose "first and most important question always concerned the absolute value and strength of the musical idea," applied to all his works. The characteristic motif germ cells of his music were among his most personal possessions. Their pregnancy and sensuous appeal, as well as their suitability for development and transformation, are always infectious—one need only think of the sensuous verve of the themes of "Don Juan" (like "champagne corks shooting up to the ceiling," as Berrsche once wrote) and the frolicsome, "somersaulting" motif of "Till Eulenspiegel," without which the repertoire of recent music would be incomplete. Or we might think of the clarinet run-up in C♯ minor at the beginning of "Salome," a figure which at once captures the sultry atmosphere of Oscar Wilde's play, or the brilliant, impulsive opening motif of "Rosenkavalier." Even though the intensity of expression and the originality of the artistic material diminished from time to time in later works, the generation of the thematic idea at the impulse of melodic and imaginative forces, together with the art of fashioning motifs of many meanings which were understandable to all out of the sphere of a dramatic or programmatic idea, remained to Strauss until his old age. The characteristics of his thematic ideas are quite ineffaceable. Even when they are transformed they are still evident to all ears, no matter if they are embedded in a most complicated score. With him the motif sprang from the firm rhythm of a word, a name, a succession of syllables. The manner in which he used the strength of the words Agamemnon ("Elektra") and Keikobad ("Frau ohne Schatten") as the foundation stones for massive doorways into the works is as admirable as the incomparably easy-going yet perfectly aimed "Once upon a time" of the Prologue to "Till" or the witty "Teschek, bedien' dich" ("Please help yourself"), whose Magyar rhythm perfectly characterizes the unexpected suitor Mandryka in "Arabella." It is, however, above all the feminine figures in his operas, the Marschallin, Ariadne, Christine, Helena, Aminta, Maria and others, who are introduced and characterized by the art of motivic symbolism, while in the tone poems, for reasons which are not apparent, the masculine element ("Don Juan," "Till," "Zarathustra," "Don Quixote") is dominant. Themes of this nature are not the result of inspiration for which the artist has to be humbly thankful, in the sense of Pfitzner's aesthetics, but a translation of reality generated by action; they are contents, not vehicles, musical shapes which formed themselves compulsively in the composer's consciousness. Their expressive content is all the more powerful the more they have grown out of the emotions of everyday, typical characters. Figures from among the people such as the rogue Till, Sophie, Barak, Mandryka and Morosus came naturally to Strauss. On the other hand the more complex characters such as Salome or the Countess in "Capriccio" presented him with fascinating problems.

What attracted him to Wagner was only to a very small extent his example as a melodist. Strauss's melodies are most individual when they are completely un-Wagnerian, neither chromatic nor pathetic. In contrast to Wagner's "leitmotiv" Strauss developed a *motif technique* which was more a matter of feelings than of construction. Only in his early tone poems, and unmistakably in "Guntram," did he make use of Wagner's fully developed aid to composition, a precise scheme of motifs. "Feuersnot" represented a transition. For "Salome" Strauss decided upon a motif technique of psychological characterization. The original stylistic feature of this technique lies in the skilful development of the Wagnerian "leitmotiv," which Wagner had deliberately used in a rigid manner. Strauss guided its growth from the germ cell of the motif. He did not employ this motif as a mere formula intended as a guide to make the contents of the dramatic situation clear to the audience. Instead he varied and transformed it, making it serve the cause of psychological elucidation like a red thread leading into the instrumental and vocal structure. Some motifs are common to several different characters, and accompany them, either literally or in altered versions, throughout the whole opera; other figures and situations are provided with several different motifs. These motifs are not merely placed alongside one another or played simultaneously: while the motif thread is never broken they give rise to new extended melodies. Thus almost every Strauss theme, in particular the brief motif which it would appear scarcely possible to develop, is compelled to run the gauntlet of many of its fellows. In the scores of the period of mature mastery, in particular, the individual motifs are driven by a brilliant artistic intellect through a great many relationships and conflicts, to emerge more alive than ever. It is most remarkable, for example, how Strauss evolved the impressive funeral music in "Helena," one of his most powerful utterances, from the insignificant Arioso of Da-ud. So it is that, like the lyrical conclusions of his tone poems ("Tod und Verklärung," "Don Quixote," "Heldenleben" and "Alpensinfonie"), the famous finales of his operas, from the ecstatic intoxication of Salome's final monologue to Daphne's metamorphosis as she leaves the sphere of things human, are spiritual-musical transformations of what had once been utterly simple melodic ideas. These apotheoses, which Strauss illuminated by his wonderfully rich musical imagination, were less constructed than poetically conceived. Nevertheless examination shows that many of the broad arches of melody, seemingly poured out as pure inspiration, really derive from the masterly development of motifs.

Especially in the one-act operas, with their conciseness of form, Strauss often formed the entire melodic substance from a single basic idea, which he then adapted creatively to the needs of the whole work. Considering the springlike blossoming of the motif world of "Feuersnot," one notices how the flame motif in A♭ major (which also becomes the motif of love) runs through the veins of the entire work. We remember the short motifs of "Salome" and "Elektra" which, in a few bars, conjure up the morbid worlds of these musical tragedies–flaming torches which light up these most densely constructed scores. It will also be felt that the oboe motif of the lonely Daphne (a G major arpeggio with one altered note), in its bucolic simplicity, and the magical woodwind prelude which follows, not only establish the Arcadian atmosphere of the work, but become the source from which its stream of melody is to flow. The growth of a work's musical contents from initial motifs did not always occur as it did in "Daphne." In works on a larger scale the transformation of particular motifs was often restricted by what Strauss described as the need for "intensive consideration," and musical imagination became subordinate to structural strength. It should, however, be noted that Strauss often employed themes whose highly personal rhythmic formulation was not intended to be suitable for development. Two examples: the reeling "Aegistheus" motif in "Elektra" and the bold trumpet motif of Midas in "Danae." Such themes are complete in themselves.

Strauss's method of showing an apparently unpromising succession of notes in ever new and surprising aspects as the music is unfolded has been compared to the technique employed by Beethoven in connection with the opening themes of the "Eroica" and Fifth Symphony. Is it correct to mention the creative method of Beethoven the symphonist, making mere motif fragments the foundation stone of immense confrontations of spiritual forces, in the same breath as the technique employed by Strauss? The answer may be formulated thus: Beethoven's initial idea, which was not always of the same weight of musical substance (the Rondo theme of the Emperor Concerto, for example) is the thematic kernel of the work, and it was fashioned with a view to the symphonic construction which was to come. "Every idea in music has a most intimate, indivisible relationship to the work as a harmonious whole," Beethoven said to Bettina. With Strauss, on the other hand, the original "idea" represented a complete melodic embryo. In his own words his task was "to await the moment at which the imagination is able and ready" to *spin out* the idea. This fact led the young Strauss to the realm of the symphonic poem, where he could introduce his themes, born of human situations, in as individual a manner as he pleased.

Strauss the melodist was distinguished by natural warmth and a compelling sweep of emotional gestures. His melodies seem to see tender idylls and the yearning of love (as in the "Sinfonia domestica" and "Feuersnot") through the eyes of children. They

150

can, however, be of the utmost sensuality when dealing with such carnal characters as Don Juan and Salome. There are melodies which are miracles of flexible line, living streams, models of classical proportioning and noble beauty, and which are nourished by the springs of naive music allied to folksong ("Ariadne"), while others cannot deny their derivation from cosmopolitan ideals ("Alpensinfonie," "Helena"). There are themes based on extremely simple harmonic progressions ("Tod und Verklärung," "Josephslegende"), and others which have grown out of a sequence of subtle modulations ("Don Quixote," and once again "Ariadne" and "Helena"). The class of melody depends on the particular dramatic situation from which it springs. Strauss frequently referred to the difficulty he often experienced in finding his way to the new style required for each work. Many scores owe their effectiveness to the conscious exploitation of the contrasts between nervously animated and simple songlike melody, between flowing chromaticism and diatonic forms, between ornamental lines and simple, romantically conceived chord sequences ("Frau ohne Schatten," "Arabella," "Danae"). Typically Straussian are powerful initial leaps of a sixth or an octave, and the sequential soaring quality of his melodic figures. Finely-wrought and hymnic melodies and the mercurial nature of notes both short and long are emphasized by warm doubling in thirds and sixths. This sometimes rather abrupt presentation of his ideas, with a high surface polish, was often imitated, but generally with little success.

It has already been mentioned that in the choice of his melodies Strauss sometimes fell below the standard of the bulk of his work. In his attempts to provide the melody with an appeal to the senses hitherto unparalleled he turned, for example in "Die ägyptische Helena," to rather stale echoes of Mendelssohn, even of Wagner (Valhalla motif), Saint-Saëns, ("Samson et Dalila"), and even an old popular tune. This is not of very great consequence. After all, the striking motif of Salome's advances to Jokanaan largely corresponds to the passage "Nun bist du mein, nun zieh mit mir" from Loewe's "Tom der Reimer," and the cradle song from the "Sinfonia domestica" is almost identical to Mendelssohn's "Gondellied" Op. 19. Even so unmistakably Straussian a melody as the Trio of the nymphs in the Finale of "Ariadne" ("Töne, töne, süße Stimme") cannot deny its di-

151

rect descent from the opening of Schubert's song "Schlafe, schlafe, holder süßer Knabe." Then again the buoyant theme in Eb of Christine's kindness and neighbourliness in "Intermezzo" was evidently modelled on that of the apprentices in "Die Meistersinger," and the principal theme of the "Festliches Präludium," in C major, on the final Allegro of Brahms's C minor Symphony. Clearly, too, the "accursed, execrable bells" which plague old Morosus in the second act of "Die schweigsame Frau" ring out the theme of Bizet's "Carillon." Naturally Strauss decked these borrowed possessions out with all his immense artistic and technical skill. A case in a class of its own is his astonishing manipulation of motive material from "Fidelio" which (as Harald Kaufmann has demonstrated in an essay) Strauss employed most aptly in his "Friedenstag." The good-humoured literal quotations in his major works represent, for the most part, flashes of wit which go straight to their mark. Such borrowings may be mere thematic repetitions of passages already familiar. However, seen in an altered harmonic light and before a new dramatic background, they can also produce a reminiscence as subtle as the lovely, romantic Ab major them of the "opera" in "Capriccio." This first appears when the Co talks about operas of the past, and it is later extended to f an atmospheric and meaningful orchestral interlude. Nc would suspect that this moonlight music had its origins in a inent theme of the long-forgotten, sarcastic "Krämersp The opening of "Daphne" is a similar case. Examination that the initial motif, with its immense melodic potentia an exact quotation (here in Eb) of the first motif of part choral work "Die Göttin im Putzzimmer," an piece which Strauss had written a year earlier—thoug of Rückert's verses has given place to the serenely mosphere of the bucolic opera, the theme being n and at the same time more profound.

What of the ballet "Kythere," to which Strauss devote great deal of attention from about the turn of the century, and whose twenty-five very detailed sketches (like those for the opera "Lila") are interesting in many respects? Schuh has shown that here Strauss, with an astonishing degree of naive assurance, had reflected perfectly the rococo style of Watteau and his contemporaries, thus anticipating the "release from Wagner" and the relaxed serenity later characteristic of "Rosenkavalier," "Ariadne" and "Bürger als Edelmann." That is not all: study of this sketch book dating from the summer of 1900 is not only a voyage of discovery through a world of truly Straussian themes, some of them developed into lengthy phrases and formal patterns with indications of their underlying harmonies–it reveals the amazing fact that the majority of these themes are already familiar to lovers of Strauss's music. This is because the best ideas in the "Kythere" sketches were incorporated in other works written during the next decade–confirmation of their value! A peasant waltz and an adagio nocturne were used in "Feuersnot,"

"Krämerspiegel"

a minuet, a gavotte and a solemn hymn pointed to characteristic themes in the music of "Ariadne" and "Bürger als Edelmann," and two passages became dance figures in "Josephslegende." In the same book Strauss marked the first sketches for the song "Ich schwebe" (after Henckell) with the words "Sketch for 'Kythere.'" Once, at the "Entrance of the pilgrims and shepherds," Strauss looked backward–to the second theme of "Don Quixote." These sketches are a mine of information.

A curiosity of Strauss's formation of motifs which merits attention is his way of anticipating particular turns of melody. While writing music for specific poetic images and events of nature he would sometimes recall earlier settings of similar ideas and now, often after many years, would give them new and enhanced musical form. A striking example of this is provided by the passage from the second act of "Die schweigsame Frau," which dates from 1934, when Aminta sings to Morosus of "Flowers, stars, and tender green," of verdant meadows and bird-

153

song–clearly anticipating in many details the graceful music red-olent of nature in the first monologue of Daphne. Even more surprising is the phrase which follows: "Das Blau des *Himmels* niederschwingen," which reappears exactly (in G♭ major instead of F major) in the melodic line of the duet for female voices "Was *Himmels* Regen der Erde gibt" from "Danae." One might here (as in the case of Schubert) think in terms of basic motif associations with such features of nature as the sky, light, sun-shine and storms in Strauss's sub-conscious mind. We also come across connections between one work and another when similar human emotions are concerned, such as the relationship between the love scenes in "Heldenleben" and the "Sinfonia domestica." This is naturally true to an even greater extent of the songs, which are predominately lyrical in conception, and in which similar imagery often occurs.

Is it not remarkable that the master of the immensely com-plex apparatus of the modern orchestra should show a definite preference for melodic simplicity? When Strauss conducted his Symphony in F minor before Brahms, the aged composer was very careful in weighing his words of praise: "Young man, ex-amine Schubert's dances closely, and see what you can do by way of inventing simple, eight-bar melodies." Strauss remarked about that encounter: "It is mainly thanks to Johannes Brahms that I have never since then disdained a popular melody (how-ever little value may be placed on such tunes, they occur to one very seldom, and only if one is lucky) in my works. Another reproach by the master: 'Your symphony contains too much play-ing about with themes. This piling up of many themes based on a triad which differ from one another only in rhythm has no value' has always remained clear in my mind. I realized then that counterpoint is justified only when poetical necessity com-pels two or more themes which are not merely rhythmically but also harmonically contrasted to combine for the time being. . . ." Strauss referred to the same subject in a letter written to Ferdi-nand Schreiber in 1919: "The old contrapuntal practice of fash-ioning a melody in such a way that it will combine with a se-cond one has not greatly interested me. You can make fugues all day long like that, but what I really considered worthwhile was discovering how to compel two mutually antagonistic themes to come together. . . ."

154

This concentration on essentials, the use of counterpoint which "says something" and which "sounds," wholly unacademic *melodic polyphony* which does not complicate the issue but which underlines, and the avoidance of any filling-in part unrelated to the melodic substance–these were the results of long experience as a creative and interpretative musician. Seldom has polyphony more effectively served the purposes of homophony. In the mastery with which in his complex vocal pieces (for example the "Deutsche Motette" and the complicated ensembles of "Die schweigsame Frau") Strauss created tension and warmth in the polyphonic texture as though with silver threads, we see something of the wide range of his spirited yet intellectually controlled tonal language. He was a master of the art of expressing several different moods simultaneously. "Only really purposeful polyphony discloses the marvel of orchestral sound to the full," he wrote in connection with melody in the foreword to "Intermezzo." The A♭ major Interlude of that "little opera about marriage" offers a brilliant example of this almost poetically-conceived instrumental "poly-melody," when the three contrasting themes of the woman's love and longing are fashioned into an expressively tender, finely-woven arioso. He always conceived a multi-voice texture from the melodic standpoint.

"Judging by my past experience of creative activity a motif or phrase of two or four bars occurs to me. I get it down on paper and at once extend it to form a phrase of 8, 16 or 32 bars, which naturally does not remain unaltered, but which, after being laid aside for a time, gradually takes on its final shape. . . ." Strauss never made any secret of the fact that "no long melodies such as those of Mozart" came to him ready made. "Only short themes occur to me, but I do understand how to use such a theme, to paraphrase it, and to draw out all that it contains." Nevertheless it is by no means difficult to unearth innumerable Strauss melodies which extend over ten, twenty or more bars– widely-spanned cantilenas which do not appear to have been planned by the intellect and skilfully "lengthened," but have the effect on the listener of "primary discoveries." One such instance is undoubtedly the final Trio of "Rosenkavalier," that sublime inspiration which Strauss derived from the trivial Mariandl Waltz. Undoubtedly, too, the two characteristic principal themes of "Don Juan," the powerful "Hero's" theme in "Heldenleben," Barak's full-flowing song "Mir anvertraut" from the last act of "Frau ohne Schatten" and the widely-spun A♭ major Sextet from the second act of "Die schweigsame Frau" are proofs of Strauss's ability to invent themes of considerable length. In all probability too much importance is commonly attached to the question of the dimensions of the melodic ideas, whose bounds cannot possibly be laid down with certainty. The decisive factor is and remains the power and density of the inspiration, the spiritual radiance of the resulting music. It was left to Hans Pfitzner to describe his rival Richard Strauss, in one of his books, as a "poor devil" in this respect. . . .

At the heart of Strauss's operas, from the time when he left the Wagnerian music drama to pursue the ideal of the opera of pure music, there is the *singing human being*. From the time when he was fifty the vocal melos of his operatic works was to achieve increasing prominence in place of the sensuous instrumental effects of his tone poems and the bizarre, naturalistic modes of expression of his music dramas. This re-discovery of true cantabile can be found foreshadowed in the melodic element of Salome's final monologue, and in the recognition scene between Elektra and Orestes. (Although when Specht, in this connection, calls even "Elektra" a "bel canto opera" he is not to be taken seriously). The typically Straussian conversational style, which contrasts so strongly with Wagner's "Sprechsingen" with its weighty symphonic underlining by the orchestra, and which takes its dominant position between arioso lyricism and the spoken word, had as its model Kunrad's sermon in "Feuersnot," the first independent utterance of the young music dramatist, which was to exercise its influence all through his career. Thus the Marschallin's monologues in "Rosenkavalier" have their origins in melodic flexibility derived from the contours of speech, following all the human impulses of this "comedy for music." From then on the vocal lines were blended with the text to an ever-increasing extent, in lyrical as well as in dramatic contexts. The diction of speech has "passed into the music" (Mussorgsky). Strauss's method differed essentially from Janáček's use of speech motifs based closely on declamation in that his characteristic parlando, swift though it is, never leads to a mere scanning of the text in the voice parts. Even in rapid tempi, when the singers appear to "speak" ("The tempo is on no account to be misjudged, as it exactly follows the natural tempo of speech"), Strauss is concerned to employ melodic material to underline the musical-dramatic situation. His vocal lines sink to the level of pure secco recitative, or even to that of ordinary speech, only when the dramatic situation scarcely admits of any alternative. During the 'twenties the two extreme basic concepts of dramatic music came into close proximity, as represented by "Intermezzo," whose parlando comedy style is carried to its logical conclusions, and "Helena," with its full-toned lyrical pathos.

The entire history of opera has seen a constant ebb and flow of forces in the struggle for supremacy between drama and music, but the mature operatic art of Strauss, basically sensuous, placed the emphasis clearly on the "soul of opera"-melody. However, "melody is a crystallization of the spiritual life of man," as Pekrowski wrote in his study of the relationship between the dramatic element of opera and melody. "It is necessary to feel deeply with the character, to become one with him, if we are to pass on his deeper thoughts and feelings." Strauss's melodies are not "music which is beautiful in itself." They grow from the psychological and musical expressive possibility of the voice, from the human relationship and social conditions of the dramatic story. Their characters, images and conflicts determine the purpose and form of the composer's ideas. What a long succession of mainly feminine characters, from Salome to Madeleine, from Ariadne to Danae, born of a rich power of melodic invention! (Very early in Strauss's career he was aware that the feminine element would be of primary importance in his operas, as is shown by a sentence of Wagner which he quoted in a letter to Dora Wihan: "Women are our consolation, for every woman comes into the world as a human being, while every man is born a philistine, and it is a long time before he achieves real humanity, if he ever does.") What a meaningful, individually conceived and executed melos which, even if heard outside the opera house, over the radio or from a recording, can never be separated from the flow of the dramatic reality of the musical-dramatic situation which gave birth to it! Strauss's vocal melodies are the expression of beauty and truth. Their fine lines and buoyancy reveal the streams of emotion, the pulse of the thinking and feeling musician. They show unmistakably the extent to

157

which the music comes from the depths of the soul, or whether it remains on the surface of the senses. They are incorruptible.

*

"... In one chord you experience a world! ..." In *sound* there reside the secret of life and the power of the illuminating image. The composer may invent melodies, may construct forms, may be master of the structure and of the artistic handling of his materials—these factors come together and take on convincing value only through the primary ability to conceive in terms of sound. All constructive, formal, technical and stylistic elements of music are merely outward means to realize the tonal vision, to make it perceptible to others. Sound, as a phenomenon of physical acoustics, is the same in all ages. The number of available notes, of their shades of tone colour and of their possible combinations, have grown over the centuries owing to the development of instrumental music, but in essentials the notes have the same value that they had 500 years ago. The individual note, for example C, has had its place in all eras of musical history: it appears in Gregorian chant and in the "Meistersinger" Prelude, in "Das wohltemperierte Clavier" and in Schoenberg's piano pieces. The note itself does not alter, but the manner in which it is introduced and employed does alter. The note always has the same number of vibrations—but the sound which reaches the human ear, in the context of subjective concepts of music, is always new and manifold in its appearances and effects. Here is the riddle: how can anything remain the same yet constantly change? What does in fact change? The transformation applies to the significance of the sound, the context in which it appears, the spiritual content which flows from unknown springs to find expression in music.

Richard Strauss was probably the last of the great German composers who based their works on the expressive power of musical sound. His was also undoubtedly a brain which not only thought but also experienced in sounds. Owing to the fact that everything he wrote appears to be an incarnation of beautiful sound, his opponents believed, and still believe, themselves obliged to doubt the deeper significance of his music. (Since there is nothing they find more unbearable than music of blossoming

158

colourfulness which "sounds well.") It was by means of colouration that the great orchestral magician was able to give late romantic music a brilliantly festive lustre of its own. Festive music, that is to say music which *shines* as an illumination of the mind and spirit. This is still the case when Strauss abandons the instrumental apparatus a hundred strong and makes music with the chamber ensemble of Wagner's "Siegfried Idyll." What a distance separated the monster orchestras of 120 needed for "Elektra" and the "Alpensinfonie" from the refined style of "Metamorphosen" for 23 solo strings, and the Prelude to "Capriccio" for string sextet! What a contrast between the turbulent battle scenes of "Heldenleben" and the transparent filigree work of "Ariadne"! Just as there are painters the starting point of whose composition is colour, so Strauss's music glows in a thousand hues. However, a painting by Slevogt or Corinth would be inconceivable without a preliminary design (despite the artistic theory of Wölfflin), and similarly the musician's tonal feeling plays a part in forming the work as a whole. Max Reger's saying "Any composition is good if it can be played without any use of colour" (one could also say "which can be whistled") remains true in the case of Strauss. Gluck's words concerning drawing and painting in the foreword to "Alceste" are also worth remembering. It was only in a few episodes of "Heldenleben," "Salome" and "Elektra" that the element of tone colour gave rise to passages of such a degree of naturalism that the laws of "pure musical form" and of the "wonderful art of mind and spirit" were called in question.

*

It needed Strauss the *harmonist* to create the conditions required to allow the music to make its full impact. He combined all that a master of expression could achieve in the fields of melodic characterization and in the construction of a web of independent parts within the order of the romantic concept of harmony. While the classicists dominated their world of sound through the power of tonality, the romanticists and late romanticists made it their plaything, and drew out its ultimate consequences by means of tonal tension and relaxation. The extent to which the romantic harmony of Wagner's followers derived from "Tristan" has been demonstrated in great detail by Ernst Kurth.

Theirs was an art of veiled sounds, of dynamic tonal progressions and increasing colouration, of the smooth blending of chromatic note sequences and the combination of remote chords –features which have been recognized since Wagner's great tragedy as the specific marks of the neo-romantic style. It should not be forgotten that in the case of Strauss this style can be traced back by way of Liszt (first and foremost), Spohr and Weber to Mozart. It is fundamentally a concept of harmony linked with tonality. Strauss mastered the harmonic picture to the last detail, relating even the most complex harmonic procedures to the basic elements subdominant, dominant and tonic. His liquefactions of tonalities represent the farthest point reached by the psychologizing of tonal language. They are an advance into new realms of harmonic expression which result from the idealistic wanderings of certain works. They are peripheral, not fundamental. In every case the autocracy of the dissonance is confronted by the resolving principle of consonance.

Here, too, Strauss knew what he wanted and what he could do. He was conscious of Wagner's demand that one should never "allow harmonic effects to exist for their own sake." He did not shrink from really expressionistic orgies of dissonance, "cacophony" as they were called at the time, when he was intent on conjuring up in sound the ominous, sadistic atmosphere of "Salome" and "Elektra." Why should he serve the tonal realm of the "only beautiful" when what was required was to depict ugliness? Strauss was here compelled, as he was at certain places in his tone poems, to cross the border into atonality. What the young master wrote to Ritter in 1890 after the world première of "Macbeth" is worth recalling: "There were a few people there who realized that behind the frightful dissonances there lay something other than pleasure in discord for its own sake, namely an idea," and later: "Lassen and Bronsart had only heard interesting new sounds in 'Macbeth.' If only I could root out the accursed euphony!!" Even in his early days Strauss recognized in the supposedly obsolescent chords of the conventional major-minor system a means to loosen the fetters of harmonic restrictions. When we hear and see how at the beginning of "Don Juan" he boldly switches straight from the C major of the initial upward-surging motif into the principal tonality of E major, how at the end of the love scene in "Heldenleben" he modulates

160

from G minor to D minor above a sustained chord of G♭ major, or how at the close of "Zarathustra" the resolving chord of the sixth in B major is confronted by the threatening pizzicato C of the basses–we can see clearly that here is innovation.

Strauss went to extremes only in "Salome" and "Elektra." "These two operas stand on their own among my works: in them I went to the extreme limits of the harmony of psychological polyphony (Klytemnestra's Dream) and to the limits of what ears of today can accept." The flickering harmonies of the Quartet of Jews which was denounced as "ear-splitting" at the time when "Salome" appeared, or the polytonal outbursts of the orchestra in "Elektra" (with A major and E♭ minor appearing simultaneously) are complexes of sound which are scarcely to be measured by the standards of absolute beauty. "Strauss cold-bloodedly thrusts the remotest tonalities on top of each other, without giving a thought to the fact that they may cause distress, concerned only with the fact that they are 'alive,'" the shocked Debussy exclaimed. However, when Strauss was asked for a prescription against this "distress," he had a humorous answer ready, as was so often the case: "Yes, one mustn't hear that *vertically* but *horizontally,* then it can be understood. . . ." Thirty years later, when he heard "Elektra" performed under Böhm in Dresden, he is said to have exclaimed in astonishment that he himself could no longer understand how he came to write such a problematic score. . . .

In order to become familiar with the harmonic charm of his music in its sensuous nobility we must turn to "Rosenkavalier," "Ariadne," and all the works of his full maturity. The strong tensions created in the morbid spheres of the two grim tragedies gave place to a new, light and tonally firm world of harmony which remained serene even in moments of drama; this represented a conscious change of direction from dissonance to consonance, from dissolution to drawing together. Much of what gives delight in the harmonic context of the late works can be found presaged in the tone poems from the time of the breakthrough with "Don Juan," and in the popular elements of "Till" and "Feuersnot." This was artistry which unfolded and characterized the thematic idea by means of a rich inner life of harmony, which gave warmth to what were in themselves homophonic and diatonic melodies by means of chromaticism at once imaginative and controlled. Strauss demonstrated this most clearly in his "Don Quixote," in whose Introduction and individual variations he produced a series of surprising cadential resolutions on an unchanging harmonic basis. Features of this technique include the widespread use of multiple suspensions, enharmonic changes, passing notes and anticipations, although the fundamental significance of the relations between triads, augmented and diminished intervals remains evident both in the smallest harmonic units and in the structure of whole scenes and acts. There is another striking characteristic: the fairly frequent combination of major and minor elements, or of the harmonic and melodic minor used simultaneously. The result is the comprehensive *"euphony"* of a harmonic language which became ever more consciously devoted to the finest shading of the musical expression. In his later works Strauss derived the strength of his music to a striking degree from a simple concept of harmony, renouncing all chromaticism and other stimulants which had transformed the lush waves of sound of earlier works into the realm of the sensitive expression of feelings. His harmonic formulation reached its point of greatest simplicity and conciseness in the works of concerto type dating from his last creative years.

The excessive sweetness which occurs from time to time in Strauss's works has been explained as a result of their lack of harmonic tensions. It is true that the "floods of beauty" in certain scores (in particular "Helena" and the late works "Daphne" and "Danae") involve the risk of swamping the listener's senses. Strauss knew this, and he constantly sought opposing forces in his symphonic and dramatic works. In his best creations he found them, by turning aside into surprisingly fine and individual realms of harmony. The extent to which he succeeded, as his will to create both expression and effect developed, in fashioning romantic harmony into an individual tonal background is indicated by an abundance of impressive examples: in "Rosenkavalier" the impressionistic tonal mixtures which give a silvery sheen to the melody of love at the moment when the rose is presented to Sophie–an idea of melodic, sensuous and harmonic imaginative power; in the "Alpensinfonie" the uniquely mysterious introductory bars to the representation of night during which all the notes of the scale of B♭ minor are heard, in "Die Frau ohne Schatten" the strangely pale harmonic illumination at the mo-

162

ment of petrification, in "Daphne" the impressionistic twilight at the homecoming of the flocks and (a style of harmony completely new to Strauss) the sense of mystery and awe which is created when Apollo places the cloak round Daphne. How totally different were the stern military contours of "Friedenstag," written a few months earlier! Wherever one looks in the realm of Strauss's harmony one finds imagination coupled with skill. Thus, for example, the motif of the potion of memory in "Helena" proves to consist of a sequence of chords which compress a veritable labyrinth of tonalities within the space of four bars. The same technique leading to the creation of independent chord and key complexes occurs later in the significant scene of the creditors of "Danae"–new impressive examples of that pictorial quality which had especially marked out Strauss's harmony since the time of "Zarathustra."

The individual scenes are naturally influenced by the appropriate local colour. "Salome" and "Josephslegende" have an exotic atmosphere, as have some episodes of "Schlagobers" and "Helena;" the Viennese element is present in a whole series of works, and so is that of southern Italy. . . . Strauss wrote afterwards in connection with "Salome" that he had always been conscious of the absence of convincing eastern colour in operas with an Oriental setting. "Necessity provided me with a really exotic harmonic system whose colours varied, especially in strange-sounding cadences, like those of shot silk." However, Strauss never fell victim to the temptation to write in a crudely pseudo-exotic manner (even in the "Japanische Festmusik," when it would have been so easy to adopt such methods). Nor did he adopt Spanish local colouration in his tone poems "Don Juan" and "Don Quixote," with the exception of the bolero rhythm. Strauss's fine harmonic feeling also shows itself in his characteristic employment of particular keys in the service of his musical-poetic ideas. For example the opening of "Heldenleben" is in a heroic E♭ major, that of "Daphne" in a bucolic G major. A prominent feature of his heartfelt love melodies, soaring yet intimate, is the use of keys with many flats or sharps (F♯ and D♭ major). The astonishing extent to which, while composing, he conceived in particular tonalities from the outset is indicated by a remark on the back of a sketch book for "Elektra": "Elektra alone B♭ minor, against the world heightened B minor. Agamemnon Bb minor, Triumph Dance C major." Again, on one page of the original libretto of "Danae" Strauss wrote "D major" against Jupiter's "Sieh, ich rufe dich" at the end of the first act, against the "golden dreams" which follow immediately he wrote "Db major," and against the "golden rain" "Gb major" in the margin. . . . The characteristic choice of keys in the "Sinfonia domestica" is revealing: the head of the family is depicted in a masculine F major, the capricious, incalculable wife in the remote key of B major, and the baby, not yet quite steady on his feet, hovers between D major and D minor–exactly in the middle between his parents. . . . So everything has meaning and order.

*

Strauss's world of sound began where that of Wagner ended. In intoxicating yet at the same time transparent orchestral sound, and also in textures with the delicacy of chamber music he demonstrates his complete mastery of the *melos of colour.* This constructive element, in its highly developed culture and spiritual animation, is an essential part of his music. Strauss's sensuously warm sound may be ecstatic or majestic–it is loveliest in the combination of glowing colour with spiritual qualities. This particular attribute of Strauss is as inimitable as the revolutionary fire of Beethoven, the fervent poetry of Tschaikowsky, the open-air musicality of Dvořák or the wit of Offenbach. Even when Strauss writes in a vein of pathetic feeling his music is never flabby, but is a living tonal organism. (The charge made by his critics that Strauss employed "sluggish streams" of orchestral sound far removed from classical ideals is without foundation. Strauss cannot be held responsible for the bad manners of those who exploit some features of his technique without adopting his guiding principles–in particular the suppliers of music to the Hollywood film industry.) Strauss achieved something decisive with the flexible, slender, clear and graceful sound which he learned to draw from the orchestra, namely the overthrow of Wagner's musical empire. It is significant, with regard to the continuing effectiveness of his music today, that the audacities of 1900, the bitonality of "Heldenleben" and the excesses of "Elektra", have long since lost the fascination of novelty, while the aura of light surrounding so much of his more serene, buoyant and warmly-coloured music still shines undimmed, familiar though it has become, despite all changes of taste. "Only my carefully differentiated orchestral texture with its *'nervous counterpoint'* (if I may be permitted that expression) was able to venture into areas where music alone can penetrate—in the closing scene of 'Salome,' at the moments of Klytemnestra's dread, in the recognition scene between Elektra and Orestes, in the second act of 'Helena,' in the Empress's dream (second act of 'Frau ohne Schatten')." The ingeniously fashioned texture in a characteristic work of Strauss is a web of freely-flowing motifs woven with great bravura. "When I hammered out some things (from 'Salome') on the piano to my good father a few months before his death, he groaned in despair: 'God, this nervous music! It's just as though cockchafers were crawling about in one's trousers!'" Strauss wrote in his "Recollections," and he went on with an obvious wink: "He wasn't altogether wrong."

We can easily picture Strauss the musician who conceived in colour and sound amid the mountains of his Upper Bavarian homeland and in the clear air of the south. . . . Strauss, as a south German, had no need to study the Viennese atmosphere on the spot when he wrote "Rosenkavalier." On the other hand "Don Juan," "Ariadne" and many other works were possible only as the reflection of southern warmth and brightness, which probably first came to the fore, clear to everyone, in the idyllic slow movement of "Aus Italien." It was in Sicily, on Christmas eve in 1937, that Strauss completed "Daphne," which marked the meeting between Mozart's world of sound and that of Wagner beneath the Grecian sky. "I can assure you that there is sunshine in Richard Strauss's music," Debussy wrote in his critical essay. Often, in essentially lyrical works (Hölderlin hymns, last orchestral songs etc.) there is almost *too much* light, so that we feel a lack of the contrast provided by shadow. But with what inimitable skill Strauss was able to "tear down a piece of the heavens, to draw it into himself" (as Hofmannsthal once wrote in a letter), when he was concerned to adorn his art with the light of poetry and truth! Then it shone like a medieval illuminated manuscript whose golden characters were raised so that they caught the light from all directions. (It was Berlioz who discovered how to achieve this *"catching of light"* in modern instrumentation.) Strauss raised the technique to the point of absolute mastery, and for the first time extended it to vocal music. The southern, sensuous atmosphere of many of his works soon made him very popular in the Latin countries, France and Italy, but also in England. (During one of his trips to Spain he was driven to despair by constantly hearing the "Rosenkavalier" waltzes in hotels and coffee houses.) A segment of southern life viewed through a musician's temperament–Zola's familiar definition could be applied to the soaring brightness of Strauss's art. While we link Weber with painters of a similar artistic outlook such as Caspar David Friedrich and Carl Blechen, in the case of Strauss we are reminded of the glittering splendour of Slevogt or Corinth, and of the open-air work of the impressionists.

What a wide range of artistry Strauss demonstrated in his quest for beauty, significance, and descriptive qualities in his modes of musical expression! No one who listens to a work by Strauss can fail to notice his mastery in the invention of new sounds, surprising tonal combinations and fine gradations of intensity in the free treatment of the thematic material. There is no tone colour beyond the range of this master of the art of instrumentation. In his orchestra witches' cauldrons hiss and bubble, fairy stories are whispered and exercise their charm, the jester's cap and bells tinkle, and the voices of free humanity sing and rejoice. In his search for naturalistic and realistic modes of expression there was scarcely an effect of colour which Strauss neglected to employ. His goal of presenting *"images"* which were as exact and satisfying to the senses as possible was achieved through the descriptive qualities of his instrumental and vocal language. His is music to hear *and* see. Its tonal character is concrete and close to life; it is never an end in itself, but is an expression of natural forces. The means of presentation may take on highly complex forms, but their aim in each case is to reflect some general and typical characteristic. As Strauss himself put it: "The rainbow shines in seven colours, but there is always only the one rainbow."

Tonal ideals change. . . . In the full flowering of his mastery of colour Strauss tried to give each score, and even to some extent each song, its own particular tone colour, a unique *sound form.* This produced the especial "aroma" of his music, a quality which had been met with previously only in Wagner. A few chords or melodic lines of "Salome," "Ariadne" or "Helena"

166

are enough to reveal the sultry eroticism, the blossoming archaism and the hymnic expansiveness which characterize these three works respectively. Strauss was in agreement with Hofmannsthal, who wrote in 1928 while they were working together on "Arabella": "The decisive factor is the discovery of the correct tone for the entire work, a certain overall atmosphere in which the whole will live. In 'Helena,' for example, this is somewhere between the elegant and the solemn (infinitely different from the darkly ominous tone of 'Elektra,' but at the same time far removed from the elegiac tone of 'Ariadne'). The tone of 'Arabella' also clearly differentiates it from that of 'Rosenkavalier.'. . ." The diverse attributes of Strauss's tonal imagination could be demonstrated by hundreds of examples. For instance he painted the "whole first half of the 'Domestica' in water colours and pastel shades," and within a few years ventured, in his music dramas, on the boldest conquests of sound extended to proportions hitherto unheard of. Even within *the same* work ("Heldenleben") he would contrast tone pictures of elemental power and vast stature with others of a sensitive, sinewy nature. Although he soon found it necessary to discard the monster orchestra of "Salome" and "Elektra," he had, by writing those works, identified himself with the concept of overpowering theatrical music. He had indeed needed new and more intensive means to depict the dark and perverse passions of those grim one-act operas. Here was that "hypertrophy of the feelings" to which Rolland referred, and which was characteristic of many members of Wagner's generation (including Berlioz and Zola). "What do the people want?" exclaimed the composer of "Elektra" when a friend tried to console him after the work had been attacked in the press following the first performance. "When a mother's being slaughtered on the stage I can't play a violin concerto in the orchestra pit."

The manner in which, throughout his career, Strauss created transparency of sound, increasingly concerned as he was to give both voices and instruments their rights and to let them shine, creating atmosphere with new, bright colours, and drawing situations and figures with clear strokes–all these reveal in every detail the hand of a man of deep understanding. All through the finely graduated range of his music, extending as it does from tender, serene lyricism to the construction of monumental and

167

grandiose tonal edifices, we sense the presence of a born, natural musician. Rather than draw together the elements of the music drama in the Wagnerian sense, Strauss decked it out with his personal commentaries and analysed it. He represented every emotion between the extremes of tears and laughter in the symbols of music. Whether he was writing on a massive or an intimate scale he always kept within certain bounds. To go beyond these would have meant straying from artistry into artificiality. . . .

With Strauss the growing complication of the tonal picture and its later simplification represented a process which can be followed in clear stages. The line of development began in the later symphonic poems with their constant extension of the orchestral apparatus, culminating in the enormously complex scores of "Elektra," "Josephslegende," the "Alpensinfonie" and the "Festliches Präludium," with new instruments constantly being added until at last Strauss could go no further. He was in a cul-de-sac. However, while steadily increasing the size of his orchestra he had also been developing the idea of giving subtler differentiation to the tonal structure–a move in the direction of chamber music having an effect opposite to that of expanding the orchestra. The first step in this process of refinement was the subdivision of the violin parts in the mature tone poems, then Strauss divided the upper strings into three in "Elektra" (3 each violin and viola parts), and the first culminating point of this new line of development came with the scoring of "Ariadne" for a chamber orchestra. A wonderful degree of economy entered into Strauss's work. A comparison between the tonal concepts of the two Viennese comedies "Rosenkavalier" and "Arabella" shows in the one case the full power of blossoming strings and flashing brass, in the other a treatment of the full orchestra allied to chamber music, with many passages scored for a reduced ensemble sometimes as small as a solo string quartet–an art of "leaving out" which Strauss first attained in "Intermezzo" ("freed from all central European heaviness"), developed in a masterly fashion in "Capriccio," and intended to refine still further in the ballet-opera "Venus und Adonis" or "Die Rache der Aphrodite," which was to have been written "without trombones and trumpets," but which never got beyond the stage of preliminary sketches. Another noteworthy factor about Strauss's work in its most advanced stages is the degree to which (despite the use of certain naturalistic touches) he renounced non-musical elements, so that even moments of dynamic drama never go beyond the bounds of genuine music. The two lines, of the extension of the orchestra and of increasing refinement, cross each other in "Die Frau ohne Schatten." In no other work are the contrasts found in such close juxtaposition: the tonal palette of the massive orchestral apparatus (whose most unusual feature is a glass harmonica), which makes full use of every aspect of symphonic technique, stands in striking contrast to the truly intimate delineation of certain scenes by the solo violin and cello. There is an especial fascination in the way volcanic outbursts of orchestral sound and simple instrumental song are blended into a harmonious entity.

The extent of the transformation which Strauss's art underwent is made clear by a comparison between two characteristic operatic scenas. Each has a highly significant place in a one-act opera, and each is a dramatic monologue for the soprano singer of the title role. One is the impassioned monologue "Allein! Weh, ganz allein" from the tragic "Elektra," created at the zenith of Strauss's career: it is the first pillar of a musical structure seemingly made up of massive blocks of stone—no aria, but a solo scena of a stature recalling Gluck, making use of every nuance of expression from the sudden cry to a warm flood of sound, and not so much supported as driven along by the violently raging orchestra. Human passions are aflame even in this "point of repose" of a fiercely pessimistic, nerve-shattering work. ... The other is from "Daphne," the bucolic tragedy which, like "Elektra," has its roots in ancient Greek mythology, but which is full of light and the serenity which sprang from the wisdom of old age. Daphne sings her first great monologue; it is not an ecstatic outpouring but is more an address to nature. Daphne's solo is a thing of airy, lyrical enchantment, a constant flood of freely-flowing vocal melody and delicately-spun string tone which floats and sweeps ever higher, a finely woven texture of thematic relationships. This is not drama but infinite peace, a blissful longing for tranquillity and beauty, expressed at the outset in the simple woodwind introduction. The forces of nature are not poured out, they are controlled. This is not music of a woman's vengeance, but a song of Eros, of virginity. ... When the composer of "Elektra" heard his opera for the first time at the

169

rehearsals for the world première in Dresden, the orchestra could not play loudly enough to satisfy him. "As I was still infatuated with the Germanic ff at that time, I foolishly harried Schuch's fine-sounding (not threatening) brass during the rehearsals." Thirty years later, in the case of "Daphne," the situation was exactly reversed. At the dress rehearsal in Dresden Strauss was at first dissatisfied with Böhm's presentation of the work. He wanted it to sound *still more* delicate, *still more* transparent.

*

"Now at last I have learned to orchestrate," Strauss told the Dresden orchestra before they gave the world première of the "Alpensinfonie." A few years later, at the time of "Frau ohne Schatten," he declared that at last, after completing the score of this opera, he had gained complete command over all the possibilities of the art of *instrumentation*. What assurance, what clarity of mind concerning his own ability lay behind those words! Strauss's unparalleled advances in orchestral technique, the impulsive, soaring, sensuous yet transparent sound were the expression of an incomparable mastery of his material. The orchestra became to an ever increasing extent his instrument for expressing inner spiritual feelings. The orchestration, tending in Strauss's early years toward violent colouration, took on a gentler and at the same time more flexible character as the resources employed were reduced. Even from the viewpoint of sheer orchestral technique, Strauss's progress toward the ideals of Mozart and Wagner was amazing. The unique qualities of the instrumentation make it evident that Strauss did not regard tone colour simply as a decorative element to be added to his scores to enhance their melody and harmony. His art lay rather in deriving the particular orchestral tone from the atmosphere and characteristics of the moment—"orchestral thinking" as Dvořák (after hearing "Don Quixote") described the basic requirement of every composition for orchestra. It is here that virtuosity takes on a real significance.

In 1904, in the foreword to his new edition of the "Treatise on Instrumentation by Hector Berlioz," Strauss laid down his views in detail. After attributing the secret of the tonal poetry of "Tristan," "Die Meistersinger" and the "Siegfried Idyll" to their polyphonic construction, he declared that the "pronounced brittleness of colouration" in scores by Berlioz, Weber and Liszt was caused by the fact that the "chorus of accompanying and filling-in parts was not considered worthy of melodic independence by the composer...." "If only everyone who wants to write for the orchestra could be compelled to begin his career with the composition of some string quartets! He would then have to show these quartets to two violinists, a violist and a cellist, and obtain their opinions. If these four worthy instrumentalists say 'Yes, this is well written for the instruments, well-phrased and singable,' then this son of the muses should follow his inclination to write for orchestra (preferably a small one at first). If not, he had better choose a different career. When finally the call of the large orchestra can no longer be denied, then the well-meaning 'young master' should study the eleven Wagner scores (from 'Rienzi' to 'Parsifal'), and he will see how each demonstrates the simplest possible means of presentation, will appreciate the noble proportion which is preserved in the use of all resources throughout these works. On the other hand remember as a warning the example of a living composer who once showed me the score of a comedy overture in which the four Wagner tubas danced along with the rest of the brass in the liveliest rhythm (merely to strengthen the tutti)...." Such a passage indicates the educational purpose of this treatise on instrumentation, which is still indispensable to every orchestral composer. An estimable trait of character of the essentially modest Strauss: only eight of the 151 extensive musical examples in the book are taken from works of his own.

Strauss employed all the means of expression developed since the creation of the modern orchestra, with the knowledge accumulated by his predecessors, in a most personal, natural and at the same time refined manner. Instrumentation now signified the illumination of the inner events, and the translation into sound of feelings and emotional forces. The orchestra, which was consolidated and refined as an instrument of expression in the tone poems, was perfected as the vehicle for the dramatic element, the single instruments being used in an increasingly individual manner. The more Strauss committed himself to the transparent ideal of "symphonic accompaniment," which eliminates the danger of "murdering the singers," the more frequently he availed himself of the services of individual instruments as soloists—the violin, viola, cello, oboe and horn. His technique varied endlessly, suited always to the spiritual expression and atmosphere of the programmatic or dramatic content of the work. There was never a blemish, an error in the choice of tone colours or in the composition of the orchestra. Anyone who studies the nature of the composer as indicated in his scores will notice how much more freely he worked, and how he was at his most effective, when making use of simple resources and avoiding the artificial, over-emphatic and violent. Interesting in this connection are the late works in which Strauss clad ideas of a far earlier period *afresh* in a simpler garb, such as the "Rosenkavalier" Waltz Sequence of 1944, which is more transparently orchestrated than the original (though Strauss later regretted that it suffers from "a few over-abrupt modulations"). It also appears to be important that the living stream of Strauss's orchestra was not made to conform to a scheme such as we encounter in Bruckner and Reger. To Strauss the possibilities of drawing and painting in sound were always new and endless.

While he may certainly be regarded as an artist of high spiritual purpose, his listeners often saw him as a naive *illustrator in sound,* whose aim was always assured. It was the over-enthusiastic naturalist Strauss who committed himself to the statement (though it was later withdrawn): "I regard the ability to depict events outside music as the greatest triumph of musical technique." The naturalistic outlook gave rise to such virtuistic tone pictures as the bleating of the flock of sheep and the dripping of water after the hero's ducking in "Don Quixote," the essentially harmless instrumental scherzi "Ganz der Papa" and "Ganz die Mama" in the "Domestica," the waterfall in the "Alpensinfonie," the cry of the falcon in "Frau ohne Schatten," the swish of the toboggan, the newspaper rustling and the sounds of the game of skat in "Intermezzo," or the growling of the bear in "Arabella." The naturalistic elements of "Salome" and "Elektra" are completely integrated in the musical-dramatic structure—such generally crass illustrations (the sound of the night wind, the neighing of horses, the cries and the noise of fighting) can scarcely be removed from the tonal organism. The horrifying effect created by the contrabasses at one point in "Salome" (the sound is produced by short strokes of the bow on a string gripped by two fingers) was misunderstood for many years until Strauss

172

explained in his "Recollections" that it represented an impatient sigh of the Princess as she waited for the head of Jokanaan. There was nothing in the world of experiences which Strauss could not capture in sound.

It is not always possible to draw the line between the symbols of a mere representation of nature in sound, and the realistic demands of certain works. Tone pictures such as the sunrise in the "Alpensinfonie," the glittering rose, and the clock stopped "in the middle of the night" in "Rosenkavalier" or the ringing of the bells in "Friedenstag" were born of necessity out of the realistic situation of the action, and released themselves from their subservience to the purely material elements. Strauss succeeded ideally in this in the unexpected sequence of chords which characterize the magical extinguishing of the fire in "Feuersnot," and above all in the mysterious F♯ major rustling of the leaves during Daphne's transformation into a laurel. This mastery of instrumental clothing produces (as Wilhelm Kienzl once put it) "music to see with the ears." It is first and foremost *music*. Probably no one before Strauss, apart from Weber in the Wolf's Glen scene in "Freischütz," had been able to produce so tangible an evocation of forces of nature. Had Strauss been content to experiment with interesting tone colours, the results would no doubt have been different and of less lasting value.

The fact that Strauss attempted to an ever greater extent to draw the line between, on the one hand, superficial musical illustration using all the subtleties of "tone effects" true to nature, and on the other hand tonal symbols springing from the innermost content of the music, can be seen from innumerable examples of his mature works. Instruments for making mere noise, such as the wind machines in "Don Quixote" and the "Alpensinfonie," never played more than a subordinate role with Strauss. (He rejected any ultra-naturalistic device such as Respighi's use of a gramophone record of a nightingale's song in his "Pines of Rome.") To an ever increasing extent the descriptive passages were drawn into the overall texture. The composer of "Don Quixote" was right to laugh at those "sheep-headed" people who noticed nothing in the whole tone poem but the "seventeen bars of mutton." ... The natural forces which Strauss unleashed in "Elektra" with such merciless effect became an organic part of the musical structure in the storm music of "Helena." While the

173

illustration of the trickling of the gold dust in "Josephslegende," by means of a glissando of the solo violin in conjunction with harp and string harmonics, gave the impression of a cleverly devised interpolation, the tone picture of the golden rain in "Danae" is created by a fine instrumental web of sound which does not so much depict the enchantment of the gold itself as the sense of delight to which it gives rise. The result is a truly inspired sound picture.

Following the composer's orchestra to the last vibrant echoes and into the polyphony of colours and tone symbols gives increasing insight into the feelings and methods of Strauss the colourist. The mastery with which he controlled a small or large performing apparatus, aided by an ingenious technical imagination, is undisputed. . . . Naturally, however, when his contemporaries first heard certain of his works they found them positively startling in their boldness. For example after the first performance in Vienna of "Tod und Verklärung" Hanslick wrote of a "horrible battle of dissonances, in which the woodwind howl downwards chromatically in thirds while all the brass threaten and all ghosts rage," and in 1905 an equally unresponsive critic gave vent to his feelings concerning the orchestra of "Salome" as follows: "We find this orchestra very incomplete, and expect Richard Strauss to include the following musical instruments in his next opera: four of the new express locomotives with double boilers (tuned to the chord of F♯ minor), three foghorns (on high C's), and a battery of 15 cm. howitzers for enhancing the effect of the timpani. . . ." Such views on his art themselves reflect the spirit of the age.

There was never any lack of surprises in the sphere of his orchestra, with which he presented the new and many-sided contents of his symphonic and dramatic works. He began, in his tone poems, with the triple woodwind which he so loved in the score of "Lohengrin," then progressively enlarged his orchestra still further. His especial susceptibility to a blossoming string melos remained with him all his life. He adopted new instruments seldom used before in the late romantic orchestra: the oboe d'amore, heckelphone, bass clarinet, saxophone, celesta, organ, and several others; the muted trumpet added a fresh nuance to the sound of the brass. The apparatus became increasingly complex. The extreme limit in sheer size was reached by the colossal

174

orchestra of the choral work "Taillefer," with its 24 woodwind, 20 brass, 12 percussion and 90 strings. The 96 strings, quintuple woodwind, 8 horns, 6 trumpets and 4 trombones of the "Festliches Präludium" (like Mahler's orchestral arsenal) also belong to the realm of overblown enormities, on which Strauss soon turned his back. In contrast to Berlioz he did not regard extreme mass effects as being necessary in order to bring music to the general public. It was not the perfecting and increasingly virtuistic treatment of the means of expression which he considered to be decisive, although it often led him to create baroque tonal fascination, but the value of the music in its context. When at the age of seventy he let loose a whole bombardment of noise at the tormented old man in "Schweigsame Frau," his over-scored occasional pieces lay far behind him. Strauss's efforts had long been directed toward the more sparing treatment of the orchestra, allied to chamber music, which he had first tried out in "Ariadne." (It has been said that during a rehearsal of "Carmen" under Krauss in Munich Strauss shook his head and said: "Two trumpets! And I generally need at least four!") He wrote the following in 1929 when starting work on "Arabella": " I am convinced that in future dramatic effectiveness will be dependent on the employment of a smaller orchestra, which does not overwhelm the voices as a large orchestra does. Many younger composers have already realized this to some extent. The orchestra of the future is the chamber orchestra, which alone is capable, with its crystalline underlining of all that occurs on the stage, of presenting the composer's ideas with consideration for the singers and with all possible clarity. A final fact which is by no means unimportant is that the audience should not merely hear notes, but should also be able to follow the words...." There is no doubt that as Strauss grew older he devoted more and more attention to solving the problems of many of his libretti through the clarity of his music.

Although Strauss gained a thorough knowledge of almost the entire family of instruments even during his youth, he did not willingly set limits to his imagination to comply with an instrument's normal technique, and his woodwind and brass parts contain passages which can be played only after careful study and practice of the fingering. How indignant all orchestral players were when Strauss made unprecedented demands in his works, both by requiring prodigies of technique from them and by extending the compass over which they had to play! During the strenuous rehearsals for "Salome" in Dresden a principal woodwind player said to him reproachfully: "Herr Doktor, that may go on the piano, but not on my clarinet," and Strauss replied with a smile: "Don't worry, it can't be played on the piano either!" Orchestral players were helped to master the uncommon demands of his scores in a practical manner: they were issued with study books which assisted them in preparing to carry out their tasks. Today the so-called Strauss technique has long since become common property.

"I've given the soprano something to solve there! She'll simply have to *torment* herself until she gets it right!" Strauss remarked to Zweig as they looked through the "Schweigsame Frau" music together. He liked to give sopranos, in particular, some tough nuts to crack, but he was not slow to offer friendly assistance, sometimes to the most eminent singers. In any one generation Elektra and the Dyer's Wife can probably be really mastered by only a dozen sopranos of great dramatic gifts, and Zerbinetta and Aminta only by the few whose coloratura is impeccable. For the other voices, too, there are many highly taxing parts: one thinks of the low contralto E♭ of Gaea ("Daphne"), the tenor parts of Matteo ("Arabella") and Henry ("Schweigsame Frau") with their uncomfortable transitions to very high notes, the high-lying baritone parts of Kunrad ("Feuersnot"), the Barber ("Schweigsame Frau") and Jupiter ("Danae"). In the case of "Guntram" it was only with difficulty that the singer of the title role was persuaded that the part, which is longer than that of Tristan, could be sung at all. Strauss is said to have remarked of a tricky passage in "Elektra": "I couldn't get that myself," and when it comes to the "Deutsche Motette" his demands with regard to range (from the contra B♭ to C♯ above the treble clef) and breath control are far in advance of what can normally be expected of singers. Nevertheless there is good reason for numbering Strauss among the magicians of the human voice. It is only tenors who have less for which to be grateful to him. His female characters are creatures gifted with all the virtues of flowing lyrical cantilena. Many a renowned soprano has declared that her vocal artistry did not shine in the full light of international success until she appeared in the great Strauss roles. He

176

never forgot Wagner's advice to compose music in such a way that singers enjoy singing it. His ability to make the voice the bearer of melodies charged with feeling, and to create fascinating new textures by the skilful combination of, in many cases, high female voices, has seldom been called in question. It is not surprising that the favourite role of the Marschallin first fell into the hands of coloratura prima donnas. Frieda Hempel even wanted to adorn the part with fioriture, a suggestion which brought the composer's wrath down on her head. The fact that Strauss poured such an infinite wealth of beauty into the duets of "Rosenkavalier," "Helena" and "Arabella," the trios and ensembles of "Ariadne," "Schweigsame Frau" and "Danae" may perhaps be attributed to the influence of the exquisite female voice duets between the Countess and Susanna and between Fiordiligi and Dorabella in Mozart's operas. Like Mozart, Strauss had a masterly understanding of how to depict different emotions in characters singing at the same time.

A glance at his *orchestra* shows us a vision of Strauss's musical imagination. It would be out of the question to give any indication of it in mere words. . . . A selection of a few of the cases in which individual instruments are used with instinctive assurance to create symbols in sound must suffice. His instrumentation is, incidentally, a treasure store of characteristic solo effects. "The Hero's helpmate" in "Heldenleben" owes its character to extended, brilliantly effervescent violin solo passages, while lyrical solo violin cantabile depicts the ethereal world of the Empress and the magically swaying lyricism of the scene at the spring in "Die Frau ohne Schatten." Following the example of Berlioz's "Harold in Italy," Strauss created the inglorious character of Sancho Panza in "Don Quixote" through the medium of a solo viola. The same tone poem also provides, above all, brilliant opportunities for the hero himself—the virtuistic "title role" of the solo cello; the soulful song of the cello in the scene at the Falconer's house in "Frau ohne Schatten" also remains in the memory. The vivid naturalism of the contrabasses in "Salome" has already been mentioned. The woodwind are employed with great delicacy. How graceful are the flute runs in "Till," how sweetly the oboe sings its sensual song in "Don Juan," and how much the oboe d'amore in the "Sinfonia domestica" tells us about the sunshine of the child's life. How peaceful is the elegiac shepherd's melody of the cor anglais in "Heldenleben"! Clarinet, basset horn, bass clarinet, heckelphone and bassoon—all have their characteristic tone colours which Strauss put to individual use. With what radiance the victorious trumpet carries all before it in "Don Juan"! The horns seem to want to blow themselves straight in the pandemonium at the exit of Ochs in the last act of "Rosenkavalier"–but in the wonderfully spacious cantilena of the moonlight music in "Capriccio" they sing with contented warmth. Trombones and tuba intone the solemn mountain motif in the "Alpensinfonie." Harp and celesta chords shine through the silvery texture of "Rosenkavalier." The piano sparkles in the chamber music of "Ariadne"–and wittily portrays the dancing master in the music to "Der Bürger als Edelmann." The organ appears in "Zarathustra." The timpani make their mark in the early "Burleske." There was a steady increase in the freedom and eloquence with which Strauss employed his musical resources. As his art grew in realistic power of expression he used the instruments in an increasingly individual manner. Thus it is not surprising that during his last years he showed a new interest in works of concerto type.

What the young master wrote to his father after the first sectional rehearsals of "Don Juan" in Weimar expressed the justifiable pride of the discoverer of a new tone world: "Especially beautiful was the passage in G major for the oboe with basses divided into four parts, divisi cellos and violas, all muted, also the horns all muted; it sounded quite magical, and so did the dejection passage with harp bisbigliando and violas ponticelli. Our first trumpeter had never seen anything like it–an old, ponderous man who had never been expected to be so agile up to high B natural. . . . Our first clarinettist had never played a passage going up to the top F♯ either, and the bass players didn't trust themselves to reach the high B natural, but it sounded wonderfully characteristic. . . ." A few days later, after a two-hour full rehearsal, he wrote: "The orchestra puffed and blew, but pulled their weight famously. After 'Don Juan' a horn player who was sitting there sweating and quite out of breath gasped: 'O God, what have we done wrong that you have sent us this rod to beat us (meaning me)! We won't get rid of *him* in a hurry.' We laughed till we cried. The horns certainly blew as though they weren't afraid of death!"

The animated flow of the music is matched by the vibrant flexibility of Strauss's *rhythm*. It is significant that the young late-romanticist could feel satisfied neither with the strictness of Schumann's rhythmic schemes nor with the structural principles of the finales of the symphonies of Brahms and Bruckner (". . . so much pointless running about, especially in the transition sections"). The Mozartian lightness and serenity of his musical language favoured a buoyant, springy, variable rhythm whose point of balance frequently varied, and which was far removed from the static richness of Wagnerian music drama. It would have been strange if Strauss the vital had not always been in search of new nuances of rhythm. His waltzes released all the good fairies of three-four time. The march, polka, gavotte, polonaise and other dance forms add rhythmical verve to his scores. On occasion, too (in certain dances of "Josephslegende" and "Schlagobers," and in the scene of the kings and queens in "Danae") he would employ fascinating five-four and seven-four rhythms. Stravinsky's polyrhythms seem to have been anticipated when the composer of "Rosenkavalier" derives the erotic fluidity of the first scene from a constant alternation of duple and triple time. While Strauss based the rhythmic patterns of his operas and songs on the flow of speech, he solved the problems posed by this procedure in many original ways.

*

Artistic *form?* . . . Strauss several times made statements which indicated "that he is a musician first and last and all the time, to whom all 'programmes' are only the spur to create new forms, and nothing more. . . ." "A poetic programme can certainly lead to the establishment of new forms, but if the music does not develop logically out of itself the result is 'Literaturmusik'. . . ." "New ideas must seek new forms; that basic principle of Liszt's symphonic works, in which the poetic idea was at the same time the form-creating element, became from then on the guiding light for my own work in the symphonic medium." And finally: "Only when content and form match one another perfectly, as in the really great works, is perfect art achieved." These are significant statements by a musician who has often been suspected of forcing musical form into slavish subservience to programmes. The detailed formal analyses of the early tone poems and operas (such as "Don Juan," "Guntram" and "Frau ohne Schatten") by Alfred Lorenz, Edmund Wachten and Heinz Röttger have long since revealed the strict order of the symphonic and dramatic architecture of these works. The *"formal impetus"* to which Lorenz refers is a prominent feature of the general musical picture. Despite all originality in the musical language, the form of the programmatic composer remains firm and secure, even though pictorial features have their place in the music and often make their way to the fore. "Till Eulenspiegel," "Don Quixote" and the "Sinfonia domestica" are all compositions of organic growth, of whose brilliant formal layout the listener is probably quite unaware (this is no bad thing!). Strauss was never for a moment in doubt that each of these scores, which grew steadily in length from the fifteen or so minutes of "Don Juan" to the fifty minutes of the "Alpensinfonie," needed a particular formal tie if it was to appear as a complete entity of spirit and mind. More or less strict forms were no strait-jacket for his poetic or more concrete subjects. On the contrary, it was only through their well-designed "clothing" that the strong emotional contents of these tone poems were given essential shape. "Don Juan," which Hanslick described as a "tumult of blinding daubs of colour, a stuttering delirium of sound," proves on close examination to be constructed in free sonata form. Strauss the destroyer of form simply did not exist. Each of the tone poems can be shown to obey the fundamental laws of an established form (sonata form, rondo, variations etc.).

The manner in which Strauss built up a musical-dramatic scene was unparalleled since Wagner's "Tristan." He complied with the Beethoven-Wagnerian law of dialectic development. A wise gardener, he assisted the growth of strong plants from the motif seed. He succeeded in achieving a co-ordination of musical and dramatic form, in the creation of a vehicle both for the expression of feeling and for illustrating the events of his subject, primarily through an abundance of thematic relationships. Every scene in the Strauss operas is an entity in itself; the division into "numbers" in the Wagnerian sense is only veiled, or in some cases is perfectly obvious. Nevertheless the individual sections are skilfully linked together—right on to the finales of his acts and operas, conceived and fashioned with particular love—an astonishingly large number of which form quiet, resigned conclusions. ("The present ending to the act is very pretty," Strauss wrote to Hofmannsthal after reading the first draft of "Arabella," "but not effective enough for an opera. Cosima Wagner once said to me: 'The ends of the acts are the main thing!'") His ability to "through-compose" operas with no evident joins, though in fact creating well-balanced formal structures, was developed still further in his old age. It is always what is well-conceived and skilfully fashioned, in the highest sense artistic, that proves compelling, and when planning "Semiramis" in 1935 Strauss's assurance in matters of form was so great that he had "nothing whatever against making two evenings of it." It can easily be seen how the choice of tonalities in his operas gave rise to particular formal complexes, and how the scheme of modulations had a real significance on the creation of form. At the same time Strauss made equally adroit use of the dramaturgic factor of contrasts and of the logical evolution of particular tonal spheres.

"Salome" and "Elektra" were still the products of eruptive forces which created each of them, as it were, in a piece, and the various excerpts which can be taken from them always remain mere splinters of a monolithic structure. This was no longer true of "Rosenkavalier," "Frau ohne Schatten" or "Danae," in which the structural power of the musical-dramatic whole by no means excluded the presence of individual musical forms on a smaller scale. Strauss recognized the validity of the other great possibility of post-Wagnerian opera (above all in "Ariadne," his opera-play), and by adopting the self-contained forms of aria, song, duet, trio and larger ensemble he prevented his music from becoming formless. With the formal clarity and proportional beauty of his mature operatic works Strauss combined the invention of such ingenious ensembles as the sextet, septet and nonet of "Die Schweigsame Frau," and the "laughing" and "squabbling" octet in "Capriccio," which was conceived in a mood of scintillating good humour. With ever increasing virtuosity and consciousness of his powers he developed for himself the technique which had enabled Mozart to make different characters express very different sentiments simultaneously. He made increasing use of the chorus ("Friedenstag," "Danae"). It was a logical consequence of the spirit of his operas of pure music, commencing with "Rosenkavalier," that he should en-

181

hance the value of the various formal elements, both individually and collectively. He lavished all his mastery in the constructive field on "Capriccio," which is a veritable compendium of musical forms. Strauss knew precisely why he always emphasized to his librettists that at such and such a point he needed this or that: an aria, a duet, a larger ensemble. This practice, which according to Wagner's theory of the "Gesamtkunstwerk" would have prejudiced the "truth" of the work, corresponds to the deeper truth of modern opera psychology.

The mastery with which, in his symphonic and dramatic scores, Strauss combined strict constructive elements with those of full-blooded emotion is evident from hundreds of examples. His concern was to fashion the most complex forms in the simplest possible manner. Note, for example, the Sonnet from "Capriccio," which is constructed with the highest artistry in five-bar phrases, but which gives the impression in performance of being improvised. Then there is the astonishingly flexible way in which fugal form was employed in certain orchestral works ("Zarathustra," "Domestica" etc.) and operas (prelude to the third act of "Rosenkavalier," "Capriccio" ensemble). Consider the complete mastery of the rondo in "Till" and in Zerbinetta's Aria from "Ariadne," of the passacaglia in "Schlagobers" and "Panathenäenzug," and of the canon in the description of science in "Zarathustra" and in the quartet of Jupiter's lady loves in "Danae." How effortlessly the traditional types of overture flowed from Strauss's pen, from the classically noble overture of "Ariadne" to the variegated pot-pourri overture of "Die schweigsame Frau!" (Although in most of the stage works a few orchestral chords were sufficient for him to establish the atmosphere, and he sometimes went straight into the first scene). How brilliantly he could command the various dance forms of ancient and more recent times, from the sarabande and gavotte to the Viennese Waltz! Whether on a small or large scale, in a straightforward song with piano accompaniment of a few minutes' duration or in the highly polyphonic, multi-coloured symphonic structure of "Metamorphosen," which plays for half an hour, clarity and lightness mark the formal structure.

The opinion has often been expressed that after the time of his early symphonies the "progressive musician" Strauss (in contrast to Brahms and his school) avoided classical symphonic form.

This idea does not stand up to examination. Both "Helden-leben" and "Sinfonia domestica" are constructed as symphonies, each in a number of major sections, with development, recapitulation and coda. Later (in 1913), when the operatic composer had finally gained the upper hand over the symphonist, Strauss criticised the classical forms, in particular the sonata and quartet. "They no longer attract me as they did. . . . I am convinced that the last Beethoven quartets attained the highest pitch of perfection. To attempt to overstep these boundaries seems to me to be folly. Musical forms come into being, evolve, then die, in order to make way for new forms. . . ." It is above all the music of Strauss's old age which demonstrates most clearly his ability to create music of classical clarity and perfection of form. A certain diminution of his powers of invention seems to have been balanced in these works (Horn and Oboe Concertos, the two Sonatinas for Wind etc.) by an even greater feeling for classical proportions. The themes are not, indeed, so much "unfolded" in the classical sense as "illuminated" from different angles. It is to be regretted that Strauss never completed the project, which dated from about 1925, of writing a "Symphony on three themes in E♭ major" (making use of the dialectic methods of the great masters).

A basic problem of his music is its occasional contradiction between *form* and *content*. His joy in being able to express himself with the abundant tonal resources of the modern orchestra led him along the path of tonal expansiveness even in tone poems whose content really called for a somewhat different manner of expression. The grandiloquent monumentalism of the symphonic self-portraits in "Heldenleben" and the "Sinfonia domestica" undoubtedly led to stylistic errors. Similar weaknesses in the relationship between the simplicity of the original concept and its elaborate execution are to be found in the "Alpensinfonie." Such discrepancies are also to be met with in the dramatic works, for example the fact that the tale of "Die Frau ohne Schatten," instead of being narrated simply, is weighed down by orchestral interludes which open the sluices for a symphonic flood, while in the "Deutsche Motette" the element of simple solemnity is prejudiced by the complexity of the structure. On the other hand Strauss understood how to re-establish a balance between the conflicting elements even of such works as these by the inclusion of lyrical points of repose and chamber music episodes. In the one-act operas, which were strongly influenced by Ritter, there is a remarkable unity of content and form. This is true of the popular-styled "Feuersnot," of the darkly tragic "Salome" and "Elektra," and finally of "Daphne," although the lyrical and pathetically expressive gestures of this music do not always appear to be reconcilable. When Strauss conceived the brilliant tonal scenario of "Ariadne" with its 37 instruments he nearly made the mistake of rejecting the intimate form at the apotheosis, and decided "to go over to the 'full orchestra,' although behind the scenes" at the entrance of Bacchus. "A very silly idea indeed," as Strauss later admitted. Even without the larger orchestra the "bath of sound" at the conclusion of the work represents a stylistic solecism which is to be regretted. Unfortunately, too, Strauss did not always succeed in upholding the dramatic form with equal intensity from beginning to end in the operas laid out in several acts. It is not difficult to see that even a masterwork like "Rosenkavalier" falls into definite high spots (first act, beginning of the second and end of the third) and weaker parts, that in the case of both "Arabella" and "Schweigsame Frau" the first act is superior to those which follow in profile and content, and that in "Danae" the last act contains the most powerful streams of musical invention. Strauss's way of flinging himself with the greatest elan into the first scene of an opera, and of applying his self-critical faculties as the work progressed probably made it impossible completely to eliminate such differences of the formal substance within a work. Wagner, too, was unable to prevent the appearance of similar differences ("Walküre," second act).

The question of *"cuts"* is very important in the case of Strauss. As the young Court Conductor at Weimar he had fought energetically against the traditional "cutting down" of the Wagner operas. He presented "Lohengrin" in 1889 and both "Tannhäuser" and "Tristan" during the following years almost without omissions. When people asked at that time: "What is Strauss doing?" the answer was always: "Strauss is taking out cuts!" He wanted his respect for the original form of a work of art, his concept of unconditional fidelity to the work, to be applied to his own music. The fierce disputes in which he became involved at the time of the first performances of "Rosenkavalier" and

"Ariadne" have become part of operatic history. In the case of the "comedy for music" which Strauss had "composed as it stood, unaltered" although "even the librettist had expected omissions to be made," he had as partner Schuch, who had "never yet conducted an opera without cuts." Strauss would not accept the omissions specified by Schuch. "I will not tolerate these cuts under any circumstances. Please send me your prompt copy vocal score immediately, and I will mark in it exactly which cuts I authorize for Dresden.... The ensemble of squabbling in the second act must be restored completely, and Ochs's narration in the first act at least in its essentials...." Thirty years later (in his "Recollections") Strauss saw the humorous side of the argument: "It is not correct to say that a well composed and dramatically well balanced opera is made *shorter* by cuts. An example: After a year Baroness K., a friend of Seebach, saw *my* 'Rosenkavalier' in Berlin. She told me afterwards that the opera had seemed to her shorter than it had in Dresden. I replied: 'Yes, because less was cut out!' Therefore the proportions were more correct, and light and shade better distributed.... After I had been annoyed for some time by the Schuch cuts which had become irremovable I wrote to him saying that he had forgotten one important cut, as the Trio in the third act merely held up the action, and I suggested the following cut: D major 'Ich weiß nix, aber gar nix' to G major: beginning of the final duet! He was furious!–but he recovered to some extent from the Dresden disease...."

In this respect, as in others, Strauss's feeling for proportion and form changed over the years. Certain cuts in the monster part of "Elektra" have long since become generally accepted, and it is also a long time since Strauss produced the second version of "Ariadne," with its new scenic Prologue, to overcome the difficulty of the formidable length of the work in its original form. An important compression of the (dramatically imperfect) second act of "Helena" was authorized by the composer in 1933. In "Arabella" he agreed to the omission of the foolish flirtation-skirmishing between Adelaide and the young Domenik, as well as of the final bars of the second act. In the case of the Finale of "Friedenstag," too, he had recourse to a red pencil shortly before the world première.... Always conscious of form, he developed at the height of his powers a complete sense of proportion, of giving everything its due prominence and no more. He used

185

to say that one must not "have too much feeling for one's own music," as "the effect determines everything!" When, during the last ten years of his life, Strauss encountered his "Ariadne," either as conductor or merely as a listener, he particularly enjoyed the point in the Prologue at which the "Composer" wrathfully makes the required cuts. "In *this* opera at least I've composed the cuts."

STRAUSS THE MAN

SOCIETY HAS ITS OWN PRE-CONCEIVED NOTIONS CONcerning the private life of prominent artists. It sees in a great musician first and foremost the "brilliance" and "abnormality" of his personality. It would prefer him to unite all the typical characteristics of the epoch in his musical nature. There was little brilliance apparent in the externals of the man Strauss. Specht referred long ago to the "contrast between the calm solidity and simplicity of the composer himself, and the raging power of his creations and the tumult which they arouse." Strauss was neither an extraordinary nor an everyday man–he was quite simply a *man*– one who possessed all the qualities which shine through his works: imagination, clarity, steadiness, confidence, fire, awareness of life. He himself declared that he owed "the constitution of his brain and nervous system" to his mother, and his "vivacious, passionate temperament" to his father. At the end of the romantic age he was distinguished by his healthy personality and attitude to the beauties of life.

His very appearance set him apart from other renowned artists of his time. Those who saw Strauss, particularly in his earlier years, were liable to be somewhat disappointed. One would scarcely have supposed that this tall, lanky man with his spherical head, fair moustache and marine-blue eyes was the composer of "Don Juan" and "Elektra." Romain Rolland described him thus: "This figure with the pale, somewhat feverish-looking face, the remarkably light eyes with their indeterminate yet firm gaze, the childish mouth with a fair, almost white moustache, the fine, curly hair which forms a crown above the temples and the arched forehead." However, his face seemed to gain in expressiveness as he grew older. The massive bald skull, the heavy countenance of old age with the purposeful lines of mouth, nose

187

and forehead, the fine hands, all reflected the content and meaning of a life full of creative work. The jovial unceremoniousness of the young Strauss gave place to the physiognomy of mature wisdom and experience. Even in old age his figure was slender and his step elastic, his gestures simple rather than patriarchal. To a far greater extent than formerly his eyes reflected his feelings. "In the rare moments when his eyes flash," wrote Stefan Zweig, "one senses that something demonical lies concealed in this remarkable man, something which first makes one a trifle mistrustful when one sees the precision, the method, the solid craftsmanship, the apparent nervelessness of his way of working. . . ."

The man without nerves . . . Immediately after Strauss had completed yet another page of score which was to excite others, he would become a fanatical card player. Continually springing from one artistic task to another, this well-balanced personality managed to preserve his Bavarian calm despite the great exertions of travelling and rehearsing. The rare abilities to concentrate on what was important at the moment, and to prevent himself from being turned aside from his real artistic mission even in the international confusion of hotels and festivals, are almost unique in the proportions they assumed with Strauss. (During the period of unrest following the First World War he sketched out his "Intermezzo" in the hotel rooms of three continents.) During the final rehearsals prior to the world première of an opera, when others were losing their nerves, he would radiate sunny cheerfulness. It was fascinating to observe this "certainty of self-control," this "laziness of his eyes and general attitude, a fine feeling for the progress of events which leaves nothing more for him to do except to radiate all his acquired charm. He has achieved such an easy manner and such good order in things material that there are neither contradictions nor restrictions but only a balance of avowal and narration, of question and answer . . ." (Bie). When Strauss raised his tenor voice in a stream of broad Bavarian dialect, when he made his demands on the work and those concerned with it, he constantly displayed the characteristics of "genial bonhomie" (Rolland). Strauss the man was at the same time naive and subtle, modest and self-assured.

It is hardly surprising that Strauss the satirist was a *cheerful* person in his private life. Beside the deep seriousness of most of his works the roguish Strauss comes into his own. Anecdotes attributed to him (though some are probably spurious) bear witness to a wit remarkably unerring in its aim. When Strauss once called his "Salome" a "scherzo with a fatal conclusion," when he mentioned on occasion that he always learned from the producers what had been in his own mind when writing new works, such statements reflected a good measure of self-irony. His ability to come up with a good, dry south-German joke at the right

Richard Strauss offering his "Rosenkavalier"
Sketch by Enrico Caruso

moment is illustrated by the following examples. . . . During an early orchestral rehearsal of "Elektra" Schuch was disturbed by a sudden gust of wind. He saw a solitary charwoman in the gallery, and called out "What are you doing there?" whereupon Strauss replied from the stalls: "Looking for a common chord." . . . At a social function in London a gentleman was poking fun at the entirely insignificant compositions of the last German Kaiser. Strauss remarked maliciously "It is neither refined nor very

189

intelligent to make fun of the composition of crowned heads, because one never knows *who* has composed them." ... One last joke: At a rehearsal of "Frau ohne Schatten" in Breslau Strauss was perturbed by the fact that so little was to be heard from the dramatic contralto. He turned to the leader of the orchestra, on his left, and said: "Children's nurses are certainly good at producing *silence.*"

Strauss's vein of humour was evident in his personal life, his wit often being directed against the reactionary servility of the world around. He liked to tilt a verbal lance at narrow-mindedness, and his naturally cheerful disposition was opposed to dreary pessimism wherever he found it. At one time he intended to give "Zarathustra" the sub-title "Symphonic Optimism in fin-de-siècle form, dedicated to the 20th century." He revenged himself on the stupidity of some of his dull-witted critics by means of the song "Wenn," which first appeared in the Munich publication "Jugend," and which is in D♭ major, but ends in D major. At the transition to the new key Strauss wrote: "The composer advises singers who intend to perform this song in public before the end of the 19th century to sing the remainder from here onward a semitone lower (in D♭ major), so that they end it in the key in which it began!" As a result of this harmless pleasantry he was reproved by the Munich Opera Director von Perfall, who told Strauss that a Royal Bavarian Court Conductor must not behave in such a way in public. ... *One* joke appears particularly characteristic of his biting irony in his contacts with the brainless officialdom around him. In 1933 Strauss had to fill in a questionnaire sent out by the "Reichsmusikkammer," and he came upon the question: "How can you prove your standing as a composer? (Name two composers as references. Submission of manuscripts can be required.)" His reply in his own handwriting was "Mozart and Richard Wagner."

In his relation with people, artists and others, he was courteous and good natured. After he had introduced himself at Meiningen, at the age of twenty-one, Bülow was able to report on the "extremely good impression" which the "unassuming entrance" of the future Court Conductor had made everywhere, so that "even the ladies of the choral society were glad to make the acquaintance of their new conductor." Josef B. Foerster told of his meeting at Bayreuth with the young composer of "Don

Juan," who (as we also gather from his letters to his parents) talked so "naturally and without shyness, but very respectfully and with an almost childlike communicativeness." It was Debussy who referred to the "winning power of the man" whose "openness and determination remind one of the great explorers who travel through the territories of savage tribes with a smile on their lips." Hermann Bahr spoke of a "steadfast, weather-beaten, remarkably composed man, calm and joyous . . . gardeners look like that, so do people who use a microscope a great deal—people who are accustomed to observing things at close quarters and contemplating their meaning, and who bring love, patience and fidelity to their work," a description which amounts to about the same thing. . . . The American Sidney S. Bloch gave a vivid description of Strauss the conductor, making it clear that he could be "rude in the true Bavarian manner" if a singer left him in the lurch at a rehearsal. "His face became bright red, and he didn't mind what he said or to whom. With the members of his orchestra, on the other hand, he was always on very friendly terms, even when something in the performance displeased him, and they would follow him blindly. . . ." He would, however, always take care to avoid upsetting people of importance needlessly through unguarded remarks.

Despite the high honours and undisputed successes which soon came his way, Strauss never locked himself up behind a wall of stiff formality. Nevertheless he placed a certain distance between himself and mediocrity, whether in or out of uniform, especially at official receptions and similar functions, by comporting himself with a personal dignity which excluded any undue familiarity. He did not wish to be honoured or decorated, but merely treated in a fitting manner. "I am afraid you have not sufficient diplomacy," Bülow had written to the young Strauss. In his later life, however, he appeared to possess this quality to a great extent. Despite his formidable reserve toward anything which would be to his discredit, he was an understanding friend and colleague who, in this respect as in others, asserted his artistic authority to good effect. Always willing to help, he was, for example, an unenvious promoter of the art of Reger, for whom he negotiated with his first Munich publisher Aibl. When Pfitzner was in difficulties with his publishers in connection with the revised version of his "Christelflein," Strauss offered to help. He was one of the first to bring the early symphonies of Mahler to performance, and in Weimar he helped Humperdinck's "Hänsel und Gretel" to win worldwide success. The young Schoenberg, too, had much to thank him for. His assistance to colleagues extended to the giving of very carefully considered advice, as for example when he recommended muted trombones to Schillings for one of his music dramas, even before Strauss himself had used them. On another occasion he expressed his willingness to obtain extra-large thirty-four stave manuscript music paper in Leipzig for his friend.

It was inevitable that a man in such a position, of such influence, should often be misunderstood. He was sometimes described as cool and probably even arrogant. He was said to be calculating and egocentric, and to show signs of a "striving for power" (Rolland). This picture is superficial, and is rejected outright by those who knew Strauss as a man, and who emphasize his fundamental goodness, human warmth, and gentleness of nature. It is also far too often overlooked that all through his life Strauss was concerned not only with his *own* works but with German culture in its *entirety*. Conversations throughout his years of maturity were concerned to an ever increasing extent with *all* the questions of humanitarian culture, the place of music in western cultural history, the theatre, literature, the visual arts and science; his own works and his own person were of far less account to him. He was always concerned with the *cause* he had to represent–but he never rode a hobby-horse. When it seemed necessary to him he did not hesitate to speak forcefully in order to attain his goal–as in connection with the question of rebuilding and restoring the house of Goethe and Liszt in Weimar. "I would never consider it beneath my dignity to box the ears of a few scoundrels and enemies of art," he wrote to Krauss during work on "Capriccio." He asserted his place in the social community when, as a young opera conductor in Munich and Berlin, he published his songs based on poems of social criticism, and later (even when he was Director of Opera in Vienna) he exerted himself energetically on behalf of the material safeguarding of the musical profession. While he was at Weimar he offered 1000 marks out of his own pocket to provide new décor for "Lohengrin" after the Bayreuth model–a gesture reflecting a sense of personal responsibility for the music of the western world which we can scarcely comprehend. Later, as a composer of worldwide renown, Strauss never neglected opportunities for patronage, although on a limited scale.

*

Strauss the artist would have been unable to complete his life's work had Strauss the man not possessed so intimate a relationship with all the intellectual and musical movements of his time. His classical *education,* which he obtained as a "not particularly good scholar" of the Ludwigsgymnasium in Munich and during his period at the University which followed, but above all through the powerful impressions of his journeys to Italy, Greece and Egypt, raised him high above the cultural level of the average creative musician. "The November sojourn (1892) in Corfu, Olympia and Athens was of decisive importance to my whole relationship with Grecian civilization, and in particular with its art during the fourth and fifth centuries B. C.," he wrote in his "Recollections." With Strauss, regarding his actions and work, we find ourselves contemplating the fruits of a really great range of formative experience. His imposing mental stature was demonstrated by a lifelong striving for "perfection" in the sense of Goethe. The spiritual and artistic worlds in which Strauss's mind was active encompassed, in essentials, everything which belongs to the concept of classicism. "The Viennese classicists, antiquity, Goethe's Weimar, the works of Wagner–those were the temple of the spirit which was sacred to him" (Schuh). His detailed knowledge in the realms of literature, the visual arts, and above all cultural history, astonished many who conversed and corresponded with him. A man both of eye and ear, he "took in life through his eyes" (as Rolland once said of Handel), attempting, even in his youth, to follow Goethe's example by "turning his attention away from the restricted interests of the German musician to regard *everything* in the world ..." He attempted, as he wrote, to "put on the large spectacles through which our greatest artists saw the world ... and even to make such spectacles myself–my own artistic production." There is also good reason to assume that his general knowledge did not stop short of the really new elements in the creative world of his time.

Strauss was unusually receptive to the attractions of the visual arts. Thus, for example, he never left Dresden without visiting the famous picture gallery in the "Zwinger" to study works by Italian masters, and without examining the collection of porcelain in great detail. He was also one of the most frequent visitors to the Pinakothek (the great Munich picture gallery), the art collections of Vienna, Paris and elsewhere. He needed no catalogues, as he was fully conversant not only with the painters but with the contents of their works. Even during his last visit to London in October 1947 he spent several hours almost every day in the British Museum, the National Gallery, Tate Gallery and Wallace Collection. (On that occasion, as Schuh reported, while standing before Veronese's "Santa Helena," he mentioned the fact that shortly after the turn of the century he had conceived the idea of writing a "symphony of paintings," although he had soon given up the plan. The Adagio was to have been based on Veronese, and the Scherzo on Hogarth.) Time and again he derived inspiration from the visual arts: in the case of "Rosenkavalier" from contemporary illustrations by Hogarth, and in that of a projected ballet from Watteau's painting "Embarquement pour Cythère." When Strauss was working on his "Daphne" he had in his mind's eye the statue "Apollo and Daphne" by Lorenzo Bernini, which he had often viewed at the Villa Borghese in Rome, and the "Primavera" of Botticelli. With the eye of an art connoisseur he adorned his schloss in Vienna, a building full of light and designed in imitation of baroque originals, with a great many valuable old masters, some of them originals. On the other hand his home at Garmisch contains a carefully and lovingly assembled collection of Bavarian and Tyrolean peasant pictures, paintings on glass, old crib figures, gothic and baroque madonnas, pewter jugs–together with products of other lands which the wide-ranging traveller had brought back from countries as far away as Portugal. His study, with its especially valuable pieces of old porcelain, resembled the room of an art collector. Shortly before his death he had Ludwig Sievert's Munich stage design for the apotheosis of "Ariadne" hung above his bed.

Strauss's profound knowledge of literature is demonstrated by the extensive library which he left to future generations. The classical and romantic masterpieces were among his spiritual possessions; in Munich and Meiningen he profited by the performances of classical plays, which he attended regularly. Strauss felt himself particularly at home with Goethe (whose name he spelt in a way of his own: Göthe)–he read Herman Grimm's biography of the poet during the last years of his life. However, he also had a remarkable appreciation of the works of such men as Stifter and Anzengruber. He was so widely read that he frequently referred Hofmannsthal to the work of a writer whose environment was far removed from theirs, for example the Russians Tolstoy or Turgenyev. When Krauss gave him ten volumes of works for the French theatre, by Sardou, Dumas and others, he read them avidly. His delight in reading can be judged from the correspondence with his friend the publisher Anton Kippenberg: "Please send a small selection of books, preferably 'artistic history or memoirs' to Bad Nauheim, where I am staying for a three-week cure, and have nothing left that's worth reading," he wrote from Düsseldorf in 1925, and on another occasion he asked for the "Chinese robber novel" ("Die Räuber vom Liang schan Moor"). . . . Strauss once acted as a literary historian. With his accustomed tenacity he pressed for the reprinting of the "really epoch-making article 'I want to learn to read' (i.e. to read scores)" written by Ferdinand Kürnberger in 1848, which "belongs on the bedside table of every German"–a wish which was fulfilled by Insel-Verlag in 1940, when they issued a private print of sixteen pages. His relations with poetry were not always so certain, as will be shown in the chapter dealing with his songs.

The mature Strauss was drawn to an increasing extent to historical studies, which he regarded as the "only occupation worthy of an educated man." Much of his attitude to the warlike developments of his lifetime sprang from his understanding, based on extensive knowledge, of earlier epochs. During the last years of his life he wrote: "I am reading with interest Raumer's history of the Hohenstaufen dynasty. It is particularly instructive, as hardly any other historical period demonstrates so clearly and unambiguously the fact that history consists almost entirely of a succession of stupid and wicked deeds, vulgarity, greed, deception, murder and destruction." Strauss came to recognize a great failing of the Nazi regime; as he put it: "One might almost say that the study of history is superfluous when one perceives how little those who are called upon to make history have learned from it!"

There can hardly have been a writer, painter–or of course musician–of his time with whom Strauss did not come into close contact. As early as 1883/84, when, at the age of nineteen, he made his first visit to Berlin, he moved "in fascinating circles, introduced through kind recommendations," mixing with the artistic group around Menzel, Werner, Knaus and Begas. During his first trip to Rome he became acquainted with Lenbach. Later, when he had established a firm footing in the German capital, he came into close contact with the "secession" movement. Max Slevogt, who in his early days painted Salome dancing, was close to him as artist and friend. He was associated with Lovis Corinth, who drew a typical cover illustration for the libretto of "Elektra." He had a high regard for Max Liebermann, who produced two oil paintings, a lithograph and an etching of Strauss at about the age of fifty. When we come to writers and musicians their number is so great that it becomes difficult to select a few for mention. The representative of musical "progress" at the turn of the century was soon in touch with the literary "modernists" Dehmel, Henckell, Bierbaum and others. Strangely enough he never set a line by Gerhart Hauptmann to music, but he was close to the humanism of that poet, especially in the later days of his evocation of antiquity. The writings of Romain Rolland, the great French littérateur, moved him deeply. (He dedicated songs of personal significance, to words by Goethe, to both men.) However, it was the cultivated nature of the Austrian Hofmannsthal, with whom he became acquainted in Paris in 1900, which first aroused in him the feeling of a real community of creative aims. When they first came to an agreement over the libretto of "Elektra," Strauss wrote to Hofmannsthal: "You are the born librettist, in my eyes the greatest compliment I could pay, since I consider it far more difficult to write a good opera text than a fine play." The poet replied: "I am quite sure that all our life long the two of us will come to an understanding quickly and simply over everything." The fact that this close intellectual association, like those with Bahr and with the later librettists Zweig and Gregor, did not lead to intimate friendship, that despite close collaboration and the frequent use of such terms as "My dear friend" a certain distance could still be felt, appears particularly revealing in the case of Strauss. ("My personal relations with Strauss, as always, casual, but charming,"

Hofmannsthal once wrote.) There were not many people with whom the mature master was linked by really close personal ties as artist and man. Among those few these names could hardly be omitted: the musicians Max von Schillings and Friedrich Rösch, the scenic artists and costume designers Alfred Roller and Leonhard Fanto, the bass singer Paul Knüpfer, the critic Oscar Bie, the physician Friedrich Lönne, the banker Willy Levin, and among his immediate neighbours in Garmisch Karl Alwin and his wife Elisabeth Schumann. During the last ten years of his life the old man found particularly understanding friends in the artistic couple Clemens Krauss and Viorica Ursuleac, in Rudolf Hartmann, Willi Schuh and Karl Böhm.

He liked to dedicate his works to people who were in some way close to him, to whom he felt deeply grateful. He dedicated several volumes of songs to his wife, "Intermezzo" to his only son, and the "Sinfonia domestica" to both of them. He dedicated important operas and orchestral works to his friends Rösch, Levin, the theatre directors Seebach, Reucker and Tietjen, and the conductors Busch, Krauss and Böhm. However, the picture is not so simple as it appears. While, for example, he dedicated "Salome" to the proprietor of an English banking house, the masterly interpreter of his first operas to achieve worldwide success, his "personal conductor," his "dear and only Schuch" went away empty-handed. In this connection it may be worth mentioning that Strauss never once wrote a work in memory of a person near to him whose loss he mourned. Neither the death of his parents nor the tragic deaths of Hofmannsthal and Zweig left a creative mark–quite unlike, for example, the cases of Berlioz and Verdi. We remember the words of Wilde in "Salome:" "The mystery of love is greater than the mystery of death," and recognize in this fact the expression of a positive attitude to life. Only in the case of a minor work, the "Parergon zur Sinfonia domestica" for piano (left hand) and orchestra, written for the one-armed pianist Paul Wittgenstein, did the serious illness and recovery of his son Franz provide the impulse for composition.

Strauss knew that during the years of his artistic maturity he was the world's foremost composer. He was not lacking in a healthy sense of his position, but like all other really important people he did not allow fame to go to his head. It was clear to him that the creative spirit attained its true value only through

197

his striving after ever higher achievements, not as a result of self-satisfaction but through the correct estimation of the extent of his artistic abilities. His unfailing sense of proportion and historical perspectives was made evident on many occasions. Considering a Tintoretto, for example, he remarked that his music was related to that of Wagner as the art of Tintoretto was to Titian—he had ventured upon the "extreme, the limits of what is possible." It was this modest pride which enabled Strauss to allow his music to flow along (even when he was conducting) almost without passion, and to regard adulatory praise with scepticism. "Please criticize severely, I am not in the least touchy," he once wrote to Hermann Bahr; similarly he considered that he had the right to expose without pity the weaknesses which he detected in certain composers contemporary with him. Any showing off, whether of his own person or of his ability, was repugnant to Strauss. He had no high opinion, in particular, of the feuilleton gossip of the boulevard papers, and it was "only to kill time" that he ever read even the reviews of well-informed critics. "Only good music criticisms are always right," he asserted following the largely favourable reception of his free adaptation of "Idomeneo" in Vienna ... Far from seeking interviews with inquisitive newspaper reporters, he avoided them. There has seldom been a conductor less prone to vanity.

He was deeply conscious of the need to be entirely honest with himself concerning the value of his music. The following passage, written in 1908, bears witness to a remarkable power of *self-judgment:* "If my works are good and of any significance toward the possible future development of our beloved art, then they will maintain their place even if they are rejected outright by the critics, and despite all dark suspicions of my artistic intentions. If, however, they are worthless, even the most gratifying momentary success and the enthusiastic approval of the arbiters of fashion will not keep them alive. The music will go into the pulping machines, as so much has already gone, whether I agree or not, and I shall not shed any tears over it. For a time my son will piously play my tone poems from my private copies of the piano duet arrangements, then they too will disappear, and the world will go on!" ... With regard to the masters of the classical tradition he said: "If each of these great men has conquered a mountain nine thousand feet high among the principal works in the sphere in which he excelled, while I have ascended one of only four thousand five hundred feet in each of these classes of music, I can be content, and may look back with satisfaction on my life's work" (1919). . . . "Formerly I was in the vanguard. Today I am almost in the rearguard" (1923). . . . "Without being immodest may I finally–naturally at a fitting distance–also mention my own life's work, as possibly the last offshoot of the world theatre development in the realm of music" (1935, to Gregor). . . . "I know quite well that my symphonic works do not approach Beethoven's tremendous genius, I know exactly the distance which separates my operas (in breadth of conception, primary melodic invention, cultural wisdom) from the immortal works of Richard Wagner–but the . . . history of the development of theatrical art entitles me, I believe, to the modestly gratifying consciousness that in the diversity of my dramatic subjects, in the manner of their treatment, my operas will retain an honourable place in world history in relation to all earlier creations for the theatre (Wagner excepted) at the end of the 'rainbow,' and if new territory is still to be opened up in the sphere of opera, then good foundation stones have been laid along this "Avenue of Sphinxes" (1945, after reading Gregor's "World History of the Theatre"). . . . And in 1942, in his "Recollections": "Many now consider 'Elektra' the highspot of my work! Others vote for 'Die Frau ohne Schatten'! The general public swears by 'Rosenkavalier'! One must be content, as a German composer, to have got so far . . ."

What a scrupulously careful watch Strauss kept, during all periods of his life, over his own creative power! With what positively scientific factualness this eminent musician held the balance at the height of his career! "I prefer it when the understanding controls the feelings, not the reverse"–such a remark was typical of him. In a letter written in 1918, in which he encouraged Hofmannsthal to consider new joint projects, he wrote: "I am fifty-four years old, and who can say how long my creative energy will continue to bring forth anything good? We two could still give the world some beautiful things . . . every few years a charming little Singspiel, alternated by a comedy with music (like the 'Bourgeois'), then a satirical operetta, then–as in 'Die Zauberflöte'–comes a little Papageno, then comes another Papagena, until the spring is dried up" . . . It was more than

199

twenty years before the spring dried up ... Sometimes Strauss's pronouncements were made in a typically forthright Bavarian manner–for example when reporting to his uncle Carl Hörburger the meagre success of "Aus Italien" he wrote that no one had become a great artist who "had not been considered mad by thousands of his fellow men." On another occasion he excused himself to Hofmannsthal on the grounds that "provincial musicians are well known for their lack of taste in matters of aesthetics." Strauss's healthy and genuine modesty is demonstrated by his attitude to the venerable masters of his art. He told an admirer of his "Salome" that basically "the old gentleman" (Wagner) had done it all before. His modesty concerning his own work enabled him to pen an acknowledgment as generous as that in the letter in which he told Reger that he envied him the possession of such immense ability. Nor did Strauss hesitate to ask the advice of Thuille, as the "greater contrapuntist," concerning the concluding fugue of his "Sinfonia domestica."

"As we well know, it is very hard for anyone to be conscious of his own weaknesses, so that the benefit ... of self-criticism, if any is exercised at all, is nullified," Strauss wrote in his preface to Leopold Schmidt's "Musical Life of the Present Day" ... Was it really hard for him to exercise the necessary self-criticism? Did he not rather strive until his old age to carry it still further? Zweig referred to this trait of Strauss's character in his "World of Yesterday": "I have met many great artists during my lifetime, but never one who was able to preserve such abstract and cool objectivity toward himself. Thus Strauss confessed freely during our first hour together that he knew quite well that a musician of seventy no longer possessed his original power of musical invention. He would scarcely be able to create symphonic works like 'Till Eulenspiegel' or 'Tod und Verklärung' any longer, since pure music required the highest degree of creative freshness. However, he said that the word still gave him as much inspiration as ever. He could compose music for a subject already to hand, because with him musical themes developed spontaneously out of situations and words. That was the reason he said, why he had turned exclusively to opera during his later years."

Constantly exercised criticism of his own products was a principle of life to Strauss. His inborn leaning toward self-control

("I am never satisfied") practically never allowed him, he confessed, to listen to the last act of "Rosenkavalier," with its mixture of styles, entirely untroubled in mind. Whenever possible he avoided certain of his popular songs. Zweig, a keen observer, wrote as follows about a rehearsal of "Helena" in the Salzburg Festspielhaus: "No one else was in the auditorium, which was completely dark all round us. Strauss was listening. Suddenly I noticed him tapping lightly and impatiently with his fingers on the arm of his seat. Then he whispered to me: 'Bad! Very bad! Nothing occurred to me there.' A few minutes later: 'You see, that's good!' He judged his own work as factually and impartially as though he were hearing this music for the first time, as though it had been written by a complete stranger, and this astonishing sense of his own true measure never deserted him..." Schuh wrote of an occasion when he was turning over for Strauss, who was playing the piano accompaniments for a broadcast recording of some songs in Vienna. Suddenly Strauss stopped during one of the Brentano Songs. "Is that right?" he exclaimed, then, after a moment's hesitation: "Dreadful, an impossible modulation!" Once, when the subject of the wonderful simplicity of the "Ariadne" music cropped up in conversation, Strauss remarked that in other works, unfortunately, he "put far too much into them," and that this "often spoilt them." "I always write in too complex a way–it's because I have a complicated brain..."

Strauss sent Schuh an account of his impressions of the dress rehearsal of "Danae" at Salzburg which is incomparable as a document of balanced self-criticism. In it we read: "So here is the composer's criticism: very lively opening, plastic choral scenes in grey-brown colours, with the strongest contrast provided by the Golden Magic, with Jupiter's radiant brilliance of trumpets and trombones, and the women's duet, which went excellently, shimmering in a glitter of gold ... everything very well shaped dramatically, with good contrast, fresh in tempo and invention. Then a certain deterioration after the entry of Midas– perhaps dramaturgically apt and necessary for the exposition of new themes which are to be important later, but not, to me, satisfactorily fashioned except at the 'golden garment' passage. Perhaps the rather dry text is responsible. No doubt Hofmannsthal would have provided me with something more stimulating here ... To go on: nothing better occurred to me for the dialogue between Danae and Midas despite laborious racking of my brains. However, probably no one but myself noticed this, perhaps because of the fine tenor, and it was soon over ... On the other hand the end of the act, despite some apprehension on my part, was very effective ... I have nothing more to criticize in the third act, but can say with satisfaction (which probably no one would begrudge me) that it is among the best things I have ever written. It is something of which a man of seventy-five can be proud. Beautiful, poetic melody flows through the whole act with mature youthfulness ..."

Strauss reacted in different ways to his successes, which were of remarkable proportions in their day. It is reported that at the world première of "Salome" his mood was one of "indifference." At the end of the dress rehearsal of "Elektra," while everyone else was still speechless with excitement, Strauss is said to have broken the tense silence by saying in a contented voice from his seat in the front stalls "I liked it." Often it was not the most inspired works for which Strauss had especial affection. He regarded the "Alpensinfonie" ("... really a good work!") particularly highly among his orchestral compositions. He repeatedly described the contented, lyrical concluding monologue of the old noise-hater Morosus in "Die schweigsame Frau" as one of his "most successful ideas." With "Capriccio" he bade farewell to the opera stage. At the dress rehearsal in Munich he expressed his feelings with tears in his eyes as the last D♭ major chord died away: "I can't do anything better than that."

*

His inborn *practical sense* expressed itself in the maxim which he adopted for life, that he always "wanted to get the most out of his work." Strauss, who began young both as a creative and as an interpretative artist, at first considering himself primarily a conductor and secondly a composer, soon strove for a secure economic basis of his career which would give him financial independence even purely as a composer. He made no bones about the fact that he wished not only to be free to engage in creative work, but to earn money by it. It was a tenet of Strauss's epicureanism that art was, to him, primarily a product of ability based on knowledge, also involving economics. He expected substantial, in fact very substantial payments for his music, and in this respect he was undoubtedly a child of the capitalist era. However, it is an historical fact that such masters as Handel, Gluck, Meyerbeer and Wagner laid their idealism aside when it came to the question of earning money. We should not overlook the fact that Strauss was neither a shrewd stock exchange speculator nor a smart owner of large estates or racing stables, but a man who saved money diligently during every period of his life, and who took pains to act with scrupulous correctness in material as well as in artistic matters. Three times, as a result of the turbulent period through which he lived, he lost most of his money: at the beginning of the First World War, during the years of inflation, and after 1945. "On the 1st August 1914 the English seized my capital which was in the keeping of Edgar Speyer in London–the savings of thirty years' work. For eight days I was in the depths of depression, but then I got down to work on 'Die Frau ohne Schatten,' which I had just started, and embarked once again on a life of laboriously earning money, just when I had hoped that from my fiftieth year onward I would be able to devote myself exclusively to composition," he wrote in his "Recollections." Again and again healthy optimism triumphed over a threatening situation, and only Goebbels disconcerted him seriously when he ordered the German theatres to be closed in 1944. ("Just, imagine, since the 1st September 1944 I haven't earned a pfennig in performing fees.") Even then, however, luck did not desert him: the London publishing house of Boosey & Hawkes took over the majority of his works. At the end of his life he could say that nothing was still owing to him by the troubled world in which he had lived. He had known profit and loss, and had balanced his account.

Strauss certainly had not Wagner's talent for running up debts, nor did he (like Verdi) order his economic affairs for the benefit of the community as a whole. He was a man of sound business sense, who made good use of his money and kept his financial affairs under strict control. Publishers, theatres and orchestras got on best with him if they reached a satisfactory understanding in these practical matters. His language in correspondence of this kind was as determined as it was blunt. "So 1500 marks is still too much," he wrote to Schuch before the Dresden "Feuersnot." "Oh, this theatre! The devil take the composition of operas! What more do you want? Am I to give you something else? Per-

haps a fire engine? So as to extinguish the Feuers-money-not . . .
I'll re-christen myself Ricardo Straussino and have Sonzogno as
my publisher, then you'll agree to everything . . ." In contrast to
his justifiable claims as a composer, Strauss was more generous
in his demands as a conductor. During the last decades of his
life, in particular, he expressed his willingness to conduct his less
popular operas without a fee at theatres with whose management
he was on friendly terms.

The financial proceeds from his first great works are often
over-estimated. Some of them made a fortune–but it was for
the publishers, not the composer. It is difficult to reconcile with
the unfavourable picture of the "adroit man of business" the fact
that Strauss sold his first popular tone poems and songs, with all
the performing and other rights for all time, for a trifling sum of
a few thousand marks in all to his first publisher Eugen Spitzweg (Josef Aibl) in Munich, thereby cutting himself off from any
future financial benefit from these works. He later mentioned
the sums paid to him: "A volume of five songs 200 marks, 'Aus
Italien' 500 marks, 'Don Juan' 800 marks, 'Tod und Verklärung'
1600 marks, 'Guntram' 5000 marks (plus 'Eulenspiegel' 1000
marks), all inclusive of the original manuscripts." Strauss was
later angry, with good reason, when Universal Edition, Vienna,
sold the original score of "Don Juan" in Switzerland for
12,000 francs. It was only from about the time of the "Sinfonia
domestica" that payments became really substantial. Following
the world première of this work in America Strauss conducted
two matinée performances in the vast New York Wannemaker
Department Store, whose first floor had been converted especially into a concert hall. When the German press criticized him
for this he replied promptly: "True art ennobles every place of
performance, and earning money honestly for wife and child
is no disgrace even to an artist!" (In 1956 a recording of the "Sinfonia domestica" was made by the Dresden State Orchestra in
the Kreuzkirche, Dresden.) Strauss mentioned in an interview
given in America that he had been paid exactly 30 shillings by
his publisher for "Traum durch die Dämmerung," but that this
popular song had earned the publisher 400 pounds during the
first year alone. "I have done far better with the 'Domestica.' I
have been paid 1750 pounds for it, almost 9000 dollars in your
currency." The fees he received then grew to record proportions,

equalled in the field of serious music prior to Strauss only by those commanded by Verdi, Massenet and Puccini. In common with these composers, however, Strauss was no "fee hunter." The fact that, in agreement with his publisher, he had "Rosenkavalier" published first in Paris, so that outside Germany at least the work would enjoy the 50 year copyright protection period, was an intelligent demonstration against governmental unreasonableness. Strauss accepted without bitterness the fact that his early works "Don Juan," "Tod und Verklärung" and "Till" did not bring him in a cent in fees for performances in the U.S.A., owing to the dubious structure of American copyright law. It was only in the cases of a very few works that financial considerations were decisive, and this was not so even of the labour which Strauss, urged on by Hofmannsthal, reluctantly undertook in connection with the "Rosenkavalier" film made by an English company. A composer who wanted to exploit his art for material rewards certainly would not have accepted opera libretti of so little immediate popular appeal as those of "Frau ohne Schatten" and "Helena," and would not have written so many vocal works which address themselves only to a small circle of connoisseurs. A musician who was "always calculating" is hardly likely, either, to have made the often all-too generous gestures of giving away his precious and irreplaceable manuscripts (not only small sketch books but also the scores of some of his masterworks) to friends in Germany and elsewhere... That may provide food for thought.

*

Anyone who wished to see Strauss completely relaxed and free from formality did well to seek him out in the circle of his family and friends. In his large but by no means luxuriously appointed houses in Weimar, Munich, and Berlin-Charlottenburg, from 1909 onward in his country house at Garmisch, and in the charmingly situated little schloss with a view of the Belvedere which the city of Vienna presented to him in 1924–there he could live in the privacy he loved. With him was his clearheaded wife, who, after a promising career as an opera and lieder singer, was the faithful companion and "real helpmate" of her famous husband's long life (she survived him for only about eight months). When Strauss composed his "Heldenleben" he

205

wrote the following commentary on the scintillating violin solo "The Hero's helpmate": "I intended here to portray my wife. She is very complex, a little perverse, a little coquettish, never the same twice, changing from minute to minute ..." Alfred Kerr described her as follows in 1946: "A magnificent woman, blossoming, sound of constitution, outspoken to the point of bluntness, not to be downed in argument." Also close by were the "children": their only son Franz and their daughter-in-law Alice, and later the grandsons Richard and Christian. Full of the heartfelt concern of a husband and father, Strauss was happiest when in the midst of his immediate family. He also kept in close contact, right to the end, with his only sister Johanna von Rauchenberger in Munich. He never willingly left his home for any long period. It was principally at Garmisch, in the "peace of this white house" during the summer months, that he found the necessary leisure for his composing. When he was once asked which production of "Elektra" had given him most pleasure he replied candidly: "Its production at Garmisch, when I was completely immersed in the work, and surrounded by my family." Nevertheless Strauss liked to interrupt his life at Garmisch by making lengthy visits to friends in Dresden, Karlsbad and (as a still active old man) Switzerland. He was particularly fond of Dresden, with its magnificent orchestra and its art treasures. Well on into old age he would ask "What's going on in good old Dresden?," and he had poignant memories of his "dear Dresdeners" who had helped him to achieve his greatest opera triumphs.

"Strauss knows how to relax," wrote Rolland. "There is a touch of Bavarian indolence about him. I am sure that after hours of intensive life, when his energy is strained to the utmost, he spends hours of empty nothingness ..." This ability to escape from the day's activity, quickly to change the evening dress of a man of the world for the comfortable Bavarian house coat of a child of nature, to come straight down from the conductor's rostrum to his own rose garden, was among his many fortunate characteristics. All the tension of his artistic career found its natural release in complete tranquillity. The creative artist was transformed almost instantaneously into an everyday figure with a "talent for dozing off and idling the time away." His intensive preoccupation with great literature, with questions of art and scientific knowledge, enriched his hours of leisure increasingly as he grew older; it was only during his exile in Switzerland toward the end of his life that he was compelled to forego the discussion of artistic matters. A wonderful story teller, he kept himself young at heart through his close links with his grandchildren. Photographs show him giving his grandson Richard piano lessons and playing chess with him. He was in his element, whether at home or on his travels, playing his "beloved skat," which Thuille had taught him to appreciate in his early years. Strauss made his operatic representative Storch in "Intermezzo" say: "Ah, a game of skat is such a pleasure, the only recreation after music"—while we hear in the orchestra the adroit shuffling and dealing of the cards. Strauss really found the evening foursome game a necessary natural reaction to the overburdening of his brain brought on by his artistic work. (He later stated laconically that during his time at Weimar, which was "not very productive" as regards composition, but which was "the happiest time of his life," he had devoted the time to his bride and the theatre, "together with card playing.") If his "passion for cards" contributed to his worldwide fame, that was part of the overall picture: everything he set his mind to was *completely* successful . . . "How beautiful life is," sings old Morosus in his concluding monologue. "But it is so beautiful only when one is no fool and knows how to live." Strauss knew how to live.

PROGRAMME MUSIC

THERE IS NO SUCH THING AS A PIECE OF MUSIC OF ANY value in which the attempt is not made, to a greater or lesser degree, to give expression to some kind of feeling. Even so-called "absolute" music such as a Prelude or Fugue from Bach's "Well-tempered Clavier," a sonata movement by Mozart or Beethoven, a Schubert Impromptu or a Chopin Nocturne, to mention but a few examples, expresses a particular feeling, and the germ of a "programme" can be found in the directions to the performer. Music which has no content, no programmatic ideas, no thoughts and feelings, which merely dances past the ear as a "play of animated musical shapes," is not music in the fullest sense of the word. We could scarcely imagine a composer who thought about absolutely *nothing* at the moment of artistic creation. All thinking and recalling leads of necessity to a definite concept. The only question is whether the content of the musical work in question is clearly recognizable and openly expressed.

Genuine *programme* music on a large or small scale deals with a particular subject from life, history, or literature. Its nature depends on that of the subject. Confusion is caused by the fact that the vital impulse behind the composition, the emotion underlying the music, is often obscured by the overplaying of naturalistic details which are not of paramount importance to the character of the work as a whole. It is only in a limited number of illustrative symphonic works of recent times that the expression of ideas from the sphere of human life is *completely* lacking. The decisive factor is still the question of the depth of the experience and the human ideas mirrored in the work.

Programme music, which not only expresses but above all depicts, is generally regarded as an "invention" of nineteenth century composers. In fact, however, musical works based on the representation of specific events or ideas can be traced back much further—almost as far back as our knowledge of musical literature extends. Only a few particularly characteristic instances need be mentioned here. Among the subjects chosen over and over again for musical representation pride of place probably goes to battles. We know that in ancient Greece Apollo's fight with the serpent was depicted in music played by flautists at the games held at Delphi. A great many vocal battle scenes, by Jannequin and others, have come down to us from the 16th century, the golden age of *a cappella* music. Apart from the fruits of this remarkable love of the depicting of warlike events, many concerts of birds and hunting scenes of the same period have come down to us. Johannes Eccard, the great polyphonic master of the age before Bach, attempted to depict in music the varied activities in the square before St. Mark's in Venice. At the close of that epoch programme music began to experience a time of rapid development. Explanatory words were now omitted, and the music was presented with different tasks. Works for organ and harpsichord made use of the new opportunities for musical description. Other solo instruments (lute, violin) gradually came on the scene, and finally the orchestra as a whole adopted these means of expression. There is room here to mention as important examples of baroque programme music only the harpsichord pieces of Couperin and Rameau, with their great diversity of contents, the delightfully naive "Biblical Histories" of Kuhnau, and Bach's humorous "Capriccio on the departure of the beloved brother," pieces which found an echo later in Beethoven's Rondo "Rage over a lost penny." Other model examples of classical programme music include Vivaldi's concerti grossi "The Four Seasons," the graceful symphonies of Dittersdorf and Stamitz, Haydn's charming early symphonies "Le Matin," "Le Midi" and "Le Soir," and his "Creation." At the crossroads between two ages of music there stood Beethoven, the great musician of ideas. It is not only the "Pastoral Symphony" and the piano sonata "Les Adieux" which are based on detailed programmes—the majority of his other symphonies and sonatas, and the overtures to "Egmont" and "Coriolanus," among others, are direct expressions of his relationship to the reality around him. These strongly humanistic or even revolutionary manifestations of Beethoven's creative will formed the real basis of the programmatic course which music took during the 19th century.

210

The breakthrough to what Bülow later described as *"instrumental drama"* was achieved by Berlioz. Through the descriptive power of his musical language and his bold use of new means of tonal expression he raised the concept of programme music to the stature of a "stylistic principle." In his brilliant "Fantastic Symphony," with its sub-title "Episodes from the life of an artist," Berlioz made use for the first time of the poetic "leitmotiv," the "idée fixe" as a form-creating element of musical language. "I visualized an artist gifted with a lively imagination who found himself in the state of mind described so incomparably by Châteaubriand in his 'René,' that of a man who for the first time has seen a woman possessing such beauty and charm that she fills his mind as an ideal. Strangely enough his thoughts of her are always accompanied by a musical theme which seems to him to have the same adorable and exalted character as the object of his love herself. This 'idée fixe' follows him incessantly, and that is the reason why it appears in every movement of the Symphony from the subsidiary theme of the first Allegro onward ... The object of thus setting out the programme in words is not, as many seem to believe, to repeat exactly what the composer has exerted himself to illustrate with the help of the orchestra. Indeed, the reverse is the case: in order to make the plan of the Symphony comprehensible and to justify it he had to have recourse to the written word, in order to fill in the gaps which were bound to occur in the development of the dramatic ideas ..."

The first composer to adopt the ideas of Berlioz in Germany was Liszt, whose "symphonic poems" were historic documents of the new movement. The Lisztian tone poem draws its fundamental strength from the *"poetic idea."* "A programme or title is justified," Liszt said, "only when it is a poetic necessity, indissolubly attached to the work, and indispensible to its understanding." In this sense Liszt was content to adhere generally to the programmes of his thirteen "poems," turning the listener's imagination toward a historical subject, a dominant character or a picture without, however, shackling it. "In programme music one theme does not call the other into being at the dictate of form; here the motifs are not the results of stereotyped relationships or contrasts of tone colour, and colouration as such does not determine how the ideas are grouped ... The artist who chooses this artistic form enjoys the advantage of being able to relate all the emotions which the orchestra can express with such great power to a poetic subject . . ." The seed scattered by Liszt fell on particularly fertile ground in Russia. The nationalistic Russian composers believed that in programme music they had discovered the means best suited to the musical expression of their ideas. The fantasy overtures "Romeo and Juliet" and "Francesca da Rimini" by Tschaikowsky and the orchestral works of Rimsky-Korsakoff are full of strongly-felt musical pictures. Mussorgsky created a model of exceptionally rich programme music in his cycle of piano pieces "Pictures at an Exhibition." In a very similar way Czech national music was distinguished by the melodious tone poems of Smetana and Dvořák. Programme music has recently experienced an unexpected renaissance in some of the symphonies of Shostakovich, in particular his Eleventh and Twelfth. ("Programme music is an especially interesting musical genre.")

Robert Schumann, who regarded a close connection between literature and music as natural and fruitful in his piano works, stated in one of his critical essays that the words with which Beethoven prefaced the score of his "Pastoral Symphony" went to the very heart of the subject of programme music. "In the few words 'More the expression of feeling than tone painting'," he wrote, "Beethoven summed up an aesthetic principle for composers, and it is utterly ridiculous for painters to depict him sitting by a brook, one hand supporting his head as he listens to its rippling." Berlioz was thinking along the same lines when he wrote: "As for the imitation of sounds in nature Beethoven, Gluck and Rossini have demonstrated by means of brilliant examples that these belong to music's sphere of expression. However, the composer of this (Fantastic) Symphony, being convinced that the misuse of such imitation is always dangerous, and that its use is permissible only in moderation, regards this form of art not as an end in itself but merely as a means to an end . . ." Berlioz here attempted to differentiate between pure programme music and tone painting. He recognized the questionable value of translating non-musical noises into musical sounds through tone painting. He appreciated the difficulty of presenting the musical illustration so vividly before the listeners that they could visualize the scene which the composer had in mind without knowledge of his title or guide to the work. Who would be bold enough to continue this line of development toward such venturesome goals? . . .

*

Goethe: "It requires no art to imitate thunder in music, but the musician who could awaken in me the feeling that I have when hearing thunder would be an artist of great merit. Creating an inner mood without making use of commonplace outward means is the great and noble prerogative of music."

Schlegel: "It seems strange and ridiculous to some people when musicians talk about ideas in their works, and it is often to be observed that they have more ideas in their music than they have about it . . . Is it not necessary for purely instrumental music to create its own text?"

E. T. A. Hoffmann: "Poetic truth is not created by the outward form, which is adopted by chance; it springs rather from the innermost being of the poem, and this being shapes for itself the form in which it is to come to life and, with its distinct characteristics, addresses people like an acquaintance, making them believe what it will."

Novalis: "The musician derives the nature of his art from himself—he cannot be suspected of plagiarism even in the slightest degree."

Schumann: "If a composer holds out a programme to us in front of his music I say: 'First let me hear that you have written beautiful music; after that I will find your programme agreeable as well.'"

Mendelssohn on his "Songs without words": "The message which I receive from music which I love is not too indistinct but on the contrary too distinct. While in the case of one song or another I have had a particular word or words in mind, I do not wish to reveal them to anyone, since the same word has different meanings to different people; a song can say the same thing to everyone and arouse the same feeling in them—but they would not all express that feeling in the same words."

Bülow saw the expression of a poetic idea in all music: "The immediate tonal effect must give rise, as it were, to a transcendental effect which is not bound up with the subject being depicted in sound."

Tschaikowsky: "My (Fourth) Symphony is naturally programmatic, but the programme is such that it cannot be formulated in words. They would give rise to mockery, and appear ridiculous. I must confess I was sufficiently naive to believe that the course of the ideas in my Symphony would be so clearly understandable that its broad outlines would be understood by everyone even without a programme. . . ."

Mahler: "There is no modern music, from Beethoven onward, which is without an inner programme. But no music is worth anything if one has first to tell the listener what experience is re-lived in it or what experience it is intended to give him. So once more: pereat–every programme! One has to bring ears and a heart, and–last but not least–give oneself over willingly to the rhapsodies of the music. A vestige of mystery always remains . . ."

Reger: "Music should not, like programme music, need the participation of a third person before it is generally understandable. Music should be, in its own right, the expression of pure feeling."

C. D. Friedrich: "The painter should not paint merely what he sees before him, but also what he sees within himself. If, however, he sees nothing in himself, then he should refrain from painting what he sees before him. Otherwise his paintings become like screens behind which only invalids or even corpses are to be found."

Menzel: "Not everything is true to nature which is most carefully copied from nature."

Rodin: "Be truthful, you youngsters! But that doesn't mean simply be exact. There is a low form of exactitude, that of the photograph and casting mould. Art begins with inner truth. All your forms, all your colours must express feelings."

Liebermann: "Only he who views nature with his own eyes, and at the same time possesses the ability to pass on what he has witnessed, is an artist . . . Art is clarity, not mysterious, monastic Latin which means something different to each person who hears it."

*

The decisive impulse for the further development of the symphonic poem came through Richard Strauss. It was in this field that his quickly established musical personality with its astonishing self-assurance first came on the scene, and it first gave him a worldwide reputation. A new note came into the correspondence of the twenty-four-year-old composer of "Tod und Verklärung." He wrote to Dora Wihan: "With Ritter's help I am now armed with a forceful view of art and life; after feeling my way for a long time I now have firm ground under my feet... Just think of it, I am now one of the Lisztians, and in short a more advanced standpoint than that which I have now taken up is scarcely conceivable..." Throughout his tone poems are we not in a world of daring adventure which nourished the imagination of this composer who was imprisoned in the bourgeois world? Berlioz drew the subjects of his programmatic works from a bizarre romantic world of feeling which had little to do with the world of reality. Liszt was a confirmed idealist, open to lyrical feelings and philosophical ideas. With Strauss a strong wind, the breath of a zestful feeling for life, and a realistic creative will were evident right from the bright opening fanfare of "Don Juan." At a time when music was still regarded as a refuge from life, Strauss, the musician of the day and of the present, declared himself for unmetaphysical, vital *music of reality.* He later chose the path of musical subjectivity. "Programme music" proper, symphonic music with its primarily spiritual world as opposed to the primarily sensuous world of opera, was released from its ties with naturalistic subjects, musical representation in sound was released from illustrative tone painting, and graphic characterization from factual reporting. It is easily seen that the question of the subject chosen, of the programme, is of fundamental significance as regards the real musical value of a tone poem. The way in which he follows the programme, too, offers a composer unlimited possibilities for creating music which is lifelike and realistic, or on the other hand passively clinging to the subject. The facts that from the standpoint of critical realism Strauss's programmes are seldom completely satisfactory, that the essential content of a work is often overshadowed by the material element of the subject, and that the themes remain rooted to their times–all these were factors far more dangerous in works of this class than in operas.

A number of common objections to his "symphonic poems" can be shown to be invalid. Certainly Strauss went beyond Liszt in the art of plastic illustration–but his skill in tonal characterization had its roots deep in the soil of music. The pictorial, descriptive element became increasingly prominent—but Strauss's programmatic indications are merely a guide to musical ideas, to melodic evolutions. The best of his programmatic works always understand how to leave their programmes behind and stand on their own feet as absolute music. We sense the fine irony with which Strauss once said in this connection: "Do you know what absolute music is? I don't," or with which he called programme music a "derogatory word in the mouths of all those who have no ideas of their own . . ." In 1929 he defended himself energetically against the charge that the quality of his melodic invention varied from work to work. "Programme music, like other kinds of music, is possible, and is raised to the level of art, only when its creator is first and foremost a musician with ideas and the ability to build structures. Otherwise he is a charlatan, because even in programme music the first and most important question is that concerning the real value and strength of the musical idea . . ." We should consider the full significance of the sentence which he wrote at the time of "Zarathustra": "I am a musician first and last, for whom all 'programmes' are merely the stimulus to the creation of new forms, and nothing more."

The letter which the young composer sent to Bülow from Munich in August 1888 deserves notice on account of the significant statements which it contains. He wrote: "A link with the Beethoven of the 'Coriolanus,' 'Egmont,' 'Leonora No. 3' Overtures, of 'Les Adieux,' and above all with the last works of Beethoven, all of whose music, in my opinion, could probably never have existed without a poetic subject, now seems to me the only course by which further development of instrumental music in its own right is still possible. If I have not the artistic power and talent to achieve something worthwhile in this direction, it is no doubt best to leave the field to the great Nine and their four renowned followers; I don't see why, before we have tested our strength to see whether we can create independently and possibly advance our art by a small step, we immediately want to talk ourselves into decadence and assume the attitude of decadence in advance; if it is of no avail—well, I still think it may be better to have taken a wrong turning and said something wrong, but in pursuit of one's genuine artistic conviction, than to have said something superfluous on the old, well-trodden road . . .

From the F minor Symphony onwards I have found myself in a gradually increasing contradiction between the musical-poetic content which I wish to convey and the ternary sonata form inherited from the classical composers. In the case of Beethoven the musical-poetic content was generally wholly covered by this very 'sonata form,' which he raised to its highest point of perfection ... If one wants to create a work of art which is unified in its mood and consistent in its structure, and if it is to give the listener a clear and precise impression, then what the author intends to say must have been equally clear and definite in his own mind. This is made possible only by inspiration through a poetic idea, whether it is introduced as a programme or not. I consider it a legitimate artistic method to create an appropriate new form for each new subject, to shape which finely and completely, although very difficult, is all the more fascinating for that very reason ..."

One final letter worth quoting in this connection is that relating to "absolute" and "expressive" music which the young programmatic composer addressed to Johann L. Bella in March 1890: "The representatives of music here fall into two groups, the first consisting of those to whom music is 'expression', and who treat it as a language as precise as the language of words, but for use where words are inadequate as a means of communication. To the others music is "form in sound", that is to say they establish the basic amosphere of the work to be composed ... and develop the themes which they evolve in accordance with a wholly superficial, musical logic which I cannot comprehend, now that I recognize only poetic logic. Programme music: real music! Absolute music: it can be put together with the aid of routine and rule-of-thumb technique by everybody who is at all musical! First: true art! Second: artificiality! Oddly enough our present-day music has adopted No. 2 as its starting point, and the true position has been demonstrated only by Wagner and Liszt. Therefore we young musicians of today still always begin with No. 2, until we realize that this is not really music at all, but that 'the most precise expression of a musical idea,' which must create its own form, each new idea its unique new form, is the basic requirement of a musical work."

The young "espressivo" musician was frequently to be found following the scent of Beethoven's "poetic idea." (The fact that

217

as a composer of ripe maturity he later accepted Schering's view of Beethoven's hermeneutics, which he decribed as the "only correct and true" estimation, fits in with this fact.) Nevertheless it can be seen that in the symphonic handling of his programme music he proceeded in a manner quite different from that of Beethoven. Strauss sought musical forms suited to the programmatic contents of his works–with Beethoven, on the other hand, the programme, or rather the headings to the movements, had scarcely any influence on the formal construction of the work. This is clearly a fundamental difference.

Although many people refuse to accept the fact, it is undoubtedly true that Strauss placed no great importance on the publication of an explanatory "programme." "I don't like programmes at all. They promise one person too much, they exercise too great an influence on another, a third protests that the programme has stifled his own imagination, a fourth would rather not think at all than try to rethink what someone else has already worked out, and the fifth has another objection ready–in short–programmes are inopportune" (1907). Strangely enough the situation was different in actual practice. Even where it was clear that a detailed summary of events could only be vague and of dubious value, as in the cases of "Tod und Verklärung" and "Till," the "programmes" of which were added after the works had been composed, Strauss's views on the drawbacks of printed guides were not accepted. It can, however, be said that he failed to make his wishes in this important matter sufficiently clear. In his desire to give the broad mass of the lay public some assistance to help them appreciate the music he allowed too much importance to be attached to illustrative details–thereby damaging his own position. Anyone who wishes to understand his tone poems need only bear the titles of the works in mind: "Don Juan," "Don Quixote," "Sinfonia domestica," "Alpensinfonie" ... They should suffice to transform musical impressions into concrete pictures.

In July 1905, Anno Salomae, Strauss wrote a letter to Romain Rolland which throws a great deal of light on this subject. Even in this persuasively worded letter, though, Strauss avoided the ultimate conclusions ... The complete letter runs as follows: "Dear Friend! Heartfelt thanks for your letter. You may be right about the programme of the 'Domestica.' In this you agree with

G. Mahler, who condemns the programme out of hand. But in fact 1. I have given no programme for the S. Domestica, 2. you yourself have, I believe, an incorrect idea of the purpose of such a programme ... To me the poetic programme is no more than the basis of form and the origin of the purely musical development of my feelings–not, as you believe, a *musical description* of certain events of life. That would be quite contrary to the spirit of music. Nevertheless, in order that music should not lose itself in pure wilfulness and wallow out of its depth it needs certain formal restrictions, and these are provided by a programme. To the listener, too, such an analytical programme should not be more than a pointer which can be used by those who so desire. Those who really understand how to listen to music probably don't need it at all ... I will gladly follow your advice to provide no programme of the work in Paris. But do you believe the Paris audience is capable of listening to a symphony lasting three quarters of an hour without a signpost? ... Grateful thanks in advance and cordial greetings, Yours very sincerely, Dr. R. S."

The programme is not set to music, but it is an element which gives rise to the musical inspiration. The programme is, however, the touchstone for the work's content of ideas and feelings, for the question whether it is a realistic or a naturalistic work of art. In the best of Strauss's tone poems ("Don Juan," "Till Eulenspiegel," "Don Quixote") realistic features and impressions are *represented* in living musical pictures within a literary programme. In these works Strauss made only limited use of descriptive elements, always giving pride of place to the music in its own right. The objections raised from time to time against the few purely naturalistic episodes of these scores (such as the noise of breaking pots and the execution on the scaffold in "Till" and later, in "Don Quixote," the bleating of the sheep and the fight with the windmills) got on Strauss's nerves all his life long. In reality this aesthetically questionable kind of *"tone painting"* tied to its subject occurs only sporadically. At the time of "Aus Italien" Strauss dealt with attacks of this nature in a letter to Karl Wolff. "It is really too ridiculous to suppose that a composer of today, who has learned from the classics, especially late Beethoven, and from Wagner and Liszt, would write a work lasting for three quarters of an hour merely in order to show off

219

a few piquant effects of tone painting and dazzling instrumentation which every advanced music student has at his command." It was only in later tone poems, with the self-glorification which often lay at their heart, that the subject attained predominance over the musical content. Only in the monster self-portraits of "Heldenleben" and the "Domestica," as well as in the nature panorama of the "Alpensinfonie," was the poetic-realistic idea obscured by the larger-than-life private experience. In his later tone poems Strauss concerned himself solely with his own person and his immediate surroundings, so he was inevitably running contrary to the view of the theoretician of naturalism Arno Holz: "Art has the tendency to return to nature. It becomes natural in accordance with the measure of its means of expression." While there is no room in Holz's concept for the individual ego of the artist, whose function is merely that of a spectator or observer, in Strauss's case any description of nature is a subjective statement, a personal experience. Strauss recognized the difference which undoubtedly exists between nature and art as follows: the view of the onlooker is deliberately directed toward one part of the subject under consideration, therefore only one aspect of reality "returned to nature." In his tone poems (in contrast to his operas) the means of representation became not simpler but more complex as time went on. Inner necessity became outward effect, and the tone picture became a vast canvas.

Strauss was very conscious of the dangers of tone painting which was unduly "real." It was also clear to him that the listener had more chance to perceive the purely musical value of his programmatic symphonies if the effects of tone painting as such did not push themselves to the fore. As late as 1911 he had written in reply to a question: "In my opinion *everything* can be composed, if the musician has the necessary talent," but when he was sixty-seven he expressed a different opinion. "It is simply not true to say that one can compose '*everything*', if by 'composing' we mean the translation of an expression of ideas or feelings into the symbolical language of music. It is naturally correct that one can paint in notes and sounds (especially with motifs depicting animation), but there is always the danger of entrusting *too much* to music and falling into the error of a barren imitation of nature. In that case, however much spirit and technical ability has gone into the music, it will always remain second-class."

Caricature by Olaf Gulbransson

It may be regretted that Strauss so often gave vent to spontaneous statements which cast doubt on his attitude in this respect. However, a distinction should be drawn here. There is no reason to doubt the accuracy of the character drawn by the Viennese impresario Albert Gutmann, throwing light on a unique blend of self-assurance and naivety. "Once when Strauss dined with us–it was shortly after the performance of his 'Sinfonia domestica' by the Philharmonic–the conversation turned to 'musical illustration,' and he expressed himself, to my astonishment, as follows: 'I regard the ability to express outward events as the

221

highest triumph of musical technique,' and he demonstrated his point by placing his knife and fork side by side on the table. 'You see, that makes a slight noise; to be able to reproduce such trifling sounds so that the listener can be in no doubt about their nature requires great artistic technique. I should like to carry it that far!'" ... What Strauss was here expressing was his delight in his own technical skill, in his ability to draw music even from essentially unmusical noises ranging from the sound of gargling to the roaring of a waterfall. Difficulties did not daunt him, in fact he enjoyed them, because to Strauss art meant "being able, and even able to do everything; to quote a jocular expression 'Anyone who wants to be a real musician must be able to compose a menu'" (Zweig). All such ironical statements should, however, be taken with a grain of salt, as they were often merely the result of high-spirited improvisations. Even in serious works on musical history one still constantly comes across the famous "glass of beer" which Strauss said he wanted to depict so accurately in music that every listener would be able to tell whether it was a Pilsener or Kulmbacher beer. Equally indestructible in Strauss literature is the "table of logarithms" whose setting in easily understandable music he said he considered a rewarding task. His witty "bon mots" can and should be recognized for what they are. He told an American reporter, who was pestering him with unneccessary questions about the contents of the "Domestica," that the symphony showed him working in his study, and also "standing on the balcony in my shirt-sleeves." On another occasion he explained to Mottl that he had illustrated one of the seducer's victims in "Don Juan" with such accuracy that everyone must be able to see that she had red hair ... Till Strauss!

It was certainly a fact that his music always sprang from perception of the senses. Music to be seen with the ears ... In its pictorial quality, its ability to form images in detail, it is indeed the ideal "film music." (It was only on account of the chaos at the end of the war that the project of producing a musical film based on the "Alpensinfonie" was abandoned.) Even Debussy had spoken of a "picture book, a film" in connection with "Heldenleben." New musical aesthetics give preference to those works in which the illustrative elements are not unduly prominent, and in which, instead of purely optical impressions, the

222

programmatic idea gives rise to realistic musical forms. The material elements should be matched to the content of a work. The problem of Strauss's pictorial tone symbols lies not in their existence but in their *function*. ("A wind machine?," Dvořák remarked during a discussion of "Don Quixote." "Why not? The only thing that matters is whether the composer of a work achieves the desired result.") What did Strauss intend to express through his sound pictures? Certainly nothing of overwhelming immensity, no drama despite "Macbeth," no philosophy despite "Zarathustra," and no idyll despite the "Domestica," but the sense of life of a modern bourgeois human being at the turn of the century. This was not art for its own sake, but artistic impression and human experience, not random playfulness, but striving and exertion! Thuille, the friend of Strauss's youth, seems to have had a premonition of the operas which were to come when he said: "Whoever writes symphonic poems today does so merely because of an artistic urge to imitate; Strauss is the only one who has been led along this road by inner necessity and severe struggles within himself . . . It will be surprising to see where this man eventually finds his goal."

"THE FIERY PULSE OF YOUTH"

The young "musician of expression," not yet twenty-two years old, took his "first step towards independence": *"Aus Italien"* was composed as a result of the first journey to Rome and Naples. The tall, lanky third conductor at the Court Opera of his native town had to go south on account of lung trouble, and he summed up his musical impressions of the trip in this "symphonic fantasy." Anyone who listens with alert senses to this work, which is still full of the mood painting of earlier programme music, will not find very much that is "Italian" in it apart from the "Neapolitan folk life" of the concluding movement with the immense verve of "Funiculi-funicula." What the young composer captured of the experiences of his first journey to central and southern Italy with the aid of a full, though not yet unusually large, orchestra was a reflection of his receptiveness to the vivacity of life in the south—a piece of colourful and exuberant Munich "secession" artistry. A good deal of natural Bavarian strength went into this fantasy, whose music does not come from the depths but from just below the surface, so that it reflects objects around it. This is a transitional work. Strauss could not yet free himself from the traditional four-movement form which he had tried out in his two youthful symphonies, and he also retained the customary descriptions of the movements. He did, however, add highly characteristic phrases which at once arouse the listener's imagination: "In Campagna," Andante—"In the ruins of Rome, fantasy pictures of vanished glory, feelings of sadness and melancholy in today's bright sunlight," Allegro molto con brio—"On the shore at Sorrento," Andantino, and "Neapolitan folk life," Finale: Allegro con brio, Presto. (He wrote a detailed analysis of the work in 1889 for the "Allgemeine Musikzeitung.")

"The work is somewhat new and revolutionary," Strauss wrote to Lotti Speyer after the world première at Munich in 1887, "and the last movement has aroused great opposition, or at least shaking of heads, among both old and young. I naturally got the most pleasure out of it; it was a 'Hatz' as the Viennese say. Some people applauded lustily, others hissed loudly, but finally the applause won the day. My opponents have declared me to be half mad, talk about wrong paths and all kinds of similar nonsense. I was immensely proud; this is the first work of mine to have met with opposition from the mob, so it must be of some importance . . ." The Munich audience certainly seem to have taken exception to the carefree audacity of the last movement. Strauss himself later enjoyed repeating the joke of the pianist Giehrl: One can hear from the Finale that the composer was in Naples immediately after an outbreak of cholera . . . Strauss defended himself against the misunderstandings which had arisen a few months after the première with its mixed reception. He hit out at the "frightful lack of judgment and understanding" of that part of the public which, led astray by "possibly dazzling, purely superficial elements" of his work, had allowed itself to be blinded to its real content. "This consists of feelings on witnessing the splendid natural beauties of Rome and Naples, not descriptions of them–I have even been given a musical Baedeker of southern Italy to read!"

"Aus Italien" must be rated as a youthful work related to Mendelssohn (A major Symphony) and Brahms. It is not a document of maturity, but at most a fresh beginning. Its reverberations were such that the name of the young Munich composer now had a good ring in the international world of music. Time has, however, decided against this Italian fantasy–because greater music, more abundantly alive, soon followed to occupy the attentions of conductors. Nevertheless this work, which grows out of the quiet meditation of the "Campagna" movement with increasing animation until in the Finale it plays brilliantly and humorously with Neapolitan folk music (Strauss heard the Tarantella motif of the Coda at Sorrento), contains an abundance of charming features. The road from merely formal beauty to beauty created by character and musical significance here reached its initial goal. For the first time Strauss the colourist made his bow, with the style which he was later to employ with such na-

226

tural assurance. ("The work is among the most difficult examples of modern concert music, and unfortunately it can be really mastered only by a brilliant conductor and a *first-rate* orchestra," the young composer wrote to Schuch in 1887.) The second movement, "In the ruins of Rome," which Strauss actually sketched at the thermal springs of Caracalla, casts its spell on the listener through the power of its impulsively springing trumpet theme which is reminiscent of the theme of nature in "Zarathustra." "On the shore at Sorrento," the third, slow movement, is music full of sunlight glittering on the waves. Even the master of such musical impressions, Debussy, was enchanted by the "salutary colour" of this study in sound, which demonstrated for the first time the broadly-flowing cantabile characteristic of the later Strauss. At the same time he consciously refrained from direct pictorial description in sound, instead approaching the concept expressed by Beethoven in connection with the "Pastoral Symphony." Bülow's unfavourable remark when asked to accept the dedication of "this symphonic fantasy embellished by local opposition," that the composer had here "gone to the extreme limits of the possibilities of sound (in the realm of beauty)" was balanced by his admiration for its "exuberance of ideas, its richness in relationships." The weaknesses of these symphonic "character pieces" reside in their naive mixture of sentimental nature observation and popular music at its most unbuttoned. Aestheticians will never find them wholly acceptable.

*

The young man who strode into life with exuberant energy intoxicated himself and his listeners with his *"Don Juan"* after Lenau. "Off and away toward ever new conquests, as long as the fiery pulse of youth is racing!" Under this banner the hymn to passion and symphony of incandescent love went round the world. Listening to Strauss's "Don Juan" means submitting once again to the seductive picture in sound of this "tone poem for large orchestra" which is slender, flexible, springy in rhythm, rapidly changing in expression, and shining in many colours–the first real stroke of genius of its twenty-four-year-old composer. Later, backed by the experience of his full maturity, he reached this level of achievement again from time to time, but he never exceeded it. Here we have the quintescence of his musicality which has overcome all the stylistic changes of the times right down to the present day, and which has outlived a great deal that has claimed greater validity in the meantime. A stroke of youthful mastery full of overflowing vitality and the expression of boundless optimism! A work full of the bliss of love, not sexual satiety as one might imagine when reading the verses by the poet of "Weltschmerz," Nikolaus Lenau, which inspired Strauss to the composition of his "Don Juan." It is a work in which the young "storm and stress" composer challenged the bigotted stagnation of social life in the "barren beer swamp" of Munich, proving with the volcanic force of his mind that the power of life is stronger than habitual dissatisfaction and decay –a work which holds the mirror up to its age! The first fire-drunk bars open up a new world. That was the experience of Strauss's contemporaries, and the work has retained its magic to this day.

Nevertheless the impulsive longing, desire, fulfilment and controlled ardour of this music can be understood only with reference to the three sections of Lenau's poem of the same name chosen by the composer. (Strauss asked that the programme book of the Berlin Philharmonic should contain "only the verses by Lenau printed at the beginning of the score, with all the dashes indicating deletions," but "no thematic analysis.") Lenau's dramatic fragment presents his hero as being driven by insatiable desire, until he meets his end not at the hands of the Commendatore, but as a result of his own disgust at love. His demoniac craving for love is summed up as follows:

> The magic circle, the measureless bounds
> Of enchanting, beautiful womankind
> I would transverse in a storm of enjoyment,
> And die in a kiss at the lips of the last.
> Oh friend, if I could but fly everywhere,
> Wherever beauty blossoms, kneel before all,
> And, if only for a moment, triumph . . .
> Ah, passion is always only for the new;
> It cannot be transferred from one to another,
> It can only die here, spring up again there,
> And knowing itself, know nothing of repentance . . .

The poet's intention is clear: he made willpower grown beyond all bounds confront the social order; the superman with his compulsive urge to go on to ever fresh conquests challenges the stagnation of the community. Strauss was scarcely influenced by Lenau's metaphysical idea "... that the unconquerable spirit finally subdues material things." His "Don Juan" is also no symphonic picture of the sensual hero of Mozart's opera or of the works by Calderón, Molière, E. T. A. Hoffmann, Pushkin or Shaw. His Don Juan is a portrait not à la Lenau but after Slevogt–painted with the glowing colours of the joy of existence, filled with all the elemental power of Eros. A Don Juan who tastes life in all its diversity, who conquers reality and triumphs in a "storm of enjoyment," afire with ever new passion until the "fuel is consumed, the hearth is cold and dark ..." In this poetic idea, which by no means ignores the dark side of its subject, Strauss found the luminous tonal language of his fascinating work. In "Don Juan" he developed the Berlioz-Liszt concept of the symphonic poem with youthfully unbridled strength. He avoided mere description. He did not "depict" a narrative of his hero's sensuality in action with naturalistic means, but vividly suggested its effects. The thematic values of the "Don Juan" music are strong enough to guard against a descent into mere pictorialism. The finest among these extraordinarily plastic themes occurred to Strauss under blue southern skies. The dazzling conviction with which they are introduced into the symphonic texture and developed demonstrates his mastery in the combination of poetic content and musical structure. "Don Juan" was conceived in free sonata form–its broad sweep is fiery yet restrained, sensual yet not sultry, vital yet perfectly controlled. It was to remain Strauss's most compact tone poem.

What an abundance of melodic figures! What Dionysian sparks! The situation of the impulsive hero is presented perfectly in the boldly modulating opening bars, whose meteoric ascent brings to mind the opening of the "Euryanthe" Overture. Then the seducer, hastening "from desire to enjoyment," appears with a triumphant gesture (first theme in E major). Three women fall under Don Juan's spell: Zerlina approaches shyly and sweetly. The charming violin solo at the top of the instrument's compass indicates a beautiful, sentimental woman, an easy prey to the bold adventurer. He professes his love to the infatuated cantilena of the violin and noble horn counterpoint. A gently sighing oboe melody (the real second theme) characterizes Donna Anna, who now captivates Don Juan. This episode is suddenly interrupted by the second Don Juan theme, of Beethovenian stature, which is presented by the horns in unison, "very energetically," a persuasive image of the victorious life force, and one of the most brilliant of all Strauss's melodic ideas. The climax of the work is reached; Don Juan comes to his senses. The conclusion, the Coda, marks the extinction of the ecstasy of desire. After dynamic crescendi which rise to a climax formed by the entire thematic material strongly concentrated, the final dying fall in the minor comes as a relief from almost incessant tension.

A young German composer had found his feet. The fact that the Munich conductor felt and thought with all the "clarity which has now come to me" when he had been appointed to Weimar, corresponds to the striving of the composer of "Don Juan" toward new, higher artistic goals. In the handling of the full modern orchestra, too, he was now at the height of his powers. All this at the age of 24! He was immensely gratified that, attacking with the full vigour of youth, he had reached his first objective. Audiences and experts were on his side—although not a few people were shocked. (Hanslick referred in 1891 to a "non plus ultra of a wrong, unbridled trend.") This was approximately the result he had hoped to achieve through the composition of tone poems. "The sound was wonderful, immensely glowing and exuberant," he wrote to his father after the first rehearsals at Weimar in 1889. "The story will make a tremendous stir here," and "fortunately the whole thing isn't really difficult; it's only very strenuous, and fifty notes more or less won't make much difference." Two days later: "A great joke!" It was not until after the first performance had taken place under his direction that all his justifiable pride found expression: "Dear Papa! So the 'Don Juan' success was tremendous, the piece sounded magical, went excellently, and met with a storm of applause unheard of in Weimar."

*

The step from the shameless brio of "Don Juan" to the unsensual *"Macbeth"* may be compared with that from "Salome" to "Elektra." The rich colour and the glow of chromaticism were here replaced by rugged melodic contours. The new "Tone poem (after Shakespeare's drama) for full orchestra" had a complicated early history. In its definitive form "Macbeth" is not the first of Strauss's symphonic poems, which were composed in a sequence between 1886 and 1898, but the third. Nevertheless this Shakespearian subject was the first which had aroused the imagination of the young Strauss after his conversion to the ideas of Liszt and the "New German" school. He later used most of the version sketched at Munich in 1886, giving it an altered conclusion. This work, full of echoes of "Tristan," but also influenced by Brahms in its almost abstract thematic workmanship, is among the scores whose rhythms and harmonies fascinate the expert, without ever having conquered the public. In its dark colouring (skilful use is made of the bass trumpet) and the consequence of its progression of ideas it stands, perhaps, on a higher level of artistry than "Tod und Verklärung." However the victorious, radiant, truly Straussian element of "Don Juan" is missing. This may be the reason for its neglect by conductors and orchestras.

Strauss, an enthusiastic theatregoer in his early years, was deeply impressed by Shakespeare's tragedy. The musician's imaginative power was richly nourished by this drama of the great English playwright. What he had in mind was a musical compression of Shakespeare's five acts into a "tone picture" at whose centre were the two principal figures of the action: the demoniac hero Macbeth, whom tragic fate turns into a murderer, and Lady Macbeth, as the motive force behind her husband's crimes. In his "Macbeth" Strauss decided against a detailed "programme," merely indicating the significance of two important passages. At the appearance of Macbeth's defiant principal theme, with the bass instruments leaping over wide intervals to sinister effect, the name of the hero is given. Later, at the dissembling theme of Lady Macbeth, played by the woodwind, the following lines of the poet are quoted:

> Hie thee hither,
> That I may pour my spirits in thine ear;
> And chastise with the valour of my tongue
> All that impedes thee from the golden round,
> Which fate and metaphysical aid doth seem
> To have thee crown'd withal.

Further themes of married love and the destructive power of war, of dread and doubt, make their appearance. The combination of the motifs of love and vengeance, the contrapuntal treatment of the uncommonly characteristic material, are highly artistic. The darkly sinister quality of this music makes itself felt in tone pictures with a greyness of their own (Strauss was using triple woodwind for the first time)–but there is no falling back on purely naturalistic-illustrative methods. A certain ruthlessness reminiscent of Berlioz characterizes this work, probably owing to the uncompromising realism of the subject which could hardly give rise to beauty of line: a "Macbethian witches' kitchen" Bülow called it after studying the original version. Strauss himself was well aware of what he was doing. "I am at present working on an orchestral piece, 'Macbeth,' which is naturally very wild in character," he wrote, not without pride, to his friend Lotti Speyer, and to Bülow he described the new score with its "violent and gruesome content" as the "most independent and purposeful work" which he had composed until then.

Was "Macbeth" written too soon? Strauss confessed that it had to be "revised on the advice of Bülow so that it would correspond to the correct stylistic principles of true programme music ..." The question of an orthodox principle arose because the original "Macbeth" concluded with a triumphant march of Macduff. "Bülow was horrified by the dissonances of 'Macbeth,' and at the (D major Triumphant) March of Macduff, the original ending, he remarked quite rightly that it was nonsense! An 'Egmont' Overture could certainly conclude with a triumph march of Egmont, but a symphonic poem 'Macbeth' could not end with the triumph of Macduff." Strauss followed his mentor's advice by writing a totally new ending to the score (an exception among his works in this respect) based on Macbeth's tragic death. He had already told Ritter that he was "no longer entirely satisfied" with the instrumentation. "There are too many inner parts, so that in some places the principal themes do not stand out as clearly as I intended, and I have more or less made up my mind to revise the whole piece completely ..." This second "Macbeth," which was first performed at Weimar in 1890, convinced Bülow, and the letters to his wife at the time of the Hamburg performance contain the following expressions of enthusiasm: "'Macbeth' is, for the most part, extravagant and deafening, but brilliant in summo gradu... The sound of the work was overwhelming." Nevertheless we should not shut our eyes to the fact that behind Strauss's original conception there had been a very bold realistic idea: to help the forces of life to assert themselves again after the tragic, manly downfall of the hero.

*

The tone poem *"Tod und Verklärung"* is redolent of the mood of weariness at the end of the 19th century from which creative artists were not immune. Strauss, by now possessing the complete assurance of his young mastery, certainly went through a spiritual crisis during his period as a conductor in Munich, with the stagnation of the operatic situation there. His healthy personality was not untouched by the sadness of "Tristan." His concern with Schopenhauer and other pessimistic philosophical writers temporarily endangered his inner strength. Strangely enough in a musician of 25, his gaze wandered over the threshold of death. Still following in the footsteps of Brahms, he found himself captured by the spirit of the dying century in which "deep melancholy is mixed with all we do." " 'Macbeth' lies buried in my desk, silent and resigned," he wrote to Bülow in August 1888. External circumstances such as the separation from his early girl friend Dora Wihan (in one of the few surviving letters to her he wrote of the "new orchestral piece" which "contains more dissonances than your little ears can bear"), illness of himself or of friends cannot be shown to have any bearing on "Tod und Verklärung." "Tod is purely a product of the imagination—no experience lies behind it, I was not ill until two years later. An idea like any other—in the last analysis the product of a musical need. After Macbeth (begins and ends in D minor) and Don Juan (begins in E major and ends in E minor), a piece which begins in C minor and ends in C major." These words from a letter to Wilhelm Bopp, who had asked the composer about the programmatic idea, really tell us all we need to know. This work, which was completed at Weimar, does not represent recollection but a vision of an idealistic "deliverance and transfiguration of the world."

For the first time Strauss had not created his new "tone poem for orchestra" on the basis of sensuous impressions or a literary work. The subject was of his own invention: the agony and death of a man who longs for his extinction, and before whose eyes pass pictures of happy youth. The poem by Alexander Ritter which was published with the programme when this work received its world première at Eisenach in 1890 clothes Strauss's idea in really banal words. The unusual fact of the matter is that the poem was not the inspiration for the composition, as Ritter's verses were written only *after* hearing the completed work; after the third performance Ritter produced a revised version of his text, which was published at the beginning of the score. (In a more recent facsimile print the text appears in a version further significantly shortened and altered.) Not only Hanslick, who cannot be considered an authoritative critic where Strauss is concerned, but also Rolland overlooked this. The fact that the poem was written after the music does not prove that Strauss, who thought in terms of the struggle between two opposing forces in a man's body, did *not* compose "Tod und Verklärung" with particular images in mind. Beside the poetic idea a vision of reality can be seen in almost every bar. Strauss represented not only death but the process of dying in this music. ("Six years ago I had the idea of illustrating the dying moments of a man who has striven toward the highest idealistic aims–probably an artist–in a tone poem," he wrote in 1894 in a letter to Hausegger.) He describes the death struggle with clinical accuracy: the knocking, dragging rhythms of the opening leave nothing to be desired as regards clarity. The hallucinations, the gradually weakening heartbeat of the fever-stricken invalid can be felt in an almost physical sense. This symphonic sickbed, which points forward unmistakably to the operas, leaves the listener with a somewhat uneasy feeling, which is not lessened by the fact that in the second version of the poem, which Strauss chose, the dying man lies "in the wretched little room, feebly lit by the stump of a candle . . ."

With that reservation, "Tod und Verklärung" contains an abundance of deeply-felt music, not without soaring energy, but deriving most of its effectiveness from the sphere of solemn, hymnic expression. The layout in three sections suggesting a symphony movement (with an introduction and an epilogue in which a great deal of tension is discharged) makes this work unusually clear-cut in its thematic and structural aspects. Strauss here created the "new form" which he always sought, by introducing

234

"the principal theme only at the culminating point in the middle of the work." The broad pathos of this score based on the model of Liszt's "Tasso," the solemn dignity of the death and transfiguration here depicted, were largely responsible for the fact that many people regarded this work, when it appeared, as Strauss's bid for success with the broad public. In view of this universally understandable, fine-sounding ideal picture of a man's release from his struggle with death, many share Rolland's view that "Tod und Verklärung" is "one of Strauss's most deeply affecting works . . . the summit of an epoch of his life." (Only the carping Hanslick objected that Strauss's magic lantern gave out a very feeble light.) In fact the broadly-conceived "transfiguration" theme rises to a C major apotheosis of sensuous radiance, whose "moving effect" even Strauss's conservative father could appreciate. In contrast to the earlier tone poems, the novel aspects in the instrumentation were to be found in the more even blend of colours . . . A few years later, when the "Prima donna Nikisch" performed "Tod und Verklärung" with the Berlin Philharmonic, and "misused it so shamelessly" that Strauss was seriously concerned for the work and the public's reaction to it, he finally came to the conclusion, as he put it in a letter to his father, that "the work seems to be indestructible!"

The ideas which serve as Strauss's thematic material are not "great," but they are of remarkable plasticity and suggestive power (one need only think of the oppressive death motif). The idealistic aspect appears to be completely integrated with the images of reality—here, perhaps, is the reason for the immediacy of the work's effect. It is difficult to describe this emotion-charged music, which contains so many echoes of Wagner: how in the opening Largo with the two final chords of what is to become the transfiguration motif, here heard in the minor, the indeterminate syncopations trail away into uncertainty, how the magical flute theme rises above the heavy, oppressive atmosphere with calm poignancy, spreading endless peace—until a fortissimo timpani stroke releases a flood of passion. The preparation for this is impressive, while the fever rises gradually from the tremolo of the basses, but does not become frenzied even in the Agitato. It is only gradually that power builds up. Then, amid the happy reminiscences and anxious fantasies of the fever-stricken man, the motif of transfiguration rises up, played by the brass and basses against a harp background. (Strauss never lost sight of this thematic idea, which was based, significantly enough, on the final phrase of Ritter's tone poem "Olaf's Hochzeits-reigen;" he quoted it in several later works, including "Helden-leben," "Krämerspiegel," and "Im Abendrot," one of the Last Songs.) Once again recollections of childhood fill the dying man's dreams; this motif appeared at the beginning as a "melancholy smile." The dreadful warning of approaching death is heard from the trombones. Finally there is the "transfiguration," a tre-mendous climax of expression, and solemn extinction. The hym-nic, majestic ending is the first example of the lyrically flowing conclusions with which Strauss crowned most of his tone poems from then on. He never again approached so near to the region of mysticism as in this work, but even in his naive vision of the passing of a human soul Strauss remained tied to the life of this world, clearly opposed to Schopenhauer. He could not go against his nature.

*

Next came a Scherzo—*"Till Eulenspiegel's lustige Streiche."* Here was humour, which had not yet had its say in the tone poems, the open, happy smile so much at home on the face of a Bavarian musician. "Till" is the artistic reflection of Strauss's eventful years at Weimar, which Seidl later referred to as bring-ing about a "period of blossoming achievement" such as had not been seen since the time of Liszt. It contains boundless joie de vivre, exuberance and satire. How many people there were with whom the young composer had a bone to pick at that stage of his career!—the narrow-minded and reactionary, the "aesthetes" and perpetual "followers," the dull-witted and the "clever boys!" He wrote "Till" with the satisfied feeling that he had now shaken the "old dust of Weimar tradition" off his feet. He also wanted to pour scorn on that part of the unresponsive Munich public, "made up of bankers and tradesmen of low tastes," which had shown not the slightest appreciation of his first dramatic work "Guntram." So Strauss determined to express unmistak-ably his contempt for humdrum society and its narrow view of life, contempt for the "land of the philistines, of stupidity and slow-wittedness" from which the young enthusiast for Greece

236

had told Bülow (in a letter written from Athens two years earlier) he was glad to have escaped. Nevertheless there was nothing irreconcilable about this wittily brilliant piece of programme music. The rogue Till, as the teller of unpalatable truths, a rebel –that was how Strauss wanted to introduce into his own world of sound the stories of Till collected by the Franciscan monk Thomas Murner, written in old German, and later revised by Simrock: always laughing, and with a jest on his lips. There is no indication that Strauss also used as a model Charles de Coster's Till Ulenspiegel, a popular figure from the time of the Netherlands' wars of independence. Even Strauss's sub-title is entertaining: "After an old rogue's tune–in Rondeau form–set for full orchestra." We can see this deliberately stilted, old-fashioned wording (Rondeau instead of Rondo) on the score. The work is an amusing round song made up of musical Eulenspiegel tales–but naturally it is far removed from the traditional form as taught in schools. The artful intriguer who made fun of his fellow men, who sometimes pointed out their folly by obeying their instructions to the letter, and who was afraid of nothing–this Till created his own brilliant musical form with his principal theme returning again and again, together with numerous variants and elaborations. When Strauss, in his old age, was asked by Gregor whether he was aware that in "Till" he had reached the metaphysical bounds of great humour, he replied promptly: "Oh no–I only wanted to give the people in the concert hall a good laugh for once." A somersaulting mixture of persiflage and impudence, not broad comedy but "the most triumphant laughter in music"–in the words of Wilhelm Furtwängler a "stroke of genius, worthy of Beethoven."

Naturally it is no mere chance that the figure of the rebellious "Arch-knave by the Grace of God," who was born in Brunswick about the year 1300, occupied Strauss's attention for many years. His interest in the subject was aroused when he heard the "Eulenspiegel" opera by Cyrill Kistler at Würzburg in 1889 or thereabouts, a work the clumsiness of whose libretto amused him. Strauss started to sketch his own libretto for a comic opera, shortly after completing "Guntram," but he did not get beyond the first act. He decided on the more compact form of a symphonic poem. The universal success of this tone poem renewed his desire to write a "Eulenspiegel" opera. A five-act opera "Die

237

Schildbürger" to a text by Ferdinand von Sporck? "Friend Sporck's excellent book is gradually beginning to find echoes in my mind and heart, to awaken new ideas which may 'perhaps' be able to live" (letter to Schillings). Once again the plan came to nothing. "Feuersnot" took its place.

The problem of this class of work, that of accommodating a literary programme in a compact musical form, is solved perfectly in the case of "Till Eulenspiegel." Here the musician's flights of fancy became the content of the work. By restoring the rogue Till's cheerfulness at the end, allowing him to triumph over all the dissonances of existence, he clearly lifted the work out of the realm of the description of material events into that of realism. Strauss intended at first to withhold the exact content of the work from the public. Even at the time of the world première at Cologne in 1895 he refused to give Wüllner a detailed explanation. "It is impossible for me to give a programme to 'Eulenspiegel': what I had in mind when writing the various sections, if put into words, would often seem peculiar, and would possibly even give offence. So let us, this time, leave it to the audience to crack the nuts which the rogue has prepared for them. All that is necessary for the understanding of the work is to indicate the two Eulenspiegel themes which are run right through the work in all manner of disguises, moods and situations until the catastrophe, when Till is strung up, after sentence has been passed on him. Apart from that let the gay Cologners guess what a rogue has done to them by way of musical tricks ..." Later, though, Strauss revealed what scenes he had had in mind during the composition: he gave Mauke information for the latter's analysis of the work, and he authorized Klatte's guide to it. It is not concerned with motifs and scenes derived from literary sources, but with traditional heroic and hilarious adventures of the popular figure Till, whose relation to the thinking and feeling of the ordinary people called for realistic musical representation. Till's story was told in the lightest musical tones. A "modern Papa Haydn" (Busoni), he not only sparkles with wit and good humour; he is also simple, convincing, and not averse to whistling a popular tune. Just as, later, the tragedy of "Elektra" was followed by the comedy of "Rosenkavalier," so the idealistic heights of "Tod und Verklärung" gave place to the lively popular style of "Till." It is quite natural

that the cheeky rogue's adventures should have been presented
several times on the ballet stage.

This work is a masterpiece of humour, blended with slightly
ironical characteristics, which glows with uncommon warmth and

*The popular tune from "Till Eulenspiegel": Copy of the score
by the composer (1944) "To the worthy Till on his 50th birthday"*

sympathy ... The technique of the thirty-one-year-old composer
here shows completely new features: a highly developed art of
tonal perception, a dazzling mastery of detail, deft juggling with
motifs, laughing and chuckling of the instruments, a sure feeling
for both drastic and charming effects–in short an orchestral buffo
style which magically matches the mischievous philosophy of the

popular hero Till, yet which never destroys the feeling of a logical sequence and natural order of events. Strauss had at his command not only his full power of musical invention but a new "golden abundance" of instrumental ideas. Hanslick wrote in Vienna of a "real world exhibition of sound effects and contrasts of mood." (The old Bruckner had a different opinion: he at once wanted to hear this "delightful humoresque" a second time in Vienna.) The rarely employed D clarinet seems to laugh and chuckle, the horns apparently want to blow themselves straight, trumpets whine "lamentingly," and "in the lowest part, the contra bassoon, Till's big toe sticks out." For the first time the orchestral virtuoso, now using a really large scoring with quadruple woodwind, eight horns and six trumpets, let nothing escape him. Till seems to want to run the gauntlet of an enormous mass of instruments. This famous piece of buffo artistry, to a greater extent than almost any other work of recent musical history, cannot be ignored by any conductor, orchestra or recording company. It is always with us.

What happens in the story? A great deal, but it is no more than a succession of pranks and clashes with authority, whose details are not essential. After the story-teller Strauss has commenced with his "Once upon a time there was a buffoon named Till Eulenspiegel," which has the simplicity of folk music, the hero skips in with his impudent principal motifs: the first bold and assertive, brilliantly conceived for the solo horn, the second, the really characteristic Eulenspiegel motif, played cheekily by the high clarinet. Till arrives on horseback at the pot market, where the outcry of the market women above the breaking of pots (cymbals and rattle) quickly puts him to flight. He now amuses himself by dressing as an unctuous wandering preacher, beneath whose cassock we catch a glimpse of the jester's motley. Till is involved in an affair of gallantry. However, his ardent wooing ("glowing with love" Strauss wrote above the string melody) is rewarded only by a rebuff, which enrages him. He vents his fury on some learned men–the "cream of the philistines, the professors and savants" are depicted most "drily" by three bassoons, bass clarinet and contra bassoon. With a cheeky popular song, which the composer obtained from among the ordinary people, Till goes on. But the day of reckoning arrives, and Till sees his last hour approaching. He is captured and dragged before the court of justice. When asked whether he pleads guilty, he boldly whistles his theme in answer, but then he laments the turn events have taken. The threatening trombones announce the verdict: death–with the last flute trill the mocker meets his fate. Then, however, the short epilogue says that Till has never died in the heart of the people. The rogue lives on.

*

The distance between this and Strauss's next tone poem is very great. The young follower of Nietzsche experienced the need to express his feelings and reflections on reading *"Also sprach Zarathustra"* in a programmatic work. His vociferous contemporaries soon came to realize that this had nothing to do with "philosophy set to music." What they heard in this new, fiery tone poem was neither a musical picture of the "superman" nor the reflection of the pathologically overblown view of the world held by the poet-philosopher whose influence on music at the turn of the century had so dangerous an effect. Strauss did not here translate Nietzsche's philosophy into terms of music, but merely adopted as the starting point of his work the lyrical, hymnic atmosphere of the Zarathustra book. His was only a distant and general view of Nietzsche, the exact opposite to an intellectual score precisely modelled on every nuance of the original. The great prophet descends from the mountain–but he descends so far that he arrives on the plain of totally unphilosophical, healthily atmospheric music of this world. The hymn to life of "Zarathustra" is genuine Strauss. This is a glowing score, with pronounced southern colouring, and it is prefaced, significantly, by Nietzsche's lines: "Too long has music been dreaming; now let us awaken. We wandered by night, now let us walk by day."

The contradiction between what is in this instance a purely abstract programme of ideas by the philosophic poet, and the inspiration which it gave the musician, is unmistakable. While Nietzsche dreamed himself painfully into a longed-for reality, out of his infirmity, the sense of repression and intoxication with life, Strauss strode straight to this view of the world with the healthy vitality of his spiritual and physical nature. While the dithyrambic, ecstatic language of Nietzsche and some of his ideas aroused the composer's imagination, any such "Tone poem (freely after Nietzsche) for full orchestra" could represent no more than "a venture" in the context of his complete output–a quest for new forms of expression. Undoubtedly Strauss was not referring to himself in his musical evocation of Nietzsche's "superman." This work, which was completed in Munich in August 1896, and first performed at Frankfurt on Main later in the same year, contains nothing to support any such interpretation. No statement concerning this work is known to have been made by Nietzsche, who was already incurably ill at the time, but he had been sceptical about the possibility of a setting of "Zarathustra." He had, however, made the following significant remark about his book to Peter Gast in 1883: "To what category does this 'Zarathustra' really belong? I almost believe it belongs among symphonies."

Of all Strauss's works this is the one most fettered to its age. It could and can be understood fully only by those who find the way into Nietzsche's nebulous house of ideas, and they were probably few even in the year when this tone poem appeared. (Hugo Wolf called it a "success as a great joke" in Vienna). Rolland was certainly right when he wrote: "The programme which Strauss chose does not lose itself in insignificant pictorial and anecdotal details, but is outlined in a few expressions and majestic strokes." However, he, who later referred to this as a "feeble work," overlooked the fact that this popular-style compendium of worldliness and mysticism, of solved and unsolved riddles, also perplexes the listeners and makes their access to the work's musical beauties difficult. At the same time in this piece, whose structure demands to be heard rather than seen, the hand of the formal architect and tonal magician Strauss is most important, and the work's tonal fascination has won for it a greater measure of appreciation during recent years. The form is clearly that of a symphonic fantasy, inspired by various sections of the book.

The basic problem with which Nietzsche and Strauss were concerned was the relationship of man to the world–to nature. The poetry of the sunrise, following on the first part of the Hymn to the Sun which is used as a preface, opens the score–this Introduction, with its swift changes between major and minor and extreme contrasts of light and shadow, grows out of the lapidary motif of nature played by the trumpets, in fact an octave divided at the fifth. There follow eight self-contained but skilfully linked musical scenes. By contrast to the most unphilosophically simple tone symbols of the shining sun (Strauss used the organ for the first time), longing, delight, and the passions, there are darker representations of loneliness and mystery. The manner in which, in the concluding "Night Wanderer's Song," the composer sets the B major brightness of the descant against the humming C of the basses, the basic note of nature, is most impressive. The horns intone the "Credo in unum Deum," suggesting the inhabitants of "the unseen world," and Strauss pours out a song of faith through the medium of the melos of strings divided into many parts. "The great longing" has the musical character of irresistible upward striving. The glorification of things terrestrial ("Of joys and passions") is followed by the funereal "Dirge." In the irony of the Fugue, which has been quoted in all seriousness as an early example of the use of the twelve-note system, the music becomes "scholastic," as befits the subject "Of Science." The "Convalescent" turns again to the happy confidence of life, and at the rhythmic "Dance-Song," with its pronounced Viennese flavour, the musician comes on the scene with his naively carefree joie de vivre. But even this "Dance of light feet" was unable to bring Nietzsche to the ordinary man.

TONE PAINTINGS

THE MUSICAL FORM BECAME MORE AND MORE EXPAN-
sive. The "symphonic poems" took on ever greater proportions,
until they were "tone paintings" on the grand scale, with a duration of up to almost an hour. Strauss commenced the new phase
of his orchestral writing in Munich in the summer of 1897 with
"Don Quixote." This work has, unjustly, been assigned to a place
somewhat in the background among his symphonic works. The
bold idea of making the "Knight of the Woeful Countenance,"
from the world-famous novel by Cervantes "Don Quixote de la
Mancha," which appeared in 1605, the hero of symphonic variations could only come to a musician of Strauss's brilliant in-
ventiveness and technical skill. He was attracted by the tragic
foolishness and worldly wisdom of the unpractical Quixote, a
highly contradictory character whose nature contained elements
of caricature, the grotesque and pathological. The genial satire
on the vanishing Spanish feudalism, a reflection of 16th century
reality, stirred his imagination. Strauss went his own way, by
making the erratic individualist, who built castles in the air without realizing that they existed only in his own mind, the symbol
of all those who live their lives under a delusion. Strauss's "Quixote," with its mocking grimaces, contains less criticism of society than self-irony. ("It is very original, entirely new in colour,
and a really comic presentation of all sheeps' heads–who, however, have not understood, and have even laughed at it," the
composer wrote to his mother in 1898.) Now, at last, recognized
and admired, full of vigour and rich in experience of the world,
"preparing to create the heavy brigades of 'Heldenleben' and the
'Domestica' and the hurricane of 'Salome',"–Strauss was really
a philosopher, a laughing philosopher of music.

Before reaching this sparkling work one must get through its full title: "Introduzione, Tema con variazioni e Finale, fantastic variations on a theme of knightly character for full orchestra." This sounds neither graceful nor a popular title, and it is not even accurate. It would be more correct if worded "on a double theme," since this attempt, undertaken with sovereign assurance, to present Cervantes in the form of orchestral variations which go technically beyond anything attempted hitherto, was based on the wittily contrasting themes of the hero and of his companion Sancho Panza. (Many years later Strauss referred to the "variation form taken ad absurdum" of "Quixote"). The manner in which the composer depicts the wandering knight and his companion with uncommonly characteristic motifs capable of numerous transformations, the deluded Quixote by the solo cello, his cunning squire by the bass clarinet, tenor tuba and–in view of Sancho Panza's habit of gossiping–solo viola, gives rise to a fantasy picture of delightful romantic irony. "Whether he was a fool or a wise man is not clear, but obviously he went to heaven," as Cervantes wrote.

A turning point! Strauss based "Don Juan" and "Till" on ideas which provided the inspiration he needed to create his most unified tone poems. "Don Quixote" is Cervantes composed at length–nothing is omitted which can help to realize the fantastic subject in music vividly and completely. The consciousness that the late-romantic means of musical expression were not yet by any means played out turned the Goya of music in the direction of instrumental ornamentation and drastic satire. Modern ears, accustomed to greater economy of materials and stronger intellectual discipline, cannot fail to be aware of a certain overloading and garrulity of effect. Many take exception to the fact that Strauss unconcernedly incorporated in his score such naturalistic features as the sound of sheep (muted brass "bleating") and a description of the knight being whirled through the air (played by flutes, "flutter-tongued," with glissandi of the harps and the rushing of the wind machine). Rolland wrote that people believed they were "being made fun of . . . it seems to be all the same to the sly, mocking Strauss." Is it not, however, a fact that such earlier composers as Telemann, Purcell and the Russian Anton Rubinstein (whose orchestral humoresque of the same name Strauss scarcely knew) were inspired to compose by the epic of Cervantes, each attempting with his own means to create as graphic a portrait of the grotesque knight as possible? Strauss remains a genuine, imaginative inventor even when the musical substance is dissipated in purely pittoresque description, and the polyphony of colours approaches the realm of purely decorative art. (In his "Versuchen" Bertolt Brecht wrote that the "realistic manner of writing does not imply a renunciation either of imagination or of true artistry. Nothing prevents the realists Cervantes and Swift from seeing knights tilting at windmills and horses founding states.") Nevertheless the excursions into naturalism are certainly not the essential features of the score–Strauss used to sail through them "con grandezza" when conducting. This is a work of suggestion, of the capricious alternation of moods and feelings ranging from contented laughter to sad resignation. When, after this continuous sequence of bold adventures, the satirist Strauss lays down his arms, he provides one of his warm-blooded, lyrically meditative epilogues, all the more conciliatory after the bizarre events which have gone before. With the song of the solo cello the master bids an affectionate farewell to his shipwrecked hero, who has ceased to be an adventurer cut off from the world of reality, and is now a responsible human being.

Once again it was not until after the world première had taken place in Cologne in 1898 that Strauss provided details of the content of the new tone poem. In this case one could, undoubtedly, concentrate entirely on the spirited and colourful music for its own sake, but complete enjoyment is reserved for the listener with a knowledge of the story-preferably having read the relevant passages in Cervantes beforehand. The "programme," which can only be indicated briefly here, identifies the episodes in detail . . . After Quixote has been introduced in the Introduction, which skilfully suggests his knightly, elegant and tragic characteristics ("Don Quixote, who spends his time reading tales of chivalry, loses his reason, and determines to travel the world as an itinerant knight"), the variations depict his adventures. The departure of the clanking hero and Sancho Panza, the battle with the windmills and flocks of sheep, Panza's desires, figures of speech and sayings, Quixote's tale of the fantastic kingdom, the adventure with the procession, the knight's vigil on a summer night, his affair of the heart, his ride through the air, the boat journey, the attack on the mill and the mendicant friars, and finally the single combat and homecoming—almost too much happens for the uninitiated ear to take it all in. Strauss used Quixote's adventures to present the knightly theme in a great variety of forms; indeed, even the wonderfully beautiful, calming melody of the Epilogue is merely a variant of the principal theme which has been proved in so many battles. It is reminiscent of the "Idée fixe" of Berlioz, but only in the sense that Strauss did not stay in one place. "Don Quixote" is a piece of world literature in music—so elegant, virtuistic and adventurous in its positively acrobatic gestures that it has scarcely an equal in all Strauss's work. It is at the same time the most "objective" of all the tone poems. It is elastic and finely-wrought, and the Dulcinea episode has a magical luminosity. It is also, however, loquacious, and not free from the danger of crumbling to pieces as a formal structure. As in the case of "Don Juan," there is scarcely any Spanish local colour despite its southern brightness—the composer addresses us rather as a cosmopolitan man of the world. This reduces the work's value somewhat. It was still in manuscript when the first performance took place. Strauss was then already deeply immersed in his next task, with which (as can be seen from a sketch book of 1897) he occupied himself at the same time. After an ironic look at the world he turned his attention to his own "hero's life."

*

After the last barline of the score of *"Ein Heldenleben"* Strauss wrote: "Berlin-Charlottenburg, 27th December 1898." Shortly before that the already famous Bavarian musician had gone to Prussia, to the German capital. The newly-appointed Berlin Court Conductor saw the century coming to its close, and sensed instinctively the contradictions of the changing times. His artistic will sought the glorious tonal splendour of a brilliant epoch, into whose centre he drew the creative artist, represented by himself. In contrast to the earlier symphonic works, the new "Tone poem for full orchestra" was to represent nothing less than the man and musician Strauss at the height of his creative power. "Ein Heldenleben" has in fact nothing to do with the great patriotic ideas of the heroic symphonies of Beethoven and, in recent years, Shostakovich. It was Strauss's first acknowledgment to the "new subjective style" to which he referred in his last writings a few weeks before his death. "Why do people not see what is new in my works, how . . . the man becomes visible in the music?" It is fortunate, at least, that Strauss dropped the idea of calling this work a "new tone poem 'Eroica'," which he mentioned as late as the summer of 1898.

There was no lack of voices attacking the "megalomania" of this most voluminous and even monumental of Strauss's orchestral works to date when it received its first performance at Frankfurt on Main in 1899, and the concert management were given the well-meant advice to place the work at the end of the programme so that members of the audience could get out of the hall before it began. The period of more than sixty years which has elapsed since then has removed the shock effect of this heady fin-de-siècle vintage. It has, however, opened some eyes to the other side of the picture in this musical autobiography: the hero realizes that he has conquered in vain. He sees that what he has achieved is misunderstood by his "adversaries." He renounces his claims and goes, as Strauss once put it, "to grow cabbages." The heroic glorification of his own artistry gives place to "heroic disgust" (Rolland)—"something of Nero is in the air." That could be nothing but the expression of the artist's relationship to the spiritual emptiness and stagnation of the age. The French writer also expressed himself as follows in his important essay of 1904 concerning the composer of "Heldenleben": "The hero's victory has made him aware of his strength: his pride is now boundless; he exalts himself, no longer able to distinguish between reality and his grandiloquent dreams, just like the nation which he represents. There are germs of disease in Germany: a delirium of arrogance, a belief in self and contempt for others . . . Germany had hardly become a world power when it found the voice of Nietzsche . . . and the secession. The grandiose music of Richard Strauss now has that appearance . . ."

A document of its age—but also a part of Strauss's own personality . . . he knew that innumerable statesmen, artists and scientists, conscious of their abilities, had used their own careers as the basis of important autobiographical works. He was tempted, seventy years after Berlioz's "Fantastic Symphony," to depict an artist's life, using *his* means of expression. He did not choose the traditional classical or romantic forms for his private Eroica, but decided in favour of an oversize instrumental structure with quadruple woodwind, eight horns, five trumpets–a colossal symphonic portrait larger than life. Is it possible to represent the essentially quiet private life of an artist, his development and struggles, even his joy in past achievements, in a welter of overlarge and therefore coarsened orchestral sound? Why so much noise? Such questions inevitably arise as a result of the sheer force of this music. With its tendency towards excessive volume of sound this score appears to sum up the artistic ideals of the period of Strauss's youth. Nevertheless it would be a mistake to regard Strauss's subjective concern with his own life as the equivalent of Makart's empty blaze of colour. A more apt comparison is with Corinth's sensuously vital self-portrait with a female model. The same power of healthy artistry, the same blend of genuine pathos and naive human feeling, and the same discernment in the use of rich colours! While Strauss's orchestra was enlarged by the addition of new instruments, his tone world was being enriched in the direction of chamber music. The musical qualities of "Heldenleben" clearly make their presence felt behind the aberrations of the "programme."

With the exception of "Elektra" there is no other work of Strauss in which musical representations of ugliness and flowing melody are heard in such close juxtaposition. The composer presents the "hero" with broad, energetic strokes–the first bars form one of the most powerful openings which Strauss ever penned, in the "Eroica" key of E♭. Then, however, with the bickering of the wind, caricaturing the army of "adversaries," he destroys the splendid verve of the opening, and at the same time, unfortunately, the structural unity of the work. Shrieking and chattering woodwind figures and the empty pomposity of open fifths in the brass point to the example of "Die Meistersinger." (The initiated professed to hear in this passage the name of a well-known Berlin critic.) Then we are introduced to "the hero's helpmate" in the great lyrical Intermezzo of the score which leads into the broadly flowing love scene in G♭ major, with the technically difficult solo violin part depicting the capricious "Pauline." The composer-husband used an amusing vocabulary of expressions, ranging from "ingratiatingly flattering" to "frivolous" and "scolding," to describe all the shades of feminine behaviour which he knew so well from personal experience. (Steinitzer aptly remarked that this section of the work ought to

250

be entitled "The Wooing of the Hero".) This single-movement work, in three clear-cut sections, now gets somewhat out of hand from the viewpoint of formal aesthetics. While Strauss has hitherto identified himself with the hero, he now unexpectedly depicts "The hero's battleground." This fierce warlike scene (which had a precursor in the brassy "Battle of Lützen" in the Weimar "Festmusik" of 1892) comes to a climax in the relentless "cacophonies" resulting from the head-on clash of the motifs of the hero and of his adversaries, until the love theme heralds the transition to the victoriously radiant Recapitulation. A new section, "The hero's works of peace," contains, as in a symphonic Development, quotations from earlier works, which establish links with the new "Heldenleben" motifs ("Don Juan," "Tod und Verklärung," "Guntram," the song "Traum durch die Dämmerung" among others). Finally "The hero's retreat from the world and his fulfilment"–a pastoral, peaceful conclusion in which the voices of the adversaries are heard only from afar off; the attention is turned inward. The orchestra's fury is spent, and the road to melodic beauty is open. By the time the work comes to its end with a short wind fanfare based on the hero's theme, greatly broadened (Strauss added these heroic closing bars as the result of experience gained at the rehearsals for the world première at Frankfurt), the listener, too, is somewhat exhausted.

As was so often the case, Strauss later added further explanations to the programme of "Heldenleben" which were designed to make this massive work more readily comprehensible. He was originally of a different opinion. To Rolland he said: "You need not read my programme. It is enough to know that it describes a hero in conflict with his enemies . . ." On another occasion he referred to the "remarkable man" who regains his "inner stability" during his progress through life. Is that an idea which still has anything to offer people of today? The world against which the artist then had to fight in his struggle to assert himself is no more. The warlike experiences of his artistic spirit can hardly arouse historical or sociological interest. Nevertheless "Ein Heldenleben," in its essence one of the simplest of the tone poems and conceived as a "direct pendant" to "Don Quixote," became a monument in sound to the turn of the century. It was *thus* that musical revolutions were brought about in those days. (Strauss wrote scathingly to his father about the reception of this work by

the conservative audience at the Berlin Opera concerts, how "the
nobility and numerous old maids" reacted sourly, and the "fault-
finders ... heard nothing of the forty minute work except those
ugly passages, totalling at most seven minutes, which were necessary to provide contrast.") The work brought out to a far
greater extent than hitherto the powerful elan of Strauss's impetuous temperament. The undisguisedly Caesarean gestures and
the decorative pathos of the tone painting are both disturbing.
"Heldenleben," dedicated to Willem Mengelberg and the Concertgebouw Orchestra, is Strauss's most personal creation—by no
means his most popular, although it has of late been taken on
concert tours by eminent conductors and orchestras as a showpiece. The composer later indicated a degree of displeasure with
this work ("I have no particular liking for it").

*

After the heroizing of his own life there was a return to the
idyll of bourgeois domestic happiness; after the proud self-as-
sertion and the conflict with the outside world the intimate contemplation of his private existence ... *"Sinfonia domestica"* is
a reflection of Strauss the citizen and family man, during whose
years in Berlin all the bitter struggles on behalf of artistic ideals
were overshadowed by his happiness with "my dear wife and
our son," to whom the work is dedicated. In April 1902 Strauss,
who had been compelled to rest his eyes for some time, "slowly
began to compose a little again: worked ... peu à peu on a large-
scale symphonic poem" (to his parents). In a serene frame of
mind, having meanwhile returned to the musical stage with the
"little opera" "Feuersnot," he set about his "principal task" of
the "Domestic Symphony," his "musical picture of marriage."
Scarcely anything in this contemplative, warm-blooded score
leads us to believe that it was completed (on New Year's Eve,
1903) at a time when Strauss was already working on "Salome."
It was, naturally, a charming idea to capture the little world
of domestic life, with the child's games and the happiness of
his parents, in a symphonic work. The man, his wife and their
(at that time six-year-old) son are set to music of photographic
accuracy; we are shown familiar household scenes, the happiness
and cares of the married couple—not to mention some disputes,
though the whole is an idyll, lavishly produced. (Even Goethe

252

did not shun the publication of details concerning his private life.) If, nevertheless, there is "something difficult to bear" in this work it has its origin in the contradiction between content and form which is clear to everybody in the "Domestica." There is a striking disparity between the intimacy of the programmatic design and the full-toned performance by an orchestra of more than a hundred (with quadruple woodwind, four saxophones for the first time, eight horns etc.), between the simplicity of the programme and the monumentalism of the execution. The delicate offspring of the parents became a giant symphonic baby. The pleasant genre picture of life in Berlin-Charlottenburg took on the proportions of a vast theatrical scene in which "kitchen, living room and bedroom are open to all and sundry" (Rolland). "One can hardly make such a lot of noise at home," Strauss's father had objected, also expressing doubts about the title and dimensions of the work, and a critic wrote that one could undoubtedly identify the three members of the family in the music, but that an important fourth character had been forgotten: the landlord, who would have come to give notice to quit if such a din had been made in the house ... Strauss himself may have sensed this discrepancy between the harmlessness of the basic idea and the over-rich tonal resources employed. He attempted to minimize it by an enchanting lightening of the texture approaching chamber music, and by employing themes some of which were naively songlike. Despite these efforts the "Domestica" (how much more successful is the solution of the tonal problems presented by the related Fourth Symphony of Mahler!) represents, strictly speaking, an error of aesthetic judgment. Not everything in it makes the effect it may once have made.

"My next tone poem will represent a day in the life of my family. It will be part lyrical, part humorous—a triple fugue will bring the Papa, Mama and baby together," Strauss told the press in America, far from the spot where the work was being written ... Humorous? The composer soon found it advisable to state that he "did not intend to be facetious" when he wrote the "Domestica." "What can be more serious than married life? Marriage is the most serious event of a lifetime, and the sublime joy of such a union is increased by the arrival of the child. This life naturally has its humorous side, which I have also introduced into the work to brighten it, but I want the symphony to be

253

taken seriously . . ." This attitude is typical of Strauss. Undoubtedly much of this work, which is made up of four linked movements (Allegro, Scherzo, Adagio and Fugal Finale), is highly
enjoyable, above all the "lusty squabble" of the technically virtuistic double fugue which depicts an all-too human matrimonial
row. There is, however, something uncommonly serious and even
solemn about the music when Strauss refers to the loving mother
or the child. A sense of heartfelt emotion dominates the "Domestica," while the opera "Intermezzo," written twenty years
later, shows off the burlesque side of marriage. He wrote to his
parents after the world première, which took place in 1904 during a Strauss festival at the Carnegie Hall in New York, "that
'Domestica' . . . had a tremendously enthusiastic reception. After
a great deal of annoyance caused by that band of anarchists the
New York musicians, I obtained a brilliant performance following 15 rehearsals, which used up a great deal of energy and curses. 'Domestica' is a success, sounds splendid, but is very difficult
(especially for the horns, which squeaked out their top A) . . .
The reception was stupendous, perhaps eight calls, two laurel
wreaths, and the critics, who had been very hostile here in New
York, changed their tone . . ."

Basically a very simple programme! The course of an ordinary
day in the composer's life with all its prosaic details: the child
plays, and his parents join in his games, then they get him off to
sleep. A romantic idyll of the husband and wife is followed,
after their child has woken next morning, by a lively scene of
domesticity as the "gay conclusion." Strauss originally provided
explanatory headings for the individual sections of the score,
but he withdrew these before the work was printed, in his desire
to avoid the publication of unduly revealing programmes. By an
oversight a few unimportant remarks remained in the score, and
these were at once seized upon by Strauss's opponents. (The jocular "Ganz der Papa" (Papa all over) and "Ganz die Mama"
still appear in the score.) What were formerly identified as "The
husband," "The wife" and "The child" are now described merely
as the first, second and third themes. All these melodic ideas are
of a particularly popular character. Take, for example, the four
"masculine" themes at the beginning: first a "comfortable" entrance of the cellos and bassoons, then a "dreamy idea" of the
oboe, marked by a rising seventh, a "grumpy" clarinet figure,

254

and finally a "fiery" phrase of the violins–all heard within the first few bars. Natural vivacity and warmth mark the themes of the wife, whose volatile temperament ("lively and gay–giocoso–wrathful") bears an unmistakable resemblance to that of the "helpmate" in "Heldenleben"; the first motif, aptly enough, is an inversion of the husband's theme. Strauss called the "very tender theme" of the child an idea of "Haydnesque simplicity," and he gave it, unexpectedly but very effectively, to the oboe d'amore(!).

The way Strauss "plays" with these themes, never violating the laws of musical beauty despite all the constructive workmanship involved, is remarkable. Balanced dynamic proportions, clear outlines and easily appreciated construction provide the work with its natural effectiveness. Only at the close, in the "virtuistic Coda with a colossal crescendo" which crowns the double fugue, is the composer's voice obscured by excessive pomp à la Makart. The fact that right at the end, at the height of the unruly Stretta, the voice of the "husband" again comes powerfully to the fore, does something to mend matters. Busoni made the criticism of this Epilogue that Strauss "does not leave off when he should. He fails to recognize the mastery of the incomplete..." (If he had a collaborator when writing his tone poems, as he had with the operas, such errors in the overall conception would have been avoided.) In individual episodes of the Scherzo and Adagio passages of less originality go side by side with music of great depth and reflective calm such as the "Cradle Song" which is opened by two clarinets, the Notturno "Creation and Observation," and the gratifyingly unsentimental "Love Scene." Strauss added the last two of these titles only after the first German performance. Such clearly descriptive passages need only be *heard,* although illustrative features like the bell sounding in the evening and morning have their part to play. All nervous and agitated elements were banished from this score. When the master celebrated his eightieth birthday at Vienna in 1944, he conducted his Pastorale yet again with the Vienna Philharmonic. A recording has captured that performance for posterity.

*

During the second year of the Great War there appeared *"Eine Alpensinfonie."* More than ten years had elapsed since the completion of the "Domestica," and it was widely believed that Strauss had finally turned his back on symphonic music, to devote himself entirely to the opera stage. Later it was learned that he had in fact been engaged upon the composition of this work, which he was determined should be a particularly fine example of its class, for a long time, though with many interruptions. It seems scarcely credible that the first sketches for the sensuously pictorial "Alpensinfonie" date from 1911, the time of "Ariadne" with its classical elimination of inessentials. (Strauss wrote to Hofmannsthal: "I am waiting for you, and meanwhile torment myself with a symphony, which is giving me even less pleasure than shaking off cockchafers.") Equally incomprehensible is this work's proximity to the romantic mysticism of "Die Frau ohne Schatten" and to the meditative "Deutsche Motette," which occupied the composer at the same time as his Alpine poem. There are clearer resemblances between it and the decorative ballet "Josephslegende." Never again were contrasting styles to cross in Strauss's work as they did during this period. Never again was his aim so clear: to create a synthesis between, on the one hand psychological, descriptive music, and on the other self-sufficient music of classical simplicity. After it had been on the stocks for years, he surprised his friends by orchestrating this work of nearly an hour's duration, concerned with the beauties of life, in exactly a hundred days in the winter of 1914/15, during a creative pause between writing the second and third acts of "Frau ohne Schatten."

Just as the first tone poem "Aus Italien" had its origins in the experiences of nature in the south, the fifty-year-old composer here dealt with pictures and atmosphere of the beloved mountain world of his Upper Bavarian homeland. Long Alpine tours were unnecessary, as he had a beautiful view of the Zugspitze and the massive Wettersteingebirge from the windows of his country house at Garmisch, but the work naturally also contains impressions of the district around Berchtesgaden and other Alpine features. This is no musical work of Beethovenian feeling for nature, no paen of an ethical relationship between man and nature (any comparison with the "Pastoral Symphony" is misleading), but an imposing Alpine panorama made up of features of the landscape and experiences of nature. The misunderstanding with which this pleasant tableau of journeys amid

256

nature, a counterpart to Hodler's mountain landscapes, was received from the outset, arose on account of the unfortunate description "Symphony." This suggests a spiritual coming to grips with the mountain world which would have to show something of spiritual "heights" and "depths," and of elemental forces. (Gysi suggested that "A day amid the mountain peaks" would be a better title). In this respect the thoroughly naively planned "Alpensinfonie" cannot even be compared with Liszt's romantic "Bergsinfonie." Strauss kept to visible, factual objects. Spiritual reflection is restricted to the short episode of the "Elegy," which gives the wanderer a clue to the meaning of nature's riddles. Apart from that this richly melodic music, which is full of life, is characterized by its colourful outward effect. Everything appertaining to a mountain climb is to be found here, described in wholly unliterary music–although the tone poet Strauss had undoubtedly conquered far higher peaks in the past. The complete absence of eroticism is noticeable. The traveller remains alone with nature. He seeks refuge in isolation.

Description of nature? The painter Renoir wrote: "How difficult it is not to miss the exact moment when one must cease to imitate nature in a painting. The picture must not smell of the model, but one must sense nature through it." The musician Strauss went on making music, unconcerned with such aesthetic considerations. In his attempt to "paint" nature as exactly as possible he descended to naturalistic effects–the Alpine picture really "smells" of the "model." Not only when he uses cow bells, wind and thunder machines to illustrate sounds of nature (the sensation-seeking listener is denied only a rain machine), but also in other musical pictures which the listener feels he can almost touch with his hands, no purely fresco-like detail is missing. By this time Strauss had no scruples about introducing explanatory words in the score. The work opens with the mysterious atmosphere of "Night:" solemn chords herald the mountain motif, played by the brass. The sun rises in a radiant A major; it is daybreak. After a short walk across the plain the "ascent" begins. Hunting horns are heard in the distance–the traveller enters the woods with horns and trombones. The "stroll by the brook" leads to the "waterfall," which rushes and glistens in the violins (spiccato), harps and celesta. The mountain lover strides across "flowery meadows" and up to "mountain pastureland." He continues to ascend "through thicket and underwood" in a fugato, until he arrives "on the glacier." (The sparkling of the everlasting snow is depicted with masterly skill by the trumpets at the top of their compass.) "Dangerous moments" have to be gone through. At last, however, the "summit" is reached: a hesitant oboe melody represents the oppressive feeling in the traveller's breast. The experience becomes transformed into a "vision" of the lonely nobility of nature. "Mists gather" (portrayed by the heckelphone). "The sun gradually becomes darkened" to the soft sound of the organ; the cor anglais plays its "Elegy." Silence is all around, the "calm before the storm." "Thunder and storm" (a tumultuous orchestral deluge) unexpectedly catch the traveller during his "descent." His route again takes him past the waterfall, but he does not stop there. Finally "Dusk," a sumptuous sound picture, a contemplative dying fall, and once again "Night," with a descending scale in B♭ minor: tranquillity after danger and exertion. The ring has closed.

After Schuch's death the score of the "Alpensinfonie" was dedicated to "Count Seebach and the Royal Orchestra at Dresden, in gratitude;" unfortunately the composer gave the manuscript to the French nation, which he admired, amid the turmoil of the months following the end of the Second World War. Technically an amazing achievement; it is in one movement, but contains the elements of the four movements of a conventional symphony with interwoven variations, and at the same time an example of mastery in the use of an oversize instrumental apparatus, together with a "distant orchestra," which could scarcely be excelled. The glow of colour and the transparency of a really live tonal imagination give the basically unexciting subject light and shade. (Strauss published a simplified version of the monster score, omitting the organ, in 1934). When the work was given its first performance by the Dresden Orchestra, in Berlin in 1915, the principal objection was to the striking diatonic simplicity, indeed banality, of certain turns of melody. Can it be doubted that in this nature idyll (how much closer to nature the music to "Daphne" is!) Strauss consciously sought simplicity? In innumerable places he wrote naively happy melodies in the bright dress of luscious string euphony, easily appreciated and uncomplicated. Before the Berlin première he declared: "I wanted to compose, for once, as a cow gives milk."   *

It almost seemed as though, with the nature pictures of his mountain symphony, Strauss had turned away from his youthful love of symphonic poems. The plan of an "Antichrist," which was to follow that work, came to nothing. Only a few sketches survive of a new "absolute" Symphony in E♭, the first since the early work in F minor. Opera held him in its grip. Nevertheless Strauss later thought in terms of a new tone poem from time to time. In 1929 he wrote: "Time and again I wanted to return to symphonic literature, which occupied me so much during my early years, but so far nothing worthwhile has occurred to me." This remained the case until 1939, when, in company with several Anglo-Saxon and French composers, he received a commission to compose a festive work for the celebration of the 2600th anniversary of the foundation of the Japanese Empire. Strauss, who was then occupied with the completion of the score of "Danae," accepted the commission after some hesitation, and wrote his *"Japanische Festmusik,"* whose duration is about that of "Don Juan," within a short space of time, so that the first performance in Tokyo could take place in 1940 as planned. Undoubtedly this late symphonic work with its themes which are remote from the experience of present-day listeners belongs to the sphere of programme music. It is equally clear that this last composition of Strauss for a very large orchestra is an occasional piece, in which he was not greatly concerned with subjective personal statements. In any event, he hit on the required basic note of joyful festivity. He wrote a work which is not lacking in natural verve, but which avoids cheap exotic effects, despite considerable use of temple gongs. Constructed as a symphonic movement, it consists of five sections which the composer entitled as follows: Seascape, Cherryblossom Festival, Volcanic Eruption, Attack of the Samurai, and Hymn of the Emperor; tone painting proper is restricted to the description of an erupting volcano.

It is greatly to be regretted that at the age of seventy-eight Strauss felt himself unable to bring to fruition the happy idea of a tone poem *"Die Donau."* He gave the first information concerning this work "for full orchestra, chorus and organ" when writing in February 1942 to congratulate the Vienna Philharmonic Orchestra on its hundredth anniversary. "The musical gift which I had in mind for my dear friends and artistic colleagues

"Die Donau": *Sketch for the uncompleted tone poem (1942)*

on the occasion of this jubilee cannot, unfortunately, be ready by the desired date, however much I exert myself. Feeling does not become transformed into melodies as quickly as it did with the great old masters ... I therefore ask you to have patience until my gift is worthy of its recipients, so that it will remain in your memories as a living expression of my love and admiration ..." Why did Strauss evidently find it increasingly difficult to proceed with this composition? The fact that he was engaged on other tasks (including the composition of the new horn concerto) at the same time points to deep-lying reasons. The cares of that time, with the war threatening the spiritual life of the nation to an ever increasing extent, told against this idyllic work. It was undoubtedly suggested by Smetana's "Vltava," but Strauss cannot have known Janáček's "Donau" fragment. The time of "Die Donau" was soon over for ever. When Strauss thanked the Vienna Philharmonic for their congratulations on his 85th birthday he sent them a page of the sketches with the dedication: "A few drops from the dried-up source of the Danube." Rolf Wilhelm has written that the work was to have lasted about half an hour, according to a reconstruction of the four extant sketch books and two piano sketches with detailed indications of the instrumentation. As in the case of the "Alpensinfonie," Strauss intended to produce a linked succession of landscape scenes: Donaueschingen Castle, The Source, Town Views, Narrows and Rapids, Woodland, Cornfields, Ingolstadt (here the theme of the wife from the "Domestica" was to be introduced, as Pauline Strauss was born in Ingolstadt), Regensburg, Passau, The Danube Nibelungs, Wachau Vintage Festival, and Vienna, with chorus singing words of Weinheber. Strauss is said to have considered seriously the possibility of the score being completed by another hand from his sketches. A sense of responsibility to Strauss's memory can only prompt one to warn against any such attempt. There can be no doubt that Strauss's project represented an attempt to extend the lighter, transparent style of his old age to the sphere of programme music.

*

Beethoven's Overture "The Consecration of the House" may have been in Strauss's mind when he wrote his *Festliches Präludium"* in 1913 on the occasion of the opening of the new Konzerthaus in Vienna. This work for large orchestra and organ is pompous and radiant, with an air of "Die Meistersinger" about it and in a diatonic C major. It is massively and decoratively effective–but in its overblown scoring (for an even larger orchestra than the "Alpensinfonie") it expresses a bloated concept of music which is very much a product of the age. This work, an "occasional composition written to order," demands no fewer than 96 strings, corresponding wind, eight timpani and a dozen trumpets in the distance–demands which, naturally, have hardly ever been met. Sheer sound is the decisive element of the piece, which says virtually nothing about Strauss the man–a rare occurrence among his works.

Human feeling makes up for this in two minor works of concerto type. The world-famous composer wrote them in the years 1924/27 for the Viennese pianist Paul Wittgenstein, who had lost his right arm in the First World War. The two works for left hand alone with orchestra, which were printed privately and have only recently become generally available, were marked "Exclusive property of Herr Paul Wittgenstein." While the *"Parergon zur Sinfonia domestica"* is to be numbered, in a sense,

261

among the autobiographical works, the *"Panathenäenzug,"* symphonic etudes in the form of a Passacaglia, must be considered a programmatic work. "Parergon" commences with a troubled Introduction representing feelings of anxiety on account of the illness of Strauss's son; the main body of the work then consists of idyllic pictures of happy childhood, for which Strauss employed themes from the "Domestica." "Panathenäenzug," with its strict formal structure founded on a succession of notes in the bass, has a festive character. (The title refers to the greatest and most glittering festival in honour of the goddess Athene, with games, competitions and sacrifices.) Here again Strauss chose a symphonic style, treating the technically brilliant solo line as an obbligato orchestral part: this procedure was far removed from the classical ideals of his last instrumental concertos. Among the concert works composed for Wittgenstein neither the occasional pieces by Strauss nor those of the Viennese composers Franz Schmidt and Korngold have proved to possess lasting life. There remain the Fourth Concerto by Prokofieff, which appeared in 1931, and the bitter-sweet poem which Ravel completed shortly before his death.

SONGS AND CHORAL WORKS

Long before Strauss reached the realm of opera he was regarded in the musical world primarily as a *lyricist*. Bie called his exuberant springtime of song "a pre-echo of the great works," and the songs of the mature master, with equal justification, an "after-echo." The most successful of his early songs, "Zueignung," "Morgen," "Heimliche Aufforderung," "Cäcilie" and others, were taken into the programmes of lieder recitals to such an extent that one could really talk of "popular hit songs" —not to mention "Ständchen," whose "invincible popularity was later to wring so many sighs from him." These melodically expressive, universally sung but frequently over-ingratiating and unadventurous lieder were often received with pleasure by those who stood out against Strauss's early symphonic works. Appearances are, however, deceptive. The song writer Strauss is by no means really well-known. Among his 150 or so published songs it is always the same twenty dead certain successes which are performed, with at most another twenty occasionally chosen. The music lover who is solely a listener has hardly any idea of the extent and scope of Strauss's output of songs, about which he declared to Tenschert towards the end of his life that in its "variety, particularly with regard to the characteristic and humorous songs . . ." it had "not yet received its due recognition." His compositions in this medium, ranging from the Christmas song he wrote at the age of six to the Four Last Songs, mark the beginning and end of his creative career.

Was Strauss a born lyricist? He certainly lacked a restless inner will impelling him to dream in colours and notes. He was not a lyricist whose magic constantly turned everyday things into symbols of things spiritual. His poetic preserve lay in the actuality and reality of subjective experience, and this experience was

263

expressed in music markedly conservative in flavour. His most beautiful songs were written for his young wife, or later for particular performers who were in close contact with his art. It is an art which, to a greater extent than his works in other classes, cannot be exonerated from the charge of conforming to the taste of the times to an extent which was almost dangerous. Overtones of a certain "salon" romanticism cannot go unnoticed, at least in the earlier songs. It is unmistakable that Strauss the lyricist based himself on Schubert, Schumann and above all Liszt, rather than on the psychological or declamatory song. Before the *"melodic song"* proper was superseded by the more varied powers and new expressive possibilities of musical declamation, it found a truly lyrical exponent in Strauss. What melodic richness within this world of poetic miniatures! What a sense of form and feeling for spiritually sublimated sensations! What lively imagination, joy in pictorial imagery and sensuous richness! Nevertheless the strong personality of the composer did not assert itself so markedly in the lyrical sphere as in his works in other categories. Was that because Strauss confronted the homely song of Schubertian romanticism with the assured effectiveness of the concert song, because, unlike Brahms and Hugo Wolf, he underlined the contrast by forcing songs into the evening dress of the concert platform? Then again, most of his songs were born as an offspring of the mood of the moment, often while he was engaged upon the composition of large-scale works.

It is therefore understandable that Strauss did not choose the song *texts* with the same exercise of his powers of literary judgement which marked his work in the field of opera. The lyricist turned unconcernedly to poems by writers of his time. The generation of writers with whom he grew up, and in many cases came into personal contact, provided his raw material. That would have been quite in order, and a model even for present-day composers, had Strauss shown more discernment in his choice of poems. Many of his song texts by Gilm, Liliencron, Bodman, Schack and others appear wholly representative of the beauty-drunk lyricism of field, woodland and meadow, devoid of inner meaning, which has its being either in sickly nature mood-painting ("Kennst du die Blume, die märchenhafte?") or in an excessive outpouring of feeling ("Ich trage meine Minne von Wonne stumm"). The essence of such examples lies in raising reality to the idealistic level through invoking the sense of the hymnic and of "Weltschmerz." One must differentiate between the poets. For example the Scot John Henry Mackay, author of the contemplative "Morgen" and "Verführung" with its glow of colour, stands incomparably higher than Felix Dahn with his sentimentally pointed "Mädchenblumen." Naturally one also comes across treasures, songs like Otto Julius Bierbaum's "Traum durch die Dämmerung," which pours forth poignant melancholy, reflecting the artistic atmosphere of the dying century and its society:

> Broad meadows in the grey of dusk;
> The sun has gone, the stars appear,
> Now I go to the loveliest woman . . .
> I do not go quickly, I hasten not,
> Drawn by a delicate silken band
> Through the twilight to the land of love
> In a blue, gentle light.

Songs in a class of their own are those based on the young *Soziallyrik* of the 'nineties, to words by Richard Dehmel and Karl Henckell. Here the young Court Conductor showed clearly that he was not only at home in the artistic salons of Munich-Schwabing and Berlin-W. Strauss was the first lyrical composer of recent times who ventured away from his bourgeois milieu into the realm of social criticism. It cannot be doubted that at that time he felt himself greatly attracted to the progressive ideas of Dehmel and Henckell. It is therefore all the more to be regretted that he got no further than the four famous examples of this class of song; in all other cases he selected less significant poems by these authors ("Befreit," "Waldseligkeit," "Ruhe, meine Seele" and others). It was in the "Arbeitsmann" and "Lied an meinen Sohn" of Dehmel that the new note of challenge was sounded for the first time: "Der Sturm behorcht mein Vaterhaus . . ." Then, at the dawn of the new century, came the moving "Blindenklage" of Henckell: "Wenn ich dich frage, dem das Leben blüht." Above all there was the stirring "Lied des Steinklopfers," which raises Henckell's words "Ich bin kein Minister . . ." to the level of a social indictment by means of a grippingly realistic mode of expression:

265

Today, a pauper,
I have eaten nothing,
The All-Merciful
Has sent nothing.
Of golden wine
I have dreamed,
And break stones
For the Fatherland . . .

There is scarcely any connection between this great humanistic art (which deserves to be rescued from oblivion) and the contents of the perfumed Biedermeier artistry of Dahn and Busse, or the "Germanistic songs" whose existence can be explained only as a product of the unbridled spirit of the age. Strauss's choice of poetic forms is happier in pieces of folksong character: the cradle songs, whose words themselves are charming ("Träume du, mein süßes Leben," "Muttertändelei" and others), or the little gems of humour which correspond so well to the sparkling exuberance of Strauss's nature ("Für fünfzehn Pfennig" from "Des Knaben Wunderhorn," "Ach, weh mir unglückhaftem Mann" etc.). Sometimes, too, Strauss liked to indulge in satire. But where could he find a satirist whose verses hit the bull's eye, whose irony went beyond the sphere of private jokes between like-minded artists? Some excellent opportunities for effective literary-musical collaboration were lost here.

Strauss did not avoid the German classics-but he set their poems far less frequently than those of contemporary writers. There were long intervals between the isolated appearances among his songs of the great classical names, Goethe, Schiller and Heine, while Eichendorff, Mörike, Keller and others were conspicuous by their absence. It must be recognized that Strauss was not primarily interested in "setting to music" a text which had already been "composed" as a song by the poet. The verses of such men as Klopstock, Uhland and Rückert appeared to him better suited to his purpose. Many unspoken things from the world of Rückert called forth some of Strauss's loveliest lyrical inspirations (first and foremost the profound tone poetry of the "Deutsche Motette"). He was similarly attracted to Brentano: in the whole range of his vocal art there is scarcely anything more precious than the fragrant and intimate Six Songs Op. 68. With

Goethe, whose "Pilger's Morgenlied" and "Gefunden" he had set rather non-committally in his early years, he almost always had a sense of personal communication during the years of his maturity. Significantly enough his Goethe settings were, without exception, occasional pieces (including the three songs from the "Bücher des Unmuts" with which the fifty-four-year-old composer intended to annoy his publishers)–not lieder in the traditional sense but reflections, not without a tinge of Goethe's profundity. Strauss, who proclaimed the greatness of Goethe throughout his life, and who judged all art by Goethe's standards, had, as a composer, a natural reluctance to try to match the poet's genius.

The question whether Hölderlin's rather obscure language could or should be used as the basis of a vocal composition became acute in the case of the Hölderlin Hymns. They enchant the ear, while presenting only the superficial outlines of the poet's craggy spiritual landscape. The meaning and shape of Hölderlin's meditations are not to be illustrated by a carefree setting which flows smoothly along from word to word. While Hölderlin may be regarded as particularly unsuited to musical treatment, as his heightened speech-melody in itself reaches the extreme bounds of musical prosody, it may well be that simple rhymed verses which would otherwise have been forgotten long ago have proved to be excellent moulds to contain outpourings of musical feeling. The contrast between Mackay and Hölderlin demonstrates this point very clearly. When, shortly before his death, Strauss turned to Eichendorff and to the poems of Hermann Hesse, wonderfully clear expressions of ideas concerning the departure from this beautiful world, he probably regretted his neglect of other masters of the word.

*

Strauss's *song style* can provide no surprises if it is considered in conjuction with what has been said concerning his personal style in general. Everything that he later undertook in the large-scale forms of the musical stage he tried out in his early songs with piano. While following Liszt in the expression of late romantic feeling, he formed his song style on the basis of melodic impulse. With one great proviso, however–that the melodic line is really free only in a few youthful pieces. The melodic flow of

267

his typical songs demonstrates the greatest diversity in the division of vocal line and instrumental accompaniment. Strauss complied strictly with the principle of exact word accentuation. (When he paid insufficient attention to this, as in "Ständchen," he was most dissatisfied with the result.) He followed the contours of every word, every alteration of the poetic idea, without ever allowing the cantabile phrases to descend to the level of declamation. In the formation of the vocal line, the modulations and changes of key, a Strauss song is the sensitive tonal vessel for the text. Its colour and atmosphere derive from the words; the "verse governs the melody of the song," as Strauss once remarked, and the piano's completely independent function is to add depth and inwardness of feeling to the content of the song. Examination of the character of his melodies shows that they can never be separated from the poetic word. The fact that so many of his songs (for example "Morgen," "Traum durch die Dämmerung", and "Freundliche Vision") represent an absolute musical-poetic entity in the minds of those who know them, emphasizes this. The manner in which Strauss apparently reduced every poem to prose and employed a heightened form of the declamation pattern thus obtained gave rise to a good deal of unjust criticism.

The astonishing fact is that despite the mosaic of brilliant details and the pronounced textual illustration, this art of lieder writing almost always preserves the natural verve of the melody. This lyrical flow normally seems to proceed from the spirit of vocalization. As a rule a basic melodic motif runs throughout the song, especial importance often being attached to a particular upbeat (as in the famous "Auf, hebe die funkelnde Schale"). It is only in a few songs that the sonorous piano accompaniment with its full chords endangers the proportion and form of the composition. Strauss was never for a moment in doubt that only what had to be said could be given convincing colour. Moments of unduly sentimental pathos occurred from time to time. More than once, however, surprise was caused when songs considered dense in construction were performed with the orchestral accompaniment which Strauss arranged later, and now appeared loose and transparent in texture. In a great many Strauss songs less emphasis should be placed on the romantic, decorative element, and even the "New-German ardent lyricism" (Weissmann) can be interpreted in a more relaxed, baroque manner. (Strauss himself, in his early years, often played the accompaniments in a finely poetic, decidedly "free" manner.) The way he transformed the word which established the atmosphere into a musical symbol and incorporated it into a picture in sound sheds light on the art of the later tone poet. Whether he had to illustrate such ideas as the sun, rain or the soughing of wind, silver birches or a slow mountain descent, to make bees hum or depict the rustling of treetops, Strauss did not consider it a burden, but a task for which he was well equipped. Sometimes in such illustrations of nature, such as the stormy night of "Lied an meinen Sohn" and the thundery atmosphere in "Lied der Frauen," the piano accompaniment is extremely difficult to play. In Strauss's later songs illustrative modes of expression became less important than an intensive spiritualization of the relationship between words and music. Strauss had long since turned his attention primarily to that species of vocal music which offers the greatest opportunities to the development of musical ideas from verbal inspiration, resulting in the freest and most varied effects—opera.

The songs fall stylistically into three groups. The first category is serious in character, and derives its mood content from the combination of arioso lyricism and a background of piano tone colour. Such songs, in which voice and piano together create a lyrical poem (particularly successful in this respect are "Traum durch die Dämmerung," "Ich trage meine Minne," "Befreit," and "Ruhe, meine Seele"), are regarded by many as the essence of his song style. It was his ambition to create as perfectly harmonious a bond as possible between music and words; he was greatly talented in this respect, and deserved to succeed. The lively melodic lines of many of the songs suggest the lyrical element of the operas, although Strauss never achieved in his songs the melodic and declamatory conciseness of his dramatic works. The romantically coloured song of popular cut often consists merely of atmospheric music, so it is always in danger of becoming superficial. The standard of taste at the turn of the century is reflected all-too accurately by the rhapsodic "Cäcilie" and the sentimental "Allerseelen" ... (though it should be mentioned that excellent lieder singers have recently raised their performances of these songs to a far higher artistic level by the stylistic purity of their interpretations). The second class of song

269

is of far more account: the aquarelle inspired by a relaxed poetic idea, light and delicately fashioned, in which romanticism appears stylized in bright colours. Pieces of this serene nature are already to be met with in the "Schlichte Weisen" Op. 21 (the light-footed "All mein Gedanken, mein Herz und mein Sinn") and later in the graceful "Schlagende Herzen," the sprightly songs from "Des Knaben Wunderhorn," the "Wiegenliedchen" and many others. Such pieces may be less melodically striking than the most popular songs, as capricious, gaily exuberant elements necessitate a refinement of melody and a reduction of the romantic emphasis placed on crucial words. Thus the Brentano songs, most of which are written for coloratura soprano, as true children of the muse of charming artistry, include many pearls of this scherzando genre: the tender "Säusle, liebe Myrte," the naive "Ich wollt' ein Sträußlein binden," and "Amor" with its birdlike twittering ... Finally there is the category of vigorous songs reflecting earthly, sensuous joy in which the mature master, possessed by now of all the opera composer's means of expression, shows his hand clearly. The melos is even more radiant than hitherto, at the same time completely free of pathos or heaviness. Such songs include "Als mir dein Lied erklang," ringing triumphantly through the night, the fiery "Pokal," and the boldly rhythmic idyll "Schlechtes Wetter."

For his wife, whom Strauss often described as the best interpreter of his lieder, he orchestrated a considerable number of his songs with piano. The next step was to compose original *songs with orchestra*, which were not merely songs with piano superficially enlarged. Before "Don Quixote" he wrote the "Four Songs for solo voice with orchestral accompaniment," after poems by Mackay, Bodman, Schiller and Goethe–a cycle of extraordinary literary diversity, unified only in its acknowledgment to the spirit of earthly joy. (The "Gesang der Apollo-priesterin" represents a remarkable mixture of antique nobility, "Parsifal" mysticism, and the characteristics of Strauss's youthful style.) The two orchestral songs which followed were of strong musical characterization: the sadly sweet "Notturno" to words by Dehmel, and Rückert's "Nächtlicher Gang," painted with dark realism. A first conclusion to the works of this type was provided by the Three Hymns written in the 'twenties, despite the contradiction, already mentioned, of settings of Hölderlin by an extrovert south-German composer. Almost classical in their clarity of form, with baroque turns of melody, these songs ("Hymne an die Liebe," "Rückkehr in die Heimat," and "Die Liebe") bear witness to imaginative powers scarcely lessened by the passage of time. The last four orchestral songs to words by Eichendorff and Hesse, with the flowing melismas of their vocal lines, represent a lyrical epilogue to Strauss's work–music written on the brink of death, whose poignant sense of bidding farewell can be matched only by that of Brahms's "Vier ernste Gesänge." In few scores of the twentieth century has the demand for beauty been so truly fulfilled.

Even before the young Strauss had given the world his first set of songs Op. 10, including "Zueignung" and "Allerseelen," he had written a great many songs. (Steinitzer gave details of some of them in his biography.) The flood of songs which followed was poured out, with only short breaks, over the periods 1885/88 and 1894/98–interrupted by the years during which Strauss devoted himself to the composition of symphonic poems. After he had moved to Berlin there was a further harvest of song with Opp. 46 to 49 ("Waldseligkeit" and "Lied des Steinklopfers"). The period of the "Domestica" saw the appearance of the cycle Op. 56 including "Blindenklage" and "Frühlingsfeier." Then it was not until after "Die Frau ohne Schatten" that Strauss returned to song writing with the twelve perfectly aimed satirical songs of the "Krämerspiegel" to words by Kerr, dedicated "in a gay mood" to Friedrich Rösch, his companion in the struggle for composers' rights. The magical Brentano songs (later orchestrated) and the five short songs to poems by Heine and Arnim were really the last fruits of this autumn of song at a time of full maturity. What followed, the five artistically exotic "Gesänge des Orients" from the Chinese, and the various isolated pieces to texts by Goethe and Weinheber, lacked that power of conviction which returned to such immense effect in the last songs with orchestra.

*

The Strauss song–the world of the musical dramatist in miniature ... Who would assert that any such song, however unassuming, was merely poured out as the composer felt it and not formed? The laws of poetry and music can be seen at work in

Strauss as clearly as in any song writer who has employed other stylistic elements and has perhaps entered regions of profounder expression. An excellent example of this fact is offered by *"Freundliche Vision,"* a setting of a beautiful poem by Bierbaum which runs as follows:

> Nicht im Schlafe hab' ich geträumt.
> Hell am Tage sah ich's schön vor mir:
>> Eine Wiese voller Margariten.
>> tief ein weißes Haus in grünen Büschen,
>> Götterbilder leuchten aus dem Laube.
>> Und ich geh' mit einer, die mich lieb hat
>> ruhigen Gemütes in die Kühle
>> dieses weißen Hauses,
>> in den Frieden,
>> der voll Schönheit wartet,
>> daß wir kommen.

> I did not dream of it by night,
> I saw it before me in bright daylight:
>> A meadow full of marguerites.
>> A white house deep in the green bushes,
>> Divine forms shine through the foliage,
>> And I walk with one who loves me
>> At peace into the cool
>> Of this white house,
>> Into the peace
>> Which waits, full of beauty,
>> Until we come.

The text, poetry in sound from the realm of subjective experience of nature, falls into two parts: a short explanatory introduction of two lines, and the vision itself of seven lines. The music is based on a rhythmically flowing semiquaver motif which persists from beginning to end. The curve of the melody forms a unified entity. (Strauss did not regard as a practical possibility a division of the piece into a recitative and aria in miniature.) The two introductory lines give rise to effective modulations from B major to the principal tonality of C major. This harmonic contrast corresponds to the images reproduced in the music: "Nicht im Schlafe" (B major) and "Hell am Tage" (C major).

September (Hermann Hesse)   Richard Strauss.

"September"
Beginning and end of the score of the last of the four songs with orchestra
of 1948, the 84-year-old composer's last completed work

In the main body of the piece the melos flows even more broadly; the cantilena attempts to overstep the natural breaks at the ends of lines by means of tied-over notes. At the end of the first section ("Götterbilder leuchten aus dem Laube") the dominant key of G major is reached, but it immediately assumes the role of the fifth in C major. At the end of the setting of the text proper Strauss, following Schubert's example, repeats certain key words of the poem as a kind of coda to sum up the content of the song: "Und ich geh' mit einer, die mich lieb hat–in den Frieden–voll Schönheit." The seven-bar epilogue, built up on a pedal point C, exudes peace and quiet. No vocal effect running counter to the words has been admitted. A few subtle poetic points deserve especial mention: the words "eine Wiese" and "tief" are matched by particularly convincing musical images. The solemn setting of the word "Götterbilder" and the unusual turn of harmony at "Kühle" are also noteworthy. A little work of art in itself: the simple structure of suspensions with the diminished seventh on B which gives an unexpected colour to the word "Schönheit." Hardly anyone listening to this song, with its duration of only a few minutes, will have any inkling of the range and diversity of the means of expression employed.

*

In any consideration of the *choral works* the attention is drawn to a work which represents one of Strauss's most profound utterances: the *"Deutsche Motette."* This nobly conceived humanistic document of 1913, composed between "Ariadne" and "Frau ohne Schatten" in the "great" creative period, is among those works which bring a glow of happiness wherever they are heard, but which have never become widely known on account of their difficulty. Strauss had sensed the beauties of Rückert's language fifteen years earlier when (together with Schiller's "Abend") he set the poet's "Hymne" "Jakob, dein verlorener Sohn kehret wieder" as one of the "Two Songs for sixteen-part mixed-voice chorus a cappella." The unusual combination of a fervent glow of colour and skilful polyphony which aroused admiration in that instance created a really deep impression when similar characteristics were given, by means of enhanced spiritual and colouristic resources, to a work related in content, the "Deutsche Motette" for four solo voices and sixteen-part mixed voice chorus a cappella. This rapt evening hymn with the trusting appeal "Wach in mir, du Licht, o wach in mir" is full of deep spiritual strength. The complex structure of this score seems wholly based on the works of 17th-century masters, while the use of modern chromatic and enharmonic techniques has greatly extended the range of harmonic expression. Like all the fruits of Strauss's creative technique, the contrapuntal effects here are logical and dependent on the work's content. The planned economy of the layout is not affected by the elements of tone painting which appear. The "Motette" points forward to the choral Finale of "Friedenstag," but its basic character of hymnic devotion is far removed from the sphere of opera . . . Strauss himself called this latter-day masterpiece of the art of motet composition, with its profound spiritual quality, a "really good piece." Outstanding among the few vocal ensembles which venture upon performing it from time to time is the Dresden Kreuzchor.

The other choral works are of less consequence. *"Wandrers Sturmlied"* for six-part chorus and large orchestra, which still sometimes appears in the programmes of large municipal choirs in Germany, has been mentioned in the context of the youthful works. The ballad *"Taillefer"* for mixed chorus, soli and orchestra, after Uhland, was composed by the young honorary Doctor of the University of Heidelberg as a pompous gift of gratitude. Here Strauss was clearly following in the wake of Loewe's ballad style. What a curiosity in the literature of choral music is this piece for a colossal instrumental apparatus reminiscent of the wildest dreams of Berlioz, and a giant chorus! (Strauss prefaced the score of this "Doctorate work" with the words: "'Taillefer' is intended for performance in large halls, as will be seen from the layout and orchestral scoring.") In other occasional pieces in this class, too, Strauss experimented with sound effects on such a heroic scale that the results were artistically negligible. While acting as adjudicator at several important competitive festivals around the turn of the century he became interested in music for male voice chorus. Both the male voice choruses a cappella after Herder's "Stimmen der Völker" and the Teutonic "Bardengesang" after Klopstock's "Hermannsschlacht" for male voice chorus and orchestra gave offence on account of their unconcealed bombast typical of the Kaiser's era. It may appear doubtful whether Strauss's "dear Father" was particularly pleased by the dedication to him of the martial "Schlachtgesang."

Strauss's personality was reflected to a far greater extent by a number of vocal works of his middle and later creative periods. From the short cantata of 1914, whose poetic text by Hofmannsthal raises it to a high artistic level, to the male voice chorus "Durch Einsamkeit" of 1940, after Wildgans, Strauss frequently demonstrated his understanding of the possibilities of the choral work for men's voices. In his song cycle *"Die Tageszeiten"* after Eichendorff for male voice chorus and orchestra, dating from the Schubert year 1928, he sought a Renaissance of the romantic spirit in a vocal symphony of inner companionship with nature. "Der Morgen," "Mittagsruh" and, particularly lovely, "Abend" giving place to "Nacht"–all glow with the magic of a warm summer day. This work, whose diversity of invention owes much to folk music, makes unusual demands on the singers, as the voices are used to provide quasi-instrumental tone colour. The orchestra unfolds no unnecessary volume of sound. Traces of Mendelssohn, Brahms, and of Strauss's own earlier works are constantly to be heard in this music depicting the transformation of nature during a day. Ten years later a choral work which Eugen Papst had asked him to write got no further than the planning stage. With his last choral work, the vocal Epilogue to the opera "Daphne," written in 1946, Strauss turned in this medium, as in others, to a classical "last period" style in the gentle twilight of romanticism. This Epilogue *"An den Baum Daphne"* for nine-part chorus a cappella is a piece of immense technical difficulty. Strauss wrote this expression of mankind's homage to the evergreen laurel for the Concert Association of the Vienna State Opera Chorus. It is certainly no conventional item of the choral repertoire, but a late affirmation of subjective beauty which makes very free use of words which Gregor originally intended to appear in the opera. (In the extended concluding section the singers vocalize). The whole is the most interesting example of a characteristic of Strauss–his ability to return to a mood-picture created earlier and, using the same thematic material, to "compose it afresh." The eighty-two-year-old composer sought the peace of solitary nature.

THE CURTAIN RISES

EVERYONE MUST START SOMEWHERE, AND ONLY IF WE know the beginnings can we judge the conclusion. *"Guntram,"* with which the young Strauss (who was, however, as old as Mozart at the time of "Figaro") entered the opera scene, has never, as the master's "youthful indiscretion," established a firm place for itself in the opera repertoire. Nevertheless it represents the fateful transformation of the symphonic into the dramatic composer. With "Guntram" he was drawn (though not as yet finally) into the orbit of his sun—opera. He had soon found his way to the opera stage as a conductor, he had arranged Gluck's "Iphigénie en Tauride," and now he made his debut as an opera composer. As Strauss often acknowledged, the decisive influence was that of Alexander Ritter. "I owe it to him that he discovered my dramatic gift. Without his urging and his collaboration, incurable enthusiast for the mighty works of Richard Wagner that I was, I would scarcely have had the idea of writing an opera, as librettists were not available or, like Eberhard König (who later wrote for Hans Sommer), did not inspire me."

It was almost inevitable that the twenty-three-year-old Munich opera conductor should still be hopelessly under the influence of Wagner and Schopenhauer at the time of the original conception of his music drama. Saturated with the ideas of the Wagnerian "Gesamtkunstwerk" and its dominant theme of redemption, engrossed by the vision of "Tod und Verklärung," Strauss felt himself impelled, during the years which saw his mastery developing, toward his own idealistic utterance in the tradition of "Tristan" and "Parsifal." Although "unfortunately" he felt himself to possess "no 'poetic' talent," he wrote his own text, as befitted a true Wagnerian. (In his old age he described this libretto not as a "masterpiece" but as a "journeyman's piece".) However, it was several years before he began the composition, at Weimar early in 1892 (". . . a wonderful time! There I won my beloved Pauline . . ."). When Strauss finally started work on the music of the first act he did not, surprisingly enough, release himself from the spell of Wagner. Although in the meantime he had created the musically individualistic tone poems, documents of radical (so-called) "progress" of the epoch, "Don Juan," "Macbeth" and "Tod und Verklärung," Strauss remained true to the Wagnerian ideal in "Guntram." "Freshly Wagnerized" as the libretto was, as a musician he made no attempt to escape from the power of his great predecessor.

How did Strauss come upon the unusual subject of his first opera? He read in the Vienna "Neue Freie Presse" an historical account of a mysterious order of minnesingers founded in Austria during the middle ages, whose members called themselves "Contenders for love," since they fought on behalf of love. The subject blazed up in Strauss. He was filled with the Christian altruism of the idea of the "Band," and he realized clearly the possibility of the confrontation of the peaceable hero and the ethical community . . . The course of the action, set in the 13th century and freely invented, is briefly as follows: Guntram, the minnesinger, saves Freihild, the daughter of an old Duke who has given his child and the land to an unworthy noble, from death at her own hand. He tries to move the husband's heart, but that tyrant draws his sword, and Guntram strikes him down in self-defence. On the Duke's orders Guntram is thrown into a dungeon, there to await death. His companion Friedhold, the emissary of the Band, and Freihild, open the way to freedom for him. Guntram accepts their assistance, but not for his love of the woman or in order to rejoin the Band; he means to live in isolation as his conscience demands. This conclusion, inspired by a reading of Max Stirner's chef d'œuvre "Der Einzige und sein Eigentum," in which the "superman" of Nietzsche clearly makes his presence felt, was preceded by a different version which was superseded before the world première at Weimar in May 1894. In that version Guntram sacrificed his desire for isolation to his vow, and returned to the Band: ". . . my God speaks to me through myself!" During the composition of the last act Strauss decided on the change of the originally altruistic character of Guntram, making him an anarchistic lone wanderer when he was "suddenly filled with disgust by the self-destruction of the will" (Rolland). The reproach of Ritter, who was closely identified with the idealistic world of this work, that the altered conclusion was "Unchristian" and the hero's character "impious," was a hard blow to the young composer. "Through the new form of the third act you have thoroughly spoilt your work, because 1. the work is now robbed of all tragedy. 2. The very minimum, indispensable element of artistic unity has been removed. 3. The character of the hero has become a patched-up, psychologically quite impossible absence of character. 4. The tendency of the work is now highly immoral, mocking at all ethics... Dear friend, come to your senses! Do not totally ruin your work whose first two acts are so beautiful ..." Strauss still tried to win over the faithful Ritter to his own views. "I am doing nothing with the third act until I have played it over to you; I still cherish the hope that its music will reconcile you to it ..." "Ritter never quite forgave me for the repudiation of the minnesinger Band (third act, scene between Guntram and Friedhold), in which Guntram passes judgment on himself and denies the Band the right to punish him," Strauss confessed in the account of his youth and formative years.

Time has decided against "Guntram." Too much immature idealism weighs down the concept of the "Germanic troubadour troupe" (Gysi), whose resigned hero has about him hardly anything of the gay vigour of the young "storm and stress" tone poet. It would naturally be a mistake to search for connections with Strauss's personal or family life in "Guntram." Strauss himself repeatedly denied the existence of any such significance (except that Friedhold possesses characteristics of Alexander Ritter). Guntram is altogether the "title hero" in the sense of the Wagnerian music dramas, and it is significant that the "eternal womanly element," emphasized even in the titles of almost all the later operas, is, for the first and last time, not dominant in "Guntram" ... In two motifs of the text, however, there is undoubtedly youthful, exuberant conviction: Guntram's enthusiastic account of his vision of peace, and his realistic description of the fury of war. (Forty years later Strauss was to repeat this affirmation of the ideal of peace in a different context in "Friedenstag.") Guntram's song of peace, the dramatic heart of the work, culminates in the words "I see peace in the roseate evening sky . . ." and "From afar what wrathful fury! A fiery storm wind blows towards me . . . Must I call it the demon of war? With a bloody scourge it whips up hatred . . ." Lines of this nature do not depart from the Wagnerian pattern. Nevertheless the assured mastery of Wagnerian alliteration by the young composer (who soon recognized the artificiality of this elevated literary diction) is remarkable:

> Hohen Gesanges
> göttliche Gabe.
> Im heil'gen Gewande
> göttliche Lehre
> leite zu Gott . . .

"The music will be extremely simple," he wrote in a letter to Ritter, "very melodious, only cantilenas for the singers; when setting my own text it is only thus that the music flows from my pen . . ." And to his parents: "You'll be surprised how simple and melodious the music is; I have now exhausted my fury in symphonic poems of all kinds, and have become frightfully straightforward . . ." Is that really true to the extent suggested? Is not "Guntram," more than any other work of Strauss, dominated by Wagner and his tonal concepts? Nothing in this music drama springing from the sphere of neo-romantic feeling gives any indication that the greater part of the score was written in Cairo and Luxor. Strauss had formed so clear a concept of Wagnerian medievalism that even the bright colours of the Orient could not influence the character of the work. From the unfolding of the motifs (particularly frequent use is made of a phrase with the "Rienzi" turn) to the spiritual volatilization, with breadth of dialogue and monologue backed by feeling but no real content, often merely an effective tonal façade–over the whole canvas the influence of Wagner is paramount. "Lacking in experience," Strauss in fact created not an essentially vocal but an orchestral work, without regard to the limitations of the human voice. Later, in the foreword to his "Intermezzo," he candidly admitted that he had "almost completely neglected the separate development of purely lyrical passages, to which Richard Wagner devoted careful attention." The young music dramatist felt most at home in the great ariosi in the manner of his hymnic songs with orchestra. In Guntram's (overlong) message of peace the unfolding of the contrasts between war and peace is impressively successful—a song which streams with life despite the employment of tried and trusted stylistic means. In other parts of the score the retrospective element comes into its own: the succulently sweet "Lohengrin" magic of the orchestral Prelude, the concluding ensemble of the first act which is based on the first sextet from "Tannhäuser," and Guntram's melody of love with all the dramatic tensions of the harmony of "Tristan." Such passages, like the leitmotiv technique taken over in its entirety from the Bayreuth master, belong to the spiritual character of "Guntram." With its Wagnerian echoes this work clearly looks to the past. At the same time, however, several important features, especially at the close, are undoubtedly fruits of Strauss's own personality.

It was in the late summer of 1887 that Strauss started preparatory work on his first opera. The earliest mention of it was in a letter to Bülow: "I am also working on—don't be alarmed—an original, tragic opera on a text of my own, in three acts!!" Bülow replied by return of post: "Your interesting information that you are going around with a 'dramma lirico' has greatly astonished me. I have confidence in your youthful creative power, and wish you the amount of artistic somnambulism which you will need for success." Six months later Strauss could already write that he had "a complete first draft of an opera text ready," and that he was "quite satisfied" with it . . . There the matter rested, as new symphonic projects occupied his mind. Not until November 1889 did Strauss "again begin to work on the opera text and knead it about," so that "the sweat of anxiety bathed my forehead . . . but I'll get it into shape" (to his parents). Finally in October 1890 he was able to send the newly revised draft text to his father, asking for his "most severe and merciless criticism." This was clear and detailed; his suggestions led to important alterations, and the deletion of the scene with a mystical seductress. In March 1892 Strauss could write to his mother that he had begun the composition. He wrote to Bülow in June of that year: "Longing for fresh holiday air I am furiously glaring at my four walls, and composing, out of boredom, the second act of my opera (the first is already complete), and fretting at the same time over my dear Opera Director . . ." Meanwhile Strauss had commenced his journey south, taking "Guntram" with him. Entries in his

281

diary give details of the progress of the work. On the 19th November in Athens, the day before visiting the Acropolis: "After dinner the scene between Guntram and Friedhold, third act, completed in outline;" on the 23rd November: "Third act 'Guntram' text (second final version) finished;" then in Cairo on the 1st December: "Short score third act begun," and finally: "Christmas Eve, 'Guntram' ready."

However, the time-consuming activity of instrumentation still lay before him—and the third act, which occupied Strauss until September 1893 on account of its revision. He was more informative than during any other period of his career. "Guntram's Monologue is ready, 56 pages of score (some of two systems) already written in full, I think the first act will be ready at the beginning of March," he wrote to his father from Luxor. Four weeks later: "I'll make a huge cut in the Prelude to the second act, as that symphonic poem takes too long ... I look forward to beginning the instrumentation of the second act in a few days, and hope to reach the Narration of Peace in Cairo; then I'll cross the sea and collect new impressions in Sicily ..." And finally, from Taormina: "The second act is already somewhat thicker, I've just finished the War Narrative, this has become real Strauss! ... The last scenes will be written in Palermo!" Shortly before his return home, Strauss summed up his activities in a letter to Bülow from Ramacca: "You will believe that I have not been loafing musically all the time when I tell you that I have completely orchestrated the first two acts of my opera 'Guntram,' and have composed the third. It has become somewhat fiery music—but 40° Réaumur in the sunlight are, in any case, more than the evening temperature in the Weimar Court Theatre when Lassen is conducting 'Hiarne' (by Ingeborg von Bronsart)."

Thus six eventful years had elapsed since he first encountered the story which gave rise to "Guntram," before (following abortive negotiations with Karlsruhe) the opera received its world première at Weimar in May 1894, at the end of Strauss's period of activity as a conductor there. He conducted the performance himself with his fiancée as Freihild. He wrote to Ritter that apart from the absence of a covered orchestra pit the work produced exactly the effect he had intended. He was not, however, to experience much pleasure in connection with his operatic firstborn. In Munich, after a long delay, a single performance took place in 1895. Its failure in his native town long rankled with Strauss. He wrote in his "Recollections": "The principal singers had refused the roles, the orchestra went on strike under the leadership of my own cousin and violin teacher, Konzertmeister Benno Walter, and a deputation asked the General Director Perfall to free the orchestra from this 'scourge of the gods.' The tenor, whose memory had failed him at times during the première, declared afterwards that he would sing at further performances only if he received an increased pension . . ." Justifiable wrath overcame the young dramatic composer after this unedifying Munich intermezzo. "It is incredible how many enemies 'Guntram' has made for me . . . it makes me feel like a criminal. People will forgive anything, even the most blatant lie, except the fact that one has written what is in one's heart" (to Arthur Seidl). Performances under Strauss which had already been announced in Dresden and Berlin did not take place. However, certain people of consequence showed their respect for the work, among them Verdi, whose letter of appreciation Strauss treasured.

Indeed, the "honourable and virtuous youth Guntram," to whom his begetter, as a piece of humour at his own expense, had put up a monument in the garden of his house at Garmisch, was to be brought back to life fifty years later. When the Berlin Radio presented a broadcast performance of the work in honour of the composer's seventieth birthday, Strauss expressed the opinion that the "amount of beautiful music . . . would probably justify a revival." A few years later he roused the sleeping beauty, his "young love, now somewhat aged," from her long sleep, hoping that "she would not need too much make-up." This "make-up" consisted of a little rhythmic tightening-up in the voice parts, retouching of the instrumentation, and above all making substantial cuts. The old vocal score consisted of 230 pages, the new (unaltered in layout) of only 147. This indicates how energetically the cutting pencil had been applied, and it transpired, when the opera was again produced at Weimar in 1940, that the new concentration had revealed a good deal of life in "Guntram." The poet-composer, when asked to write a foreword for the programme, declined to do so on the ground that "the whole of 'Guntram' is itself a foreword . . ."

"Now I am curious to know which way the boat will head, for one is really propelled along, while believing one is rowing oneself," Strauss wrote to Ritter after the world première of "Guntram." The composer was certainly disappointed by the poor reception of his first opera, but it is a great exaggeration to assert that Strauss lost his will to compose another opera. Time would tell—and the greater part of his life still lay before him. Fire had been kindled in him, and the stage never let him out of its grip. Even while he was still at work on "Guntram" new opera subjects were brought to his notice. Bülow drew his attention to Ibsen in 1888. "On reading Ibsen's latest romantic drama (actually some years old, but only now published in German), 'Das Fest auf Solhaug,' I repeatedly thought of you. An excellent subject for an opera, although in my opinion it should be altered to end tragically!" Strauss's answer is typical: "I have read Ibsen's 'Fest auf Solhaug:' a good opera subject, but the love of two sisters for the same man, which has already become somewhat stale from 'Opfer um Opfer,' 'Die Hexe' etc., does not greatly appeal to me personally. On the other hand I find 'Kaiser und Galiläer' at least very interesting and finely laid out," to which Bülow replied: "There should be no disputes over questions of taste. It would be confoundedly boring in the world if B was always the echo of A. I cannot share your antipathy for the idea of two sopranos in rivalry for the love of the same tenor or baritone..." During his visit to Egypt Strauss seems to have seriously considered an opera subject of his own. On the 10th November 1892 he wrote in his diary: "Read 'State and Religion' (by Wagner); impelled by it to plan a new drama..." The sketch of "Das erhabene Leid der Könige" was found among Strauss's papers at his death.

While still at Weimar, Strauss was considering the idea of a Eulenspiegel opera. To put Till on the opera stage, the rogue who infuriates the philistines and makes fools of the narrow-minded—that was something to appeal to the taste of the thirty-year-old composer. He wrote in a letter to his father in 1893: "I am already working on a new opera text in my head. I think 'it'll go'," and in a letter written to an unknown correspondent a few months later: "Now I'm concerned with getting a 'Till Eulenspiegel with the burgesses' into shape. I've already invented a very nice plot, except that I can't yet see the figure of Herr Till

Eulenspiegel clearly in front of me; the book of folk tales has given us only a rascal, who is too shallow for a dramatic figure –but a deepening of the character from the point of view of his scorn for other people presents great difficulties . . ." The draft scenario of a first act (some notes indicate that Strauss originally conceived the piece in one act) ends with the strife among the burgesses. The attempt to contrast the "mocker at the world, who scorns people because at heart he loves them" and the mean-minded citizens of Schilda, who founder through their own stupidity, was probably *too* bold for the young music dramatist. Once again the orchestra triumphed over the stage; the projected opera became the symphonic "Till."

Two years later, when Strauss came into close contact with the leading literary figures of Munich, his desire for a gay, popular opera text became increasingly strong. It was to be an echo of "Meistersinger," a parodistic product of a youthful heart. It is not surprising that the new Eulenspiegel book by Strauss's friend Ferdinand von Sporck remained unused, in view of the widespread popular success of the tone poem. The new "Till" opera was to have five acts, and to be set in Schilda like Strauss's own projected version; the hero appeared in the character of a "Jewish merchant." In a sketchbook dating from 1897 there are even some themes for a two-act scenario "Die verlassenen Weiber von Schilda." He could summon up no enthusiasm for Bierbaum's dramatically unpromising fairy-tale libretti "Lobetanz" and "Gugeline," and he passed both of them on to Thuille. Other dramatic projects of that period which never came to fruition despite the existence of a remarkable number of substantial sketches include an opera "Lila" after Goethe, for which he asked Cosima Wagner's advice and help, and an extensive ballet "Kythere" after Watteau; there was also the scenario of a one-act ballet "Kometentanz." (Further details are given in the chapter entitled "The Dance"). Strauss told Rolland during that period that for the moment he was more intersted in gentle, happy music than in heroics. Who would write him *the* opera libretto which he needed in order to free himself from the power of the Wagnerian music drama?

*

Experience had taught Strauss that he should himself seek a suitable subject. "The Flemish saga 'The Extinguished Fire of Oudenaarde' came into my hands," he recalled in 1942, "and gave me the idea of writing a little intermezzo *against* the theatre, with personal motifs and a touch of revenge on my dear native town where I, like the great Richard thirty years earlier... had had so few encouraging experiences." Strauss saw clearly that this subject from an old collection of "Netherlands Sagas" contained opportunities to strike a blow at the reactionary spirit of the Athens on the Isar. Long before, in 1888, the young Munich opera conductor had complained to Bülow: "I have gradually come to realize that this is ground on which a prosperous musical life simply cannot exist. On my own I can never drag the cart out of the mire in which I find everything here..." However quaintly harmless the "Singgedicht" *"Feuersnot"* with its strange title (literally "Fire Famine") may appear to the modern listener, we should not lose sight of the spirit of passionate opposition which animated Strauss when he wrote the piece, an expression of his anger at the unfriendly reception of his "Guntram" at the Munich Opera. "In 'Feuersnot,' even stronger than hitherto, there is confirmed that spirit of opposition which, together with my considerable creative gift and my inborn ability, was clearly marked in me from my earliest youth."

In Ernst von Wolzogen, who was later to found and direct the "Überbrettl" theatre in Berlin, based on the Parisian model, the new Royal Prussian Conductor found a like-minded colleague. The author of the Liszt novel "Der Kraft-Mayr" seemed to him a man of suitable wit and spirit for the carrying out of his plan. Wolzogen wrote in his autobiography: "During the last weeks of my stay in Munich I met Richard Strauss, who, on account of the unfavourable reception which his native town had given to his first operatic work 'Guntram,' was as ill-disposed towards it as I was. So we set to work and devised a plan for revenge, which later took on artistic form in 'Feuersnot'..." The old Flemish saga tells of a proud maiden who leaves a wooer hanging in a basket outside her house at night, so that he becomes the laughing stock of all. Thereupon, in revenge, an old magician extinguishes all the fires and lights in the town, and will not re-kindle them until the girl has repented. As early as March 1899 the librettist could write, following a performance of "Zarathustra" in Munich: "It has given me a powerful incentive to get on at once with our opera. I now have the following idea: 'Feuersnot' in one act –setting old Munich in a legendary Renaissance period. The young romantic hero is *himself* a magician; the great old magician, his teacher, whom the worthy citizens of Munich once threw out, does not himself appear. At the end, in order to free the town from its dearth of fire, the town council and citizens beg the heartless girl to offer her maidenhood to the young magician, which she does. When love is combined with the magic of genius, then even the worst philistine must see the light . . . !" That sounded less decorous than frivolous, and the philistines found plenty to complain about in what they considered the playful attitude adopted to the obscenities of an immoral text. Wolzogen wrote his libretto "in a few days" in the summer of 1900 on the island of Rügen, "in the fresh enthusiasm of a delightful love affair." He had modified the moral laxity of the saga, but unfortunately he failed to show the amorous aspect of the story from a naive, spontaneous viewpoint. Strauss, who recognized this fact even before the world première, advised Schuch in a letter "to give due emphasis to the burlesque, impudent, brazen, parodistic element throughout the work." The glorification of Eros expressed in the hymnic conclusion of the work seems rather too solemn after so much frivolity:

> All warmth springs from the woman,
> All light proceeds from love –
> From hot, young womanly love
> Alone comes the re-kindling fire.

To Strauss and Wolzogen "Kunrad the Ebner" was Strauss himself, who voiced his criticism of his native town. His "Master Reichart, the Ancient of Laim" was Wagner, whom the people of Munich had driven out of their gates in the days of King Ludwig II of Bavaria. Strauss felt himself as Wagner did in the character of the Mastersinger who beats his arch-enemy Hanslick in the guise of Beckmesser. The result was the fiery address of Kunrad, which has lost some of its interest over the years on account of its local Munich allusions, and its polemics relating to events familiar at the time of its creation but long since forgotten. (It is not, however, surprising that to Strauss this "sermon" was the "main thing, and the rest of the action amusing

287

subsidiary material"). Strauss particularly asked the singer of Kunrad to present "his entire monologue in a really commanding, authoritative tone"–certainly no easy matter ... All this now appears to have been no more that an episode in a private literary and musical feud which has long since died out; Strauss later settled down not far from Munich and made his native town a present of the original score of "Feuersnot" (which was, however, written in Berlin).

Wagner did not merely figure in the story of "Feuersnot"–in style and manner of expression he dominated the whole work, despite the growing independence of the composer. The text which Wolzogen put together on the basis of old Munich dialect expressions reminds one constantly of "Die Meistersinger:" the "Solstitial Fire" of the Munich citizens could not have existed without the Nuremberg St. John's Eve in "Meistersinger." There is a great deal of alliteration in these often affected lines, as though one were in the middle of "The Ring." Such expressions as "Im Düstern Neidaugen zur Wacht," "träumenden Tor," "gaukelnden Geck," "weichen, winselnden Wicht" and "wunderwirkendem Wein" abound, while the love duet ("Feuersnot! Minnegebot!") could be from "Tristan." At other times, though, Wolzogen, in his "boisterous, rather archaic style," hits on lines of boldly satirical humour from the sphere of his "Überbrettl:" "Läßt wo ein Pfaff seinem Windlein Lauf, schobert's der gleich wie ein Hündlein auf." As could be expected, objections to such phrases were raised by those concerned even before the first performance. This example was replaced in the printed libretto by two harmless lines: "Er läuft den Frommen wohl hinterdrein, kommt darum doch net in Himmel 'nein." Only in the vocal score (and naturally also in the full score) can one find these "objectionable" phrases: "Kann der nimmer sein Zeit erpassen? Hündlein frei'n auf off'ner Gassen!" and "Soll'n wir verrecken, hols die Pest? Weil sich ein Mädel nit lirumlarum läßt?" Strauss himself altered a number of verbal infelicities of his own accord: Urschel became Ursula and Hochgezeit Hochzeit, while he replaced Mädlein by the simple Mädel. Nevertheless the verbal undergrowth of this "Singgedicht" contains a good deal that is mannered and unintentionally funny.

Strauss did not hesitate for long. "... I am hard at work; I have already begun the composition of the opera ..." he wrote

In the prime of life
Lithograph by Max Liebermann (1918)

"Die ägyptische Helena"

Scenic design for the first act by Ludwig Sievert (Berlin State Opera, 1935)

in a letter sent to his parents at the beginning of October 1900. Equally impulsive are the next reports from his workshop: "Since Wednesday I have been free, and am working industriously at the composition of the opera, a fifth of whose text is already sketched in music ... the opera, which will be very simple–and, insofar as anything occurs to me–also melodic–is giving me a tolerable amount of pleasure ..." "I compose day and night: 'Feuersnot' is already nearly half finished. It is scarcely possible to orchestrate without triple woodwind any longer ..." " 'Feuersnot' will be pure Lortzing," and " 'Feuersnot' will be ready this year. Extremely popular-sounding and melodious. I believe I have succeeded!" Punctually on New Year's Day 1901 Strauss could begin on the instrumentation. "I have to conduct four or five times a week ..., every day I sit for almost ten hours over my score, which I hope to have completed in about a fortnight's time. I even do without my walks, but when everything is ready I shall be able to relax all the more contentedly."

Strauss the music dramatist still lived under the spell of Wagner, but he was here stretching out the first feelers of his personality–for this reason a Strauss cycle would have to begin with "Feuersnot," as a Wagner cycle does with "Rienzi." (His "Guntram" corresponds approximately to Wagner's "Liebesverbot" or "Die Feen"). In the score of "Guntram" the diction of "Tristan" and "Parsifal" is predominant, in "Feuersnot," with its many Wagner quotations, that of "Die Meistersinger." A "Meistersinger" texture is everywhere in evidence. At Kunrad's Address, which already contains many seeds of Strauss's future operatic development, one thinks immediately of the great speech of Sachs. Nevertheless the transition to the Strauss of "Salome," the subtle differentiation of the orchestra, the lightening of the texture in favour of a new birth of the opera of the voice and of pure music–all these are to be found in "Feuersnot," shining through a score which is still largely Wagnerian in cut. In particular Strauss the melodist came into his own in all the crowd scenes and episodes involving children, and in the musical joy of the Waltz (the first Strauss waltz!). What an abundance of really beautiful, freshly-flowing music! The stuffy townsfolk are depicted with telling humour, while the antics of the children are the product of an understanding heart–the music is so lively and exuberant. When one hears the old Munich choral songs, bathed in shimmering orchestral colours, the scenes in which they occur seem unusually fresh. Here, where Strauss was clearly addressing himself to the Volkstheater with its hard-working artisan and lower middle class audiences, his talent is illuminated from a remarkably attractive side. It was a pity that the enchanting flavour of Bavarian folk music in this one-act work remained almost unique in the realm of his operas. What horizons are opened up by the thought that Strauss might have worked further along the lines of this "Munich baby" with its simple, popular-sounding melodic style! He made the attempt twenty-eight years later, when, following the intellectual beauty of "Helena," he determined to pursue a different ideal, seeking the road to a new "Meistersinger." Left on his own by his librettist, he failed to find it.

The dazzling, scorching glow of the "Feuersnot" music, from the midsummer night of love to the flickering radiance of the fire, springs from a different impulse. When Kunrad begins to work magic, when the fire myth grows to become the driving force of human action dominated by Eros, and when Diemut is compelled to sink into her lover's arms, then the composer of "Don Juan" is wholly in command. (The love scene turns out to have been based on an Adagio Notturno taken from the abandoned "Kythere") ... The work's weaknesses? They lie in the musical-dramatic sphere. Even in the dialogues between the lovers there is some dead wood, showing that Strauss the scenic dramatist was not yet the equal of Strauss the composer. Then again the contrasts between the popular-style songs, dances and choruses, and the symphonic sections with their brilliant orchestration reminiscent of "Till" are very marked. The young dramatic composer (who had, however, by that time reached an age which neither Mozart nor Schubert lived to see) tried to express almost too much in words and sound. We hear echoes of the Hall of the Gibichungs in close proximity to music of the beer halls—while the satirical, Offenbachian element has dropped into the background. On the homeward journey after the world première under Schuch, which took place at Dresden in November 1901, Bie asked Strauss whether he had really approached the setting of Wolzogen's libretto primarily from the serious or from the comic side. Strauss replied: "I just composed it as it stands!"

"Feuersnot" ushered in the Strauss era at the Dresden Opera. He gave that renowned institution, which he called the "El Dorado for world premières," the preference over the court theatres of Berlin and Vienna, whose first reaction to the work had been one of reservation on moral grounds. "Schuch is a marvel," he wrote, "Schuch has let me see my work as it really is, the old opera cobwebs have been swept away, and suddenly there is the comedy in music." Even in Dresden trouble arose over certain situations of the opera. ("The alterations which the General Management insist on making to the libretto are quite unacceptable...") The fact that it was not an undisputed success may

The Dresden Theatre (Semper's building, destroyed in 1945)

have been due to the difficulty which those who were not born and bred in Munich found in attempting to follow the work's local allusions. Outside Dresden its reception varied. It was an unexpected success under Mahler in Vienna: at the end of the performance Strauss had to appear in front of the curtain almost a hundred times. Despite this triumph, interest in "Feuersnot" soon began to die down–to the composer's great grief, as a strong bond of fatherly love linked him with this opera. Was it, as he feared at the ill-chosen time of the Berlin première, to appeal only to "connoisseurs and those of cultured taste," and only "gradually win over the general public? He pressed the claims of this opera in letters to opera directors and conductors more insistently than was ever the case with any other work of his. "What about

'Feuersnot?'"—that was the refrain of innumerable letters to Schuch and other musicians. ("How was 'Feuersnot' attended? If you particularly want to do me a favour, please see that it does not disappear from the repertoire again," to Schuch in 1909). Even after fifty years, in his last diary entry, the aged composer reverted to this "Singgedicht." It seemed to him in retrospect to be the "first attempt (also on account of the text) to approach the theatre in my own way, dealing with a quasi personal subject on a 'smaller scale' . . . It is forgotten that this undoubtedly imperfect work . . . at the very beginning of the century represented a new subjective style in the nature of the old opera, an upbeat . . . It was precisely on account of the not-to-be-deleted Address of Kunrad that the whole little non-opera was written."

*

There was another projected opera with which Strauss concerned himself for several years, although it never took on tangible form. Shortly before he set to work on Wolzogen's "Feuersnot" libretto, he made another attempt to write a text of his own, a thieves' comedy "Ekke und Schnittlein" after Cervantes. The sketch of April 1899 was revised in December of the same year, after which Strauss's father described his son's draft text as "frivolous." When Strauss, very pleased with the "attractive, really popular text" of "Feuersnot," asked Wolzogen for a new comedy libretto, he gave his colleague the plan of the thieves' comedy. Wolzogen at once agreed to develop it. "I have a splendid title for your robber story, 'Coábbradibosimpúr,' a wonderful mouthful! This wild monstrosity of a word is to be the day's password of the robber band. Their leader makes it his business to invent a remarkable password like that every day. I should very much like to turn the whole thing into verse for you at once . . . I may get a charming singspiel theatre built on the Schiffbauerdamm . . . The robber farce would fit splendidly into my programme, and I would produce and rehearse it with absolutely bold realism. But you would have to be satisfied with an orchestra of 36!" . . . Indeed, in July 1903 Wolzogen sent "part of the text," and promised to send the remaining sections in quick successions. "The affair is giving me many more headaches than I had supposed, and it proceeds far more slowly than 'Feuersnot' did . . . The subject is very fragile and unpromising for the dramatic action, because it only describes the milieu, with neither lyrical points of repose nor dramatic events ... The whole joke must not last longer than an hour–or it won't be a joke at all ..." Strauss made only a brief reference to this episode in his "Recollections": "Ernst von Wolzogen ... later also arranged a robber novel by Cervantes, which I myself had sketched out as a one-act opera. I mislaid the libretto, I don't know where." In the meantime Schuh has discovered the manuscript. It bears the title: "Coábbbradibosimpúr oder Die bösen Buben von Sevilla. A robber piece in one act after Cervantes by Ernst von Wolzogen. Music by Richard Strauss." It is not known whether Strauss got to the point of sketching any of the music.

At the same time Wolzogen tried to interest Strauss in the idea of a historical comic opera "König Ragnar Rauhbeins Tochter." "Read Andersen's story 'The Swamp King's Daughter.' This most psychologically fascinating story combines the milieu of the Vikings with the realistically humorous figure of King Ragnar Lodbrock, who killed the fierce serpent. I believe the combination of these elements would be extremely fruitful for both of us. I'll get round the difficulty of the mocking at Christianity if I play my cards right. Then there's the Eskimo slave Sgnirpr–what a sweet name, and what a role for Lieban!" This plan, too, came to nothing, like that of a "Heilige Einfalt" with which Wolzogen's wife hoped to make her mark as a writer. Strauss rightly hesitated during those years. He felt that the world expected something remarkable from him. Was it "Salome?"

ABYSSES

THE AGE WHICH REACHED OUT ITS ARMS TO SEIZE THE forty-year-old composer was characterized by pathos and the desire for sensations. What the bourgeois public of the Kaiser's Germany regarded as high art was in fact the questionable spirit of beauty-saturated, empty "secessionism." Until the First World War it was believed that dreadful deeds could be transformed by the power of music, and sultry excesses concealed by the employment of highly refined musical-dramatic technique. Driven on by the false spirit of the times, influenced by art and literature, by the whole bubbling, fermenting atmosphere of "modernity," Strauss plunged into the human abysses of his two most famous one-act operas. It was no wonder that with regard to subject matter, action and artistic temperament, "Salome" and "Elektra" were typical products of an age on which the present day turns its back. The nature of both works can be understood only with reference to the social structure of opera at the dawn of the present century, and the question of their lasting life is first and foremost sociological. Operas such as "Salome" and "Elektra" will always retain their power over the public in a bourgeois-capitalist society. In both works Strauss skilfully employed decadent forms of expression to present socially negative elements of dissolution within the sphere of modern opera. However much life still remains in the music, the typical features of that morbid age of decadence, with its craving for sensual satiety and its blindness to reality, now appear as products of soul-destroying luxury. In "Salome" as in "Elektra" the individual is all-important, the people are ignored, and the characters entangle themselves in webs of perversely exaggerated passions which distort their view of the world and make normal relationships with other people impossible. Over-emphasis of the

Biblical and classical originals was bound to lead to a decom-
position of their ethos. Even if Strauss did no more than depict
human degradation from the outside, without falling victim to
his subjects, what is monstrous remains monstrous. No one
should attempt to regard it otherwise.

*

Strauss's attention was virtually bound to be attracted by
Oscar Wilde's *"Salome."* From 1901 onward this poetic drama
of the Irish writer who had died in 1900 created a great stir on
the stage in Germany; Strauss saw the Reinhardt production with
Gertrud Eysoldt at the Berlin "Kleines Theater" in November 1902. He wrote about the occasion in his "Recollections":
"After the performance I met Heinrich Grünfeld, who said to
me: 'Strauss, that would be an opera subject for you.' I was able
to reply: 'I'm already composing it.' The Viennese poet Anton
Lindner had already sent me the exquisite piece, and had offered
to make an 'opera text' out of it for me. When I had agreed to
his proposal he sent me a few cleverly versified opening scenes,
but I could not make up my mind to take the composition in
hand until one day the thought occurred to me: why not simply
compose the text, beginning 'Wie schön ist die Prinzessin Salome
heute Nacht?' From that point onward it was not difficult to
make the fine literature into something which was more than a
very good 'libretto.' And now, after the Dance and in particular
the whole closing scene have been clothed in music, it does not
require much perception to declare that the piece 'cried out for
music.' Certainly, but one had to see it!" There seems to be no
doubt that shortly after the recommendation from Lindner
(whose "Hochzeitlich Lied" he set to music) Strauss began
sketching a "Salome" after Wilde, but serious work on this project began only after the completion of the short score of the
"Domestica" in August 1903.

Wilde, a contemporary not of Picasso but of Makart, wrote
his dramatic poem in 1892 in richly glowing French; the world
première took place in Paris in 1896, and the printed text, which
first appeared in Paris in 1893, was embellished in 1897 with the
pen and ink sketches and vignettes of Aubrey Beardsley. Wilde
had been drawn to the subject by Flaubert's story "Herodias"
and Huysmans' novel "A Rebours," with its description of the

picture "Salome's Dance" by Moreau. A prose poem of exciting brilliance in the spirit of over-sensitive "fin-de-siècle" art, filled with luxuriant verbal imagery from the sphere of Wilde's famous story "The Picture of Dorian Gray!" Strauss was particularly attracted by Wilde's polished prose, with which he became familiar in the German translation by Hedwig Lachmann. "I like setting good, clear prose," he often said right into his old age. At the same time he recognized the need to simplify a great deal of elaborate imagery and much of the Biblical phraseology. He turned to Romain Rolland for help concerning the translation and pronunciation of certain names. (When Strauss wrote that the laws of the French language had been treated arbitrarily, Rolland retorted with a reference to German pride and arrogance.) Tenschert has studied the copy of Lachmann's translation which Strauss used, and has detailed the composer's many alterations and omissions. He was probably guided to an equal degree by considerations of personal taste and those of verbal-musical diction. Minor figures such as Tigellinus, a young Roman, the Nubian, and Salome's slaves were omitted, while the account by the Nazarenes of Christ's miracles, together with the discussions on religious philosophy, seemed to Strauss to be unnecessary in a highly concentrated opera, and even Narraboth, who figures prominently in Wilde, was relegated to a subsidiary position. The statement, constantly repeated in print, that Strauss set Wilde's text "word for word," is therefore not correct. The libretto of the opera "Salome" is barely half the length of the complete play. Nevertheless "Salome," together with Debussy's "Pelléas et Mélisande," may be regarded as the first works for the musical stage to represent the category of the "literary opera," opera based directly on a literary work, such has since been widely cultivated.

"In the meantime I have completed my one-act opera 'Salome' . . . in rough (it has become very fine), and hope to be able to let you have the complete score in the autumn of 1905 . . .," Strauss wrote to Schuch, who was eagerly awaiting news, in September 1904. What was it that so fascinated Strauss in "Salome," which he wrote during a single burst of creative activity at the Villa de Ahna in Marquartstein, Upper Bavaria? First and foremost the mysterious, exotic atmosphere of the picture which it presents of the Court of the Tetrarch of Galilee and Peraea,

Herod Antipas (the son of Herod the Great), who is living in incestuous union with his brother's wife, and, already tired of her, lusts after her daughter; insane luxury, excessive love of pleasure and enervation of the senses have resulted in a complete decay of the concept of morality. (Gysi pointed out the strange irony of the fact that the same Strauss who had made himself an advocate for conventional married life in the "Sinfonia domestica," composed shortly before, now, as a dramatic composer, painted a picture of shattered marriage ties at the Court of Herod; it is sufficient to show how erroneous it would be to identify the composer of "Salome" with the unnatural world of Salome). The dramatic conflict arises from the fact that Salome, the "daughter of sin," wildly desiring first the living body and then the head of the prophet Jokanaan, feels the first stirrings of genuine love at the moment of the gratification of her perverse longing. These new motives, adopted by Wilde from Flaubert, make his account very different from that of the Bible, in which the Evangelists Matthew and Mark tell how the Princess of Judaea demanded the Baptist's head at the instigation of her vengeful mother. It was probably Heine, in his "Atta Troll," who first made rejected love the reason for the prophet's execution . . . Did Salome, that dangerously seductive beast of prey, not appear to the musician like an object in a dream? Perhaps he was scarcely aware that in this musical monument to lustful and destructive love, which "is greater than the mystery of death," he was seeking to achieve ecstasy of the senses to so alarming an extent. Undoubtedly Strauss was captivated by the idea of the confrontation of Roman Cæsarism, the inwardly decaying world of the Old Testament, and the rising tide of Christianity, with its initial purity of purpose. The impact of these latter two epochs was embodied in Salome and Jokanaan. She was a creature of impulse, depraved, at once inquisitive and knowing, seeking experience even past the threshold of death; he on the other hand, the prophet held prisoner in the cistern, vainly preached the moral laws of Christianity. (Strauss originally intended a grotesque portrayal of Jokanaan).

The vision of the musician completely absorbed that of the poet. It gave a higher meaning to the marsh flower of Wilde's original, liberating and beautifying—a procedure which could only occur once with such perfection, but which misled many after Strauss into attempting, in vain, to emulate his example. In the gallery of other dramatic and symphonic works on the subject of Salome one comes across the names of Massenet, Glazunov, Florent Schmitt and others; almost simultaneously with Strauss the French composer Mariotte wrote a "Salomé," also after Wilde. Undoubtedly music made Salome a thing of fanatical horror (the character was originally free from fanaticism). The monstrous woman gave rise to a picture of glittering eroticism. Horror was to be represented through the medium of beauty. Even the sinister, evil elements of "Salome" were transformed into opalescent tone pictures. Its by no means exalted content seems to be veiled in splendidly intoxicating music, whose power conceals the hideous things behind it. It is important to realize this fact. Strauss's "Salome" is, to a great extent, hysteria become music. Such hysteria can infect people wholly unmusical by nature. Music of this kind demands cool nerves, demands the full consciousness of the human being who is able to feel clearly.

"It is the symphony in the medium of drama, and is psychological, like all music," Strauss asserted in connection with the "Salome" music. (Only a misunderstanding could lead to the concept of this as a "symphony with accompanying voices," though). Strauss turned the play "Salome" into a dramatic tone poem full of vain beauty and luxuriant sound—which, strangely enough, signified ugliness and discord to the generation of the turn of the century. The troubled waters of this sea of sound, its exotic eroticism and overpowering sultriness, the sinister and evil, are the expression of an over-ripe intellectual culture coming into contact with the naive naturalness of the musician. In "Salome" Strauss outdid Wagner, and despite its shock effect people of perception including such composers as Mahler, Reger and Busoni realized that he had put himself in Wagner's place. He himself described this as the one among his works about which one "could perhaps speak of progress beyond Wagner." The music takes on a new function: to capture and overpower the listener. From the first languishing words of Narraboth to Salome's "Liebestod" there is a gradual dynamic crescendo of intensity, a flaming brand of orchestral sound which never overwhelms the voices. "Salome" is primarily a thing of colour. The atmosphere, the vibration in the air and the vapours of a tropical night (which Strauss often experienced in the Near East) have never again been so powerfully conveyed as in this complex score with its polyphony of motifs and rhythms, its well-

"Salome": First page of the original score (1904)

judged harmonic and instrumental attractions, and its great dynamic curves. Salome's shuddering pleasure at the sight of the Prophet is painted as suggestively in sound as the fluctuating drunkenness of Herod. The pale C♯ minor organ chord, with tremolo strings and convulsive wind figures, heard when Salome kisses the head of Jokanaan, remains as firmly fixed in the memory as the iridescent play of colours at the mention of the "schönsten Smaragds" and of the "Opale, die immer funkeln, mit einem Feuer, kalt wie Eis." What a conquest of sound from the warmth of "Wie süß ist hier die Luft," with the pale moon and soughing night wind, to the naturalistic sounds of brooding, moaning, screeching nature conjured up by motifs on almost every page of the score! Never before had Strauss's tonal palette been so varied: to the strings and normal wind instruments, treated with complete mastery, were added the individual tone colours of the heckelphone, the celesta, and an abundance of percussion instruments. The music follows the subtlest impulses of the drama, which the composer made entirely his own. Only in the Quintet of Jews and in the "Dance of the Seven Veils" do the thematic materials of the opera come together to form self-contained structures. The "Dance," musically weaker than the rest of the work, was, significantly enough, added after the rest of the opera. ("With the exception of the Dance 'Salome' is being engraved in full score and vocal score," July 1905). By the end of August the work was complete.

Experience and ability are hidden behind this score, which extends the sounds produced by a giant orchestra over a hundred strong to the extreme limits of its expressive possibilities, depicting vividly every mood and state of mind between rapture and disgust, desire and satiety, the fire of life and the blackness of death. For the first time Strauss had carried his personal style to the level of the highest mastery in a work for the stage. He achieved his effects by the use of three means of expression: a crystal-clear, polished motif technique which descends to sentimentality only on occasion during Jokanaan's calls to repentance; a highly artistic "nervous counterpoint" in the skilful alternation of the voices and instrumental parts; and finally an ecstatic espressivo style which, in Salome's concluding monologue with its fervour grown to the point of insanity, gave the musician an opportunity to develop far beyond the range of the poet. Only the categorical "Man töte dieses Weib!" could put an end to this repulsive scene. The balance of the various elements was not yet perfect. The first ten minutes (there is no instrumental prelude) are taken up by love music of nervous tonal finesse, of radiant transparency. The world of Salome and Narraboth–a romance of sweet melancholy! Later (especially in the powerful orchestral

301

interludes) the pathetic element is predominant. Salome, the exotic flower, blossoms in a riot of colours during her three seductive songs, and horror comes into its own quite mercilessly at each repetition of her "Ich will den Kopf des Jochanaan." For the first time Strauss had created one of the great, dominating female roles which were to be typical of him from then on. For the first time, too, he had mastered the form of the one-act opera of sufficient stature to fill an evening. He often remarked in later years that the caesura at the end of an act disturbed him.

The fact that the young symphonist, in his creative enthusiasm, sometimes laid on the orchestral colour very thickly did not escape the notice of the highly experienced, practical man of the theatre in later years. Not every conductor possessed his ability to give a crystal-clear performance of this work. ("Conduct 'Salome' and 'Elektra' as though they were by Mendelssohn: fairy music," Strauss wrote in his "Golden Rules"). Some tonal modifications which Strauss made in 1930 for a surprisingly light-toned, lyrical Salome in Dresden correspond to a changed relationship to the work and its presentation; before that he had, albeit reluctantly, authorized a "reduced version" of the wind parts for use in moderate-sized opera houses. His concept of Salome herself altered in that he now thought less in terms of a woman of heroic passions than of a fascinating, almost childlike princess. (An "ill-bred child," as he called her in a letter to the author). The experience of his many later operas also gave him new ideas concerning the production of "Salome." "In contrast to the excited music, the acting of the performers must be restricted to the greatest simplicity, in particular Herod must guard against rushing about like a victim of neurasthenia, remembering that despite his moments of erotic instability he is an Oriental parvenu, intent on impressing his Roman guests, and assuming the composed dignity of the great Caesar in Rome. Fury *on* and *before* the stage at the same time—that's too much! The orchestra does all that is necessary," he wrote in his "Recollections." Any exaggeration is detrimental to this already blatant opera. This is true of Salome's Dance, which was originally performed by a ballet dancer resembling the Salome. "A purely Oriental dance, as serious and controlled as possible, thoroughly restrained, preferably on *one* spot such as a prayer mat—greater movement only in the C♯ minor passage, and in the last two-

302

four a rather orgiastic climax ...": Strauss wanted it thus. But what are we usually offered! Salome as an unbridled vamp–the "exotic café chantant type, waving Jokanaan's head about in the air with snakelike movements" seems a complete contrast to the human light in which the musician bathed his Salome, who still possessed a certain childlike attractiveness even in her hysterical excesses. ("Anyone who has been in the Orient and has observed the decorum of the women there will understand that Salome, as a chaste virgin, an Oriental princess, can be portrayed only by

Caricature of the Paris première of "Salome" (1907)
To the right Gabriel Astrud, director of the Chatelêt-Theatre

using the simplest, most refined gestures, otherwise her destruction by the forces which she discovers in the world around her will arouse not pity but only disgust and horror.")

Strauss's intention of portraying in his opera people of his own time in the guise of characters from a remote period of history, to hold the mirror up to a society which had come to a halt, was the sensation of the year 1905. Who now remembers the opposition of the older Wagnerians, who wanted to allow only three performances to take place of the original Dresden production of "Salome" under Schuch? Who remembers the reply of an older Bayreuth musician when asked whether he knew "Salome": "I don't concern myself with filth!"? Before the first really triumphant Strauss première (this time Vienna and Leipzig had also tried to obtain the new work) the rehearsals in Dresden went far from smoothly. No wonder, when we read in letters that six weeks before the first performance even Schuch "has not yet seen the full score, and has no idea at all what is in store for him." In these circumstances none of the worthy Court Opera Singers, with the exception of the Herod, showed any inclination to study the parts assigned to them; the first Salome, who accepted the part of the "sixteen-year-old princess with the Isolde voice" only after a great deal of hesitation, and who reduced Strauss to despair with her continual "I won't do that, I am a respectable woman," had had enough after three performances.

Furthermore the "musical understanding of His Catholic Majesty" the King of Saxony could not possibly suffice for this unusual opera. In Berlin, where the Kaiser was "very, very reserved" on the subject of this work, in Vienna, England and the U.S.A., people felt it incumbent on them to display moral indignation. (In London the Lord Chamberlain ordered the singer of the part of Salome not to appear with the head; she had to be content with a bloodstained sword at the dress rehearsal, with an empty platter at the première, and later, following a complaint, with a blood-filled silver bowl) ... Tempi passati! Today the Princess, Herod and Jokanaan are among the most coveted operatic roles, and half a century after its appearance "Salome," the "horrible masterwork with an Isolde become a Jewish prostitute" (Rolland in his "Jean-Christophe"), represents to a great many opera-goers a nervous-eccentric "musician's opera" standing between "Tristan" and "Wozzeck," which skilful producers and scenic designers attempt to bring nearer to the feelings of a new age. Musical-dramatic form can so overshadow the content of a work that the pathological "Salome case" has become something very near to an artistic work of genius.

*

Only a new opera could come into consideration after "Salome." "Symphonic poems no longer give me any pleasure," Strauss remarked about that time. He would have preferred to

304

write a comic opera, but who was to provide him with a suitable subject? Then, shortly before the completion of "Salome," a friend drew his attention to the tragedy *"Elektra"* which Hugo von Hofmannsthal had published in 1903, and Strauss attended a performance of it in Berlin, produced by Reinhardt, with Gertrud Eysoldt in the title role. He at once sensed the great possibilities for the opera stage of this startling night piece from the ancient world, and he decided to get into contact with the Austrian playwright, who was ten years younger than himself, and in whose mime play "Der Triumph der Zeit" he had shown little interest four years previously, regarding the setting of "Elektra" to music. "You have awakened in me, so unexpectedly, the hope of no small degree of pleasure . . . The more I considered it, the more clearly detailed it seemed to me–perhaps you have seen it quite differently" replied Hofmannsthal, at once showing himself open to the idea. A few months later he made the surprising admission: "'Elektra,' proceeding toward triumph and purification–can be presented incomparably more powerfully in music than in the poem." The basis was thus established for fruitful collaboration between the two men. Although Strauss determined to write "Elektra" in 1906 ("Already at work," he reported in June, after a long delay), more than three years were to elapse before the score was completed. The delays were caused by Strauss's many engagements as a guest conductor–a tour of Europe in the summer of 1907 with 31 concerts in 31 days in the same number of towns . . . But he determined to get on with the composition: "I won't tire myself with so much conducting during the winter, and want to work solidly on 'Elektra,' so you have something to look forward to again," he told Schuch.

What was it that so attracted the enthusiast for Greece in this tragedy, far removed from the spirit of antiquity, of a poet who was sensitive and Apollonian in spirit rather than genuinely heroic in his thinking and feeling? It was certainly not the ideal of a light, clear Hellenism which he had encountered fifteen years earlier in the collection of vases and terra-cotta work at Athens and which (in the words of Hölderlin) was of the "colour of his heart." He was drawn rather by the grim, ruthless world of the Atrides with their dark compulsions and bloody forces, the impact of psychology and myth. While Strauss experienced the boundless fears of these figures in an almost physical sense, their hatred and love, their immeasurable life-denying passions, he proclaimed in this work a "concept of the demoniacal Greeks of the fifth century B. C." which contrasted with the ideas generally current. (In the foreword to his "Birth of tragedy out of the spirit of music" Nietzsche had referred, similarly, to the "good, strong inclination of the ancient Greeks toward pessimism, tragic myths, and the concept of everything dreadful, evil, mysterious, destructive and ominous on the foundations of existence.") The mythological story, preserved in the shadowy regions of the human soul, of the murder of Agamemnon, the return of Orestes and his deed of retribution on his degenerate mother and her paramour lies wholly in a sphere of emotional experience bordering on the perverse. What was this horrifying evocation of antiquity but a costume allowing two artists of the dawning century to satisfy their thirst for tangible reality? "Elektra," with its wild and pathological driving forces of hate by which the matriarchal rule in the household is destroyed, contains nothing whatever of the feeling of warmth which the public is accustomed to expect of the art form of opera, particularly as a radiation of the power of Eros. What has survived of the classical proportions of the Greek tragedy of Aeschylus, Euripides and Sophocles? Over-excited nerves made the doom-laden human being an unrestrained beast, the feeling of guilt becoming a spiritual complex and the subject of psychoanalysis. Strauss succumbed to this atmosphere during the pre-war years, although " 'Elektra' had to have the great tragic sweep." "Triumph and purification . . . ?" Both can be recognized to some extent at the end of the work when, after Elektra's words ". . . und diese Stunde bin ich das Feuer des Lebens, und meine Flamme verbrennt die Finsternis der Welt," Strauss conceived the all-destroying dance of vengeance and joy (significantly ending in the major) as self-release from the degradation and stupor of the brooding avenger.

Like the music drama "Salome," the musical tragedy "Elektra" represents the fashioning of an historical subject from the viewpoint of a modern, decadent literary concept. We now know that the new interest in the classical subject was aroused when the discoveries of Heinrich Schliemann pointed to the reality of the world of the Atrides. Hofmannsthal, who had never seen Mycenae, came near to its spirit in his own figurative and imaginative language, with its antitheses of ideas; his poetic drama,

306

in its close connection with Siegmund Freud ("Studies of hysteria") was the real starting point for the neo-psychological variations of the theme by writers from Hauptmann to O'Neill, Giraudoux and Sartre. In Hofmannsthal's work Elektra is always at the centre of the story of guilt and expiation: a hate-filled fury, a crazed maenad right up to her lonely, ecstatic death, concerned only to avenge the blood of King Agamemnon, treacherously shed. The fact is, however, that although Elektra speaks incessantly of the "deed" she fails at the decisive moment, and the axe with which her father was murdered remains where it was hidden. Klytemnestra, her opponent: "In the garish light of the torches her sallow, bloated face appears even paler over her scarlet robe . . ." (Strauss later stated that she "should not be an old, disintegrating witch, but a beautiful, proud woman of fifty, whose degeneration is the result of spiritual, not physical corruption.") Does the contrast between the "demoniacal fury and the flightiness of her worldly sister" Chrysothemis really create the effect which Strauss intended? In her craving for love and motherhood she is far more attractive than Elektra, but the only straightforward and truly sympathetic human character is Orestes, whose mission it is to deal the death blow. The others, including the Queen's paramour Aegistheus, are mere foils. The changes for which Strauss asked were not far-reaching. They concerned only a few points in the recognition scene between Elektra and Orestes, and the ending of the work, it being agreed at first to omit Aegistheus in the opera version. Strauss soon changed his mind on this point, however: "He is necessary to the action, and must also be slain, if possible in view of the audience." The readiness with which Hofmannsthal at once complied with Strauss's requests to make the necessary alterations to "Elektra" came as a surprise to the musician. Two men dissimilar by nature came close together in their first creative encounter. "Today Richard Strauss played and sang large parts of 'Elektra' to me. It is *very* fine, and it adds to the play instead of detracting from it," Hofmannsthal acknowledged. And shortly before the completion of the composition: ". . . your music gives me something very fine in addition, something which is naturally far more than actors and scenic designers can ever give me."

Corresponding to the over-wrought condition of the figures on the stage, and to the horror engendered by the ancient story, the music resembles a fearful nightmare. Outwardly a virtuistic command of words and music creates a maximum of artistic tension; inwardly there is a descent into the depths of a bestial underworld, into the driving passions of depraved human nature. In "Elektra" Strauss plunged into the abyss on the dark side of existence with all the vehemence of his vital musical nature, although he later asserted that he had approached the subject "very coolly and at a distance." Disease here is not restricted to Klytemnestra's liver; everything in this snake pit is rotten, putrid, decaying, while the music, in its unprecedented demands on the orchestra, a truly gigantic apparatus even larger than that of "Salome," glitters, shines, seduces, underlines every word and gesture. It slavers, tingles, spits, reels and chokes. Only once does it touch the listener's heart: in the recognition scene between Elektra and her brother. Here, at the decisive point of the spiritual converse between them, the heroine's character rises from hysteria to the superhuman level. At this moment overwhelming emotion enters into the sphere of profound ethics: "Was willst du fremder Mensch?" Here the music clearly leaves the neurasthenia of Hofmannsthal's drama far behind in content and form. ("I need a great climax after Elektra's first cry 'Orest.' I will introduce a tenderly trembling orchestral interlude... I must have material for the required crescendo: the best lines you can give me, and all in the same ecstatic mood, always increasing in intensity... Your lines at Elektra's recognition of Orestes are wonderful, and are already composed..."). The clarity, nobility and the breadth of the lyrical landscape at this encounter remain almost unparalleled in Strauss's works.

Strauss was conscious of the difficulty which confronted him in the composition of this "Elektra." Immediately after his first contact with Hofmannsthal's play he recognized, as he had in the case of "Salome," the "powerful increase of musical intensity right up to the end: in 'Elektra' the recognition scene, whose possibilities could be realized to the full only by music, is followed by the hideous apotheosis... At first I was alarmed by the thought that the two subjects had many similarities in their psychical contents, so that I doubted whether I had the power to rise for a second time to the height of intensity required to match the subject. However, my desire to confront Winkelmann's Roman imitations and Goethe's humanity with this demoniacal, ecstatic Hellenism of the sixth century gained the upper hand over my doubts, and in the event 'Elektra' even represented an advance in overall unity of construction, in the power of the climaxes—I would almost say that its relationship to 'Salome' is that of the more perfect, more stylistically unified 'Lohengrin' to the brilliant first attempt of 'Tannhäuser.' The two operas stand alone among all my works: in them I went to the extreme limits of harmony, psychical polyphony (Klytemnestra's dream) and the receptive ability of modern ears" (in the "Recollections," concerning "Elektra") ... By "psychical polyphony" Strauss undoubtedly meant the "extreme differentiation of the modern orchestra," that reached a degree in "Elektra" from which Strauss himself later considered it necessary to withdraw. A certain disparity with the stage action gave rise to a piece of symphonic-theatrical super-music which endangered the balance of the component parts of the dramatic "Gesamtkunstwerk." Here, undoubtedly, the self-glorifying symphonic opera had reached its ultimate point of development. A simplification of the tonal picture was an immediate necessity. Strauss made the great change in his works from "Rosenkavalier" onward.

"Salome" is all colour and atmosphere, "Elektra" monumental form, with its construction based on massive pillars of sound. From the moment when the Agamemnon theme stands out above the swirling sounds of the orchestra like a mighty fragment of rock, the lapidary musical style of the one-act tragedy is established. The "style has the sound at its command," as Bie sagely remarked. This style had to correspond to the ecstatic elements of a grim world of emotions: the wild flames of pathos and passion, frenzied fury and eruptive force had to determine the expressive values of the composition. Going beyond Wagner, Strauss boldly released the bonds of harmony, in this way giving a wide scope to the psychological depths of the work. The result was a novel, at times atonal, orchestral sound picture of often threatening raggedness (Interlude following the scene of Elektra's recognition of Orestes). Even the appearance of the score shows an immense advance into the realm of unusual combinations of sounds. One remarkable feature is the almost mathematically calculated division of instrumental weight, in which the exactly specified balance between the numbers of string and wind instruments is of particular importance. The strings, each part divisi in 3, are confronted by forty wind instruments (including eight clarinets of various kinds, heckelphone, contra bassoon and Wagner tubas), and a whole battery of percussion. In face of such orchestral forces, the fact that both in declamatory and in arioso passages the voices are not swallowed up by floods of sound, and (provided that the markings in the score are strictly observed) remain understandable, appears to be one of the greatest secrets of the composer, whose intentions and ability left nothing to chance in "Elektra." Never again did he emphasize the fluttering half-light of blood-red tone colours and the rhythmic and harmonic accents of an immense orchestra with such alarming openness of feeling. He flung wide the doors of expressionism.

The whole is held together by broad-spanned arches: the boldly-formed architecture of a single-movement dramatic symphony. The tragedy is summed up in four great musical-dramatic scenes which are filled to the brim with powerful feeling: Elektra's Monologue, the Klytemnestra scene, the Recognition scene, and the liberating ecstasy with which Elektra dances herself to death in a frenzy of self-destruction. The ear, which has just been allowed to bathe in the warm, sentimentally diatonic song of Chrysothemis in E♭ major (a piece whose Viennese flavour earned for it the ironic description "Chrysothemis Waltz"), is suddenly shocked by the hectic hysteria of Klytemnestra's entrance. Is this still music? The drawing of a sickly mind tormenting itself, the face of a being haunted by dreams and shaken by dread, reeking with blood and full of ghastly superstition, shows Strauss on the borders of musical naturalism. (Contemporary criticism rose to its climax in the words "This music smells," and in the "Signale" there were satirical references to libretti for "opera composers of Straussian tendencies" such as the music dramas "Incest," "Lynch Justice" and "The Bloodthirsty Gorilla"). Following the dramatic contours of the score, one becomes aware of the fact that it is not the wild, unruly elements, which in the composer's own words "go beyond all music," which trouble the ear today. More questionable are the episodes of Chrysothemis, and Strauss's mundane idealisation of anti-human elements in Elektra's triumphant dithyrambic dance of vengeance–today, to a greater extent than formerly, we are aware of the fact that even at such moments of harshness Strauss did not depart from his well-tried opulence of sound. (Stravinsky and Orff have since revealed a new concept of antiquity). Taken as a whole this work, in which Strauss appeared as a tragedian for the first and last time, is an oppressive, breathtaking outburst and outcry of a music dramatist at the turn of the century. No "opera of the future" in the Wagnerian sense, but a revolutionary, monumental document of its time for the opera stage, a work of unique brilliance, its composer's "most unified, compact, but also most spiritually powerful creation" (Schuh). Here was the "wonderful, furious, grandiose music" which Hofmannsthal had in mind a few years later for a dance drama "Orest und die Furien." Strauss, who had turned, from the time of "Ariadne" onward, to the new, ancient Hellenic ideal of "noble simplicity and tranquil greatness," would have none of it.

In September 1908 Strauss was at last able to write to his friend Schuh (this time only the Dresden Opera came into consideration for the world première), from the new house at Garmisch into which he had just moved: "'Elektra' is ready, and the end is juicy! The principal role must now undoubtedly be given to the most highly dramatic soprano you have . . ." Then, shortly before the eventful première in January 1909: "I am wildly eager to hear the 'Elektra' orchestra for the first time on the 18th." The opera was probably less strikingly successful than the electrifying "Salome." (Angelo Neumann even telegraphed to Prague that it had "flopped.") Not until thirty years later was this opera of great conductors and tragic actor-singers to achieve a come back. Since then it has reverberated like thunder round the world's larger opera houses at regular intervals. But although the fascination of sinister antiquity remains almost as strong as ever, this dark actus tragicus of decadence now appears as a detour away from the otherwise light-filled path along which Strauss travelled. Enough of tormenting passions which two thousand years could not placate. Enough of the inferno.

REALISTIC SCENES FROM LIFE

THE INEVITABLE CHANGE CAME WITH THE VIENNESE comedy *"Der Rosenkavalier."* Strauss, weary of the nervous sensations and uproar of his tragic operas, felt instinctively that he must turn to something else–something serene and full of life, not inhumanity but human warmth, not dissolution but bringing together, a reversion to simplicity, a consideration of the values inherent in opera form. Had he not, in "Salome" and "Elektra," represented merely the negative side of life in highly sophisticated garments? Were those operas not restricted, fundamentally, to illustrating the disintegration of former civilizations, without indicating any chance of a rebirth? In the long run they provided no solution. Escape into Biblical or classical antiquity must not be to a society sinking into a morass of degeneration–just as it would be a mistake to leave opera in a world of unreality, of beautiful mirages and false concepts of life. While it is true that Strauss was able to create warm-blooded figures in the realms of aesthetic literature with its mythology, divinities and kings, of the popular world of the theatre and the representation of history, a new positive movement also appeared in his work (above all in "Rosenkavalier," "Arabella" and "Schweigsame Frau")–toward the concept of opera as an expression of *festivity*, a feast of beauty! He did not devote his attention to imponderables, but, as his philosophy demanded, to subjects whose foundations were firmly established–seeking what was, sociologically speaking, security. It would be misleading to seek clear social intentions in these basically humorous works. They are "colourful reflections" of eras of German and Austrian cultural history, pictures of their times with a good, realistic feeling for the typical characteristics of the world around, spotlights turned on society, and in particular on human weaknesses and illusions.

313

("No intentional criticism of the age, but its unintentional mirror," in the words of Karl Laux). Instead of the barren factual descriptions of naturalistic artists he created fine dramatic action, with "pointed" instead of "photographically natural" dialogue. It must be recognized that this operatic art for "lovers of pleasure," with its air of opulence and enjoyment, is at the same time something for "thinking" people. We should not lose sight of the fact that Strauss contrasted the so-called upper classes, whose members do not by any means always cut a good figure, with representatives of the ordinary people: men and women of a Viennese tavern and of the Fiaker Ball, and strolling players in old England. This fact makes these works (to quote "Capriccio") the "symbol of life," "life striding forward" as Goethe conceived it. "The material is evident to all, but only he who has something to show discovers its meaning, and the form is a mystery to most people."

Strauss's leaning towards the rococo in "Rosenkavalier" is strange only to those who overlook the historical parallels between the heyday of rococo culture and the years prior to 1914. Both in the Louis-Quinze period and in the pre-war years mankind had a foreboding that the world was approaching a turning point. People shut their eyes to the threatening storm clouds, and preferred to feel their way back to the spirit of an epoch in which that alone appeared to be important and worthy of consideration which promised to increase the enjoyment of an existence long since shaken to its foundations. During that decade before the First World War Molière was re-discovered for the stage; the delicate charm of the paintings of Watteau, Boucher and Fragonard counteracted the violence of modern pictorial art, and Max Reinhardt achieved sold-out houses with Beaumarchais' comedy "Figaro." Fine artistry of delicacy and heartiness, a new brilliance of cultivated operatic art appeared, and deluded the public of that day concerning the true situation. Only from such soil of an era slipping downhill could the silver rose sprout ... Nevertheless it should not be overlooked that Strauss and Hofmannsthal did not show the whole of the age of Maria Theresa. Only in connection with the character of Ochs does "Rosenkavalier" give any indication of the powerful social tensions of the age, with the growing struggle for freedom from the bonds of feudalism.

314

When we think of a creative artist there generally comes to mind a particular, significant aspect of his nature or work. We think of Rembrandt's "Night Watch," Goethe's "Faust," Bach's "St. Matthew Passion," and Strauss's "Rosenkavalier." This brilliant concept of a Viennese comedy in music which the Bavarian master hit upon while at the height of his powers, having been drawn to the milieu by choice and intuition, is a slice of history become music–the last opera to be a really worldwide success. (As early as April 1909 Strauss could write exultantly to Hofmannsthal: "We shall smite as many tens of thousands with the new comedy as we have smitten thousands with 'Elektra,' as it says in the Bible about Saul and David.") What a surprise for the musical world eagerly awaiting the next milestone along the road of Strauss's development! Here was a "Viennese masquerade" which laughed at wisdom with its waltzes; no retreat into romanticism as some imagined, and at the same time no speculation or compromise with a public which had been unable to listen with Grecian ears, but a piece of human life giving rich pleasure, in which the gaiety of a healthy man, the wit of a brilliant mind, and the instinct of sensual feeling vibrate in a serene, crystal-clear firmament. Strauss was preaching no moral attitude, he was concerned to make music with all the resources of the theatre. The white and gold, the glittering silver rose of this score coloured by south-German culture have conquered all, right down to the present day. This festive opera (a characteristic which Hofmannsthal frequently emphasized) is acknowledged to be a classic of its time and style.

"Next time I'll write a Mozart opera!" Strauss did in fact correspond with Hofmannsthal about the possibilities of a buffo opera. The synopsis of a "Semiramis" based by the composer on Calderón's "Daughter of the Air" was rejected by the poet with the cool words that he was writing "for himself" at the moment, and could make nothing out of the plot of the Calderón work. Nevertheless this project remained in being until the autumn of 1910, and it was taken up again by Gregor in 1935. Hofmannsthal, on the other hand, attempted to win Strauss over for a comic opera based on a "Casanova" story (which later became the prose comedy "Christinas Heimkehr"). Then something else came to the surface, and at the beginning of 1909, shortly after the première of "Elektra," the ice was broken. A memorable letter arrived from Hofmannsthal in Weimar: "In three quiet afternoons here I have made a complete, entirely fresh synopsis of an opera ... Period: Maria Theresa." It was "Der Rosenkavalier!" As amusing as the work itself (which, until the completion of the composition, was still known as "Ochs von Lerchenau," or, for a time, "Die Frau Marschallin") is the poet's description of its birth that March. "The scenario was really evolved in conversation with the friend to whom the libretto is dedicated, Count Harry Kessler. The figures existed and acted before us even before we had names for them: the buffo, the old man, the girl, the lady, the 'Cherubino.' They were types which could not as yet be given real individuality. The always typical relationships between the characters gave rise to the action, almost without our knowing how ... The scene of these fruitful discussions was Weimar; I went to Berlin, without a word in writing except a note of the characters scribbled on the back of a namecard, but with a plot in my head coherent enough to relate. I remember the effect this account had on Strauss as though it were yesterday ... He said: 'Go home quickly and send me the first act as soon as possible!' ... Those enthusiastic discussions in Weimar, that playing with typical, unnamed figures and the possible combinations into which they could be drawn would have been insufficient in themselves to have conjured up a little world of living people, but in the background was the unspoken wish to create a half imaginary, half real picture of Vienna in 1740, a whole city with its different estates of the realm which confront each other and intermingle, its ceremonial, its classes of society, their mode of speech—or rather the different mode of speech of each class in the social order—with a sense of the proximity of the great Court, and above all an ever-present awareness of the ordinary people. Thus the bustling throng of minor figures came into being: a duenna, a police commissioner, an innkeeper, lackeys and a major-domo, intriguers, parasites, tradesmen, hairdressers, messengers, waiters, sedan-chair men, policemen, idlers ..." (As the poet saw them from his standpoint, one must add.)

Now work commenced, "with tempestuous animation" like the impulsive opening of the orchestral Prelude ..." First act received yesterday, am simply delighted" Strauss wrote at the beginning of May from Garmisch, where he was enjoying the annual leave from the Berlin Opera allowed him since the previous autumn. "It is really fascinating beyond all measure: so fine, perhaps a little too fine for the multitude, but that doesn't matter. The middle section (ante-chamber) not easy to construct, but I'll manage it. I've got the whole summer in front of me. Closing scene splendid, I have already done some exploratory work on it today. I wish I had got as far as that, but as I have to compose in the correct order on account of symphonic unity, I must just have patience. End of the act delightful; you are a

"*Der Rosenkavalier*": *Sketch for the introduction to the first act (1909)*

splendid fellow. When shall I get the rest? All the characters are fine, clearly drawn, but unfortunately I need very good actors again, once more it won't go with ordinary opera singers..." Twelve days later: "My work is flowing like the Loisach, I am composing everything in full as I reach it. Tomorrow I'll begin the levée. The scene with the Baron is already finished, but you must write me some more text: at the end of the Baron's Aria, after the phrase 'muss halt ein Heu in der Nähe dabei sein,' I need a big musical conclusion in the form of a Trio... If it goes on like this the first act can be ready in sketches at the beginning of June..." A few weeks later the mention of "hay" (in which village girls could be tumbled) gave rise to a vigorous protest

317

from the sensitive poet, who objected to the fact that Ochs boasted of his erotic adventures in a coarse fortissimo. "The line 'muss halt ein Heu hier in der Nähe sein' is conceivable only in a light tone of voice, from both the dramatic and musical points of view ... The fact that Ochs bellows 'Heu' *ff* gives me a stab of pain. I implore you to alter that"... "You are Da Ponte and Scribe in one!" ... So the work went forward rapidly, and at the end of May Bahr received the news: "The first act was finished in sketches yesterday: I believe I have succeeded in creating the Viennese milieu in atmosphere and melodic line."

The second act saw a temporary rift in the harmonious collaboration. On reading the text Strauss found it "excellent until the Baron's entrance," but felt that after that there was "something wrong," that the act "is flat and feeble, lacking the necessary increases of dramatic intensity." For the first time there occurred the situation which was to become the rule in each joint work from then on: the musician took over the reins himself ... "Three days of snow, rain and fog have today germinated a decision in my mind which I won't keep back from you any longer. Now this is how I imagine the second act ..." He proceeded to outline to his friend all the familiar events from the entrance of Ochs, who rushes in as a result of the outcry raised by the Italian intriguers, with the duel in which Octavian wounds him in the arm ... "One more thing: as you will now have to rewrite this section thoroughly, please revise the whole dialogue between the Baron and Sophie again. This dialogue is not on the level of the first act ..." Hofmannsthal accepted this "very helpful and fruitful criticism" in good part, not allowing it to "dishearten" him in the least. At the end of September Strauss finished the composition of this act, and began work on the instrumentation of the first two acts. By the end of April 1910 he completed this "hard grind," for which the publishers Fürstner in Berlin and the printers were already waiting ... And not even the text of the third act was yet ready! ("I am at Garmisch, waiting in agony.") He received it, though with omissions, early in May. Again Strauss, the demanding, raised objections: "The last piece which you have sent me doesn't please me at all in its disposition ..." "The entrance of the Marschallin and the scene which follows must be the focal point of the action, with the greatest tension and concentration. When the Baron and all the crowd have gone everything must gradually become lyrical, and return to gentle melodic lines." Hofmannsthal readily complied with his wishes, and confessed that he had here "learned something fundamental and not to be forgotten regarding dramatic writing for music ..." "Your alteration and compression is excellent; I am following it exactly, and am merely attempting to match the various situations with the most characteristic and comical turns of phrase (especially in the mouth of the Baron) ..." "So I hope you are satisfied–I have so enjoyed working on this project that I was almost sad when I had to write 'Curtain' at the end ..." Was the poet, whose attention was drawn by friends to longueurs after the exit of Ochs, right in thinking that the final scene would appear unduly protracted? "I have not failed to consider your letter, but for your peace of mind I can tell you that: 1. I have shortened various things at the end on my own account, and 2. neither you nor Herr von Salten can judge at this stage what the musical effect of this ending will be. The fact that it seems flat in reading is obvious. On the other hand, provided that anything occurs to the musician, it is precisely at the conclusion that he can aim to achieve his best and greatest effects–you can leave it to me to judge this. I am nearly ready, and I believe the last third has turned out brilliantly successful ... I will be guarantor for the ending from the Baron's exit, if you will guarantee the other parts of the work." How completely justified Strauss's self-assurance was in this instance! ... The score was completed at the end of September 1910.

Hofmannsthal himself summed up the story of the opera, which is not in itself complicated, in a letter to Strauss: "A fat, elderly, arrogant suitor, favoured by the father, is ousted by a handsome youth." The manner in which the doltish Baron Ochs auf Lerchenau, greedy for money and women, is adroitly robbed of the fruits of his vain machinations, how a mature woman renounces the love of a youth in favour of a budding young girl, so that the laws of morality are re-established and the impression remains that true love is not to be bought, and that youth belongs to youth–those are the contents of a bright, humanistic opera in the classical tradition. But what poet and composer have made out of this "non plus ultra of simplicity!" The development is really "completely removed from the trivial and conventional..." As Hofmannsthal wrote to Strauss "The lively atmosphere of the whole, with contrasting figures full of life" made use of all the "requirements, possibilities and stylistic laws of an operatic comedy." On the other hand the musician, who intended to compose a comic opera, was vigorous in making his demands. He did not want the "dramatic-comic" element to be neglected. "Don't forget that the public should also laugh! *Laugh,* not smile and smirk!" A glance at the score shows that Strauss did, however, seek a relaxed, Mozartian serenity which is as far removed from the middle-class comedy of situations of Lortzing or Nicolai as it is from the burlesque operetta style of Offenbach. (It is known that about that time Strauss several times went to the National Theatre in Prague to see performances of "The Two Widows," which Smetana had written with somewhat similar musical and dramatic aims in mind.)

Hofmansthal knew his people; he caricatured the figures a little when the subject demanded this treatment, and he was a thought over-gentle when he, the Viennese, was concerned with emotions. The division of the work into three acts of approximately equal length, the delight in ornamentation, and the sensitive play of moods are characteristic of the poet with whom Strauss readily–perhaps a little too readily–went into partnership from then on. His verse certainly demands music, while possessing music of its own. The work's virtues include its close contact with the Viennese popular comedy, its wholly successful creation of the "milieu" of Vienna in the days of Maria Theresa with its levée, its ceremonial, mysterious intriguers and a "God-damned private room," with "a hundred living links from the palace by way of the world of lackeys to the farmyard." Then there is the charm of the language: the fine gradations between the speech of the nobility, with their widespread use of foreign words, and the naive local jargon of the ordinary people. (No dialect can be translated convincingly into a foreign language.) The torrent of words used by Hofmannsthal's opera characters is sometimes dangerous. This is accentuated by the fact that Strauss lost a little of his control over the dimensions and form of the whole work through his desire to get on with the composition at once, although he often received acts and scenes of the libretto in instalments. A certain amount of verbiage, especially in the account of Ochs's amorous adventures and in the highly complex intrigues of the third act, might otherwise have been pruned considerably, and certain musical nuances might have been suited even more exactly to the libretto's differentiation in speech and characterization between the various social classes.

The sources of this work, which is basically a little "more than a farce," are to be found in a great many Viennese comedies and pieces of buffoonery. It is not difficult to detect relationships with "Figaro" (the Countess and Cherubino), and above all with the work of the English painter, copper-plate engraver and satirist Hogarth, with his famous engravings "The Toilette" and "Marriage à la Mode." Do we not find Ochs prefigured in the oafish provincial aristocrat from Limoges in Molière's ballet-comedy "Monsieur de Pourceaugnac," and Octavian in the figure of the young nobleman who disguises himself as a girl in Louvet de Couvray's "Faubias"? These two motifs were the basis of the first draft of the opera libretto, which Strauss evidently never saw. The idea for the final act was provided, apart from Molière, by the Viennese writer Hafner; even the stock figures of the opera buffa, the notary, doctor etc., were not omitted. Other things, such as the central scene of the presentation of the rose and the conclusion of the work, were products of Hofmannsthal's own imagination. Improbabilities such as the assembling of all the principal characters in a tavern of ill repute have to be accepted as operatic conventions. This is a fundamentally musical, poetic opera libretto poised between broad popular appeal and a study of deep human feelings–indeed a "comedy *for* music!" It is the fulfilment of a musical-poetic collaboration on a high artistic level, a weaving together of the work of two men striving toward the same goal, although the then foremost poet of Austria found himself subject to misunderstandings and attacks even from his friends on its account. The creators of "Rosenkavalier" never had cause to regret their hours of happiness. "When I had Hofmannsthal's libretto read to my Opera Director in Berlin, Count Hülsen," Strauss later wrote, "he advised me against it: he said it was no text for me! He regretted that he had 'so little time,' otherwise he himself would have written a 'genuine German text' for me! After the hundredth Berlin performance he came to me in the artists' room and congratulated me with the words: 'But it's also a delightful libretto!'. . ."

The characters of this comedy of music and action . . . There is scarcely another opera in musical history the dramaturgical significance of whose characters has been so extensively considered and written about. At the centre of the human scene stands the Marschallin–her Christian names Marie Theres are certainly no mere chance. Many people have thought of her, with her goodness of heart and spiritual stature, tied to an older husband and leading a useless life, as movingly typifying the tragedy of those who are growing old and faded. That is an understandable exaggeration, which has its origin in the relative lack of spiritual depth in the other figures (a shortcoming of comedy, whose characters remain as they are established at the outset). One generally hears and sees the Marschallin, who undoubtedly personifies declining feudalistic society in Austria, as a woman filled with resignation. How did Strauss wish the Marschallin to be imagined? He wrote in his "Recollections": ". . . A young, beautiful woman, at most 32 years old, who once, in a moment of bad temper, appears to the seventeen-year-old Octavian as an 'ageing woman,' but is by no means David's Magdalena–who is also frequently presented too old. Octavian is neither the first nor the last lover of the beautiful Marschallin, who also must not play her first act conclusion sentimentally as a tragic farewell for life, but still with Viennese grace and charm, with one eye damp, the other dry . . ." "She was only annoyed with the hairdresser," he once said with a touch of irony about that often misunderstood scene. Quite clearly Strauss ensured that this unsentimental view prevailed with regard to the Princess Werdenberg of the unfortunate "Rosenkavalier" film of 1926: a lonely young woman who, scarcely escaped from her convent education, has been forced by her parents to marry the famous field marshal (also young), who appears in the film version.

The other principal figure is Ochs. "The success of the opera depends on Ochs," Strauss wrote to Schuch shortly before the world première in Dresden. In this boorish hunter of wealth and women, who brags about his "aristocratic" origins, the author and composer have turned their backs on aestheticism and drawn a crude, insensitive member of the landed gentry to the life. The Marschallin sums up the situation when she sings:

> There he goes,
> the bloated, evil man,
> and gets the pretty young thing
> and a rich dowry with her.

Here, too, Strauss had his own sound views, but unfortunately they are seldom put into practice in the opera house. "Most bass singers have always presented a hideous monster with a ghastly make-up, a figure whom civilized audiences (French and Italian) have rightly found repulsive. This is completely incorrect. Ochs must be a handsome country Don Juan about 35 years old, a nobleman (though somewhat coarsened by country life) who can behave himself correctly enough in the Marschallin's salon, so that she does not have him thrown out by her servants after five minutes. *Inwardly* he is utterly coarse, but he is presentable enough outwardly or Faninal would have rejected him at first glance. In particular the first scene of Ochs in the bedroom must be played with the utmost delicacy and discretion if it is not to be as revolting as the flirtation of an old general's wife with a second lieutenant. Comedy, not–low Berlin farce!"

While Hofmannsthal, in his "unwritten foreword to 'Der Rosenkavalier,'" also described Ochs as "at any event still a nobleman of a kind," and the Marschallin as "still, as it were, a person of distinction," he saw in Sophie, the young daughter of the purse-proud, newly ennobled parvenu Faninal, only a "pretty, everyday girl . . . of bourgeois silliness, affected, the product of her education." Did he really ignore the fact that it is to this charming bud of a girl ("My mother is dead, and I am all alone. I must stand for myself . . .") that the future belongs? Strauss's characterization of Sophie by the same motif of a fourth and sixth which he used for the Marschallin is a fine example of his art of psychological character drawing. All the decorative magic of the work is concentrated on "Octavian, called Quinquin, a young gentleman of noble family," the boyish Count Rofrano and immediate successor of Mozart's Cherubino–a woman plays a youth, who in turn dresses up as a girl; a woman in man's clothes thus has to give the impression of a young man in disguise. When Octavian sees Sophie "he is struck dumb." One must watch and listen very closely in order to recognize, behind the spectacle of an attractive breeches role, the youth who, as the possessor of great personal gifts but still half a child, is already deep in the swamp of feudal society, lives a dream of love, and chances to light on the little Sophie . . . In his essay on Hofmannsthal and Strauss Hans Mayer wrote that Strauss, with Cherubino in mind, had "developed but also blunted" the title figure; on the other hand he had, with his own unique means, "exalted" Sophie.

This operatic comedy, composed in just under seventeen months, is a feast of melody. One could imagine many of the orchestra's melodies, unaltered, being sung, and what are the voice parts in the Trio Finale of the third act but lines of the score, three among many, in a texture out of whose fragrant clouds radiant sound ascends, floating more delicately than the tenderest voice! There is scarcely another opera (apart from "Daphne") in which instruments and voices are so sensuously and ethereally blended, so united in their purpose. That is probably the really novel feature of "Rosenkavalier": its return to the melodic principle of pure "opera," which constantly breaks through the spirited parlando phrases of its conversational style. Its sweetly luxuriant melodies delighted audiences from the first. The tender melancholy which occurs at times has moved all hearts, the immense verve of the Viennese three-four time has carried all before it. The return to diatonic harmony is matched by the re-introduction of self-contained musical forms. Spirit, wit, irony, dancelike animation and blissful emotion—the music is a single crescendo of feeling, bathed in the glowing colours of the orchestra restored to its normal size and to its normal accompanying function. Such sparkling happiness had been lacking in German opera since Mozart. In the richness of its musical figures this work reflects the living rococo spirit which has come down to us not in painted ceilings and ornate paintings in heavy gilt frames, but in graceful, silver-framed pastels.

This work has been called a "waltz-opera" (just as "Die Meistersinger" has been described as a "march opera.") It was a brilliant idea of Strauss to intensify the Viennese atmosphere by means of the 19th century waltz, and at the same time to smuggle the waltz, which was still forbidden at the Court of Wilhelm II, into serious opera through the back door of a disreputable tavern. Some people, with scruples worthy of Beckmesser, have regarded the waltz melodies as stylistically out of place, demanding instead dance forms of Maria Theresia's Vienna (Minuet, Gavotte, Sarabande etc.). Gysi retorted: "In that case a work like 'Tannhäuser' ought to be written in medieval neumes." The Richard Strauss Waltz with its rhythmic and harmonic attractions is a child of the 20th century, and is well suited

324

to helping to establish the tone of this "comedy for music" with its joy of living turned into sensuous sound. Other anachronisms found their way into the score, but it is to the remarkable mixture of the swaying bliss of vigorous waltzes (Ochs Finale of the second act), silvery-tender rococo magic (presentation of the rose), old Italian cantabile (Tenor Aria) and naive tunes reminiscent of folksong (Concluding Duet) that the score owes much of its charm. After all, the most diverse elements are brought together as an entity in Mozart's "Zauberflöte." Contemporary criticism made the most extraordinary suggestions for eliminating the "stylistic discrepancies." Probably the oddest was the proposal to cut out the last act completely, adding a "happy ending" to the second act . . .

There is no space to mention more than a few of the gems of melodic invention which Strauss strewed, though not altogether evenly, over this opera with its superabundance of life. As the poet wrote shortly before the première, it is "like a garland made entirely of flowers." First act: the Prelude sweeps by with the impulsive, seventeen-year-old ardour of Octavian. In ninety bars it gives an exact and unmistakable picture of the erotic content of the work, an introduction to its world of feelings. What a richly animated opening scene between the Marschallin and her young lover, followed by the sweet archaism of the Breakfast Minuet and the turbulent entrance and narration of Ochs, with his boasting of his sexual exploits in hay lofts! The specifically Viennese note, with its impudently ironical undertone, is intuitively struck right away. The levée, skilfully constructed from a diversity of elements including the Italian Tenor Canzona, leads into the lyrically lustrous, poignantly coloured Monologues of the Marschallin, which give an early hint of the renunciation which must follow. Second act: everything builds up to the presentation of the rose in the light of shimmering, silvery sound, with the grandeur of a splendid ceremony. (The finely-pointed chord sequences in F♯ major of the three flutes, three solo violins, harps and celesta create an unforgettable impression). The lyrical duet of the young couple is of a wonderfully fine intimacy of spirit. The musical flow is halted for a time by the drastic comedy of Ochs, his lackeys and other minor figures, culminating in the Duel, until the Finale with the great "Lerchenau" Waltz, which Strauss himself described as a "hit of the first order." The third act opens with the orchestra's virtuistic, will-o'-the-wisp Presto Fugato. The music played during the Baron's supper at the tavern while he plans to seduce the supposed maid Mariandl, with its sensual waltzes, is perhaps a trifle too close to the world of operetta. Then, however, the broadly-flowing lyricism of the renowned Trio for female voices descends on the listener–Strauss evolved this enthralling combination of the voices of the Marschallin, Octavian and Sophie from the parodistic waltz of Mariandl with amazingly rich inspiration. A chef d'œuvre comparable only to the "Meistersinger" Quintet! (During the composition of this brilliantly laid-out piece Strauss's wife is said to have pressed him to spin out the thematic threads more and more). The Closing Duet of the two young lovers, Mozartian and reminiscent of folksong, has the task of bringing the work to a sweetly poetic ending of intimate delicacy. Strauss never felt and formed music so intensively as in this Finale. Never since Wagner has the opera stage experienced such a moving and deeply satisfying apotheosis.

While Strauss was still working on the last, "merriest" and "most songlike" act of his opera the preparations for the latest "Strauss Première" began in Dresden. It was to be in January 1911, the "last entirely carefree international event of the European theatre before the war" (Gregor). Once again Schuch conducted a Strauss world première–probably the most dazzling of all. As the production of this piquant comedy proved too much for the theatre's resident producer, Strauss brought Max Reinhardt in to save the ship, later writing "Ariadne" for him as an act of gratitude. ("There is now such an accumulation of inflammable material directed against me and my poor 'Rosenkavalier' that I will probably not let myself be seen at the première.") Thus there came together in Dresden the foremost exponents of the musical theatre in pre-war days: apart from Schuch and Reinhardt the Viennese scenic artist Alfred Roller, whose designs were later constantly quoted as "models." Strauss was angry when the broad canvas of the comedy was later slashed by unnecessary cuts. Dark clouds around a happy opera! "Der Rosenkavalier," which Strauss dedicated in a spirit of bonhomie to "My dear kinsfolk the Pschorr Family in Munich," and whose original score was later presented to the National Library in Vienna, brilliantly weathered all the storms with its "shattering

Poster for the Dresden World Première of "Der Rosenkavalier"

success, extra trains to Dresden etc." A special post office even had to be set up in the Semper building of the Opera House. It has always given most pleasure on the stage when the lilting Viennese element has been emphasized by the cast, and also from the conductor's desk. ("So light, flowing tempi, without compelling the singers to rattle off the text . . . in a word: Mozart–not Lehár," Strauss later wrote in a letter to Schuh). The waltzes have reached the broadest public in a variety of concert versions, to a greater extent than music from any other opera of recent times. "Rosenkavalier" is the most important cultural offspring of German comedy in music since "Figaro" and "Meistersinger." With it Strauss really "spread happiness."

*

The worldwide success of the "comedy for music" soon tempted Strauss to venture on a similar undertaking in a popular vein. While still occupied with the naively harmless "Intermezzo" to his own text, he began to look around for suitable new subjects. In the autumn of 1918 Hofmannsthal suggested a "bucolic opera." The poet noted: "Festival of flowers, almost pagan-mythical, as the centrepiece, or a peasant wedding . . . the whole a ceremony: mysterious and comic figures." What a strange scenario, when one reflects that Hofmannsthal was affected more than many of his compatriots by the downfall of the Austrian Empire! Strauss seems to have been more attracted to a suggestion for a comedy made by Alfred Kerr, the author of the "Krämerspiegel": a comic opera entitled "Peregrin." "Peregrin–the philosophizing world-improver of ancient times–who finally, tormented by his craving to achieve something startling, jumps on to a self-built pyre–and is burned to ashes. Its combination of biting humour and death seems to me to make it an excellent theme . . . The ineffectual striver after a high aim. The farcical hero, tragic hero. The idiot blundering in a tragic drama" (Kerr). The plan fell through owing to the fact that the Berlin critic never completed his libretto.

An imperialistic world war had changed the people and their social conditions. The human climate had become cooler, the milieu more sordid. The glitter of the silver rose remained undimmed, but the figures around it appeared in a new light. Nevertheless the composer first used a significant phrase in 1922:

a "second 'Rosenkavalier.'" "Nothing can be experienced a second time," replied Hofmannsthal, but that was not to be the last word on the subject. Already in 1924 the poet mentioned in a letter a "Viennese comedy" suitable for setting to music, and only three more years elapsed before the plan for a continuation and further development of this popular class of opera had proceeded so far that a decision by the two artists (who had meanwhile collaborated in the creation of "Helena," a work of a totally different kind) was in the air.

Then, in 1927, there was a remarkable encounter with Wagner's "Meistersinger" which might have been as significant for Strauss as his visit to a performance of the play "Elektra." Strauss wrote Hofmannsthal a really astonishing letter concerning the effect of this Munich "Meistersinger," which illuminates the situation perfectly. "I recently heard 'Meistersinger' again, a fabulous work. Since then the wish has never left me to write another work of this nature–unfortunately, of course, at a fitting distance. But at all events a really German work, a good piece for the theatre and at the same time a genuine document of German culture. The best background to the subject seems to me to be the age-old contrast between Latin and German art–which must be personified in three representatives of music and poetry corresponding to the three types Walther, Sachs and Beckmesser." At what other time did Strauss the musical dramatist approach so near to the characteristics of national realistic art? Tireless in passing on promising ideas to his colleague, Strauss suggested the following three types to present the antithesis Latin-German on the stage: "1. the German artist who adopts foreign, Bohemian ideas, 2. the artist creating on the basis of both cultures, represented at best by Mozart, and most recently by my own humble efforts, 3. the so-called Boche-type... He would finally have to be developed ad absurdum à la Beckmesser, or represent the disgraced intriguant of the piece..." Strauss also mentioned literary works which he wanted Hofmannsthal to study (Hagen's "Minnesingers," R. von Liliencron's "German life in folk songs," Fürstenau's "History of the Dresden Opera" and others), and mentioned events of his own life of which use could be made in the action of the opera. He visualized a "long, five-hour opera with choruses and ballet," and concluded: "It would be splendid if anything better occurred to

329

you, but it must be *'Meistersinger No. III'* (there can't be a second 'Meistersinger,' a thought freely adapted from Bülow)...
I now have time and leisure, and still feel tolerably fit to tackle such a vast work!"

His friend's reaction was not surprising. He could not find anything in Wagner's realistic, historical comedy which would nourish his own creative processes. An idea useful to the composer was, he wrote, a great blessing, which was more likely to be frittered away than stimulated by such models. The great charm and great strength of "Die Meistersinger" (purely as a literary work) lay, for him, in its indestructible reality, as it presents "German municipal life and its changes," and "gives new life to a true, compact world which once existed..." However, such a realistic view of bourgeois life, 16th century Germany reflected in a picture of Nuremberg, was "not to be imitated" –even as a national document. ("The national epic was the product of a temporary increase of national feeling brought about by the unification of Germany.") Nor could he accept the idea of autobiographical elements. Hofmannsthal's conclusion was that such a work could not be copied or repeated, that at most it could be taken as a general model. "Although far removed from its model there is, however, a fairly successful opera which owes a great deal to 'Meistersinger,' the only one so far as I know: 'Der Rosenkavalier!' There it is the Nuremberg of 1500, here the Vienna of Maria Theresa ... which really forms the basis of the whole work, and through which the characters take on life..." Such figures as Ulrich von Liechtenstein (whom Strauss had in mind) were as uninviting to him as the whole world of the decaying middle ages–something, perhaps, for Gerhart Hauptmann, whom he recommended to Strauss, not without a touch of irony. "My imagination was drawn to the atmosphere, suited to comedy, of a far more recent period–possibly 1840 or 1850." Meanwhile Strauss had made another proposal: Turgenyev's novel "Mist," but he was not yet satisfied; he felt himself misunderstood by the poet, and went into detail: "Between Puccini and Pfitzner, with three original feminine figures who produce a tangled web of envy and jealousy" ... Now Hofmannsthal was offended, and he pointed out to Strauss the difference between Puccini's librettists and himself, "as I am compelled by my nature ... to produce something of stature." He made himself even clearer: "I might just as well bang on the table with my knuckles and say to you: there you have the thematic material for a symphony." The plan of a gay one-act opera with ballet, "Achilles auf Skyros," in which Hofmannsthal attempted to interest his friend, was also abandoned.

*

Troubled times! On no other occasion did Strauss and a writer have such difficulty in agreeing on the subject of a new opera. The background was the vague idea, which remained alive for many years, of renewing the success of "Rosenkavalier," while producing something which was both outwardly and inwardly entirely fresh in effect. There could be no doubt that the "Meistersinger" project, an attempt along these lines, had been killed by Hofmannsthal's unfavourable attitude. The turning point came with a letter which Strauss wrote at the end of June 1927: "After 'Helena' I should like to write a short one-acter," then, in September, a call for help followed: "In a week's time I will have finished the score of 'Helena,' . . . but now I have nothing more to work on: totally burned out! So please write! It may even be a 'second Rosenkavalier' if nothing better occurs to you. At worst a little stop-gap work–a one-acter–practice in dexterity–oil to prevent the imagination from becoming rusty . . ." This time the spark started a fire. Hofmannsthal wrote about a comedy idea with a ballroom, a charming female character and several young men, period 1860 or 1880. A little later he wrote: "The figures of the new comedy opera dance before my eyes almost importunately. They are spirits I have conjured up for you, and now I cannot get rid of them. The comedy can be better than 'Rosenkavalier.' The figures stand perfectly clearly before me, and they are very well contrasted. The two girls (sopranos) can be splendid roles (for singing) . . . A tenorino and a baritone as lovers. The latter is the most remarkable figure in the piece, from a half-foreign world (Croatia), half a buffo, and at the same time a splendid fellow, capable of deep feelings, wild and gentle, almost demoniacal . . . The principal figure is female . . ."

What the poet here outlined was the long-promised second "Viennese book," the "lyrical comedy" in three acts *Arabella* or The Fiaker Ball." The characters and motives mentioned by Hofmannsthal appeared in the novel "Lucidor, figures from an unwritten comedy," published in 1910, a work whose first draft dates from the same time as the "Rosenkavalier" libretto, and a "Lucidor" scenario of the summer of 1910; this comedy plan occupied him at regular intervals until 1926 (on the last occasion as a "Vaudeville" for Gustav Waldau). In addition Hofmannsthal used elements from the projected light comedy "Der Fiaker als Graf," whose rather bloodless plot appeared to him to be "too slender" to provide an opera subject on its own, but which could be "linked with motifs from another unwritten comedy." The combination of the "Lucidor" story with the Viennese "Fiaker" atmosphere provided a suitable basis for a three-act operatic comedy, "almost an operetta," which was to rank in its humorous aspects not only with "Rosenkavalier" but also with "Fledermaus" ...

Six months elapsed before Hofmannsthal had got the libretto into shape. Strauss had at once realized that for the opera the principal emphasis would have to be transferred from the love affair of the girl disguised as a boy to Arabella and her mysterious suitor Mandryka; Zdenko (Lucidor) and Matteo (Wladimir) should provide the secondary plot. The milieu of Vienna in the 'sixties was also to be given greater emphasis, and to be integrated with the action. The Fiaker Ball, with the historical figure of Fiakermilli, the coachmen etc., offered a good opportunity for presenting glimpses of everyday life in Vienna at that time. When the completed libretto finally arrived at Garmisch, Strauss was by no means entirely satisfied. "I have just received 'Arabella,' have already read it through carefully three times, and find the first act as a whole capital. The figures are very good and plastic, the 'landowner' especially attractive and original. So far I find only Arabella a little less clearly drawn, and her short dialogues with the three Counts (for Hofmannsthal) rather unimportant and commonplace. Only the end of the act seems unfortunate to me. In my opinion it must definitely conclude with a solo, an aria, a lyrical outpouring of Arabella ..." "As I say, the architecture of the last seven pages isn't good, has no musical line, too much confusion in the dialogue; it would be difficult to compose, and could hardly be formed into unified musical structures ..." (And Strauss directed the poet's attention to the great aria for Katharina in Goetz' "Taming of the Shrew").

332

A new note had entered into the artistic collaboration of the two men. A picture of the new opera did not form itself as quickly in Strauss's mind as was generally the case, and when he returned to the first act, after some time had elapsed, it would not "begin to turn into sound, and to be frank, the characters don't interest me at all . . . in particular the principal figure Arabella, who does not go through the slightest spiritual conflict throughout the whole three acts . . . harmlessness personified . . . everything will be weaker and more conventional than in 'Rosenkavalier' unless you succeed in making Arabella a really interesting figure like our good Marschallin . . ." When had Strauss found one of his operatic heroines so unsatisfactory? A feeling of uncertainty beset the composer, who even suggested a scene showing that Arabella had really loved Matteo, and considered the possibility of a tragic ending to the opera. "It must not be a frivolous comedy, particularly as it now contains nothing really amusing or witty, everything pointing towards tragi-comedy . . . How would it be if, at the moment when the temperamental Mandryka believes Arabella to have been proved faithless to him, he shoots himself, and Arabella gives him the 'glass of water' as he lies dying?" . . . Hofmannsthal succeeded in persuading Strauss to abandon this unhappy denouement, but there was still no agreement concerning the complete revision of the first act, whose satisfactory construction Strauss regarded as determining the question of the composition. He also considered the title "Arabella" too colourless . . . Hofmannsthal: "I will keep your demands in front of me as a rule to be observed strictly." Strauss: "Your appreciation of exactly what else I would like the new piece to contain convinces me that you will . . . find the right solution. Take as much time as you like–I am patient, and am concerning myself with Mandryka, who must, after all, establish the tone of the whole and determine the style." This struggle to put "Arabella" into shape lasted for eighteen months; as late as June 1929 Strauss was still dissatisfied with certain points–and he had still not composed a note . . .

Really a new edition of "Rosenkavalier?" Were not both composer and librettist visualizing something far more popular in style, close to operetta? Strauss wrote pressingly: "A year ago I asked you for a great subject à la 'Meistersinger'; if I cannot have this, then a little Scribe, Sardou or even Lortzing in the garb of Hofmannsthal" ... The poet, allowing that he "can do with an injection of Scribe and Sardou from time to time," wrote: "You have helped me to go beyond my natural satisfaction with the characteristics of the dramatic figures, making me seek their final justification in the action." He paid his friend back in the same coin by asking him, on this occasion, to "think and feel" himself into the personalities of the contemporaries for whom the work was, after all, to be written. He expected a great deal of the planned realistic comedy opera, "if, as a new stylistic undertaking, not diminishing power but increased artistic insight leads to a reduction of the volume of sound, if the primary element, the melody, is allotted to a rather greater extent to the voice, and the orchestra, at least for long stretches, is not treated symphonically but is subordinated to the voice in an accompanying role (not as regards volume of tone, but in a different distribution of the 'leadership')." He believed that in this way operetta could be robbed of the "magic circle" which it had cast round the hearts of the public. "If one could only get away from the spirit of intellectual music, that element which is unduly prominent in German musical life ... yes, if as a fully mature composer one could reach right out of oneself, perhaps something really enchanting could be attained ..." At the time when Strauss began to concern himself with the music of the new work he wrote that he was studying with great interest Kuhač's collection of South-Slavonic folk songs and dances, with the intention of making use of them in the opera. Hofmannsthal's reply is very revealing: he said he had nothing in principle against the use of folk melodies, but he warned expressly against drawing on them for a ballet episode in the Fiaker Ball of the second act, as that would endanger the historical validity of the score.

The year 1929 saw the libretto of "Arabella" arrive at its final shape, but it also saw the sudden end of the artistic collaboration with Hofmannsthal's tragic death on the 15th July. During the previous summer Strauss had written to his friend in terms which proved to be prophetic: "I find that we understand one another better from year to year; what a pity that such good work of steadily increasing perfection must some day come to an end, and others will have to start again from the beginning ..." When Strauss received the libretto in its final form he was so pleased with it that he sent Hofmannsthal an enthusiastic telegram of thanks. This telegram arrived at Rodaun a few hours before the funeral of Hofmannsthal's eldest son, who had taken his own life. It remained unnoticed on the writing desk–together with the messages of sympathy on the loss of the son. It was not opened until days after the death of the poet, whose delicate constitution had been unable to bear the blow. A "young man again, in eternal grace," as Thomas Mann called him in his commemorative words, had passed away . . . Strauss took up the new work, certainly not with a light heart, retaining the title chosen by the poet, "Arabella . . ."

"Vienna, about the year 1860 . . ." So it was, indeed, to be something in the nature of a "second Rosenkavalier." However, the "pleasure-craving, frivolous, debt-contracting" Vienna of that time with its "questionable modes of existence," its tarnished brilliance, is even more remote from modern feeling than the historical enchantment of Vienna under Maria Theresia. The Vienna of 1860 had long since forfeited its "golden" glory. It had become threadbare and musty, and shabbiness ought to be clearly indicated as contributing to the "atmosphere" of this work, although producers often fail to do this. "Arabella" did not originate in the late Biedermeier period of Franz Joseph, it only "plays" in it. At the same time poet and musician introduce something of the resigned fatalism of an aristrocratic society already in decline: "The position is hopeless, but not serious." It is good to find that in this instance there is an abundance of historical satire (although Hofmannsthal anxiously avoided any contact with the wars around 1860), with a clear view of elements of the decadent world, and of those which were strong enough to hold out against it. Figures such as Count Waldner, the retired cavalry officer whose passion for gambling has brought him to the brink of bankruptcy, and his Victorian wife, possess all the characteristics of an aristocratic society corroded by capitalism. This man of breeding will stop at nothing in his efforts to marry his elder daughter Arabella to a rich husband. He sends a picture of her to a wealthy brother officer of his regiment, hoping that, "fool that he is," he might marry the girl. Arabella is a mixture of Chrysothemis and Sophie, a lovable, proud creature who dreams in all humility of the "right man, if there is one for me in this world"–"the queen of the whole piece." But she is, fundamentally, as far removed from this haute volée withering in luxury, in which one merely makes a show of being "top drawer," as is her suitor from Walachia, the well-to-do Mandryka: a member of the landed gentry, but "half a peasant," who, in his vigorous strength of character (allied to humour) is wholesomeness personified. One of the few real bon vivants in operatic literature! Other figures are less sharply drawn. Zdenka, devoted by nature, forced to wear boy's clothes because their father can provide for only *one* daughter "in something like the fitting manner," represents a new, attractive type of breeches role, but the idea of a girl brought up as a boy has more of the romantic novel than of realistic comedy about it. (In "Lucidor" Hofmannsthal wrote that Lucile had "some masculine characteristics": her hair had been kept short since an attack of typhus, and her hips were slender). The not exactly intelligent cavalry officer Matteo, and Fiakermilli, copied rather weakly from a character of popular tradition, remain marginal figures.

The poet, to whom this work represented a concession after the venture into the mythological world of "Helena," did not here write from the depths of his heart, composing rather than feeling, returning to the atmosphere of the old Austria, this time to the world of a declining aristocracy, whose typical modes of speech he captured. "Romanticism in a sinking world" (H. Mayer)! Many of the motifs and characteristics in the plot of this work seem like weaker offshoots of the great baroque comedy of love. Frequently the variation of elements of proved effectiveness can only be felt, not established in detail. Nevertheless it exists. Widespread use is made of historical material of the 'sixties, typical Viennese features, and figures from society and everyday life of the period, producing rich humour in the scene of the Fiaker Ball (though this is, unfortunately, dramatically weak). Even when Hofmannsthal approached the sphere of the operetta which had long given the world a false picture of Vienna, he demonstrated his own experience in the drawing of human beings, in the art of spinning threads, tying and untying them. In the foreground, for him, are the two events of "the fullest experience of life" which determine the destiny of the two pairs of lovers: the initial encounter, and the transformation it brings to each. The libretto does, however, contain longueurs, recalling its literary origin, which were dangerous to the composer. (Although Strauss often expressed the wish for lyrically expansive passages.) The

336

unravelling of Zdenka's improbable plot concerning the key of Arabella's room, for example, is unduly protracted, as is the resulting episode with the revolver. But what poetry there is in the closing scene, when Arabella descends the stairs towards the reconciled Mandryka, holding in her hand the glass of water which (unlike Scribe) Hofmannsthal employed as the symbol of bridal chastity! Hofmannsthal's artistry as a poet of opera exercised its magic once again.

"... and in fact the whole of Vienna is nothing but a mixture of opera and operetta." Opera in the garb of operetta–that demanded from the outset a new outlook on the part of the composer who had referred in a letter written to Hofmannsthal in 1916 to his "great talent for operetta," and had been a Viennese by choice for ten years: light, melodious music as a reflection of the morbid "haut goût" of this bourgeois, frivolous, hidebound Vienna, which creates a sense of reality without upsetting the formal balance. Strauss, who, strangely enough, never got to the point of writing a real operetta, here succeeded in establishing the correct atmosphere. The Slavonic folk melodies stand out like gems in the conversational setting of the "lyrical comedy;" the rustic melodies of Mandryka, the poignant duet between Arabella and her wooer, in which skilful entwining of the two voices grows into an impressive hymn, and above all the duet of the sisters Arabella and Zdenka, whose melody, played by the horns in conjunction with the voice lines, has a charm of its own which no one could overlook. This element of folksong, which fits in so admirably with the satirical aspects of the work, is the best thing in a score of full maturity. Strauss was undoubtedly looking back; his sweetly melodious lyricism abounds in passages in thirds and sixths, while some things give the impression of being mere sensuous decor. It should, however, be noted that Strauss handled the orchestra and the ensembles with new mastery, and that everything has become slender and simple by comparison with "Rosenkavalier." The transparency of the orchestral sound, which often approaches the quality of chamber music (the wind generally appearing only in tuttis and interludes), the economy shown in the use of chromatic harmony, the feathery buoyancy learned from Mozart–all these show Strauss at the summit of his technical powers. The tone picture of "Arabella" never becomes monotonous. The orchestra (middle-period

Wagner in size) is characterized by warm melodies in the inner parts (violas) above sustained bass lines, with bright, animated upper parts.

Would the dramatic and also musical weaknesses which "Arabella" undoubtedly contains have been eliminated during further intensive work by author and composer to establish its most perfect possible form? The sudden death of Hofmannsthal certainly prevented the making of many more alterations–he had put only the first act into its final form. ("Hofmannsthal's last word–one has no choice but to follow" Strauss wrote to Anton Kippenberg) . . . Virtually the whole first act is captivating, with its mixture of "prose" and "lyricism," its crystalline clarity and its air of effortless mastery. The opening with the fortune teller, the amusing scene between Waldner and his daughter's suitor with the wittily pointed "Teschek, bedien' dich" (Please help yourself–to banknotes!) and finally Arabella's poignantly lyrical monologue, with its prominent viola solo–these all glow with a diversity of colours. By contrast the second act, after the tender meeting of the lovers, contains a certain amount of inferior material, with rather artificial waltzes and the quick polka of Fiakermilli. Strauss did not hit on a wholly convincing note for this section of pure operetta, with its after-echo of the ballroom act of "Fledermaus." The conclusion to the act is no conclusion at all, but a device to get out of an awkward situation. (The "Munich version," in which the Finale, abbreviated, leads straight into the stormy, unambiguous orchestral prelude to the last act, is a later attempt to improve the construction of the work at this point.) The lengthy final act draws at first on musical motifs of the preceding acts. The style is conversational, melodically supported, and embellished with highly artistic contrapuntal lines, but without striking individuality at dramatic moments. At the climax of the dramatic conflict the "sprechgesang" gives place to spoken dialogue–the parlando is so lively that it casts the music off. The Finale, introduced by the same impressive descending sequence of chords which accompany the moment in the second act when Arabella is introduced to her lover in the ball scene, expresses the joy of unfulfilled longing in a fine poetic manner. Once again the ear is regaled with rare delights.

The composition of the opera was delayed when Strauss found pleasure in a totally different labour: the revision of Mozart's

338

"Idomeneo." In 1931 he wrote to Erich Engel in Dresden: "'Arabella' is nearly ready in the piano sketches! But please don't ask me for the score! There is no time at all for such works now: I'm not in any hurry at all. Until people are half way to understanding a little about 'Frau ohne Schatten,' 'Intermezzo' and 'Helena' they need not hear anything more . . ." Three months later he wrote to Busch that the "first hundred pages of the 'Arabella' score are written, and the opera can be launched down the slipway in September 1933," but he sounded a different note in May: "It is not easy for me to decide to give up a performance of 'Arabella,' but firstly I have become rather weary of the labour, and would like to interrupt it with a new work, provided that my powers of invention continue to function reasonably well as my seventieth birthday approaches, and secondly the circumstances (neither the publisher, the theatre nor the public have any money) have become so unfavourable that I believe it would be foolish to launch a major work into such uncertain waters now . . ." Nevertheless, partly thanks to the urging of the vigorous Dresden Opera Director, "Arabella" was completed by mid-October 1932. Then, when the brownshirts took over control of the State in the following year, and the period of cultural crises began, the composer felt little desire for a Strauss première at Dresden under the aegis of the new regime–he wanted to put the opera "back into its box." Only when he could see no way out of his existing contractual obligations did he give permission for the world première to take place under Clemens Krauss in July 1933. Hofmannsthal was not the only person missing: Busch and Reucker, to whom the work is dedicated jointly, were absent on account of the new political circumstances. The unanimously favourable reception of the work reflects the extent to which lovers of Strauss had been longing for a happy work in a popular style such as this. The fact that "Arabella" is now the most frequently performed Strauss opera in Germany after "Rosenkavalier" (some way ahead of "Ariadne" and "Salome"), and continues to create its full effect (despite a certain amount of criticism) demonstrates how successfully the spirit of the older type of operatic comedy was here renewed. Much of the superficiality of operetta which seemed to weaken the work becomes transformed in the lyrical, human shimmer of the musical portrait of its heroine.

*

The "new work" with which Strauss wanted to interrupt the instrumentation of "Arabella," and which he in fact began to sketch out twelve days before the completion of the score of the earlier work, was the comic opera *"Die schweigsame Frau."* When he received the libretto from Stefan Zweig he was fired with enthusiasm. At a time when there was a great deal to sour his life here was a buffo text after his own heart—a little frivolous and very human. In a "History of the Silent Woman" which was among the papers left at his death he wrote: "After the death of the faithful, genial Hofmannsthal I had to resign myself to the thought that my work in the field of opera was ended ... I had given up hope of finding another librettist, when Anton Kippenberg came to visit us, before going on to join Stefan Zweig at Salzburg next day. I had previously enjoyed Zweig's adaptation of Ben Jonson's 'Volpone,' and his very amusing comedy 'Das Lamm des Armen' in Vienna. So I said casually to Kippenberg: 'Ask Zweig (whom I did not know personally) whether he hasn't an opera libretto for me.' This was in the winter of 1931/32." The result was the beginning of correspondence between the two. They met for the first time at Munich in November, and discussed plans for a large-scale ballet and a "gay, lively opera buffa"—a humorous work based on Jonson's "The silent woman." The poet later wrote of this first encounter in his "World of yesterday" that he felt "the honour of such a commission ..." "Since Max Reger set my first poems I had always lived in music and with musicians ... But I knew of no creative musician of our time to whom I would more willingly have been of service than Strauss."

Zweig was still busy with the completion of his book on Marie-Antoinette, and Strauss had to write several times asking for the promised draft text and the first scenes of "Sir Morosus" (as the work was originally entitled). Finally, in June 1932, they were sent: "This is only the first section—molto vivace—now the lyrical passage in which Morosus laments his loneliness will follow at once, then comes the Barber's canzona concerning women, and a duet. You will have all that by the end of the week at the latest ... It goes without saying that all this is merely a basis for work, and if you want changes I will revise everything." Strauss replied enthusiastically from Switzerland: "Many heartfelt thanks for the delivery of the Morosus rough draft. I repeat sincerely that it is delightful–the born comic opera–a buffo idea to be set beside the best examples of its kind–more suited to music than either Figaro or the Barber of Seville. I beg you to complete the first act as quickly as your other important work allows–I am burning to get started on it in earnest . . ." So now the matter was really in hand. As early as December Strauss could confirm the receipt of the second act: "The second stanza has succeeded too! The ending, which is as original as it is poetic, is especially good." His enthusiasm rose to a positive fever pitch of musical-poetic fervour when, in his letter acknowledging receipt of the third act, he quoted the first eight significant bars of his song "Ich trage meine Minne": "Yes, that I have found you, you dear child, I will be glad all the days that are granted to me." Zweig wrote about this fruitful and harmonious collaboration in his memoirs: "Thus the most cordial relationship imaginable came to exist between us; he visited our house and I went to his at Garmisch, where, with his long, slender fingers, he played the whole opera over to me on the piano, bit by bit, from the sketches. Without any contract or obligation it was taken for granted that after completing this opera I would at once plan out a second, whose basic idea he had already agreed to." Strauss often said afterwards that there was no other opera text, either earlier or later, in which he had been forced to make so few improvements. The alterations were restricted to a small cut in the second act and minor verbal additions in a few "complex pieces." "The composition of none of my previous operas had proved so easy to the musician, and had given me such unmixed pleasure," Strauss wrote in the paper left among his effects to which reference has already been made. Apart from a slight dispute concerning the possibility of an ironical confusion of feelings during the scene prior to the "marriage ceremony," there was no hint of the frayed tempers on both sides which had characterized Strauss's relationship with Hofmannsthal. The opera was completed at the end of October 1934, and its Overture, which was composed later, in January 1935.

The text is of great historical and literary interest. With the exception of the superfluous divorce scene in the last act, a by no means prudish repetition of the preceding scene with the notary, it is well constructed, and rises at times to the level of poetry, although there is sometimes an over-abundance of words. Strauss was so pleased by the "delightful opera buffa libretto" with the "touch of Scribe" that he described it as the "best text of a really comic opera to be written since 'Figaro'." It is founded on the comedy "Epicoene or the silent woman" by Ben Jonson (1609), which had already served Mark Lothar as the subject for his noisy "anti-noise" opera "Lord Spleen" (1930). While Shakespeare (with Marlowe) must be regarded as proclaiming the new age of the individual, Jonson brought the medieval comedy of representative types to its fulfilment. This almost forgotten writer, who began life as a bricklayer, led an adventurous life as a soldier, actor and poet, finally to die in poverty. He had been introduced to the German stage by Zweig's frequently performed adaptation of "Volpone." What did the story of "Epicoene" signify to Strauss? How had Zweig transformed the play, which had previously existed in German only in Tieck's translation? The original was basically a comedy of masks, belonging to the class of entertainment which had provided opera buffa with one of its basic plots: that concerning a pair of young lovers and a blustering old man, who is finally deceived and defeated. The heartlessness of such buffo texts often seems, to the more susceptible tastes of later generations, to verge on utter lack of feeling, and in this respect Zweig, without removing the satire on an outdated society, made changes and deepened the psychology of the work. His Aminta-Timidia, who leads the old man such a dance (in Jonson "she" is actually a boy disguised as a young woman), is no unscrupulous deceiver. His "silent woman," actually the wife of the nephew whom Morosus has threatened to disinherit and who, with Aminta, is a member of an opera troupe, is a woman fighting for her love. She therefore agrees to pretend to be a domineering, vituperative spitfire–quite contrary to her real nature. On the other hand Morosus, in Jonson a woman-hater who cannot endure noise, becomes a touching character: an old retired admiral and freebooter whose ear-drums, have been pierced in action with the enemy, a good-hearted man who needs peace and quiet, but who is brought to the verge of despair by the tumult around him. The fact that Aminta clearly has some sympathy with him makes her "scene" and the "horse cure" (a whole series of "false emotions") seem rather heartless. The quarrelsome nautical hero to whom Zweig gave the rather un-English name Sir Morosus does, however, possess all the prejudices of his class against everything considered lowering, and he has a truly English dislike of the theatre: "It's scandalous that our honourable name should be besmirched because a Morosus prostitutes himself for money in public, with castrati and buffoons, and has a noisy woman, an ear-splitter, an actress, as his wife."

The principal attraction of the libretto to Strauss probably lay in the development of the fascinating principal character who is tricked into a Don Pasquale situation by a crafty barber, by Aminta and her languishing amoroso, and who, touched by "sweet love and music," finds his way to a new acceptance of the world. It lay in the self-reflecting wisdom of the "poor fellow" who is transformed from a crotchety misanthropist into a happy, cured man, who so formulates his philosophy of old age:

> How beautiful music is,
> But so beautiful only when it is over!
> How wonderful is a young, silent woman,
> But so wonderful only when she remains the wife of another!
> How beautiful life is,
> But it is so beautiful only when one is no fool,
> and knows how to live!

Here the comedy takes on a deeper meaning: complete, ironic self-perception and the praise of life based on the wisdom of ripe maturity. When at the conclusion the hero sings his contentedly serene Epilogue all can sense that Strauss had a soft spot for him, the old, crusty, sympathetic sea dog Morosus. Not quiet resignation but happy tranquillity of spirit, laughter at human folly and a smile at perversity which can change into human kindness—those are what "Die schweigsame Frau" leaves with the listener. Not only the style of comedy but also the historical background were new among Strauss's works. No one can doubt that Strauss, who made so many centuries his own, could have created a realistic musical picture of Shakespearean England with its troupes of strolling players, legacy hunters and barbers. In order to introduce an opera company, however, Zweig moved the action by about two centuries, not altogether convincingly. "Room of Sir Morosus in a London suburb about the year 1780"–the date is close to that of "Rosenkavalier," and indeed the new comedy of disguises has much in common with the earlier one: the

343

abundance of characters from different classes of society, the Hogarthian view of humanity–and also a few stylistic infelicities. Zweig and Strauss between them introduced something of Daumier's fierce satire, and a few unnecessarily startling effects ... A significant phrase of Zweig which applied to both authors: "The age provides the pictures, I merely write the words for them."

The music had finally struck the flexible, gay note of opera buffa. In this score (which Strauss wrote without interruption in two years) the orchestral language and vocal part-writing were carried with great bravura through a cross-fire of styles and colours. None of Strauss's other operas had anticipated, to any considerable extent, the buffo style of "Die schweigsame Frau" –in its grace and lightness of touch it is really a song in praise of the brio of Italian comic opera. It almost seems that the seventy-year-old composer now wished to turn his mastery to forms which he had wholly or partially eliminated from his previous operas. Having done without overtures (except in "Ariadne"), he now wrote a thoroughgoing comedy overture, a self-contained piece which whirls wittily along, and which Strauss himself described as a "Potpourri." He led off at once with a large orchestra, which was later only occasionally employed at full strength. Strauss made use, on the basis of his profound knowledge of early English and Italian music, of pieces by Peerson, Monteverdi, Legrenzi and others, instrumental and vocal "numbers" in which, unconcerned with historical veracity, he stylized the music of Jonson's day in a most fascinating manner–a spirited pointillism of varied styles. Nevertheless the really outstanding aspect of this score is the brilliance of its construction: by contrast to the two Viennese comedies Strauss placed large-scale vocal ensembles at the climactic points of the musical and dramatic action. The first act, which is invented and shaped with particular mastery, sparkles like jewellery from the brilliant "Sechzig-, siebzigtausend Pfund" of the opera singers in waltz time, by way of the intimate verve of the great A major Septet ("Nicht an mich, Geliebter, denke") to the vivacious Stretta of the Rossinian Finale. In the other two acts, too, in which solo numbers occupy the foreground, the delightfully blossoming Sextet in A♭ ("Wunderbar, sie anzuschauen") in the second act and the triumphant Nonet ("Alles Frohe, alles Schöne, Sir Morosus, immerdar!") are pearls

344

"Die schweigsame Frau"
Sketch for the opening scene of the third act (1933)

of the art of ensemble writing; many similar gems adorn the work
right through to the "tender and intimate" concluding song. Possibly the inventive power no longer flows as it did in the earlier
works, and dozens of conscious or unconscious references to
works by Strauss himself and other composers can be detected
–this lyricism of old age blends into the style of the folksong,
whose spirit Strauss adopted in the hearty popular acclamation
"Hoch soll er leben!", in the frequently varied "Freut euch des
Lebens" and in many other instances, while he was also successful in his springy, dancelike rhythms, delicious reminders of the
harlequinade scenes in "Ariadne." Natural lyricism containing
true feeling also distinguishes the charming Arietta of Aminta,
a Mozartian creature whom Strauss handled with particular
affection; her dialogue with Morosus, richly upholstered with
opulent harmony of thirds and sixths, and the tender duet between the two young lovers which concludes the second act are
highlights of the score. This lyricism also glows in the amorous
cantilenas of Henry, shows off the Figaro-like figure of the "Barber of London" in his rapid songs, and offers effective contrast
to the buffo antics of the troupe of singers. What Strauss later
remarked about the content and spirit of the libretto is true of the

345

whole work: "In its combination of fine lyricism and comedy it represents an entirely new genre in the world of 'opera buffa'."

Strauss balanced on a razor's edge: he neither abandoned the symphonic, through-composed style nor made the divisions between recitative and aria unnatural breaks, despite some use of spoken dialogue. The type of prose recitative employed here, characterized by orchestral interjections, corresponds to a suggestion made by Zweig. ("I consider prose dialogue to be the natural thing in subordinate passages, but I feel that the music should underline points from time to time, ironic, illustrative and paraphrasing, instead of dying out altogether during the prose dialogue—otherwise every musical entry sounds like an 'Aria'.") Strauss illustrated the types, motives and situations taken from the old opera buffa. He provided an instrumental commentary to moments of drama and emotion, and always caused a hearty laugh at the right moment. He was not now writing a weighty German comedy, but a light-footed "comic opera" in the spirit of well-tried, immortal italianità. Nevertheless he poured out so many notes that the orchestral score and vocal score are more voluminous than those of any of his other operas. He was naturally tempted to make much of the "noise" which is so important an element in the story: from banging doors to the ringing of bells, from the housekeeper's chattering to exploding ammunition. The seventy-year-old composer would not give up *that* joke.

The Dresden world première in June 1935 of this opera written under threatening political skies needed the utmost diplomacy: "So the black day dawned for National Socialist Germany when an opera was performed which caused the despised name Stefan Zweig to be paraded on all the poster hoardings" (Zweig). Silenced after four performances, Aminta found her voice again only after 1945, under democratic stars. This character comedy with music contains so much light dexterity and smiling humanity that, like Verdi's "Falstaff," it really needs to be seen far more frequently. Does the length of the work, of the third act in particular, restrict the number of performances? When this "charming and wise work" received its belated Berlin première at the Komische Oper in December 1954, Walter Felsenstein unexpectedly succeeded in reducing the piece to the length of a normal opera performance, thereby giving it a fresh lease of life.

346

It was, however, especially after the Salzburg performances under Böhm (who had conducted the world première) in 1959 that this opera really began to gain ground in Germany and other countries. Strauss several times recommended cuts, and a revision of the dramaturgical structure. The recipe for success was given in the work itself:

> Real humour remains amusing
> only if it does not go on too long . . .

While the composition of this opera was still in progress Zweig tried to interest Strauss in a new comedy subject. "I have just been to Vienna to see whether Goldoni's 'Mirandolina' could be adapted as an opera. The milieu, 18th century Venice, is fascinating, and the hostess who attracts all, but whose heart belongs to one alone, is as charming a theatrical figure as any, but the piece is too slender as it stands, and would have to be combined with a sub-plot: perhaps Casanova himself could be brought in, to be outwitted by this one woman. At any event I am now also looking for German versions of the other pieces (by Goldoni), and perhaps something will prove suitable. I have some other ideas too—but the fine days in Vienna are shattered by artillery fire . . ." Despite his pleasure in collaborating with Zweig, Strauss did not look with favour on this comic union between Mirandolina and Casanova.

None of these plans could come to fruition. Knowing nothing about the letter which Strauss had sent shortly before the première of "Die schweigsame Frau" asking Zweig to write another libretto for him, but which had been seized by the Nazi authorities, Zweig sent the composer a highly significant letter at the end of June, writing that in view of the position in which he (as a Jew) found himself he proposed Joseph Gregor as Strauss's new literary colleague. "I have given careful thought to the question of the kind of text which would be the best for a new work for you. I feel more and more clearly that something in the middle of the road is out of the question—it should either be something really noble and strict in form, or something very light or even ironic. A merely theatrical opera without either a profound moral purpose or a gay, relaxed atmosphere would not seem to me suitable as a crowning piece . . . I have already said how it grieves me that I myself cannot write such a libretto for you . . ." In the last letter which Zweig sent Strauss, in December 1935, signing himself "Morosus," the talk is still of "Die schweigsame Frau," and of the attempts to get it produced in Vienna.

*

At the time when the "Third Reich" was making its first war-like preparations the now seventy-year-old master wrote his *"Friedenstag."* This fact should be appreciated in its full significance: it shows the composer to have had his own firm views on the decisive issue of the idea of peace. "Friedenstag" is a serious opera with a conscious ideological basis, though no direct reference to current circumstances. It is an echo of the classical "liberation operas," Strauss's first "heroic" opera, in many respects a late successor to the early "Guntram," and his first one-act opera since "Elektra." The libretto is by the Viennese cultural historian and theatrical expert Joseph Gregor. What no one could be allowed to know during the years when the work was being written and at its first performance is no longer a secret: the fact that it was the librettist of "Die schweigsame Frau," Stefan Zweig, who had suggested the subject to Strauss. He, an outcast, was even concerned with the rewriting of the "scene of the meeting between the two commanders."

Friedenstag–Peace Day? The action takes place on the 24th October 1648 in the citadel of a beleaguered town. The bells which begin to ring out at the beginning of the last third of the opera proclaim the Peace of Westphalia, the end of the Thirty Years' War, that most devastating war ever fought on German soil, whose effect on the life of the German people was catastrophic. Driven on by religious differences and the private interests of numerous petty princelings, German had fought ferociously against German. The Commandant receives an order from the Emperor to hold the town at all costs. He is deaf to the appeals of the suffering townsfolk. He appears stern and unyielding even to his young wife. In order to avoid the shame of surrender he determines to blow the fortress sky high. In this last precious hour of preparation for death all living strength is summoned up once again, and man and wife find their way back to each other. The powder store is about to be set on fire when canon shots and the pealing of bells bring about the great transformation: peace has been signed, peace which a whole generation

348

know about only from hearsay. A drawbridge is lowered, symbolically, to show a landscape freed from the scourge of war, and jubilant crowds of people.

A basically simple, easily understandable story, well laid out and developed by Gregor, though with some verbal obscurities. Apart from the Commandant and his wife the librettist created an abundance of less important and less productive characters who certainly gave the composer ample opportunities to exercise his talent in descriptive writing, but who unduly overburden the sung drama. The main doubt about the work lies deeper, concerning as it does the question of the listener's sympathy. The Commandant is a wholly rigid slave of duty. This fanatical warrior may be moved briefly by the plight of those under his command, but there is scarcely any conflict in his mind between the demands of duty and human love (the relationship between him and his wife was intended to reflect the whole spiritual situation). True, there are the marksman who "hates fighting and war," Maria, who exclaims "Curses on you, war!", and the "woman of the people" who, as the most outspoken representative of the despairing townsfolk, accuses the Commandant of being their "murderer." On the other hand the passive attitude of the majority of the soldiers, uncouth yet genuinely moved by their hope, glorifies blind obedience to the death in its senseless extreme. There are suggestions of pacifism. ("I have seen the enemy . . . they are men like us, they suffer, out there in their trenches, just as we do . . ."). The great failing is that the conclusion does not carry dramatic conviction. Had peace not come like a bolt from the blue at the crucial moment, bringing an end to thirty years of fratricidal slaughter, catastrophe would have been unavoidable. The proclamation of peace is nothing but an all-too well-timed "miracle." Gregor's statement that the miracle was prepared for by the inner transformation of Maria does nothing to alter this fact.

There had long been dormant in Strauss the artistic vision of the "Proclamation of world peace by the Emperor Henry II of Germany as the background to a one-act opera." Zweig told Strauss the outline story of this work in the summer of 1935. The composer considered it "excellent," and asked Zweig to draft a scenario—but the project got no further at that time as the political circumstances compelled Zweig to drop out of the picture.

Nevertheless he expressed his willingness to give advice concerning the work. Strauss could summon up no enthusiasm for Zweig's suggestion that Gregor should take his place as librettist. "Give my greetings to dear Gregor, but as for 'libretti,' I prefer to sit on a–branch!" (a play on the name Zweig, Strauss intentionally using the other German word for branch, Ast). A few weeks later, with reference to "Friedenstag" and "Capriccio," which was already under consideration: "Please, please work out for me the two subjects which you alone have devised, without Gregor, whose collaboration in this I absolutely forbid–I will compose no disguised operas!" But despite this objection Gregor was soon on the scene–Strauss was at that time reading Gregor's "World History of the Theatre," and had come across the famous painting "The surrender of Breda" which Velasquez painted after Calderón's drama. Gregor wrote in detail about his meeting with Strauss and the origins of "Friedenstag": "The invitation to submit a draft scenario to the master reached me in the summer of 1935. He had already decided that the work was to extol peace; we know of this idea from 'Guntram,' where it was formulated at some length . . . thought had already been given to some historical incidents concerning peace, in particular the conclusion of peace between Frederick I and the Lombardian league of cities (Constance, 1183); the choice of this subject would have concerned a peace between north and south. However, Strauss had cut himself off from the middle ages since his first two music dramas, piously regarding that period as the personal domain of Wagner. So our attention turned to the Peace of Westphalia in 1648, less because this brought us back to the baroque age than because it concerned peace between Germans. I found myself in perfect agreement with Strauss that the historical facts, which are here generally familiar and easily grasped, should be employed only as a general background, while the opera–the new work was simply to be so described–would have to enjoy complete freedom. As the incident of the signing of peace at Münster and Osnabrück is generally dated to the day, the title was originally to be '24th October 1648,' but this was changed in favour of the more generally applicable title which the work now bears."

The collaboration between Strauss and his new librettist proved to be fruitful. Simultaneously with the "military" opera,

350

plans were discussed for work on "Semiramis" (which never got beyond the stage of sketches), and the nature poem "Daphne." "I worked at the text of 'Friedenstag' during the summer and autumn of 1935 in close contact with the master in a beautiful room in a tower of his country house at Garmisch, several times interrupting the work when I had to travel elsewhere, and always going back there afterwards." As always, Strauss did not restrict himself to criticizing the librettist's literary sketches and exposés, but at once made counter-proposals, showing his colleague a better way to proceed. After making a series of alterations, most of which were intended to create particular moods by the use of new verbal images, Strauss demonstrated his remarkable knowledge of dramaturgy in the necessary improvements which he made at the end of the opera. He alone was responsible for all the events of the libretto of "Friedenstag" following the dramatic change of situation brought about by the "canon shot from afar": "Message! At its close short dramatic dialogue, until the duel, the embrace. Then the people press in. Then official proclamation of the Emperor's message. Solemn silence. Then Maria begins ... song of peace, in which all gradually join, rising to the highest jubilation." But at the beginning of September, when Strauss was in possession of the complete libretto, the significant moment of creative criticism arrived. "These are not real people: the Commandant and his wife–it's all on stilts. I don't believe any field captain in the Thirty Years' War referred to the 'splendid thought of war.' This is a kind of 'poetry' which fails completely in the theatre. Our friend (Stefan Zweig!) probably feels this too. Then the whole scene from the entry of the Holsteiner is badly constructed: two school teachers might talk like that on the subject of 'The Thirty Years' War' ... Will you try to revise the whole thing in heightened prose, but as people really speak–no stage figures ..." However: "The last corrections are enormous improvements, and get nearer to the heart of the matter. The ending must be quite different from the point at which the two commanders embrace each other. At this moment of silence the people's hymn of peace must be heard very quietly from outside; only a song of praise with no reminder of the war. Maria, the two commanders, and all those present gradually take up the hymn, while the tower slowly sinks down. When this is done and all the people are seen outside, there must be a single

351

crescendo to the end, purely lyrical. It can only be so . . ." And so it was. Gregor had suggested a "double fugue," but Strauss replied "Stretta, only stretta!"

Although Strauss threw himself into the work with alacrity as soon as he had received the first draft text ("a first sketch extends to the departure of the 'deportation'"), and although he wrote to the librettist as early as January 1936 "No. 1 is ready in rough sketches, and the fair copy will be completed in about a fortnight," he could not summon up the creative energy which hastened the composition of his masterpieces. "I have now been busy with the composition for several weeks, but it refuses to become music such as I must demand of myself," he complained to Zweig. "The whole subject is a little too prosaic–soldiers–war–hunger–middle-age heroism–dying together–with the best will in the world I can't get the feeling for it." Such an expression of doubts concerning the composition inevitably reminds one of similar uneasiness in connection with "Josephslegende," the "Alpensinfonie" and "Schlagobers," among other works. However, "I believe the concluding hymn has turned out very well," he wrote on completing the short score, and then, at the end of June 1936: "The score is ready." He did not show any great excitement, as his mind was already full of a new comic or even grotesque subject.

Like "Fidelio," the opera "Friedenstag" concludes with a kind of scenic cantata. The powerful, steadily growing final hymn, taken up by all the soloists, choral groups and instruments, with the popular appeal of its stretta construction, has a more healthy directness about it than the vague and highflown text to which it is set, and which calls on an abstract "Ruling spirit." This Finale would, in fact, be inconceivable without the example of the Ode to Joy in "Fidelio;" the pronounced simplicity of the melody is also reminiscent of the diatonic directness of the "Olympische Hymne." (The parallelism with "Fidelio" goes far beyond thematic relationships; the structural plan and key symbolism of the Finale are astonishingly reminiscent of those of Beethoven's opera.) Despite its strictness and ruggedness of outline unusual in Strauss (there is little of the shapely grace of the stylized operas "Ariadne" and "Helena"), the music of "Friedenstag" does not really appear pathetic; it seems to spring from a somewhat detached relationship to the subject and its significance. March rhythms, short soldiers' songs and the like abound. Never before had the composer made such extensive use of the expressive powers of the chorus in any of his operas. The choruses of the hungry townspeople, grimly holding out without solace or hope, which are heard from afar, the multi-voice message of peace, the antiphony of choruses behind the scenes and on stage, and the powerful combination of all the vocal forces in the Finale give this score a new individual character. On the other hand the orchestra only occasionally comes to the fore in its own right, and, as befits the austere overall style, merely beautiful sound is avoided. The skill displayed in the work's construction generally exceeds the wealth of invention, about which Strauss later expressed doubts on occassion. Nevertheless the score has its strong points. One of these is the darkly atmospheric opening, from whose ominous string chords the heavy march rhythm gradually emerges. Others include the tonally bold, lamenting march of the deported, only twenty bars long, the strongly expressive duet between the Commandant and his wife, the warmly radiant chorus of thanksgiving "Segen über Euch," and the link between the orchestral interlude depicting the waiting for death and the bell chorus of the message of peace. The familiar blossoming Strauss style depicts the character of Maria in extensive, technically demanding soprano gestures; in her (somewhat artificially contrived) solo scene the love which his wife bears the Commandant inspires a great lyrical outpouring. The through-composed texture of the musical scenes also contains a number of other solo numbers of intentionally popular style: the Italian canzonetta of the young Piedmontese, the Commandant's song about the cavalry battle of Magdeburg, and the military march of the Holsteiner's troops. All these things are fashioned and built up with the hand of complete mastery, and have behind them a cool perception of the breadth and depth of this heroic opera-ballad, for which Strauss considered the description "Drama" or "Bühnenweihspiel."

The world première took place in July 1938 under the conductorship of Clemens Krauss, to whom, jointly with his wife Viorica Ursuleac, the first Maria, the work is dedicated. This was the first Strauss première in his native town; the evening opened with Beethoven's "Prometheus" ballet. A few months later the opera was performed in Dresden and Berlin in a double bill with

"Daphne." "Friedenstag," which is undoubtedly of greater account by reason of its affirmation of the idea of peace than for its musical-dramatic substance, was to be the last sign of Strauss's concern with the threatening world around. ("When one looks at Europe the piece becomes increasingly symbolic," wrote Gregor on the completion of the composition.) A year after the work's appearance the Germany of that time had little regard for peace between nations ... Since then very little has been heard about "Friedenstag."

THE GRECIAN STRAUSS

Strauss's work in the field of opera was intima-
tely connected with Hellenism. In its psychological isolation, at
least in the sphere of opera, the 19th century was far removed
from the Grecian spirit. Ancient mythological subjects vanished
from the opera stage as the ideals of the Renaissance lost ground
and the national epics of Europe were rediscovered. Strauss, who
was undoubtedly linked with the spirit of late romanticism,
found his way back to Antiquity at a comparatively early age as
a result of his visits to Greece. The experience of Hellenism led
him, after the grim excursion through the mythological abysses
of "Elektra," to classical Greek myths, which certainly brought
a spirit of bright serenity into his work, but which also led him
away from the firm ground of reality. The fact remains that one
must recognize in Strauss's concern with Antiquity from "Elektra" to "Danae" an important field of his endeavours in the
realm of dramatic music, the natural complement to his realistic
operas based on German and Austrian historical subjects.

The first work of the "Grecian" Strauss, whose new, serene
classicism began to be increasingly prominent from about his
fiftieth year, pointing back to the beginnings of opera more than
three hundred years earlier, is *"Ariadne auf Naxos,"* with its two
greatly contrasting "layers" of action. In his encounters with
mythology Strauss the classicist did not derive inspiration only
from Ancient Greece; the eye also seems to catch passing glimpses
of Botticelli, Bernini, Tiepolo, Poussin, Handel, Gluck and
Mozart, Canova, Moreau and Böcklin. None of these elements
could be omitted without weakening the effect of the easily comprehensible and at the same time deeply sensuous "antique"
sound created by Strauss with the assistance of his literary
colleagues Hofmannsthal and, finally, Gregor. Strauss once re-

marked that real opera subjects could be found only in Greek Antiquity. He gave post-Wagnerian opera in Germany a renewed form of expression whose human content has been preserved in numerous works of operatic history, except that in Strauss's case the mythological stories were combined with modern psychology to a degree hitherto unknown. Gregor himself once doubted the value of these subjects at the present time, but for the fact that they were supported by the power of Strauss's music. Naturally it was advisable to free a baroque-mythological theme from the restrictions of period costumes, to show the human being behind

Strauss and Hofmannsthal: Cut-out by W. Bithorn

the mask. Only *transformation* could form the basis for this illumination of ancient stories—in Strauss's own words the "last fulfilment of Grecian longing."

It would even appear that this spiritual heart of "Ariadne," the mystery of transformation, had exercised an influence outside the work itself, affecting its fate. In 1912 "Der Bürger als Edelmann," a German version of Molière's "Le Bourgeois gentilhomme," with Hofmannsthal's "Ariadne auf Naxos" taking the place of the original Turkish Ceremony as the divertissement concluding the play, formed a stage entertainment in which, despite a brilliant musical and scenic presentation, each work detracted from the effect of the other. Weighed in the balance and

356

found too much! The farce of Molière's "Bourgeois gentilhomme" coupled with the leaden weight of a mythological opera–the project was doomed from the start. Hofmannsthal, the Viennese aesthetic poet, tried to do too much when he interwove three wholly dissimilar elements: the satirical comedy concerning the foolish Parisian nouveau riche Jourdain, the harlequinade of the "Unfaithful Zerbinetta with her four lovers," and the mystical transformation of the lamenting Ariadne. The authors are known, however, to have retained their love for this original version of "Ariadne." "The first idea was charming," the composer wrote as late as 1942, "beginning with spoken comedy, elevated by ballet and commedia dell'arte to the height of the purest wordless music, but it finally failed . . . with the public. The audience for plays did not come, to its cost, and the opera audience had little interest in the Molière. The management had to employ casts of actors and singers at the same performance, but instead of the takings of two good productions they received the proceeds of only one, and even that was a doubtful draw at the box office!"

The superficial motive for the creation of this work was one of gratitude. Max Reinhardt had rendered invaluable assistance at the time of the première of "Rosenkavalier" in Dresden, and Strauss and Hofmannsthal offered to write a play with music for his Deutsches Theater in Berlin. The choice fell on Molière's comedy about the newly enriched cloth merchant Jourdain, who accepts people as human beings only if they have titles, who fails to see that he is being duped, and ignores the voices of the ordinary people, his maid and his sensible wife–a mediocre comedy despite its aggressiveness typical of Molière. It did, however, provide scope for attractive music suggesting historical models, following examples such as that of Lully, who had written the original songs, dances and concluding ballet. The Court Composer of Louis XIV was replaced two and a half centuries later by the brilliant modern musician. Hofmannsthal, with his sensitive artistic imagination, carried his ideas further: ". . . I am summoning up all my powers for a small but by no means easy task." Simultaneously with the plan of a work intended as a mark of gratitude to the great Berlin producer there dawned at the end of March 1911 the idea of a "thirty-minute opera for a small chamber orchestra . . . entitled 'Ariadne auf Naxos,' compounded from heroic-mythological figures in 18th-century costume with hooped petticoats and ostrich feathers, and figures from the Commedia dell'arte, Harlequin, Scaramuccio and others, who interweave a buffo element into the heroic story . . . That is how I imagine it. Not as a slavish imitation, but as a spirited paraphrase of the old heroic style, intermingled with buffo comedy . . ."

The musician's first reaction was cool, and the poet replied that he could leave the text "uncomposed, with no hard feelings," if the idea did not interest him in principle. However, even in the first joint work on this artistically fascinating combination of heroic baroque opera and gay comedy, an amalgamation of two contrasting worlds never before experienced in the history of opera (a procedure which many people mistakenly regarded as demonstrating the bankruptcy of the drama), the original conception underwent a change. What the poet now had in mind was an "opera with a subtle fusion of styles, with a deep underlying meaning . . ." "It was suddenly clear to me what an excellent thing it would be to insert just such an operatic divertissement in 'Bourgeois gentilhomme'." Between the Molière play (reduced from five acts to two by wholesale cutting of the story of the bourgeois lovers Cléonte and Lucile, and of the Turkish Ceremony) and the one-act opera he inserted a kind of Intermezzo concerning the preparation for the theatrical performance, and culminating in the Major Domo's ridiculous order that the serious opera and the comedy of the buffo troupe are to be presented to the guests simultaneously. A final idea was to conclude the opera with a burlesque epilogue for Zerbinetta. Although Strauss was sceptical about the Molière from the first ("I feel the piece lacks any real point"), Hofmannsthal continued to insist on his idea of a necessary combination of play and opera. "I'll stake my reputation on it: only if the whole thing is produced will my linking of the two pieces be an intelligent joke . . ." So the "minor work" became a major project, the "little Molière affair" an immense undertaking. The future was to prove that the mixture of spoken comedy and opera lacked vital strength, but that the tragi-comic opera, with the musical "Prologue in the theatre" composed later (based on the Intermezzo, which was cut almost out of existence at the world première), was destined to give pleasure to discerning audiences on a steadily increasing scale. .

358

The mythological story was merely the starting point for the subject matter of the opera proper. The myth of Ariadne has appeared many times in opera, from the birth of the art form at the beginning of the 17th century, when it inspired Monteverdi, up to modern settings by Milhaud, Orff and Martinu. (Monteverdi's "L'Incoronazione di Poppea," incidentally, contains a very early example of the intermingling of serious and burlesque elements). The interest of "Ariadne" for Hofmannsthal is best summed up in these phrases: "It is concerned with a simple and immense problem of life: that of fidelity. Whether to cling to what is lost, to remain faithful unto death–or to live and go on living, to break away, transform oneself, to sacrifice one's spiritual unity, and yet in the transformation to preserve oneself, remaining a human being instead of sinking to the level of a beast that has no memory . . ." Equally illuminating are these words: "Transformation is life itself, the essential mystery of the creative nature; clinging to the past is numbness and death. Nevertheless all human values are linked with fidelity to what has been, and a refusal to forget. This is one of the chasms of contradiction above which our existence is built . . . So here Ariadne confronts Zerbinetta, as Elektra confronted Chrysothemis. Nothing remained for Elektra but death. Ariadne, too, determines to give herself to death; 'her boat sinks, and sinks to new seas.' This is transformation, the wonder of all wonders, the real secret of love . . ." At a moment when she is most receptive, Ariadne meets Bacchus. She believes him to be death, to whom alone she has sworn to give herself. Nevertheless she breaks her oath, deeply sincere heroine though she is, when Bacchus is revealed as a god, and she accepts life and love with him. Meanwhile Zerbinetta flits in and out of the story, making mocking interjections, well pleased with her "lovers of all kinds," the symbol of frivolous, earthly love with worldly-wise irony on her lips–the wealthy patron of the arts naturally doesn't want to miss the buffoonery of the harlequinade characters surrounding Zerbinetta . . . In his letters Hofmannsthal sought to throw light on the characters and their motivation with increasingly persuasive power. The work was to show the creative artist in his relations with the real and ideal worlds, and the transformation brought about by love. But the figures are too remote from life; they do not become people of flesh and blood, and cannot quite conceal the dramatic weaknesses of the action. The best element of the text is its high poetic quality, sometimes suggesting Goethe.

As Strauss concerned himself to an increasing extent with the intellectually artistic combination of reflective drama and playful harlequinade, this remarkable fusion of the serious and comic, of profundity and frivolity, psychological complexity and simplicity, he became increasingly attracted to the idea of such a setting. He regarded the real opera "Ariadne" as his principal task. To him it was a fascinating blend of old musical forms and new spirit, full of delightful ideas in a colourful framework encompassing parody and deep significance. He visualized an opera somewhat after the 18th-century style with arias, duets and ensembles, in which "irreconcilables are reconciled in the unity of a work of art" (Schuh)... At the end of May in the year of "Rosenkavalier" he began to devote himself intensively to the idea. "'Ariadne' can become very beautiful. As the dramatic skeleton as such is thin, everything depends on the poetic realization. With you there is no need to wonder whether the verses will be full of fire. But saddle up Pegasus. I imagine Ariadne... contralto, Bacchus... lyric tenor, Zerbinetta... high coloratura soprano..." The composer then began to influence the construction of the libretto, marking out the individual "numbers" carefully, adopting the old-fashioned operatic terms Recitative and Aria, Rondeau, Theme with Variations, Buffo Terzetto, and he referred to "coloratura frolics and showpieces..." Hofmannsthal understood what he had in mind. "Everything is to be like a wire framework on which to hang the music," and Strauss, for his part, advised his friend to have coloratura arias from "La Sonnambula," "Lucia di Lammermoor" and Hérold's "Le Pré aux clercs" played over to him. "Dionysus enlighten you! I am waiting!" The work proceeded apace. The libretto was ready by July 1911; at the beginning of 1912 Strauss wrote: "The score of 'Ariadne' is half complete. Everything will be ready by the 1st April. Now I must soon have the complete text of the Molière in order to write the preludes and interludes, songs etc.–but believe me, the success will be determined by the ending, and that is now the Hofmannsthal-Strauss opera, not the Molière-Reinhardt..."

The result was inevitable: opera and play did not go together. The first performance took place in October 1912 in the newly-completed Kleines Haus at Stuttgart (which had been preferred to the Deutsches Theater in Berlin). Savage cuts had been made to reduce the combined works to a reasonable length, but even so they ran to between four and five hours, and met with very little understanding–despite the composer's own participation as conductor, with Reinhardt's production, the employment of specialist Strauss singers from Berlin, Vienna and Dresden, and a first-rate orchestra playing valuable old instruments! (Strauss rejected Reinhardt's suggestion that the chamber orchestra should be placed on the stage, as was done in the case of Stravinsky's "Soldier's Tale" a few years later.) One of the participants remarked sarcastically that he had seen a different "Ariadne" at each rehearsal . . . Even after the private performance before invited guests which preceded the première, further last-minute cuts were proposed. Most unfortunately the King of Wurtemberg gave two audiences of fifty minutes each in the intervals during and after the play, which postponed the beginning of the opera still further. "The excellent idea had not justified itself in practice . . . So four years later Hofmannsthal and I . . . saw ourselves obliged to wield the axe and separate Molière from Hofmannsthal–Strauss," the composer wrote later. However, the poet had been the first to revert to the painful subject. In the summer of 1913, after the completion of "Josephslegende," and at a time when "Frau ohne Schatten" was demanding all their creative energy, Hofmannsthal suffered from "pangs of heartache caused by the unfortunate Molière . . . To me the most unpleasant thing in the world is pouring out my strength for a lost cause–what use is all the patching up? . . ." But the next words in the letter run: "The only solution has lain in my desk for a week." It was only after long hesitation that Strauss, who had struggled for four years "against any separation of the opera from the comedy," decided in July 1916 on the composition of the new scenic Prologue, through whose existence alone Hofmannsthal now regarded "the whole work 'Ariadne' to be complete." Hofmannsthal considered the music "the most beautiful you have ever written," and wrote: "It will be an enchanting surprise for the whole world!" On the contrary, after the world première of the "New Version" had taken place at Vienna under Schalk early in the third winter of the war, in October 1916, the world was neither enchanted nor surprised. It took very little notice, so that the disappointed poet again lost his confidence and spoke of a "linking of the dead with the living which is contrary to nature . . ." Ten years later there was no longer anything problematic about this second "Ariadne."

The Prologue of this version which was soon described by its creator as "definitive" is a delightful idea. It is no spoken comedy (Hofmannsthal originally thought in terms of a comic piece of his own), but a little opera, composed by Strauss in the feathery-light, strongly rhythmical parlando style which was to distinguish "Intermezzo," written soon afterwards. Little, almost too little, remains of Molière. The action now takes place in the palace of a Count, the "richest man in Vienna," and this eminent personage, a product of the socially unworthy Prince Eugène period, is represented by his Major Domo, the only speaking part. In this way a direct link was created between mythology and the life of society. The principal character, the young, enthusiastic Composer, was originally visualized by Hofmannsthal in a realistic light: "At the centre of the picture, to an even greater extent than before, I place the destiny of the musician . . . The Composer is a purely symbolical figure, half tragic, half comic; the contradictions of the whole piece are now rooted in him . . ." Hofmannsthal certainly did not imagine the character as possessing the charm with which what became a breeches role (the idea came from Leo Blech) is generally presented; to him the idea of the "Composer as a woman" was quite simply "appalling." The fact was, though, that Strauss's instinct, backed by the examples of Cherubino and Octavian, proved to be right. Both in human feeling and musical import the open-hearted young Composer, with his dawning capacity for love, dominates the Prologue, which owes its spiritual stature to him. He represents the artist freeing himself from the bonds of feudalism, and determined to create his works in accordance with his own conviction. These splendid words of the Composer end the Prologue:

> What is music? Music is a holy art, to assemble all the qualities like cherubim round a shining throne, and thus it is the most divine of the arts—holy music!

All that is known of the irreparable weaknesses of the original "Ariadne" has not prevented certain music critics from continuing to demand the "first version." It is difficult to sympathize

362

with any such unrealistic idea: the Prologue is now deeply rooted in operatic life. The organic connection between the Prologue and the opera proper, although actually fashioned only from thin threads of artificial silk, appears to be absolutely firm in the theatre. A performance of "Ariadne" without this scenic Introduction, the product of a new flexibility in the setting of words, is a rarity. Without this Prologue we would be the poorer by some notable music. The brilliance displayed in its construction is not confined to the musical relationships and self-quotations, but comprises the art by which (especially in connection with the ingratiating melody of the "Venus" song, which comes into the young Composer's mind in stages) an existing basic structure is made to yield something completely new, its elements contrasting yet belonging together–and with only the right amount of music, "so that the ear is fresh for the opera." Strauss skilfully characterizes each of the personalities with a few strokes: he introduces the Composer with an impulsively fiery motif, shows Zerbinetta as she is in a few gaily flirtatious bars, and points an ironic finger at the mentality of the minions of the rich man who have so little appreciation of what the serious opera signifies. In addition the Prologue, in which almost all the characters of the opera appear, throws fresh light on Zerbinetta. One need only remember the duet between her and the Composer. In this briefest and most blossoming love scene which Strauss ever wrote, which "contains his best ideas," he strikes a note of enchantingly pure feeling for Zerbinetta. She is not really the faithless butterfly of the opera proper. She appears, although perhaps only in a moment of self-deception, worthy of the devotion of true love.

"I am changed from what I was": these words of Bacchus could be used as a motto for the score of the delectable opera "Ariadne." The composer's world of sound has become wholly bright and clear; the symphonic weight of music drama has given place to weightless grace, an evocation of tragedy and lighthearted comedy in one, illuminated in many colours. Aesthetically speaking, "Ariadne" contains Strauss's most beautiful, most euphonious and, as he himself said, most "modern" music. At once popular in style and exclusive, it embodies not the oversensational view of Antiquity represented in Strauss's early music dramas, but the ideal of a classically radiant Hellenism. Wagnerian pathos has been reduced to classical proportions and

363

simplicity. Ariadne is far closer to a heroic Pamina than to Brünn-hilde. Only a musician who knew the laws of music drama in every detail, as well as being thoroughly familiar with the formal processes and expressive possibilities of opera, could have composed "Ariadne" with such sparkling elegance of spirit (the finest heritage of Mozart). No opera music since that of "Così fan tutte" had been at once so light-hearted and so profoundly wise. The total effect is of highly polished dramatic chamber music of typically southern grace and finesse of texture–the gateway to a new quality of lyrical nobility. The return to the old self-contained musical numbers is matched by the remarkably flexible and expressive use made of the orchestra. After the violent cataracts of sound in "Salome" and "Elektra," 37 musicians here weave an instrumental tapestry of transparent lines and colour, delightfully imitating the contrasts between soli and tutti in early works of concerto type. (A particular pleasure in itself is provided by the exuberant freedom of the solo violin, the woodwind, horns, and above all the piano.) The instruments make witty individual comments on the stage action, a moment later combining to provide the firm basis of a jubilant vocal melody. In face of such musical delights who would not feel, with pleasure, that the composer has triumphed over the dramatist, as the inner riches overshadow the outward events? Who does not himself experience the "mystery of transformation" through this work? (Another transformation was Strauss's development of a series of comic and dramatic themes in this work from musical sketches for his ballet "Kythere" of 1900.) This is really the "realm where everything is pure"–but it is not the realm of death about which Ariadne dreams. It is the sphere of profound human joy, free from restrictions of time and place yet brought close to reality by the singing voice–the realm of melody.

Ironical seriousness, serious irony . . . It is difficult to describe the music of this opera semiseria even approximately: its fervour and grace, its richness of ideas and serenity, its skilful combination of stylistic elements from very different periods, a synthesis rather than a mere mixture, in which the seria aspect is represented by homophony, the buffa by polyphony. Cecil Gray wrote amusingly about this boldly imaginative amalgamation of styles: "In 'Ariadne' Mozart and Mascagni, Handel and Offenbach dance a minuet." The baroque atmosphere which lies over the score at once establishes the basic tone of the Opera Overture. (The Overture to the Prologue written later is based on themes of the opera which follows.) When the curtain rises the nature idyll of the Trio of nymphs sets the scene impressively for Ariadne's great Monologue with its classical purity of style. Harlequin tries to cheer her up with his captivating F major Canzonetta "Lieben, Hassen, Hoffen, Fangen." Ariadne, prima donna seria, pours out her heart in the moving lament "Es gibt ein Reich, wo alles rein ist." What eloquence of melody! Again there comes the contrast of the burlesque element: the Dance Quartet of the harlequinade figures, formed as a polka, and the great bravura coloratura aria of the prima donna buffa, Zerbinetta's Recitative and Rondo "Grossmächtige Prinzessin." Strauss originally wrote this brilliantly virtuistic yet sweetly expressive piece, which is coloured by the use of the modern piano as obbligato instrument, for Frieda Hempel; he simplified it even before the première. This dramatic highspot stands exactly at the centre of the work. Witty chatter leads into the resumption of the buffo comedy, to a boisterous waltz. Then the atmosphere changes abruptly; the violins create a sense of supernatural mystery, and the radiant trumpet calls heighten the feeling of expectancy: the "creatures of nature," in their second Trio (into which is woven a fine reminiscence of the motif of longing from "Tristan"), announce the approach of the young god whom Ariadne takes to be the messenger of death. Then the composer raises the work to its final heights in the dithyrambic fire of Bacchus's music, and the wonderful interweaving of the voices of the lovers in their great Duet. With the rich euphony of the Apotheosis in D♭ major, interrupted only by the Arcadian sweetness of the Trio of the nymphs with its Schubertian nature poetry, and by Zerbinetta's brief appearance, Strauss crowns the work with the miracle of transformation, giving promise of a new life of blissful joy ... He made few changes in the revised version of the opera, but they are not insignificant. Zerbinetta's fiendishly difficult Aria was shortened by 57 bars, and its second part was transposed down a tone; later, however, he willingly added a few coloratura passages of immense difficulty to this showpiece for a "German nightingale." The second Buffo Quintet was re-set in a more concise form. Regrettable (as regards the musical content) is the omission of the Zerbinetta episode at the arrival of Bacchus, and the orchestral Interlude which followed it. The Apotheosis was radically shortened, so that Zerbinetta now sings only a few fleeting bars; on the other hand Strauss wrote a new orchestral conclusion to the rapturous Duet of Ariadne and Bacchus–a makeshift ending which sets the seal of triumph on the final scene, but which is, unfortunately, rather pompous and thickly flowing. The work of revision probably met with the greatest difficulty at this point.

What became of the Molière? As a result of the separation of the two parts of the original work, Hofmannsthal's adaptation of "Le Bourgeois gentilhomme" was produced in April 1918 at the Deutsches Theater in Berlin as a play with incidental music. The poet, who was unnamed in the play's billing, had restored the third act with its Turkish Ceremony, previously omitted, in 1917. The composer returned to his incidental music: the amusingly characteristic Overture headed "Jourdain the Bourgeois," the Shepherds' Duet, the parodistic Song of Jourdain, the witty picture of the Fencing Master, the gay Polonaise and Tailor's Dance, the graceful Prelude to the second act, and the enchantingly illustrative Dinner Music. A few newly adapted pieces of Lully's original music for the play, including a Courante and a Finale to the first act, were added. The concluding act offered the composer opportunities to provide a Dance of Sylphs, Spirits' Music, and the "Turkish" music with soli and chorus. Strauss never made music with greater ease and facility than when thus decking out Molière, writing "with the left hand, quite casually" music which is wholly successful. With his frequently polyphonic workmanship and expressive language of diverse colouristic effects Strauss here presents an ornately interwoven and transparent texture which, despite the capricious use made of modern techniques, is full of witty references to musical styles of the baroque and rococo periods ... Was this work still too subtle to be appreciated? Or was the failure of the first performance due to the chaotic background of a time of revolution? Whatever the reason, no success was forthcoming, and in August 1918, after a time of hard work, worry, stress, hope and joy, Hofmannsthal finally had to admit to "failure": "I must describe it so, there is no point in trying to delude myself, and if anyone is to blame it is I ... The opposition to 'Bourgeois' came, I am convinced, from the public ... Might it be better, painful though such a course of action would be, to keep this work back for special occasions?" ... Strauss remained devoted to the Molière throughout the rest of his life–"a work whose production would enrich every theatre of quality which can mount operas, plays and ballets ... in a manner which is first-class in *all* respects ..." "Belongs in the sad chapter concerned with cultural endeavours on the German opera stage!" he added to the "Ariadne" section of his "Recollections of the first performances of my operas".... On the other hand the Orchestral Suite which he put together in 1920 from the nine most effective pieces of the incidental music to "Le Bourgeois gentilhomme" quickly found its way to the concert hall. One never tires of listening to the Mozartian delights of this chamber music score, a gem of the recent orchestral repertoire. Both the complete incidental music and the Concert Suite have since been used for ballets.

So "Ariadne," whose early career was so fraught with difficulties, now lives in six different forms on the opera, drama and ballet stage and in the concert hall. In its mature second operatic version it has entered the international repertoire; it has long since been taken out of the sphere of imitation baroque art, being presented in a classical setting as its composer intended. (In 1943 Strauss expressed the wish to Heinz Arnold to see the work performed in Dresden in the "strict Grecian style, possibly that of Racine tragedy.") This is the most genial and ingenious fruit of the collaboration between Strauss and Hofmannsthal, in the way the life of opera seria was fused with that of opera buffa in accordance with the orders of the "rich gentleman ..." "I know quite definitely," the poet wrote to the composer in 1918, "that although it is rejected by today's audiences, it will conquer those of tomorrow." After the first Amsterdam performance in 1924 the composer was convinced: "Now I believe in 'Ariadne'." He had every reason to do so.

*

The successor to "Ariadne" was not "Die ägyptische Helena," with its romantic pathos sprung from bourgeois roots, but *"Daphne."* Once again, after deriving inspiration from other sources and striving toward other goals for many years, Strauss returned to the Grecian ideal. As in the earlier work, this picture of Antiquity reflects the Renaissance spirit. It is early-Grecian

367

in conception, mythology related in human terms. In "Daphne," which Strauss wrote at the age of seventy-three, the theme of "transformation" recurs. He had made use of it for the first time in "Ariadne" when the heroine, alone in her grief, was transformed by her encounter with a god. In "Daphne" it appears in a double form—expressed musically in double counterpoint and in stretta. Daphne is turned into a tree, and the god changes into a cowherd. His veins do not contain "balsam and ether," like those of Bacchus, but blood. He is not proof against the enchantment of love: he has become a man, and as such he is responsible for his actions. The myth mentions nothing about the transformation of the god into a cowherd. It was Strauss, not the librettist Gregor, who introduced the motif of the god's transformation into the story of Daphne. He humanized the myth, lending it spiritual and psychological depth. This alone gave the subject, as a symbol of the peace of untouched, life-giving nature, significance on the opera stage.

The one-act "Bucolic Tragedy" by Strauss and Gregor is far removed from Peri's "Dafne." Their Daphne is not to be found in Ovid; she is not merely a nymph, but has to pay dearly for her chastity. The dramatic values of the story are changed. In the possibility of her surrender the blossoming innocence of Daphne takes on an erotic potentiality. She remains the pole around which the love of Apollo and of Leukippos circles, but as the drama approaches its climax Daphne's passive suffering gives place more and more to suffering expressed in action. From the basic story of the myth, whose human content had born fruit on the opera stage over the centuries (Gagliano, Schütz, Handel etc.) Gregor formed the scenario and libretto of the new "Daphne," following a long exchange of opinions with the composer. The text, in which the librettist's fine feeling for the musical aspect of this bucolic subject is beneficial to the overall effect, is as wordy, and tends towards pathos, as much as that of "Friedenstag," which dates from about the same time; its mythological symbolism is not easily understood. Gregor did not attain the level of Hofmannsthal's best poetic and realistic opera texts, although he was successful in depicting the simple life of peasants, shepherds and huntsmen. His psychology, too, is by no means always convincing. For example in Daphne's first lament for the dead Leukippos she regrets the fact that she has refused

In Dresden at the age of eighty

(hier bricht der Strahl des Mondes durch und beleuchtet den Wipfel
des Lorbeerbaumes)

    Apollo... Bruder...

    Nimm mein... Gezweige...

    Wind... Wind....

    Spiele mit mir....

    Selige... Vögel...

    Wohnet in mir....

    Menschen... Freunde...

    Nehmt mich als Zeichen...

    Unsterblicher Liebe.

(so wie sich das Licht über den ganzen Baum gebreitet hat, fällt
der Vorhang)

"Daphne"

Last page of Gregor's libretto with the composer's marginal remarks (1936) to be his, or has failed to save his life by consenting to Apollo, although, enraged by the "proud lords" of Olympus, she is found, after her transformation, to be well-disposed towards her "brother" Apollo. This change of relationship is not made dramatically convincing.

How great the musician's direct influence was, in this instance, on the final shape of the work! Nevertheless the idea came originally from Gregor, who had been strongly influenced by a chance encounter with Chassériau's lithograph "Apollo and Daphne." At the Berchtesgaden meeting in July 1935, to which reference has already been made, Gregor gave Strauss the exposé of a "one-act tragedy with dances and choruses." "Lovely Grecian landscape," it reads. "People, identified with nature and gods . . . Two suitors: the cowherd Apollo . . . and the young . . . shepherd Leukippos . . ." "Daphne" was agreed upon, and Strauss, deriving inspiration from paintings on the subject by Bernini and Botticelli, at once threw himself into the project wholeheartedly. During that summer Gregor began work on the libretto, keeping in close touch with Zweig. ("Please be sure to adopt our friend's suggestions . . .") He worked at a "Bucolic Tragedy" which soon diverged from the naive nature poem of the first sketch. The transformation at the conclusion is already mentioned at this stage: "The music depicts the rustling of the foliage as Daphne is transformed into the tree." But Strauss raised objections, as letters of the period show: "I am quite pleased with 'Daphne,' though I would have wished for more dramatic concentration in action and language . . ." "It is a mere succession of events, no sign of any tightening of the dramatic knot; there is absolutely no big dramatic conflict between Apollo, Leukippos and Daphne . . . this would have to be a Kleistian scene, dark and full of mystery. Nothing must occur off-stage, not even the murder of Leukippos. In short: the whole thing, as it is now taking shape in not always successful pseudo-Homeric jargon, won't attract a hundred people into the theatre . . . Everything is written, not visualized on the stage . . ." Later, after Gregor had made a number of improvements: "In general the draft is splendid. The figure of Daphne, her monologue, excellent. Peneios should now be somewhat more prominent—not too much evocation of nature—Peneios's vision from the first draft, the gods who have flown—could be used in part. The whole scenario gives rise to the highest hopes..." All Strauss's self-confidence was expressed in a letter written at the New Year: "Happy New Year! 'Daphne' promises to be excellent, if the two principal scenes are successful. Congratulations!"

Strauss now lived wholly in the Grecian myth of Daphne. He felt the work coming gradually within his grasp, and began the composition in the summer of 1936. The original idea of the opera as a great nature poem came back more and more into the foreground. Did Strauss's visit to Italy early in 1936 have a decisive influence? Gregor received a letter from Milan containing the following: "Could Daphne not represent the human embodiment of nature itself, touched upon by the two divinities Apollo and Dionysus, the contrasting elements of art? She has an inkling of them but cannot comprehend them, and only through death does she become a symbol of the eternal work of art: she can rise again as the perfect laurel tree..." And immediately afterwards: "Apollo transgresses against his godhead by approaching Daphne with the feelings of Dionysus, and she senses the falsehood in his kiss... So he must... also purify himself, a process which culminates in the fact that in Leukippos he slays the Dionysian element in himself. The symbol of this self-purification would be the deliverance of Daphne by her transformation into the laurel..."

From this point it was only a short step to the final concept of the origin of the "immortal, evergreen" tree as the dominant symbol at the conclusion of the work. Gregor, now also advised by Lothar Wallerstein, fashioned the definitive third version of the text, for which Daphne's great introductory scene and her dialogue with Leukippos already existed. The Dionysian festival, the "feast of the ripened grape," was made to form the background to the crucial encounter, so that the contrast between the "Apollonian" and "Dionysian" elements, which Strauss described as being particularly fine in the text, could be presented with the greatest effect on the stage. "I have thought it over, and Clemens Krauss, to whom I gave 'Daphne' to read, agrees with me that the idea of Leukippos being dressed as a maiden must not be altered. Naturally Leukippos says nothing while so disguised... Last confrontation of Daphne, Apollo and Leukippos–his death!... Daphne, too, cannot continue to live once she has been untrue to her real nature through the potion of Dionysus... This last en-

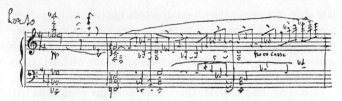

"Daphne": Copy of the short score of the Kissscene (1936)

counter of the three, the farewell words of the penitent god and the lament for Leukippos, must be very beautiful..." But Strauss's mind was still concerned with the construction of the work's conclusion, which attracted him irresistibly. (Transformation into a laurel tree to be the "self-purification" of the god and Daphne's "deliverance"–as he wrote in a letter after his discussion with Krauss in Paris.) The Finale was still merely the "human embodiment of nature," a "theatrical necessity" forming part of an otherwise purely choral conclusion to the work, not the miraculous voice of a moonlit Thessalian night... Then Krauss had a revealing idea, and Gregor's conclusion, which was already complete, was now rejected by Strauss: "We are in agreement that after Apollo's final song no human being can appear on the stage apart from Daphne, no Peneios, no solo singer–no chorus–in short no oratorio: that would weaken the effect... In the moonlight, but entirely visible, the miracle of transformation is slowly worked on her, with the orchestra alone. Daphne might, at most, say a few words, which merge into a murmur and then into wordless melody... All disturbing elements are eliminated –the solitary tree–it sings!" Now at last Daphne's wonderful poetry could unfold itself.

When the opening bars of "Daphne" are heard one might believe that Strauss had intended to write another chamber opera in the style of "Ariadne," but the tender melodic polyphony of the pastoral Introduction for woodwind, in which the cor anglais and basset horn are employed to heighten the bucolic atmosphere, does not last for long. At the rise of the curtain, after an alphorn call, the full orchestra makes itself heard, and it introduces the characterizing musical-dramatic technique of thematic construction and instrumentation familiar from works on a larger scale. This score of full maturity combines all the lyrical and dramatic characteristics of form and expression which marked Strauss's

24*

late style. Whenever the action demands finely sensitive feeling, playful baroque expression, or great pathos and dramatic excitement, there is a change of style in this music, most of which was written in Italy amid the "silvery grace" of the Mediterranean landscape.

However, the particular characteristic of this score is its lyrical, delicately animated musical picture. Daphne, that creature suggesting the breeze, the rustling foliage or spring, exists in a sphere of intimate, poetic chamber music. Where else in Strauss can one find anything as sensitive and weightless as Daphne's gently flowing introductory Monologue "O bleib, geliebter Tag?" Here, as in the poignantly lyrical, at times highly dramatic lament of the chaste nymph for the dead Leukippos, Strauss adopted a suggestive form, in which the voice is interwoven with individual instruments, principally woodwind. The feelings and moods of a close awareness of nature are caught in music which is not easily forgotten. Where else among Strauss's works is there a sound picture to compare with the chroma of the tranquillity of nature during Daphne's transformation into the laurel tree? The manner in which this metamorphosis occurs in tenderly veiled music in F♯ major, the sound growing from that of a woodwind ensemble until the whole foliage of the tree seems to spread itself out, shimmering gently in the divided strings, harp and other instruments, finally to be taken up and developed by the soprano, now freely vocalizing coloratura passages like a bird—all this creates the effect of a great "marriage of nature." The baroque concept of operatic art was here re-established with assured mastery of form, although there are also moments when the hothouse atmosphere of over-ripe late-romantic artistry is in evidence. (The original ending of the text for chorus later inspired Strauss to his Epilogue to "Daphne," a setting of Gregor's words). It was certainly clear to Strauss that a mythological opera idyll based *solely* on the "Apollonian" spirit would have wearied the ear. So he created the contrast of the "Dionysian" elements in the festival dances. He depicted the spiritual events of the encounter between Daphne and Apollo in music of great profundity. (Strauss himself once described the "Kiss scene" as the "basic idea" of the work). He varied the musical scene by means of the Valhalla pathos of Peneios and Gaea, the Bacchic brilliance of Apollo, employing his colourful orchestral apparatus and making sparing use of the chorus to depict wind and wave, thunderstorms, and the sounds of the homecoming flocks. The effect would probably have been even more impressive had these episodes been further removed from the sphere of the illustrative elements familiar from lyrical opera.

"Taormina, 24th December 1937" Strauss noted on the last page of the score, and on the following day he wrote in a letter to Gregor: "The score of 'Daphne' was completed yesterday, but please do not tell anyone..." During the following October "Daphne" received its world première at the Dresden State Opera. Karl Böhm, to whom it is dedicated, was the conductor. Daphne's costume suggested Botticelli–but a few weeks later Strauss came out in favour of a design in the spirit of Bernini. ("'Daphne' is very beautiful, noble in effect, and animated; general admiration for libretto and music," Strauss wrote to Gregor after the dress rehearsal). The composer's original intention to have the two contrasting one-act operas, the soldierly "Friedenstag" and the loftily poetic "Daphne," presented as a double bill at the same performance was given up after the premières in Dresden and Berlin. Krauss later proposed alterations to this "Bucolic Tragedy": in Berlin he wanted the opening scene to be omitted, and in Munich, on the other hand, he tried to persuade Strauss to extend the work to the length of a "normal" opera evening. Fortunately neither suggestion was acted upon. The composer did, however, retouch the instrumentation of certain passages in the score. "Daphne" marked the coming to full maturity of Strauss's serene, Hellenic style. The mild glow of a warm, clear, autumn evening lies over this opera, which Rolland praised enthusiastically on its appearance as "the most melodious creation of the aged master." Gratified by its success, Strauss declared in 1939 that he would remain with the "old Greeks" for the rest of his life...

*

Meanwhile this tireless creative artist had begun work on a new opera: *"Die Liebe der Danae."* After the two single-act music dramas concerned with heroism and virginity respectively, the ethos and eros, Strauss felt drawn to the idea of a mythological subject which could be treated lightly. "After 'Daphne' I should like to write something gay! No more tragedy!" he wrote to Gre-

gor in June 1936, and at the beginning of 1937: "A light mythological operetta would be very much to my taste after your two
serious subjects"–he scarcely realized that another historical
turning point lay ahead. For while the composer lost himself in
the world of Grecian Antiquity at Garmisch for the last time,
working on his "gay mythology," and as, with advancing age, he
came ever closer to the figures and scenes of Greek legend, the
German people were being propelled towards the abyss of a new
world war. In 1938 the Nazis seized Austria, and in 1939 they
occupied Czechoslovakia. A year before the completion of the
score of "Danae" the war broke out, and Hitler's army overran
Poland . . . Strauss, who had just reached the age of seventy-five,
quite rightly perturbed by these developments, had only one desire: to complete the new opera as soon as possible.

The history of "Danae" dates right back to 1920. As a reaction to " Die Frau ohne Schatten" Strauss had long wanted to
write a "satirical operetta in late-Antique costumes." Hofmannsthal at once understood what was in the musician's mind:
". . . Then I should like to offer you the draft of a light, three-act
piece akin to operetta and very close to the world of Lucian,
'Danae oder Die Vernunftheirat;' perhaps you will find the necessary clear water ahead of you so that you can let your beautiful little ship set sail" (February 1920). The proposed opera combined the story of Danae, whom Jupiter approached in the form
of golden rain, with that of King Midas, who turned everything
he touched to gold. The poet was quite right when he wrote to
the composer a few months later: " 'Danae' continues the line of
'Rosenkavalier,' 'Ariadne' Prologue and 'Bourgeois gentilhomme.' It demands light, spirited music such as only you, and
in the present phase of your life, can provide. The subject is set
in the early Antiquity of myths, and it is treated with a cheerful
irreverence suggesting Lucian. The more Gallic your approach
to it the better–at heart it remains Germanic in its depth, just as
I remain at heart lyrical, with a lyricism which conceals symbolical and metaphysical elements . . ." Strauss was genuinely
interested in the scenario which Hofmannsthal enclosed, and
which even indicated the various musical numbers of the first
two acts. His marginal notes on this draft show clearly how the
musician exercised an even greater influence than hitherto on the
shaping of the libretto. For example he made such notes as these:

"Entrée and short Ballet, Duo Scene, Conversation, Grand Narration," or later, in the second act: "Ballet, Letter Scene, March, Grand Scena, Conversation, then more and more song, Finale, Grand Duet..." It is not known why Strauss gave up the project at this advanced stage of joint work. Instead he wrote the equally cheerful but wholly dissimilar everyday conversation piece "Intermezzo," then, as the result of another wide swing of the pendulum, the heavily baroque "Ägyptische Helena." In his essay on "Helena," which dates from 1929, Hofmannsthal wrote: "Let us make mythological operas, theirs is the truest of all forms." At that time all his energies were devoted to bringing to full fruition the light "third style" which he had initiated in "Arabella." It was a tragedy that he himself could not take part in the eventual realization of his "Danae" plan.

Four years after Hofmannsthal's death his scenario for "Danae" was published in the magazine "Corona," but Strauss forgot all about it until Schuh drew his attention to it in 1936. He was so captivated by the idea that he asked his literary colleague of that period Joseph Gregor, with whom he was then discussing various ballet plans, to transform Hofmannsthal's scenario into a complete libretto. "A fascinating subject which I should like to compose... Perhaps you can at once get down to 'Danae' (treating it lightly, even parodistically, which would also improve the rather banal ending)... If I don't live long enough to compose the music you will always find others who are grateful for the text." He was to base himself on the existing plan of a first and second act with its "innumerable suggestions for this enchanting piece." A "dramatic Jupiter Symphony," but also a "Grecian Götterdämmerung" was the ideal of the composer, who had written to Hofmannsthal as early as 1916 that he felt himself called to be the "Offenbach of the 20th century," and now, virtually for the first time, wanted an "operetta of the finest kind... the whole thing light, simple and graceful" ... Such a concept could not easily appeal to Gregor, a learned man of the theatre whose style was essentially weighty. He attempted to revert to a synopsis of his own which he had shown to Strauss during their meeting at Berchtesgaden a year before. But the composer was quite certain what he wanted from "Danae": "I should not like to diverge so far from the Hofmannsthal line and the character of a delicate, lightly ironical singspiel . . . Your synopsis is too heavy–you want to go too deep again, and the subject could not bear the weight . . . Won't you try to elaborate Hofmannsthal's idea as it stands . . . With pretty couplets, a gay feast, elegant dances, for which I could write light stage music. And finally a simple, affectionate duet for the muleteer couple . . ."

It is very surprising to learn from Gregor that when he wrote the first two-act version of the text of the new opera he "did not know Hofmannsthal's synopsis," and "had not pursued any mythological and historical studies." Gregor gave a detailed account of this original "Danae," how it was fashioned, then, following a visit to Italy early in 1937, transformed in accordance with Strauss's wishes: "What appealed to me was the god's amorous approach to the maiden, who was the first and only person to oppose him. The love of gold was the dominant theme here. I saw Danae as the seventy-year-old Titian had seen her, and wanted to offer her so to the composer who was equally at the height of his powers, though equally old. A woman at once strong and dreamy, her gaze is fixed expectantly on the golden cloud. Amor turns away, shocked. The Danae of my original synopsis would have been far more serious . . . The first alteration of the glittering, rebellious figure of my imagination occurred as the result of a joint visit to the Villa Borghese, which Strauss loved as much as Goethe had. We visited the Daphne of Bernini, which he admired, and soon found ourselves before the Danae of Correggio. That was something different. A thirty-year-old artist, brilliantly successful, had created a work in which all tensions were dissolved into grace. Danae, a blossoming maiden, gazes with eager happiness at the gold, which she is collecting in a cloth on her lap–not at the cloud! Before Correggio's Danae Strauss said: 'You see, this lightness, this happiness is what I am after. Read Hofmannsthal's synopsis' . . ."

Surprisingly enough something quite different resulted–namely what Krauss once aptly described as a "great baroque picture with many theatrical features." Was Gregor really unable to make anything of Hofmannsthal's graceful scenario with its ironically witty rococo spirit akin to that of French operetta? Or did the dramaturgical suggestions evidently received from outside the "workshop" during the writing of "Danae" introduce other concepts of the myth into the text? Undoubtedly Krauss and Wallerstein tended to strengthen Gregor in his opinion that "even in this delicate and light matter one must go rather deeper ..." "The whole thing must approach the style of Spanish drama, so that the result is not a parody of the gods," was Krauss's opinion. Almost unnoticeably the originally merely graceful picture of Danae was transformed into something more richly human and even "heroic." This change corresponded to the dramatic accents produced by Gregor's introduction of Jupiter into the action. The god is Danae's suitor, using the muleteer Midas to woo in his stead, and giving him the power to change everything he touches into gold. Despite many warnings, Danae and Midas fall in love. Danae's transformation into a golden statue, her return to life and flight with her beloved leave the god defeated and wrathful, until he tries to console himself by means of a supper with the four queens ... "For this ending I need a fine, long farewell speech of Jupiter, like that of Hans Sachs at the end of 'Meistersinger!' Content: cheerful resignation, farewell for ever to the old love ... Following the failure of the adventure with Danae, doubt about the almighty power of the gods. The serene, beautiful gods give place to darker spirits ..."

Author and composer covered a great deal of ground before the work was complete. Reading the correspondence of those years, one can easily see how the situation had changed by comparison with that concerning "Rosenkavalier" or "Schweigsame Frau" (to mention two striking examples). The composer's "brutal criticisms" of his colleague's work were even more in evidence, and he often felt it necessary to make particular demands on the writer as regards poetic form or points of verbal accentuation. In August 1937, for example, he complained that the "verbal construction still leaves much to be desired," writing that the second act was far too "drawn-out and unnecessarily pathetic," and referring to the "whole long, boring opera." Later: "The writing in elevated language leads all too easily to hollow phrases, mere 'filling in' which says nothing, and the empty jingle of rhymes ... No 'opera text!' I'll make it that when I compose it! ..." Other points to be considered, according to Strauss, were that the opera lacked what was most important—the "soprano aria for the prima donna and the tenor aria for Midas;" the ending, whose "leanness" made it something of a falling off, should conclude on a "purely human" note without the "bed of roses"

377

whose effect was merely that of a repetition. At the beginning of the last scene Danae should be given a "simple, reflective cavatina suggesting folksong."

"The second act is now ready in rough sketches and, I believe, is good, especially the ending. Duration 40 minutes, the first act 49 minutes, so I can spread myself as much as I like in the third act." What third act? Early in 1938 a situation had arisen in the joint work which had shown "Danae" in a new light. Krauss expressed the hitherto unspoken feeling that the second Finale, which originally concluded the opera, could not satisfactorily fulfil that function. "Why do you really want to write this opera? It is concerned with a completely unsuccessful adventure of Jupiter, and one cannot conclude a piece in which Jupiter appears by making him retreat to Olympus, his thunder having been stolen—that would make the god cut a ridiculous figure..." The suggestion of a new, third act, depicting the poverty of Danae and Midas as well as Jupiter's parting from the four queens and the human nature taken on by the god, was accepted. Particularly affectionate, as always, was the conception of the conclusion to the work, which was also strongly influenced by Krauss: Jupiter goes away; Danae gazes after him in a long postlude, and turns slowly to the animals—at that moment the orchestra announces the arrival of Midas, whom Danae rushes to meet..."
"This ending is much finer, more Gallic," Strauss declared, "and I can continue the farewell mood of Jupiter without a break to the end." Then finally, when he had received Gregor's final version: "Heartfelt thanks and congratulations. All the pains you have taken have been splendidly rewarded. I am very happy." The score was completed shortly after Strauss's 76th birthday.

> Whatever you touch,
> take to your lips—
> blessed or curs'd—
> be changed to gold!

This is the real motto of "Die Liebe der Danae"... (After this opera had been known at first by the working title "King Midas," and Strauss had referred to it on occasion as "The deceived Jupiter" or "Jupiter's Last Love," Viorica Ursuleac's better idea for a title—The Love of Danae— was finally accepted.) Wagner was concerned with the curse of gold, Strauss with the overcoming of gold by love. The fact that Danae renounces Jupiter's gold and an "exalted destiny" in favour of "human happiness" is an attractive and powerful idea. Midas, the proxy "suitor as bringer of gold," forgets his vow to Jupiter. Danae, compelled to choose between god and man, riches and poverty, chooses the man she loves, and finds happiness in "peaceful pleasures." Unfortunately the presentation on the stage of the various significant relationships between love and gold until the final victory of the human couple over a "restless god" poses several problems for audiences to solve. In particular Gregor did not succeed in making the most of the social-critical possibilities of the subject, or its bearing on the present day. The "dance round the golden calf" in the opening scene at the Court of King Pollux, which rises to its climax with the repeated cry "Gold!", seems to be only remotely connected with the personal destiny of Danae. Is the human character strong enough to banish the curse of gold? Gregor's libretto, which is often obscure in ideas, language and dramatic construction (especially in the third act) does not make this sufficiently clear.

"Danae" has many links with the music of earlier Strauss operas. His dramatic works come within two categories: one is based on historical or mythological subjects and is influenced by Wagner, commencing with "Guntram" and "Elektra," the other is bathed in the sunlight of Mozart and embodied in the silvery sheen of "Rosenkavalier." "Danae," the "Cheerful Mythology," purest Hellenism, combines these two elements with great artistry, though not in perfect harmony. Regarded in this light, it is the composer's most festive and colourful operatic work after the "Comedy for Music," and after "Die Frau ohne Schatten" (ignoring in this connection the more outwardly representational "Helena") the second real "grand opera." As a creation of the mind and spirit, however, it expresses itself less directly than several of Strauss's earlier works, despite the formal beauty of the individual acts. All that glitters here is not gold, and the experience of a long lifetime was sometimes needed to get the music off the ground. (Strauss felt that in certain weak and sugary passages he had been let down by his librettist.) Nevertheless the lively unity of action of romantically shaped line, expression and gesture, the skilful varying and exploitation of the thematic material, and the attributes of a tonal language which encompasses

379

all qualities from exuberant wit to deeply-felt solemnity are captivating.

The most strikingly new aspect of "Danae" is its wealth of melodic beauty, which Strauss cultivated with great care. With its strongly constructed solo numbers and ensembles it is an act of homage to melody based on rich harmony, which has a graceful flow rather than highly energetic vitality. A German belcanto opera seeking the land of the Greeks with its vocal chords! It is undoubtedly true that blossoming lyricism comes to the fore to an increasing extent as the opera proceeds, until toward the end of the last act, in the simple pathos of the orchestral interlude "Jupiter's Renunciation," the Schubertian purity of Danae's Cavatina in B♭, and the melodically intimate farewell scene between Danae and Jupiter, it achieves a nobility which produces a deep impression. Strauss himself told Schuh with satisfaction that this was really "no falling off," that in the "undiminished creative power" of the third act he had written music which he could "place beside the best ideas in 'Rosenkavalier,' 'Ariadne' and 'Arabella'." Strauss here consciously chose as his starting point straightforward, folklike, often sensitively simple effects. (As in the case of "Helena," a certain influence of Saint-Saëns is evident.) There is scarcely anything in the whole of Strauss's operatic output to compare with the captivating, songlike duet "So führ ich dich mit sanfter Hand." The melodic riches of the score also include the lovely canon-quartet of the four queens, with the delicate ornamentation of springlike, radiant female voices in a loosely-knit texture, and the flowing "Narration of Maia's Story" which remained in every version of the work from the original draft text onward. The parlando style of earlier Strauss operas appears to have been largely relegated to the background. Instead Wagnerian elements are in evidence to a greater extent than had been the case in any but Strauss's earliest stage works: an orchestral flood coloured by the brass, with rich chords (which Strauss was to avoid in "Capriccio," his next opera) recalling the Nibelung world. A certain loquacity in the scheme of modulations is noticeable. The facts that the moderately large orchestra, whose scope ranges from delicate arabesques to richly sonorous sound, spreads an iridescent lustre over the fairy-tale events of the story (golden rain), and that the chorus is used with uncommon bite and effectiveness in the opening scene of the creditors

380

"Die Liebe der Danae"
Sketch for the creditors' scene in the first act (1938)

complete the stylistic picture of this unique "opera semiseria." Undoubtedly the Olympian composer would have recognized the dramaturgical weaknesses of his work during later critical examination, and would have eliminated some of them.

He wanted the world première of this major work to be postponed until after the war. ("In view of the unpleasant experiences concerning 'Frau ohne Schatten,' the first performance of 'Danae' cannot take place until at least two years have elapsed after the definite conclusion of peace, i. e. after my death ... In the state of the world today, 'Danae' will therefore probably be an 'œuvre posthume' ...") However, as the prospects of a worthy première soon after the war became increasingly remote owing to the destruction of the major opera houses, Strauss accepted Clemens Krauss's proposal that "Die Liebe der Danae" should be included in the programme of the 1944 Salzburg Festival. The sudden closing of all German and Austrian theatres meant that the project did not get beyond the memorable dress rehearsal that August. The composer was then eighty–who could tell whether he would ever see the work performed? After the war he turned down applications from the opera houses of Berlin,

Vienna, Munich and Dresden ... "The time for it is still not yet ripe, and painful though this renunciation is to me, for the sake of the work's future I must resist the temptation. The right thing for 'Danae' is therefore to wait patiently, and if I do not live to see the première in five or ten years' time, I can at least close my eyes in peace with the thought that I am leaving the work in the best hands. A pity! But one must be sensible! ... Perhaps the new Vienna Opera can open with it." When Hartmann later asked the dying composer for his decision, the final choice was Salzburg ... Eight whole years were to elapse before, in August 1952, "Danae" received its world première under Krauss in the same theatre which had witnessed the historic dress rehearsal: thirty-two years after Hofmannsthal's first synopsis, twenty-three years after his death, about ten years after the completion of the score, and three after the death of the composer. In accordance with his expressed wish, Hofmannsthal's name appeared together with that of Gregor on the programme. In the version produced by the Munich Opera in 1953 attempts were made to strengthen the work dramaturgically by reversing the order of two scenes in the first act and by tightening up the action elsewhere; nevertheless many psychologically unclear points remained as production problems (e. g. the golden drapery). "Danae," the most underrated of all Strauss's later operas, still awaits rebirth.

Strauss sent Heinz Tietjen, to whom the work is dedicated but who could not be present at the unique pre-performance of "Danae" in the shadow of ominous wartime events, the following lines in an attempt at consolation: "It was a great pity that you could not attend the splendid performance of 'Danae' ... After the second act a storm of spontaneous applause broke out, and the third act was really moving, my last acknowledgment to Greece, and the final meeting of German music with the Grecian spirit ..."

*

This is the place to mention the opera plans drawn from the "inexhaustible storehouse of Greece" which Strauss attempted to bring to fruition during the decade between 1935 and 1945. "Perhaps another beautiful child of the gods will come out of the egg ..." In May 1935, at the suggestion of Zweig, Gregor began to study the possibility of basing an opera on the once popular subject of Semiramis, the passionate, mythical Queen of Assyria. "I am naturally quite carried away by the 'Daughter of the Air,' indeed, I believe that no other subject can come into consideration." There was certainly something in the "air" . . . Strauss, too, devoted himself with remarkable energy to this opera plan. "Do you know the sketches of 'Semiramis' left by Hofmannsthal? They contain much valuable material concerning the demoniac side of the character of the 'Daughter of the Air.' Hofmannsthal had the right feeling that the story would have to be taken out of the sphere of state affairs into that of the imagination . . ." And two days later: "I would have nothing against making *two* evenings of it . . . The main thing is to take full advantage of all the possibilities inherent in the subject; it can well be in the form of "Wallenstein': I. Prelude and tragedy of Menon, three or four scenes, II. Semiramis, three acts . . ." But on closer consideration of Gregor's synopsis Strauss had second thoughts. ". . . I can see no possibility of its becoming a real work for the theatre, let alone a serviceable opera text. The old Wagnerian gods can hardly be represented by human singers, and kindly Asiatic gods, of whom no mortal man has any conception, not at all . . . It would be easier to base a workmanlike grand opera on old Calderón himself . . . Action and characters! No ideas! No poetry! Theatre! . . . And don't forget that the audience scarcely understand a third of the text of an opera, and if they can't follow they at once become bored . . . Calderón and still more Calderón . . ." The struggle with this vast subject went on for another year until, despite Gregor's repeated attempts to keep it alive, Strauss wrote in June 1936 that he wanted the idea "to be dropped for good."

Strauss was already busy with the first plans for "Capriccio" when "Semiramis" again appeared to become a practical proposition, and from then on references to it never completely disappeared from the correspondence between Strauss and Gregor until shortly before the former's death . . . An almost painful love of "Semiramis" (a subject which had earlier attracted Mozart and Rossini) accompanied those years. Nevertheless Strauss retreated before the prospect of a "five-act opera with a more or less interesting plot." "If you read Hofmannsthal's sketches again you will see how he considered the problem but did not master it. I imagine: four decisive moments from the life of Semiramis, flashlight photos (10 to 15 minutes each) from 'The Daughter of the Air' . . . The whole thing could last about 45 minutes: no orchestral interludes, short expositions before each scene . . ." While engaged upon the final stages of work on "Capriccio," Strauss made a resumé of the situation: ". . . I cannot do anything with it now! Too late, and in any case more or less an unsympathetic 'Aida'–i. e. grand opera!"; then again in May 1941: "We must give up 'Semiramis'–I haven't enough time or creative energy left. Besides, it is no subject for a man of seventy-seven . . ." Nevertheless Gregor sent him further draft plots in March 1942 and June 1944, the whole subject now being compressed into six scenes. The last reference to the project occurred in a letter sent by Gregor in April 1948: "The most regrettable thing of all is probably the fact that nothing came of 'Semiramis'."

All other plans for operas were of less account. "Celestina," a "large-scale Spanish piece" in three acts after Lope de Vega, came under consideration while Strauss was still working on "Friedenstag" and "Daphne." Passages in his letters to Gregor throw sufficient light on the subject: it could have been a "splendid, gruesome tragi-comedy," in which the "poetic figures of the piece: the parents, Fabio and the two lovers, could be treated parodistically." The story of the crafty Spanish brothel-keeper would have had to be handled with the "spirit of acute irony"–as a "continuation of the ironic style of 'Così fan tutte' and the completion of the joke begun in 'Feuersnot'." "The very fact that Celestina comes from such a depth of infamy gives her a strange dignity, but she remains a perfectly real bawd, not a metaphysical procuress intended for symbolical purposes like the Nurse . . ." And finally in June 1936: "I am very pleased with your 'Celestina'"–but there the matter rested. The fact that at that period of his career Strauss frequently toyed with the idea of an "Amphitryon" opera, at first in conjunction with Zweig, that he often considered including "Nausikaa" among his Grecian heroines, and that he became interested for a time in Tieck and the "old English writers"–all these bore witness to the admirable mental agility of the aged composer, who wished to encompass within the sphere of his art every aspect of the classical theatre.

*

Der dem Bilde gefolgt

Mit goldenem Segel

Und liebendem Sehnen -

Midas - grüsst dich !

(er verlässt das Schiff)

D a n a e :   Ich erschaue dich,

Midas, grosser König !

Dein Bote umgab mich

Herrlich mit dem Golde,

Mit deiner Macht !

J u p i t e r :   Mein Bote - war es ?

Nur Chrysopher ? -

Was im Traum dich umfloss

Mit ehrendem Glanz,

Der du gejubelt,

Herrliche Danae !

Aller Träume Sinn -

Sieh nun vor dir !

D a n a e :   Ich erkenne dich,

Wie ich dich geahnt :

Herr ewiger Räume -

Herr goldener Träume -

J u p i t e r :   Nicht goldnen Regens

Sinnbild umfasst dich !

Nicht Mantel, nicht Zelt -

Nur dieser Arme

Lebende Kraft !

D a n a e :   Herr goldener Träume -
(weicht zurück)

Bist du auch meiner Liebe

Allmächtiger Herr ?

J u p i t e r :
(verwundert, dann stark zu Midas)

Träger des Goldes !

Dies - mein Gebot ?

(er richtet sich gross auf, goldschimmerndes Licht trifft ihn, es
donnert leise)

Danae - Danae - Braut !

(er sucht sie zu umfassen, Danae sinkt in die Arme ihrer Begleiterinnen)

V o r h a n g !

"Die Liebe der Danae"
A page of Gregor's libretto with the composer's marginal notes
(Finale to the first act) (1938)

"Die Liebe der Danae"
First page of the score of the Prelude to the third act (1939)

Three years before his first visit to Greece, the twenty-five-year-old Strauss was first drawn to Antiquity. Following the example of Wagner's new version of "Iphigénie en Aulide," the budding music dramatist, who had just completed "Tod und Verklärung" and was working on "Guntram," produced for the Weimar Court Theatre a new translation and arrangement of Gluck's *"Iphigénie en Tauride."* The young conductor thus achieved for his own theatre, although not until after he had left it (1900), a success which, slowly overcoming critical objections, was repeated in other towns. Today, at a time when interest is concentrated on authentic original versions, we have a different view of works of the past, especially when they still possess the power to move modern audiences. The young Strauss showed remarkable patience in his detailed work (his translation is carefully matched to the metre of the French original) and a fine feeling for maintaining the broad sweep of the drama, but attitudes to the past have since changed. Fascinating though it is when Strauss takes the recitative "Ach arme Polopiden," with which Gluck followed the chorus of priestesses, and sets it to music of his own simultaneous with that chorus, however dramaturgically skilful his anticipation of the first Scythian chorus before the opening Recitative of Thoas as an off-stage song, like his re-positioning of Iphigénie's A major Aria, and however admirable in its depth of feeling is the newly composed Trio of the three principal characters Iphigénie, Orestes and Pylades, accompanied by the chorus of Greeks–such things, and the improved motivation of Thoas's death, produce unnecessary divergencies from the original score, emphasizing elements foreign to Gluck's practice, and showing him in a false light.

The festival play with dances and choruses *"Die Ruinen von Athen"* bears all the marks of an occasional work. Strauss wrote it during his period as Director of the Vienna Opera, making use of the play of the same name by August von Kotzebue and the ballet "Die Geschöpfe des Prometheus," both with music by Beethoven, to a new text by Hofmannsthal. The union of two works very different in style and quality, linked by a rather styleless "Melodramatic Scene" for which Strauss employed themes from the Third and Fifth Symphonies, produced what cannot be considered a really artistic whole. Kotzebue-Hofmannsthal, Beethoven-Strauss–the sum would not add up. There was in fact no deep reason at all for this modernization of two classical documents. Conceived by its author and musical arranger as a symbol of their experience of Greece, the work's effect was almost wholly restricted to Vienna, where it was produced under Strauss's baton in 1924, together with Gluck's "Don Juan."

Strauss's new arrangement of Mozart's *"Idomeneo"* can only be described correctly as a curiosity of musical history. Strauss the Mozart lover had always felt a deep affection for this troublesome child of the master's storm and stress period. The plan for a reawakening of the opera originated with Clemens Krauss, who had the promising idea of entrusting the musical revision to Strauss, while Lothar Wallerstein was to undertake the textual and dramaturgical rearrangement. What Strauss had in mind was to give new life to Mozart's early evocation of Antiquity. What he presented at the Vienna State Opera in April 1931 (while he was working on "Arabella"), to the astonishment of the musical world, included whole sections which he had composed afresh; this is a paraphrase, a rewriting of the work as a whole, in which for long stretches only Strauss is to be heard–the Strauss who, in "Helena," believed himself to have established a new link between the modern world and Grecian Antiquity. It goes without saying that these alterations by Strauss cannot be justified from the viewpoint of musicological purity of style. One hears ethereal "Ariadne" chords and intoxicating ensembles, while the whole work is coloured by the tonal accents of Strauss's distinctive musical language. The recitatives, the weak point of opera seria, are filled out with modern turns of phrase (there is one direct quotation from "Helena")–the whole score now appears to be through-composed. Strauss also revised the arias. Before the second act he added an entirely new orchestral Interlude in C minor which depicts, with late-romantic means, the emotions of the people at the appearance of the sea monster. Also new, although based on motifs by Mozart, is the Finale–a rapturous Apotheosis in E♭, a last act of homage to the spirit of Mozart painted with the palette of the modern master, who produced ever new, unexpected effects with the melos of the Strauss orchestra, the chorus and solo voices.

Wallerstein's libretto transformed Elektra, with her outbursts of unbridled passion, into a priestess named Ismene, who once loved Idamante, but is now in the service of Poseidon. Her wrath is directed not against the successful rival Ilia, but against the union of the Grecian prince with a Trojan princess. When (in Mozart) Elektra surprises the lovers she hisses wrathfully "Ah, what ingratitude!," while in the Strauss version Ismene thunders "Shame to Greece!" The character of Ismene is undoubtedly weaker than that of Elektra. The change is probably due to the fact that having once solved the problem of Elektra at great depth, Strauss did not want to tackle it again in another man's work. As he used a soprano for the (originally castrato) role of Idamante, the unusual ratio of three sopranos to one tenor remained unaltered. When the work was put into rehearsal again for the Vienna Mozart Week in 1941, Strauss decided to redress the balance by assigning the part of Idamante to a tenor, but this plan did not come to fruition. (During the same period, at Gregor's suggestion, Strauss considered making a new version of Spohr's "Jessonda," a task which was finally undertaken by Hermann Zilcher). The attempt at a musical reconciliation between masters of the 18th and 20th centuries has proved to be an aesthetic-stylistic error related to self-glorifying subjectivity. Mozart's music, as touched up by Strauss with great affection, "sounds" well, but it creates no warm spiritual life. Such treatment does not reduce the distance which the years have placed between Mozart and the present day–indeed, it increases that distance.

"LITERATURE"

Without true-to-life libretti opera cannot really live. Ever since the baroque age composers have been demanding texts which are good, poetic, and at the same time close to reality, and in numerous cases they have of necessity been their own librettists. Many great masters—one need only remember Weber, Verdi, Tschaikowsky and Smetana—sometimes set libretti whose literary merit clearly did not match up to the significance of the music. (It was not until Verdi was nearing the end of his long life that he found in Boito a congenial colleague who enabled him to create "Otello" and "Falstaff.") Other composers kept a constant lookout for writers of the time, from whom they hoped to receive inspiration for their dramatic works. The real turning point for opera came with the worldwide success of "Salome" by Strauss and Wilde; the subjects adopted from then on were not limited to realistic dramas and comedies of the spoken theatre which clamoured to be set to music, and plays were often used as opera libretti basically unaltered. Many subjects, however, came from literary sources remote from everyday life, intellectual rather than theatrical, of very different periods. This approach by opera to a wide range of literary production is undoubtedly a typical feature of the musical theatre of the present century. It represents an advance over the rigid scheme of the old-style opera, but at the same time it involves danger! "Opera has been linked with literature" (Ruppel). Strauss experienced the advantages and disadvantages of this fact more than almost any other creative artist.

It is a regrettable fact that at a crucial stage of his life Strauss had not sufficient strength of purpose to prevent his operatic works from sinking into the regions of pure aestheticism and mysticism. In his struggles to shatter the conventional forms of

389

the bourgeois theatre he found his way to new conventional forms remote from realistic drama. The quest for poetically varied, psychologically constructed subjects suited to musical treatment led him to the symbolical fairy tale and baroque myth. His two great baroque operas of 1919 and 1928, in which the cultivated musician filled the problematic verbal images of weightily philosophical texts with musical beauty and euphony, are a closed book to a great many listeners. They represent, unmistakably, a dying species of literary-individualistic opera. It is very revealing to see how Hofmannsthal quite openly acknowledged his liking for "incomprehensibility" in opera. "You should be glad," he wrote at the end of the First World War, "that I provide the element which will alienate people and give rise to a certain amount of opposition. You have too many adherents already, you are already the master of the moment to too great an extent, accepted on all sides; they can be angry with me, the 'incomprehensible', for giving them something which needs digesting: we are raising a mortgage on the coming generation—as in the problematical elements of 'Ariadne', about which people still growl their indignant 'Why?' and 'What for?'..." On another occasion he wrote, equally unrealistically, that the question of understanding something like the great new fairy-tale opera was not one of a "nauseating 'demand to understand,' in the sense of $2 \times 2 = 4$," but of "attaining something higher, with the mystery lying below..." Influenced by such ideas, Strauss was in serious danger of losing touch with the solid ground under his feet. Not until the time of "Daphne" did he recognize his road clearly, when he demanded of Gregor "Not literature—Theatre!"

How could Strauss and Hofmannsthal, with their contrasting natures, work together? How could the naturally cheerful, robust, down-to-earth musician seek a close association with the precious, over-refined littérateur remote from reality, who described himself as a "poet, but no man of the theatre?" The writer, half-Austrian, half-Italian, who created out of a world of pure feelings, aesthetic and "sentimental" in the sense of Schiller—and the Bavarian musician of the people, with whom everything sprang from vital observation and a living relationship with reality? "He is not exactly easy on librettists, he has his firmly fixed ideas and wishes—and is certainly stubborn," Hofmannsthal once complained, and on another occasion he wrote to Strauss: "I am far more bizarre than you imagine; you know little about me, only the surface. What attracts me lies in places where you would not expect to find it . . ." But despite the contrasts between their personalities they had certain things in common: they came from the same Alpine region, each had enjoyed a comprehensive humanistic education, which directed his gaze toward all manifestations of world culture, and each possessed a clear relationship to the multi-coloured expressions of the theatre. Hofmannsthal's life and work, too, were in a state of constant transformation. "Elektra" created the bridge to Strauss. There followed the libretti of "Rosenkavalier," "Ariadne" and "Frau ohne Schatten." For Reinhardt he wrote the great mystery plays "Jedermann" and "Welttheater." He adapted Calderón into German, and presented "Oedipus" in modern terms. He began as a lyric poet, then produced various prose works, while his earlier verse dramas were followed by the social play "Der Schwierige" and, as his great, crowning achievement, the tragedy "Der Turm" of 1925. The fine idea which linked him firmly with Strauss was: "The poetic work always intends to mirror the great totality of existence." While the collaboration was frequently overcast by "profound misunderstandings and violent differences of basic conception" (H. Mayer), Hofmannsthal's feeling for realism found convincing expression in the Viennese comedies which he wrote for Strauss at different stages of his career. Here the poet did not shut his eyes to "things around," and he escaped from the world of dreams.

Writers of stature left dramatic composers in the lurch far too long. The ungrateful task of a librettist was considered to be beneath the dignity of most of them. It seemed scarcely conceivable that a poet of repute could find fulfilment in joint work with an opera composer. (Stefan George regarded participation in the writing of an opera, the "most vulgar" theatrical form, to be an absolute "profanation.") "I know," Hofmannsthal wrote in a letter concerning "Ariadne," "that for generations no writer of stature has gladly and willingly worked for a musician . . ." However, the musician in this case was Richard Strauss, and to Hofmannsthal it was "something more than mere chance" which had brought him in contact with the greatest master of modern opera. Without really being "musical", the poet demonstrated an astonishing insight into the dramatic values of music, which has such power "to bring beautiful images to life." "Modest though my knowledge of music is, I can recognize very well everything relating to the style of the work," he wrote to Strauss in 1924, and after hearing their latest work played over on the piano: "This 'Helena' music fills me with pleasure which is, I believe, greater than that created by any of your earlier compositions, and I feel I am right in this, although I have no way of expressing myself lucidly. But however imperfect my ear, I evidently have some sense of the attributes of music, and this sense was most deeply moved by what I heard yesterday . . ."

As for Strauss, whose feeling for literary quality was by no means always certain (vide his songs), we can see from his unpublished papers what so greatly drew him to Hofmannsthal. "It was not only that he had a gift for inventing musical subjects, he had . . . an instinctive sense of what subject fulfilled my current requirements which was simply astonishing." This striking ability to feel his way into music expressed itself in Hofmannsthal's conviction that it was necessary in opera to give way to the music, to enable the music to capture what could not be said in words. The poet instinctively sought to create scenes for the musician in which his words and images could grow into the stuff of music. Bertolt Brecht has since referred to the "eminent composability" of Hofmannsthal's opera texts. Regarded in that light the poet's contribution to the partnership was not limited to the fact that he wrote a series of good libretti, which have their own literary value and do not need the composer's work to demonstrate their artistic standing. It lay above all in the fact that Hofmannsthal was able, through his poetry, to set the musician's strings vibrating. ("I respond very strongly to well chosen words!") Hofmannsthal's "poems for music" summoned up the language of sound on a broad scale. "It is necessary not only to work together but really to work *within each other* . . ." or, as Hofmannsthal wrote in his "Unwritten foreword to 'Der Rosenkavalier':" "A work is a whole, and even the work of two people can become one whole . . . Anyone who divides it is doing wrong. He who considers one element alone forgets that it is always the whole work which is heard. The music should not be torn away from the text or the words from the life of the theatre. The work is created for the stage, not for reading as a book or for one person at his piano." Strauss did not compose *any* "Elektra" or "Rosenkavalier;" his work is inseparable from that of Hofmannsthal. One might say that he composed the poet's psychology in musical notes, and in *this* respect, even in the case of his operas weighed down by symbolism, the musician could certainly be satisfied with "his dear Scribe," to whom he was indebted for the "first libretti since Richard Wagner to attain a high artistic and literary standard." "I have negotiated with the foremost German writers, even with d'Annunzio," he wrote in his notes concerning "Die schweigsame Frau," "repeatedly with Gerhart Hauptmann—and in fifty years I have found only the wonderful Hofmannsthal."

In the world of the musical theatre the long artistic collaboration between Strauss and Hofmannsthal, with the mutual growth which it fostered, and the "gently determining influence of the poet on the musician" (Schuh), and indeed of the musician on the poet, was remarkable. (Only in the association of the writer Paul Claudel with the composers Milhaud and Honegger in France did something similar occur.) For example during work on his great fairy-tale opera Strauss wrote: "Please do not let my criticism discourage you; I can only judge by myself, to whom nothing does so much good, promoting and fructifying both my ambition and my creative power, as an adverse criticism from one whose judgement I value. My criticism is meant to spur you on, not to discourage you . . ." Hofmannsthal's reply: "A perfect collaboration between two mature human beings would be something extremely rare, but we both have goodwill, a serious purpose and sense of responsibility, which is more important than the 'talent' with which every wretched fellow is equipped nowadays. (I am naturally also glad that you continue to work with me—it gives me a feeling of warmth and binds me to you more firmly, as does every revelation of a new aspect of your talent, such as this present lightness and spirit . . .)" The poet wrote of his collaboration with Strauss in a letter congratulating the composer on his 60th birthday. "It seems to me something great and even necessary in my life that you approached me eighteen years ago with your wishes and needs. I felt then that—within the limits of my ability—I could fulfil those wishes, and that such fulfilment would satisfy a deep need of my own. Many things which I produced in the isolation of youth, entirely for myself, scarcely

393

thinking even of readers, were fantastic little operas and operettas—without music. Your wishes set a target, without restricting
my freedom. Filled with the thought, to an increasing extent with
mature insight, that nothing lasting can be produced in isolation,
cut off from tradition, I have learned far more from earlier works
of a similar nature than from those which seemed to fulfil the
'demands of the present day . . .' If there was anyone who recognized the value of everything, took it up joyfully, creatively, and
gave it a higher life, that was you . . ." And finally the grief-
filled words which Strauss wrote to Gerty von Hofmannsthal
when he heard of his friend's death: ". . . This genial human
being, this great poet, this fine-feeling colleague, this warm-
hearted friend, this unique talent! No one will be able to replace
him for me and for the world of music! Posterity will create the
monument worthy of him which he has always possessed in my
heart . . ."

This collaboration of artists of equal standing could not be
re-established in the works written in conjunction with Gregor.
The entire correspondence between Strauss and his librettist is a
revealing document throwing light on an altered artistic and
human situation: here the dramatic composer with his demands
matured by experience and profound knowledge, there the poet
and expert on the subject of the historical-mythological drama,
whose work frequently lacked the necessary precision and fulness
of poetic expression, and whose verse more than once lured
Strauss back into the sphere of Wagnerian pathos. As early as
the summer of 1935, when contact was established regarding the
planned "Semiramis", Strauss protested: "No, that won't do.
Don't be offended by my bluntness, but if anything is really to
come of the collaboration between us you must allow me to
accompany your first steps in the classroom of opera with the
gentle chastisements of an experienced, grey-haired schoolmaster . . ." Again and again Strauss demanded that his colleague should use fewer "striking phrases" and "favourite expressions," should "act the schoolmaster" less, and should compress
everything still further to enhance the "strength of the verse
construction." "I see it in the way you read your texts aloud!
You allow yourself to be intoxicated too easily by words which
sound impressive, thereby losing touch with a consistent dramatic
content." Although Gregor was several times disconcerted by

such drastic criticism (Strauss himself dismissed it as "unpleasant workshop jargon"), he always acknowledged the leading position of the composer when it came to the point: "One should not strive to have one's own way when under the guidance of such a hand . . ." At all events, in the cases of three important opera projects the joint labours of Gregor and Strauss were brought to a satisfactory conclusion.

*

The work to which Hofmannsthal referred in his congratulatory letter on Strauss's birthday, and in which, unfortunately, he largely ignored the "demands of the present day," was his vast humanistic, fairy-tale opera *"Die Frau ohne Schatten."* An exceptional work, if not Strauss's most outstanding creation, in which author and composer wanted to give of their "richest and most exalted," and which is, to many people, undoubtedly the most important work Strauss ever wrote. Nevertheless here, where the writer's ideas and verbal resources were wholly literary in spirit, with his imagination soaring into the realm of mysticism and symbolism, here (to Rolland's regret) the strong bond which linked the essentially realistic composer with the librettist drew him into unduly deep water. It was soon clear that the excessive subtleties of Hofmannsthal's fable made it extremely difficult to understand the events on the stage. Without detailed knowledge of the libretto, the listener is faced with an insoluble problem of opera dramaturgy. Even if he is helped through the strange sequence of events by the guiding threads provided in the libretto, he cannot shake off the feeling that the bounds of opera have been overstepped, that the composer has had to hack his way through the undergrowth of the text in order to reach an imposing mountain range. Here, where the poet preferred to express aspects of human nature in rich metaphors of Faustian mystery, instead of bringing them to life on the stage, there occurred for the first time in Strauss's operas a gulf between the work and its audiences which the unprepared listeners of the period immediately after the Great War found it extremely difficult to bridge.

Strauss was forced rather than tempted into the intellectual-humanistic sphere of "Die Frau ohne Schatten." It can be seen that Hofmannsthal gave way to the composer only in certain details, and apparently with great hesitation. Text and music: it took a very long time, and involved much hard struggle, before the representatives of these two basically contrasting worlds came close enough for agreement to be reached. Soon after the première of "Rosenkavalier," when questioned about a new libretto, Hofmannsthal referred to the "material of a fantastic play," a "simple action in three acts, with strong contrasts and impressive conclusions to the acts, the whole with dark undertones but free from monotony." The first definite references to this work are an entry made at the end of February 1911 in a notebook of Hofmannsthal's, and a passage in the same letter written during March of that year in which he outlined the first plan of "Ariadne." "I have something quite unusual in mind: a magical tale in which two men and two women confront one another . . . the one a supernatural being, the other earthly, a bizarre woman who is fundamentally very good-hearted, incalculable, self-willed and domineering, yet sympathetic . . . all full of contrasts, with palace and hut, priests, sailors, flaming torches, rocky crags, choruses, children; the whole idea . . . grips me even while I am working, and has pushed the other plan, 'The Stone Heart,' right into the background, because it is so much brighter and more joyful. Incidentally the whole thing, as I visualize it, would be related to 'Zauberflöte' as 'Rosenkavalier' is to 'Figaro'. . ." Unfortunately Hofmannstahl's original idea of making the "buffo couple" a "Viennese jobbing tailor and his beautiful, dissatisfied wife," and of letting these "lower-class characters speak in dialect," was given up in the early stages of the librettist's work in favour of a more symbolical concept.

So Hofmannsthal had already referred to Mozart's "Zauberflöte," and he once remarked that "Die Frau ohne Schatten" was dominated by a "heroic-spiritual situation whose atmosphere was akin to that of 'Fidelio' or 'Die Zauberflöte'." The composer, too, described this work as a continuation of Mozart's last operatic creation. It is a fact that this subject, which extols peace between human beings, contains basic elements linking Strauss's work, beyond Wagner, with the world of "Die Zauberflöte." Just as in Schikaneder's fairy-tale libretto, human and spiritual elements are combined. A supernatural power (in "Die Frau ohne Schatten" that of Keikobad) dominates the relationship between the two worlds; the human beings have to undergo tests. Hofmannsthal loaded the naive story (which he made progressively more literary and complex) with a great deal of philosophical ballast. A comparison with "Die Zauberflöte" reveals the weaknesses of this work as a whole: so much psychological knowledge was incorporated in it that the resulting impression is blurred.

The essential element here is the mystery of motherhood, and the "shadow" as the ancient biblical symbol of woman's fertility. The work is a hymn to true married love, glorification of the wife and mother. Fertility is given an ethical significance: without human purification no blessing of the bond of love–here, probably under the influence of Schopenhauer's philosophy, purification is equated with pity. It is through pity that the Empress finds her way to the dyer Barak. But she cannot make up her mind to save her beloved husband in his peril, and to attain her own happiness, at the cost of the destruction of the marriage of the industrious dyer and his wife, and she leaves the decisive word, by which she could obtain the "shadow" of Barak's wife, unspoken. The opera concludes with the jubilation of the "unborn," the children of the future who are to spring from the happily reunited couples–the Emperor and Empress, the dyer and his wife. It is they who give a meaning to existence. The voices of the watchmen in the streets by night at the end of the first act express this idea:

> You married couples lying lovingly in each others' arms,
> You are the bridge spanning the chasm
> Across which the dead advance to life!
> Blessed be the work of your love!

In order that the profound relationships between one human being and another could be shown to exist on this side of the threshold of conscious experience, the need was for a fairy-tale action, a colourful alternation of scenes. Hofmannsthal (who wrote a prose form of the story after the completion of the libretto) acquired ideas from many literary sources: from "Arabian Nights" stories, from Indian, Persian and Chinese tales, from the brothers Grimm, Raimund, Novalis and Lenau, as well as from his own youthful "Tale of the 672nd Night." Gregor also found a striking parallel to the conflict between the socially unequal couples in Rückert's Oriental Epics. Nevertheless the course of the action, divided into three acts of eleven

397

scenes all told, and set in a far-eastern island realm, is entirely Hofmannsthal's invention. As his imagination fashioned artificial blossoms he lost his way, amid countless verbal beauties, in the sphere of dark, personal subjectivity. He made things not easy but, on the contrary, very difficult for the spectator. He sank himself, above all, in a personal outlook on the world and the ethos of Goethe, in the strange life of fairy tales, and in the phantasmagoria of a continuation of "Die Zauberflöte" and the second part of "Faust." (Hans Mayer pointed out the essence of Hofmannsthal's approach to Goethe: the character of the Nurse as Mephistopheles and of the Empress as Faust in the dramatic constellation, and the close parallels of structure and content between the chorus of the "unborn" and the chorus which concludes the second part of "Faust.") The "camera-obscura" of a fairy-tale opera which renders the fundamental artistic idea visible to only an insufficient extent evidently did not greatly disturb Strauss. "At the point where the understanding fails, music begins to come into its own, as it is always the expression of the immeasurable," he declared in an interview in 1935. "When a poet has to use word upon word to bring out his meaning, the composer can express everything in a single chord–even more: he can say in notes all that will for ever remain out of the reach of language". On the same occasion he dealt with the problematic nature of the text of this work: "Yes, people are still constantly saying to me 'That's so difficult to understand–we don't understand it!' Is it really so difficult? Are they not quite simple symbols–the Emperor who must be turned to stone, the woman who casts no shadow–they are all things that one can see and understand . . ."

In his close association with the author of "Frau ohne Schatten" Strauss, the musician of practical experience who generally thought so realistically, soon embraced the project with character-istic vehemence. However, it was not until the autumn of 1912 that Hofmannsthal could write to his friend that the opera was clear in his mind's eye. "I now really have the material at my command, limb for limb, scene for scene . . ." Strauss sent his heartfelt congratulations. A meeting of author and composer "in the moonlight, between San Michele and Bozen," enabled the plan to ripen. Another six months elapsed; "Josephslegende" was almost complete–and still Strauss had nothing of the great fairy-tale opera in his hands. Another visit to Italy was proposed—the poet felt that he was under pressure: "For heaven's sake don't be impatient now ... Otherwise you will endanger not only my nerves but also the work" (1913). Finally, in April of the following year, a few months before the outbreak of the war, Strauss received part of the text. "It is simply wonderful in its beauty, and so concentrated and unified that I cannot yet think of cutting out or altering the smallest point. What I have to do is to find a new, simple style which will enable me to present your beautiful poem to the listeners in complete purity and clarity," and a mere sixteen days afterwards: "The opening is already in shape, and the Emperor's Aria is very spirited and successful ... In general I am slowly finding my way to the required style and melodic character." As the work progressed Strauss soon revised his original opinion: he suggested a simplified opening to the opera and some cuts. Hofmannsthal agreed, only asking his colleague to bear in mind that "the Empress is the principal character in the spiritual sense, and her destiny is the leaven of the whole. The dyer and his wife are certainly the strongest figures, but they do not dominate the story; their destiny is subordinated to that of the Empress." In fact the Empress is the "woman without a shadow"— in her there is demonstrated the overcoming of self which raises her to a high plane of human dignity through suffering and a sense of duty ... Within three months Strauss had the rough draft of the first act, the "tale" proper, down on paper.

Meanwhile he had received the text of the second act, the "act of trials," and he was not sparing in his praise: "At any event you have never in your life written anything more beautiful and finely-fashioned, and I consider that I have done well by causing you, through our work together, to create it. I hope my music will be worthy of your lovely poem." In the thick of the work, during October, he informed Hofmannsthal that "the solo scene is complete, and contains a great deal of fervent music. The Emperor's scene has also turned out very well, and Barak's 'banquet' is merry and lively ... Everything full of contrasts ... This really is your masterpiece." Clearly Strauss was satisfied with himself. "The second act is ready, according to programme, and, I hope, hasn't turned out badly ..." Hofmannsthal, too, who had at one time doubted whether Strauss would find the right spiritual

399

mood for this unworldly subject (". . . if I had a composer who was less renowned but nearer to my heart, more in tune with my way of thought, I confess I would feel happier," he had written to Eberhard von Bodenhausen in 1914), was now intoxicated by the beauties of the music. He wrote to Bodenhausen: "Strauss visited me and played me the 1st and 2nd acts of 'Frau ohne Schatten'–for which he has succeeded in creating really wonderful music." To Strauss he spoke of the "biggest and most promising of all the works we have ever undertaken together."

But now, with the war darkening the European horizon, with thrones tottering and falling in the political as in the artistic sphere, the composer was overcome by a kind of weariness of his creative faculties. He could sense all too clearly the far-reaching effects of the catastrophic struggle in which the world had been caught up. The poet tried to encourage him–principally by justifying his work. Strauss turned to other tasks for a while: the "Alpensinfonie," the new version of "Ariadne" and the augmentation of the incidental music to "Le Bourgeois gentilhomme." At that time Hofmannsthal, too, was distracted by his war service as a diplomat, which involved a great deal of travelling. He had to console his composer: "A very detailed sketch of Act III exists, with much of the text. The act will be very beautiful and short. It concludes with a mighty upsurge in which something of the tremendous events of this year has been caught up, in a way mysterious even to me," and six months later: "The act will please you; it is full of music, music without opposition and at the same time rich, colourful and concise." In April 1915 the entire libretto was ready. "Your third act is splendid: words, construction and content equally wonderful." When he got down to composition, however, Strauss found this concluding act with its many problems lacking in text; he asked for new verses so that he could add further self-contained lyrical numbers to the score. There was another heated struggle by the two partners in their quest for the most effective form possible. While Strauss now concentrated on the utmost comprehensibility of text and content, without being able to avoid "over-excitement" of the means of musical expression (which he himself detected), Hofmannsthal was enraptured at that stage of their collaboration by the pure beauties of a tonal atmosphere "like silver exultation" which existed in his imagination. Finally, in June 1917, Strauss mastered the

400

enormous and laborious task of writing his most extensive score in "sorrow and worry during the war." Seven years had elapsed since the initial idea for the work. At such a time of war the first performance could wait ... "I have definitely decided that the world première of the work will take place after peace has returned, for purely artistic reasons."

The music of "Frau ohne Schatten" undoubtedly represents a new stage of creative development with regard to invention, technical accomplishment, dramatic force and spiritual significance. A work with such an abundance of broadly-flowing, rich-sounding music, which pours forth "like golden honey out of the dark honeycomb," signified a new summit in the sphere of dramatic music. Strauss was here in territory where "music and poetry" should "really float hand in hand"–the realm of the "opera of feeling and of humanity," leaving the theatrical effects of "Salome" and the obvious popular style of "Rosenkavalier" far behind. It is therefore all the more regrettable that this music was to lose its way in the metaphysical labyrinth of Hofmannsthal's verse drama. Strauss sought a synthesis of the oppressive weight of "Elektra" and the enchanting lightness of "Ariadne"– or one might say of Wagner and Mozart. He summed up his experiences with earlier works, and established a common denominator. "Die Frau ohne Schatten" has something of the dark glow of "Don Giovanni." Nevertheless Strauss had never been so "Wagnerian"–that is to say he had never before so completely adopted the laws of music drama on the grand scale which Wagner had established at the end of a long process of historical development. The nervous music-psychology of earlier scores no longer has a place in this work aimed at nobility and depth of feeling. Elements of chamber music are more than interesting details intended to provide contrast. (Strauss originally intended to represent the "upper world with the 'Ariadne' orchestra, the more solid and varied reality of the earth with the full orchestra.") It is essentially "grand opera." This is clear above all from the three act conclusions, which rise to the stature of mighty ensembles. The third act, beginning with the deeply moving Duet of the dyer and his wife "Mir anvertraut," is of such breadth and singing polyphony, steadily increasing in intensity, that no opera had risen to such a conclusion since "Götterdämmerung." When the voices of the reunited couples blend with the chorus, this opera takes on a grandiose breadth of feeling. It cannot be overlooked, however, that this act strives towards its end amid clear indications of diminishing energy.

How plastic the tone symbols of this music are! What melodic and rhythmic power is contained in the remarkably characteristic motifs of Keikobad, the falcon, the Emperor and others! The composer here managed to create a certain amount of clarity in the half-darkness—a burst of light illumines the scene from time to time. The novelty of this score glowing with colour lies in its expression of mystery, the characteristic of the supernatural realm in which the action takes place. While the songs of the dyer, that man of the people, the Emperor's wonderfully inspired hymn of love, and the folksong-like chorus of watchmen are all richly euphonic, the characterization of the diabolical Nurse is marked by boldly jagged harmonies and instrumentation, and the music of the "unborn" really appears transcendental. The "source of life," the thunderstorm, the scenes of the Nurse's wiles, and the petrification of the Emperor are represented in dazzlingly illustrative music, and in other places Strauss goes very deep. It needed his tonal magic, sometimes raging furiously, sometimes seeking harmonic simplicity, to differentiate between the spiritual world and the world of human beings. The music speaks in its own right in eight symphonic Interludes, which sometimes swirl powerfully with the brilliance of a heavily scored orchestra (including numerous percussion instruments, Chinese gongs, xylophone, celesta, organ and glass harmonica), sometimes taking on the gentle colours of a concertino, with violin and cello solos rising to magical effect. In this opulent tonal world fiery, brassy accents of "Elektra" are contrasted by glassy, nocturnally cold sounds frequently possessing the captivating subtlety of chamber music. Strauss also adopted new methods in the creation of musical-dramatic elements. For example in the part of the Nurse, which, with those of the dyer and his wife, had the greatest appeal to him, he attempted, "with the accompaniment of a largely solo-scored orchestra which underlines only lightly, to give fresh life to the style and tempo of the old secco recitative." The ingeniousness of this artistry is evident from the absolute clarity of the structural forms in the musical architecture of the second act, with its five scenes—a solution with which Strauss was never entirely satisfied. The music rises far above the literary aestheti-

402

cism of the text. One has to keep a grip on the simple human symbols "in the realm of Keikobad". But can that be done? Was Strauss admitting defeat when, during the last years of his life, he wrote an orchestral fantasy on the best themes of the work, using the reduced tonal resources of his final period?

At all events, the birth of his really "grand" and "romantic" opera in October 1919, during the crisis years following the end of the "accursed war," with their attendant economic chaos, was a major event thanks to the brilliant resources of the Vienna State Opera. More than thirty stage rehearsals preceded the première; Strauss, who was then opera director, entrusted the conducting to his colleague Schalk. The majority of those who reviewed the work saw in this magnificent ethical music drama a synthesis of elements developed in the composer's many earlier works, raised to new heights of effectiveness. The experiences of the early performances in Germany which followed, and which scarcely corresponded to the exceptional character of the work, compelled Strauss to acknowledge that it had been a "serious mistake" to entrust this "work, which is difficult to cast and so demanding scenically, to medium-sized and smaller theatres immediately after the war." Well-equipped companies such as the Berlin, Dresden and Munich Operas could not ignore this work which had long since aroused the "admiration of the best;" no repertoire work but something comparable with "Tristan," a permanent goal and broad field of action for great Strauss conductors, for scenic designers such as Roller, Aravantinos and Sievert. At Vienna in 1931 Krauss first presented the dyer's hut episodes of the second act as two scenes instead of three. When the opera was revived in the Munich Festival of 1939, Strauss decided to re-orchestrate the episode of the "Keeper of the Gates of the Temple;" later, at Stuttgart in 1954, the concentration of the second act into four scenes proved its value. As early as 1915 the author and composer had expressed their confidence in the effectiveness of "Die Frau ohne Schatten," agreeing that "after the war, at first in Germany," there would be "a very definite atmosphere" in which this work, "by virtue both of the theme and of its execution, could assert itself extremely well." In 1918, however, Strauss's tone changed: "The work is good–but perhaps above the level of the cultural world of today, at least as far as filling the theatre goes . . ." What a worthwhile task, to bring the humanistic, peaceful message underlying this song in praise of love and the brotherhood of man to those who are now finding their way to opera! "Only from afar was all confusion," the Emperor sings, "listen carefully, this sound is human!"

*

The related work *"Die ägyptische Helena"* can scarcely be saved. Once again Hofmannsthal searched the world's literature and history for a subject demanding the romantic enchantment of music. "Since 1920 there has flickered in my imagination –sparkling and intangible, like half-hidden, flowing water–a story, a grouping of figures." The poet wrote what he had in mind in his incomparable style: "During the night when the Greeks forced their way through blazing Troy, Menelaus must have found his wife in one of the burning palaces, and must have carried her out between crumbling walls–this woman who was his beloved, stolen wife, the cause of the war, of those dreadful ten years, the plain strewn with corpses, and the conflagration. She was also the widow of Paris, and had been the mistress of ten or twelve other young sons of Priam, all of whom now lay dead or dying–so she was the widow of these ten or twelve young princes as well! What a situation for a husband! It beggars the imagination–and it is safe from all dramatists; no text, even by a Shakespeare, could do justice to it, and I am certain that Menelaus carried this woman, even in such a situation the world's greatest beauty, back to his ship in silence. We do not know what happened after that, but several years later the son of Odysseus travelled through the Grecian kingdoms seeking news of his vanished father. He reached Sparta. There he found Menelaus in his palace, a noble and hospitable ruler, 'as handsome as a god', and Helen with him as chatelaine of the palace, as beautiful as ever, the queen of that peaceful land. One is bound to ask what had happened in the meantime. What lay between that dreadful night and the complete reconciliation which followed . . . ? What can have helped to rebuild this marriage as a true companionship on which the sun shone? . . . Here was a subject–if the question could be put to a productive purpose –possibly the basis of a lyrical work demanding music, but I did not at once recognize it as such . . ."

404

How would Strauss react to the idea of a large-scale mythological opera following in the wake of Salieri, Gluck and Offenbach? Would his instinct, aroused by the justified objections to the libretto of "Die Frau ohne Schatten," not warn him against venturing again into the undramatic world of Hofmannsthal's symbolism? Would it not seem suspicious to him that so much subtly worded persuasion on the part of the poet was needed in order to make the new idea with its literary background plausible to him? When Hofmannsthal first broached the subject to Strauss early in 1923, "Helena" was still a totally different proposition: "I frequently think about a late-Antique, somewhat irreverent comedy with much parlando and light, attractive ceremonial, a festival or the like." He attempted to win the musician over for a work which would be, in the highest sense, "operetta-like . . . in a far lighter style than 'Ariadne'." As time went on the poet decided instead on a tragic, heavily meaningful form of the myth, and gave the composer details of the action. Strauss, eager for a libretto which would take him back to the realm of the large-scale opera of ideas after the prosaic conversation piece "Intermezzo," seized the opportunity. During the discussion which (contrary to their usual practice) preceded the commencement of work on the project, the composer exclaimed: "Yes, that's an opera. At least an opera for me, perhaps not for someone else . . . You haven't told a soul about the idea? . . ." A tragic misunderstanding of a classical-mythical-operatic subject whose very existence was illusory!

There was abundant source material: Hofmannsthal went back to the fourth song of Homer's "Odyssey," to Herodotus, who made Helen travel from Sparta to Egypt, and to Euripides and Steisichoros with their versions involving two Helens. Since then Schuh has discovered as a further ancient source of the modern dramatic situation two verses from the "Lysistrata" of Aristophenes. Euripides treated the subject more seriously, in accordance with his nature. To him Menelaus was a truly tragic figure, and only to be freed from his anguish of soul by the revelation that the unfaithful Helen was a mere phantom, while the real Helen of flesh and blood, untouched and true to her Menelaus, had remained at her husband's palace in Egypt. Hofmannsthal, however, the learned adaptor of existing material, made the story dark with metaphysical elements. He borrowed the

405

potion of forgetfulness from Homer and the phantom Helen from Euripides, making an Egyptian sorceress Aithra transform the Trojan into the Egyptian Helen. Menelaus rediscovers in the real Helen his wife to whom he had remained indissolubly bound through a thousand griefs. Overjoyed at possessing her again, he takes her back to his native land. The complex spiritual events leading up to this reunion form the content of Hofmannsthal's poem, laden with a great weight of learned ballast.

The minimum requirement of an opera text is that it should be generally understandable to people who have not previously read the libretto. What, then, of an opera whose action remains incomprehensible even to those who have read the libretto or the synopsis of the work which preceded it? The opera-goer demands clarity of motives, and above all self-explanatory action. ("The essential elements of the subject must always be understandable and clear almost without the help of words" wrote Serow.) Here everything is merely suggested, not carried out. The mythology remains mere decoration. The inner drama of the two human beings with which the work is concerned is so obscured by verbiage that everything which occurs is shrouded in a poetic mist or even darkness. The cardinal error of this libretto, which is so badly split at the dramatic seams (although Hofmannsthal expressed the opinion that as "a poem for music, as opera" it was the best thing he had ever done) is that it attempts to present both the myth *and* its meaning, that while the story is being enacted the characters step outside its frame and begin to philosophise about their destinies in modern phraseology. There is also a considerable lack of balance between the two acts. The first is set in the palace of Aithra, and shows the existence of a new bond of love between Helen and Menelaus. However, as this bond came into existence under the influence of various dramaturgical "drugs," it has to be given a new natural basis, and this occurs, as a process of purification, in the second act, which is set in a palm grove at the foot of the Atlas mountains. While the first act at least has baroque colour and a lively flow, Hofmannsthal appears to be far out of his depth as a dramatist in the second. No verbal music, however harmonious (its direct dependence on Wagner is evident in almost every line) can conceal the lack of any intimate, logical and psychological development linking the magical and the tragically heroic con-

406

tents of the two contrasting acts. Only the conclusion is believable: the glorification of the marriage after so many doubts, self-deceptions and temptations. Strauss especially welcomed the problem which had been avoided even by Euripides and Goethe, "of leading Helen and Menelaus to a final moral solution." Such characters as the "Omniscient Sea-shell," the elves, representing "critical subconsciousness," and the desert sheik Altair with his languishing son Da-ud (originally conceived by the composer as

Strauss and Hofmannsthal in a Viennese coffee house.
In the background their friends Arthur Schnitzler
and Richard Beer-Hofmann: Drawing by B. F. Dolbin (1927)

a breeches role for a soprano) are highly unrealistic additions by Hofmannsthal. When the story of "Helena" was related to Strauss for the first time he said, not without justification, after the first act: "And surely that's the end of the piece. What else could happen in the second act?

The collaboration between Strauss and Hofmannsthal was particularly close and cordial during the creation of "Helena." There was complete understanding during every phase of the artistic planning and its realization between the poet, who worked

407

on this opera text with "as much determination and seriousness as satisfaction and good humour," and the musician, who
considered himself most fortunate in "this poem especially well
suited to music;" it was composed "seemingly by itself for the
most part," "unbelievably quickly." As early as the autumn of
1923, after Strauss's visit to South America, he was able to get
down to the new work: "I have already begun to sketch 'Helena';
particularly easy to compose are such pieces as the hymnic 'Bei
jener Nacht, der keuschen einzig einen' or the little duet 'Ich
laufe und hole das Fläschchen!'... Vederemo! At all events
please continue in the splendid style of the first scenes..." The
work went ahead at a rapid pace, but the composer's alert mind
was soon troubled by dramaturgical failings of the text. He wrote
at the end of 1923: "Three days in bed have now, I believe,
revealed to me the principal shortcoming of the first act as a
drama for music, from the second entry of Menelaus until
Aithra's narration. Fine though your psychological concept and
motivation is, if it is not to be pure prose it would produce a rat's
tail of tedious music..." There followed specific suggestions for
the dramatic activation of the scene. Strauss could not feel happy
about the elves either, although he considered "some fine choruses of elves and spirits," and even "pretty ballet episodes." In
July 1924 he reported: "'Helena' first act is ready in sketches,
and has a good concluding climax. I am constantly busy with the
work, and am receptive and grateful for any remark or suggestion which occurs to you."

The crisis concerning the directorship of the Vienna Opera,
together with work on minor projects, caused a delay of six
months, and after that the composition refused to go ahead
smoothly. Strauss travelled to Spain, hoping "to receive inspiration for the Prince of the Desert in Granada," but in July 1925 he
had to confess: "I have been stuck for a long time at the entry
of Altair, and can make no progress... For this entry of the
sons of the desert it is especially difficult to invent music which
is still sufficiently characteristic for ears of 1925, without falling
into the so-called realism of 'Salome', or the eccentric ways of
the moderns who hear only with American ears. However,
I expect I shall get over this obstacle too!" The score of the first
act was completed on the 1st May 1926, then, after a visit to
Greece, Strauss at last began to make progress on the difficult

second act. The librettist suggested that the conclusion should be enhanced by the union of Poseidon and Aithra, but Strauss had no relish for any such poetic variant, as it would "place the main emphasis at the conclusion on a subsidiary character of the piece." The great musical apotheosis of the (originally more simply constructed) duet of the loving couple derives from a suggestion by Fritz Busch. After a hard struggle to arrive at the best possible solution, Strauss wrote in September 1927: "Finally, after much hesitating, rejecting and refashioning, rewriting and experiencing numerous agreeable birth pangs, the Finale is very beautiful, brilliant and yet simple."

"Helena" was to be a document of the highest classical maturity, or, as Strauss put it: "My music aspires to a noble, Grecian character, somewhat after the manner in which Goethe visualized the Greeks in his 'Iphigenie'." It approaches the "purified ideal of beauty of Goethe-Winckelmann Hellenism." In fact, however, it is merely a modern, unauthentic paraphrase of genuine Hellenism, close to the baroque "Frau ohne Schatten" and to the related "Josephslegende," remote from the lucid world of "Ariadne." Even Helen's costume has bourgeois drapery, and insofar as she possesses a soul it stems from the romantic, Nordic imagination. Helen is closely related to the Empress in "Frau ohne Schatten"—here as there married fidelity is shaken by trials. Aithra's lands are dominated by the same turgid symbolism as the realm of Keikobad. Also un-Grecian is the swollen pathos of the music. It glows in sumptuous tonal garments with a wealth of exotic fragrance, and it is eminently "Straussian"—but it is so, one has to admit, in a strongly voluptuous sense without the bright consciousness, the free animation of the genuine seeker after the spirit of Greece. In the composer's own, unmistakably ironic words it is "melodious, sounds well, and unfortunately poses no problems at all to ears which have developed beyond the nineteenth century . . ." How far the composer had diverged from the original conception!

A musical and vocal opera . . . What inevitably attracted Strauss, at that stage of his career, to this libretto which he always defended with astonishing tenacity, were the opportunities it offered for an outpouring of melody, flowing bel canto, and a female role developed wholly out of the prima donna sphere. Cantilena passages extending over many bars, as in Helen's softly radiant Monologue in B major "Zweite Brautnacht" or the effective closing Duet of the second act, clearly aim at the development of pure vocalization, and usher in a new stage of Strauss's work, despite reminiscences of cantabile modes of expression in earlier operas (close of "Salome", seria passages of "Ariadne," third act of "Frau ohne Schatten"), and of Wagner. Strauss built and painted the musical scenes with intoxicating splendour and fascinating colouration. The basic characteristic is not sparkling lyricism, such as Hofmannsthal had visualized when he described the overall style of the music as lying "between the elegant and the solemn," but a flood of beautiful sound of a cosmopolitan, hymnic nature. Another feature of the "Helena" music is the lyrical character of the masterly recitative, which places great emphasis on the finely graded transitions from the parlando style to the heroic aria. There is a plethora of triads, adorned and unadorned, and oceans of flat euphony lead to melodic and harmonic stagnation, as when "Helen's awakening" is depicted by a sugary horn solo above static E major chords. There are, however, episodes of fascinating charm such as the finely stylized music of Aithra, the promising opening scene, and the delightful scene of falling asleep in the first act, in which something of the original "elegant" concept of the work is still evident. However, at Helen's entry high Nibelung pathos at once comes into its own, the atmosphere veering into that of "Tristan" at the brooding of Menelaus. ("Wagnerian, you think? Yes–but this is a Grecian Wagner . . .") A highspot of this mode of expression is the powerfully conceived and constructed mourning music. All the musical elements, including the storm music, the highly artificial elves and the Oriental desert magic, are parts of a whole in which the lack of inner balance and the tendency toward less inspired forms cannot be ignored. Episodes intended to convey an inner message often merely appear flat on the stage. A great deal in this most eclectic opera score since "Guntram" remains mere décor. It is undoubtedly nearer in spirit to Meyerbeer than to Gluck–or to Offenbach, whose name was originally quoted in this connection.

Was Strauss quite sure of the effectiveness of his "Helena?" ". . . I only hope that the dangerous Helen, who brought about the carnage of the Trojan War, still has something of her legendary capacity to give pleasure left for the author and composer of this opera, telling of her destiny after she left Troy," Strauss said at the end of an interview which he gave over the Vienna Radio before the world première. The musical world, completely under the sway of Strauss's operas following the death of Puccini, waited expectantly for the new work. Two cities, Dresden and Vienna, with their prima donnas, contended vigorously for the honour of presenting the first performance, to the annoyance of Strauss, who generally gave his permission quite casually. Preference finally went to the Dresden State Opera, where the gala première took place under Busch in June 1928. (The first Vienna performance took place under Strauss shortly afterwards.) It was only in the larger theatres that "Helena" had a brief period of glory. At Salzburg in 1933 Krauss presented a "New arrangement for the Vienna State Opera" in which the attempt was made, by tightening up the Da-ud episodes and re-positioning others, to give greater clarity to the feeble second act. Later, in Berlin and Munich (where the first act was divided into two scenes), Sievert tried to achieve a realistic presentation of the allegorical events, but without succeeding in recapturing the spirit of Antiquity; the Munich revival in 1959 also presented no new picture of the work, which is strangely split between the musician's neo-baroque concept and the perplexities of a not particularly gripping spiritual drama of Antiquity. As an opera "Helena" remains a phantom.

WORDS AND MUSIC

ALMOST EVERY OPERATIC WORK BY STRAUSS CONTAINS
the name of a woman in its title, and even in the others this theme
is varied in a way which is always fascinating. Only on two
occasions did he diverge from this practice: in "Intermezzo,"
which appeared during the years following the First World War,
and in "Capriccio," his last opera. In both cases the less clear-
cut, neutral title was chosen with regard to both content and
style, and in both cases a descriptive sub-title was added. In his
concern for authenticity in performance Strauss also wrote a
substantial foreword to each score. "Intermezzo," the "Bourgeois
Comedy with Symphonic Interludes," represented a bold and
surprisingly successful attempt to discover a conversational style
for opera roughly corresponding to the natural flow of modern
comedy. "Capriccio," the "Conversation Piece with Music,"
turned out to be a cross between intellectual comedy and opera
of feeling, fashioned with the resources of wise old age. The two-
act "Intermezzo," with its conscious avoidance of the historical
and mythological worlds and its concentration on banal everyday
life, can only be regarded as an experiment which could scarcely
take on general significance. On the other hand the one-act
"Capriccio" is an operatic work whose warm human story, before
a background of musical history brought to life, assures it of universal interest. The word "Intermezzo" signifies an interlude,
and this opera has no greater significance among Strauss's stage
works as a whole. "Capriccio" suggests a whim, fancy or original
idea, a spirited piece by a great artist once again bringing together
the experiences of a long lifetime. Both works, greatly though
they differ in weight, show the composer seeking new realistic
means of operatic expression in the sphere of charm and warmth
of feeling, irony and sentiment. Both are fascinating pieces in a

413

class apart, outside the main stream of stage works, and are therefore typical of the "spirit of opposition."

*

The audibility of words on the opera stage is an age-old stylistic problem. The relationship between *words and music* is said to be the basic question of opera—indeed, one can go further and describe it as the problem of *all* vocal music. In opera, however, a new and important factor comes into the picture: visual action. The difficulties of the composition and performance of an opera lie in striking a balance between the demands of the music, the voices, the verbal declamation and the stage action, so that all the elements of the words and music are component parts of the dramatic idea. (The old argument whether music should serve the words or words the music can be pursued ad absurdum.) This balance was achieved comparatively easily in the old opera in separate numbers, as the action was clarified and carried forward in recitatives or dialogue, while it was not even expected that the text would be clear in the arias, duets and ensembles. In contrast to this the novelty of the Wagnerian music drama lay in the co-ordination and blending together of recitative passages and musical set pieces. Strict musical declamation, about which Wagner wrote in his famous essays on "Opera and Drama," had been born. At the same time the orchestra grew in size. The human voice had to fight an often hopeless battle against the masses of orchestral sound. A conflict between words and music was unavoidable. Nevertheless this conflict in post-Wagnerian opera should not be attributed solely to the increased dimensions of the symphony orchestra. Even in completely unaccompanied vocal scenes (in Orff's "Antigone," for example) the text can be incomprehensible—because the declamation is set at uncomfortable pitches or because too little attention has been paid to vocal diction.

Strauss confessed: "My vocal style has the tempo of spoken drama, and often conflicts with the figuration and polyphony of the orchestra; only outstanding conductors, who understand something about singing, can here create the dynamic and rhythmic balance between the performer on the stage and the orchestra. The battle between words and music has been the problem of my life from the beginning, and I leave it with

414

'Capriccio,' a question mark!" ... To a greater extent than any other composer of his time, Strauss struggled with the problem, constantly and ever more clearly attempting to solve it. Such an attempt was not new. The Russian realist Mussorgsky had had the same intention in his setting of Gogol's comedy "The Marriage" as an "Opera in prose." The relationship between voice and orchestra, freed from all musical-dramatic heaviness, was to appear in a new light, the words being given the most flowing melodic form possible, with sparing accompaniment, and the prosody was to be tightened up. (Even before that the French writer Diderot had pointed out the power to form melody possessed by the expressively spoken word.) The most important things which Strauss had to say in the much-quoted forewords to his two conversational operas were concerned with these questions:

"I have devoted the greatest attention, with a degree of success growing from work to work, to meaningful declamation and a lively, conversational tempo ... Since one can seldom reckon on ideal performances in the theatre, I have found myself increasingly compelled to safeguard the balance between singers and orchestra at the outset, so that even in a performance which is less than perfect at least the essentials of the action will be generally understandable, and the work will not be presented in a manner contrary to its nature, or grossly misunderstood. The scores of 'Frau ohne Schatten' and 'Ariadne' bear witness to these efforts ... It may be that owing to misjudgments on my part even this extremely thin and transparent orchestration is too polyphonic in character, too restless in its figuration, and therefore a hindrance to the audibility of the words on the stage, or it may be that the faulty diction of our average opera singers or the unfortunately often mouthy German tone production and excessive volume of sound heard in our large theatres are to blame. Orchestral polyphony, even in the gentlest colours, in the softest pianissimo, is the death of words on the stage, and the devil has given us Germans counterpoint in our cradles, in order that we should not do too well on the opera stage ..."

"Anyone who knows my later opera scores well must agree that if the singers enunciate clearly, and if the orchestral markings are observed most scrupulously, the audience must be able to hear the words without difficulty–except in a few passages in which a necessary powerful orchestral crescendo is intended to overwhelm the voices. There is no praise which pleases me more than when a conductor of my 'Elektra' reports: 'This evening I understood every word.' If this is not the case it is safe to conclude that the orchestra did not play in accordance with my very carefully judged markings. While on this subject, I should like to mention the very particular character of my marking of orchestral dynamics; these are frequently not restricted to indicating the level of tone pp, p, f or ff for the entire orchestra, as different groups of instruments, and even individual instruments, often have very different markings. Their exact observation–the principal requirement for the correct orchestral playing of my scores–does, admittedly, pre-suppose a degree of orchestral discipline which is still somewhat unusual, but it is the basic condition for ensuring that my scores really sound as I conceived them. Especial attention has to be given to a scrupulous execution of fp markings, and of every 'espressivo' intended to give a single part precedence over the others, even though this is often scarcely noticeable. Only in this way can finely-woven polyphony be brought out clearly . . . However dazzling the huge orchestral sound produced by many of our conductors who, unfortunately, direct operas in addition to their concert work, this cannot silence the justified complaints about such ear-splitting noise at the cost of the comprehensibility of the action and of the poet's words. It is to this need that the score of 'Ariadne' owes its creation. While the orchestra here is not condemned to a merely supporting role, the notes and words of the singers *must* always remain understandable in every performance despite the expressive power of the 'chamber orchestra,' however heartless the officiating conductor . . ."

"The listener must be able to follow the naturally flowing conversation uninterruptedly, and perceive clearly the subtle developments of the characters represented in the piece, otherwise the result will be intolerably tedious, as orgies of symphonic sound will not make up for the fact that the incomprehensibility of the words makes it impossible to follow the action in every detail. Singers should remember especially that properly formed consonants can penetrate even the most brutal orchestral sound, while the human voice, however powerful, can easily be overwhelmed by an orchestra of eighty or a hundred playing no

416

louder than mezzo-forte if the singer concentrates solely on vowels. The singer has only one weapon with which to defend himself against a polyphonic and indiscreet orchestra: the consonant ... Practical experience teaches us that when singers are producing their maximum tone the clarity of enunciation, in particular the formation of consonants, suffers considerably ..." ("Intermezzo").

"The secco recitative (broken up only by chords of the strings and harpsichord) is the most primitive of art forms, but it enables a fairly complicated comedy plot to be presented clearly. The moment even one orchestral instrument sings in opposition the damage is done! ... I know that my orchestra, frequently playing in the upper register, presents more difficulties to the voices than the dark velvet carpet of the Wagnerian strings, and that even an independent flute part above a soprano can hinder the understanding of the text–I also know quite well that the bringing out of my complex polyphony on the one hand, and the discretion required in accompanying singers on the other, present the conductor with difficult problems; all the more reason for the scrupulous observation of my markings which control the relationship between voices and orchestra! I know of cases in which a solo violin (Mozart aria, first scene of 'Daphne') can scarcely hold its own against a soprano singing too loudly, while on the other hand strings and woodwind lying fairly high, even though they are playing pp, can cover a soprano voice singing in the middle register. How often, from bar to bar, conductor and singer have to hold the balance of forces by bringing this out, keeping that down, in order that the tone picture which the composer had in mind should be fashioned correctly! The fragments of the leading melody assigned to instrumental groups and single instruments have to be blended with the voice to form a smoothly-flowing melodic line ... 'What I want is stated exactly in the score!' The task of conductor and producer, to translate such a libretto and score into the reality visualized by the author and composer, is so immense and many-sided that no praise on the part of audiences and critics can be too high when a production is completely successful. Interpretation true to the notes and words, and congenial improvisation, are 'brother and sister like words and music'!" ("Capriccio").

*

During the First World War Strauss unexpectedly descended from the lofty heights of his humanistic fairy-tale opera to the down-to-earth level of his *"Intermezzo."* "The journey into the realm of romantic fairy tales and the over-stimulation of the imagination by the imposing subject of 'Die Frau ohne Schatten' reawakened the desire for a modern, wholly realistic opera, which I had long cherished in secret, and a stay of a week in Dr. Krecke's Sanatorium (in Munich) gave me the opportunity to write 'Intermezzo'. . ." This symphonic "Commedia domestica," this amusing illustration of pages from a creative musician's diary, should not be taken too seriously. The most personal experiences of the "three most hectic days," which brought Strauss "almost to the point of insanity," are depicted in a cheerfully whimsical mood. What is open to criticism is not the fact that an eminent composer presented a slice of his own family life on the stage in a sublime spirit of self-irony, taking events out of the privacy of the home and inviting laughter–indeed, there were many earlier fascinating examples of artists basing works on their own experiences. What is questionable, however, is the unduly naive, private, almost petty-bourgeois aspect which Strauss here showed of his art. He could not expect that his frivolous "Marriage Intermezzo," set in the year 1907 or there-abouts, with its soothing refrain "That can certainly be called a happy marriage," after a series of violent family rows, would be of universal interest, apart from the fact that autobiographies are naturally fascinating: this was how the world-famous man saw himself . . . This comic presentation of most personal and intimate events lacks universal validity and an ethical basis, although the author-composer once referred in connection with this piece to the "hardest spiritual struggles which can disturb a human heart." What Strauss, as librettist and composer, here represents with unsparing candour is a photographically true-to-life picture ("A photograph, but with music," he once remarked) of the family of the composer and court conductor "Robert Storch" in his villa by the "Grundlsee."

It was nothing new for Strauss to depict his family life in music, but while in his tone poems and isolated operas he had masked his identity to some extent, he modelled this harmless comedy, full of "everyday prose," on "real life" virtually undis-guised. The plot springs from the fact that the quick-tempered

418

but charming Christine is incensed on opening a love letter addressed to her famous husband, but actually intended for a Berlin colleague with a similar name. It is, however, improbable (and therefore unrealistic) that the composer's experienced wife would go straight to a lawyer demanding a divorce on the strength of what little Mieze Maier has written, without for a moment considering the character of the man whom she ought to know well enough, and who has shown so much tolerance and understanding for her own flirtation with a stupid baron. The original of this Baron Lummer, a playboy of the turn of the century, was, according to Strauss, a "shy young man of few words, whose character as an adventurer came out only when he half-shamefacedly tried to get money from my wife; until then he had been extremely modest and shy, and had aroused her sympathy . . ." The original of the man responsible for the tragi-comic confusion appears to have been not the Berlin opera conductor Edmund von Strauß but the Prague conductor Josef Stransky, who was appearing as a guest artist in Berlin, while Mieze Maier is actually supposed to have been named Mitze Mücke . . .

Who would write this prosaic text for Strauss? As early as May 1916 he cautiously sounded out Hofmannsthal. He said he wanted a "realistic comedy with genuine, interesting people, whether more lyrical or burlesqued, approaching the parodistic style of Offenbach." What he visualized at that time was "either an entirely modern, absolutely realistic comedy of character and domestic life . . . or a charming comedy of love and intrigue, somewhere between Schnitzler's 'Liebelei' and . . . Scribe's 'Glass of water'." The highly artistic poet of "Die Frau ohne Schatten" had no feeling for such a piece. To him such suggestions were "really abominable," and "with the best will in the world" he could "never take part." However, he put Strauss in touch with Hermann Bahr, the author of the successful comedy "The Concert." A discussion that autumn produced a certain amount of clarity concerning the future piece based on experiences of Strauss's own life. With scrupulous exactitude he described his character, and that of his wife, to Bahr. Strauss commented on the first draft: ". . . leave more to the music than you attempt to present and motivate through the text alone. I am sending you herewith a succession of scenes I have thought out, little more than cinema pictures, in which the music says everything, the writer contributing only a few cue words which carry the action steadily forward." Even that was none too easy: "... because it is *your* piece, the idea comes from you, and you can evidently already see and hear it complete in your mind ... I admire the way, in the few sketches you have sent me in letters, you have been able to invent ... entirely unpersonal dialogue, betraying nothing about the characters, but most delightful; I am so full of admiration for the fascination of what you have done, and enjoy it so much, that even if you were in agreement I would on no account substitute my dialogue, which is wholly based on characters, for yours, independent of a formal structure but strangely compelling for that very reason. I cannot create *your* dialogue, and I imagine that no one but you could do so. My suggestion is, therefore, that this time you must write your own text ..."

Once again, during the war, Strauss attempted to obtain the Viennese writer's collaboration, but then, one day, he began to "hack out the first scene, writing everything that occurred to me without careful selection or poetic frills ... I believe the outward form of my dialogue is quite good and lively, sometimes trivial in content (but in real life we don't talk in verse), and capable of improvement, though it must always remain natural. Please let me know whether you think it has been worth the trouble taken over it ... If the idea is successful I shall need more of this kind of thing, and if you would supply me with another piece of this nature, genuine Bahr, I should be overjoyed." Strauss then pursued this idea with all the power of conviction at his command: "I am planning a cycle: The Wife, about five comedies showing her from various sides. As you obviously see my gracious spouse in a different light from that in which I see her, a second piece from you would be delightful. Ten pieces could be written about my wife–I see that, now I am beginning to analyse her for this work: add another comedy to the cycle, that would be splendid ..." Without following up this suggestion, Bahr was full of praise for the text of "Intermezzo:" "... excellent, really astonishingly good ... Now I know for the first time what you have in mind, and I also know what I always secretly suspected, that you yourself are the only man to write this libretto! So on you go ..." The author-composer later enjoyed relating, proudly, that Reinhardt had also been lavish in his praise, writing that "Intermezzo" was so well written that he would gladly produce it as a spoken comedy . . . Now Strauss, too, was convinced, and in the summer of 1918, shortly before the end of the war, he reported to Hofmannsthal that the "little marriage opera" was proceeding excellently. "The whole thing is very well laid out, and architecture and music will probably help to overcome the literary shortcomings. I am going on with it . . ." (The fact that Hofmannsthal never forgave him the "Intermezzo" escapade, which he described as "uncultured," is not surprising.)

When considering this "Bourgeois Comedy with Symphonic Interludes" one has to forget all about music drama derived from Gluck and Wagner. What we see is an almost filmlike succession of thirteen everyday scenes in prose dialogue, linked by appropriate orchestral Interludes, with innumerable descriptions of common domestic happenings: servant trouble, the telephone ringing, letting a room, tobogganing, a game of skat, ten hard-boiled eggs, a milk bottle, raspberry juice, pills, and a gargle for the husband while he is travelling. "Anna, Anna, where's the silly goose?" "Which blouse? The blue silk one? Yes, the yellow one is better!" "You ass, can't you see there's tobogganing going on?" "Therese, you must wipe all the drawers over with a damp rag!" "Ah, you don't know them, Attorney! He is a charming fellow, but the wife–simply shocking." All these phrases occur in the text of "Intermezzo," put together from the private life of a great man. Quite apart from these trivialities suggesting the world of farce the libretto has an obvious failing: at the end of each act it suddenly descends into sentimentality. Strauss did all he could to show the volatile and capricious but by no means unsympathetic character of Christine-Pauline in all lights–"no dragon, please!" he had written as a precaution in an opera producer's album. (The piece might well be entitled "The Taming of the Shrew" or "Those who tease love one another"). However, the comedy dissolves in sentimentality when Christine bursts into tears at the bedside of little Franzl: "Papa is always good to you, you are cruel to Papa," and at the end domestic peace is established quite humourlessly at the breakfast table with coffee and rolls. Strangely enough Strauss ignored the opportunity for a gay, parodistically turbulent ending in the style of the boisterous opening scene in the dressing room, together with all detailed criticism of society à la Offenbach. It is certainly impossible to think in terms of the original intention to write a "political-satirical parody of the sharpest style." When the author writes in his brilliant foreword "This new work, in its rejection of the subjects of love and murder familiar from the typical opera libretto, with its possibly over-audacious probe 'into the whole of human life,' opens up a new road to operatic construction," his diagnosis and prognosis are correct to only a very limited extent. It is, however, a remarkable fact that within a few years of Strauss's venture into a light-footed, everyday conversational style two modernistic composers, Schoenberg in his "Von heute auf morgen" and Hindemith in his "Neues vom Tage," based their operas on banal marital crises from everyday life.

The "cinema pictures" of "Intermezzo" are not as novel in style as one is often led to believe. The transference of the scene of an opera's action from the historical past into the "ordinary life" of the present day (as a reaction to the "bird's eye view" theory of Serow, according to which an opera subject must be remote from the present-day world), had been tried out and had become reality long before the time of Strauss. On the other hand the music of "Intermezzo," with its separation and at the same time linking, of elements of purely dramatic recitative and symphonic form, appears to be merely the ultimate consequence of Strauss's earlier development. This comedy style had its roots in the Prologue added to "Ariadne": the elevation of everyday dialogue to the point of song, its rise and fall astonishingly true to nature, the gentle transitions from spoken by way of half spoken to half or completely sung words, the discreet commentary provided by the orchestra (smaller than that of any of the other operas apart from "Ariadne"), which plays a prominent part with its pointillistic wit, and adds greater weight to the proceedings by means of the expressive Interludes. The style of the dialogue derives originally from the scene between Sachs and Eva in the second act of "Meistersinger", and in the transformation of speech into melody it was to be extended with bold logic in Janáček's "Jenufa." Regarded in this light, "Intermezzo" must be considered as a new "attempt at dramatic music in prose" in the recent history of opera, following the stylistic reforms of Mussorgsky and Rimsky-Korsakow—except that the musician in

422

Strauss was so powerful that he was constantly undermining the work of the theoretician, making the music blossom and soar, careful though he was in matters of rhythmical refinement and in capturing the required conversational tone with great precision. (Strauss referred to the "scale of dialogue colours" forming a graduated link between parlando and expressive song.)

"Tempo, tempo, my husband always says, tempo is everything..." And tempo is also the driving factor of this virtuistically fashioned score, in which the musical farce is blended with charming Allegro graciousness. Whatever happens on the stage, from packing a suitcase to a domestic row, complete clarity and the desired effect are achieved. It is fascinating to observe how the agile motifs of the husband and wife (the "Robert" motif which opens the opera undergoes hundreds of transformations during the work) depict the characters, and are finally brought together in a conciliatory "marriage theme." The symphonic element gains the upper hand at times in the remarkably beautiful, in some cases very extensive Interludes which cover the changes of scene. A mischievous critic even suggested that a better sub-title would be "Symphonic Poem with Bourgeois Interludes." To quote again from the foreword: "In no other work of mine is the importance of the dialogue greater than in this bourgeois comedy which offers so-called cantilena few opportunities to develop... The lyrical element, the representation of the spiritual experiences of the characters, comes to full fruition principally in the longer orchestral Interludes. It is really only in the closing scenes of the first and second acts that the singer is given opportunities to unfold extended cantilena phrases..." Fortunately it was *only* in those two episodes that Strauss allowed himself to become sentimental. On the other hand what wonderfully tender, soaring music occurs when the wife dreams of her husband, and here really opens her whole heart (Interlude in A♭ major!). How full of life is the Waltz, with its charming opening played by the piano, and its interweaving of native Bavarian and popular-style melodies! How brightly jubilant the enthralling Interlude in E major before the last scene, and how astonishingly true to life is the film-strip skat scene, with the various corporative tricks of "gamesmanship" and clever counterfeits! (Those familiar with the personalities concerned quickly recognized the skat players as particular friends of Strauss in Berlin.) In general

423

it can be said that these Interludes, full of life and colour, show the influence of the earlier tone poems.

It is difficult to imagine "Intermezzo" in the present-day opera repertoire. Times have changed, and have seen progress. When this piece (which was not completed until 1923, during Strauss's visit to South America) received its world première under Busch at the Dresden State Theatre (normally the home of plays) in November 1924, curiosity contended with surprise and pleasure. The autobiographical element was carried so far that the singer appearing as Storch was made up to resemble Strauss, and the interior of his country house at Garmisch was reproduced accurately on the stage. The fact that the composer chose as the first Christine not an eccentric star but Lotte Lehmann, who embodied the healthy bourgeois qualities of her native Vienna, is characteristic of his attitude to his work—and to his wife. During later years he recognized the weaknesses which lay in the "piquancy" of the "representation of an episode in my own life" of this work which he had dedicated "to my dear son Franz," and advocated a more impersonal interpretation. The idea of a new version of "Intermezzo," thoroughly revised in its dramatic content, came to the fore when a new production was planned in Munich toward the end of the Krauss era there. The intention was to divide the comedy into three parts, the feeble scene of the wife at her son's bedside no longer ending the first act. However, the events of wartime prevented this. A further attempt in the same direction did not interest the composer, and the result was first tried out after his death, at Zürich in 1951. Since then this piece has found a place for itself as a festival intermezzo at the intimate Cuvilliés-theater in Munich ... Should the orchestral interludes not be performed more frequently in the concert hall? They deserve to be.

*

"Capriccio" is, to quote Nietzsche, "music about music". In it Strauss made the relationship between words and music the subject of an operatic work. The question is whether a verbal idea inspires the imagination to musical creation, or whether, on the contrary, the "freely" working creative imagination seeks the words, the poetry, the action to which it can attach itself. By choosing the subject of opera itself, Strauss aroused the contradictions of the form in his own mind. The success of this venture,

424

undertaken during the first years of a war which was to plunge the world into fresh chaos, and the fact that it was not only a spirited by a vigorously alive child of the recent history of opera were due in no small degree to Strauss's close association with Krauss, a highly experienced man of the theatre. This work is described on the title page as "A conversation piece for music by Clemens Krauss and Richard Strauss." Anyone who knows (from the correspondence) how carefully such expressions were worded may well conclude that Strauss placed particular importance on the close relationship of author and composer indicated by the conjunction "and."

This last of all Strauss's operas to be completed has a complicated history. As early as May 1935, when he came into contact with Gregor, there was some talk of a "cheerful work in one act." It was Stefan Zweig who drew attention to the short opera "Prima le parole–dopo la musica" (First the text, then the music), with words by the Abbé Giambattista de Casti, which had received its first performance at Schönbrunn, near Vienna, in 1786, in a double bill with Mozart's "Schauspieldirektor." However, weary and pessimistic about the political situation as he was, he felt unable to take the subject in hand himself. Gregor, too, was drawn more strongly to "Friedenstag" and "Daphne," and indeed "Parole–musica" was put aside in favour of the two tragic one-act operas.

While he was orchestrating "Danae," Strauss, who by then had almost reached the age at which Verdi wrote "Falstaff," experienced his old feeling of disquiet: what was he to do next? Who would supply his next libretto? Two suggestions by Gregor failed to meet with his approval: "Good old Viola has already fallen through often enough as an opera, and the ghost story is too thin and insignificant..." But what about the Casti? "The title is excellent and the problem very fascinating, if it were worked out contrapuntally with the talent of Scribe..." In an amusing letter of May 1939 he attempted to interest Gregor in the idea: an "ingenious dramatic paraphrase of the theme First the words, then the music (Wagner) or First the music, then the words (Verdi) or Only words, no music (Goethe), or Only music, no words (Mozart). Naturally there are many intermediate stages between those extremes! What I visualize is to represent this in various characters, comedy figures who become entangled in the action!... First the conductor–then the producer is as much a subject as the writer, then the composer . . . It would take at least ten actors and singers to represent this theme alone! To work this out in attractive, graceful action would be a task worthy of a Beaumarchais, Scribe and Hofmannsthal . . ."

What drew Strauss so strongly to Casti's idea was the possibility of concluding his life's work in the theatre with a play on the various stylistic elements of opera to which he had devoted his attention at different stages of his career. He, who had become aware of a "bacillus against the theatre," once again wanted to compose something "wholly spirited and original," a really "attractive" stage piece providing food for thought–an "opera about opera." "I really ought to write something of this sort, no lyricism, no arias, but dry wit, intelligent dialogue–a theatrical fugue," Straus wrote in September 1933 to Krauss, in whom he had possessed a partner of like mind on all questions of opera dramaturgy since their joint preparation of the première of "Arabella" at Dresden. (In one of his many workshop letters Strauss addressed his friend as "My dear Baton.") Strauss next thought of a kind of scenic "Interlude" between "Daphne" and "Friedenstag;" later, when this became impracticable owing to the excessive length of such an evening, he considered a gay Prologue to the one-act bucolic tragedy . . . "Our Casti must become for 1932 (after Mozart, Puccini, Lehár) what Goethe's 'Prologue in the Theatre' was for 1832 (after Shakespeare, Lessing, Schiller, Kotzebue, Iffland)." (Letter to Gregor.) This gave a fairly complete programme for the later "conversation piece," running wholly contrary to the espressivo spirit of romantic opera. The principal problem was not the action but the musical setting. The actual events of the piece, which were naturally vital to its setting in time and place, remained a symbolical frame for the dialogue of this "metamorphosis of the arts." Meanwhile Casti's old libretto (" . . . an Intermezzo of a few pages, with four characters") had undergone several transformations at Gregor's hands. In 1935 the allegorical figures became living men and women of opera. A troupe of actors blunder on a delicate situation: the beautiful, romantic chatelaine is courted both by a poet and by a musician . . . However, it was not until 1939 that Gregor's ideas could be fashioned into anything like a complete scenario: "a little comedy in the style of Eichendorff," against the background of a "mansion in the heart of the country" somewhere in Germany. The sonnet idea, the cardinal-point of the whole, was born at that time. In Strauss's opinion it should be a "sketch concerning artistic questions which interest me." "At the conclusion no happy ending, but everything to be left in the balance . . . , also the personal relationships of the couples: whether the Count marries the actress, whether the Countess decides in favour of the poet or the musician, or neither of them! In short, a large question mark!"

Now "Capriccio" was taken in hand seriously. Strauss, who had long lived intimately with all the motives and characters of the piece, pressed Gregor to transform the project from the planning stage to that of dramatic reality. Time and place: naturally rococo or Viennese Empire, on no account the Weimar of Goethe and Frau von Stein, which Gregor had suggested (with all manner of tedious cultural-historical references). "Why not the period 1815 to 1820?" Gregor's first drafts did not satisfy Strauss: ". . . dialogue which does not correspond to my taste either in form or content . . . Too much sentiment and feeling, too much poetry, while I preach Molière or Oscar Wilde . . ." Diderot was also invoked. The musician now took the initiative completely in establishing the basis of the project. "The more I think about the Casti the more clearly I see the whole piece in only four scenes . . . It seems to me that the most important thing is to create a good tightening of the dramatic knot up to the moment when poet and musician decide to write a new piece . . . The build-up I visualize would have to be in the nature of the second act Finale of 'Figaro' with its highly effective ending–a new piece which should satisfy everyone." At that time the entrance of the Italians, the burlesque Intermezzo of the servants (personifying the "real general public" in its various social strata) and the Countess's Finale took on tangible form. But how was Gregor, the non-musician, to write these conversations about opera? "Perhaps a logical, sober French mind could do it! Hermann Bahr might have been able to, or 'the silent one'."

Krauss had begun to take part, unnoticed, in the deliberations concerning the "little discussion opera." He saw clearly the weaknesses both of Gregor's draft and of Strauss's dialogue sketches. Nevertheless he considered that Strauss would best get to the heart of the problems of his beloved art if he wrote the text

427

himself. Strauss disagreed. "I can paint well-polished scores, but I need help for words..." He appealed for his friend's assistance with increasing urgency: "You have already advised me so often and so well, have diverted this project into new channels dramaturgically... you know best what I need, what corresponds to my nature... Write the libretto *yourself*..." Krauss agreed, and before the end of 1939 he delivered the first draft libretto. It was possible to take the characters from the earlier scenario. The time and place were soon chosen: "A château near Paris at the time when Gluck was beginning his work on the reform of opera there, about 1775..." "The Countess no pale German girl but an enlightened Frenchwoman of twenty-seven with free views in matters concerning love, more serious and aspiring in her ideas than her brother the philosophical theatre patron and dilettante..." The "problem of love" was thus to be made to run parallel with the problems of words and music. It was agreed that this work from the world of opera should contain examples of all the principal musical forms associated with the musical theatre. How energetically Strauss devoted himself to the new task! There was as much forceful and fruitful discussion of musical and theatrical-historical details as there was about verse and prose styles—Strauss once remarked that "I myself am always so possessed by the work that I often neglect the form." There was no need, he wrote, for the whole thing to be too tame; after all, "Die Meistersinger" had its scene of a civil brawl. "So please don't be so dignified, in my name... Reflect: you are more naturally conciliatory than I am, an Austrian with better manners, while a rough Bavarian likes to hit out at something with a flail..." From July 1940 onwards Strauss worked at the music in close contact with Krauss: "I beg to advise you that I have just sketched the introductory music to our masterwork, and the first scene up to the point at which the director wakes up." In the incredibly short period of less than eight months the composition was completed in rough, having proceeded step by step with the final form of the libretto, almost unhampered by wartime conditions. At the end of July 1941 Strauss wrote "that the whole score will be ready this week, and that I am concerned with making the instrumentation of the last scene especially beautiful for our dear friend (Viorica Ursuleac)..." Strauss wanted the flowing cantabile of the ending to

428

counteract the danger that the lyrical element would have too little scope in the discussion. It was at a comparatively late stage that agreement was reached concerning the title and descriptive sub-title of the work. The ideas extended from "The language of notes, a theatrical fugue in one act" and "The Countess's Sonnet, a stage piece with a puzzle" to the rather colourless "Capriccio," a suggestion by Krauss. There were also differences of opinion concerning the sub-title. Krauss recommended "Theatrical discussion in one act;" Strauss thought of "Musical-dramatic questions of the heart" or "Theatrical Fugue on the theme of words and music," to which Krauss responded with the formulation "A theatre piece for music," but this did not meet with Strauss's approval. Finally they agreed on "A conversation piece for music."

The aesthetic dispute between the adherents of Piccinni and those of Gluck, between the enthusiasts for Italian bel canto opera and the supporters of the new operatic ideal of higher dramatic truth and of the intimate relationship between words and music–this dispute is reflected in the conversation of the guests at the château of the beautiful Countess Madeleine and her art-loving brother. The dramatically significant conflict places the Countess in the predicament of a fondness both for the poet Olivier and for the musician Flamand. The verses of the one charm her, but the music of the other brings to full consciousness things which can never be expressed by the poetic word. Which is she to favour? In a sonnet by Ronsard, here put into the mouth of Olivier and composed by Flamand, poetry and music are blended into the higher unity of which Madeleine, as a true follower of Gluck, fervently approves. It therefore becomes even more difficult for her to make her purely human decision. Finally left alone, she vainly asks her mirror image to decide for her whether she should give her hand to the poet or to the musician. The question remains open. However, her renunciation of the fulfilment of her longing as a woman demands and finally makes possible the fulfilment of her ardent desire for an opera observed from real life. At the fall of the curtain Olivier, Flamand and the theatre director La Roche are already busy with plans for the new work. Meanwhile, however, the audience have all along been seeing the opera, which is to present these events in an artistic manner, as a "theatrical fact."

At a time when opera everywhere was seeking to re-establish its fundamental principles, it is understandable that Strauss the music dramatist took the opportunity to present some of his own views. Who was better qualified to do so than he who had given the theatre more than a dozen highly stageworthy works, and whose thoughts constantly revolved round the problems of opera right up to the end of his life? In La Roche the libretto introduced *the* figure who, although compelled for the purposes of the plot to represent grand Italian opera, at the same time has a good deal to say, as a symbolic figure of the theatre, which Strauss himself "had it in my heart to declare." The statements of this wholly serious theatre director (Strauss soon gave up the idea of a "smart Aleck" director of the calibre of the Munich operetta man Fritz Fischer in favour of a more responsible type of man with characteristics of Possart and Reinhardt) are often very telling or highly entertaining. "Give the aria its due! Have consideration for the singers. Orchestra not too loud," he says. "A grave defect of our operas is the deafening noise of the orchestra. Its bellowing and raging swallows up the voices . . ." However, it is the woman who has the finest and deepest things to say concerning opera. Words and music, "the beautiful thought in noble melody–I think there is no better union." Or Madeleine's decision:

Vain attempt
to part the two.
Blended in one are words and notes–
united as a new whole.
The mystery of the hour–
one art redeemed by the *other!*

The unusually colourful and skilful libretto, though it reaches the level of poetry only in the Ronsard sonnet and the sensitive ending, demanded the all-embracing knowledge of theatre matters and of all problems of the creation of opera which only men of great practical experience could possess. The basic idea of the work in its final form undoubtedly derives from Strauss. The figures were invented, including the two "dear enemies, friendly opponents" the poet Olivier and the musician Flamand, and also the almost ghostly figure of the prompter Taupe; only the actress Clairon had an historical model in the famous heroine of the

430

In old age: Drawing by Gerda von Stengel (1949)

Comédie Française. True, this is not an elemental piece of theatre—rather an informative work of great historical and artistic charm, a genre for which Strauss had had a weakness since "Ariadne." It is not aimed (as Strauss himself acknowledged) at an "audience of eighteen hundred people per evening." It requires prior knowledge of musical history. But why should only the "connoisseur of culture" possess such knowledge? Why not the ordinary music lover who, after all, follows David's explanations concerning the vocal art of the mastersingers with interest? The subject dealt with here will have something to say to all who feel themselves drawn to opera as an art form.

The fact that it is people, not abstractions, who here appear in a region between reality and art, between life and abstract ideas, is achieved to such a degree through the magical resources of music. They stand there plastic and warm with life, firmly outlined and finely shaded with the flexible technique of characterization which, since "Rosenkavalier," had constantly renewed itself through delight in transformation. The characters are in their own world, the salon of the ancien régime; the spirit of the age of enlightenment is recaptured by a virtuistic mastery of the technique of stylized imitation, while Gigue and Gavotte, strings, harpsichord and harp conjure up the chamber music spirit of the rococo age. Only in the distance, as though from outside, does the great innovator Gluck knock at the door of the age. (Between the early arrangement of "Iphigénie" and the quotations from Gluck in "Capriccio" there lay half a century of dramatic endeavour and creation.) The comic elements of the work reach their summit in the masterly Octet in two parts, a piece unparalleled in the whole of musical literature, which strikingly contrasts the voices of six people who are quarrelling with the lyricism of two Italian singers. However, the centrepiece of the work is the extended Fugue "Discussion on the theme Words and Music." Here speaks the creator of the "Sinfonia domestica" Fugue, who was fascinated by the idea of planting in the theatre this musical form alien to the stage. Verdi, too, finally arrived at the Fugue which concludes "Falstaff." These strict ensemble forms, including also the delightfully parodistic servant Intermezzo, are merely the dramatic point of junction ("I am steadily moving away from simultaneous composition . . ."). Strauss surrounded the fluid conversational style of his music, growing out of the comedy parlando of "Intermezzo," with a lyrical shimmer.

Its beautiful fragrance and gentle glow of feeling make "Capriccio" a precious gift of aged serenity, despite its wit and animation. It is really a document of final maturity, especially remarkable when one remembers how Strauss's vitality had been poured out and transformed since "Guntram" of 1894. Following the Wagnerian weightiness of some parts of earlier scores, it is also the last delicious "turn to Mozart" in his work in the operatic sphere. The Andante con moto Introduction for string sextet is gentle and restrained, the F♯ major Sonnet ("Kein Andres, das mir so im Herzen loht"), with which poet and musician together do homage to the Countess, is brightly radiant, the Moonlight Music, with its melody which had lain dormant in the "Krämerspiegel," is sensuously romantic, while the closing scene of Madeleine, with its great melodic refinement and revelation of every step between sensitive feeling and roguishness, reveals a character who is half Marschallin, half Arabella, and at the same time wholly individual. The music of "Capriccio" is akin to that of the "Ariadne" Prologue, except for its enrichment by certain pliant features of the later Strauss. The fairly large orchestra appears at full strength in only a few places in this dialogue opera. It is generally treated in the manner of chamber music, the solistic use of the instruments radiating a magical enchantment. It is actually possible to hear almost every word—a vital consideration in a conversational opera. How, at the final summit of his mastery, Strauss transformed this conversation into scenes of vocal and instrumental music, how he made the voices chatter, attaining the tempo of high comedy despite a wealth of delicate lyricism, and how skilfully he wove the voices into large ensembles—these are difficult to describe in a few words. The work can only be experienced and savoured. Thus "Capriccio" confirms once again the principles of a great lifetime of music. The animation of youth has become spiritualized. What was once drama related to its times is now timeless aesthetic discussion. Has "Capriccio" not proved conclusively that discussions are possible in opera? Not only Madeleine but also the musician Strauss concludes the "dispute" with a superior smile. The work ends with a repeated question posed by his beloved solo horn.

In 1942, contrary to his original intention to postpone the world premières of his operas until after the war, Strauss gave permission for his "friend and colleague," to whom this happy "caprice" of final operatic wisdom is dedicated, to give the first performance. In October of that year at the Munich National Theatre (at a private showing for invited guests and then at the première itself) the work delighted those who were able to make the journey to southern Germany in wartime. Since then, especially after 1945, it has continued to demonstrate its living power both in the international repertoire and in festival productions. At each fairly satisfactory realization of the work's individual conversational style there is no danger of the audience losing interest at any time during the 130 minutes of its single act. Cuts, above all in the closing scene, appear to be unjustified. (It is also difficult to see the necessity for the division of the work into two acts which Rudolf Hartmann tried out in 1957 at Hamburg and Paris, and later at Munich) ... What about another opera? Strauss probably considered Krauss's new suggestions, but his response was not what might have been expected: "As for a 'new opera,' it can at least be pleasant if you 'think about it!' But do you really believe that after the Capriccio of Fugue or Muse or Muse Madeleine or Erato or ... anything better or even as good can follow? Isn't this D♭ major the best conclusion to my life's work in the theatre? After all, it's only possible to leave *one* will!"

THE DANCE

THE ELEMENT OF THE DANCE PLAYS AN ESSENTIAL PART in Strauss's music. How could it be otherwise in the case of a composer like Strauss to whom a sense of rhythm and colour was an inborn gift? It was only in recent times that ballet, cultivated for centuries merely as an entr'acte or at best an organic "number" in opera, had been developed as a self-contained art form. Strauss, who later described the dance as "mother of the arts," observed with close attention the decay of the traditional ballet divertissement. The dance is intellectual-expressive art, and its problems attracted him as early as the 'nineties. Among the suggestions he considered around the year 1897 was one by Wedekind, the story of a flea which found its way under a lady's hooped petticoat. As yet, however, Strauss possessed no clear idea of the laws of motive and gesture, and he did not proceed beyond a few sketches. He was also fascinated for a while by the scenario of a one-act "Kometentanz." ("The writer Paul Scheerbart has sent me a very attractive plan for a ballet: Dance of Comets, an astral pantomime, for which I will at once write the music. No need here to worry about singers, and one can rage at will in the orchestra.") When the Berlin Opera showed no interest in the idea the Dance of Comets was laid aside.

The plan of a three-act ballet "Kythere" seemed more likely to come to fruition. The extensive, sumptuous scenario by Strauss himself derives from impressions which he received from paintings by Watteau and his contemporaries Boucher and Fragonard when he visited the Louvre with Rolland in 1900. "Ideas for the ballet 'The Island Cythère' after Antoine Watteau," he wrote in a notebook that May. However, it is known from diary entries and annotations made in various art books that this meeting in Paris had been preceded by extensive studies of Watteau since

1896. At the end of September Strauss read the complete scenario to Rösch and Bie, who were "both very satisfied," and Hofmannstahl too, to whom he showed it in the "Rosenkavalier" year 1909, long after "Kythere" had been pushed aside by "Feuersnot" and the "Sinfonia domestica," found it "very attractive and artistically conceived." Not only the scenario but also the very detailed and extensive musical sketches (representing a contact with the rococo world astonishing at that stage of his life and work) lift "Kythere" above the level of the other ballet plans. The fact that this project finally came to nothing is probably due to the scale on which the work was conceived—it would have far exceeded the length of the normal ballet. "Kythere is much too long. Fills three ballet evenings," Strauss later commented on this abortive project. Not until January 1945 did the figures of the second act, Diana, Endymion and Venus, again come before his eyes ... Salome's "Dance of the Seven Veils" must be considered his first significant contribution to the modern expressive dance. This no longer has anything to do with the conventional ballet insertion unconnected with the drama proper: it is a dance poem which intoxicates the senses and in which everything is dominated by the inner turmoil of a corrupt female psyche. From then onward Strauss's road was clear. In this sphere too, as the first important German composer since Beethoven, he wanted to create something of real stature, but his efforts in this direction were never really successful.

Strauss had a revealing experience: "During the last years before the First World War the Russian Ballet under its brilliant director Diaghilev, with the incomparable Nijinsky, made a great stir in Germany. A visit of theirs to Berlin so enchanted me that I gladly followed up a suggestion by Hofmannsthal and Count Harry Kessler that I should write a work for this unique ensemble ..." In the "Ballets Russes" of Serge Diaghilev, who inspired almost all the great composers of his time, the Russian and French traditions were combined. Of striking ability in every aspect of ballet, these artists, who were then appearing for the first time in western Europe, were striving toward new goals. What Strauss visualized he expressed as follows on the occasion of a Munich production of *"Josephslegende"* in 1941: "I wanted ... to renew the dance. The dance as an expression of drama—but not exclusively. Dance in the modern manner, which is only

436

action paraphrased or converted into rhythm, unfortunately too often leads us far away from the heart of the true dance, purely inspirational, dedicated to movement and absolute beauty–the ballet. That was what I wanted to rejuvenate ... My 'Joseph' contains both elements: dance as drama and dance as–dance. The pure possession of sheer gracefulness must not be thrown away; just as in music, alongside characteristic, programmatic and elemental features, the line of absolute beauty must never be ignored ..."

A strange work, scarcely suggesting the rarified air of "Ariadne" and, like Strauss's other pieces in this genre, a mere "occasional work," parergon! It is not at all easy to find oneself stylistically in "Josephslegende" (which the authors originally entitled "Josephs Legende"). There can certainly be no talk of a "legend" in the sense of Liszt's "St. Elizabeth." Nothing on the stage immediately points to the biblical story. We see the ornate hall of an Italian Renaissance palace, with people in 16th-century costumes feasting at a richly appointed table, and only after a considerable time do we guess that the man in Oriental and the woman in Venetian dress who watch the proceedings with an air of boredom from seats on a dais beneath a baldachin are Potiphar and his wife. Hofmannsthal and Kessler, as authors of the scenario, could scarcely explain convincingly why the legend was removed from its original setting and transplanted to these uncharacteristic surroundings. No particular conflict remote from the psyche of the Ancient Egyptians but a product of Renaissance life is to be found in this version of the story. The splendour and the fibre-softening luxury which mark the decadence and per-version of Potiphar's household could have been introduced without difficulty into a genuine or imitated picture of life in the house of a nobleman in the Egypt of the Pharaohs. Potiphar's wife suffers under the same destiny which Wilde showed at work in Salome and Hofmannsthal in Elektra: her overwhelming sensual desire, which was uncontrolled but perfectly simple in the biblical narrative, has become complex, transformed into terms of modern decadence, clearly alienating the humanistic basis of the story of Joseph. The long sequence of events prior to the entry of Joseph, the erotic dances of veiled and unveiled women, Sulamith's dance of love-longing, the boxing matches depicted with the utmost naturalism–all these can have no signif-

437

icance in relation to the real subject of attempted seduction through dance except to explain the abandoned nature of the woman by illustrating the immorality of society around her. The enticement scene itself and the fury of the rebuffed temptress are based on the biblical account, while the episode in which Joseph is saved by an archangel is a poetic addition.

In no other instance did the basic idea of a work by Strauss form itself so slowly and laboriously, and the creation of no other stage work of his was accompanied by such expressions of irritation. Did Strauss, with his alert mind, in fact realize that this ballet, aimed at the "festive and splendid," no longer had a place in an age which was soon to be sucked down in the maelstrom of a world war? . . . In June 1912 Hofmannsthal announced the plan: "In conjunction with Kessler, who has a really productive imagination, especially as regards decorative art, I have devised a short ballet for the Russians, 'Joseph in Egypt'. . ." Strauss replied without hesitation: "So once again, 'Joseph' is excellent–it's being swallowed up! I have already begun sketching; Count Kessler's (cultural-philosophical) views do not altogether convince me, but no matter, I'll soon round the headland, particularly if the scenario contains (perhaps with the list of characters) a very exact description of the character of Potiphar's wife . . ." When the composer expressed doubts on account of the similar relationship between Salome and Jokanaan, the poet replied: "I can really find no similarity except that in both works a woman demands something of a man which, on the stage, we are only accustomed to seeing a man demand and a woman either give or refuse to give . . ." Then the joint authors began to raise all kinds of philosophical, profound and almost religious considerations, and Strauss, with his genial naivety, replied bluntly: " 'Joseph' is not getting on as quickly as I expected . . . If anything bores me I cannot easily find music for it. Such a Joseph who seeks God–I have a devil of a time with him. Oh well, perhaps in some atavistic corner of my mind I'll find a pious melody for the virtuous Joseph . . ." That scarcely sounded very respectful, and it brought in reply an admonitory letter from Hofmannsthal full of lofty poetic diction and worthy sentiments: "I am surprised that you find particular difficulty with the figure of Joseph, which appears to me to be the best and most successfully conceived . . . As I see the figure you would

438

have to seek the music for it . . . in the purest region of your brain, where uplift, the clear glacier air of the highest peaks, and absolute spiritual freedom are to be found . . . This shepherd lad, a gifted child of a race from the hills who has been transplanted among the people of the rich delta land, appears to me far more like a noble, unbridled colt than a pious student of theology. His quest of the Divine, in wild upward leaps, is nothing but a fierce urge to reach inspiration hanging beyond his grasp . . . I cannot believe that you are unable to find a bridge linking this young man Joseph with recollections of your own youth–Potiphar or no Potiphar, something higher, sparkling, hard to reach was above–and was to be plucked down: that is Joseph's dance . . ." Not until ten months later did Strauss write to the poet that he had "now had the leisure to sketch out Joseph's dance successfully, and hope the matter will now go forward smoothly, the sketches to be completed in the autumn, and the score in the spring of 1914 . . ." "It means a great deal of hard work." He later said he had written this ballet "on an impulse . . . without seeking any particular style."

Uplift, clear glacier air, inspiration . . . What trace of these is to be found in the score? What does this music, with its decorative, broad flood of sound, express of the literary-aesthetic reforms of the writers, who, in this case, were more mentally active than the composer? The contrast to which Kessler referred "between the costume and the intimate spiritual life of the characters revealed by gestures and music" hardly makes its point with Strauss. The score is limited to pompous ornamentation, although (as every choreographer would admit) it is uncommonly danceable. The themes are of pronounced simplicity. The few leading motifs are far more rarely altered, transformed or pointed with fresh meanings than is customary in other Strauss works. As in "Salome" he depicted the contrast between the purity of soul of the man of God and the hysteria of the woman overwhelmed by carnal desire, against the background of a wholly decadent, lascivious society. However, while in "Salome" he had found a modern musical formula for the description of ecstatic sexual longing, and fashioned it into sung drama, the danced "Josephslegende" is merely a work of decorative splendour in a setting of baroque unreality and mystical transfiguration. A gigantic orchestra (with the division of the violins into three groups taken over from "Elektra," together with heckel-phone, four harps and celestas, piano and organ) is employed, without creating the sensuous glow characteristic of other Strauss works. The erotic element has an insipid effect, and fails to stir. Joseph's major tonality is like a dazzlingly white wall on which the bright colours of a rich palette play. No doubt the instrumental colouration was intended to create its effect by means of associations of mime and subject (the "trickling" of the gold dust, the "greyhounds," the "boxers"). No doubt, too, that Joseph's dance, one of the longest solos in ballet literature, has a certain idyllic charm, but the elemental spiritual power of music, its ability not only to depict but to evaluate and analyse, has been dammed up. This pantomime of a good hour's duration is no purifying vision but merely a perplexing dream. Hofmannsthal soon recognized the weaknesses of this ballet score. "The music has great allure, a real fresco style, that is its best feature," he wrote to Bodenhausen. "In spiritual content it leaves much to be desired."

Time has played its tricks with the work. As "La Légende de Joseph" it received its successful world première at the Paris Grand Opéra in May 1914. It was conducted by the composer, wearing the rosette of the Legion of Honour, the choreography was by Fokine, with the beautiful Maria Kusnetzova from St. Petersburg and the young Massine from Moscow (replacing Nijinsky who was originally to have created the part of Joseph) in the principal roles. On the same day Strauss's greatest exponent Ernst von Schuch was carried to his grave in Dresden. The Russian Ballet also presented the work during a season in London–then the war broke out, and no one had the time or inclination to concern themselves with a ballet which was all splendour, luxury and sensuality. The fact that it had first been performed in Paris, at that time the centre of the world of dance (the unusually attractive evening had produced the sum of 511,000 francs, the largest ever received at the Grand Opéra), did not facilitate the spread of the work under the changed conditions which soon prevailed. So its influence on the reform of a "music drama without words" to which Strauss had aspired remained unrealized; seven years elapsed before performances took place in Vienna and Berlin; there the desired style of the period of Paolo Veronese was adopted for the first time. In 1947 Strauss brought the

440

most effective parts of the score together into a "Symphonic Fragment" for concert use. Today the erotic dance drama "Josephslegende" is scarcely a document of the renewal of ballet–not even a really cultural endeavour; at best it is a decorative piece of assured effectiveness for a well-equipped ballet company in a large city.

*

"Schlagobers," the unpretentious "Gay Viennese Ballet in two acts" owes its existence to a mere whim. A work of relaxation written during the period when Strauss was director of the Vienna Opera, it was intended as a gift for Golden Vienna. In this ballet, a return to the spirit of the old, unassuming divertissement, he wanted to do homage to the genius of the city on the Danube. The fact that the piece was concerned only with Vienna's "genius" for hearty eating and enjoying sweets was unfortunate, and as a result the sweetmeats it has to offer leave a rather sour taste behind. Why not an artistic glorification of all things Viennese springing from the true spirit of ballet? A new story from the Vienna Prater with the vitality of the "Rosenkavalier" Waltz? But in fact the piece was no more substantial than "schlagobers"–whipped cream. The ordinary people of the immediate post-war period, who were certainly not wallowing in whipped cream, referred to the "Millionaires' Ballet" in Vienna and turned away. Only the free form of the "Schlagobers" Suite, for which Strauss picked the choice (sugar) plums of the ballet score, is still an occasional reminder of the existence of this occasional piece without deeper significance.

In the summer of 1921, while his work on "Intermezzo" was going ahead, Strauss drafted his own scenario for a ballet. (Hofmannsthal, to whom he mentioned the project, wrote: "A ballet of your own devising! That is splendid. You have the ability for it, in the sense of a Bavarian baroque-theatrical talent for the stage. Even the mythological ballets you showed me years ago were good, possibly a little over-loaded; now in your maturity it will certainly become something excellent.") The gaily culinary atmosphere of this Vienna is best created by the Introduction to the libretto: "Anyone who strolls on a sunny Whit-Sunday along the principal avenue of the Vienna Prater, shaded by fine chestnut trees, will encounter a great many carriages, each drawn by

441

two smart little horses, decorated with white elder and roses, which are taking swarms of white-frocked girls and black-jerseyed boys, accompanied by aunts and uncles, to the famous pleasure house of the great Empress Maria Theresa. These are the confirmation candidates who, after a festive meal, enjoy for what in most cases is the first time in their young lives the pleasure of a trip in one of the beloved old Viennese fiakers. Where could this delightful excursion end but in that El Dorado of youth, one of the no less famous confectioner's shops, eating Sacher-, Linzer-, Bischinger- and Dobosch-tarts with 'Schlagobers'. . ." The events of the ballet tell of the troubles of one of the boys, who has a particularly healthy appetite. The scene becomes darkened: he sees black before his eyes, and the sweetstuffs which he has enjoyed, but which have created havoc in his stomach, come to life in the tangible reality of ballet. To this story Strauss wrote animated and to some extent distinctive music whose qualities bear no relation to the unimportance of the whole. It is conceived as characteristic music rather than as a poetic ballet. There are a series of finely imagined tone pictures, the eastern-flavoured dances of Princess Teablossom, Don Zuccero, Prince Coffee and Prince Cocoa. Witty, somewhat mundane use is made of conventions of the popular Austrian waltz, traced back as far as Lanner in the actual Schlagobers Waltz and the Slow Waltz of Princess Praliné. March, Minuet, Gavotte and even Polka (shades of Strauss the boy-composer!) make their appearance. Viennese, Upper-Bavarian and exotic elements are mixed equally in this musical confectioner's shop, whose unruly animated sweetstuffs are brought back to reason by a brilliantly constructed Passacaglia. The unproblematic nature of the music is rooted in the subject. At least a splendid "Rêverie" in A♭ with an extended violin solo reflects deeper feeling. "A ballet for ballerinas' feet and not for the heads of philosophers" (Elsa Bienenfeld). A rejuvenation, a revolution of the ballet, such as Strauss had in mind when he planned the "danced music drama" of his Legend, was not to be expected here.

"Schlagobers," completed in October 1922, received its first performance at the Vienna State Opera in May 1924 as the festive opening to the celebrations marking Strauss's sixtieth birthday. The unenthusiastic reception which the work met with caused him to alter certain features of the original Vienna version.

442

For German theatres the naive story was described as a "Gay dance comedy in nine scenes." The appearance of the German equivalent of the Viennese dialect title, "Schlagsahne," on the occasion of the German première at Breslau was a poor joke. (The French translation "Colonel battu," mentioned in the Paris press reports, was, however, more amusing.) "Schlagobers" had so little success at its few performances that the composer later made no effort to promote the work. As early as the first Breslau performance of what was now "Schlagsahne" it seemed to him to have lost its humour. He once asked the opera director "perfectly ingenuously:" "Are we playing this evening?" The director: "Certainly, Herr Doktor! We are performing your 'Schlagobers'." Strauss, smiling: "Who's talking about *that?* I only want to know whether we're playing skat this evening..." This irony was probably lost on the worthy director. Thus Strauss was not particularly interested when, in the war year 1943 of all times, the completed plans of a "Schlagobers" film were submitted to him. He examined the exposé, and his criticism was devastating: "The film scenario is...unworthy rubbish! Heavens above, what a low level! By comparison my harmless, unassuming Schlagobers plot is pure Goethe. Impossible to allow a note of my music to be used for it..." Although agreement on the subject was finally reached during the last winter of the war, through the mediation and help of Gregor, this Viennese musical film was never "born."

When Strauss resigned from the directorship of the Vienna Opera in the autumn of 1924, "wearied by the struggle against... malicious opposition and the impotence of tradition," he recalled with especial gratitude in a farewell letter to Roller the performances of "Josephslegende" and of the "beautiful 'Ruinen von Athen,' which the Viennese failed to appreciate." He might also have mentioned the *"Couperin-Tanzsuite"* after keyboard pieces by the French master—a charming gift for the ballet company of the Vienna State Opera, which first performed this new evocation of the past under Strauss's baton in 1923, in the Redoutensaal of the Vienna Hofburg. Demonstrating his joy in the ornamental finesse of these pre-classical courtly dance pieces, a great artist of the twentieth century has here put a new and tasteful polish on creations of the past. They are elegant sound pictures, to which the string tone of Strauss's 30-strong chamber orchestra

443

gives a character quite distinct from that of the original harp-sichord or clavichord. Among the eight pieces in the Suite the most charming are the Carillon, with celesta, bells and harp, the virtuistic Tourbillon, and the Final March with its quiet conclusion. This Dance Suite has become widely known in the concert hall. Strauss's love of Couperin was to find expression again during the Second World War when he added six new sections to this work, again based on keyboard pieces by Couperin, to form a historical dance vision *"Verklungene Feste,"* following a choreography by the early French ballet master Le Feuillet. The first performance took place at the Munich Opera in April 1941. Strauss's creative imagination went further in this instance, seeking an amalgamation of the styles of the rococo age and the present day in the content of the work. Shortly afterwards Strauss published the new pieces of the Couperin Ballet (whose proximity to "Ariadne" can often be felt clearly), augmented by two further numbers, under the title "Divertimento for Small Orchestra." Again he displayed an admirable gift of historical feeling in such pieces as the charming Rondeau "Le tic-toc-choc," the graceful "Brimborions" (trinkets) and others. We sense the pleasure in "re-grouping" pieces, most of them intended for dancing, which were thus made accessible to far wider audiences. Art is intended for life.

*

After the mature master had achieved so fruitful a relationship to the ancient world, a new love for the forms of ballet awoke in him. Only a many-sided mind like that of Strauss, well-versed in literature, could move so imaginatively in the realm of mythological ballet—what a joy to witness Strauss, at the age of seventy-five, spreading his wings in that direction! He had been captivated by the element of dance in "Daphne," and in 1936, when first coming to grips with "Danae," he asked Gregor: "What would you think of 'Danae' in pantomime? With great dances on the subject of gold? Both serious and parodied?" In the autumn of 1938 Strauss thought it worth while considering the composition of a classical ballet to supplement the one-act operas originally intended for performance as a double bill, but which Strauss later decided should be presented separately. "We already have a lever de rideau for 'Daphne': my half-hour

444

Couperin Suite! How would it be if you also devised a short ballet for me, suitable to go with 'Friedenstag?' What subject? Something Nordic, Celtic? Perhaps you will think of something. Medieval Spanish? Something like Calderón?"

"It is a very long time since I have written anything for ballet..." At that period Strauss had an almost uncontrollable desire for a "light" dance subject in which he could combine agreeableness with practical usefulness. He hoped Gregor could devise a "short ballet (about half an hour), if possible only dances–a minimum of action, restricted to a few decisive moments." "I don't want to interrupt 'Danae' by undertaking anything else very extensive." Gregor, who was at home in all corners of the world of mythology, at once made four suggestions, and it is very interesting to see how Strauss, who quickly made up his mind about them, reacted to these ideas. About "Nausikaa" he wrote that he could not imagine the character of the poetic Nausikaa being portrayed in dance, asking only whether the whole thing would not make a little two-act opera instead... Then Gregor drew his attention to the "greatest 'kulturkampf' in all history so far, Nefertiti and Echnaton," but the musician feared that the subject would be too close to that of "Aida." Next a "Zenobia," freely adapted from Calderón's drama, was thrown into the debate: "Collision between Roman civilization and the Orient"–Strauss considered that it contained too much warfare for it to go with "Friedenstag." He showed most interest in an "Alkestis" which had been suggested to Gregor by the painting of Herakles by Rubens in the Dresden Gallery: "...gives me great pleasure...on no account timeless, no southern Italy, no baroque, but genuine ancient Hellenism, fifth or sixth century B.C., with which I am slowly beginning to reconcile myself since the Dresden 'Daphne'!" His enthusiasm soon cooled down: the subject was too well known and outworn; a title part who "only dies and is carried about instead of dancing–impossible;" he considered male dancers unpopular with the public. However, he did not give up. "Can you not find a subject whose principal figure is actually a female dancer, e.g. Guinard in the painting by Lancret? Isn't there a similar subject in Wieland? Can't anything be made of the famous Lais? Eleusinian Festival? Perhaps you will hit on a subject..." The dancer to whom Strauss referred was the renowned French ballerina

Maria Cenergo; Gregor quickly devised a scene to take place between her and Sallé, "Die Feindinnen"—an idea which Strauss followed up for a time as late as 1943. There were also two suggestions for a "Pandora," and a "Phaeton" was proposed for performance on a double stage, the chariot of the sun with its driver above, parching humanity below. "Less plot—plenty of dancing" was now his ideal—the return to classical ballet.

So all his efforts to create a new, light and loosely constructed classical dance poem remained without practical results. This musician in whose nature it was to react so spontaneously (one need only think of "Salome" and "Frau ohne Schatten") had become slower in making decisions. "My work for the theatre is definitely finished..." Definitely? There was still "Die Rache der Aphrodite," the object of all his love. It was during the last, dreadfully turbulent winter of the war that (as he wrote to Gregor), Strauss had a notable dream: "After breakfast in the house of a great man, who was not, however, present himself, Hofmannsthal came up to me with the words 'I have a one-act opera subject for you, very tender—nymphs!' While trying to learn more about it I awoke. I considered the whole 'tender' Greek mythology of nymphs, naiads and dryads, have studied the whole subject in Vollmer's Mythology, and have finished up with Endymion and our old friend Diana. You know I have an old three-act ballet scenario 'Kythere' after Watteau's famous picture at Sanssouci... I also have an uncomposed ballet synopsis by Haas-Heye 'Philomela' in my drawer: Apollo, Daphnis, Philomela, pairs of lovers—pantomime with singing..." Then came the revealing suggestion: "Do you consider it possible to make something similar out of Diana and Endymion (as conclusion); only Diana singing, with off-stage female chorus... The *handsome* men not singing, only miming..." Within a few days Gregor was able to submit the first sketches, and Strauss telegraphed laconically: "Continue not Semiramis but Aphrodite." This really was a subject which greatly attracted him: a danced and sung contest between a voluptuous Aphrodite and a reserved, almost malicious Artemis, resulting from an experience of love. "Under Sodom and Gomorrha," in chaotic wartime days, joint work on the project began with the confrontation of the two goddesses in the second act. The musician was tireless in urging his wishes: the scene between Venus and Diana was to have a

446

"small core of comedy," a "very finely polished, somewhat satirical dialogue . . . no 'Biedermeierei': Wilde–not Gessner," a "dialogue of goddesses through suggestions, on which the orchestra comments . . ." "Please think over my fleeting ideas. I am waiting eagerly until a beautiful little comedy occurs to you, in which the figures are better interwoven than in your draft. I repeat: *one* great, witty principal scene: Mary and Elizabeth– everything else introduction and coda . . ."

Occasional work on "Venus and Adonis" or "Die Rache der Aphrodite" can be traced as far as the beginning of 1946. Strauss had asked for a second version of the text, but owing to the chaotic postal connections during those post-war days Gregor could not be sure whether Strauss had received the text as far as the lament of Adonis in the third scene . . . The original idea of a short companion piece to "Friedenstag" had long since given place to the bold plan of a renewal of the classical "tragédie-ballet," the sung ballet or danced opera . . . The aged master wanted to demonstrate his "audacity" once again in a "mythological ballet with soli and choruses." Nevertheless the "comedy without words" vanished from his field of vision just as it had appeared to him in a dream. Aphrodite remained dumb.

FAREWELL

Suddenly Strauss found his eightieth birthday upon him. Torn asunder by five years of a new devastating war, the world had undergone an enormous transformation. The dream of existence amid happiness, peace and beauty was shattered for the time being. A well-preserved life devoted to music, accompanied by triumphs and the glory of splendid premières, could no longer be isolated from an age which was shaking bourgeois life, long threatened, to its foundations. Since the world première of "Capriccio" in 1942 little had been heard of Strauss. Although his mind was still active, he was not spared the burdens of old age. Pain led more and more frequently to doubts and resignation; living in retirement at Garmisch and Vienna, he tried to make the best he could of the oppressive circumstances surrounding him. During that period he felt himself linked particularly closely with the Munich Opera, whose new productions conducted by Krauss, under the composer's eye, were authentic to the last degree, and were the "fulfilment of their creator's most sanguine dreams." In the sphere of active work Strauss, who considered himself by then the "last representative of the development of the world theatre in the realm of music," looked back to his youth. For his grandsons he made fresh manuscript copies of his three most popular tone poems "Don Juan," "Tod und Verklärung" and "Till" (the original manuscripts of which he had "handed over to the publisher unconcerned")–and the labour was "even a source of enjoyment" to him. There were also large-scale new works, the Second Horn Concerto, the choral Epilogue to "Daphne" and the Sonatina in F for wind . . . "I go on quietly working for myself (following Goethe's noble example)."

The aged composer felt the dissolution of the world he had

known in an almost bodily sense. Around his eightieth birthday he was able to enjoy a number of performances given in his honour by the Dresden and Vienna Operas. (He took his last farewell of Dresden, where he experienced an air-raid alarm in the Hotel Bellevue, with a strange sense of foreboding.) He was also able to record almost all his orchestral works on tape with the Vienna Philharmonic Orchestra, although only the recording of the "Sinfonia domestica" survived the war. Then, however, came the days in Salzburg which cast a blight on his spirit: Goebbels ordered the Festival to be abandoned, and he was convinced that "Die Liebe der Danae" would never again be heard in his lifetime ... Rudolf Hartmann, the producer of "Danae," has written about the atmosphere of those days at Salzburg, which remained vividly alive in the memories of all those who were present. "It was about a week before the memorable dress rehearsal (16th August 1944) when, shortly before the beginning of the orchestral rehearsal, Richard Strauss entered the darkened auditorium of the Festspielhaus and joined me at the producer's table as was his custom. He followed the course of the rehearsal with close attention, nodded from time to time in agreement with Clemens Krauss's corrections or indications to the performers, hummed a few notes, and occasionally made a characteristic remark. He particularly appreciated the performance of the scene with Jupiter and the four queens. However, by contrast to many similar meetings in Munich, Berlin and Vienna, all signs of his participation were overshadowed by deep seriousness; it had been announced that morning that under the pressure of external events the Festival was being abandoned, and that the work on 'Liebe der Danae' could be continued only up to the dress rehearsal ... Towards the end of the second scene Strauss stood up and went to a seat in the front row of the stalls. The silhouette of his striking head stood out, alone, against the light from the orchestra pit. The Vienna Philharmonic played the wonderful Interlude before the last scene with incomparable beauty ... motionless, lost in his own thoughts, he heard the final echoes of his splendid work ... Moments of profound silence passed after the last notes had died away. Then, visibly moved by what he had just experienced, Krauss summed up in a few sentences the significance of those last days in Salzburg. Then Strauss walked to the rail of the orchestra pit, raised his hands

450

in gratitude, and spoke to the Philharmonic in a voice choked with tears: 'Perhaps we'll meet again in a better world!' He was unable to say any more. All those present waited, tense with emotion, as I led him carefully out of the auditorium. A little while later, leaning on my arm, he walked back through Salzburg in bright sunlight. He pointed out the route he had in mind: 'Let's go that way, past my beloved Mozart!'. . ."

How deeply he felt the events of those days is shown by two letters. "Since the 1st September my life is at an end; it would have been best if the great geniuses of Olympus had called me to them on the 17th August!" he wrote to Hartmann, and under the influence of the same events he sent Tietjen this poignant message of despair: "This 16th August, with your Bayreuth 'Meistersinger,' marked the last flickering of the flame of German operatic culture. Since the 1st September the flower of German music, which had bloomed for two hundred years, has been withering away, its spirit has been caught up in the machine, and its crowning glory, German opera, cut off for ever; most of its homes are reduced to rubble and ashes, and some of those not destroyed are already degraded as cinemas (Vienna Städtische Oper). My life's work is in ruins; I shall never again hear my operas, which have attained a high level of artistic maturity in the past decades, and which I have been privileged to see performed with a rare degree of perfection by fine artistic ensembles, great conductors and producers, and masterly orchestras . . . In poor Munich the house in which I was born by the lovely Court Church of St. Michael has already been bombed. In short my life is at an end, and I can only wait with resignation until my blessed namesake calls me to him in the waltz heaven. During the past weeks, in order to pass the time without brooding on the worries and tribulations of these days, I have carried out a task which I long had in mind: I have taken the Rosenkavalier Waltzes, which have been so unjustly vulgarized, and whose poor arrangement by Singer always displeased me, and by adding the Introduction to the opera I have made a new piece for full orchestra with a longer, brilliant conclusion. It is to be my farewell to this beautiful world . . ."

This is the place to consider the remarkable document, already mentioned, which, in the farewell mood of those years, Strauss described as "a kind of testament: my artistic will," and in which he concerned himself with the "significance of opera and the future which I desire for it, particularly in Vienna, the cultural centre of Europe". In April 1945, fully conscious of the fact that the end of the war would mark the beginning of a new era for the world's opera houses, Strauss wrote a six-page letter to his close friend the conductor Karl Böhm, who had moved from Dresden to Vienna. It is certainly no "testament" in the sense that Strauss was here stating his last wishes for the whole future of opera, but his very subjective views and suggestions, which he recommended to future generations, using the example of Vienna. Who could resent the fact in this document Strauss dealt to a greater extent than usual with *his own* works?

In the first part of the letter Strauss gave "in lapidary style" an outline of the development of Western music. "German music was created by Johann Sebastian Bach. The birth of Mozartian melody is the revelation of the human soul sought by all philosophers. The orchestra, founded by Joseph Haydn, given a language of its own and perfected by Weber, Berlioz and Richard Wagner, rendered possible in music drama the supreme artistic achievements of the human spirit, as the highest pinnacle and completion of a 2000-year cultural development." Then Strauss expressed his ideas concerning a *National Opera* devoted solely to the great masterworks of the history of opera, supplemented by a second theatre with a more broadly popular repertoire. He wrote: "Just as the State has set up museums of the visual arts which contain only the greatest works of art of past ages, unmixed with works in lower categories and inferior quality, in order to meet the needs of art lovers, so, in view of the damaging effect of the present system of day-to-day repertory performances of opera, it should be recommended or demanded that cities such as Vienna, Berlin, Hamburg, Munich and Dresden should each have at least two opera houses for performances of works in different categories. The large theatre would house a permanent repertoire of the greatest works performed in a first-rate manner, and kept at the same level through regular rehearsals, by the best artists and orchestral players, who would not be hampered by having to perform inferior works for much of the time. It would not be necessary to have a performance every single day." Then followed a list of the works which would have to be performed in any such "opera museum, to which the educated world has the same right as it has to the Pinakothek, the Prado and the Louvre": five works by Gluck, five by Mozart, two by Verdi (strangely enough only "Simone Boccanegra" and "Aida"), two by Berlioz ("Benvenuto Cellini" and "The Trojans"), one each by Beethoven and Bizet, all the operas of Wagner (except "Parsifal," reserved for Bayreuth) and nine operas by Strauss; in addition, "for the sake of historical knowledge," certain "so-called grand operas dating from early in the last century" (Meyerbeer, Halévy) could be presented occasionally. For the smaller theatre Strauss compiled a more extensive list, set out alphabetically from Adam to Verdi, also containing Russian and Czech classical masterpieces, and more recent works by Pfitzner, Schillings, Korngold, Charpentier, Chabrier and other composers. Here, and in the third theatre, a "Volksoper," which should also be established if possible, "new works should be performed. They should be selected with great care, not merely for the prestige of giving world premières, and they should not place unnecessarily heavy burdens on those taking part." This "testament" differs in the English version which was published in 1950. In that second version the list of operas to be performed at the smaller theatre also includes works by Flotow, Rossini, Puccini, Saint-Saëns, Massenet and others, while "The Barber of Bagdad," "Hänsel and Gretel" and "Palestrina" are transferred to the opera museum. In contrast to the German text, the English version of the list of works for the smaller theatre contains none of Strauss's own stage works–he wanted to avoid naming works by living composers, and the number of his operas and ballets in the repertoire of the large theatre is here reduced to eight.

*

Strauss's feelings during the last months of the war were expressed in the moving lament of *"Metamorphosen."* While catastrophe swept irresistibly across Germany he wrote this "Study for 23 solo strings" in "an absent state of mind." (On the manuscript he worded the title "Studie für Streicher, 23stimmig.") This is a last-period spiritual utterance–but not, as the choice of the title derived from the aged Goethe would suggest, a piece of absolute music. Indeed, it is full of deep programmatic significance: grief at the loss of irreplaceable cultural riches destroyed by the most barbaric of all wars, German towns, architectural

453

"Metamorphosen"–extract from a sketch book (1944)

masterpieces and theatres. "Mourning for Munich" Strauss had written above a sketch for the work; others were headed by quotations from Goethe. In February 1945, shortly before he completed the actual composition, he heard the news of the destruction of the Lindenoper in Berlin and of Semper's theatre in Dresden, the building in which his best-known operas had received their first performances. A few weeks later, in March, he received the equally tragic news of the loss of the Vienna Opera. ("God protect my dear, beautiful Vienna!" he had written to Gregor a little earlier.) What a cry from a wounded heart was

454

this letter to the Viennese librettist: "I am inconsolable! The Goethe House, the most sacred place on earth, destroyed! My lovely Dresden–Weimar–Munich, all gone!" With a deep sense of pain Strauss completed the score of "Metamorphosen," in which, unusually among his works, minor keys predominate, at Garmisch three weeks before the end of the war. Despite the comparatively short time taken in its composition, the aged master had to struggle hard to complete the score as he wanted it, refusing to give even his intimate friends details of the purpose and nature of the new work. Nevertheless resignation is not the characteristic of this music. Even when prostrated by grief, Strauss made an affirmation of his love for the beauties of the world, sweet fulfilment and transfiguration, a living exhortation.

The work as a whole? A symphonic slow movement with a duration of almost half an hour; there had been nothing like that since Bruckner's Eighth Symphony and the torso of Mahler's uncompleted Tenth, and even from the formal point of view it was a remarkable document of the musical outlook of an eighty-year-old composer. Then again the fact that Strauss employed the strict modes of expression of the string orchestra used as a body of soloists was (apart from the Introduction to "Capriccio") a feature new to his works. Metamorphoses are transformations. In three inter-related movements, two Adagios flanking a more animated middle section, there is unfolded a broad symphonic tapestry based on three groups of themes, which are constantly subject to variation. While the slow, tensely elegiac sections are eloquent with impassioned sorrow, the Agitato episode is animated by living forces which present a challenge to apathy. The concluding section, in the tempo of the opening, is once again full of deeply moving tragedy. The real thematic backbone of this stream of blossoming polyphonic music is undoubtedly formed by the first four bars of the Funeral March in the "Eroica." The dotted rhythm of this Beethoven motif, with its brooding quality, appears in the violas and cellos until, like the sun breaking through clouds, it is borne aloft by a contrapuntal texture of growing complexity. Strauss surprised the admirers of this masterpiece of tonal substance by remarking that during its composition he was virtually unaware of following in Beethoven's footsteps. Only very slowly did the literal quotation from the "Eroica" fashion itself out of his second theme. Not until nine bars before the end is it played in unison by the lower instruments. It is not difficult to recognize as the source of this richly solemn euphony of string tone the voluptuous sweetness of certain episodes in "Zarathustra" ("Song of Belief"). In the warm, velvety sound of the strings we hear choice cadences and intoxicating harmonic echoes of "Ariadne." Who but Strauss could have created such a lyrical polyphony from the spiritual sphere of "Tristan," at the same time incorporating in the masterly workmanship of the tonal tapestry creative elements of his own? This music is really "symphonic," if by that term we are referring not to the traditional form but to a spiritual quality of the tonal structure not previously attained by Strauss. In his combination of inspired imagination and carefully considered formal technique there is something of the "remarkable German artistic spirit" which, in the words of Shaw, "began with Johann Sebastian Bach, and is still alive in Richard Strauss." He could not have expressed the "Memento mori," the "thought that you are mortal," more impressively in sound.

Strauss was in no hurry to introduce these "Metamorphosen" to the world, which was preoccupied with other things; he did not expect much of the work's outward effectiveness. "Ready for its first performance, if so desired," he wrote to Schuh. Then, in January 1946, he sent the score to the Collegium Musicum, Zürich, at the request of whose conductor Paul Sacher the work had been written. (It is, however, doubtful whether, as Herbert von Karajan believes, the restriction of the scoring to 23 solo strings was merely a concession to the small Zürich ensemble.) The plan for a private first performance in a house in Zürich was soon abandoned. A public concert was decided upon. Strauss attended the later rehearsals, and himself conducted parts of the final rehearsal. "He excelled in bringing out the main lines of development by means of powerful dynamic and tempo increases—an unforgettable experience for the conductor, the Collegium musicians and the few listeners who were present!" (Schuh). Strauss later dedicated the score, in gratitude, to his Swiss friends; he asked Gustave Samazeuilh to make a piano arrangement for him. Although leading conductors and orchestras still frequently pass the "Metamorphosen" by, blind to the significance of this late work, the world cherishes it as a particularly precious bequest.   *

Strauss was in Garmisch during the last days of the war. The "puffed-up frog Prussia, also known as Greater Germany" had been "burst." At the end of April American troops occupied the town. When they were about to enter his house the old man of eighty-one confronted them, saying in English "I am Richard Strauss, the composer of the 'Rosenkavalier'!" At that they left the house. Next day he wrote in his diary: "A total victory of the spirit over raw materialism." Johanna von Rauchenberger has given a moving account of how her brother listened to the announcement of the end of the war broadcast shortly afterwards by the Swiss Radio, and how, after listening to the "Eroica," he expressed his emotion in the words "And *yet* Beethoven was a German . . ." A few months later he wrote revealingly to Kippenberg: ". . . But one must be content to be still alive, if existence in poor ruined Germany can still be called life. The parallel with Athens after its destruction by Sulla is shattering. But Germany has fulfilled its last and highest cultural mission with the creation of German music, and I shall keep this thought in mind until I am called to my gods in Olympus–the 'religion of classicism' in my heart . . . I am now waiting for permission to enter Switzerland, where, for the sake of my wife's health, we want to spend the winter in the mild climate of Lugano . . ."

Faithful friends took Richard and Pauline Strauss to Switzerland in mid-October 1945–and in view of the more agreeable living conditions there the one winter became three and a half years. Baden-bei-Zürich, Ouchy and Pontresina were the first places of refuge. Later Strauss made the Palace Hotel in Montreux his asylum:". . . very well appointed but rather cut off from the world." He wrote: "My life's work was completed with 'Liebe der Danae' and 'Capriccio' "–but anyone who believed that he had finally laid down his pen was to learn that in fact he was still at work. During his years in Switzerland he wrote, in addition to the Last Songs, two new works of concerto type and the orchestral fantasias "Frau ohne Schatten" and "Josephslegende," both of which are clearly marked by the stylistic characteristics of his last period. Only in the cases of Goethe, Verdi or Titian can we find comparable creative power in ripe old age. "Wrist exercises" Strauss called his late instrumental and vocal works with a smile in 1945; "craftsmanlike study material for our worthy instrumentalists and self-sacrificing a cappella choruses–studio

457

work to prevent the wrist and mind from becoming too flabby" (to Schuh), and "A legacy without musical-historical significance" (to Kippenberg). "They are workshop labours intended to prevent my right wrist, freed from conducting, from going to sleep prematurely . . ." Almost all of them are still to be discovered by concert promoters.

During his last creative period it was believed that after so often proving his ability to direct his art along fresh channels, Strauss had found his way to a classical late style distinguished less by boldness of invention and in the use of tonal resources, than by the wise exploitation of all his creative experiences. His last works confirm this belief. The successful music dramatist and composer of weighty tone poems now returned to the writing of "unliterary" instrumental works which had no pretentions to be anything but beautiful and easily appreciated music. Strauss was therefore completing the circle back to the works of his youth. The characteristic features of this late style are easy to describe. They consist of a relaxed, transparent structure with a great reduction of the instrumental apparatus, which is used with new finesse. The themes, which in their strongly stylized character are sometimes of no great "weight," are of a slender and graceful lightness which is almost Mozartian. They stand out from a straightforward harmonic background and engage in virtuistic arabesques. Real symphonic development is excluded in favour of a naively joyous interplay of themes. All metaphysical and mystical elements which could point to a tragic relationship to events in the world around are banished from these last works "without musical-historical significance." The wisdom of old age has given them an aura of absolute serenity. ("Motto: very tender–Moonlight Sonata . . ." Strauss wrote in the letter dealing with his planned ballet-opera "Die Rache der Aphrodite.") Fierce ardour has given place to gentle warmth, the storms of springtime to autumnal mellowness. Passion has been turned into clarity, the prevailing shade being that of evening. "I want to spread joy." At the same time Strauss gave new expression to his love for various wind instruments, the oboe, clarinet and horn, whose particular tonal atmosphere he had been able to capture in a masterly manner throughout his whole career. It may be assumed that he would have written further concert works in his late manner if sufficient time had remained to him.

458

The succession of these last documents, which Strauss regarded as "occasional works," commences with the *Second Horn Concerto* in E♭ major of 1942. Strauss had composed his First Horn Concerto for his father at the age of seventeen, and he was seventy-eight when he wrote his second, in the same key. This work was written in the happy aftermath of the successful première of "Capriccio" in Munich, with the serene virtuosity of Strauss's late style. It has its basis in the character of the solo instrument, which he, his father's son, had mastered to a greater extent than almost any other composer, with luxuriant cantilenas and dazzling passage work. The orchestra plays a sometimes lively part in the proceedings. A bold, fanfare-like cadence for the soloist opens the work, as in the case of the First Concerto, and establishes the concerto character of the first movement, with its alternations between rapidly flowing and more tranquil passages, and its prominent use of the woodwind. The Andante into which it leads also uses the woodwind to create its mood of idyllic lyricism. It almost looks as though the composer temporarily forgot he was writing a horn concerto! The Finale, as so often in works of this character, is a vivacious, effervescent six-eight Rondo, which "has turned out very nicely," as Strauss wrote from Vienna to Viorica Ursuleac, telling her of the completion of the work. The whole piece is full of the cool serenity of old age.

"Je ne travaille pas, je m'amuse." Joy in relaxation also gave birth to the two *Sonatinas for 16 Wind Instruments*. Both undoubtedly originated in recollections of the Suite and Serenade which Strauss had written in his youth. Both belong in the sphere of private music making rather than on the concert platform, although considerable technical demands are made on the players. Both works are improvisatory as regards the sequence of movements: when writing them Strauss did not bother about an overall symphonic plan. (The title "Sinfonie für Bläser" chosen for the second of these pieces after Strauss's death is most unsuitable). The material is based not on real "themes" but on short "motifs," which are passed to and fro among the instruments only slightly varied, in rising and falling sequential patterns. Drawing on experiences gained from his early wind pieces, the eighty-year-old composer enlarged the group of wind instruments by the addition of a third clarinet, basset horn and bass clarinet. Strauss wrote the First Sonatina in F major, with the humorous

459

sub-title "From the workshop of an invalid," smiling beneath tears, while convalescing after an attack of influenza in the spring and summer of 1943. The first of the three movements to be written was the central one, the two-part "Romance and Minuet." This is artistically-formed, playful music full of southern clarity and animation–music which seems to be engraved, although sometimes with too small a needle. After the world première in Dresden Strauss determined that its performance during his lifetime was to be restricted "once and for all to the meritorious Tonkünstler-Verein." The Second Sonatina in E♭, "Merry Workshop," which was originally in one movement, is founded on the complete contrast between an Introduction from the harmonic realm of the lamenting Rhine Maidens of "Götterdämmerung" and an elastic, springy Allegro. (Strauss seems to have been very fond of this light-footed idea, which was to recur in a different rhythm as the Rondo theme of the Duet Concertino). Shortly after he had completed this single-movement piece, which he dedicated to the memory of Mozart, in January 1944, he decided to extend it to three movements, and later to four. Related melodic material, founded on a signal-like motif of a fourth, formed the basis of the balancing Allegro con brio, which clearly exceeded the structural proportions of the Sonatina. A year later, a few weeks after the end of the war, there followed an Andantino as a contemplative Intermezzo. But the form was to be extended still further. In the final version, which included a new Minuet, Strauss stood the Sonatina on its head: the original "Introduction and Allegro" was placed at the end of the work, and the original Finale became the opening movement. By contrast to the flanking movements the two inner movements are very short. Strauss was here remembering the rococo style of the wind music in "Le Bourgeois gentilhomme." Unfortunately the repeated additions to this Sonatina, which thus grew to a duration of forty minutes, extended it "beyond the bounds of form . . ." Shavings from the workshop of old age, without making any great claims–but intending to entertain.

The *Concerto for Oboe and Small Orchestra* dating from 1945, the first fruit of Strauss's stay in Switzerland, was the earliest of these works to make its way through the world's concert halls. It was the leading oboist of the Philadelphia Orchestra, stationed in Garmisch as an American soldier, who suggested to Strauss that he should write "a piece for oboe." Solo oboists must be grateful to Strauss for the brilliant, heart-refreshing work which he created for them in this neglected field. How well he understood how to exploit the technical and tonal characteristics of the oboe in virtuistic scale passages and witty leaps, and to make the instrument "sing!" Three interlinked movements create an Arcadian atmosphere of shimmering transparency. An orchestra, chosen for its delicate tonal balance (woodwind, two horns and strings), produces short episodes of polyphonic colour. From the introductory Allegro onward the themes of the solo oboe, often charmingly interwoven with flute and clarinet melodies, sound like a greeting to Mozart. The thematically widely-spun Andante depends wholly on the sweet tone of the oboe. The Rondo Finale is a thing of genuine buffo brio. With the Oboe Concerto Strauss overcame the heavy-heartedness of "Metamorphosen." These two works have in common a masterly command of form, and a predominance of spiritual elements over those of strong animation.

In the case of his last instrumental work, the *Duet Concertino* for clarinet and bassoon with string orchestra and harp, written at the end of 1947 for the small ensemble of Radio Svizzera Italiana, Strauss again seems to have been returning to an earlier project. In December 1885 Bülow, who was then on a concert tour in Russia, drew the young composer's attention to a posthumous Trio pathétique for piano, clarinet and bassoon by Michael Glinka, a copy of which had been sent to him by the composer's daughter. He wrote: "I will send it to you through a music dealer. Perhaps the combination of instruments will inspire you to something of your own. I have always found the ensemble of piano and wind instruments pleasing to the ear, and it seems to me that there might be something both possible and worthwhile to be done in this field ..." Strauss did in fact find renewed pleasure in the combination of two widely contrasting woodwind instruments against the fragrant background of a string orchestra. He enriched the accompaniment by separating a solo sextet from the main body of strings. Whole stretches of this charming work, whose three movements follow each other without a break, thus take on the character of chamber music. The balance of the soloists with each other and with the orchestra is skilfully managed. In the first of the three movements moder-

461

ate in tempo (Strauss was more meditative during his last years), the clarinet has the leading word, while in the second, a slow, lyrical monologue above whispers from the solo violin and harp, it is the bassoon. In the Finale, a Rondo of the most straightforward kind on a babbling six-eight theme, the two solo instruments are in complete accord. The whole work is marked by naive pleasure in music making and carefully planned economy, in which what is left out is almost more important than what is said.

The light and shadow of a lifetime devoted to music found their last noble expression in the four wonderful *Songs with Orchestra,* settings of poems by Eichendorff and Hermann Hesse. They are symbols in sound of the fulfilment of old age, and were published only after the composer's death. What a process of artistic purification and refinement there had been since the early songs with their striving after broad melodic and harmonic effects! This last-period lyricism created an exalted, crystalline world hovering between light and darkness. These songs, their composer's swan-song and a really perfect "last work," are full of a mellow, golden mood of farewell in the evening twilight. They are songs of life slipping away, sung sadly, yet full of confidence in what is to come. Their melody is no longer material, it is all flowing melisma, and soars on "free wings" (Hesse) above all material connections. The crown of these "Last Songs," with their serenity and radiant instrumentation, is "Im Abendrot," to verses by Eichendorff, which was composed separately from the rest of the group, and which was placed at the end of the cycle when they were published. The earliest sketches for this song are contained in a sketch book dating from the end of 1946 or the beginning of 1947. "Wie sind wir wandermüde–Ist das etwa der Tod?" are the final lines, and at the reference to death, like a tender recollection, the horn plays the principal theme of "Tod und Verklärung." Nevertheless it is noteworthy that Strauss did not end this song on a note of Schubertian melancholy, instead re-introducing, after the fateful question, the programmatic suggestion of larksong. Right to the end the gently jubilant trills of the piccolos, recalling the two birds soaring aloft into the evening sky earlier in the poem, "nachträumend in den Duft," shine out like a glitter of silver in the valley of death. The other songs are based on poems by Hesse, whose finely

462

atmospheric poetry an admirer of his art had given to Strauss. "Frühling," the first of the group, is a picture of springtime bathed in radiant light. "Beim Schlafengehen," placed at the beginning in many performances in accordance with a last wish of the composer, clothes a sense of leavetaking ("Nun der Tag mich müd gemacht") in a gently modulating melodic line which is carried further by the solo violin and the soprano voice–this is the most inspired piece in the sweetness of its melos. The last, "September," sings in an intimate, hope-seeking tone of the growing life of nature in the garden. It was in fact September when Strauss completed this song at Montreux–the same autumn month in which he died a year later. The final words of this legacy are:

> . . . sehnt sich nach Ruh,
> langsam tut er die großen,
> müdgewordenen Augen zu.
>
> . . . longing for peace,
> slowly he closes his great,
> wearied eyes.

*

There was much that was comforting in this epilogue, a farewell without bitterness. The four years in Switzerland were a time of retrospective meditation. Strauss was fully aware that he stood on the threshold of death, and he was ready for his call. As the grand old man put the finishing touches to his work at the end of (in his own words) an "eighty-year industrious, honourable and good German artistic life," he saw the dawning light of a better future. All accounts of his years in Switzerland emphasize his awareness of his age and his determination to complete his work with his mind still clear. (It is good to know that he was scarcely troubled by the shameful tragi-comedy of an attempt to start "Denazification" proceedings against him. In May 1948 he was finally declared to be outside the operation of these laws; what other outcome could there have been to the affair?). When, a few months before his death, Strauss borrowed from Schuh a copy of Grimm's classical book on Goethe, he marked the following passages, among others, as he read them: "The length of his

463

life was important; Goethe had a double lifetime, whose second half was so important for the completion of what was begun in the first half." Strauss made use of the time which remained to him. "Everyone lives until he–is exhausted! At least the great do," he had written in the diary of his journey to Greece and Egypt more than fifty years earlier ... Nothing could be more wretched than a comfortable man with no work–that thought of Goethe appealed to him. Indeed, throughout his lifetime, during which his essentially practical, craftsmanlike attitude to life had gradually changed to the wisdom of Goethe's old age, work always came first. Nevertheless his was now the life of a man alone, under no illusions about the fact that "his world" had been shattered. Few of his creative colleagues were still alive. After Hofmannsthal, Zweig had died in 1942; a man at odds with the times, he had been broken by his fate as an exile in far-off Brazil. ("Greetings to all my friends! I hope they may see the dawn. Being too impatient, I go before them," he wrote in his farewell letter). The last winter of the war saw the death of Rolland, whose fight for peace and progress Strauss had followed sympathetically. The eldest had outlived them.

He read a great deal, and read thoroughly–Goethe above all. "You find me at my favourite occupation–my favourite at the moment," he said when receiving a visitor at Garmisch. "I am reading Goethe, in the way that I have wanted to all my life–although writing down notes and composing operas has always prevented me from doing so. I am reading the whole of Goethe as he developed and as he finally became, not tasting here and there, every so often a passage from 'Faust,' 'Hermann and Dorothea' or 'Wilhelm Meister' as the fancy takes me, but thoroughly and systematically. I began with volume one, and now I have reached the Goethe of the Wetzlar period. Now that I am old myself I will be young again with Goethe and then once again old with him–in his way, with his eyes. For he was a man of the eye–he saw what I heard ..." Strauss certainly read a great deal, tirelessly in Wagner's "Opera and Drama," the "book of all books on music," and biographical works, and he loved conversations with stimulating companions. Discussions of the masterpieces of world literature were illuminated by his tireless mind –above all when they concerned the themes of his "creed: Mozartian melody as the purest revelation of the human spirit,

464

Dichter: Doch das Leid zu deuten
vermag sie allein.
Nie vermag es Musik
die ganze Tiefe
des Tragischen auszudrücken.
Dies ist allein
nur der Dichtkunst gegeben.

Comtesse: Das sagt Ihr jetzt,
in dem Augenblick,
wo ein Genie uns lehrt,
dass es eine musikalische
Tragödie gibt ?

Graf: Halt ! noch einen Schritt
und wir stehen vor dem Abgrund.
Schon stehen wir der "Oper"
Aug' in Aug' gegenüber.

"Capriccio"
A page of the libretto with manuscript improvements by the author and composer, and a page of the piano sketches (1940)

"Capriccio"
Final page of the score (1941)

and Wagner's operas, which he considered to represent the pinnacle of the development of Western culture" (Schuh). His thoughts constantly returned to his love of Hellenic civilization, to classical humanism as the basis of education. The manuscript of an essay "Art, artistic history, history," dating from 1945, unfortunately remained incomplete.

He watched pensively the first flickering of the re-kindled fire of German culture, the first signs of life from the opera companies in Dresden, Berlin and Munich. "I am very glad to hear from you that poor dear Dresden is making serious efforts to build up a worthy operatic life again ... I readily believe that the excellent Keilberth conducts 'Ariadne' splendidly; who are singing now? Are the Strauss old guard still at work? And is the wonderful orchestra still intact?", Strauss wrote to the author in July 1946. He always replied in the same sense to enquiries about "Danae," which was still unperformed: there was plenty of time for that. Fifteen other stage works were already available for every tolerably well-appointed theatre ... On occasion he would attend performances of his operas in Zürich, including "Ariadne" and "Arabella." He followed with evident sympathy the plans of his Dresden friend Alfred Reucker to realize, with wider aims, Wagner's idea of a "Zürich Festival Theatre" as the scene of exemplary productions of the works of both masters. The time was not yet ripe for a project of that nature, which had been born in another form as early as 1925 as the bold idea of a Strauss Festival Theatre in Athens, and which may eventually materialize at Garmisch. "Please tell Reucker, with heartfelt greetings," he wrote in the same letter to the author, "that I am exerting myself on behalf of our (Zürich) festival idea, but it isn't easy in the land of the kantönli, and the significance of serious operatic culture has not yet really impressed itself upon the people and the theatre bureaux ..."

In October 1947 the vigorous eighty-three-year-old composer surprised the world by undertaking a strenuous four-week visit to England. The initiative came from Strauss's old admirer Sir Thomas Beecham and the publisher Ernst Roth, who considered it advisable and even necessary to bring the German master, who was still regarded with scepticism in some quarters in England, in personal contact with the international world of music again. The plan of a concert performance of "Daphne" under the composer's direction was soon given up; instead "Elektra" was performed (though under Beecham). "I am very much looking forward to October!" wrote Strauss in May to Roth, who has written about this last journey in detail. "I am very pleased with Beecham's excellent plans. As regards programmes I will fall in with Beecham's wishes completely, he shall decide what he would like to conduct; in any case I'll gladly leave the brilliant 'Heldenleben' to him. I would most like to conduct the 'Alpensinfonie'...." The B.B.C., which took over the sponsorship of the entire Strauss month, wanted a new work, if possible the Oboe Concerto. But Strauss objected: "I won't make a ridiculous figure of myself, beating away in the air when half the audience cannot hear what is being played! I have nothing against the 'Rosenkavalier Waltzes' being included in the programme though, possibly 'Zarathustra' or the 'Alpensinfonie,' 'Salome's Dance,' 'Till Eulenspiegel,' 'Rosenkavalier Waltzes'." (He was referring to the so-called "First Waltz Sequence," published in 1946.) Later he wrote that he could "on no account remain in London for four weeks," then finally, from Pontresina in July: "As regards my stay in London, do whatever you think best."

So on a lovely autumn day, accompanied by friends, but not by his infirm wife, Strauss left by air for London. That same evening he heard an act of "Figaro" performed by the Vienna State Opera Company at Covent Garden. The old Strauss of the headlines, long since apparently forgotten, was lionized once again—at many events from the highly official reception to the press interview, borne with stoical equanimity. ("No hostile discord in the press, ceremonial reception and dinner of the Philharmonic Society—in short real pleasure.") Most of his words were extremely modest in tone. "I am only an unimportant man, standing, moreover, at a lost post, and having no more than a few inconsequential words to say in the last act of the drama," he told a newspaper reporter. When a young lady of the press asked him, as the last of her innumerable questions, "What are your plans for the future?" he replied: "Why, just to die!..." In the evenings, however, this "unimportant man" conducted two of the leading London orchestras, and met with receptions as tumultuous as ever. "Don Juan," "Burleske," "Sinfonia domestica" and "Rosenkavalier Waltzes"—that was the astonishingly full programme of the first festival concert which he conducted

466

in the vast Royal Albert Hall. On the second evening, however, he restricted himself to conducting "Till." When it was time for Strauss to go to the rostrum he remarked: "So now the old horse ambles out of his stable once again . . ." Still a devotee of great paintings, he spent the mornings in long visits to the London galleries. One more episode from Roth's account: "Strauss followed the rehearsal (under Beecham) tensely, and was satisfied with everything. However, during the trumpet fanfare at the beginning of 'Don Quixote,' after listening intently for some time, he turned to me with a look of despair, and asked: 'Did you hear the trumpets? I can't hear them any more' . . ." On the evening of the 1st November Strauss returned to Switzerland, in good health, and conscious that he had carried out a mission on behalf of a better Germany.

It had been like the last stretching up of a naturally healthy, leaf-bearing tree. During 1948 Strauss began to suffer from bodily ailments, and in December of that year (after caecum trouble) he had to undergo a complicated bladder operation in the Clinique Cécil, Lausanne. Pauline, too, was separated from her husband's sickbed by illness. "I am lying here convalescent. I am quite well, in the circumstances, but I ask myself why I am being called back into an existence in which I have outlived myself"–that was a tone new to Strauss, however serious the situation. He recovered only slowly, filling sleepless nights by studying classical chamber music, Beethoven's Second Symphony and, naturally, "Tristan." "Now I have got through a bladder operation, but there is no longer any skat for recreation," he wrote to Friedrich von Schuch. His burning desire was to return to his dear Garmisch, to his family, before his approaching 85th birthday. At the beginning of May he was finally able to begin the return journey with Pauline, after a stay in Zürich. Strauss, who had been made an honorary citizen of Austria in 1945, was home again. And his homeland was happy to have one of its greatest sons back.

A glance at the sketch books shows how Strauss occupied himself during the years in Switzerland. According to Schuh they are full of motifs, cadences, themes and studies of the most diverse kinds, including figuration and harmonization studies on a theme from Beethoven's String Quartet Op. 132. There are also sketches for a violin concerto, an old plan–with the solemn, Bruckner-like theme of a slow movement... Among the projects to which Strauss returned frequently from the beginning of 1945 onward was the plan for the "Aphrodite" ballet-opera, to an almost complete scenario by Gregor. However, work on the music had scarcely been begun when, in February 1947, it was dropped in favour of another idea. He wrote to Gregor that he had lost all desire to write a ballet, but that he would like to make the Ettal monastery, where his son and younger grandson had studied, the present of a school opera or play with music. A friend of children, as always, he wanted to write as simple a little work as possible, which would be sung and played by young people, his grandsons among them, at Ettal. What about a Hans Sachs piece? Gregor made counter-proposals: he referred to Wieland's tale about the donkey and his shadow in the "Geschichten der Abderiten," and drafted two scenarios entitled "Des Esels Schatten." "Eselsschatten excellent idea, singspiel form with songs, duets, witty spoken dialogue, possibly doggerel verse" Strauss cabled enthusiastically. A letter followed a few days later: "I am very pleased with your draft. I again recommend singspiel form: 'Entführung aus dem Serail,' Lortzing, with a great deal of dialogue, which would not burden the children as much as Straussian songs, duets etc., and above all a school orchestra, for which I have never been accustomed to write, and to whose primitive nature I would have to adapt myself (even a *good* pianist with a weaker string orchestra)... In the dialogue of the famous council meeting with the sycophantic speeches you can give free rein to your wit... Once again, I beg you, no opera text, no verses with 'Rhyme or I'll eat you!'... Little, very comic stanzas à la Wilhelm Busch. As though that were so simple, you'll reply—but the attempt must be made..." Gregor's reply raised practical questions: "Is there any way of making use of this work? In my first draft, a singspiel to be performed by boys, it would be something for the Vienna Boys' Choir, which could go all round the world. In the version as a prose comedy which you want that naturally wouldn't be possible. Please let me know, too, how long the 'Eselsschatten' should be. You wrote mentioning a school celebration, thus an hour at most... but we have already got to two and a half hours without intervals..." For six months Gregor did his best with the ironical, turbulent, mythological subject until Strauss, who was still not satisfied, acted

468

on a suggestion of Bernhard Paumgartner and transferred the work to the Viennese writer Hans Adler, who died in 1959. Strauss was delighted with the libretto which he soon received from Adler. The resulting contributions by the composer did not amount to much, but a few rough sketches and notes, a tenor aria and a chorus found among his effects are among the charming and tenderly human musical ideas of his old age. As his eighty-fifth birthday approached he returned to the impressions of childhood. (The same spirit is reflected in the "Recollections and Reflections," edited by Schuh and published in 1949). Already overshadowed by the threatening signs of a general deterioration of his condition, he noted down parts of a new Hesse setting, the choral work "Besinnung," which remained fragmentary: "Divine and eternal is the spirit . . ." It was to be in a clear, diatonic C major, with a fugal section in eight parts–the last music Strauss noted down, shortly before he left Montreux.

Strauss spent his last birthday among his family at Garmisch. His condition did not permit him to take part in the Strauss celebrations in Paris at the beginning of June, as he had intended, and he was also unable to conduct the "Domestica" at Wies-

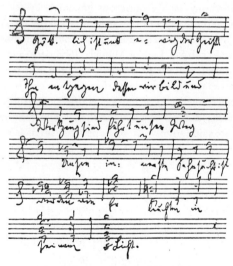

One of the last sketches: "Besinnung"
after Hermann Hesse (1949)

baden about that time. He wrote to his friend Gustave Samazeuilh: "After seventeen months of suffering the doctors declared me to be fully recovered a few days ago, and until the last
few hours I fully intended to come to the wonderful festival
which Paris wants to prepare for me. But cold reason finally won
the day ... The fact that the broadcast of 'Friedenstag' co-in-
cides with the Paris conference of foreign ministers is perhaps an
omen, and I regard it as a fine reward that my artistic vision
of 1938 is to mark the creation of a peace which will really make
the world happy in the city of light, Paris ..." On the eve of his
birthday, however, Strauss unexpectedly attended the dress
rehearsal of a new production of "Rosenkavalier" in Munich,
and asked to be allowed to conduct the Waltz Finale to the second act and the conclusion of the third. As he left the Prince
Regent Theatre, the chronicler relates that many people were
surprised to see not a weary, bent old man but an upright figure
walk firmly to the car. Scenes for a Richard Strauss film "A Life
for Music," of which unfortunately few copies exist, were also
shot at that time in Munich and Garmisch. The Presentation of
the Silver Rose was performed under the baton of its composer
once again. How beautiful it all was!

On the birthday itself Strauss was honoured by the Bavarian
government and the town of Garmisch-Partenkirchen. A tanagra
statuette, the creation of a Strauss Foundation, an honorary doctorate of the Faculty of Law of Munich University, and the deed
of his honorary freedom of Garmisch were the gifts presented to
him. (Unfortunately the excellent idea of a concert to be played
by an ensemble made up of musicians drawn from all the German orchestras did not come to fruition.) The recipient of all
these honours said in reply: "I am happy that it has been granted
to my wife and me to return, at least for the summer months, to
our old homeland, in the circle of my family and the enjoyment
of my own house and garden ... In hospitable Switzerland and
the mild air of Lake Geneva I was very well looked after, my
wife and I were freed from the cares of everyday life, and I was
in the fortunate position of being able to render some slight
assistance to my family and suffering fellow-countrymen, but I
was always conscious, with great grief, of the hard lot of my dear
native town, with which the most beautiful memories of my life
are inseparably linked ... Permit me," Strauss went on, address-

470

ing himself to the official representatives, "as a memento of this day on which I have been so greatly honoured, to present you with a modest answering gift, a little manuscript for the Bavarian State Library. It is the score of a Concert Waltz entitled 'München,' which I wrote some years ago for a film that never materialized. It has not been printed or performed, and can sleep on in a suitable spot. And once again a thousand thanks for all your goodness and friendship!" . . . The climax of the days of festivity in Munich was provided by a new production of "Le Bourgeois gentilhomme" with Strauss's delightful music. This fulfilled a cherished wish: ("It is a long time since I have enjoyed any performance as much as this. It's a pity that Hofmannsthal cannot see it too")–especially as the poet's name was at last mentioned beside that of Molière on the playbills. Strauss spent a most stimulating evening at the Gärtnerplatz Theatre–his last visit to a theatre! "How he expressed his thanks to those taking part, smiling and evidently moved from his place in the circle! –he was a phenomenon of vigour. Afterwards his car (unfortunately there were no horses to draw him away!) had difficulty in getting through the crowd of people still applauding him outside the theatre."

Eight days after his eighty-fifth birthday, influenced by the articles which had appeared in the press, Strauss wrote the "last notes" to which reference has been made earlier. This paper is concerned mainly with "Feuersnot," and reads: "In the biographical essays, a great many of which are reaching me, I miss almost everywhere a correct appreciation of 'Feuersnot,' including its libretto. It is forgotten that this undoubtedly imperfect work (imperfect especially in its all-too unbalanced handling of the orchestra), at the very beginning of the century, represented a new subjective style in the nature of the old opera, an upbeat! With Goethe, in particular, all literary historians search in almost every work and every sentence for relationships of the author's personality and experiences to the work, so why do people not see what is new in my works, how in them, as with Beethoven, the man is visible in the work?–this begins in the third act of 'Guntram' (renunciation of collectivism), 'Heldenleben,' 'Don Quixote,' 'Domestica'–and in 'Feuersnot' the tone of mockery, irony and protest against the opera texts of the time is the individualistic novelty. Hence the gay persiflage on Wagnerian diction; it was precisely on account of the not-to-be-deleted Address of Kunrad that the whole little non-opera was written! The affirmation of 'Intermezzo' and 'Capriccio' is what makes my dramatic works different from the general run of operas, masses and variations, in the direct succession from Beethoven, through Berlioz and Liszt. Music of the twentieth century. The Grecian German!"

Strauss was to leave Garmisch and raise his baton in Munich once more. On the 13th July his careful hands guided the Radio Orchestra in a performance of the Moonlight music from "Capriccio." He was not in the best of health, but when he spoke about art and new plans his mind was as lively as ever. During those July days the grand old man was still busy writing notes for discussions with the Munich Opera Director Alois Johannes Lippl and Rudolf Hartmann about the reconstruction of the Munich Opera. Strauss's dearest wish that his "master producer," to whom he had entrusted the artistic and technical training of his elder grandson, would return as head of the Munich Theatre, was not to be fulfilled until after his death ... His garden gave him pleasure, his beloved flower-bed. "They will still blossom when I am no longer here," he said as though to himself.

In the first days of August Strauss, who had often felt tired and giddy during the fatiguing weeks of his birthday celebrations, suffered from bouts of weakness which kept him in bed. Heart attacks led to a worsening of his condition. His life force was still unbroken, though, and his illness ran a fluctuating course ... Hartmann gave a moving account of his visit to Garmisch at the end of August, after Strauss had asked to see him. "... I enter the bedroom. In the room, which seems to be filled with light, the white bed stands with its head facing the doorway. Richard Strauss has turned his head a little, he reaches out his right hand to me and greets me: 'I am glad you've come. Sit down beside me.' While I bring the chair close to the bed I notice the large oxygen apparatus which stands nearby, ready for use, and I remember with a sinking feeling what I have just been told about the course of his illness during the past few days. He replies only with a slight, meaningful gesture to my carefully worded question about his health. As he remains silent I want to say something comforting to him, but in the emotional tension of the moment I cannot find the right words–he gives me a long

The handwriting of the eighty-five-year-old composer:
Last page of the draft of the address delivered at Garmisch
on the 11th June 1949

look, and I feel I must remain silent before the knowing expression of those bright, unclouded eyes. Then he says: 'Death has dealt me the first hard blow, given me the first sign.' Immediately after that his mood changes, however, and he asks about personal matters, showing his deep interest as always. His facial expression is scarcely altered, but the paleness and weariness of his features is something new. His thoughts pass to matters which have always concerned him. He lies there calmly, propped up fairly high, and his hands glide over the blanket in brief, emphatic gestures. I hear the deep, rather hoarse voice speaking about his ever-recurring concern for the future development of the European Theatre . . . 'So much for me to do still–but I believe that some of the seed I began to scatter has fallen on fertile soil . . .' I am afraid of over-tiring him, but he insists on saying what is in his mind: 'Who knows when we shall be able to talk together again?' A few deep, rather gasping breaths fill me with quickly-growing alarm . . . He is grief-stricken over the destruction of so many theatres, speaks about the interior and exterior reconstruction which has already been begun, and goes further and further into plans. He mentions people he would like to see in particular positions, surveys the possibilities of the major opera organizations still functioning, and concludes, smiling: 'We would have divided that world up quite well–our world.' Then he is silent for a long time, pursuing a train of thought which I can follow in an almost tangible sense. After a while he goes on quietly, in a very different tone of voice: 'Grüß mir die Welt' –my greeting to the world. He stops, asks 'Where does that come from?' I think at once of the similar words from 'Walküre,' and say so, but he shakes his head: 'No, no, it's not that, this phrase occurs somewhere else,' and repeats: 'Grüß mir die Welt.' He remains silent for a long time, I see that his face is showing signs of fatigue, and feel that it is time to leave him. Richard Strauss lies there quite peacefully . . . The time has come. I get up to take my leave. I turn hesitantly away. He again reaches out both hands to my right hand and holds me back: 'Perhaps we'll see each other again; if not, you know everything.' A last powerful grip, his hands release me, and I quickly leave the room. On my way out I hear Richard Strauss sob heavily, and then call loudly for his son . . ."

It might have been meant in a double sense, that "Grüß mir

die Welt" from the first act of his beloved "Tristan." Out there was the great and beautiful world which he had to leave, but that other little inner world remained behind . . . At the beginning of September, gravely ill, he dictated his last letters–that to François-Poncet (" . . . unfortunately I am ill") no longer bore his finely characteristic signature. He had periods of unconsciousness. At other times he would sit up in bed, lifting his arm as though to conduct ("Tristan?") . . . On the 8th September 1949, shortly after two in the afternoon, Richard Strauss died peacefully and without pain. The two doctors in attendance stated the cause of death to have been uraemia. The kidney stone, which it had not been possible to remove at the last serious operation owing to the patient's advanced age, had brought about a fatal infection of the urinary passages.

"Slowly he closed his great, wearied eyes . . ." During the afternoon the news of the great composer's death was flashed round the world–and that still troubled world of the early post-war years held its breath for a moment. Almost all radio stations altered their programmes that evening, the leading conductors and orchestras remembered Strauss. The family had a death mask prepared by an artist; it showed the countenance serene and relaxed, the features free from bitterness. In the afternoon of the 12th September, in accordance with Strauss's wishes, his body was cremated in Munich. Only a few of his closest friends were able to get there from long distances, but a great many of the people of Munich went to pay their last respects. In compliance with a wish which Strauss had expressed, the Trio from "Rosenkavalier," which he had loved so deeply, was performed once again–this time as a rapt farewell–by the same singers whom he had conducted face to face three months earlier: "I have vowed to love him in the right way." Pauline Strauss and the closest relatives accompanied the urn to Garmisch. There it was placed in the room where the master had died, not far from his garden, his mountains . . . State and city hastened to pay tribute to his memory in worthy ceremonies. Four weeks later, at Bayreuth, "Tod und Verklärung" and "Metamorphosen" blossomed in the rich, full tone of his Dresden Orchestra . . . "In memoriam," as Strauss had written, with a wealth of meaning, by the quotation from Beethoven at the end of the latter work–music which glows even at the moment of parting, and remains radiant.

APPENDIX

BRIEF BIOGRAPHY

1864 Richard Georg Strauss born at 6 a.m. on 11. 6. at Altheimer Eck 2, Munich. His parents are the principal horn player and "Hofmusikus" of the Court Orchestra Franz Joseph Strauss (b. 1822) and his second wife Josephine, née Pschorr (b. 1837).

1867 Sister Johanna born (9. 6.).

1868 Piano lessons with A. Tombo.

1870 First compositions (Schneider Polka, Christmas song). Elementary schooling (1870–1874).

1871 First opera visits with his mother to the Munich National Theatre ("Freischütz" and "Zauberflöte"). Father professor of the Akademie der Tonkunst.

1872 Violin instruction with B. Walter (1872–1882).

1874 Hofmannsthal born (1. 2.). Royal Ludwigsgymnasium Munich (1874–1882).

1875 Study of musical theory, composition and instrumentation with F. W. Meyer (1875–1880) and of piano pláying with A. Niest in Munich.

1881 Symphony in D minor (30. 3. Munich). Festmarsch published as Op. 1 by Breitkopf & Härtel.

1882 Study at Munich University (philosophy, aesthetics, art history, 1882/83). First visit to Bayreuth with his father (August). Wind Serenade (27. 11. Dresden) and Violin Concerto (5. 12. Vienna).

1883 Wagner died (13. 2.). First visits to Berlin and Dresden (19. 12. Cello Sonata, Tonkünstlerverein). Winter in Berlin (Leipziger Strasse 96).

1884 First meeting with Bülow. Summer in Feldafing near Munich. Debut as conductor at the Munich world première of the Wind Suite (18. 11). Symphony in F minor (13. 12. New York).

1885 Engaged as musical director, with Bülow, at Meiningen (1. 10.). From 1. 11. sole conductor of the Court Orchestra. Friendship with Ritter. Meeting with Brahms. Prize for Piano Quartet.

1886 Left Meiningen (1. 4.). First visit to Italy (Rome and Naples, April/May). Visit to Bayreuth ("Tristan" and "Parsifal," July). Engagement as third conductor at the Munich Court Opera (1. 8. 1886 until 31. 7. 1889). First opera conducted by him: "Jean de Paris."

1887 Visit to Bülow in Hamburg (January). World première of "Aus Italien" (2. 3. Munich) and of "Wandrers Sturmlied" (8. 3. Cologne). Acquaintance with Pauline de Ahna in Feldafing (August/ September). First meeting with Mahler in Leipzig (October). 2nd visit to Italy (2nd Symphony in Milan, December). "Ständchen."

1888 Visit to Italy (Lake Garda, Verona, Bologna, "Tristan," May/June.)

1889 Musical assistant at Bayreuth ("Parsifal"). Appointment as conductor at Weimar, with Lassen (1. 10. 1889 until June 1894). Rehearsed "Tannhäuser," "Lohengrin" etc., "Don Juan" (11. 11. Weimar). Father retired.

1890 Guest conductor of the Berlin Philharmonic Orchestra ("Don Juan," February). "Burleske" and "Tod und Verklärung" (21. 6. Eisenach ADMV Festival). "Macbeth" (13. 10. Weimar).

1891 Life endangered by severe inflammation of the lungs (May). Stay at Feldafing (June). Visit to Bayreuth ("Tannhäuser," with Pauline de Ahna as Elisabeth). Christmas with Cosima Wagner at Bayreuth.

1892 "Tristan" at Weimar (17. 1.). First meeting with Gerhart Hauptmann. Severe pleurisy and bronchitis (June). Feldafing (June/July). Trip to Greece and Egypt (beginning November) for the restoration of his health. Work on "Guntram."

1893 Egypt, Sicily, Corfu (until June). Summer at Marquartstein in Upper Bavaria, Villa de Ahna. World première of Humperdinck's "Hänsel und Gretel" (23. 12. Weimar, with Pauline de Ahna).

1894 Last meetings with Bülow in Hamburg and Berlin (January). Bülow's death (13. 2.). Engagement to Pauline de Ahna (10. 5. Weimar). "Guntram" (12. 5. Weimar, with Pauline as Freihild). First Bayreuth appearance as conductor: "Tannhäuser" (with Pauline as Elisabeth); orchestral rehearsals of "Tristan" and "Parsifal." Mozart cycle and "Tristan" in Munich (August). Married to Pauline de Ahna (10. 9. Weimar). Song volume ("Morgen," "Heimliche Aufforderung") for Pauline. Appointment as Court Conductor in Munich, at first with Levi (1. 10. 1894 until 1. 11. 1898). Residences in Munich: Hildegardstr. 2, later Herzog-Rudolf-Str. 2. Conductor of Munich Akademie concerts (Odeon) and of the Berlin Philharmonic Orchestra (1894/95).

1895 "Till Eulenspiegel" (5. 11. Cologne). "Guntram" in Munich (16. 11. with Pauline). Visits to Switzerland and Hungary (December).

The face of fulfilment
A picture taken in Garmisch a few weeks before Strauss's death

1896   Mozart and Wagner performances in Munich. Resignation of Levi. New contract as Court Conductor for two years. Holiday in Marquartstein (September). "Also sprach Zarathustra" (27. 11. Frankfort on Main). Concert tour to Russia (Moscow). Concerts in Düsseldorf (Niederrheinisches Musikfest), Brussels, Liège etc.

1897   Extensive concert tours to Amsterdam, Barcelona, Brussels and London. First time in Paris (Colonne concert with "Tod und Verklärung" and "Till," February). Son Franz Strauss born (12. 4.). "Der Arbeitsmann" (Dehmel).

1898   "Don Quixote" (8. 3. Cologne). Concerts in Zürich, Madrid, London, Prague, Amsterdam etc. Summer in Marquartstein. Departure from Munich: appointed for 10 years Royal Prussian Court Conductor at the Berlin Court Opera (at first with Muck, later also Blech, 11. 11. 1898 until autumn 1918). First Berlin residence: Knesebeckstr. 30. Foundation of the Genossenschaft deutscher Tonsetzer (jointly with Rösch and Sommer).

1899   "Heldenleben" (3. 3. Frankfurt on Main). First meeting with Rolland in Berlin (April). "Zarathustra" in Paris. "Tod und Verklärung" in London. Niederrheinisches Musikfest, Düsseldorf ("Heldenleben," May). "Ring" and "Fledermaus" at the Berlin Opera.

1900   First meeting with Hofmannsthal in Paris (Lamoureux concerts with "Don Quixote" and "Heldenleben," March). "Iphigénie en Tauride" (9. 6. Weimar). Summer in Marquartstein. Concerts in Brussels (October).

1901   First Strauss concert in Vienna (Kaim Orchestra, January). Visit to Spain (March). Tonkünstlerfest, Heidelberg (June); accepted chairmanship of ADMV (from F. Steinbach, until 1909). "Guntram" in Prague (October). Concerts with the Berlin Tonkünstler Orchestra, which he directs from October 1901 until Summer 1903. Concerts with the Berlin Philharmonic. First Dresden Strauss world première and collaboration with Schuch: "Feuersnot" (21. 11.).

1902   "Feuersnot" in Vienna (January, Mahler). Concerts in Amsterdam and Paris. Concert tour with the Berlin Tonkünstler Orchestra (southern Germany, Austria, Italy, southern France, Switzerland, February/March). Prater concerts in Vienna (June).

1903   Foundation of "AFMA." Strauss Festival in London (Amsterdam Concertgebouw Orchestra, June). Slight illness, convalescence on the Isle of Wight (June/July). Marquartstein (July/August). Honorary doctorate (Dr. phil.) of Heidelberg University. "Taillefer" (26. 10. Heidelberg). Concert visits to England and Poland (December). New Berlin residence: Joachimsthaler Str. 17.

1904 First concert tour of North America with his wife (35 orchestral concerts and lieder recitals, February/April). Strauss Festival in New York with the "Sinfonia domestica" (31. 3.). Tonkünstlerfest, Frankfurt on Main ("Domestica," 1. 6.). Summer in Marquartstein, 6th Swiss Tonkünstlerfest, Solothurn and Zürich, and 2nd Bavarian Music Festival, Regensburg ("Taillefer"). Visits to Holland, Poland and England (October/December).

1905 Concerts in London ("Domestica," February and April). 1st Alsace-Lorraine Music Festival, Strasbourg (May). Tonkünstlerfest, Graz ("Heldenleben," May/June). While there receives news of father's death (31. 5., lung complaint). Summer in Marquartstein. Order of the Crown, 3rd class. New edition of Berlioz's treatise on instrumentation. "Salome" (9. 12. Dresden).

1906 "Salome" in Prague, Berlin (5. 12.), Turin, Milan etc., "Domestica" in Paris (March). Tonkünstlerfest, Dresden ("Salome," June). First concert in Salzburg with the Vienna Philharmonic (Mozart, August). Summer in Marquartstein.

1907 He conducts six performances of "Salome" at the Paris Opéra (May). Officer of the Legion of Honour. Extensive tours in Italy, France, Holland etc. Cure at Bad Nauheim (June/July). Regular guest conductor of the Vienna Philharmonic (1907/08). Editor (for three months) of the periodical "Der Morgen."

1908 Concerts in Rome and Paris (February/March). Concert tour with the Berlin Philharmonic to France, Spain, Portugal, Italy and southern Germany (May). Accepts the conductorship of the symphony concerts of the Berlin Court Orchestra (following Weingartner) for ten years following the Pension Fund Concert (15. 5.; in force from autumn 1909 until 1920). Strauss week in Wiesbaden (August). Construction of the country house at Garmisch, Zoeppritzstr. 42 (architect: Emanuel Seidl). Move in in September. Completion of "Elektra." Appointed General Musical Director of the Berlin Court Opera (2. 10. 1908 until autumn 1918). Special leave from the Berlin Opera (October 1908 until 1. 9. 1909).

1909 1st Strauss week in Dresden with "Elektra" (25. 1.). "Elektra" in Berlin (15. 2.) and Vienna (24. 3.). Member of the Academy of Arts, Berlin. Tonkünstlerfest, Stuttgart (June): relinquishes chairmanship of the ADMV (successor Schillings); honorary director.

1910 "Elektra" in London, Prague, Budapest etc. Mother dies (16. 5.). Conducted Vienna Opera for the first time: "Elektra" (June). Strauss weeks in Frankfort on Main and Munich. Relinquishes conductorship of the Berlin Opera (1. 10.); from then on contract as regular guest conductor (some 25 opera performances and the concerts given in each season until 1918). Knight of the Order of Maximilian. New Berlin residence: Hohenzollernstr. 7. At St. Moritz for the New Year.

1911 "Rosenkavalier" (26. 1. Dresden); at Milan in March. Strauss weeks in Krefeld, Cologne and The Hague. Munich Festival ("Figaro" and "Tristan," August). "Rosenkavalier" in Berlin (14. 11.). First Strauss biography (Steinitzer).

1912 Strauss week in Stuttgart with "Ariadne auf Naxos" (25. 10.).

1913 Visit to Italy with Hofmannsthal (concert in Rome, spring). Munich Festival ("Ariadne," August). "Festliches Präludium" (19. 10. Vienna). "Deutsche Motette" (2. 12. Berlin). New Berlin residence: Heerstr. 2 (until 1917).

1914 Death of Schuch (10. 5.). "Josephslegende" in Paris (14. 5.) and London (June, both times Diaghilev). While returning home surprised by outbreak of war at S. Martino di Castrozzo. His money banked in London confiscated. To mark his 50th birthday plaque erected on his birthplace and Strauss-Strasse in Munich, honorary doctorate at Oxford.

1915 Schuch memorial concert in Dresden (7. 1.). Strauss week in Dresden (May). "Alpensinfonie" (28. 10. Berlin, Dresden Court Orchestra). Foundation of "GEMA."

1916 Honorary member of the Gesellschaft der Musikfreunde, Vienna. "Ariadne auf Naxos," 2nd version (4. 10. Vienna). "Till Eulenspiegel" as a ballet (23. 10. New York).

1917 Visit to Switzerland (February). Co-founder of the Salzburg Festival Association. Takes master class for composition at the Berlin Academy of Arts (until 1920). Conducts the 100th Dresden "Rosenkavalier" (13. 12.).

1918 700th concert of the Berlin Court Orchestra ("Don Quixote," March). "Bourgeois gentilhomme" (9. 4. Berlin). 1st Strauss week in Vienna (April). Conflict with Hülsen-Haeseler (May): departure from the Berlin Court Opera. Armistice, revolution: temporary director of the Berlin Opera (October until autumn 1919). "Salome" at the Vienna State Opera (October). Vienna "revolt" against Strauss.

1919 Appointment as opera director (with Schalk) at the Vienna State Opera (1. 12. 1919 until November 1924). Prior to that festive month "50 years of the Vienna Opera" (Zauberflöte," "Fidelio," "Tristan," May). "Frau ohne Schatten" (10. 10. Vienna and 22. 10. Dresden). Move to Vienna (Mozartplatz 4).

1920 Last concert as conductor of the Berlin Kapelle (formerly Court Orchestra–2. 3., successor Furtwängler). "Frau ohne Schatten" in Berlin (18. 4.). Festive month "Master performances of music in

Vienna" ("Così fan tutte," "Salome," "Elektra," May). First South American tour with the Vienna Philharmonic, together with Schalk (concerts, "Salome," "Elektra," August/November).

1921   "Josephslegende" in Berlin (4. 2.). Visit to Hungary and Rumania (March). 1st Donaueschingen Music Festival (Strauss-Esche, August). Biography by Specht.

1922   Visit to Hungary (March). Salzburg Festival ("Così fan tutte," "Don Giovanni," Mozart concert). Honorary member of the Salzburg Festival Association. Second and last concert tour of North America (New York Philharmonic and Philadelphia Orchestra, autumn). Publication of the correspondence with Hofmannsthal.

1923   "Couperin-Tanzsuite" (17. 2. Vienna). Honorary member of the Vienna Philharmonic. Second South American tour with the Vienna State Opera, Argentine and Brazil ("Salome," "Elektra," concerts, June/August).

1924   Marriage of Dr. Franz Strauss in Vienna (15. 1.). Visit to Italy ("Salome," Rome). Strauss Festival in Vienna on his 60th birthday with "Schlagobers" (9. 5.). Strauss weeks in Berlin, Munich, Dresden, Breslau etc. Honorary citizen of Vienna and Munich; Strauss-Platz in Dresden; honorary lectorship of the Musikhochschule Vienna; honorary director of the Salzburg Festival. "Ruinen von Athen" (20. 9. Vienna). Conflict with Schalk. Resignation as director of the Vienna Opera. "Bourgeois gentilhomme" (1. 10.). Move into the Belvedere-Schlössel (Jacquingasse, architect: Michael Rosenauer). "Schlagobers" in Breslau (9. 10.). Strauss week in Dresden with "Intermezzo" (4. 11.).

1925   Visits to Spain (February) and to Italy and Greece (October/November). Strauss week in Hamburg (April). Cure at Bad Nauheim (May). Munich Festival ("Così fan tutte" and "Tristan").

1926   Strauss weeks in Dresden ("Rosenkavalier" film, 9. 1.) and Leipzig. Visits to Greece and Karlsbad (June/July). Salzburg Festival ("Ariadne"). Reconciliation with the Vienna Opera ("Elektra," December).

1927   "Intermezzo" in Vienna (15. 1.). "Rosenkavalier" for the first time at the Paris Opéra (February). Strauss weeks in Dresden and Frankfort on Main. Strauss conducts the "Ninth" in Dresden on the 100th anniversary of Beethoven's death (27. 3.). Grandson Richard Strauss born (1. 11.).

1928   Cure at Karlsbad (May). "Ägyptische Helena" (6. 6. Dresden, Opera Festival). Strauss weeks with "Helena" in Vienna (June) and Berlin (November). "Tageszeiten" (21. 7. Vienna). Summer in Pontresina (August).

1929 Illness (April). Visit to Italy (May). Hofmannsthal dies (15. 7.). Munich Festival ("Figaro," "Così fan tutte" and "Tristan").

1930 Strauss week in Dresden (May). Cure at Karlsbad (August). Visit to Paris (September/October).

1931 Winter in Vienna. "Idomeneo" (16. 4. Vienna). Visit to Switzerland (July). Munich Festival ("Così fan tutte," concert).

1932 Strauss week in Munich (February). Grandson Christian Strauss born (27. 2.) Summer in Switzerland. Salzburg Festival ("Fidelio," two concerts).

1933 On the 50th anniversary of Wagner's death Strauss conducts "Tristan" in Dresden (13. 2.), and in the summer (for Toscanini) "Parsifal" at Bayreuth. "Arabella" (1. 7. Dresden, Opera Festival). "Ägyptische Helena," new version (14. 8. Salzburg). "Arabella" in Berlin (12. 10.). President of the Reichsmusikkammer (15. 11. 1933 until June 1935).

1934 Cure at Kissingen (April/May). 1st National Theatre Festival Week in Dresden with "Arabella" (May). Tonkünstlerfest in Wiesbaden (June). Foundation and presidency of the Permanent Council for the International "Zusammenarbeit der Komponisten" (June 1934 until 1945). 70th birthday in Dresden (special ceremony and "Rosenkavalier"), Strauss weeks in Berlin, Dresden, Vienna and Munich; honorary member of the Dresden State Opera, honorary citizen of Dresden. Radio cycle with "Guntram." Bayreuth: "Parsifal" again; declined Salzburg engagement. Music Festival in Venice (Vienna production of "Frau ohne Schatten," September). Concert in Amsterdam (December).

1935 Vienna "Ariadne" in Rome (March). Cure at Kissingen (May and September). "Schweigsame Frau" (24. 6. Dresden). Severe conflict with the Nazi regime (Zweig). Resignation as president of the Reichsmusikkammer (June, successor P. Raabe). First discussion with Gregor (July, Berchtesgaden). Strauss week in Munich (August). Dukas memorial concerts in Vichy and Paris (August/September).

1936 "Schweigsame Frau" in Milan (March) and Prague. Guest performances in Italy, Belgium and France (March/April). "Olympische Hymne" for Berlin (July). Munich Festival ("Don Giovanni," "Così fan tutte," concert). Cure at Baden-Baden and Kissingen autumn). Visit to London: "Ariadne" (Dresden State Opera) and concert of the Royal Philharmonic Society, whose Gold Medal he receives (November). Concerts in Rome (November).

1937   Visit to Italy and Sicily (March). Honorary member of the Vienna
       Konzerthaus-Gesellschaft. Beginning of the succession of model
       performances of the Krauss-Hartmann-Sievert era in Munich with
       "Salome" (18. 5.). Dresden Musical Festival ("Elektra," May).
       Strauss week in Frankfort on Main. Munich Festival ("Flying
       Dutchman," concert). Slight illness, cancelled Paris visit (World
       Fair, "Rosenkavalier" and "Ariadne," given under Krauss in Sep-
       tember). Winter in Italy (Merano, Florence, Rome, from October).
       Christmas at Taormina: completion of "Daphne."

1938   Italy (Taormina, Nervi, Rome, Merano, until April). 1st National
       Music Festival at Düsseldorf ("Festliches Präludium," "Arabella,"
       May). "Friedenstag" (24. 7. Munich, Festival). Cure at Baden bei
       Zürich (September). "Daphne" (15. 10. Dresden). Further journey
       to Italy (Milan, Merano, November).

1939   Cure at Kissingen (April/May). 75th birthday in Vienna (celebra-
       tion concert with "Domestica" and "Friedenstag," National
       Theatre Festival Week). Strauss weeks in Dresden (June, nine
       operas and two ballets), Vienna, Berlin and Munich ("Arabella",
       new version, 16. 7.). Gold Ring of Honour of Garmisch-Parten-
       kirchen. Salzburg: "Bourgeois gentilhomme." At outbreak of war
       cure at Baden bei Zürich (rheumatic complaint, August/September).
       100th "Salome" in Paris.

1940   Stay in Merano (March/April). "Daphne" in Vienna (25. 4.).
       "Helena" new version in Munich (15. 6.). "Guntram" new
       arrangement (29. 10. Weimar). Strauss cycle in Berlin (November).
       "Japanische Festmusik" (11. 12. Tokyo).

1941   "Verklungene Feste" (5. 4.) and "Daphne" (24. 5.) in Munich.
       Destruction of the Lindenoper, Berlin (9./10. 4.). Mozart festival
       week in Vienna with "Idomeneo" (December).

1942   Death of Zweig (22. 2.). Concert celebrating the centenary of the
       Vienna Philharmonic ("Alpensinfonie," 16. 4.). Week of contem-
       porary music in Vienna ("Daphne," May). "Guntram" in Berlin
       (13. 6. Krolloper). Salzburg Festival (Mozart concert). Cure at
       Baden bei Zürich (July). "Capriccio" (28. 10. Munich). Conducted
       at the Munich National Theatre for the last time: "Daphne"
       (20. 10.) Beethoven Prize of the city of Vienna (December). In-
       fluenza.

1943   Winter in Vienna. Salzburg Festival (Mozart concert). 2nd Horn
       Concerto (11. 8. Salzburg). Destruction of the Munich National
       Theatre (2. 10.), which he last visited for a performance of
       "Helena." Cure at Baden bei Zürich (October). Winter in Vienna.

1944 80th birthday in Vienna (celebrations with "Sinfonia domestica" and "Ariadne"). Strauss weeks in Dresden and Vienna: farewell to both cities (May/June). Honorary member of the Academy of Arts, Vienna. Tape recording of almost all orchestral works (Vienna Philharmonic, destroyed in 1945). "Liebe der Danae" (dress rehearsal 16. 8., Salzburg Festival). All German and Austrian theatres closed—"total war." Golden wedding (10. 9.). Death of Rolland (30. 12.).

1945 Destruction of the Lindenoper in Berlin (recently rebuilt) (3. 2.), Semper's Opera House in Dresden (13. 2.) and the Vienna Opera (March). "Artistic Testament" (April to Böhm). In Garmisch at end of war. Move to Switzerland (15. 10. Baden bei Zürich). First German Strauss performances after the war. "Ariadne" in Dresden (12. 10. Tonhalle).

1946 Living at Baden, Pontresina, Ouchy and Vitznau. "Metamorphosen" (25. 1. Zürich). Caecum operation (April). "Schweigsame Frau" again in Dresden (23. 11.).

1947 Pontresina, Lugano and Montreux. Last air trip to England (4. 10. until 1. 11.). Conducts two concerts of the Royal Philharmonic Orchestra and B.B.C. Symphony Orchestra in London ("Till," "Domestica" etc.). Gold Medal of the Royal Philharmonic Society. Bladder trouble begins (November).

1948 Montreux. "Metamorphosen" in Salzburg (Festival). Severe bladder operation (5. 12. Lausanne).

1949 Lausanne and Montreux. Slow recovery. Return with Pauline to Garmisch (10. 5.). 85th birthday: ceremony in Garmisch. Strauss Foundation of the city of Munich; honorary doctorate (Dr. phil.) of Munich University; honorary citizen of Garmisch and Bayreuth. On the previous evening, at the dress rehearsal of the new "Rosenkavalier" production at the Prince Regent Theatre, Munich, Strauss conducts the Waltz Finale of the second act and the conclusion of the third. "Bourgeois gentilhomme" his last theatre visit (13. 6. Gärtnerplatz Theatre, Munich). Shots for Strauss film: Presentation of the rose from "Rosenkavalier" Act 2 (Prince Regent Theatre). Farewell to Munich: Strauss conducts the Moonlight music from "Capriccio" for the Radio (13. 7.). Severe illness at the end of August. Strauss dies at 2.10. p.m. on the 8. 9. at Garmisch. Cremation in Munich (11. 9.). Urn placed in the room where he died. Memorial concert by the Philharmonic in Vienna (18. 9. Krauss; address by Gregor). "Frau ohne Schatten" in Buenos Aires (3. 10. Kleiber). Strauss memorial concert in the Bayreuth Festspielhaus (9. 10. Dresden State Orchestra, Keilberth).

1950   Death of Pauline Strauss (13. 5. Garmisch). Four Last Songs (22. 5. London). "Capriccio" at Salzburg (Böhm).

1951   Founding of the International Richard-Strauss-Gesellschaft (17. 8. Berlin).

1952   "Liebe der Danae" (14. 8. Salzburg Festival). "Danae" in Berlin (29. 10.) and Dresden (23. 12.).

1953   "Danae" in Milan and Paris (Vienna production).

1954   Death of Krauss (16. 5.). 90th anniversary of Strauss's birth marked by cycles of works in Dresden, Munich, Hamburg etc. Memorial exhibition in Munich. Strauss postage stamp. "Schweigsame Frau" in Berlin (30. 12. Komische Oper, Felsenstein).

1955   "Frau ohne Schatten" in the Vienna Opera Festival (opening of the new State Opera, October).

1956   First Strauss première in the new Deutsche Staatsoper, Berlin: "Frau ohne Schatten" (20. 10. Konwitschny). "Capriccio" in Berlin (7. 11. Städtische Oper).

1957   "Capriccio" in Paris (1. 3.).

1959   "Schweigsame Frau" in Salzburg (Festival). 10th anniversary of death: memorial concerts in Salzburg, Munich and Berlin (August/ September).

1960   Opening of the new Salzburg Festspielhaus with "Rosenkavalier" (26. 7.). "Rosenkavalier" film (Czinner, world première 1961). "Ariadne," "Intermezzo" and "Capriccio" in the new Cuvilliés-theater, Munich (Festival). Death of Gregor (12. 10.). 500th "Rosenkavalier" in Berlin (State Opera) and Vienna.

1962   Unveiling of the Strauss fountain by Hans Wimmer in Munich (24. 6.).

1963   Opening of the new Munich National Theatre with "Frau ohne Schatten" (21. 11., Keilberth).

1964   Worldwide Strauss centenary celebrations. Cycle of lesser-known operas in Munich (Keilberth-Hartmann).

LIST OF WORKS

Abbreviations of publishers

Atlantis	Atlantis A.G., Zürich
Bauer	Otto Bauer, Berlin
B & B	Bote & Bock, Berlin-Wiesbaden
B & H	Boosey & Hawkes Ltd., London-New York-Bonn
Br & Hä	Breitkopf & Härtel, Leipzig
Bruckmann	F. Bruckmann, Munich
Cassirer	Paul Cassirer, Berlin
Challier	C. A. Challier & Co., Berlin
Eulenburg	Edition Eulenburg K.G., Stuttgart
Forberg	Robert Forberg, Bad Godesberg
Fürstner	Fürstner Ltd., London
Heinrichshofen	Heinrichshofen, Wilhelmshaven
J & D	Juncker & Dünnhaupt, Berlin
Leuckart	F. E. C. Leuckart, Munich
Lienau	Robert Lienau, Berlin
Mosse	Mosse, Berlin
Oertel	Johannes Oertel, Munich
Peters	C. F. Peters, Leipzig
Rahter	D. Rahter, Hamburg-London
Rotapfel	Rotapfel, Zürich-Leipzig
Schott	B. Schott's Söhne, Mainz
Steingräber	Steingräber, Offenbach on Main
UE	Universal Edition A.G., Vienna-Zürich-London

Omitting the early, unpublished works

1876   Op. 1   *1st Festmarsch* for Orchestra in E♭
Composed 1876. 1st perf. 26. 3. 1881, Munich, "Wilde
Gung'l" under Franz Strauss.
Published Br & Hä (1881).
"Dedicated to his dear uncle, Herr Georg Pschorr."

489

1880   Op. 2   *String Quartet* in A (four movements)
                 1879/80. 1st perf. 1881, Munich, Walter Quartet.
                 Published UE. Duration 26 mins.
                 Dedicated to the Walter Quartet.

         –   *Chorus from the "Elektra"* of Sophocles (3rd choral
                 speech) with small orchestra
                 1880. 1st perf. 1880, Munich, Ludwigsgymnasium.
                 Published Br & Hä (Schmidt: "Hilfsbuch für den Unter-
                 richt im Gesang auf Höheren Schulen," 1902).

         –   *1st Symphony* for full orchestra in D minor (four move-
                 ments)
                 1880. 1st perf. 30. 3. 1881, Munich, Academy, Court
                 Orchestra under Levi.
                 Manuscript.

1881   –   *Festchor* with piano
                 1880/81. 1st perf. 1881, Munich, Ludwigsgymnasium.
                 Manuscript.

        Op. 3   *Five Piano Pieces*
                 1880/81. Published UE.

        Op. 5   *Piano Sonata* in B minor (four movements)
                 1880/81. Published UE.
                 Dedicated to Josef Giehrl.

1882   Op. 7   *Serenade for 13 Wind Instruments* in E♭ (one movement)
                 1881/82. 1st perf. 27. 11. 1882, Dresden, Tonkünstler-
                 verein, wind of the Court Orchestra under F. Wüllner.
                 Published UE. Duration 10 mins.
                 (Arrangements for piano solo and piano duet).
                 "To his respected teacher, Herr F. W. Meyer, Royal
                 Bavarian Court Capellmeister."

        Op. 8   *Concerto for Violin and Orchestra* in D minor (three
                 movements)
                 1881/82. 1st perf. 5. 12. 1882, Vienna, Benno Walter
                 and Strauss (version with piano).
                 Published UE. Duration 29 mins.
                 (Arrangement for violin and piano).
                 Dedicated to Benno Walter.

1883   Op. 6   *Sonata for Cello and Piano* in F (three movements)
                 1881/83. 1st perf. 8. 12. 1883, Nuremberg, Hans Wihan
                 and Hildegard von Königsthal.
                 Published UE. Duration 24 mins.
                 Dedicated to Hans Wihan.

490

Op. 10 *Eight Songs* from "Letzte Blätter" by Hermann von Gilm
for voice and piano
Zueignung; Nichts; Die Nacht; Die Georgine; Geduld;
Die Verschwiegenen; Die Zeitlose; Allerseelen.
1882/83. Published UE–B & H.
(Zueignung and Allerseelen orchestrated by R. Heger,
Zueignung also by Strauss–unpublished).
Dedicated to Heinrich Vogl.

Op. 11 *1st Concerto for Horn and Orchestra* in E♭ (three movements)
1882/83. 1st perf. 4. 3. 1885, Meiningen, Gustav Leinhos
with the Court Orchestra under Bülow.
Published UE. Duration 17 mins.
Dedicated to Oscar Franz.

– *Concert Overture* for Orchestra in C minor
1883. 1st perf. 28. 11. 1883, Munich, Academy, Court
Orchestra under Levi.
Manuscript.
Dedicated to Hermann Levi.

1884 – *Three Love Songs* for voice and piano
Rote Rosen (Stieler); Die erwachte Rose (Sallet); Be-
gegnung (Gruppe).
1883/84. Published Peters (New York) (1958).
Dedicated to Lotti Speyer.

Op. 9 *Fünf Stimmungsbilder* for Piano
Auf stillem Waldespfad; An einsamer Quelle; Intermezzo; Träumerei; Heidebild.
No. 1 originally composed as "First Albumblatt," No. 3
as "Albumblatt for Dora Wihan."
1883/84. Published UE.

Op. 12 *2nd Symphony* for full orchestra in F minor (four movements)
1883/84. 1st perf. 13. 12. 1884, New York, Philharmonic Society under Th. Thomas. 1st German perf.
13. 1. 1885, Cologne, Gürzenich, Städtisches Orchester
under Wüllner.
Published Peters. Duration 45 mins.
(Arrangement for piano duet).

Op. 13 *Quartet* for Piano, Violin, Viola and Cello in C minor
(four movements)
1883/84. 1st perf. 8. 12. 1885, Weimar, Halir Quartet
and Strauss (piano).

491

Awarded the 1st prize of the Berlin Tonkünstlerverein Competition 1885.
Published UE. Duration 38 mins.
Dedicated to Georg II of Sachsen-Meiningen.

Op. 4　*Suite for 13 Wind Instruments* in B♭ (four movements)
1883/84. 1st perf. 18. 11. 1884, Munich, wind of the Meiningen Court Orchestra under Strauss.
Published Leuckart (1911). Duration 25 mins.
(Arrangement for piano duet).

Op. 14　*"Wandrers Sturmlied"* (Goethe) for six-part chorus and full orchestra
1884. 1st perf. 8. 3. 1887, Cologne, Gürzenich, Städtisches Orchester and Chorus under Strauss.
Published UE. Duration 15 mins.
Dedicated to Franz Wüllner.

–　*Improvisations and Fugue* on an original theme for piano
1884. Manuscript (Improvisations); Fugue published Bruckmann, in Bie's "Das Klavier und seine Meister."
Dedicated to Hans von Bülow.

1885　–　*Cadenzas* to Mozart's Piano Concerto in C minor, K. 491
1885. 1st perf. 20. 10. 1885, Meiningen, Strauss (piano) with Court Orchestra.
Manuscript.

–　*"Schwäbische Erbschaft"* (F. Loewe) for four-part male chorus
1885. Published Leuckart (1950).

1886　–　*"Bardengesang"* (Klopstock) for male chorus and orchestra ("Herbei, herbei, wo der Kühnsten Wunde blutet" from the "Hermannsschlacht") (1st version).
For the performance at the Meiningen Court Theatre, 1886. 1st perf. January 1886, Meiningen, Court Theatre.
Manuscript.

–　*Burleske* for piano and orchestra in D minor (one movement)
1885/86. 1st perf. 21. 6. 1890, Eisenach, Tonkünstlerfest, Eugen d'Albert under Strauss.
Published Steingräber. Duration 17 mins.
Dedicated to Eugen d'Albert.

Op. 15　*Five Songs* for medium voice and piano
Madrigal (Michelangelo); Winternacht; Lob des Leidens; Dem Herzen ähnlich; Heimkehr (von Schack)
1884/86. Published Rahter–UE.

(Heimkehr orchestrated by L. Weniger).
Dedicated to Victoria Blank and Johanna Pschorr.

Op. 16   *"Aus Italien,"* symphonic fantasy for full orchestra in G
(four movements)
1886. 1st perf. 2. 3. 1887, Munich, Academy, Court Orchestra under Strauss.
Published Peters. Duration 47 mins.
(Arrangement for piano duet).
"Dedicated to Dr. Hans von Bülow with the most profound respect and gratitude."

1887   Op. 17   *Six Songs* after poems by F. von Schack for voice and
piano. Seitdem dein Aug'; Ständchen; Das Geheimnis;
Von dunklem Schleier umsponnen; Nur Mut; Barcarole
1887. Published Rahter–UE.
(Ständchen orchestrated by F. Mottl.)

Op. 22   *"Mädchenblumen,"* four poems by Felix Dahn for voice
and piano
Kornblumen; Mohnblumen; Efeu; Wasserrose
1886/87. Published Fürstner (Schott)–B & H.
Dedicated to Hans Giessen.

–   *Incidental Music to "Romeo and Juliet"* by Shakespeare
Four pieces, fanfares etc.; some of the texts not by
Shakespeare.
1887. 1st perf. 23. 10. 1887, Munich, National Theatre.
Manuscript.

Op. 19   *Six Songs* from "Lotosblättern" by F. von Schack for
voice and piano
Wozu noch; Breit über mein Haupt; Schön sind, doch
kalt die Himmelssterne; Wie sollten wir; Hoffen; Mein
Herz ist stumm
1887. Published UE– B & H.
Dedicated to Emilie Herzog.

1888   Op. 18   *Sonata for Violin and Piano* in E♭ (three movements)
1887/88. 1st perf. 3. 10. 1888, Elberfeld, Robert Heck-
mann and Julius Buths.
Published UE. Duration 27 mins.
Dedicated to his cousin Robert Pschorr.

Op. 21   *"Schlichte Weisen,"* five poems by Felix Dahn for voice
and piano
All' mein Gedanken; Du meines Herzens Krönelein;
Ach Lieb, ich muss nun scheiden; Ach weh mir unglückhaftem Mann; Die Frauen

493

1887/88. Published UE–B & H.

"To my dear sister (Johanna)."

Op. 23   *"Macbeth"* tone poem (after Shakespeare's drama), for full orchestra

First, rejected version.

1886/88. No performance.

Manuscript. Duration 18 mins.

(Arrangement for piano duet.)

Dedicated to Alexander Ritter.

1889   Op. 20   *"Don Juan,"* tone poem (after Nikolaus Lenau) for full orchestra

1887/89. 1st perf. 11. 11. 1889, Weimar, Court Orchestra under Strauss.

Used as a ballet by F. Ashton, 1st perf. 25. 11. 1948, London, Covent Garden Opera (Sadler's Wells Ballet Co.).

Published Peters. Duration 17 mins.

Dedicated to Ludwig Thuille.

Op. 24   *"Tod und Verklärung,"* tone poem for full orchestra

1888/89. 1st perf. 21. 6. 1890, Eisenach, Tonkünstlerfest under Strauss.

Published Peters. Duration 24 mins.

Dedicated to Friedrich Rösch.

–   *Scherzquartett* for male voices: "Utan svafvel och fosfor"

1889. Manuscript.

–   *2nd Festmarsch* in C for orchestra

1889. 1st perf. 1889, Munich, "Wilde Gung'l."

Manuscript.

For the 25th anniversary of the "Wilde Gung'l."

1890   –   *"Iphigénie en Tauride"*

Opera in three acts by Christoph Willibald Gluck

Newly translated and arranged for the German stage.

Extension of the conclusion: Trio for Iphigenie, Orestes and Pylades.

1890. 1st perf. 9. 6. 1900, Weimar. Court Theatre under Krzyzonorski.

Published Fürstner (Schott)–B & H.

(Op. 23) *"Macbeth"* tone poem (after Shakespeare's drama), for full orchestra (2nd version).

1889/90. 1st perf. 13. 10. 1890, Weimar, Court Orchestra under Strauss.

494

Published Peters. Duration 18 mins.
Dedicated to Alexander Ritter.

1892 –   *Festmusik* for full orchestra
        Composed to accompany tableaux vivants on the occasion of the golden wedding of the Grand Duke and Duchess of Weimar.
        Two pieces ("Bernhard von Weimar in der Schlacht bei Lützen" and "Begegnung und Friedensschluss zwischen Oranien und Spinola"), together with a melodrama. Battle music used in the "Rosenkavalier" film, 1925. The two orchestral pieces were performed as "Kampf und Sieg" on the 3. 2. 1931 at the 8th Vienna Philharmonic Ball, and were published by Heinrichshofen in 1940.
        1892. 1st perf. 8. 10. 1892, Weimar, Court Orchestra under Strauss.

1893 Op. 25 *"Guntram"*
        In three acts. Poem and music by Strauss
        1887/93. 1st perf. 10. 5. 1894, Weimar, Court Theatre under Strauss.
        Published Fürstner (Schott)–B & H. Duration (without intervals) 3 hours 15 mins.
        "Dedicated to my dear parents."

      Op. 26 *Two Songs* after poems by N. Lenau for high voice and piano
        Frühlingsgedränge; O wärst du mein.
        1891/93. Published UE–B & H.
        Dedicated to Heinrich Zeller.

      –   *Two Pieces for Piano Quartet*
        Arabischer Tanz; Liebesliedchen
        1893. Manuscript.
        Dedicated to Georg Pschorr.

1894 Op. 27 *Four Songs* for high voice and piano
        Ruhe, meine Seele (Henckell); Cäcilie (Hart); Heimliche Aufforderung; Morgen (Mackay)
        1893/94. Published UE–B & H.
        (Cäcilie and Morgen orchestrated by Strauss, Heimliche Aufforderung by R. Heger).
        "To my beloved Pauline on the 10th September 1894."

1895 Op. 28 *"Till Eulenspiegels lustige Streiche,"* After the old rogue's tune–in Rondeau form–set for full orchestra

1894/95. 1st perf. 5. 11. 1895, Cologne, Gürzenich, Städtisches Orchester under Wüllner.
Arranged as a ballet by V. Nijinsky, 1st perf. 23. 10. 1916, New York, Manhattan Opera House.
Published Peters. Duration 18 mins.
Dedicated to Arthur Seidl.

Op. 29 *Three Songs* after poems by O. J. Bierbaum for high voice and piano
Traum durch die Dämmerung; Schlagende Herzen; Nachtgesang
1894/95. Published UE–B & H.
(Traum durch die Dämmerung orchestrated by R. Heger).
Dedicated to Eugen Gura.

1896 Op. 30 *"Also sprach Zarathustra,"* tone poem (freely after Friedrich Nietzsche) for full orchestra
1895/96. 1st perf. 27. 11. 1896, Frankfort on Main, Museum, Städtisches Orchester under Strauss.
Published Peters. Duration 33 mins.

Op. 31 *Four Songs* for voice and piano
Blauer Sommer; Wenn; Weißer Jasmin (Busse); Stiller Gang (Dehmel)
1896. Published Fürstner (Schott)–B & H. (Wenn already published in the Munich "Jugend," 1896).

– *"Wir beide wollen springen"* (Bierbaum) for voice and piano
1896. Manuscript.

Op. 32 *Five Songs* for voice and piano
Ich trage meine Minne (Henckell); Sehnsucht (Liliencron); Liebeshymnus; O süsser Mai (Henckell); Himmelsboten zu Liebchens Himmelsbett (Wunderhorn)
1896. Published UE–B & H.
(Ich trage meine Minne orchestrated by R. Heger, Liebeshymnus by Strauss).
"Dedicated to my beloved wife."

1897 Op. 33 *Four Songs* for voice and orchestra
Verführung (Mackay); Gesang der Apollopriesterin (von Bodman); Hymnus (author unknown, wrongly attributed to Schiller); Pilgers Morgenlied (Goethe)
1896/97. Published B & B.
(Arrangement for voice and piano).

496

Op. 34   *Two Songs* for 16-part mixed chorus a cappella
        Der Abend (Schiller); Hymne (Rückert)
        1897. Published UE.
        Dedicated to Julius Buths and Philipp Wolfrum.

–   *Hymne* for mixed chorus and orchestra "Licht, du ewiglich
        eines"
        For the opening of the Secession Art Exhibition in
        Munich.
        1897. 1st perf. 1. 6. 1897, Munich, Court Orchestra and
        Chorus under Strauss.
        Manuscript.

Op. 35   *"Don Quixote,"* (Introduzione, Tema con variazioni e
        Finale), fantastic variations on a theme of knightly char-
        acter for full orchestra
        1897. 1st perf. 8. 3. 1898, Cologne, Gürzenich, Städti-
        sches Orchester under Wüllner.
        Published Peters. Duration 35 mins.
        Dedicated to Joseph Dupont.

Op. 38   *"Enoch Arden"* (Tennyson), a melodrama for piano after
        the translation by A. Strodtmann
        Arrangement as a symphonic poem after the piano ver-
        sion by Adalbert Baranski (1958).
        1897. Published Forberg.
        Dedicated to Ernst von Possart.

1898   Op. 36   *Four Songs* for voice and piano
        Das Rosenband (Klopstock); Für fünfzehn Pfennig;
        Hat gesagt (Wunderhorn); Anbetung (Rückert)
        1898. Published UE–B & H.
        (Rosenband orchestrated).
        Dedicated to Marie Riemerschmid, née Hörburger, and
        Raoul Walter.

Op. 37   *Six Songs* for voice and piano
        Glückes genug; Ich liebe dich (Liliencron); Meinem
        Kinde (Falke); Mein Auge (Dehmel); Herr Lenz (von
        Bodman); Hochzeitlich Lied (Lindner)
        1897/98. Published UE–B & H.
        (Meinem Kinde and Mein Auge orchestrated.)
        "To my beloved wife on the 12th April."

Op. 39   *Five Songs* for voice and piano
        Leises Lied (Dehmel); Jung Hexenlied (Bierbaum); Der
        Arbeitsmann; Befreit; Lied an meinen Sohn (Dehmel)
        1897/98. Published Forberg.

(Arbeitsmann and Befreit orchestrated).
Dedicated to Fritz Sieger.

Op. 40　*"Ein Heldenleben,"* tone poem for full orchestra
1897/98. 1st perf. 3. 3. 1899, Frankfort on Main, Museum, Städtisches Orchester under Strauss.
Published Leuckart. Duration 40 mins.
(Reduced orchestration by G. E. Lessing, 1942.)
"Dedicated to Willem Mengelberg and the Concertgebouw Orchestra in Amsterdam."

1899　Op. 41　*Five Songs* for voice and piano
Wiegenlied (Dehmel); In der Campagna (Mackay); Am Ufer (Dehmel); Bruder Liederlich (Liliencron); Leise Lieder (Morgenstern)
1899. Published Leuckart–UE–B & H.
(Wiegenlied orchestrated).
"Dedicated to Frau Marie Rösch née Ritter in most cordial admiration."

Op. 42　*Two Male-Voice Choruses* from Herder's "Stimmen der Völker"
Liebe; Altdeutsches Schlachtlied
1899. Published Leuckart.

Op. 43　*Three Songs* after classical German poets for voice and piano
An Sie (Klopstock); Muttertändelei (Bürger); Die Ulme zu Hirsau (Uhland)
1899. Published Challier–UE.
(Muttertändelei orchestrated).
Dedicated to Ernestine Schumann-Heink.

Op. 44　*Zwei grössere Gesänge* for low voice with orchestra
Notturno (Dehmel); Nächtlicher Gang (Rückert)
1899. Published Forberg.
Dedicated to Anton van Roy and Karl Scheidemantel.

Op. 45　*Three Male-Voice Choruses* from Herder's "Stimmen der Völker"
Schlachtgesang (anon.); Lied der Freundschaft; Der Brauttanz (Dach)
1899. Published Fürstner (Schott)–B & H.
"Dedicated to my dear father."

–　　*"Das Schloss am Meer,"* melodrama after Uhland with piano
1899. Published Fürstner (Schott)–B & H (1911).

1900   Op. 46   *Five Songs* after poems by F. Rückert for voice and piano
Ein Obdach gegen Sturm; Gestern war ich Atlas; Die
sieben Siegel; Morgenrot; Ich sehe wie in einen Spiegel
1899/1900. Published Fürstner (Schott)–B & H.
"Dedicated to my dear parents-in-law."

Op. 47   *Five Songs* after poems by F. Uhland for voice and piano
Auf ein Kind; Des Dichters Abendgang; Rückleben;
Einkehr; Von den sieben Zechbrüdern
1900. Published Fürstner (Schott)–B & H.
(Dichters Abendgang orchestrated.)
Dedicated to J. G. Pflüger.

Op. 48   *Five Songs* for voice and piano
Freundliche Vision (Bierbaum); Ich schwebe; Kling;
Winterweihe; Winterliebe (Henckell)
1900. Published Fürstner (Schott)– B & H.
(Freundliche Vision, Winterweihe and Winterliebe
orchestrated).

1901   Op. 50   *"Feuersnot"*
A "Singgedicht" in one act by Ernst von Wolzogen
1900/01. 1st perf. 21. 11. 1901, Dresden, Court Opera
under Schuch.
Published Fürstner (Schott)–B & H. Duration 1 hour
25 mins.
"To my friend Friedrich Rösch."

Op. 49   *Eight Songs* for voice and piano
Waldseligkeit (Dehmel); In goldener Fülle (Renner);
Wiegenliedchen (Dehmel); Lied des Steinklopfers
(Henckell); Sie wissen's nicht (Panizza); Junggesellen-
schwur (Wunderhorn); Wer lieben will; Ach, was Kum-
mer, Qual und Schmerzen (Alsatian folk song book)
1900/01. Published Fürstner (Schott)–B & H.
(Waldseligkeit orchestrated).
Dedicated to Pauline Strauss, Ernst Kraus, Grete Kraus,
Konsul Simon, Walter Ende and A. von Stengel.

1903   Op. 52   *"Taillefer,"* ballad of Uhland for mixed chorus, soli and
orchestra
1902/03. 1st perf. 26. 10. 1903, Heidelberg, Music
Festival under Strauss.
Published Fürstner (Schott)–B & H. Duration 16 mins.
"Dedicated to the Philosophical Faculty of the University of Heidelberg."

Op. 53   *"Sinfonia domestica"* for full orchestra (one movement) 1902/03. 1st perf. 21. 3. 1904, New York, Strauss Festival, Wetzler Symphony Orchestra under Strauss. German première 1. 6. 1904, Frankfort on Main, Tonkünstlerfest, Museum, Städtisches Orchester under Strauss.
Published B & B. Duration 45 mins.
(Reduced orchestration by G. E. Lessing).
"Dedicated to my dear wife and our son."

1904 –   *Two Songs* from Calderón's "Richter von Zalamea" for mezzo-soprano or tenor and guitar or harp
Liebesliedchen; Lied der Chispa
Composed for a new production of the Calderón play at the Lessing Theatre, Berlin (Brahm).
1904. Probably not performed.
Strauss-Jahrbuch 1954 (Published B & H).

1905 Op. 54 *"Salome"*
Drama in one act after Oscár Wilde's poem of the same name in the German translation by Hedwig Lachmann 1903/05. 1st perf. 9. 12. 1905, Dresden, Court Opera under Schuch.
Published Fürstner (Schott)–B & H. Duration 1 hour 35 mins.
Dedicated to Edgar Speyer.

1906 Op. 51 *Two Songs* for low bass voice and orchestra
Das Tal (Uhland); Der Einsame (Heine)
1902 and 1906. Published Fürstner (Schott)–B & H.
No. 1 dedicated to Paul Knüpfer.

      Op. 55 *"Bardengesang"* (Klopstock) for three male choruses and orchestra ("Herbei, herbei, wo der Kühnsten Wunde blutet" from the "Hermannsschlacht")
1906. 1st perf. 6. 2. 1907, Dresden, Teachers' Choral Society and "Gewerbehauskapelle" under F. Brandes
Published Fürstner (Schott)–B & H. Duration 12 mins.
Dedicated to Gustav Wohlgemuth.

      Op. 56 *Six Songs* for voice and piano
Gefunden (Goethe); Blindenklage (Henckell); Im Spätboot (C. F. Meyer); Mit deinen blauen Augen; Frühlingsfeier; Die heiligen drei Könige (Heine)
1903/06. Published B & B–UE.
(Frühlingsfeier and Die heiligen drei Könige orchestrated).

"To my dear Pauline on the 8th August 1903" (No. 1)
and "Dedicated to my dear mother" (Nos. 2–6).

Op. 57   *Two Military Marches* for orchestra
Militärmarsch in E♭; Kriegsmarsch in C minor
1906. 1st perf. 6. 3. 1907, Berlin, Court Concert, Court
Orchestra under Strauss.
Published Peters.

–   *Six Folksong Arrangements* for male chorus a cappella
Christlicher Maien; Mißlungene; Tummele; Hüt' du
dich; Wächterlied; Kuckuck
1906. Published Peters (Folksong book for male choruses), three choruses also Leuckart (1952).

1908   Op. 58   *"Elektra"*
Tragedy in one act by Hugo von Hofmannsthal
1906/08. 1st perf. 25. 1. 1909, Dresden, Court Opera
under Schuch.
Published Fürstner (Schott)–B & H. Duration 1 hour
42 mins.
Dedicated to Willy and Natalie Levin.

1909   –   *Feierlicher Einzug der Ritter des Johanniterordens* for
three solo trumpets, twelve trumpets, four horns, four
trombones, two tubas and timpani
1909. Published Lienau–Fürstner (Schott)–B & H.
Arrangement for organ by M. Reger.

–   *Der Brandenburgsche Mars* (Presentation March) for
orchestra
1909. Published Fürstner (Schott)–B & H.

–   *Königsmarsch* for orchestra
1909. Published Fürstner (Schott)–B & H.
"Dedicated to H. M. the Emperor and King Wilhelm II
in deepest homage."

–   *Zwei Parademärsche* for the "Königsjäger zu Pferde"
Regiment and for cavalry
1909. Published Fürstner (Schott)–B & H.
Dedicated to Kaiser Wilhelm II.

–   *Soldatenlied* ("Wenn man beim Wein sitzt") by A. von Ko-
pisch for male chorus
1899. Published Bauer (1909).

1910   Op. 59   *"Der Rosenkavalier"*
Comedy for music in three acts by Hugo von Hofmannsthal

1909/10. 1st perf. 26. 1. 1911, Dresden, Court Opera
under Schuch.
Published Fürstner (Schott)–B & H. Duration (without
intervals) 2 hours 12 mins.
"Dedicated to my dear kinsfolk the Pschorr Family in
Munich."

1912 (Op. 59) *"Der Rosenkavalier,"* Waltz Sequence from Act 3 for
orchestra
Since 1944 entitled: Second Waltz Sequence (Act 3).
1912. Published Fürstner (Schott)–B & H. Duration
12 mins.

Op. 60 *"Ariadne auf Naxos"*
Opera in one act by Hugo von Hofmannsthal. To be
performed after Molière's "Le Bourgeois gentilhomme"
(incidental music)
1911/12. 1st perf. 25. 10. 1912, Stuttgart, Court Theatre
("Kleines Haus") under Strauss.
Published Fürstner (Schott)–B & H. Duration (opera)
1 hour 25 mins.
"Dedicated to Max Reinhardt in admiration and gratitude."

1913 Op. 61 *Festliches Präludium* for full orchestra and organ
For the opening of the Konzerthaus, Vienna
1913. 1st perf. 19. 10. 1913, Vienna, Konzertverein Orchestra under F. Löwe.
Published Fürstner (Schott)–B & H. Duration 12 mins.

Op. 62 *Deutsche Motette* for four solo voices and 16-part mixed
chorus a cappella after words by F. Rückert ("Die Schö-
pfung ist zur Ruh' gegangen").
1913, 1st perf. 2. 12. 1913, Berlin, Cathedral Choir
under H. Rüdel.
Published Fürstner (Schott)–B & H.
"Dedicated to Hugo Rüdel and the excellent Hof-
theater-Singechor in Berlin."

1914 – *Cantata* for male chorus a cappella ("Tüchtigen stellt das
schnelle Glück") by H. von Hofmannsthal
1914. Published J & D.
"For Nicolaus Count Seebach on his 20th anniversary
as Generalintendant of the Royal Saxon Court Theatre."

Op. 63 *"Josephslegende"*
Action in one act by Harry Count Kessler and Hugo
von Hofmannsthal

502

1912/14. 1st perf. 14. 5. 1914, Paris, Opéra, Ballets Russes (Diaghilev) under Strauss. German première 4. 2. 1921, Berlin, State Opera under Strauss.
Published Fürstner (Schott)–B & H. Duration 1 hour 5 mins.
Dedicated to Edouard Hermann.

1915   Op. 64   *Eine Alpensinfonie* for full orchestra and organ (one movement)
1911/15. 1st perf. 18. 10. 1915, Berlin, Dresden Court Orchestra under Strauss.
Published Leuckart. Duration 50 mins.
(Reduced orchestration without organ 1934.)
"Dedicated in gratitude to Count Nicolaus Seebach and the Royal Orchestra, Dresden."

1916   (Op. 60)   *"Ariadne auf Naxos"* (new version)
Opera in one act with a Prologue by Hugo von Hofmannsthal.
Prologue newly composed (40 mins). Minor changes in the Opera.
1915/16. 1st perf. 4. 10. 1916, Vienna, Court Opera under Schalk. German première 1. 11. 1916, Berlin, Court Opera under Blech.
Published Fürstner (Schott)–B & H. Duration 2 hours 5 mins.
Dedicated to Max Reinhardt.

1917   (Op. 60)   *"Le Bourgeois gentilhomme"* ("Der Bürger als Edelmann")
Comedy with dances by Molière. Free stage adaptation in three acts (by Hugo von Hofmannsthal). The original incidental music for the Molière play (extended to three acts) augmented by new pieces (Finale to Act 1, Courante, Turkish Music etc.).
1917. 1st perf. 9. 4. 1918, Berlin, Deutsches Theater (Reinhardt).
Published Fürstner (Schott)– B & H.

1918   Op. 65   *"Die Frau ohne Schatten"*
Opera in three acts by Hugo von Hofmannsthal
1914/18. 1st perf. 10. 10. 1919, Vienna, State Opera under Schalk. German première 22. 10. 1919, Dresden, Landesoper under F. Reiner.
Published Fürstner (Schott)–B & H. Duration 3 hours 21 mins.

Op. 66   *"Krämerspiegel,"* twelve songs after poems by Alfred
Kerr for voice and piano
Es war einmal ein Bock; Einst kam der Bock als Bote;
Es liebt einst ein Hase; Drei Masken; Hast du ein Ton-
gedicht vollbracht; O, lieber Künstler; Unser Feind;
Von Händlern wird die Kunst bedroht; Es war mal
eine Wanze; Die Künstler sind Schöpfer; Der Händler
und die Macher; O Schöpferschwarm
1918. Published Cassirer (de luxe edition of 120 copies,
signed by Strauss, with drawings by Fingesten, 1921)–
B & H (1959).
"Dedicated in light-hearted friendship to Dr. Friedrich Rösch."

Op. 67   *Six Songs* for voice and piano
"Lieder der Ophelia" (Shakespeare): Wie erkenn ich;
Guten Morgen; Sie trugen ihn. "Aus den Büchern des
Unmuts des Rendsch Nameh" (Goethe): Wer wird von
der Welt verlangen; Hab ich euch denn je geraten;
Wanderers Gemütsruhe.
1918. Published B & B.

Op. 68   *Six Songs* after poems by Clemens Brentano for high voice
and piano
An die Nacht; Ich wollt ein Sträußlein binden; Säusle,
liebe Myrte; Als mir dein Lied erklang; Amor; Lied
der Frauen
1918. Published Fürstner (Schott)–B & H.
Dedicated to Elisabeth Schumann.

Op. 69   *Five Little Songs* for voice and piano
Der Stern; Der Pokal; Einerlei (von Arnim); Waldes-
fahrt; Schlechtes Wetter (Heine)
1918. Published Fürstner (Schott)–B & H.

(Op. 60) *"Le Bourgeois gentilhomme,"* Orchestral Suite
Movements: Overture, Minuet, The Fencing Master,
Entry and Dance of the Tailors, Lully's Minuet, Cou-
rante, Entry of Cleonte, Prelude to Act 2, Intermezzo,
The Dinner
1918. 1st perf. 31. 1. 1920, Vienna, Philharmonic under
Strauss.
Ballet version first performed 1944, Monte Carlo,
Ballet Russe.
Published Leuckart. Duration 35 mins.

504

1919 –   *Sinnspruch* ("Alle Menschen groß und klein") by Goethe
for voice and piano
1919. Published Mosse (Almanac 1920).

1921 Op. 71 *Drei Hymnen* after poems by Hölderlin for high voice
and orchestra
Hymne an die Liebe; Rückkehr in die Heimat; Die
Liebe
1921. 1st perf. 1921, Berlin, Barbara Kemp with the
Philharmonic under G. Brecher.
Published Fürstner (Schott)–B & H.
Dedicated to Minnie Untermayr.

Op. 70 *"Schlagobers"*
Gay Viennese Ballet in two acts
1921/22. 1st perf. 9. 5. 1924, Vienna, State Opera
under Strauss. German première as "Gay Dance Play
in nine scenes" 9. 10. 1924, Breslau, Stadttheater under
Strauss.
Published Fürstner (Schott)–B & H. Duration 1 hour
30 mins.
Dedicated to Ludwig Karpath.

1923 –   *Tanzsuite* after keyboard pieces by François Couperin,
assembled and arranged for small orchestra (for ballet
and concert hall)
Movements: Pavane, Courante, Carillon, Sarabande,
Gavotte, Tourbillon, Allemande e Minuet, March
1922/23. 1st perf. of the Ballet 17. 2. 1923, Vienna,
State Opera, Hofburg (Redoutensaal) under Krauss.
1st perf. of the Concert Suite 21. 12. 1923, Dresden,
State Orchestra under Busch.
Published Leuckart. Duration 25 mins.

Op. 72 *"Intermezzo"*
A bourgeois comedy with symphonic interludes in two
acts 1918/23. 1st perf. 4. 11. 1924, Dresden, State Opera
(Schauspielhaus) under Busch.
Published Fürstner (Schott)–B & H. Duration 1 hour
55 mins.
"To my dear son Franz."

1924 –   *Hochzeitspräludium* for two wind instruments
Composed for the wedding of Dr. Franz and Alice
Strauss (15. 1. 1924, Vienna).
1924. "Neue Freie Presse," Vienna (1948).

505

—   *Wiener Philharmoniker-Fanfare* for brass instruments and
          timpani
          1924. 1st perf. Carnival Tuesday 1924. 1st Ball of the
          Vienna Philharmonic.
          Published B & H (1961).
          Dedicated to the Vienna Philharmonic.

—   *Fanfare* for wind instruments, for the opening of the Mu-
          sic Week of the city of Vienna
          1924. 1st perf. September 1924, Vienna, Rathaus tower.
          Published B & H (1961).

—   *"Die Ruinen von Athen"*
          A festival play with dances and choruses. Music, includ-
          ing parts of the ballet "Die Geschöpfe des Prometheus,"
          by Beethoven, newly edited and arranged by Hugo von
          Hofmannsthal and Strauss. Melodramatic scene newly
          composed.
          1924. 1st perf. 20. 9. 1924, Vienna, State Opera under
          Strauss.
          Published Fürstner (Schott)–B & H.

1925   Op. 73   *Parergon zur Sinfonia domestica* for piano (left hand) and
          orchestra
          "Exclusive property of Herr Paul Wittgenstein"
          1924/25. 1st perf. 16. 10. 1925, Dresden, Paul Wittgen-
          stein with the State Orchestra under Busch.
          Private print, published B & H (1950).

—   *"Durch allen Schall und Klang"* (Goethe) for voice and
          piano
          1925. Published Rotapfel ("Liber Amicorum Romain
          Rolland").
          Dedicated to Romain Rolland on his 60th birthday,
          29. 1. 1926.

(Op. 59)   *"Der Rosenkavalier,"* music to a film. Script: Hofmanns-
          thal; direction: Wiene; musical arrangement: Alwin
          and Singer.
          New musical number: Military March in F. Also parts
          of the Couperin-Tanzsuite and Schlachtmusik.
          1925. 1st perf. 10. 1. 1926, Dresden, State Opera,
          State Orchestra under Strauss.
          Manuscript. Military March published Fürstner.

1927   Op. 74   *"Panathenäenzug,"* Symphonic Etudes in the form of a
          Passacaglia for piano (left hand) and orchestra
          "Exclusive property of Herr Paul Wittgenstein"

1926/27. 1st perf. 11. 3. 1928, Vienna, Paul Wittgenstein with the Philharmonic under Schalk.
Private print, published B & H (1950). Duration
20 mins.

Op. 75 *"Die ägyptische Helena"*
Opera in two acts by Hugo von Hofmannsthal
1924/27. 1st perf. 6. 6. 1928, Dresden, State Opera
under Busch.
Published Fürstner (Schott)–B & H. Duration 2 hours
10 mins.

1928 Op. 76 *"Die Tageszeiten,"* a song cycle after poems by Eichendorff for male chorus and orchestra
Der Morgen; Mittagsruh; Der Abend; Die Nacht
1928. 1st perf. 21. 7. 1928, Vienna, Schubert-Bund
under V. Keldorfer.
Published Leuckart.
"Dedicated to the Vienna Schubert-Bund and its conductor Victor Keldorfer" (for the Schubert centenary
celebrations).

Op. 77 *Fünf Gesänge des Orients* to poems by Hans Bethge
after excerpts from the "Hafiz" and "Chinese Flute"
for voice and piano
Ihre Augen; Schwung; Liebesgeschenke; Die Allmäch-
tige; Huldigung
1928. Published Leuckart.

1929 Op. 78 *"Austria,"* Austrian song by A. Wildgans for full orchestra and male chorus
1929. 1st perf. 20. 1. 1930, Vienna, Männergesangverein under F. Grossmann.
Published B & B.
Dedicated to the Vienna Männergesangverein.

1930 – *"Idomeneo"*
Opera seria in three acts by Wolfgang Amadeus Mozart.
Completely new arrangement by Strauss and Lothar
Wallerstein
New music: altered recitatives, orchestral interlude
(Act 2) and Grand Ensemble (Act 3).
1930. 1st perf. 16. 4. 1931, Vienna, State Opera under
Strauss.
Published Heinrichshofen.

507

1932   Op. 79   *"Arabella"*

Lyrical Comedy in three acts by Hugo von Hofmannsthal

1929/32. 1st perf. 1. 7. 1933, Dresden, State Opera under Krauss.

Published Fürstner (Schott)–B & H. Duration 2 hours 35 mins.

"Dedicated to my friends Alfred Reucker and Fritz Busch."

(Op. 70) *"Schlagobers,"* Orchestral Suite from the Ballet 1932

Published Fürstner (Schott)–B & H. Duration 25 mins.

1933   (Op. 75) *"Die ägyptische Helena"* (New version of the Vienna State Opera)

Opera in two acts by Hugo von Hofmannsthal

Dramaturgical simplification of the 2nd Act.

1932/33. 1st perf. 14. 8. 1933, Salzburg, Festspielhaus under Krauss.

Published Fürstner (Schott)–B & H. Duration 2 hours 5 mins.

–   *"Das Bächlein"* for voice with piano or orchestra

Poem incorrectly attributed to Goethe.

1933 (piano) and 1935 (orchestra, for Viorica Ursuleac).

Published UE (piano), manuscript (orchestra).

Published by B & H (1964) as Op. 88, together with the Weinheber Songs (1942).

1935   Op. 80   *"Die schweigsame Frau"*

Comic Opera in three acts. Freely adapted from Ben Jonson by Stefan Zweig

1932/35. 1st perf. 24. 6. 1935, Dresden, State Opera under Böhm.

Published Fürstner (Schott)–B & H. Duration 2 hours 55 mins.

–   *"Die Göttin im Putzzimmer"* (Rückert) for eight-part mixed chorus a cappella

–   *Four Songs* for bass voice and piano

Vom künftigen Alter (Rückert); Erschaffen und Beleben (Goethe); Und dann nicht mehr; Im Sonnenschein (Rückert).

1922 (Goethe Song) and 1929/35 (Rückert). Manuscript. No. 2 published Oertel (1951) as "Adam war ein Erdenkloß."

Dedicated to Michael Bohnen (No. 2).

Published by B & H (1964) as Op. 87.

1935. 1st perf. 2. 3. 1952, Vienna, State Opera Chorus
under Krauss.
Published B & H (1958).

–   *"Zugemessene Rhythmen"* (Goethe) for voice and piano
1935. Strauss-Jahrbuch 1954 (Published B & H).
"For Peter Raabe."

–   *Three Male-Voice Choruses* a cappella after poems by
Rückert
Vor den Türen; Traumlicht; Fröhlich im Maien
1935. Published Leuckart (1958).

1936 –   *"Olympische Hymne"* (R. Lubahn) for mixed chorus and
full orchestra
1936. 1st perf. July 1936, Berlin, Olympiad, opening
ceremony with massed choirs under Strauss.
Published Fürstner (Schott)–B & H. Duration 4 mins.
Arrangements for male chorus and for voice and piano.

Op. 81   *"Friedenstag"*
Opera in one act by Joseph Gregor
1935/36. 1st perf. 24. 7. 1938, Munich, State Opera
(National Theatre) under Krauss.
Published Schott–B & H. Duration 1 hour 20 mins.
"Dedicated to my friends Viorica Ursuleac and Cle-
mens Krauss."

1937 Op. 82   *"Daphne"*
Bucolic Tragedy in one act by Joseph Gregor
1936/37. 1st perf. 15. 10. 1938, Dresden, State Opera
under Böhm.
Published Schott–B & H. Duration 1 hour 40 mins.
"Dedicated to my friend Dr. Karl Böhm."

1939 –   *"München"*
An occasional waltz for orchestra (1st version)
For a film about Munich which never materialized.
1938/39. Manuscript.
"To the Bavarian State Library as a memento of the
11th June 1949."

–   *"Durch Einsamkeiten"* (Wildgans) for male chorus a
cappella
1939. Manuscript.
For the Vienna Schubert-Bund on its 75th anniversary,
1. 4. 1939.

509

1940   (Op. 25) *"Guntram"* (new arrangement)

Action in three acts. Poem and music by Strauss.
Considerably shortened, and in part transposed.
1940. 1st perf. 29. 10. 1940, Weimar, National Theatre
under P. Sixt.
Published Fürstner (Schott)–B & H. Duration 1 hour
45 mins.

Op. 83   *"Die Liebe der Danae"*

"Heitere Mythologie" in three acts by Joseph Gregor,
using a draft by Hugo von Hofmannsthal
1938/40. 1st perf. 14. 8. 1952, Salzburg, Festspielhaus
under Krauss. German première 29. 10. 1952, Berlin,
Städtische Oper, under L. Ludwig. Dress rehearsal for
the cancelled world première in 1944 Salzburg, Festspielhaus, under Krauss, 16. 8. 1944.
Published Schott – B & H. Duration 2 hours 45 mins.
Symphonic Fragment for Orchestra arranged after
Strauss's death (14. 11. 1952, London, Vienna Philharmonic under Krauss).
"Dedicated to my friend Heinz Tietjen."

Op. 84   *Festmusik* for the celebration of the 2600th anniversary
of the Japanese Empire, for full orchestra
("Japanische Festmusik")
1940. 1st perf. 11. 12. 1940, Tokyo, United Symphony
Orchestra under H. Fellmer. European première January 1942, Vienna, Symphony Orchestra under Moralt.
Published Oertel. Duration 15 mins.

(Op. 68) *Six Songs* after poems by Brentano for high voice and
orchestra
Orchestral version of the songs with piano
1940. Published Fürstner (Schott) – B & H.

–   *"Verklungene Feste"*

Dance vision from two centuries. Music after F.
Couperin
Couperin-Tanzsuite augmented by six further pieces
1940. 1st perf. 5. 4. 1941, Munich, State Opera (Na-
tional Theatre) under Krauss.
Manuscript.

1941   Op. 85   *"Capriccio"*

A conversation piece for music in one act by Clemens
Krauss and Strauss

510

1940/41. 1st perf. 26. 10. 1942, Munich, State Opera (National Theatre) under Krauss.

Published Schott – B & H. Duration 2 hours 10 mins.

"Dedicated to my friend and colleague Clemens Krauss."

Op. 86   *Divertimento* for small orchestra after keyboard pieces by F. Couperin

The new pieces of "Verklungene Feste" augmented by two further numbers

1941. 1st perf. 31. 1. 1943, Vienna, Philharmonic under Krauss.

Published Oertel. Duration 40 mins.

1942 –   *Two Songs* after poems by J. Weinheber for voice and piano

St. Michael; Blick vom oberen Belvedere

1942. Published UE.

For Weinheber's 50th birthday, 9. 3. 1942.

Published by B & H (1964) as Op. 88, together with "Das Bächlein."

–   *2nd Concerto for Horn and Orchestra* in E♭ (three movements)

1942. 1st perf. 11. 8. 1943, Salzburg, Gottfried von Freiberg with the Vienna Philharmonic under Böhm.

Published B & H. Duration 25 mins.

–   *Xenion* ("Nichts vom Vergänglichen") by Goethe for voice and piano

1942. Strauss-Jahrbuch 1959 (Published B & H).

"To Gerhart Hauptmann, the great poet and revered friend, with heartfelt good wishes" on his 80th birthday.

1943 –   *Festmusik for the trumpeters of the city of Vienna*

1942/43. 1st perf. 9. 4. 1943, Vienna, Rathaus tower.

Manuscript.

–   *1st Sonatina for 16 Wind Instruments* in F (three movements)

"From the workshop of an invalid"

1943. 1st perf. 18. 6. 1944, Dresden, wind of the State Orchestra under K. Elmendorff.

Published B & H. (1952). Duration 20 mins.

For the 90th anniversary of the Dresden Tonkünstler-verein.

–   *"An den Baum Daphne"* (J. Gregor), Epilogue to "Daphne" for nine-part mixed chorus a cappella

511

1943. 1st perf. 5. 1. 1947, Vienna, State Opera Chorus and Boys' Choir of the Kantorei under F. Prohaska.
Published B & H (1958). Duration 15 mins.
Dedicated to the Konzertvereinigung of the Vienna State Opera Chorus on its 20th anniversary.

1944   (Op. 59) *"Der Rosenkavalier"*, First Waltz Sequence for orchestra (Acts 1 and 2)
Free symphonic version in the form of a "waltz impromptu" with new conclusion.
1944. 1st perf. 4. 8. 1946 London, London Philharmonic Orchestra under E. Leinsdorf.
Published Fürstner (Schott) – B & H (1947). Duration 12 mins.

1945   –   *"Metamorphosen,"* Study for 23 solo strings (in C minor)
1944/45. 1st perf. 25. 1. 1946, Zürich, Collegium Musicum under P. Sacher.
Published B & H. Duration 26 mins.
"Dedicated to Paul Sacher and the Collegium Musicum Zürich."

–   *2nd Sonatina for 16 Wind Instruments* in E♭ (Symphony for Wind Instruments) (four movements)
"Merry Workshop"
Originally conceived as a Sonatina in one movement (the present Finale).
1944/45. 1st perf. 25. 3. 1946, Winterthur, Musikkollegium, Stadtorchester under H. Scherchen.
Published B & H (1952). Duration 40 mins.
"To the divine Mozart at the end of a life filled with gratitude."

–   *"München,"* a Memorial Waltz for Orchestra (2nd version)
With a new section in the minor.
1945. 1st perf. 21. 3. 1951, Vienna, Symphony Orchestra under F. Lehmann.
Published Fürstner (Schott)–B & H (1951). Duration 9 mins.

–   *"Der Rosenkavalier,"* Suite for Orchestra
1945. Published B & H. Duration 22 mins.

1946   –   *Concerto for Oboe and Small Orchestra* (three movements)
1945/46. 1st perf. 26. 2. 1946, Zürich, Marcel Saillet with Tonhalle Orchestra under V. Andreae.
Published B & H. Duration 23 mins.

512

(Op. 65) *"Die Frau ohne Schatten,"* Fantasy for Orchestra
1946. 1st perf. 26. 6. 1947, Vienna, Symphony Orchestra under Böhm.
Published Fürstner (Schott)–B & H. Duration 19 mins.
Dedicated to Manfred von Mautner-Markhoff.

(Op. 85) *"Capriccio,"* Suite for Harpsichord (concert version)
1946. Manuscript.
For the Viennese harpsichordist Isolde Ahlgrimm.

1947 (Op. 63) *"Josephslegende,"* Symphonic Fragment for Orchestra
1947. 1st perf. March 1949, Cincinnati, Symphony Orchestra under Reiner.
Published Fürstner (Schott)–B & H. Duration 20 mins.

– *Duet Concertino* for Clarinet and Bassoon with String Orchestra and Harp (three movements)
1947. 1st perf. 4. 4. 1948, Lugano (Radio Monte Ceneri), Armando Basile and Bruno Bergamaschi with Orchestra della Radio Svizzera Italiana under O. Nussio.
Published B & H. Duration 20 mins.
Composed for Radio Lugano.

1948 – *"Im Abendrot"* (Eichendorff) for high voice and orchestra
1948 (6. 5.). 1st perf. 22. 5. 1950, London, Kirsten Flagstad with Philharmonia Orchestra under Furtwängler. German première 25. 9. 1950, Frankfurt on Main, Museum, Christel Goltz with Städtisches Orchester under B. Vondenhoff.
Published B & H. Duration 8 mins.
Dedicated to Ernst Roth.

– *Three Songs* after poems by Hermann Hesse for high voice and orchestra
Frühling; Beim Schlafengehen; September
1948 (20. 9.). 1st perf. 22. 5. 1950, London, Kirsten Flagstad with Philharmonia Orchestra under Furtwängler. German première 25. 9. 1950, Frankfurt on Main, Museum, Christel Goltz with Städtisches Orchester under B. Vondenhoff.
Published B & H. Duration 13 mins.
Dedicated to Dr. Willi Schuh and Frau, Adolf Jöhr and Maria Seery-Jeritza.
The last two works were published by B & H in 1950 in the order Frühling, September, Beim Schlafengehen and Im Abendrot, and are generally performed together;

recently, in accordance with a wish expressed by Strauss, they have frequently been given in the order: Beim Schlafengehen, September, Frühling and Im Abendrot.

*

Berlioz: Treatise on Instrumentation, new edition, augmented and revised (two parts)
1905. Published Peters.

Franz Strauss: Posthumous Works for Horn, edited by Strauss and Hugo Rüdel
1909/13. Published Eulenburg.

"Betrachtungen und Erinnerungen," edited by Willi Schuh
1949. Published Atlantis.
English version: "Recollections and Reflections"
Published B & H.

Guntram

Action in three acts. Poem and music by Richard Strauss

Op. 25

(New Arrangement 1940)

The Old Duke	Bass	Guntram	Heldentenor
Freihild	Dramatic Soprano	Friedhold	Bass
Duke Robert	Heldenbaritone	Fool	Tenor

12 smaller roles and chorus

Scene: Germany   Period: Middle of the 13th century

Orchestra: 92 players

3 flutes (3rd also piccolo), 3 oboes (3rd also cor anglais), 3 clarinets (3rd also bass clarinet), 3 bassoons, contra bassoon, 4 horns, 3 trumpets, bass trumpet, 2 trombones, bass trombone, bass tuba, timpani, percussion, 2 harps, lute, strings

Stage Music: 4 horns, 4 tenor horns, 4 trumpets, 3 trombones, 4 side drums

Completed: 5th September 1893, Marquartstein

"Dedicated to my dear parents"

1st perf.: 10. 5. 1894, Weimar, Court Theatre, under Strauss (conductor) and F. Wiedey (producer) with Pauline de Ahna (Freihild), Heinrich Zeller (Guntram), Schwar (Robert), Wiedey (Friedhold) and Karl Buchta (fool)

1st perf., new arrangement: 29. 10. 1940, Weimar, National Theatre under Paul Sixt, Rudolf Hesse and Moritz Schmidt

Next theatres: 1895 Munich, Prague (Deutsches Landestheater), Frankfort on Main; 1942 Berlin (State Opera Kroll)

Feuersnot

A "Singgedicht" in one act by Ernst von Wolzogen.
Music by Richard Strauss
Op. 50

Diemut	High young-dramatic Soprano	Ortolf	Bass
		Elsbeth	Mezzo-soprano
Kunrad	High Baritone	Wigelis	Contralto
Schweiker	Tenor	Margret	High Soprano

8 small roles and chorus

Scene: Munich   Time: Midsummer Day in mythical times

Orchestra: 73 players

3 flutes (3rd also piccolo), 3 oboes (2nd and 3rd also cor anglais), F clarinet (also bass clarinet), 2 A clarinets, 3 bassoons (3rd also contra bassoon), 4 horns, 3 trumpets, 3 trombones, bass tuba, timpani, percussion, 2 harps, strings

Stage Music: harp (ad lib.), glockenspiel (ad lib.), harmonium, solo violin, cello, 2 drums

Completed: 22nd May 1901, Berlin-Charlottenburg

"To my friend Friedrich Rösch"

1st perf.: 22. 11. 1901, Dresden, Court Opera under Ernst von Schuch, Maximilian Moris and Emil Rieck with Annie Krull (Diemut) and Karl Scheidemantel (Kunrad)

Next theatres: Frankfort on Main, Vienna (Court Opera), Bremen, Berlin (Court Opera); after 1945: Zürich, Munich (1958)

Salome

Drama in one act after Oscar Wilde's tragedy of the same name in the German translation by Hedwig Lachmann. Music by Richard Strauss
Op. 54

Herod	Heldentenor	Narraboth	Lyrical Tenor
Herodias	Dramatic Mezzo-soprano	Page	Alto
Salome	Soprano (Dramatic-Lyrical Soprano)	5 Jews	4 Tenors, Bass
		2 Nazarenes	Tenor, Bass
Jokanaan	Character Baritone	2 Soldiers	Basses

2 small roles—no chorus

Scene: Great terrace of   Time: Beginning of the
Herod's Palace   Christian era

516

Orchestra: 105 players

3 flutes, piccolo, 2 oboes, cor anglais, heckelphone, E♭ clarinet, 2 A clarinets, 2 B♭ clarinets, bass clarinet, 3 bassoons, contra bassoon, 6 horns,
4 trumpets, 4 trombones, bass tuba, timpani, percussion, xylophone,
glockenspiel, 2 harps, celesta, strings

Reduced version: 3 flutes (3rd also piccolo), 2 oboes, cor anglais, 2 A clarinets, bass clarinet, 3 bassoons, 4 horns, 3 trumpets, 3 trombones, bass tuba,
timpani, percussion, harp, celesta, strings

Stage Music: harmonium, organ

Completed: 10th June 1905

"To my friend Edgar Speyer"

1st perf.: 9. 12. 1905, Dresden, Court Opera under Ernst von Schuch,
Wilhelm Wirk and Emil Rieck with Marie Wittich (Salome), Irene von
Chavanne (Herodias), Karl Burrian (Herod), Carl Perron (Jokanaan) and
Rudolf Jäger (Narraboth)

Next theatres: Breslau, Prague (Deutsches Landestheater), Graz, Nuremberg, Leipzig, Cologne, Munich

Elektra

Tragedy in one act by Hugo von Hofmannsthal. Music by Richard Strauss

Op. 58

Klytemnestra	Dramatic Mezzo-soprano	Orestes	Heldenbaritone
Elektra	Dramatic Soprano	Aegisthus	Heldentenor
Chrysothemis	Dramatic Soprano	Tutor	Bass

10 small roles and chorus

Scene: Mycenae   Time: After the Trojan War

Orchestra: 111 players

3 flutes (3rd also piccolo), piccolo, 3 oboes (3rd also cor anglais), heckelphone, E♭clarinet, 4 B♭ clarinets (2 of them doubling A clarinets), 2 basset
horns, bass clarinet, 3 bassoons, contra bassoon, 4 horns, 2 B♭ tubas,
2 F tubas (also 5th-8th horns), 6 trumpets, bass trumpet, 3 trombones,
contrabass trombone, contrabass tuba, timpani, percussion, glockenspiel,
2 harps (4 if possible), celesta (ad lib.), violins and violas (3 groups of
each), cellos (2 groups), basses

Reduced version: 3 flutes, 2 oboes, cor anglais, 4 clarinets, 3 bassoons,
4 horns, 6 trumpets, 3 trombones, bass tuba, timpani, percussion, 2 harps,
strings

517

Completed: 22nd September 1908, Garmisch

"Dedicated to my friends Natalie and Willy Levin"

1st perf.: 25. 1. 1909, Dresden, Court Opera under Ernst von Schuch, Georg Toller and Emil Rieck with Annie Krull (Elektra), Margarethe Siems (Chrysothemis), Ernestine Schumann-Heink (Klytemnestra), Carl Perron (Orestes) and Johannes Sembach (Aegisthus)

Next theatres: New York, Munich, Berlin (Court Opera), Hamburg, Vienna (Court Opera), Milan

Der Rosenkavalier

Comedy for music in three acts by Hugo von Hofmannsthal.

Music by Richard Strauss

Op. 59

Marschallin	Dramatic Soprano	Valzacchi	Tenor buffo
Octavian	Mezzo-soprano	Annina	Alto
Baron Ochs	Bass	Singer	High Lyrical Tenor
Faninal	Character Baritone	Marianne	Soprano
Sophie	High Soprano		

20 small roles and chorus

Scene: Vienna   Time: In the first years of the reign of Maria Theresa

Orchestra: 93 players

3 flutes (3rd also piccolo), 3 oboes (3rd also cor anglais), 3 clarinets (in E♭, B♭ and A), basset horn (also bass clarinet), 3 bassoons (3rd also contra bassoon), 4 horns, 3 trumpets, 3 trombones, bass tuba, timpani, percussion, 2 harps, celesta, strings

Stage Music: 2 flutes, oboe, C clarinet, 2 B♭ clarinets, 2 bassoons, 2 horns, trumpet, side drum, piano, harmonium, string quintet (solo, or substantially doubled)

Completed: 26th September 1910, Garmisch

"Dedicated to my dear kinsfolk the Pschorr Family in Munich"

1st perf.: 26. 1. 1911, Dresden, Court Opera under Ernst von Schuch, Georg Toller (Max Reinhardt) and Alfred Roller with Margarethe Siems (Marschallin), Eva von der Osten (Octavian), Minnie Nast (Sophie), Carl Perron (Ochs), Karl Scheidemantel (Faninal) and Fritz Soot (Singer)

Next theatres: Nuremberg, Munich, Basel, Hamburg, Bremen, Frankfort on Main, Milan, Zürich, Prague

Ariadne auf Naxos

Opera in one act with a Prologue by Hugo von Hofmannsthal.

Music by Richard Strauss

Op. 60

(New version 1916)

Ariadne	Dramatic Soprano	Harlequin	Lyrical Baritone
Bacchus	Youthful Heldentenor	Scaramuccio	Tenor buffo
Zerbinetta	Coloratura Soprano	Truffaldino	Bass
Composer	Youthful-dramatic	Brighella	Tenor
	Soprano	Dancing Master	Tenor buffo
Naiad	High Soprano	Music Teacher	Character Baritone
Echo	Soprano	Major Domo	Speaking role

3 small roles—no chorus

Scene: In the house of a rich gentleman in Vienna   Time: End of the 17th century

Orchestra: 37 players

2 flutes (also piccolos), 2 oboes, 2 clarinets, 2 bassoons, 2 horns, trumpet, trombone, timpani, percussion, 2 harps, celesta, piano, harmonium, 6 violins, 4 violas, 4 cellos, 2 basses

Completed: 20th April 1912, Garmisch (1st version);

20th June 1916 (Prologue)

"Dedicated to Max Reinhardt in admiration and gratitude"

1st perf.: 25. 10. 1912, Stuttgart, Court Theatre (Kleines Haus) under Strauss, Max Reinhardt and Ernst Stern with Maria Jeritza (Ariadne), Margarethe Siems (Zerbinetta), Hermann Jadlowker (Bacchus) and Albin Swoboda (Harlequin)

1st perf. new version: 4. 10. 1916, Vienna, Court Opera under Franz Schalk, Erich Wymetal and Oscar Strnad with Maria Jeritza (Ariadne), Selma Kurz (Zerbinetta), Lotte Lehmann (Composer), A. von Környey (Bacchus) and Hans Duhan (Music Teacher and Harlequin)

German première: 1. 11. 1916, Berlin, Court Opera under Leo Blech

Next theatres: 1912 Dresden, Brunswick, Coburg, Munich, Berlin (Court Opera); 1916 Dresden, Munich

519

Josephslegende

Action in one act by Harry Count Kessler and Hugo von Hofmannsthal.

Music by Richard Strauss

Op. 63

Potiphar	Sulamith
Potiphar's Wife	Archangel
Joseph	

Scene: Egypt   Time: Period of the Pharaohs

Decor and costumes after the style of Veronese (1580)

Orchestra: 112 players

4 flutes (4th also piccolo), 4 oboes, heckelphone, 3 clarinets, bass clarinet, 3 bassoons, contra bassoon, 6 horns, 4 trumpets, 4 trombones, tuba, bass tuba, timpani, percussion, xylophone, 4 harps, 4 celestas, piano, organ, violins (three groups), violas (two groups), cellos, basses

Completed: 2nd February 1914, Berlin

"To my friend Edouard Hermann"

1st perf.: 14. 5. 1914, Paris, Opéra. Ballet Russe (Diaghilev) under Strauss, Michael Fokine and José Maria Sert–Léon Bakst with Maria Kusnetzova (Potiphar's Wife) and Leonid Massine (Joseph)

German première: 4. 2. 1921, Berlin, State Opera under Strauss, Heinrich Kröller and Emil Pirchan

Next theatres: 1914 London (Diaghilev); 1921 Munich, Vienna (State Opera), Dresden; after 1945: Berlin (Städtische Oper), Vienna, Munich

Die Frau ohne Schatten

Opera in three acts by Hugo von Hofmannsthal.

Music by Richard Strauss

Op. 65

Emperor	Youthful Heldentenor	Barak	Heldenbaritone
Empress	High Dramatic Soprano	His Wife	Dramatic Soprano
Nurse	Dramatic Mezzo-soprano	Spirit	
		Messenger	Bass-Baritone

10 small roles and chorus

Scene: A fairy-tale world   Time: Legendary

Orchestra: 107 players

2 flutes, 2 piccolos (also 3rd and 4th flutes), 2 oboes, cor anglais (also 3rd oboe), E♭ clarinet (also D clarinet), 2 B♭ clarinets, basset horn (also C clarinet), bass clarinet (also C clarinet), 3 bassoons, contra bassoon (also 4th bassoon), 4 horns, 2 F tubas, 2 B♭ tubas (also 5th–8th horns), 4 trumpets, 4 trombones, bass tuba, timpani, percussion, glockenspiel, 4 Chinese gongs, 2 harps, 2 celestas, glass harmonica, strings

Stage Music: 2 flutes, oboe, 2 C clarinets, bassoon, horn (to be played in the orchestra if necessary), 6 trumpets, 6 trombones, 4 tam-tams, organ

Completed: February 1918, Garmisch

1st perf.: 10. 10. 1919, Vienna, State Opera under Franz Schalk, Hans Breuer and Alfred Roller with Maria Jeritza (Empress), Lotte Lehmann (Barak's Wife), Lucy Weidt (Nurse), Aagard Oestvig (Emperor), Richard Mayr (Barak) and Josef von Manowarda (Messenger)

German première: 22. 10. 1919, Dresden, Landesoper under Fritz Reiner, Alexander d'Arnals and Alfred Roller

Next theatres: Munich, Berlin (State Opera), Stuttgart; after 1945: Bielefeld, Munich, Stuttgart, Berlin (State Opera)

Schlagobers

Gay Viennese Ballet in two acts by Richard Strauss

Op. 70

Prince Nicolo	Prince Cocoa	Ladislav Slivovitz
Princess Praliné	Prince Coffee	Mlle. Marianne Chartreuse
Don Zucchero	Princess Teablossom	Boris Vutki

Scene: A Viennese Confectioner's Shop

Orchestra: 93 players

3 flutes, piccolo (also 4th flute), 3 oboes, 3 clarinets, bass clarinet, 3 bassoons, contra bassoon, 4 horns, 3 trumpets, 3 trombones, bass tuba, timpani, percussion, 2 harps, celesta, strings

Completed: 16th October 1922, Garmisch

"To my friend Ludwig Karpath"

1st perf.: 9. 5. 1924, Vienna, State Opera under Strauss, Heinrich Kröller and Ada Nigrin

German première: 9. 10. 1924, Breslau, Stadttheater under Strauss

521

Intermezzo

A Bourgeois Comedy with Symphonic Interludes in two acts by
Richard Strauss

Op. 72

Christine	Youthful-dramatic Soprano	Conductor	Tenor buffo
Storch	Character Baritone	Kommerzienrat	Bass buffo
Anna	Soubrette	Justizrat	Bass
Baron Lummer	Lyrical Tenor	Chamber Singer	Bass

4 small roles–no chorus

Scene: Grundlsee and Vienna   Time: The Present (1907)

Orchestra: 53 players

2 flutes (2nd also piccolo), 2 oboes (2nd also cor anglais), 2 clarinets (2nd
also bass clarinet), 2 bassoons, 3 horns, 2 trumpets, 2 trombones, timpani,
percussion, harp, piano, harmonium, strings

Completed: 21st August 1923, Buenos Aires

"To my dear son Franz"

1st perf.: 4. 11. 1924, Dresden, State Opera (Schauspielhaus) under Fritz
Busch, Alois Mora and Adolph Mahnke with Lotte Lehmann (Christine),
Liesel von Schuch (Anna), Josef Correck (Storch) and Theo Strack
(Lummer)

Next theatres: Breslau, Erfurt, Brunswick, Hamburg; after 1945: Zürich,
Vienna (State Opera), Munich (Cuvilliéstheater, 1960)

Die ägyptische Helena

Opera in two acts by Hugo von Hofmannsthal.
Music by Richard Strauss

Op. 75

(Vienna version 1933)

Helen	Dramatic Soprano	Altair	Character Baritone
Aithra	High Youthful-dramatic Soprano	Da-ud	Lyrical Tenor
		Sea-shell	Contralto
Menelaus	Heldentenor		

6 small roles and chorus

Scene: Island of Aithra near Egypt and   Time: After the Trojan War
isolated palm grove near the Atlas mountains

522

Orchestra: 101 players

4 flutes (3rd and 4th also piccolos), 2 oboes, cor anglais, C clarinet, 2 B♭ clarinets, bass clarinet, 3 bassoons (3rd also contra bassoon), 6 horns, 6 trumpets, 3 trombones, bass tuba, timpani, percussion, 2 harps, celesta, organ, strings

Stage Music: 6 oboes, 6 clarinets, 4 horns, 2 trumpets, 4 trombones, percussion, wind machine

Completed: 8th October 1927, Garmisch

1st perf.: 6. 6. 1928, Dresden, State Opera under Fritz Busch, Otto Erhardt–Marie Gutheil-Schoder and Leonhard Fanto with Elisabeth Rethberg (Helena), Maria Rajdl (Aithra), Helene Jung (Sea-shell), Curt Taucher (Menelaus), Friedrich Plaschke (Altair) and Guglielmo Fazzini (Da-ud)

1st perf. of the Vienna version: 14. 8. 1933, Salzburg, Festspielhaus, under Clemens Krauss, Lothar Wallerstein and Robert Kautsky

Next theatres: 1928 Vienna (State Opera), Berlin (State Opera), Munich, Hamburg; 1933 Vienna, Berlin (State Opera), Munich; after 1945: Munich (1956)

Arabella

Lyrical Comedy in three acts by Hugo von Hofmannsthal.

Music by Richard Strauss

Op. 79

Arabella	Dramatic Soprano	Matteo	High Lyrical Tenor
Zdenka	Lyrical Soprano	Fiakermilli	Coloratura Soprano
Mandryka	Character Baritone	Elemer	Youthful Heldentenor
Waldner	Bass	Fortune Teller	Alto
Adelaide	Dramatic Mezzo-soprano		

12 small roles and chorus

Scene: Vienna   Time: 1860

Orchestra: 90 players

3 flutes (3rd also piccolo), 2 oboes, cor anglais, C clarinet, 2 B♭ clarinets (doubling A clarinets), bass clarinet, 3 bassoons (3rd also contra bassoon), 4 horns, 3 trumpets, 3 trombones, bass tuba, timpani, percussion, harp, strings

Completed: 12th October 1932, Garmisch

"Dedicated to my friends Alfred Reucker and Fritz Busch"

523

1st perf.: 1. 7. 1933, Dresden, State Opera under Clemens Krauss, Josef Gielen–Eva Plaschke-von der Osten and Leonhard Fanto with Viorica Ursuleac (Arabella), Margit Bokor (Zdenka), Camilla Kallab (Adelaide), Ellice Illiard (Fiakermilli), Alfred Jerger (Mandryka), Friedrich Plaschke (Waldner) and Martin Kremer (Matteo)

Next theatres: Berlin (State Opera), Vienna (State Opera), Frankfort on Main, Munich

Die schweigsame Frau

Comic Opera in three acts. Freely adapted from Ben Jonson by Stefan Zweig.

Music by Richard Strauss

Op. 80

Morosus	Bass	Carlotta	Mezzo-soprano
Aminta	High Lyrical Soprano	Vanuzzi	Bass
Henry	High Lyrical Tenor	Farfallo	Bass
Barber	High Lyrical Baritone	Morbio	Baritone
Isotta	Coloratura Soprano	Housekeeper	Alto

Chorus

Scene: A room in Morosus's house   Time: Around 1780
in a London suburb

Orchestra: 95 players

3 flutes (doubling piccolos), 2 oboes, cor anglais, D clarinet, 2 B♭ clarinets (doubling A clarinets), bass clarinet, 3 bassoons (3rd also contra bassoon), 4 horns, 3 trumpets, 3 trombones, bass tuba, timpani, percussion, 4 bells, harp, celesta, harpsichord, organ, strings

Completed: 20th October 1934, Garmisch (Opera);

17th January 1935, Garmisch (Overture)

1st perf.: 24. 6. 1935, Dresden, State Opera under Karl Böhm, Josef Gielen and Adolph Mahnke with Maria Cebotari (Aminta), Friedrich Plaschke (Morosus), Martin Kremer (Henry) and Mathieu Ahlersmeyer (Barber)

Next theatres: Milan, Prague (Deutsches Opernhaus), Graz, Zürich; after 1945: Dresden, Munich, Wiesbaden, Berlin (Komische Oper)

524

Friedenstag

Opera in one act by Joseph Gregor. Music by Richard Strauss

Op. 81

Commandant	Character Baritone	Holsteiner	Bass
Maria	Dramatic Soprano	Piedmontese	Lyrical Tenor
	Marksman	Youthful Heldentenor	

9 small roles and chorus

Scene: Citadel of a beleaguered town   Time: 24th October 1648

Orchestra: 94 players

3 flutes, 2 oboes, cor anglais, C clarinet, 2 Bb clarinets, bass clarinet, 3 bassoons, contra bassoon, 6 horns, 4 trumpets, 4 trombones, bass tuba, timpani, percussion, strings

Stage Music: bells, organ

Completed: 16th June 1936, Garmisch

"Dedicated to my friends Viorica Ursuleac and Clemens Krauss"

1st perf.: 24. 7. 1938, Munich, State Opera (National Theatre) under Clemens Krauss, Rudolf Hartmann and Ludwig Sievert with Viorica Ursuleac (Maria), Hans Hotter (Commandant) and Ludwig Weber (Holsteiner)

Next theatres: Dresden, Karlsruhe, Kassel, Graz; after 1945: Graz, Coburg, Munich (1961)

Daphne

Bucolic Tragedy in one act by Joseph Gregor.

Music by Richard Strauss

Op. 82

Daphne	Youthful-dramatic Soprano	Leukippos	High Lyrical Tenor
		Peneios	Bass
Apollo	Youthful Heldentenor	Gaea	Contralto

6 small roles and chorus

Scene: Outside the hut of Peneios   Time: Grecian mythology
by the river of that name

Orchestra: 93 players

3 flutes (3rd also piccolo), 2 oboes, cor anglais, C clarinet, 2 A clarinets, basset horn, bass clarinet, 3 bassoons, contra bassoon, 4 horns, 3 trumpets, 3 trombones, bass tuba, timpani, percussion, 2 harps, strings

Stage Music: Alphorn, organ

Completed: 24th December 1937, Taormina

"Dedicated to my friend Dr. Karl Böhm"

1st perf.: 15. 10. 1938, Dresden, State Opera under Karl Böhm, Max
Hofmüller and Adolph Mahnke with Margarete Teschemacher (Daphne),
Helene Jung (Gaea), Torsten Ralf (Apollo), Martin Kremer (Leukippos)
and Sven Nilsson (Peneios)

Next theatres: Kassel, Graz, Karlsruhe, Essen; after 1945: Coburg,
Dresden, Munich, Stuttgart

Die Liebe der Danae

"Heitere Mythologie" in three acts by Joseph Gregor, using a draft by
Hugo von Hofmannsthal.

Music by Richard Strauss

Op. 83

Danae	Youthful-dramatic Soprano	Xanthe	Lyrical Soprano
		Semele	Soprano
Midas	Youthful Heldentenor	Europa	Soprano
Jupiter	High Baritone	Alkmene	Mezzo-soprano
Mercury	High Lyrical Tenor	Leda	Alto
Pollux	Character Tenor		

8 small roles and chorus

Scene: Greece   Time: Mythical pre-history

Orchestra: 99 players

4 flutes (2nd–4th also piccolos), 2 oboes, cor anglais, clarinet in E♭, D
and C, 2 B♭ clarinets, basset horn, bass clarinet, 3 bassoons, contra
bassoon, 6 horns, 4 trumpets, 4 trombones, bass tuba, timpani, percussion,
2 harps, celesta, piano, strings

Completed: 28th June 1940, Garmisch

"Dedicated to my friend Heinz Tietjen"

1st perf.: 14. 8. 1952, Salzburg, Festspielhaus, under Clemens Krauss,
Rudolf Hartmann and Emil Preetorius with Annelies Kupper (Danae),
Josef Gostić (Midas) and Paul Schöffler (Jupiter)

Dress rehearsal for the cancelled world première in 1944: 16. 8. 1944,
Salzburg, Festspielhaus under Krauss, Hartmann and Preetorius with
Viorica Ursuleac (Danae), Horst Taubmann (Midas) and Hans Hotter
(Jupiter)

German première: 29. 10. 1952, Berlin, Städtische Oper under Leopold
Ludwig, Richard Strauss junior and Josef Fenneker

Next theatres: Vienna (State Opera), Milan, Bremen, Dresden, Munich

Capriccio

A conversation piece for music in one act by Clemens Krauss
and Richard Strauss

Op. 85

Countess	Youthful-dramatic Soprano	La Roche	Bass
		Clairon	Mezzo-soprano
Count	Lyrical Baritone	Female Singer	Coloratura Soprano
Flamand	Lyrical Tenor	Male Singer	Lyrical Tenor
Olivier	Character Baritone	Taupe	Tenor buffo
	Major Domo	Bass	

8 small roles (Chorus)

Scene: Château near Paris   Time: Around 1775

Orchestra: 90 players

3 flutes (3rd also piccolo), 2 oboes, cor anglais, C clarinet, 2 B♭ clarinets,
basset horn, bass clarinet, 3 bassoons (3rd also contra bassoon), 4 horns,
2 trumpets, 3 trombones, timpani, percussion, 2 harps, harpsichord, strings
Stage Music: string sextet (in the wings), violin, cello and harpsichord
(in costume)

Completed: 3rd August 1941, Garmisch

"Dedicated to my friend and colleague Clemens Krauss"

1st perf.: 26. 10. 1942, Munich, State Opera (National Theatre) under
Clemens Krauss, Rudolf Hartmann and Rochus Gliese with Viorica Ursuleac (Madeleine), Hildegard Ranczak (Clairon), Horst Taubmann (Flamand), Hans Hotter (Olivier), Walter Höfermeyer (Count) and Georg
Hann (La Roche)

Next theatres: Breslau, Hannover, Düsseldorf, Darmstadt, Wiesbaden;
after 1945: Weimar, Vienna (State Opera), Salzburg, Munich

ORCHESTRAL WORKS

Instrumentation of the principal works

Suite for 13 Wind Instruments in B♭, Op. 4
   2 flutes, 2 oboes, 2 clarinets, 2 bassoons, contra bassoon

Serenade for 13 Wind Instruments in E♭, Op. 7
   2 flutes, 2 oboes, 2 clarinets, 2 bassoons, contra bassoon (if necessary
   bass tuba or contra bass), 4 horns

Concerto for Violin and Orchestra in D minor, Op. 8
   2 flutes, 2 oboes, 2 clarinets, 2 bassoons, 4 horns, 2 trumpets, timpani,
   strings

1st Concerto for Horn and Orchestra in E♭, Op. 11
   2 flutes, 2 oboes, 2 clarinets, 2 bassoons, 2 horns, 2 trumpets, timpani,
   strings

Symphony for full orchestra in F minor, Op. 12
   2 flutes, 2 oboes, 2 B♭ clarinets, 2 horns, 2 trumpets, 3 trombones, bass
   tuba, timpani, strings

"Wandrers Sturmlied" (Goethe) for eight-part chorus and full orchestra,
   Op. 14
   2 flutes, 2 oboes, 2 clarinets, 2 bassoons, contra bassoon, 4 horns,
   2 trumpets, 3 trombones, timpani, strings

"Aus Italien," Symphonic Fantasy for full orchestra in G, Op. 16
   2 flutes, piccolo, 2 oboes (2nd also cor anglais), 2 clarinets, 2 bassoons,
   contra bassoon, 4 horns, 2 trumpets, 3 trombones, timpani, percussion,
   harp, strings

"Don Juan," tone poem (after Nikolaus Lenau) for full orchestra, Op. 20
   3 flutes (3rd also piccolo), 2 oboes, cor anglais, 2 A clarinets, 2 bassoons,
   contra bassoon, 4 horns, 3 trumpets, 3 trombones, bass tuba, timpani,
   percussion, glockenspiel, harp, strings

"Macbeth" (after Shakespeare's drama), tone poem for full orchestra,
   Op. 23
   3 flutes (3rd also piccolo), 2 oboes, cor anglais, 2 B♭ clarinets, bass

clarinet, 2 bassoons, contra bassoon, 4 horns, 3 trumpets, bass trumpet, 3 trombones, bass tuba, timpani, percussion, strings

"Tod und Verklärung," tone poem for full orchestra, Op. 24

    3 flutes, 2 oboes, cor anglais, 2 B♭ clarinets, bass clarinet, 2 bassoons, contra bassoon, 4 horns, 3 trumpets, 3 trombones, bass tuba, timpani, percussion, 2 harps, strings

"Till Eulenspiegels lustige Streiche," After the old rogue's tune–in Rondeau form–set for full orchestra, Op. 28

    3 flutes, piccolo, 3 oboes, cor anglais, D clarinet, 2 B♭ clarinets, bass clarinet, 3 bassoons, contra bassoon, 4 horns, 4 D horns (ad lib.), 6 trumpets, 3 trombones, bass tuba, timpani, percussion, strings

"Also sprach Zarathustra," tone poem (freely after Nietzsche) for full orchestra, Op. 30

    3 flutes (3rd also 2nd piccolo), piccolo, 3 oboes, cor anglais, E♭ clarinet, 2 B♭ clarinets, bass clarinet, 3 bassoons, contra bassoon, 6 horns, 4 trumpets, 3 trombones, 2 bass tubas, timpani, percussion, glockenspiel, deep bell in E♭, organ, strings

"Don Quixote" (Introduzione, Tema con variazioni e Finale), Fantastic Variations on a theme of knightly character for full orchestra, Op. 35

    2 flutes, piccolo (also 3rd flute), 2 oboes, cor anglais, 2 B♭ clarinets, bass clarinet, 3 bassoons, contra bassoon, 6 horns, 4 trumpets, 3 trombones, tenor tuba, bass tuba, timpani, percussion, wind machine, harp, solo viola, solo cello, strings

"Ein Heldenleben," tone poem for full orchestra, Op. 40

    3 flutes, piccolo, 4 oboes, E♭ clarinet, 2 B♭ clarinets, bass clarinet, 3 bassoons, contra bassoon, 8 horns, 5 trumpets, 3 trombones, tenor tuba, bass tuba, timpani, percussion, 2 harps, solo violin, strings (reduced wind scoring by G. E. Lessing)

"Taillefer," Ballad of Uhland for mixed chorus, soli and orchestra, Op. 52

    4 flutes, 2 piccolos, 4 oboes, 2 cors anglais, 2 D clarinets, 2 B♭ clarinets, 2 A clarinets, bass clarinet, 4 bassoons, contra bassoon, 8 horns, 6 trumpets, 4 trombones, 2 bass tubas, timpani, percussion, glockenspiel, 24 1st and 24 2nd violins, 16 violas, 14 cellos, 12 basses

"Sinfonia domestica" for full orchestra, Op. 53

    3 flutes, piccolo, 2 oboes, oboe d'amore, cor anglais, D clarinet, A clarinet, 2 B♭ clarinets, 4 bassoons, contra bassoon, 4 saxophones, 8 horns, 4 trumpets, 3 trombones, bass tuba, timpani, percussion, glockenspiel, 2 harps, solo violin, strings (reduced wind scoring by G. E. Lessing)

Festliches Präludium for full orchestra, Op. 61

    4 flutes, piccolo, 4 oboes, cor anglais, 4 clarinets, bass clarinet, 8 horns, 6 trumpets, 12 distant trumpets (if necessary 6), 4 trombones, bass tuba, timpani, percussion, organ, 96 strings

Eine Alpensinfonie for full orchestra and organ, Op. 64

2 flutes, 2 piccolos, 2 oboes, cor anglais, heckelphone, E♭ clarinet, 2 B♭ clarinets, C clarinet (doubling bass clarinet), 3 bassoons, contra bassoon, 4 horns, 4 tubas, 4 trumpets, 4 trombones, 2 bass tubas, timpani, percussion, glockenspiel, wind and thunder machine, 2 harps, celesta, organ (ad lib.), strings; in addition 12 horns, 2 trumpets, 2 trombones off-stage (if necessary to be taken from the orchestra). (Reduced wind scoring without organ by G. E. Lessing)

Orchestral Suite from "Le Bourgeois gentilhomme," Op. 60

2 flutes (doubling piccolos), 2 oboes, 2 clarinets, 2 bassoons, 2 horns, trumpet, trombone, timpani, percussion, glockenspiel, harp, piano (concert grand), 6 violins, 4 violas, 4 cellos, 2 basses

Tanzsuite after keyboard pieces by F. Couperin, assembled and arranged for small orchestra, without Opus No.

2 flutes, 2 oboes, cor anglais, B♭ clarinet, A clarinet, 2 bassoons, 2 horns, trumpet, trombone, glockenspiel, tambourine, harp, celesta, harpsichord, 4 1st violins, 3 2nd violins, 2 violas, 2 cellos, 2 basses

Parergon zur Sinfonia domestica for piano (left hand) and orchestra, Op. 73

2 flutes, 2 oboes, cor anglais, 2 clarinets, bass clarinet, 2 bassoons, contra bassoon, 4 horns, 2 trumpets, 3 trombones, bass tuba, timpani, percussion

"Panathenäenzug," Symphonic Etudes in the form of a Passacaglia for piano (left hand) and orchestra, Op. 74

3 flutes, 2 oboes, cor anglais, 2 clarinets, bass clarinet, 2 bassoons, contra bassoon, 4 horns, 3 trumpets, 3 trombones, bass tuba, strings

"Die Tageszeiten," a song cycle after poems by Eichendorff for male chorus and orchestra, Op. 76

2 flutes, 2 oboes, 2 A clarinets, bass clarinet, 2 bassoons, contra bassoon, 4 horns, 2 trumpets, 3 trombones, timpani, percussion, strings

2nd Concerto for Horn and Orchestra in E♭, without Opus No.

2 flutes, 2 oboes, 2 clarinets, 2 bassoons, 2 horns, 2 trumpets, timpani, strings

Sonatinas for 16 Wind Instruments in F and E♭, without Opus Nos.

2 flutes, 2 oboes, C clarinet, 2 B♭ clarinets, basset horn, bass clarinet, 2 bassoons, contra bassoon, 4 horns

"Metamorphosen," Study for 23 solo strings (in C minor), without Opus No.

10 violins, 5 violas, 5 cellos, 3 basses

Concerto for Oboe and Small Orchestra, without Opus No.

2 flutes, cor anglais, 2 clarinets, 2 bassoons, 2 horns, strings

Duet Concertino for Clarinet and Bassoon with string orchestra and harp, without Opus No.

harp, strings

RECORDS

Abbreviations of company-titles

Amadeo	Amadeo Oesterreichische Schallplatten A.G., Vienna
Ariola	Austria Vanguard, Vienna
Artists	Society of Participating Artists, USA
Boston	Boston Records, USA
Capitol	Capitol Records Inc., USA
CBS	CBS, USA
Cetra	Cetra S.A., Turin-Italia
Classic	Classic, USA
Columbia	Columbia Graphophone Company Ltd., Hayes-Great Britain
Columbia A	Columbia Phonograph Company, Bridgeport-USA
Concert Hall	Concert Hall Society, USA
Decca	The Decca Record Company Ltd., London
Decca A	Decca, USA
Delyse	Delyse, Great Britain
DG	Deutsche Grammophon GmbH, Hamburg-Hannover
Electrola	Electrola Gesellschaft mbH, Cologne
Epic	Epic, USA
Eterna	VEB Deutsche Schallplatten, Berlin
Eurodisc	Ariola-Sonopress GmbH, Hamburg
Everest	Everest, USA
Fontana	Philips, Eindhoven-Holland
Heliodor	Heliodor, Paris
HMV	His Master's Voice, The Gramophone Company Ltd., Hayes-Great Britain
Imperial	Electrola Gesellschaft mbH, Cologne
Lyricord	Lyricord, USA
MEL	Musica et litera
Mercury	Nixa Record Company, USA
Metronome	Metronome, Copenhagen-Denmark
New Records	New Records Inc., USA

Odeon		The Parlophone Company Ltd., Hayes-Great Britain
Opera		Europäischer Phonoklub, Stuttgart
Pathé		Pathé Frères, Paris
Philips		Philips, Eindhoven-Holland
Polskie N.		Polskie Nagrania, Warsaw
Polydor		Deutsche Grammophon GmbH, Hamburg-Hannover
PYE		Pye-Nixa, USA
RCA		Victor Radio Corporation of America, New York
Record Club		Off-the-air Record Club, USA
Royale		Royale, USA
USSR		Mezhdunorodnaja-Kniga, Moscow
St. And.		Standart And., USA
Supraphon		Supraphon, Prague-ČSSR
Telefunken		Teldec Telefunken-Decca Schallplatten GmbH, Hamburg
Tempo		Tempo, USA
Urania		Urania Records Inc., USA
Victor		Victor Radio Corporation of America, New York
Vox		Vox Productions Inc., New York
Westminster		Westminster, USA

Long-playing records only

This discography, completed to the 30th April 1964, includes details of recordings which are available only in certain European countries or in the USA. Records marked* are no longer on the market. St signifies a stereophonic recording, HR a historical recording. The number following the maker's name is the diameter of the record in centimetres: 30 and 25 refer to 33 r.p.m. long-playing records, and 17 to 45 r.p.m. discs.

I. Stage Works

Feuersnot

"Feuersnot! Minnegebot" (Love Scene)

DG/Eterna	25	Maria Cebotari, Schmitt-Walter/Artur Rother –Berliner Rundfunk-Sinfonie-Orchester (HR)
HMV	17	Thomas Beecham–Royal Philharmonic Orchestra London (1955)
Columbia A	25	Eugene Ormandy–Philadelphia Orchestra

Salome

Complete Opera

Concert Hall*	30	I. Joseph Keilberth–Dresdner Staatskapelle/ Goltz, Karén, Aldenhoff, Herrmann, Dittrich (1950) (2 Rec.)

534

Decca	30		II. Clemens Krauss–Wiener Philharmoniker/ Goltz, Kenney, Patzak, Braun, Dermota (1954) (2 Rec.) Excerpts 30, 25
Philips	30		III. Rudolf Moralt–Wiener Sinfoniker/Wegner, von Milinkovic, Szemere, Metternich, Kmentt (1954) (2 Rec.)
Decca	30	St	IV. Georg Solti–Wiener Philharmoniker/ Nilsson, Hoffman, Stolze, Wächter, Kmentt (1963) (2 Rec.) Excerpts 30
Electrola/ Eterna	30	St	V. Otmar Suitner–Dresdner Staatskapelle/ Goltz, Ericsdotter, Melchert, Gutstein, Hoppe (1964) (2 Rec.) Excerpts 30

Salome's Dance

DG	17		Richard Strauss–Berliner Philharmoniker (HR)
Columbia	25		Bruno Walter–Berliner Philharmoniker (HR)
Columbia	25		Eugene Ormandy–Philadelphia Orchestra (HR)
Columbia A	25		Artur Rodzinski–Cleveland Orchestra (HR)
HMV	17		Leopold Stokowski–Philadelphia Orchestra (1955)
RCA	30		Fritz Reiner–Chicago Symphony Orchestra (1955)
DG/Eterna	17		Fritz Lehmann–Bamberger Sinfoniker (1957)
Eurodisc	30	St	Franz Konwitschny–Wiener Sinfoniker (1957)
Electrola	30	St	Artur Rodzinski–Philharmonia Orchestra London (1960)
Columbia	30		Dimitri Mitropoulos–New York Philharmonic Orchestra (1960)
Everest	30	St	Leopold Stokowski–New York Stadium Symphony Orchestra (1961)
Decca	30	St	Herbert von Karajan–Wiener Philharmoniker (1961)
Mercury	30	St	Paul Paray–Detroit Symphony Orchestra (1961)
Capitol	30	St	Erich Leinsdorf–Philharmonia Orchestra London (1961)

535

DG	30	St	Karl Böhm–Berliner Philharmoniker (1963)
Telefunken	30	St	Joseph Keilberth–Münchner Staatsorchester (1963)

Finale (Salome's Solo Scene)

DG/Eterna	25	Maria Cebotari/Artur Rother–Berliner Rundfunk Sinfonie-Orchester (HR)
Capitol	25	Liselotte Enck/Robert Heger–Berliner Staatskapelle (HR)
Columbia	30	Ljuba Welitsch/Fritz Reiner–Orchestra of the Metropolitan Opera New York (1953)
Decca *	30	Inge Borkh/Josef Krips–Wiener Philharmoniker (1954)
DG	30	Christel Goltz, Hetty Plümacher, Windgassen/ Ferdinand Leitner–Stuttgarter Staatsorchester (1954)
RCA	30	Inge Borkh/Fritz Reiner–Chicago Symphony Orchestra (1957)

Elektra

Complete Opera

Cetra	30		I. Dimitri Mitropoulos–Orchestra Maggio Musicale Firenze/A. Konetzni, Ilitsch, Mödl, Braun, Klarwein (1953) (2 Rec.)
Record Club	30		II. Dimitri Mitropoulos–New York Philharmonic Symphony Orchestra/Varnay, Nicolaidi, Jagel (1954) (2 Rec.)
DG/Eterna	30	St	III. Karl Böhm–Dresdner Staatskapelle/ Borkh, Schech, Madeira, Fischer-Dieskau, Uhl (1961) (2 Rec.)

Excerpts 30

"Allein! Weh, ganz allein" (Monologue of Elektra)

DG	30	Christel Goltz/Georg Solti–Münchner Staatsorchester (1954)
RCA	30	Inge Borkh/Fritz Reiner–Chicago Symphony Orchestra (1957)

"Ich kann nicht sitzen" (Chrysothemis's Scene)

Philips	25	Hilde Zadek/Rudolf Moralt–Wiener Sinfoniker (1954)

"Ich will nichts hören" (Scene Elektra-Klytemnestra)

DG	30		Christel Goltz, Elisabeth Höngen/Georg Solti –Münchner Staatsorchester (1954) "Was willst du, fremder Mensch?" (Scene Elektra-Orestes)
DG	30		Christel Goltz, Frantz/Georg Solti–Münchner Staatsorchester (1954)
RCA	30		Inge Borkh, Schöffler/Fritz Reiner–Chicago Symphony Orchestra (1957) Finale (Elektra's Solo Scene)
HMV	30		Erna Schlüter, Ljuba Welitsch, Schöffler, Widdop/Thomas Beecham–Royal Philharmonic Orchestra London (HR)
RCA	30		Inge Borkh, Frances Yeend/Fritz Reiner–Chicago Symphony Orchestra (1957)

Der Rosenkavalier

Complete Opera

Vox	30		I. Clemens Krauss–Münchner Staatsorchester/ Ursuleac, von Milinkovic, Kern, Weber, Hann, (Concert Performance, HR) (4 Rec.) Excerpts 30 (2 Rec.)
Urania	30		II. Rudolf Kempe–Dresdner Staatskapelle/ Bäumer, Lemnitz, Richter, Walter-Sacks, Böhme, Löbel, Liebing (1950) (4 Rec.)
Decca	30		III. Erich Kleiber–Wiener Philharmoniker/ Reining, Jurinac, Güden, Rössl-Majdan, Weber, Poell, Dermota, Klein (1954) (4 Rec.) Excerpts 30, 25, 17
Columbia	30	St	IV. Herbert von Karajan–Philharmonia Orchestra London/Schwarzkopf, Ch. Ludwig, Stich-Randall, Meyer, Edelmann, Wächter, Gedda, Kuen (1958) (4 Rec.) Excerpts 30
DG/Eterna	30	St	V. Karl Böhm–Dresdner Staatskapelle/ Schech, Seefried, Streich, Wagner, Böhme, Fischer-Dieskau, Francl, Unger (1959) (4 Rec.) Excerpts 30, 17

Scenes

Electrola	30		Robert Heger–Wiener Philharmoniker/Lehmann, Olszewska, Schumann, Paalen, Mayr, Madin, Gallos (HR) (2 Rec.)

Electrola	30	Wilhelm Schüchter–Berliner Philharmoniker/ Rysanek, Grümmer, Köth, Wagner, Neidlinger, Traxel (1954)

Overture

Urania	30	Kurt Eichhorn–Münchner Staatsorchester (HR)

"Di rigori armato" (Tenor Aria)

Electrola	30	Helge Rosvaenge/Orchestra (HR)
Telefunken	30, 25	Peter Anders/Hans Schmidt-Isserstedt-Orchester Städtische Oper Berlin (1957)
DG	17	Libero de Luca/Orchestra (1960)
RCA	30	Mario Lanza/Orchestra (1960)

"Da geht er hin" (Monologue of the Marschallin and Finale 1st act)

Decca	30	Maria Reining/Hans Knappertsbusch–Züricher Tonhalle-Orchester (1951)
DG	30	Tiana Lemnitz, Georgine von Milinkovic/ Ferdinand Leitner–Stuttgarter Staatsorchester (1955)

"Mir ist die Ehre widerfahren" (Entry of the Rosenkavalier 2nd act)

Columbia	25	Elisabeth Schwarzkopf, Irmgard Seefried/ Otto Ackermann–Wiener Philharmoniker (HR)
Victor	25	Rise Stevens, Erna Berger/Fritz Reiner–RCA Victor Symphony Orchestra New York (HR)
DG/Eterna	17	Tiana Lemnitz, Maria Cebotari/Artur Rother –Berliner Rundfunk-Sinfonie-Orchester (HR)
DG	25	Georgine von Milinkovic, Elfride Trötschel/ Ferdinand Leitner–Stuttgarter Staatsorchester (1955)

"Da lieg ich" (Waltz Finale 2nd act)

Columbia	25	Weber, Dagmar Hermann/Orchestra (HR)
DG/Eterna	25	Hann, Marie-Luise Schilp/Artur Rother–Orchestra (HR)
HMV	25	Kipnis, Else Ruziczka/Orchestra (1952)
DG	25, 17	Böhme, Ruth Michaelis/Robert Heger–Münchner Philharmoniker (1955)

538

Prelude act III

Urania *	30		Kurt Eichhorn–Münchner Staatsorchester (HR)

Finale (Trio and Duet) act III

DG	25		Elisabeth Ohms, Elfriede Marherr, Adele Kern/Orchestra (HR)
Victor	25		Rise Stevens, Erna Berger/Fritz Reiner–RCA Victor Symphony Orchestra New York (HR)
DG	30, 17		Tiana Lemnitz, Georgine von Milinkovic, Elfride Trötschel/Ferdinand Leitner–Stuttgarter Staatsorchester (1955)

Waltzes 1st and 2nd act

Decca	25		Karl Rankl–Royal Philharmonic Orchestra London (HR)
HMV	25		Arthur Fiedler–Boston Promenade Orchestra (1954)
Philips	25		Eugene Ormandy–Philadelphia Orchestra (1956)

Waltzes 1st and 2nd act (New form)

Decca	25		Anthony Collins–London Philharmonic Orchestra (1951)
Supraphon	30		Hans Swarowsky–Wiener Philharmoniker (1951)
Vox	30	St	Heinrich Hollreiser–Bamberger Sinfoniker (1962)
Philips	30, 25	St	Eugen Jochum–Concertgebouw Orkest Amsterdam (1962)

Waltzes act III

DG	17		Richard Strauss–Münchner Staatsorchester (HR 1941)
Supraphon	30		Hans Swarowsky–Wiener Philharmoniker (1951)
DG/Eterna	30, 25, 17		Eugen Jochum–Berliner Philharmoniker (1955)
Telefunken	25		Franz André–Orchestre Symphonique Radio Nationale Belge Bruxelles (1957)
DG	25		Fritz Lehmann–Bamberger Sinfoniker (1958)

Imperial	25		Wilhelm Schüchter–Sinfonie-Orchester Nordwestdeutscher Rundfunk Hamburg (1960)
Decca A	30		Mishel Piastro/Orchestra (1960)
Heliodor	25		Artur Rodzinski–London Philharmonic Symphony Orchestra (1960)
Eurodisc	30	St	Franz Konwitschny–Wiener Sinfoniker (1960)
RCA	30	St	Fritz Reiner–Chicago Symphony Orchestra (1960) (Arr. Reiner)
Polydor	30, 17	St	Hans Carste–Berliner Promenaden-Orchester (1961)
Vox	30	St	Heinrich Hollreiser–Bamberger Sinfoniker (1962)
Philips	30, 25	St	Eugen Jochum–Concertgebouw Orkest Amsterdam (1962)
Capitol	25		Felix Slatkin–Hollywood Bowl Symphony Orchestra (1962)
DG	30	St	Karl Böhm–Berliner Philharmoniker (1963)

Suite

Victor	25		Eugène Goossens–Cincinnati Symphony Orchestra (HR)
Columbia	25		Eugene Ormandy–Philadelphia Orchestra (HR)
Mercury	25	St	Antal Dorati–Minneapolis Symphony Orchestra (1958)
Westminster	25		Artur Rodzinski–Philharmonia Orchestra London (1960)
Capitol	25	St	William Steinberg–Philharmonia Orchestra London (1961)

Ariadne auf Naxos

Complete Opera

DG	30	I. Karl Böhm–Wiener Philharmoniker/Reining, Noni, Seefried, Lorenz, Kunz, Schöffler, Muzzarelli (HR 1944 Performance Staatsoper Vienna) (1963) (3 Rec.)
Columbia	30	II. Herbert von Karajan–Philharmonia Orchestra London/Schwarzkopf, Streich, Seefried, Schock, Prey, Dönch, Neugebauer (1955) (3 Rec.) Excerpts 30, 17

540

| RCA | 30 | St | III. Erich Leinsdorf–Wiener Philharmoniker/ Rysanek, Peters, Jurinac, Peerce, Berry, Pre- ger (1961) (3 Rec.) Excerpts 30 |

Ariadne's Scenes (Monologues)

| Electrola | 30 | St | Lisa della Casa, Schock/Alberto Erede–Ber- liner Philharmoniker (1961) |

Overture

| DG/Eterna | 17 | | Ferdinand Leitner–Stuttgarter Staatsorche- ster (1954) |
| Electrola | 30 | St | Alberto Erede–Berliner Philharmoniker (1961) |

"Es gibt ein Reich" (Ariadne's Monologue)

DG/Eterna	17		Annelies Kupper/Ferdinand Leitner–Stuttgar- ter Staatsorchester (1954)
Philips	25		Hilde Zadek/Rudolf Moralt–Wiener Sinfoni- ker (1954)
Decca	30, 17		Lisa della Casa/Heinrich Hollreiser–Wiener Philharmoniker (1957)

"Großmächtige Prinzessin" (Zerbinetta's Aria)

Electrola	30		Maria Ivogün/Orchestra (HR)
DG	25, 17		Adele Kern/Orchestra (HR)
Decca	25, 17		Ilse Hollweg/Josef Krips–London Symphony Orchestra (1951)
Electrola	25, 17		Erika Köth/Otto Matzerath–Berliner Philhar- moniker (1957)

Josephslegende

Complete Ballet

| Urania * | 30 | | Kurt Eichhorn–Münchner Staatsorchester (1952) (2 Rec.) |

Die Frau ohne Schatten

Complete Opera

| Decca | 30 | | I. Karl Böhm–Wiener Philharmoniker/Goltz, Rysanek, Höngen, Hopf, Schöffler, Böhme (1956) (5 Rec.) Excerpts 30 |

DG	30	St	II. Joseph Keilberth–Münchner Staatsorchester/Borkh, Bjoner, Mödl, Thomas, Fischer-Dieskau, Hotter (1963 Performance Staatsoper Munich) (4 Rec.) Excerpts 30

Scenes of the Empress

St. And.	30		Eleonor Steber/Orchestra (1960)

Fantasia for Orchestra

Columbia A	30		Eugene Ormandy–Philadelphia Orchestra
Capitol	30	St	Erich Leinsdorf–Philharmonia Orchestra London (1962)

Schlagobers

Complete Ballet

Lyricord	30		Erich Kloß–Frankenland Sinfonie-Orchester Nürnberg (HR) (2 Rec.)

Waltz

DG/Eterna	25, 17		Eugen Jochum–Berliner Philharmoniker (1955)

Intermezzo

Four Interludes

Telefunken	30	St	Joseph Keilberth–Münchner Staatsorchester (1963)

Waltz-Scene

DG/Eterna	17		Fritz Lehmann–Bamberger Sinfoniker (1957)
Columbia	30		Wolfgang Sawallisch–Philharmonia Orchestra London (1959)

Interlude in A flat

HMV	17		Thomas Beecham–Royal Philharmonic Orchestra London (1955)

Arabella

Complete Opera

Decca	30	St	I. Georg Solti–Wiener Philharmoniker/della Casa, Güden, Malaniuk, Coertse, London, Dermota, Edelmann, Kmentt (1959) (4 Rec.) Excerpts 30, 25, 17
DG	30	St	II. Joseph Keilberth–Münchner Staatsorchester/della Casa, Rothenberger, Malaniuk, Rogner, Fischer-Dieskau, Paskuda, Kohn, Uhl (1963 Performance Staatsoper Munich) (3 Rec.) Excerpts 30

542

Scenes

Columbia	30		Lovro von Matačić–Philharmonia Orchestra London/Schwarzkopf, Felbermeyer, Metternich, Gedda, Schlott, Dickie (1955)

Excerpts 17

"Aber der Richtige" (Duet Arabella-Zdenka 1st act)

DG	17		Viorica Ursuleac, Margit Bokor/Berliner Staatskapelle (HR)
Telefunken	17		Marta Fuchs, Elsa Wieber/Wilhelm Franz Reuss–Berliner Philharmoniker (HR)
Decca	30,25,17		Lisa della Casa, Hilde Güden/Rudolf Moralt –Wiener Philharmoniker (1954)

"Du sollst mein Gebieter sein" (Duet Arabella-Mandryka 2nd act)

DG	17		Viorica Ursuleac, Jerger/Berliner Staatskapelle (HR)
Telefunken	17		Marta Fuchs, Schöffler/Wilhelm Franz Reuss Berliner Philharmoniker (HR)
Decca	30,25		Lisa della Casa, Schöffler/Heinrich Hollreiser–Wiener Philharmoniker (1954)

"Das war sehr gut" (Finale act III)

Decca	30,17		Lisa della Casa, Poell/Rudolf Moralt–Wiener Philharmoniker (1954)

Die schweigsame Frau

Overture

Telefunken	30	St	Joseph Keilberth–Münchner Staatsorchester (1963)

Daphne

"O bleib, geliebter Baum" (Daphne's Monologue)

DG *	30		Annelies Kupper/Fritz Lehmann–Münchner Philharmoniker (1955)

"Götter! Brüder im hohen Olympos!" (Apollo's Scene)

Victor *	25		Torsten Ralf/Karl Böhm–Dresdner Staatskapelle (HR)

"Ich komme, grünende Brüder" (Finale)

Victor *	25		Margarete Teschemacher/Karl Böhm–Dresdner Staatskapelle (HR)

543

| DG * | 30 | Annelies Kupper/Fritz Lehmann–Münchner Philharmoniker (1955) |

Die Liebe der Danae

Symphonic Fragment

| HMV | 30 | John Barbirolli–Hallé Orchestra Manchester (1957) |

Capriccio

Complete Opera

| Columbia | 30 | Wolfgang Sawallisch–Philharmonia Orchestra London/Schwarzkopf, Ch. Ludwig, Moffo, Gedda, Fischer-Dieskau, Wächter, Hotter, Christ, Troy (1960) (3 Rec.) Excerpts 30 |

"Kein anders, das mir so" (Sonnet)

| Decca | 30, 17 | Anton Dermota/Karl Böhm–Wiener Philharmoniker (1956) |

"Wo ist mein Bruder?" (Closing Scene Madeleine)

| Columbia | 30 | Elisabeth Schwarzkopf/Otto Ackermann–Philharmonia Orchestra London (with Moonlight Music) (1954) |

| Decca | 30 | Lisa della Casa, Bierbach/Heinrich Hollreiser–Wiener Philharmoniker (1954) |

II. Symphonic Works
Festmarsch

| Urania * | 30 | Kurt Eichhorn–Münchner Staatsorchester (1952) |

Serenade for Wind Instruments

Artists	25	Werner Jansen–Los Angeles Symphony Orchestra
Mercury	25	St	Frederick Fennell–Eastman Wind Ensemble
Boston	30	St	Simon–Boston Woodwind Ensemble (1961)

Violin Concerto

| Urania * | 30 | Siegfried Borries/Artur Rother–Berliner Rundfunk-Sinfonie-Orchester (1952) |

1st Horn Concerto

| Urania * | 30 | Heinz Lohan/Gerhard Wiesenhütter–Leipziger Rundfunk-Sinfonie-Orchester (1950) |
| Columbia | 30 | Dennis Brain/Wolfgang Sawallisch–Philharmonia Orchestra London (1957) |

544

2nd Symphony

Artists	30		Herbert Häfner–Wiener Sinfoniker (1950)

Suite for Wind Instruments

PYE	30		Karl Haas–London Baroque Ensemble (1961)
Boston	30	St	Simon–Boston Woodwind Ensemble (1961)

Burleske

Electrola	25	Elly Ney/Willem van Hoogstraten–Berliner Staatskapelle (HR)
Vox *	30	Gerhart Münch/Alfons Dressel–Münchner Rundfunk-Sinfonie-Orchester (HR)
Victor *	30	Claudio Arrau/Désiré Defauw–Chicago Symphony Orchestra (HR)
Odeon	30	Fabienne Jacquinot/Anatole Fistoulari–Philharmonia Orchestra London (1954)
Decca	30	Friedrich Gulda/Anthony Collins–London Symphony Orchestra (1955)
Telefunken	30	Poldi Mildner/Artur Rother–Radio-Sinfonie-Orchester Berlin (1957)
DG	30	Margrit Weber/Ferenc Fricsay–Radio-Sinfonie-Orchester Berlin (1957)
RCA	30	Byron Janis/Fritz Reiner–Chicago Symphony Orchestra (1958)
Fontana	17	Rudolf Serkin/Eugene Ormandy–Philadelphia Orchestra (1959)
Eterna	25	Werner Richter/Heinz Bongartz–Leipziger Rundfunk-Sinfonie-Orchester (1960)
USSR	30	Jakow Sak/Algis Shjuratis–State Symphony Orchestra of the USSR Moskow (1960)

Aus Italien

Victor *	25	Frederick August Stock–Chicago Symphony Orchestra (Andantino) (HR)
Westminster *	30	Henry Swoboda–Wiener Sinfoniker (1952)
Decca *	30	Clemens Krauss–Wiener Philharmoniker (1954)

Don Juan

Decca A *	25	Richard Strauss–Berliner Staatskapelle (HR)
Decca A *	25	Otto Klemperer–Berliner Staatskapelle (HR)
Decca A *	25	Karl Böhm–Dresdner Staatskapelle (HR)
Royale *	25	Hugo Balzer–Berliner Sinfonie-Orchester (HR)
Victor *	25	Fritz Busch–London Philharmonic Orchestra (HR)

Mercury	25	Willem Mengelberg–Concertgebouw Orkest Amsterdam (HR)
Decca A	25	Herbert von Karajan–Concertgebouw Orkest Amsterdam (HR)
Columbia A	25	Fritz Reiner–Pittsburgh Symphony Orchestra (HR)
Victor	25	Serge Kussewitzky–Boston Symphony Orchestra (HR)
Decca A	25	Sidney Beer–National Symphony Orchestra, London (HR)
Victor	25	Hans Kindler–Washington National Symphony Orchestra (HR)
Decca	25	Clemens Krauss–Wiener Philharmoniker (1951)
Columbia	25	Herbert von Karajan–Philharmonia Orchestra London (1952)
HMV	25	Arturo Toscanini–NBC Symphony Orchestra New York (1954)
Philip/MEL	25, 17	Eugen Jochum–Concertgebouw Orkest Amsterdam (1954)
Electrola	25	Wilhelm Furtwängler–Wiener Philharmoniker (1954)
DG	30, 25	Fritz Lehmann–Berliner Philharmoniker (1955)
Vox	30	Jascha Horenstein–Bamberger Sinfoniker (1955)
Decca	30	Hans Knappertsbusch–Conservatoire Orchestre Paris (1956)
USSR	25	Georges Georgescu–State Symphony Orchestra of the USSR Moskow (1956)
Heliodor	25	Artur Rodzinski–London Philharmonic Symphony Orchestra (1957)
Philips	25, 17	Bruno Walter–New York Philharmonic Symphony Orchestra (1957)
Supraphon	25	Karel Šejna–Philharmonia Prague (1957)
RCA	30	Fritz Reiner–Chicago Symphony Orchestra (1958)
Columbia A	25	Eugene Ormandy–Philadelphia Orchestra (1958)
Fontana	30	St George Szell–Cleveland Orchestra (1959)

546

Mercury	30	St	Antal Dorati–Minneapolis Symphony Orchestra (1959)
DG/Eterna	25		Karl Böhm–Dresdner Staatskapelle (1959)
Eurodisc	30	St	Franz Konwitschny–Wiener Sinfoniker (1960)
Capitol	25	St	William Steinberg–Philharmonia Orchestra London (1961)
Everest	30	St	Leopold Stokowski–New York Stadium Symphony Orchestra (1961)
Decca	25	St	Alceo Galliera–Philharmonia Orchestra London (1961)
Decca	30, 25	St	Herbert von Karajan–Wiener Philharmoniker (1961)
Ariola	25	St	Otto Matzerath–Sinfonie-Orchester Hessischer Rundfunk Frankfurt o. M. (1961)
Telefunken	25	St	Joseph Keilberth–Berliner Philharmoniker (1961)
Philips	30		Eugen Jochum–Concertgebouw Orkest Amsterdam (1962)
Supraphon	30	St	Karel Ančerl–Philharmonia Prague (1963)
DG	30	St	Karl Böhm–Berliner Philharmoniker (1963)
CBS	30	St	Eugene Ormandy–Philadelphia Orchestra (1963)

Macbeth

| Westminster * | 30 | | Henry Swoboda–Wiener Sinfoniker (1954) |

Tod und Verklärung

Victor	30		Wilhelm Furtwängler–Wiener Philharmoniker (HR)
Victor *	30		Leopold Stokowski–New York City Symphony Orchestra (HR)
Columbia A	30		Leopold Stokowski–All America Orchestra (HR)
Victor	30		Leopold Stokowski–Philadelphia Orchestra (HR)
Decca *	30		Clemens Krauss–Royal Philharmonic Orchestra London (HR)
Telefunken	30		Willem Mengelberg–Concertgebouw Orkest Amsterdam (HR)
Columbia A	30		Eugene Ormandy–Philadelphia Orchestra (HR)

Victor	30		Fritz Reiner–RCA Victor Symphony Orchestra New York (1952)
RCA	30		Arturo Toscanini–NBC Symphony Orchestra New York (Concert Performance 1952) (1955)
Capitol	30		William Steinberg–Pittsburgh Symphony Orchestra (1955)
Vox	30		Jascha Horenstein–Bamberger Sinfoniker (1955)
Decca	30		Hans Knappertsbusch–Conservatoire Orchestre Paris (1956)
Philips	30		Bruno Walter–New York Philharmonic Symphony Orchestra (1957)
Columbia	30		Alceo Galliera–Philharmonia Orchestra London (1957)
Supraphon	30		Georges Georgescu–Philharmonia Prague (1957)
RCA	30	St	Fritz Reiner–Wiener Philharmoniker (1958)
Fontana	30	St	George Szell–Cleveland Orchestra (1959)
Mercury	30	St	Antal Dorati–Minneapolis Symphony Orchestra (1959)
Electrola	30	St	Artur Rodzinski–Philharmonia Orchestra London (1960)
Decca	30	St	Herbert von Karajan–Wiener Philharmoniker (1961)
Columbia	30	St	Otto Klemperer–Philharmonia Orchestra London (1962)
CBS	30	St	Eugene Ormandy–Philadelphia Orchestra (1963)

Till Eulenspiegel

DG	17		Richard Strauss–Berliner Staatskapelle (HR 1939)
Telefunken	30		Clemens Krauss–Wiener Philharmoniker (HR)
Decca *	30		Clemens Krauss–Orchestra Scala Milano (HR)
Victor	25		Serge Kussewitzky–Boston Symphony Orchestra (HR)
Columbia A	25		George Szell–Cleveland Orchestra (HR)
Columbia A	25		Artur Rodzinski–Cleveland Orchestra (HR)
Victor	25		Fritz Reiner–RCA Victor Symphony Orchestra (HR)

DG	17	Wilhelm Furtwängler–Berliner Philharmoniker (HR)
Tempo	25	Vittorio Gui–Orchestra Maggio Musicale Firenze (HR)
Decca	25, 17	Clemens Krauss–Wiener Philharmoniker (1951)
Columbia	25	Herbert von Karajan–Philharmonia Orchestra London (1952)
RCA	30	Arturo Toscanini–NBC Symphony Orchestra New York (Concert Performance 1952) (1956)
Supraphon	30	Franz Konwitschny–Philharmonia Prague (1953)
Philips	25, 17	Eugen Jochum–Concertgebouw Orkest Amsterdam (1954)
Electrola	25	Wilhelm Furtwängler–Wiener Philharmoniker (1954)
DG	30, 25, 17	Ferenc Fricsay–Berliner Philharmoniker (1954)
Capitol	30	William Steinberg–Pittsburgh Symphony Orchestra (1955)
Vox	30	Jascha Horenstein–Bamberger Sinfoniker (1955)
USSR	25	Alexander Gauck–Allunion Radio Symphony-Orchestra Moscow (1956)
Philips	25	Eugene Ormandy–Philadelphia Orchestra (1956)
Heliodor	25	Artur Rodzinski–London Philharmonic Symphony Orchestra (1957)
Polskie N./ Telefunken	25	Georges Georgescu–State Philharmonia Georges Enescu Bukarest (1958)
Mercury	25 St	Antal Dorati–Minneapolis Symphony Orchestra (1958)
RCA	30, 17	Fritz Reiner–Wiener Philharmoniker (1958)
Columbia	30	Igor Markevitch–Orchestre National Radio Paris (1958)
DG/Eterna	25	Karl Böhm–Dresdner Staatskapelle (1959)
Fontana	30 St	George Szell–Cleveland Orchestra (1959)
Eurodisc	30 St	Franz Konwitschny–Wiener Sinfoniker (1960)
Electrola	30 St	Rudolf Kempe–Berliner Philharmoniker (1960)
Decca	30 St	Herbert von Karajan–Wiener Philharmoniker (1961)
Everest	30 St	Leopold Stokowski–New York Stadium Symphony Orchestra (1961)

Capitol	25	St	Erich Leinsdorf–Philharmonia Orchestra London (1961)
Ariola	25	St	Otto Matzerath–Sinfonie-Orchester Hessischer Rundfunk Frankfurt o. M. (1961)
Telefunken	25	St	Joseph Keilberth–Berliner Philharmoniker (1961)
Philips	30		Leonard Bernstein–New York Philharmonic Symphony Orchestra (1961)
Philips	30, 25	St	Eugen Jochum–Concertgebouw Orkest Amsterdam (1962)
Supraphon	30	St	Karel Ančerl–Philharmonia Prague (1962)
RCA	30	St	Charles Münch–Boston Symphony Orchestra (1962)
DG	30	St	Karl Böhm–Berliner Philharmoniker (1963)

Also sprach Zarathustra

Columbia A *	30		Frederick August Stock–Chicago Symphony Orchestra (HR)
Victor	30		Serge Kussewitzky–Boston Symphony Orchestra (HR)
Victor	30		Artur Rodzinski–Chicago Symphony Orchestra (HR)
Decca	30		Clemens Krauss–Wiener Philharmoniker (1951)
RCA	30		Fritz Reiner–Chicago Symphony Orchestra (1955)
DG	30	St	Karl Böhm–Berliner Philharmoniker (1958)
Decca	30	St	Herbert von Karajan–Wiener Philharmoniker (1961)
RCA	30	St	Fritz Reiner–Chicago Symphony Orchestra (1963)

Don Quixote

Decca A	30	Richard Strauss–Münchner Staatsorchester (HR)
Victor *	30	Thomas Beecham–New York Philharmonic Symphony Orchestra (HR)
Victor *	30	Eugene Ormandy–Philadelphia Orchestra (HR)
Columbia A *	30	Fritz Reiner–Pittsburgh Symphony Orchestra (HR)

550

RCA	30		Arturo Toscanini–NBC Symphony Orchestra New York/Frank Miller (Concert Performance 1953) (1957)
Decca	30		Clemens Krauss–Wiener Philharmoniker/Paul Fournier (1954)
HMV	30		Charles Münch–Boston Symphony Orchestra/ Gregor Piatigorsky (1955)
Electrola	30	St	Rudolf Kempe–Berliner Philharmoniker/Paul Tortelier (1959)
Epic	30	St	George Szell–Cleveland Orchestra/Pierre Fournier (1961)
RCA	30	St	Fritz Reiner–Chicago Symphony Orchestra/Antonio Janigro (1961)
Columbia	30	St	Eugene Ormandy–Philadelphia Orchestra (1963)

Ein Heldenleben

Decca A	30		Richard Strauss–Münchner Staatsorchester (HR)
Capitol	30		Willem Mengelberg–Concertgebouw Orkest Amsterdam (HR)
Victor *	30		Willem Mengelberg–New York Philharmonic Symphony Orchestra (HR)
Victor *	30		Thomas Beecham–Royal Philharmonic Orchestra London (HR)
Columbia A	30		Artur Rodzinski–Cleveland Orchestra (HR)
Decca	30		Clemens Krauss–Wiener Philharmoniker (1952)
HMV	30		Fritz Reiner–Chicago Symphony Orchestra (1955)
Philips	30		Eugene Ormandy–Philadelphia Orchestra (1955)
DG	30		Karl Böhm–Dresdner Staatskapelle (1958)
Mercury	30	St	Antal Dorati–Minneapolis Symphony Orchestra (1958)
DG	30	St	Herbert von Karajan–Berliner Philharmoniker (1959)
Electrola	30	St	Thomas Beecham–Royal Philharmonic Orchestra London (1960)
Everest	30	St	Leopold Ludwig–London Symphony Orchestra (1961)

551

| RCA | 30 | St | Erich Leinsdorf–Boston Symphony Orchestra (1963) |
| CBS | 30 | St | Eugene Ormandy–Philadelphia Orchestra (1964) |

Sinfonia domestica

Vox A	30		Richard Strauss–Wiener Philharmoniker (Concert Performance 1944) (HR)
Victor	30		Eugene Ormandy–Philadelphia Orchestra (HR)
Decca	30		Clemens Krauss–Wiener Philharmoniker (1952)
DG	30		Franz Konwitschny–Dresdner Staatskapelle (1957)
RCA	30		Fritz Reiner–Chicago Symphony Orchestra (1958)

Feierlicher Einzug

| Decca | 17 | St | Karl Pilss–Trompeterchor der Stadt Wien (Feierlicher Einzug der Ritter des Johanniterordens) |

Festliches Präludium

| DG | 30 | St | Karl Böhm–Berliner Philharmoniker (1963) |

Eine Alpensinfonie

| Urania * | 30 | | Franz Konwitschny–Münchner Staatsorchester (1952) |
| DG/Eterna | 30 | | Karl Böhm–Dresdner Staatskapelle (1959) |

Suite "Der Bürger als Edelmann"

Columbia A	30		Fritz Reiner–Pittsburgh Symphony Orchestra (HR)
Decca	30		Clemens Krauss–Wiener Philharmoniker (1953)
HMV	17		Thomas Beecham–Royal Philharmonic Orchestra London (Menuet of Lully) (1955)
DG	30		Ferdinand Leitner–Berliner Philharmoniker (1956)
RCA	30		Fritz Reiner–Chicago Symphony Orchestra (1957)
Columbia	30		Igor Markevitch–Orchestre National Radio Paris (1958)
Columbia	30		Wolfgang Sawallisch–Philharmonia Orchestra London (1959)

Couperin-Tanzsuite

Lyricord	30		Erich Kloss–Frankenland Sinfonie-Orchester Nuremberg (HR)
Electrola	30	St	Artur Rodzinski–Philharmonia Orchestra London (1959)

Parergon

Boston	30		Paul Wittgenstein/Orchestra (1959)

Divertimento

Urania	30		Artur Rother–Berliner Rundfunk-Sinfonie-Orchester (1951)

2nd Horn Concerto

Columbia	30		Dennis Brain/Wolfgang Sawallisch–Philharmonia Orchestra London (1957)

Festmusik

Decca	17	St	Karl Pilss–Trompeterchor der Stadt Wien (1960)

1st Sonatina

Boston	30	St	Simon–Boston Woodwind Ensemble (1961)

Metamorphosen

DG	30		Wilhelm Furtwängler–Berliner Philharmoniker (HR) (1964)
Pathé	30		Jascha Horenstein–Orchestre National Radio Paris (1953)
Vox	30		Heinrich Hollreiser–Bamberger Sinfoniker (1956)
Columbia	30	St	Otto Klemperer–Philharmonia Orchestra London (1962)
Eterna	30	St	Otmar Suitner–Dresdner Staatskapelle (1964)

2nd Sonatina

Odeon	30		Karl Haas–London Baroque Ensemble (1953)

Oboe Concerto

Urania *	30		Erich Ertel/Artur Rother–Berliner Rundfunk-Sinfonie-Orchester (1952)
Supraphon	30		František Hanták/Jaroslav Vogel–State Philharmonia Brno (1963)
Eterna	30		Hans-Werner Wätzig/Heinz Rögner–Berliner Rundfunk-Sinfonie-Orchester (1964)

553

Duet-Concertino

Capitol   30   Gerald Caylor, Don Christlieb/Harold Byrns-
                             Los Angeles Chamber Orchestra (1951)

III. Vocal Music

Wandrers Sturmlied

Westminster * 30   Henry Swoboda–Wiener Sinfoniker and
                             Chamber Choir (1952)

Taillefer

Urania   30   Artur Rother–Sinfonie-Orchester und Chor Ber-
                             liner Rundfunk/Maria Cebotari, Ludwig, Hotter
                             (1951)

Brentano Songs

DG   30, 25   Erna Berger–Michael Raucheisen (1954)
DG   30   St   Rita Streich–Günther Weißenborn (3 songs)
                             (1962)

Lieder des Unmuts

DG   30   St   Dietrich Fischer-Dieskau–Karl Engel (1960)

Four Last Songs

Decca   30, 25, 17 Lisa della Casa/Karl Böhm–Wiener Philharmo-
                             niker (1953)

Columbia   30, 25   Elisabeth Schwarzkopf/Otto Ackermann–Phil-
                             harmonia Orchestra London (1954)

Vox   30   Christel Goltz/Heinrich Hollreiser–Wiener Pro
                             Musica Orchester (1956)

Eterna   30   St   Hanne-Lore Kuhse/Václav Neumann–Gewand-
                             hausorchester Leipzig (1964)

Songs

HMV   30   Lotte Lehmann–Paul Ulanowsky (7 songs) (HR)
HMV   30   Elisabeth Schumann–Karl Alwin (8 songs) (HR)
Odeon   17   Richard Tauber/Orchestra (4 songs) (HR)
DG   17   Heinrich Schlusnus/Gerhard Steeger–Berliner
                             Staatskapelle (4 songs) (HR)
DG   30, 17   Heinrich Schlusnus – Otto Braun, Sebastian
                             Peschko (5 songs) (HR)
Telefunken   30   Peter Anders–Hubert Giesen (3 songs) (HR)
DG/   30, 17   Peter Anders/Walter Lutze–Berliner Philharmo-
Telefunken   niker (1953)

554

Decca	25		Suzanne Danco–Guido Agosti (5 songs) (1953)
HMV	30,17		Kirsten Flagstad–Edwin McArthur (5 songs) (1956)
DG	25		Peter Anders/Fritz Lehmann–Münchner Philharmoniker (4 songs) (1956)
Metronome	17		Antti Koskinen–Eyvind Møller (4 songs) (1956)
DG	25		Heinrich Schlusnus/Winfried Zillig–Sinfonie-Orchester Hessischer Rundfunk Frankfurt o. M. (3 songs) (1957)
Delyse	30		Helga Mott–Erik Werba (5 songs) (1957)
Columbia	30		Aase Nordmo-Lovberg–Gerald Moore (8 songs) (1957)
Electrola	30,17		Dietrich Fischer-Dieskau–Gerald Moore (16 songs) (1957)
Decca	30,17		Lisa della Casa–Karl Hudez (3 songs) (1957)
Electrola	25,17	St	Rudolf Schock–Wilhelm Schüchter–Berliner Sinfoniker (8 songs) (1958)
DG	17		Annelies Kupper–Hans Altmann (6 songs) (1958)
DG	30		Rita Streich–Erik Werba (3 songs) (1958)
DG	30,17	St	Irmgard Seefried–Erik Werba (8 songs) (1959)
Amadeo	30,17		Anny Felbermayer, Alfred Poell–Victor Graef (16 songs) (1960)
Decca	17		Hilde Güden–Friedrich Gulda (5 songs) (1960)
RCA	17		Leontyne Price–David Garvey (3 songs) (1960)
Electrola	30	St	Rudolf Schock–Adolf Stauch (4 songs) (1961)
Amadeo	30		Eberhard Wächter–Heinrich Schmidt (5 songs) (1961)
DG	30	St	Rita Streich–Günther Weißenborn (6 songs) (1962)
DG	30	St	Grace Bumbury–Erik Werba (4 songs) (1963)
Decca	30	St	Tom Krause–Penti Koskimies (8 songs) (1963)
Decca	17		Hermann Prey–Karl Engel (4 songs) (1963)
Electrola	30	St	Lisa della Casa–Sebastian Peschko (7 songs) (1963)

555

IV. Chamber Music

Klavierstücke

Artists	30	Alfred Brendel

Piano Sonata

Artists	30	Alfred Brendel

Cello Sonata

Concert Hall *	30	Raya Garbousova–E. I. Kahn
Artists	30	C. Stern–P. O'Neil
Vox	30	Joseph Schuster–Friedrich Wührer (1957)
DG	30	Ludwig Hoelscher–Hans Richter-Haaser (1957)
Odeon	30	André Navarra–Ernest Lush (1959)

Piano Quartet

New Records	25	J. Figueros, G. Ricci, F. Brieff and B. Segall

Violin Sonata

Victor *	30	Jascha Heifetz–A. Sandor (HR)
Classic *	30	J. Tyron–J. La Mountaine (HR)
Concert Hall *	30	L. Kaufmann–Carlo Bussotti (1953)
USSR	30	Leonid Kogan–Andre Mytnik (1960)

CONTEMPORARIES

Bahr, Hermann (1863–1934), Austrian dramatist, who dedicated his comedy "Das Konzert" to Strauss. Strauss wanted him to write the libretto of "Intermezzo." His wife Anna Bahr-Mildenburg was a famous Klytemnestra.

Beecham, Sir Thomas (1879–1961), leading English conductor who directed successively the London Symphony Orchestra, London Philharmonic Orchestra and Royal Philharmonic Orchestra. Achieved particular success with the works of Mozart, Delius, Sibelius, and above all Strauss, whose "Elektra" and "Don Quixote" he conducted in the composer's presence during the London Strauss Festival in October 1947.

Bierbaum, Otto Julius (1865–1910), Munich poet and novelist, who wrote the words of a number of Strauss songs ("Traum durch die Dämmerung," "Freundliche Vision" etc.). Opera libretti for Strauss failed to materialize.

Blech, Leo (1871–1958), conductor and composer. Active at the Berlin opera houses from 1906 until 1953, apart from the Nazi years. Closely connected with Strauss's works since the Berlin "Elektra" (1909).

Böhm, Karl (b. 1894), born in Graz, first studied law (Dr. jur.), opera director at Hamburg, Dresden (1934/42) and Vienna (1942/45 and 1954/56). Outstanding Strauss conductor, now active in Vienna, Berlin, Munich, Salzburg, Bayreuth, New York etc. Conducted the Dresden world premières of "Die schweigsame Frau" and "Daphne," the latter being dedicated to him. Strauss sent him his "Artistic Testament" in 1945.

Bülow, Hans Guido Freiherr von (1830–1894), originally studied jurisprudence. Pupil of Wagner in conducting and of Liszt in piano playing. From 1864 General Musical Director of the Munich Court Opera, where he conducted the world premières of "Tristan" and "Meistersinger." Later conducted in Hanover, Meiningen, Berlin and Hamburg. Gave great encouragement and assistance to the young Strauss, whom he appointed at Meiningen.

Busch, Fritz (1890–1951), prominent conductor, who, during his period at the Dresden State Opera (1922/33), conducted the world premières of "Intermezzo" and "Ägyptische Helena." Forced to emigrate in 1933; "Arabella" though dedicated to him, was conducted by Krauss.

Dehmel, Richard (1863–1920), north-German social-critical writer, whose poems set by Strauss included "Der Arbeitsmann" and "Lied an meinen Sohn."

Draeseke, Felix (1835–1913), pupil of Liszt, composer and teacher in Dresden. Wrote several music dramas and oratorios ("Christus"), eclectic in style. His essay "Die Konfusion in der Musik" (1907) gave rise to a heated dicussion about Strauss.

Gregor, Joseph (1888–1960), Viennese art historian and theatrical expert, in charge of the theatrical collection of the Austrian National Library, who wrote the libretti of "Friedenstag," "Daphne" and "Liebe der Danae" (after Hofmannsthal's draft) for Strauss.

Hanslick, Eduard (1825–1904), Viennese musical theoretician ("Vom Musikalisch-Schönen") and influential music critic. Supported Brahms, was reserved and hostile toward Wagner, Bruckner and Strauss.

Hartmann, Rudolf (b. 1900), chief producer of the Munich State Opera during the Krauss era, "Staatsintendant" since 1952. Producer at the world premières of "Friedenstag," "Capriccio" and "Danae." At the composer's request he features Strauss's works prominently in the Munich opera festivals which he directs annually.

Hauptmann, Gerhart (1862–1945), leading figure in the sphere of bourgeois realism, successful playwright ("Die Weber," "Fuhrmann Henschel" etc.). In close contact with Strauss, whose "Salome" and "Elektra" he particularly admired.

Henckell, Karl (1864–1929), social poet, whose works set by Strauss included "Lied des Steinklopfers" and "Blindenklage."

Hofmannsthal, Hugo von (1874–1929), Austrian poet and dramatist, highly artistic and also, in his best works, realistic by nature. From the time of "Elektra" closely associated with Strauss ("Rosenkavalier," "Ariadne," "Josephslegende," "Frau ohne Schatten," "Helena" and "Arabella"). He died on the 15th July 1929 at Rodaun in tragic circumstances shortly after completing the libretto of "Arabella."

Kerr, Alfred (1867–1948), Berlin theatre critic, lived in England from 1933. Wrote the satirical song cycle "Krämerspiegel" for Strauss. A proposed opera ("Peregrin") did not materialize.

Kessler, Harry Count (1868–1937), writer and politician. Wrote the libretto of "Josephslegende" with Hofmannsthal.

the works of Strauss from his youth. Opera director in Frankfort on
the works of Strauss from his youth. Opera director in Frankfort on
Main, Vienna, Berlin and Munich (1937/45), then guest conductor.
Intimate colleague and adviser of Strauss; librettist of "Capriccio,"
whose first performance, like those of "Arabella," "Friedenstag" and
"Danae," he conducted. Strauss dedicated "Friedenstag" and
"Capriccio" to him. Married to Viorica Ursuleac, the first Arabella,
Maria and Madeleine.

Mackay, John Henry (1864–1933), social-critical poet. Follower of Stirner.
Author of several of Strauss's most popular songs: "Morgen," "Heimliche Aufforderung" etc.

Reinhardt, Max (1873–1943), outstanding Berlin producer and theatre
director, who emigrated to the U.S.A. in 1933. Came to the rescue at
the original production of "Rosenkavalier" in 1911. In gratitude Strauss
dedicated "Ariadne" to him, and he was its first producer.

Ritter, Alexander (1833–1896) was one of the first disciples of Wagner,
whose niece he married. Belonged to the Weimar Liszt circle, and
lived, variously employed, at Stettin, Dresden, Schwerin and Würzburg. 1882/86 a violinist in the Meiningen Orchestra under Bülow and
Strauss, then in Munich. Fatherly friend of the young Strauss, who
dedicated "Macbeth" to him. Composer of the one-act operas "Der
faule Hans" and "Wem die Krone," as well as symphonic poems.

Rolland, Romain (1866–1944), French writer and musicologist of advanced ideas. Principal works: the musical novel "Jean-Christophe"
and books on Handel and Beethoven. Frequently wrote about Strauss,
with whom he remained on friendly terms until his death.

Roller, Alfred (1864–1933), renowned scenic artist of the Vienna Opera
during the Mahler and Strauss eras. His designs for the Dresden
"Rosenkavalier" in 1911 were models for all later productions of the work.

Rösch, Friedrich (1862–1925), Dr. jur., a friend of Strauss since his student days in Munich. Co-founder of the "Genossenschaft deutscher Tonsetzer," talented composer. Strauss dedicated "Tod und Verklärung"
and the "Krämerspiegel" to him, and delivered an address at his funeral.

Schalk, Franz (1863–1931), Viennese conductor, pupil of Bruckner, whose
symphonies he was one of the first to promote. Began as an opera conductor with Strauss in Berlin. From 1900 conductor and 1918/29 director (for a time together with Strauss) of the Vienna Opera, where he
conducted the world première of "Frau ohne Schatten."

Schillings, Max von (1863–1933), Intendant and General Music Director
in Stuttgart and Berlin (1919/25). Recognized opera composer. A friend
of Strauss, who transferred to him the libretto of "Pfeifertag," and conducted his "Mona Lisa" in Vienna. Married to Barbara Kemp, a brilliant Salome, Elektra and Dyer's Wife.

Schuch, Ernst von (1846–1914), born at Graz, went to Dresden in 1872, conducting the Dresden Court Opera and Orchestra until his death. The first notable Strauss conductor of this century, to whom the world premières of "Feuersnot," "Salome," "Elektra" and "Rosenkavalier" were entrusted.

Schuh, Willi (b. 1900), Dr. phil., lives in Zürich as a music critic. Belonged to the intimate circle of the friends of Strauss's last years. Edited Strauss's correspondence, and has written about him extensively. "Frühling," one of the Last Songs, was dedicated to him.

Sommer, Hans, real name H. F. A. Zincke (1837–1922), co-founder of the "Genossenschaft deutscher Tonsetzer," was originally a physicist and mathematician, but then turned to music. Achieved note principally as a song-writer (more than 200 songs) and as composer of fairy-tale operas.

Strauss, Franz Joseph (1822–1905), the composer's father, Royal Bavarian court musician of the Munich Court Orchestra and professor at the Academy. Renowned horn player, who also published compositions for his instrument, and worked at Bayreuth.

Strauss, Pauline, née de Ahna (1862–1950), second daughter of a Bavarian Major-General. Married to Strauss from 10. 9. 1894. Outstanding young-dramatic soprano (Weimar, Bayreuth) and interpreter of the early Strauss songs, some of which were dedicated to her.

Thuille, Ludwig (1861–1907), from 1883 teacher of composition at the Munich Academy. A friend of Strauss, who dedicated "Don Juan" to him, and transferred to him the libretti of the operas "Lobetanz" and "Gugeline," which Bierbaum had originally intended for Strauss.

Tietjen, Heinz (b. 1881), for many years Intendant of the Operas of Breslau, Berlin (Städtische Oper and State Opera) and Hamburg. Strauss dedicated "Danae" to this powerful supporter of his work.

Wedekind, Frank (1864–1918), Munich dramatist, who glorified the hostility to life and the superficial morality of the late-bourgeois era. In contact with Strauss concerning a projected ballet ("Der Floh").

Wilde, Oscar (1856–1900), Irish-born, one of the most striking phenomena of Victorian England as a dramatist and writer of short stories. His "Salome" served Strauss as the basis of the music drama of the same name.

Wolzogen, Ernst Freiherr von (1855–1934), satirical Munich writer, founder of the "Überbrettl" theatre, who wrote the text of "Feuersnot" for Strauss. Later joint opera plans remained unrealized.

Zweig, Stefan (1881–1942), Austrian novelist and dramatist who, after Hofmannsthal's death, wrote the libretto of "Die schweigsame Frau" after Ben Jonson, and remained a friendly adviser in connection with Strauss's later operas. Committed suicide while exiled in South America (Petropolis).

BIBLIOGRAPHY

Asow, Erich Hermann Mueller von: "Richard Strauss, Thematisches Ver-
zeichnis," Vienna-Wiesbaden since 1955.

Bahr, Hermann: "Meister und Meisterbriefe um Hermann Bahr," edited
by Joseph Gregor, Vienna, 1947.

Busch, Fritz: "Aus dem Leben eines Musikers," Zürich, 1949 and 1952.

Debussy, Claude: "Musik und Musiker," Potsdam, 1949.

Erhardt, Otto: "Richard Strauss, Leben, Wirken, Schaffen," Olten-Frei-
burg i. Br., 1953.

Foerster, Josef B.: "Der Pilger, Erinnerungen eines Musikers," Prague,
1955.

Gregor, Joseph: "Richard Strauss, der Meister der Oper," Munich 1939,
1943 and 1952.

Gysi, Fritz: "Richard Strauss," Potsdam, 1934.

Hofmannsthal, Hugo von: "Danae oder Die Vernunftsheirat," edited by
Willi Schuh, Frankfort on Main, 1952.
"Briefe der Freundschaft," correspondence with Eberhard von Boden-
hausen, Frankfort on Main, 1953.

Kapp, Julius: "Richard Strauss und die Berliner Oper," Berlin, 1934
and 1939.

Krüger, Karl Joachim: "Hugo von Hofmannsthal und Richard Strauss,"
Marburg, 1934.

Lindner, Dolf: "Die Liebe der Danae," with a foreword by Clemens
Krauss, Vienna, 1952.

Mayer, Hans: "Hugo von Hofmannsthal und Richard Strauss," Berlin,
1961 (Sinn und Form).

Muschler, R. Conrad: "Richard Strauss," Hildesheim, 1925.

Pfister, Kurt: "Richard Strauss," Vienna, 1949.

Rolland, Romain: "Musicien d'aujourd'hui," Paris, 1908.
"Correspondence avec Richard Strauss," edited by Gustave Samalzeuilh,
Paris, 1951.

561

Rostand, Claude: "Richard Strauss," Paris, 1949.

Schuch, Friedrich von: "Richard Strauss, Ernst von Schuch und Dresdens Oper," Dresden, 1952 and 1953.

Schuh, Willi: "Über Opern von Richard Strauss," Zürich, 1947.
"In memoriam Richard Strauss," Zürich, 1949.
"Das Bühnenwerk von Richard Strauss in den letzten unter Mitwirkung des Komponisten geschaffenen Münchner Inszenierungen," Zürich, 1954.

Specht, Richard: "Richard Strauss und sein Werk," two volumes, Leipzig, 1921.

Steinitzer, Max: "Richard Strauss," Leipzig, 1911–1927.
"Richard Strauss und seine Zeit," Leipzig, 1914.

Strauss, Richard: "Briefwechsel mit Hugo von Hofmannsthal," Vienna, 1925 (edited by Franz Strauss) and Zürich, 1952, extended 1963 (edited by Franz and Alice Strauss, revised by Willi Schuh).
"Betrachtungen und Erinnerungen" (English version "Recollections and Reflections"), edited by Willi Schuh, Zürich, 1949, extended 1957.
"Briefwechsel mit Hans von Bülow," edited by Willi Schuh and Franz Trenner, Bonn, 1953 (Strauss-Jahrbuch).
"Briefwechsel mit den Eltern," edited by Willi Schuh, Zürich, 1954.
"Briefwechsel mit Joseph Gregor," edited by Roland Tenschert, Salzburg, 1955.
"Briefwechsel mit Stefan Zweig," edited by Willi Schuh, Frankfort on Main, 1957.

Tenschert, Roland: "Dreimal sieben Variationen über das Thema Richard Strauss," Vienna, 1944.
"Richard Strauss und Wien," Vienna, 1949.

Trenner, Franz: "Richard Strauss, Dokumente seines Lebens und Schaffens," Munich, 1954.

Wolzogen, Ernst von: "Wie ich mich ums Leben brachte, Erinnerungen und Erfahrungen," Brunswick-Hamburg 1922.

Zweig, Friderike: "Stefan Zweig, wie ich ihn erlebte," Berlin, 1948.

Zweig, Stefan: "Die Welt von gestern, Erinnerungen eines Europäers," Stockholm, 1947.

– "Strauss-Jahrbücher, 1954 und 1959/60," edited by Willi Schuh, Bonn, 1954 and 1960.

– "Mitteilungen der Internationalen Richard-Strauss-Gesellschaft," edited by Julius Kopsch, Berlin, since 1953.

SOURCES OF THE ILLUSTRATIONS

The dust-cover illustration is a colour reproduction of the painting by Max Liebermann in the National Gallery, Berlin. The lithograph (after P. 288) of the composer in his fifties dates from the same wartime year 1918, and is by the same artist. Leopold von Kalckreuth's youthful portrait (after P. 48) is in the collection of Dr. Franz Strauss at Garmisch. The original of the bronze bust by Hugo Lederer, 1903 (before P. 49), several castings of which exist, is in the National Gallery, Berlin. The photograph of the eighty-year-old composer by Hildegard Jäckel (Dresden) after P. 368 was taken in June 1944 when Strauss last visited Dresden. The drawing by Gerda von Stengel (Munich) on P. 431, from the last year of Strauss's life, first appeared in the Bayreuth Festival Book of 1952. A few weeks before his death Strauss was visited at Garmisch by the photographer Karsh of Ottawa; the author is grateful to Armin Schönberg (Hamburg) for enabling the portrait after P. 480 to be reproduced. The photograph of the death mask (before P. 481) was taken by Hildegard Steinmetz, Munich.

The majority of the documents and manuscripts here reproduced, some of them for the first time, are the property of Dr. Franz Strauss. Strauss wrote the "Tristan" bars (P. 90) at the end of the chapter "Tragik und Ende" in Rudolf Bach's book "Tragik und Grösse der deutschen Romantik," which he borrowed from Dr. Willi Schuh in 1946. The "Elektra" rehearsal schedule on P. 115 is in the possession of Dr. Friedrich von Schuch; the sketch for "Die Donau" (P. 260) was presented to Dr. Roland Tenschert. The letter on the anniversary of the Dresden Orchestra (P. 132/133) is in the keeping of the Dresden State Opera. The drawings on P. 25 and 291 are by Friedrich Gäbel (Berlin). The photograph after P. 128 is by Gertrud Gröllmann (Dresden), and the photograph of a stage design before P. 289 is by Fritz Witzig (Munich). The extract from a letter to Dora Wihan on P. 92 and a number of other illustrations are from the author's Strauss collection.

INDEX

The only Appendix entries included in this Index are those of the section entitled „Contemporaries". In the Index of Works the first entry in italics refers to the page(s) of the book on which a detailed account of the work (history, content, form) is to be found. The Index of Works includes unfulfilled plans—projects, sketches and uncompleted compositions.

I. Works

Stage Works

Instrumental Works

Vocal Works

Goetz, Hermann (1840–1876) 332

Gogol, Nikolai (1809–1852) 415

Goldoni, Carlo (1707–1793) 347

Gounod, Charles (1818–1893) 128

Goya, Francisco de (1748–1828) 246

Gray, Cecil (1895–1951) 364

Gregor, Joseph (1888–1960) 44, 56, 61, 90, 91, 108, 118, 120, 125, 126, 130, 131, 140, 196, 199, 237, 275, 315, 326, 347 to 352, 354–356, 368–387, 390, 394, 395, 397, 425–428, 443 to 447, 454, 468, 560

Grimm, Herman (1828–1901) 195, 463

Grimm, Jakob (1785–1863) 397

Grimm, Wilhelm (1786–1859) 397

Grünfeld, Heinrich (1855–1924) 296

Grützner, Eduard (1846–1925) 135

Gulbransson, Olaf (1873–1958) 221

Gutmann, Albert 129, 221

Gutzkow, Karl (1811–1878) 17

Gysi, Fritz (b. 1888) 257, 279, 298, 324

Haas, Joseph (1879–1960) 99

Haas-Heye 446

Hafner, Philipp (1731–1764) 321

Hagen, August 329

Halévy, Jacques Fromental (1799 to 1862) 453

Hamsun, Knut (1859–1952) 22

Handel, George Frederick (1685 to 1759) 13, 193, 203, 355, 364, 368

Hanslick, Eduard (1825–1904) 35, 58, 71, 76, 77, 174, 180, 230, 234, 235, 240, 287, 560

Hartmann, Rudolf (b. 1900) 197, 382, 434, 450, 451, 472–474, 560

Hase, Oskar von (1846–1921) 59

Hauptmann, Gerhart (1862–1946) 21–23, 70, 74, 196, 307, 330, 393, 560

Hausegger, Siegmund von (1872 to 1948) 121, 234

Haydn, Franz Joseph (1732–1809) 210, 238, 255, 452

Hebbel, Friedrich (1813–1863) 17

Heine, Heinrich (1797–1856) 17, 266, 271, 298

Heinrich II (973–1024) 349

Hempel, Frieda (1885–1955) 177, 365

Henckell, Karl (1864–1929) 46, 153, 196, 265, 560

Henze, Hans Werner (b. 1926) 103

Herder, Johann Gottfried von 1744–1803) 274

Herod I (The Great) 298

Herod Antipas (4 B.C.–37 A.D.) 298

Herodotus (400 B.C.) 405

Hérold, Louis J. F. (1791–1833) 360

Hesse, Hermann (1877–1962) 80, 267, 271, 462, 469

Hindemith, Paul (1895–1963) 104, 422

Hitler, Adolf (1889–1945) 24, 49, 55, 374

Hochberg, Bolko Graf von (1843 to 1926) 111

Hodler, Ferdinand (1853–1918) 257

Hölderlin, Friedrich (1770–1843) 267, 270, 305

Hörburger, Carl 97, 200

576

Krauss, Clemens (1893–1954) 65,
100, 137, 140, 192, 195, 197,
339, 353, 370, 371, 373, 376 to
378, 381, 382, 386, 403, 411,
424–426, 428, 449–451, 561

Krecke (phijsician) 418

Kreutzer, Konradin (1780–1849)
111

Krupp, Alfred (1812–1887) 57

Kürnberger, Ferdinand (1821 to
1879) 195

Kuhač, Franjo K. (1834–1911)
100, 334

Kuhnau, Johann (1660–1722) 210

Kurth, Ernst (1886–1946) 159

Kusnetzova, Maria 440

Lachmann, Hedwig 297

Lancret, Nicolas (1690–1743) 445

Lanner, Joseph (1801–1843) 442

Lassen, Eduard (1830–1904) 110,
160, 282

Laux, Karl (b. 1896) 314

Le Feuillet, Raoul–see Feuillet,
Raoul le

Legrenzi, Giovanni (1626–1690)
98, 344

Lehár, Franz (1870–1948) 44, 328,
426

Lehmann, Lotte (b. 1888) 424

Lenau, Nikolaus (1802–1850) 51,
227–229, 397

Lenbach, Franz von (1836–1904)
196

Leoncavallo, Ruggiero (1858 to
1919) 53

Lessing, Gotthold Ephraim (1729
to 1781) 426

Levi, Hermann (1839–1900) 32,
111

Levin, Willy 197

Lieban, Julius (1857–1940) 293

Liebermann, Max (1847–1935) 23,
74, 196, 214

Liebknecht, Wilhelm (1826–1900)
16

Liechtenstein, Ulrich von (1200 to
1276) 330

Liliencron, Detlef von (1844 to
1909) 23, 264

Liliencron, Rochus von (1820 to
1912) 329

Lindner, Anton 296

Lippl, Alois Johannes (b. 1903)
472

Liszt, Franz (1811–1886) 12, 20,
34, 50, 83, 97, 110, 160, 171,
179, 192, 211, 212, 215, 217,
219, 229, 231, 235, 236, 257,
264, 267, 286, 437, 472

Lönne, Friedrich 197

Loewe, Carl (1796–1869) 151, 274

Lope de Vega (1562–1635) 384

Lorenz, Alfred (1868–1939) 180

Lortzing, Albert (1801–1851) 289,
320, 333, 468

Lothar, Mark (b. 1902) 342

Louis, Rudolf (1870–1914) 58

Louis XIV (1643–1715) 357

Louis XV (1710–1774) 314

Lucian (2nd cent.) 374

Ludendorff, Erich (1865–1937) 57

Ludwig II (King of Bavaria) (1864
to 1886) 24, 287

Lully, Jean-Baptiste (1632–1687)
98, 357, 366

Luther, Martin (1483–1546) 65

Mackay, John Henry (1864–1933)
265, 267, 270, 561

577

Mahler, Gustav (1860–1911) 10, 21, 37, 39, 50, 77, 78, 99, 103, 113, 118, 128, 175, 192, 214, 219, 253, 291, 299, 455

Maillol, Aristide (1861–1944) 107

Makart, Hans (1840–1884) 22, 23, 250, 255, 296

Manet, Edouard (1832–1883) 23

Mann, Heinrich (1871–1950) 22

Mann, Thomas (1875–1955) 10, 11, 20, 22, 41, 68, 73, 77, 335

Maria Theresa (Empress) (1717 to 1780) 314, 316, 320, 324, 330, 335, 442

Marie-Antoinette (Queen of France) (1755–1793) 340

Mariotte, Antoine (1875–1944) 299

Marlowe, Christopher (1564–1593) 342

Marschalk, Max (1863–1940) 101, 121

Martinu, Bohuslav (1890–1959) 359

Marx, Joseph (b. 1882) 103

Marx, Karl (1818–1883) 15, 20, 23

Mascagni, Pietro (1863–1945) 364

Massenet, Jules (1842–1912) 97, 205, 299, 453

Massine, Leonid (b. 1896) 440

Mauke, Wilhelm (1867–1930) 238

Mayer, Hans (b. 1907) 323, 336, 391, 398

Meck, Nadeshda von (1831–1893) 43

Melchinger, Siegfried (b. 1903) 57

Mell, Max (b. 1882) 87

Mendelssohn Bartholdy, Felix (1809–1847) 34, 96, 151, 213, 226, 275, 302

Mengelberg, Willem (1871–1951) 137, 252

Menzel, Adolph von (1815–1905) 196, 214

Meyer, Ernst Hermann (b. 1905) 72

Meyer, Friedrich Wilhelm 30

Meyerbeer, Giacomo (1791–1864) 24, 52, 97, 151, 203, 410, 453

Milhaud, Darius (b. 1892) 146, 359, 393

Mitropoulos, Dimitri (1896–1960) 138

Mörike, Eduard (1804–1875) 266

Molière, Jean Baptiste (1622 to 1673) 229, 314, 321, 356–358, 360–362, 366, 367, 427, 471

Monteverdi, Claudio (1567–1643) 98, 344, 359

Moreau, Gustave (1826–1898) 297, 355

Mottl, Felix (1856–1911) 110, 222

Mozart, Leopold (1719–1787) 43

Mozart, Wolfgang Amadeus (1756 to 1791) 20, 28, 34, 35, 56, 63, 66, 78, 79, 84–87, 105, 107, 117, 119, 128, 132, 136, 137, 139, 140, 146, 155, 160, 165, 170, 177, 179, 181, 190, 198, 199, 209, 229, 290, 315, 320, 321, 323–326, 328, 329, 337, 338, 341, 345, 355, 362–364, 375, 383, 384, 386, 387, 396 to 398, 401, 417, 425–427, 433, 451–453, 458, 460, 461, 464, 466, 468

Muck, Karl (1859–1940) 111

Munch, Edvard (1863–1944) 23

Murner, Thomas (1475–1537) 237

Mussorgsky, Modest (1839–1881) . 156, 212, 415, 422

579

CONTENTS

DATE DUE

O'Hogan			
DEC 18 79			